Ethics, Professional Responsibility and the Lawyer

Ethics, Professional Responsibility and the Lawyer

by

Duncan Webb LLM (Hons) VUW
Senior Lecturer in Law at
Victoria University of Wellington

Wellington
BUTTERWORTHS
2000

The Butterworth Group
A member of the Reed Elsevier Group plc

New Zealand	BUTTERWORTHS OF NEW ZEALAND LTD, 205-207 Victoria St, PO Box 472, Wellington
Australia	BUTTERWORTHS, Chatswood NSW
Canada	BUTTERWORTHS CANADA LTD, Markham ONT
France	EDITIONS DU JURIS-CLASSEUR, Paris
Hong Kong	BUTTERWORTHS ASIA, Hong Kong
India	BUTTERWORTH & CO (ASIA) PTE LTD, New Delhi
Ireland	BUTTERWORTHS (IRELAND) LTD, Dublin
Italy	DOTT A GIUFFRÈ EDITORE SPA, Milan
Malaysia	MALAYAN LAW JOURNAL Sdn Bhd, Kuala Lumpur
Poland	WYDAWNICTWA PRAWNICZE PWN, Warsaw
Singapore	BUTTERWORTHS ASIA, Singapore
South Africa	BUTTERWORTH PUBLISHERS (PTY) LTD, Durban
Switzerland	STÄMPFLI VERLAG AG, Bern
United Kingdom	BUTTERWORTHS LTD, London; BUTTERWORTHS (SCOTLAND) LTD, Edinburgh
USA	LEXIS-NEXIS, Dayton OH; LEXIS LAW PUBLISHING, Charlottesville VA

Cataloguing in Publication data (N.Z.)

Webb, Duncan A. (Duncan Alexander)
Ethics, professional responsibility and the lawyer / by Duncan Webb. - Wellington, N.Z. : Butterworths, 2000.
p. ; cm.
ISBN 0408715227
1. Legal ethics. I. Title.
174.3_dc21

Preface

Legal ethics is a subject upon which (I now discover) it is particularly difficult to write. Any area of law has problems with overlapping, vague and often non-existent boundaries with other areas. This is the case in respect of the law regarding the duties and responsibilities of lawyers. Any study of this area must touch on the law of fiduciaries, Court procedure, personal property, and contract to mention but a few. This work has attempted to do some justice to the fact that an examination of the duties of lawyers is more than just an examination and critique of the law. It requires a consideration of issues that are usually the domain of other disciplines altogether such as sociology, philosophy and politics. Decisions as to the depth of analysis and coverage in such areas is largely arbitrary and therefore any goal of completeness is illusory. This work is however aimed at lawyers and law students. The focus is therefore on the law and the context in which it exists. It seeks to inform on the content of the obligations owed by lawyers as well as providing a discussion of the foundations, critique and justifications of those obligations. It also seeks to look at the problems facing lawyers and the profession, as well as putting hard (and possibly unpopular) questions about the regulation and discipline of lawyers.

This has meant that some areas of law touching on legal practice have been ignored or dealt with in a cursory manner. I have tried to focus on the duties of lawyers to their clients and the Courts, as well as examining the role and place of the professional organisation. This has meant that I have not dealt with, for example, liens on the basis that it is more a matter of property law and raises few issues in relation to professional conduct. Similarly privilege is left to the extended discussion it requires which is usually found in evidence works. I have also devoted only one chapter of the work to the duties of practitioners to the profession and each other.

Some prefer to refer to professional responsibility and place a corresponding emphasis on the regulation of the profession. Others choose to discuss the area in terms of ethics and tend to focus on the conflicts between the personal and professional moral lives of lawyers. In fact the two are largely inseparable. Any examination of the rules must address the tensions between the rules themselves, and the norms which apply to conduct outside of the profession of law. Similarly a study of the tensions in the moral lives of lawyers cannot be undertaken without a thorough discussion of the legal and professional obligations themselves, and why they are, by and large, regarded as appropriate.

If the questions of professional conduct raised are to be properly discussed it is impossible to avoid discussing moral and legal theory. The philosophical foundations of professional ethics are a necessary part of this work. While the deep questions about why certain approaches to a lawyer's work are flawed (or not) should be addressed directly and thoroughly, an exhaustive discussion of the philosophical foundations of the various approaches to legal ethics is beyond the scope of this work. I have taken the stance that a rigorous and critical discussion is possible without encumbering the reader with too much esoteric philosophy. In essence I have attempted to write a book which tends towards the practical rather than theoretical, but does not shy away from the plainly philosophical content of the area.

Overseas criticism of the conduct of the profession suggesting a kind of crisis, while not entirely accurate, strikes a chord with many. The profession has undergone change and societal expectations have transformed the view of the profession. The halcyon days of lawyer-statesman, paternalistic guide, are gone. Lawyers are now expected to listen to their clients, respect the autonomy of their clients, and make their clients familiar with the processes and content of the law as far as possible. The public has also lost patience with closure of the profession and restrictive practices. The barriers, which have previously restricted entry to the profession, are now lower than they have ever been. The profession is now more open to people of both genders, every ethnicity and belief, and any social background. This change in the demography of the profession has meant that there is no longer a homogeneous set of interests and beliefs which cements the bonds between members of the profession. Also gone are many of the restrictions that inflated lawyers' incomes. The fixed scale of costs has been abolished, the ban on advertising relaxed, and lawyers have become altogether more prepared to meet the expectations of their various clients as regards costs and services. In short lawyering has become more open and more competitive.

The place of law has also changed. No longer is the law the preserve of the rich, and no longer is it considered an unfortunate evil if recourse to legal rights and the Courts are necessary. The Courts are regarded as the ultimate guarantors and arbiters of a myriad of legal rights of citizens. When relationships fail, contracts are breached, human rights are infringed, or wrongs are committed the matter will be dealt with in the shadow of legal process. One of the main contributors to this change has been the wide availability of legal aid to those who would not otherwise be able to afford legal assistance. This is an improvement on the exclusivity of the Courts and law in earlier times. It has however led to the growth of the legal profession, a change in the kind of assistance that lawyers render, and a change in the demography of clients.

In such a changing environment it is necessary to be aware of the changing circumstances to which the Rules of Professional Conduct and the ethical demands of professionalism apply. Some of the basic objects of the rules remain to ensure that legal advice is objective, that access to justice is provided to all, and that the interests of the client are protected, to name but a few. However there is a steady international trend to add to this list other more demanding and more specific requirements: the provision of quality advice, the protection of the client from illegitimate advantage taking, and the charging of reasonable fees. Regulation of the profession is no longer regarded as members of a closed group disciplining their own for a wrong against the group. It is a matter of governing the relationship between the providers of an essential service and the consumers of that service.

These trends and pressures have culminated in far reaching proposals for the reform of the structure and functions of the profession. At the time of writing the President of the Law Society has sent a circular letter to all practitioners outlining proposals of the then (National-led) government which were ostensibly reached in consultation with the society. Those proposals were contained in a letter from the President of the Law Society to all practitioners dated 20 October 1999 and an attached paper. The proposals, if implemented, would make membership of district law societies voluntary, and the New Zealand Law Society would retain only core functions of admission, discipline, financial assurance, and rule making. District law societies would become like trade associations devoted to the promotion of the interests of members and providing services for which member demand existed. The fidelity fund and the statutory costs review regime would be abolished. Lawyers would also be permitted to practise under the auspices of limited liability companies and in conjunction with non-lawyer professionals. Whether these reforms, or reforms like them will be implemented under the new (Labour-led) government remains to be seen. What is not in doubt is that the profession is currently in a period of considerable change.

There has also been a change in direction in the way in which the issue of ethics is dealt with in New Zealand. Previously the acquisition of knowledge of ethics by practitioners has been left to professional education, or to a process of osmosis in practice. Recent moves have formalised the teaching of ethics by prescribing it as part of the curricula taught by the universities and the Institute of Professional Legal Studies. The Council of Legal Education has resolved to make an undergraduate course in ethics a compulsory part of the admission requirements. The resolution was made after a significant study in 1996 by the New Zealand Law Society: the *Cotter-Roper Report on Education and Training in*

Ethics and Professional Responsibility. The report recognised that the pressures of modern practice and the diversity of the profession meant that it could no longer be left to the profession alone to give a consistent grounding in the ethical and professional demands of the practice of law.

Academics are traditionally squeamish about identifying the objective of legal ethics. However, the motivation for the implementation of a compulsory course in legal ethics in New Zealand universities is clear — to make lawyers more ethical. This is not the same as instilling a system of rules or even values. It requires that lawyers are aware of the issues and tensions surrounding the practice of law in a modern environment. There are, however, a number of steps to achieving this. The first step is to educate prospective lawyers in the content of lawyers' obligations to their clients, the Courts, and their colleagues. It was concluded in the Cotter-Roper report that many lawyers were ignorant of the professional rules by which they were bound and insensitive to problems of professional conduct when they arose. Such ignorance or insensitivity can be overcome by ensuring that prospective lawyers are aware of the nature and content of the rules of professional conduct, have some skill in identifying situations where there are issues of professional conduct, and have the requisite analytical skills to apply the rules to the problem in hand. This is the first objective of the current work.

The objectives of teaching ethics are broader than this. The Cotter-Roper Report concluded that the objective of ethics in legal education was to ensure that candidates for admission "have developed their attitudes and values with respect to the legal profession and professional responsibility": p 61. This is much the same as the stance taken in England by the Report of the Lord Chancellor's Advisory Committee on Legal Education and Conduct *First Report on Legal Education and Training* (London, 1996). In para 1.19 it observed "lawyers need to acquire personal and professional values and standards which are *internalised* from the earliest stage of education and training". It is this inculcation of values with which academics particularly are uneasy. Despite much rhetoric, most, though not all, law teachers adhere to the view that they present information and guide criticism in a morally neutral way. Or at worst, in a way which does not intentionally seek to change the moral viewpoint of the student. It seems that the Cotter-Roper report sees the role of a teacher of legal ethics is not only to assist in the development of moral skill in prospective lawyers, but to obtain agreement to (or at least acquiescence in) a particular set of values which underpin the legal profession.

Students and practitioners continue (or perhaps properly begin) to learn of the complexities and realities of law and legal practice outside of the university. Accordingly the teaching of ethics must continue after graduation, in the vocational training and in the profession. While there is much to be gained from enabling students to contemplate some of the hard ethical problems without the pressures of practice and personal circumstances, in reality the personal and professional pressures are an integral part of ethical problems of professional practice. While the New Zealand Law Society has responded to calls for continued education in ethics by providing courses in various areas of professional ethics, these are voluntary and therefore attended by a relatively small proportion of practitioners. It may be in the future that the recently legislated power to compel practitioner education will be exercised in the area of professional ethics.

In some areas of the law it is possible to discuss and theorise without exposing oneself to criticism other than of a scholarly kind. However there are other areas in which one's personal views and beliefs are held up for scrutiny. Nowhere is this more so than in the area of professional ethics. It is not possible to isolate a theoretical discussion of legal ethics from personal conduct. This is illustrated by an anecdote regarding a class in which I was discussing the role and theoretical justifications of pro bono work. When a student raised his hand I felt quite prepared for any subtle question or theoretical challenge, but not for the actual question "how much pro bono work do you do?". After taking some moments to think, I concluded that the question was in fact very pertinent and even justified. What right did I have to theorise about pro bono work if I was not prepared to go on record and say that I practised what I preached? Students learn ethics not only from the words of their teachers, but also from their acts. As a person who is interested in the areas of professional conduct and ethics I cannot escape the fact that my personal views and actions will be the subject of scrutiny.

Acknowledgments
This work was funded by Victoria University of Wellington. I am grateful to the Centre for Legal Practice at Exeter University and to the Law Faculty at Canterbury University for their hospitality in accommodating me for some months whilst writing. The New Zealand Law Society has kindly given permission to reproduce the *New Zealand Law Society Rules of Professional Conduct for Barristers and Solicitors* as an appendix. Cassandra Treadwell was also a great help in assisting in the initial research. Thanks also to my mother, Marion Webb, for reading through drafts, and to the many friends and colleagues who made helpful suggestions and drew my attention to recent developments. Thanks also to Tania, Albert and Lewis who supported me throughout.

Duncan Webb
Wellington
March 2000

Abbreviations

A number of sources have been used repeatedly throughout the work and have been referred to in an abbreviated manner as follows.

- The New Zealand Law Society *Rules of Professional Conduct for Barristers and Solicitors* are referred to as "The rules", and rules are cited as rule *x*.
- E-DEC Limited *Purposes, Functions and Structure of Law Societies in New Zealand — Final Report to the New Zealand Law Society* 1 September 1997, is referred to as "The E-DEC report".
- The *Guide to the Professional Conduct of Solicitors* 8th edition, 1999, is referred to as "the English *Guide*".
- The American Bar Association Model Rules of Professional Conduct are referred to as "The ABA Model Rules".

Summary of contents

Table of contents

PART ONE — THEORETICAL FOUNDATIONS

PART TWO — PROFESSIONAL ORGANISATION AND CONTROL

CHAPTER 3: THE LAW SOCIETY AND ITS ROLES

CHAPTER 4: PROFESSIONAL STANDARDS

PART FIVE — DUTIES IN LEGAL PRACTICE

CHAPTER 15: DUTIES IN THE CONDUCT OF A LEGAL PRACTICE

Table of cases

Table of statutes

Part One

Theoretical Foundations

Chapter 1

The Profession and Society

1.1 Introduction

Perspectives on professions vary. Professionals will have a different perception of their role and status from the view held by members of other competing professions. Users of professional services will have a different opinion of the usefulness of those services from those who do not or cannot employ them. Frequently these views will conflict. Professionals predictably justify their position and the continuance of the status quo. Others, not least those who would usurp the position of existing professionals, attack the privileges accorded to professionals. They argue that the maintenance of the existing environment is motivated by the self-interest of those who occupy the most privileged positions.

Lawyers in particular have been the subject of considerable criticism. They have been accused of avarice, dishonesty, amoralism, cronyism, elitism, and exclusionary practices. The traditional response of lawyers does little to allay these suspicions. Lawyers have been known to defend their position by various strategies including claims that laypersons are not sufficiently informed to criticise,[1] that monopolistic practices are justified as being in the interests of the public, that they are motivated by service, and that the level of fees is necessary to ensure that they can devote themselves to their client's cause without financial concerns. Accusations of dishonesty are dismissed as isolated cases which are punished by the profession (and if criminal by the Courts).[2]

This chapter seeks to examine the sociological foundations of the opposing approaches to the place and role of the legal profession in society. Under a sociological analysis the legal profession is viewed as a social phenomenon. Its continued existence is to be explained in terms

---

1 See for example Dal Pont [1996] NZLJ 313.

2 Though the record shows the frequency of practitioners being struck off (usually for dishonesty) is: 1988 — 8; 1989 — 8; 1990 — 6; 1991 — 1; 1992 — 8; 1993 — 4; 1994 — 4; 1995 — 5; 1996 — 6; 1997 — 3; 1998 — 7 (of the 1998 incidents all involved misdealing in client funds).

of the common features and interests of its members, the place it occupies as part of the social structure and hierarchy, its function in society, and the way in which social actors use the profession for the advancement of their own goals and interests. An important school of sociological analysis of the professions, known as structural functionalism, is founded in the thinking of Durkheim.[3] That approach focuses on the role of social actors in a transformed and transforming society. It seeks to explain the professions in terms of a positive ordering force. Common values and traditions, including a commitment to service, are used to explain the bonds between members and justify the professions' existence.

Another school of thought analyses the professions in terms of the tendency of individuals to seek common goals of wealth, power, and status. Based on the founding work of Weber[4] the profession is explained in terms of the essentially egoistic ends of its members and the creation of an insulated sphere of activity in which those ends may be pursued.[5] More recent scholarship which will be considered has tended to shun the extremes of these views and seek to analyse the professions in a more pragmatic light which might be seen as drawing on aspects of both the Weberian and structural functionalist approaches.[6]

1.2 Functionalist approach

The functionalist approach generally supports the position of the professions which are considered to be of benefit to the wider community. The approach is based on the observation that many professions are undoubtedly indispensable. It is impossible to conceive of any industrialised society that does not have functionaries that fulfil the roles of doctors, lawyers, nurses, engineers and so on. Lawyers act as important intermediaries in any society: intermediaries between clients and specialised knowledge, between contracting parties, between the citizen and the state, the litigant and the Courts, and so on. Such

3 E Durkheim *The Division of Labor in Society* (trans G Simpson) New York, Free Press, 1964.

4 M Weber *Law in Economy and Society* (Max Rheinstein (ed), trans E Shils and M Rheinstein) Cambridge, Mass, Harvard University Press, 1945.

5 M Larson *The Rise of Professionalism: A Sociological Analysis* Berkeley, University of California Press, 1977, p xvi.

6 For Marxism the position of the professions as neither clearly proletariat nor clearly capitalist is problematic. See K Marx *Capital* New York, International Publishers, 1967. The disagreement lies in whether the professions are a residue of the *petite bourgeoisie* that will eventually wither away, or a growing class of necessary intermediaries between state, capital, and labour. The fundamental disagreement of theory makes a Marxist analysis of limited use and will not be explored further in this work.

functions demand specialised knowledge and skills that cannot be efficiently acquired by those directly in need of them. The roles of professionals are, therefore, unique and serve an important societal function.[7]

One of the early (and arguably less fruitful) projects of the functionalist approach to the sociology of the professions was to try to identify the features which made any particular occupation, or body of people with a like occupation, a profession.[8] This trait approach was considered important to enable the demarcation of the professional function from other less socially important occupations. Such lists generally identify factors such as specialised knowledge, restricted admission, self-regulation, loyalty to client, and professional organisation.[9] Lawyers have traditionally adopted such an approach. By identifying such distinguishing features they are able to differentiate themselves from non-professionals, and also from other professionals who occupy less privileged positions.

An approach which focuses on the functions of the profession, as conceived by the profession, has some significant shortcomings. It inevitably appears as an apology for the status quo. By identifying certain aspects of the legal profession and classifying them as essential, they argue that they are necessary. Further, in explaining the features of an institution in terms of social need and corresponding function it is but a small leap to justify the institution which satisfies the need, regardless of how effectively it does so Such an approach highlights the development of professions from their less formed predecessors. It tends to adopt a linear view of the development of the professions. This suggests that professions are improvements on their less developed predecessors and that, if anything, their defining features such as independence, altruism, and self-regulation should be enhanced.

1.2.1 *Professional power*

A defining factor of a profession on such a view is the aggregation of professional power in the hands of its members by virtue of the importance of the societal role played, and regulation of the activity

7 Some sociologists have accorded the professions an even higher place, claiming that they are the most important element in modern social order: T Parsons, "Professions" in *12 International Encyclopaedia of Social Sciences*, New York, Macmillan, 1968, p 536; and recently H Perkin *The Third Revolution: Professional Elites in the Modern World* London, Routledge, 1996.

8 These attempts have varied between an examination of traits, process, or social recognition. See S Brint, "Eliot Freidson's Contribution to the Sociology of the Professions" (1993) 20 Work and Occupations 259, 260-262.

9 This list is drawn from the Royal Commission on Legal Services (UK), "Final Report V 1" London, Her Majesty's Stationery Office, 1979, 28, 30.

being in the hands of the profession. It is undeniable that many professions, and the legal profession especially, wield considerable influence. The legal profession justifies this power in part by claiming that it is used for the benefit of citizens generally. It is claimed that the legal profession has developed as a counterbalance to other social phenomena, and in particular the state. Lawyers claim to act as a shield from and advocate against the state for their clients. In this sense the legal profession has long seen itself as a protector of human rights and the rule of law both independent of, and as an adjunct to, the Courts. To achieve this it is asserted that independence from the state, and especially from regulation or discipline by the state, is required.

However, in global terms there is little evidence that the legal profession acts as an effective bulwark against the excesses of the state. While some lawyers accept instructions to act for clients against the state, others act for the state against citizens. In this sense it seems that lawyers are politically neutral as to the relationship between state and citizen. Moreover, it cannot be said that lawyers in general seek to limit the state's power. Lawyers are diverse in the beliefs they hold and the interests they seek to promote. It can also be observed that the profession and the state are not wholly antagonistic to each other. The legal profession assists the state in making known to citizens the limits of their rights and duties, ensuring that the systems of the state run according to the state's own rules etc.[10] Moreover, the profession relies on the state to approve and enforce the profession's continued monopoly.

1.2.2 *Altruism*

Most advocates of the functionalist view claim that, left to their own devices, the professions will act in a manner that is, in sum, in the public interest. By entering into the profession the practitioner sacrifices the right to pursue self-interest. Once a member, the professional may charge a reasonable fee, but the dominant motivation is service to the client and the community. There are other benefits to the professional such as protection from unqualified competition, availability of collegial support, and free participation in the profession's governance.

As between lawyer and client the interests of the client are paramount. The profession of lawyer has traditionally been viewed as one of service. Members entered the profession ostensibly out of a commitment to the values of justice and a devotion to the calling of law. Matters such as the generation of a comfortable living and the prestige attached to the

---

10 In some senses the profession is an extension of the state. See the discussion in S Tomsen, "Professionalism and State Engagement: Lawyers and Legal Aid Policy in Australia in the 1970s and 1980s" (1992) 28 Australian and New Zealand Journal of Sociology 307.

profession appeared to be secondary to the provision of service to those who required it.

While few lawyers today would maintain that they were wholeheartedly committed to public service above all else, there remains a strong view that the work of the legal profession, both in general and as regards the work of its individual members, is of considerable benefit to society. However, it is doubtful that most lawyers have the interests of their clients foremost in their minds when they set out for the office every day. The motives of lawyers are complex and personal and therefore defy generalisation. It is probable that motives such as a comfortable income for self and family, esteem of peers, progression in the firm, status in society, engagement in meaningful work, as well as the interests of the clients all play a part.

1.2.3 *Collegiality*

The functionalist view of the legal professions sees the group "lawyers" as a distinct entity. It is regarded as a community of individuals. Not only are lawyers perceived as sharing common traits and characteristics, but also similar objectives, ideals, and aspirations. If a social actor is autonomous from the state there is a regulatory gap which is filled by membership of the profession. Professional decisions are not made in a social vacuum, but rather with recourse to the ethic of the professional group. Central to this community view of the profession is the assumption that the members of the community have significant commonalities. If it is shown that there is no substantial agreement between lawyers about their role, then the existence of this alleged community is thrown into doubt. There are some obvious similarities between lawyers: they have a common education, similar skills, and largely similar interests in maintaining the status of the profession. While the concurrence of such interests may be sufficient to establish a trade union or professional association, it could hardly be said that alone they could be the basis of a community of individuals.

Initiation into the professional group assists lawyers in achieving a sense of community. The process of admission to the bar or entry on the roll of solicitors is a rite of passage that clearly delineates members from non-members. The process is a formal one, which requires oath-taking and entry of the candidate's name on a formal and definitive roll. Unlike some other professions or quasi-professions (such as counsellors) there is little room for argument as to whether one is entitled to claim professional membership as a lawyer. Associated with this has been the adoption of particular trappings such as the lawyer's gown (although these trappings are being eroded in many jurisdictions, and have gone entirely in others).

Exclusion of others from the community of lawyers also reinforces a sense of identity. Unlike accountants and medical practitioners, lawyers have almost uniformly shunned the formation of association with other professionals within a single firm to serve their clients. While accountants have expanded their practices to include marketing, human resources, and legal advice, lawyers have not. Indeed in many jurisdictions such a practice is prohibited by the professional rules, and lawyers are prohibited from pursuing other endeavours.[11]

Despite these outward manifestations of belonging and exclusivity, and the claims of common altruistic purpose, the suggestion that lawyers are on the whole united in such a way is generally viewed with considerable scepticism. In particular there are clear divisions which separate lawyers from each other. A lawyer who is a partner in a major national firm dealing in corporate finance has far more commonality with the directors of his or her clients than with a sole practitioner whose work is mainly in legally aided family law matters.[12] Many lawyers do not ply their trade within the confines of a legal practice. More frequently lawyers act in their capacity of lawyers as employees of businesses, public interest organisations, government, and so on. Legal academics and Judges are further categories of lawyers who have only a secondary attachment to any so-called community of lawyers.

For a long time members of the profession were drawn from more or less identical backgrounds. While regarded as a meritocracy, the profession of law has historically been dominated by the upper middle (and more recently the middle) classes. Prior to the twentieth century it was largely a gentleman's profession.[13] Only those from a moderately wealthy background could afford to undertake the lean years before formal admission, whether as an articled clerk or pupil. Women were excluded from the profession entirely.[14]

More recently, however, the legal profession has become considerably more diverse with an increase in members from low income groups, women, and ethnic minorities. Consequently, there is a multiplicity of views within the profession on almost every conceivable issue. Most

---

11 See, for example, New Zealand Law Society *Rules of Professional Conduct for Barristers and Solicitors* 5th ed, Wellington, 1998, r 2.03.

12 See J Dixon, "Stratification in the Legal Profession: Sex Sector and Salary" (1995) 29 Law & Society Review 381.

13 Indeed the early English Law Society was titled "The Society of Gentlemen Practitioners of Law".

14 Women were permitted to practise in New Zealand only by virtue of the Female Law Practitioners Act 1896 and the Law Practitioners and New Zealand Law Society Acts Amendment Act 1896. The first woman admitted in New Zealand was Ethel Benjamin in 1897. For an interesting discussion of the reform of the law in this area, see G Gatfield *Without Prejudice* Wellington, Brookers, 1996.

importantly it can no longer be said that there is real agreement about the place and task of the legal profession itself. A cursory inspection of academic and practitioner journals will demonstrate that there are sharp divisions and disagreements about the role of lawyers, how their role is best effected, the governance of lawyers, and indeed the very existence of the legal profession in its current form. Some are rightly sceptical about whether there was ever a true community of legal professionals. Few can seriously maintain that such a community exists today.

1.2.4 *Self-governance*

Historically, the legal profession has been left to regulate itself. The functionalist approach claims the legal profession requires and has been accorded autonomy to fulfil its important and specialised function in society. That autonomy enables it to devise rules that fit the work of its members, and to mete out appropriate disciplinary measures to those who breach the rules.[15] If we accept the functionalist view, the claim that lawyers should be free from outside regulation seems a reasonable one.

Self-regulation is also justified by the claim that such regulation requires complete and specialised knowledge held only by lawyers. The functionalist view sees the lawyer as fulfilling particular roles within a given social structure. It is undoubtedly true that lawyers fill an indispensable social role and that their expertise is needed because the law and its associated procedures are complex. However, lawyers make a leap of logic and claim that the nature of a lawyer's role is similarly complex, and that lay people cannot understand the subtleties of the lawyer's role and therefore ought not be entitled to participate in any rule-making process. It is claimed:[16]

> As one of the hallmarks of professionalism is special skill and learning, it is difficult to see how those without such skill and learning can understand the role and responsibilities of lawyers and draft rules that reflect this.

The second justification for self-regulation is the need for an independent legal profession to protect citizens against excesses of the

---

15 See R Angal and S Payne, "The Law: Professional Autonomy and the Public Interest" in P Boreham et al (eds) *The Professions in Australia — A Critical Appraisal* St Lucia, University of Queensland Press, 1976, 110-133 where the authors reject the suggestion that uncontrolled self-regulation is in the public interest.

16 G Dal Pont, "Drafting Rules of Professional Conduct" [1996] NZLJ 313, 313. See also P Thomas and G Mungham, "Solicitors and Clients: Altruism of Self Interest" in *The Sociology of the Professions Lawyers Doctors and Others* (R Dingwall and P Lewis eds) London, MacMillan, 1983, 131, 149.

state.[17] It has already been noted that it is by no means clear that lawyers do act in any concerted way as a protector of citizens against the state. They act for both citizen and state, and have an interest in cooperating with the state to ensure the continuance of their legislatively endorsed monopoly.

Any justification of self-governance is dependent on the truth of the claim that the prime motivation for lawyers is the protection of the public interest. If democratically elected politicians or appointed bureaucrats are more likely to regulate the legal profession in the public interest, then the governance of the legal profession should be in the hands of those actors rather than the lawyers themselves. There is a natural suspicion that lawyers will make rules which will be in their own interest in the long run. It is clear that some rules for the protection of the public from unscrupulous lawyers do exist — if this were not the case the state would be quick to step in and fill the regulatory gap. It is arguable that lawyers' rules do little more than weed out unwanted members of the profession, and protect the status quo. An historical view would suggest that until recently lawyers have been incredibly successful in eliminating or incorporating competitors, keeping rules protecting the public to a minimum, and excluding the public from easy access to the law.[18]

1.2.5 *Professional autonomy*

Not only is the profession in general free from outside interference, but to a large degree each lawyer acts autonomously. On this view, the role of a professional requires a degree of independence in professional life which is absent in most other commercial or bureaucratic relationships. Each member of the profession is individually responsible to the profession for his or her actions, whether acting within a firm of professionals, as a member of a business organisation, or as a sole practitioner. The decision making of professionals is considered to be

---

17 See for example the preamble to the New York State Bar Association Code of Professional Responsibility as amended in 1996 (New York State Bar Association, New York, 1970) [http://www.nysba.org/opinions/codes/anchor1.html]. This view was also articulated by A N Whitehead in *Adventures of Ideas* Cambridge, Cambridge University Press, 1933, 73.

18 Indeed Max Weber observed of lawyers that: "Whenever legal education has been in the hands of practitioners, especially attorneys, who have made admission to practise a guild monopoly, an economic factor, namely their pecuniary interest, brings to bear as strong influence upon the process not only of stabilising the official law and of adapting it to changing needs in an exclusively empirical way of also presenting its rationalisation through legislation or legal science" Max Weber *Law in Economy and Society* (trans A M Henderson et al) Cambridge, Mass, Harvard University Press, 1954, 202. M Larson *The Rise of Professionalism: a Sociological Analysis* Berkeley, University of California Press, 1977.

independent from the organisation within which they work. A lawyer is answerable to the profession for acts undertaken on a client's instructions. A lawyer, therefore, is expected to exercise independent professional judgment when accepting or rejecting the instructions of a client.

1.2.6 *Conclusion*

The structural functionalist view of the profession has increasingly come under attack. However, the ideal of professionalism at the centre of this view has proven surprisingly resilient. It seems that the concept may be adjusted to fit modern conditions, but it is not likely to disappear altogether immediately. The predictions of one commentator, made in 1988, so far seem accurate:[19]

> Professionals — in the sense that both champions and critics have used the concept during the last two centuries — will not disappear. It will persist as both a nostalgic ideal and a source of legitimisation for increasingly anachronistic practices, although it will lose considerable credibility. It will continue to reflect the experience of a dwindling elite. ... For the mass of lawyers, however, occupational life will mean either employment by a large bureaucracy, dependence on a public paymaster, or competition within an increasingly free market. Whichever they choose, these lawyers no longer will enjoy the distinctive privileges of professionals — control over the market for their services and high social status. The age of professionalism is ending.

1.3 Market model — Weberian perspectives

1.3.1 *Introduction*

A more sceptical view of the motivations of lawyers starts from the assumption that lawyers have motivations similar to any other social actor: they are presumed to seek to satisfy their own preferences. Overall these preferences will tend towards the maximisation of things commonly regarded as advantages: wealth, status, and social and political power. Such a view strikes at the foundations of a functionalist approach. Any purportedly altruistic action is recast in terms of long-run benefits, and claims to self-regulation are viewed as efforts to effect the perpetuation of hegemony and the exclusion of competition. Moreover, there is a deep-rooted suspicion that the immense complexity of the law and its procedures is at least in part generated and maintained by lawyers as a disincentive to the public from proceeding without legal assistance. Similarly, professional associations and the accompanying affectations of office collapse into a facade, which has been used to elevate the status of members of the profession on illusory grounds.

---

19 R Abel, "England and Wales: A Comparison of the Professional Projects of Barristers and Solicitors" in R Abel and P Lewis *Lawyers in Society vol 1: The Common Law World* Berkeley, University of California Press, 1988, 66.

There is no suggestion of any conspiratorial collusion on this analysis. While it is suggested that the efforts of lawyers tend in general to strengthen their own position, any coordination of individuals is created by naturally similar preferences. This has inevitably led to the forming of groups such as law societies and bar associations that assist in the coordination of lawyers' efforts. Many of the members of the profession are likely to agree with the functional/altruistic analysis of the lawyer's role — few would overtly identify themselves as self-centred egoists. However, the altruistic model is inevitably used and developed in a way which, perhaps unconsciously, serves the interests of those who have control of the rule-making process. There may well be a degree of innocent self-deception on the part of members of a profession who perceive the protection of their own position as in the public interest.

1.3.2 *Creation of demand*

The law is substantively and procedurally complex and has been largely developed by lawyers. Lawyers benefit considerably from this complexity because it creates a considerable demand for their services. While there have been some moves to make it easier for non-lawyers to be aware of and exercise their rights[20] the law remains largely inaccessible to most citizens. This is not to say that lawyers complicate the law in a calculated fashion. Certainly some areas of the law, such as the law of secured transactions, are necessarily complex. However, even in non-technical areas of the law the language developed by lawyers is jargonistic and the concepts frequently complicated. Important areas of the law have arguably been rendered obscure and difficult by the development of technical language and fine distinctions, when it is essential that it be knowable to all citizens. The complexity of the criminal law and the proliferation of offences created by rule and regulation is a prime example.

Professional services are dependent on the recipient having a high regard for the deliverers of the service and perceiving a need for the service itself. If the profession is lowly regarded, consumers will be reluctant to pay high fees, and be suspicious of the quality of the advice or other service delivered. Conversely, if the profession and its members are highly regarded and membership of the profession is considered a mark of rank or class, then it is likely that the profession will be successful and its members left to conduct their own affairs. Prospective clients have to believe that they will be better off with the assistance of a lawyer than

20 One example is the conscious shift to "plain English" in law drafting wherever possible. Similarly the Disputes Tribunal, constituted under the Disputes Tribunals Act 1988, prohibits the attendance of lawyers under s 38(2) unless exceptional circumstances exist. Also there has been a growth in do-it-yourself guides on some areas of the law such as will drafting, and trusts.

without. The market for legal services is enhanced if lay people are overawed by legal problems, and they consider that lawyers are able to effect positive results where they would be unable to by themselves. It is at least arguable that there are situations in which a lawyer's assistance is either not helpful, or in fact detrimental: where the claim is small the costs of legal assistance may exceed the benefit of enforcing rights; where the problem is simple and the client, could effectively resolve it themselves; where lawyerly intervention is an impediment to settlement. While some lawyers will advise in such situations that their assistance is an unnecessary expense, it is obviously difficult for lawyers to recognise their own superfluity.

While adherents to the functional approach accept unquestioningly that there is a need for professional assistance, others question whether the need for such specialised knowledge is not itself a result of the existence of the professionals themselves.[21] It is in the interests of any profession to persuade the public that the skill and knowledge possessed is both needed by the public and unattainable without the assistance of the professional. The previous flourishing of a number of professions which provided little real assistance bears testimony to the ability of a well organised group to persuade the public of the utility of its services which proves illusory.[22]

1.3.3 *Limiting entry*

It is widely believed that the legal profession is a route to wealth, power, and status. There will, therefore, be a large number of people seeking to become lawyers. The more lawyers who are available to provide a professional service, the lower the price for such a professional service will be. A similar reduction in the status of the profession and its influence is also likely. The realist argues, therefore, that lawyers move to protect their market by limiting the entry of new members. Weber observed in respect of this aspect of professions:[23]

> Both the extent and the methods of regulation and exclusion in relation to outsiders may vary widely, so that the transition from a state of openness to one of regulation and closure is gradual. Various conditions of participation may be laid down: qualifying tests, a period of probation, requirement of

---

21 E Freidson *Professional Powers: A study of the Institutionalization of Formal Knowledge* Chicago, Chicago University Press, 1986.

22 A prime example is the medical profession prior to the turn of the century when any improvement in a patient's condition was more likely due to chance than the doctor's intervention: W J Goode, "Encroachment, Charlatanism, and the Emerging Professions: Psychology, Sociology and Medicine" (1960) 25 American Sociological Review 902, 912. In pre-industrial society the role of the witchdoctor or cleric might similarly be questioned.

23 M Weber *The Theory of Social and Economic Organisation* (A M Henderson and T Parsons trans) New York, Free Press, 1947, 142.

> possession of a share which can be purchased under certain conditions, election of new members by ballot or eligibility by birth or by virtues of achievements open to anyone.

Certainly, it is easier to become qualified as a lawyer today than it has been in the past. Significant formal and informal barriers still exist. The abundance of would-be lawyers is readily apparent from the proportionately high enrolments (and high rejection rate of aspiring students) in law schools in comparison with the size of the legal profession.[24] Although New Zealand barriers to entry in to the profession are not high by international standards, they still pose considerable hurdles to aspiring lawyers.[25] Once candidates have completed the university study they must still undergo a 13-week intensive professional course.[26]

Moreover, the content of the university education has often been criticised as theoretical and esoteric. Much of the information taught in law schools is not used in everyday practice. It is arguable that university legal education is not aimed at providing skills for practice notwithstanding that the Council for Legal Education (which is composed more or less entirely of lawyers) determines the content of the degree.[27] Little of a solicitor's practice involves the application of legal knowledge gained at university. Far more frequently employed are skills that have been acquired on-the-job such as drafting, negotiating, interviewing, delegating, and marketing.

If this is true, it must be asked what benefit aspiring lawyers and the public get from the arduous academic barriers to becoming a lawyer. Weber was forthright in rejecting the usefulness of formal educational

---

24 C Parker, "An Oversupply of Law Graduates: Putting the Statistics in Context" (1993) 4 Legal Education Review 255 (for an Australian perspective).

25 These include high fees, limitation of entry into courses and the length of time taken to complete the degree. The UN *Basic Principles on the Role of Lawyers* provides "There is to be no discrimination of any kind against a person with respect to entry into or continued practice within the legal profession, except that a requirement that a lawyer must be a national of the country concerned shall not be considered discriminatory". An earlier draft had provided that discrimination should include the grounds of race, colour, sex, ethnic origin, religion, political or other opinion, national or social origin, economic or other status.

26 Costing $3800 plus GST in 1999.

27 Section 31 of the Law Practitioners Act 1982 provided that the Council will comprise: two Judges of the High Court, a District Court Judge, four persons to be appointed on the recommendation of the Council of the New Zealand Law Society, the Deans of the Faculties of Law, and one person to be appointed on the recommendation of the Council of the New Zealand Law Students' Association Incorporated.

requirements with strict curriculum. He claimed that the reason for such claims was:[28]

> ... not a suddenly awakened "thirst for education" but the desire for restricting the supply of these positions and their monopolization by the owners of educational certificates. Today the "examination" is the universal means of this monopolization, and therefore examinations irresistibly advance.

In any event qualification for admission by no means guarantees a career in legal practice. It is necessary to secure employment in a law firm. Many law firms have a hierarchical structure and few junior lawyers are expected to progress far up the hierarchy.[29] It is in the interests of law firms that there is a large pool of graduates available the best of which they can select as employees. It is expected that many lawyers who begin work in a law firm will find that they do not have the required qualities for law practice (at least in that environment) and will seek to use their talents elsewhere. There is a significant attrition of lawyers who leave the profession in the first few years of practice.

At the top of the profession the main tool of closure is the partnership. A common conception is that an employed lawyer in a firm is working towards being a partner in a law firm. The idea of a lawyer perpetually being an employee is not one that the culture of the profession has readily adopted. To reach the full professional status of a partner it is necessary to be accepted by the existing partners and frequently to buy a portion of the value of the firm. This has predictably led to a perpetuation of existing gender and ethnicity imbalances in established law firms. For example, surveys consistently show men to be far more likely to stay in the profession and become partners in firms than their women counterparts.[30]

1.3.4 *Limiting substitutable services*

Lawyers are also seen as protecting their dominance in the market for legal services by excluding others from providing similar services and

---

28 M Weber *From Max Weber* (H H Gerth and C W Mills eds) London, Routledge, 1964, p 241.

29 There is a particularly high rate of exit from the profession at an early stage for women. See G Gatfield *Without Prejudice* Wellington, Brookers, 1996, 157 which shows rates of up to 18.85 women leaving the profession (in 1990) for every 100 practising certificates held. This compares with the high of 7.94 (in 1989) for men.

30 G Gatfield and Alison Gray *Women Lawyers in New Zealand* 1993 shows that men were three times as likely to be partners in a law firm than women. In 1995 practising certificates issued by the New Zealand Law Society show that 88.7% of principals (partners or sole practitioners) were men and 11.3% women: G Gatfield *Without Prejudice* Wellington, Brookers, 1996, 135.

thus ensuring that its members are the only people able to provide the services required. From the turn of the century up until a few years ago lawyers had been particularly effective at precluding other professionals from providing the services supplied by lawyers. Indeed s 63 of the Law Practitioners Act 1982 makes it an offence to practise as a solicitor unless properly admitted — a prohibition that the Law Society has been quick to enforce.[31] Historically, there was a number of law-related professionals including doctors of law, serjeants, barristers, scriveners, attorneys, procurators, conveyancers, pleaders, solicitors and notaries. The domain of these various professionals was determined according to their professed skills and the Court jurisdiction in which they operated. These roles had, by the turn of the century either withered away or been enveloped by the professions of barrister and solicitor.[32] Lawyers have managed to expand their domain into areas of activity traditionally occupied by others, and seek to continue this trend as they expand their own practices, and limit the expansion of non-lawyers.[33]

The reasons for the eventual dominance of barristers and solicitors are difficult to explain in terms of benefit to the public. While previously there was considerable specialisation in legal tasks, and some competition between the professions, such inter-profession rivalry no longer exists. There was, of course, a massive rationalisation of the legal system of England in the latter part of the nineteenth century prompted by serious problems that had become apparent. Predominance of barristers and solicitors may also be attributable to their superior organisation (by the Inns of Court and the Society of Gentlemen Practisers respectively) and the legislative recognition and control of solicitors.[34]

It is interesting to observe the apparent rise of new legal professionals. There are moves to reintroduce a profession of conveyancers who can undertake property transactions outside a firm of solicitors.[35]

---

31 See for example *Auckland District Law Society v Dempster* [1995] 1 NZLR 210 where the Auckland District Law Society had injuncted Dempster from acting as a solicitor in land conveyances. See also *Dempster v Registrar-General of Land* [1997] 2 NZLR 609. See also ss 54 and 64-67 of the Law Practitioners Act 1982.

32 T Plucknutt *A Concise History of the Common Law* London, Butterworth & Co, 5th ed, 1956, 215-230.

33 N D Israel, "Multidisciplinary Practices" [1996] NZLJ 381, J W Hayes *Multi-Disciplinary Practices* Proceedings of the 9th Commonwealth Law Conference.

34 2 Geo II (1729). See generally W S Holdsworth *A History of English Law* London, Methuen & Co, 1937, vol XII, 54.

35 Conveyancers Bill 1998, recent proposals for the reform of the structure and functions of the law society would also see the introduction of a separate profession of conveyancers regulated initially by the law society, see Letter, President of the Law Society to all practitioners, 20 October 1999 and the attached paper.

Accountants have also made incursions into the role of lawyers in the area of legal advice concerning taxation and business planning. In response to this lawyers have also sought to extend their own areas of practice into that of other professionals though not without resistance from those other professionals. An ongoing area of dispute is the objection of real estate agents to lawyers acting as agents in the sale of real estate pursuant to an exception in the statutory monopoly given to real estate agents.[36] The existence of such disputes is indicative of the tensions between professional groups who seek to protect, and if possible expand, their monopoly markets.

The clearest monopoly of lawyers in New Zealand is the right of audience in the Courts. While a litigant who is a natural person may appear on his or her own behalf, only barristers may act as the agent for another in Court proceedings.[37] Indeed any body corporate must employ the services of a barrister to be heard in a Court and may not be represented by an employee or officer.[38] The claimed justification of these limits is the difficulty of establishing the authority of an employee or officer to bind the litigant, and the need for advocates to be experts. Justifications for such limitations are generally phrased in terms of protecting the administration of justice and ensuring that advocates are versed in the procedures of the Court and certified as fit persons to represent others.

1.3.5 *Enhancing status*

Status is widely regarded as intrinsically valuable. Indeed, it is sometimes difficult to understand why there are so many aspiring lawyers who embark on the arduous qualification process except in terms of the status of the mantle "lawyer". Adam Smith (a lawyer himself and a defender of the professions) commented:[39]

> To excel in any profession, in which but few arrive at mediocrity, is the most decisive mark of what is called genius or superior talents. The public admiration which attends upon such distinguished abilities makes always a part of their reward; a greater or smaller in proportion as it is higher or lower in degree. It makes a considerable part of that reward in the profession of physic; a still greater perhaps in that of law; in poetry and philosophy it makes almost the whole.

---

36 Section 16, Real Estate Agents Act 1976. See, for example, *Lewis v Real Estate Institute of New Zealand* [1995] 3 NZLR 385.

37 Sections 54 and 61, Law Practitioners Act 1982. Occasionally a litigant may be assisted by a "McKenzie Friend": *Mihaka v Police* [1981] 1 NZLR 54; *McKenzie v McKenzie* [1970] 3 All ER 1034; *Collier v Hicks* (1831) 2 B & Ad 663.

38 See *Harrison v Guardian Assurance Co Ltd* [1988] 1 NZLR 59; *Re G J Mannix Ltd* [1984] 1 NZLR 309 (CA); *Tritonia Ltd v Equity and Law Life Assurance Society* [1943] AC 584.

39 *The Wealth of Nations* Book 1 Chapter X.

Professionals defend their claim to status as necessary to effectively discharge their functions. To gain the trust of clients and the ear of a Judge, lawyers must be recognised as trustworthy. Associated to status is a need for a commensurate income.[40]

The factors that contribute to the status of lawyers are many and varied and include distinctive dress, admission procedures, and clear position in a hierarchical professional organisation. The perception of the work undertaken as intellectually demanding, requiring skill and special judgment will also be a factor. In fact, most of the work of lawyers does not fit such a description; arguably this is largely how clients perceive it. The fact that it is difficult to become a lawyer will also contribute to the status. There are numerous people who failed to reach the standard required for admission to the bar, or partnership in a firm, suggesting (not necessarily accurately) that those who did reach the standards imposed are of a better calibre than those who did not.

The nature of the professionals' clients will also affect the way in which they are perceived. Lawyers have generally acted for individuals rather than the state or other professionals. It has been suggested that this has given them considerably more status than other professionals such as social workers or nurses.[41] Also relevant is the fact that clients of lawyers have traditionally been wealthy and influential individuals or organisations. This is perhaps mirrored in the way in which various practitioners are viewed by their peers. Those who practise in large law firms regard themselves as working in the "premier" segment of the legal market. Conversely, sole and criminal practitioners with largely legally-aided criminal clients are regarded by some as of a generally lower standing.

Adding to the prestige of the profession is the fact that its members often rise to positions of considerable power and influence in government and public life. In particular, politics has traditionally had a large proportion of legally qualified participants. Lawyers have also led a number of extremely high-profile political and civil rights causes. Such achievements of lawyers in the public eye undoubtedly reflect well on the way lawyers are perceived in general.

---

40 Adam Smith argued: "We trust our health to the physician: our fortune and sometimes our life and reputation to the lawyer and attorney. Such confidence could not safely be reposed in people of a very mean or low condition. Their reward must be such, therefore, as may give them that rank in the society which so important a trust requires." *The Wealth of Nations* Book 1 Chapter X.

41 M S Larson *The Rise of Professionalism* Berkeley, University of California Press, 1977.

The other side of lawyers' status is the widespread belief that lawyers are poorly regarded by clients. While it is true that lawyers in general are not as highly regarded as a number of other professionals, paradoxically, individual lawyers are held in particularly high esteem by their own clients. While members of the public may disparage lawyers, their own lawyer is usually excluded from such generalisations.[42] This discrimination by the public between lawyers can be turned to lawyers' advantage. When there are instances of misconduct they are labelled as exceptional cases and blame is placed on the moral flaws of the individuals concerned rather than the role of lawyers generally, or the system of rules within which they act. Some deny that instances of defalcation and the like are at the heart of the way in which lawyers are viewed, calling this a fallacy.[43]

1.3.6 *Conclusion*

On the Weberian approach, the professions generally and the legal profession in particular are seen as a vehicle used by members to effect particular ends. The legal profession can be said to be engaged in an ongoing project to enhance the wealth, status, and power of its members. The problem with this Weberian approach is twofold. First, it is not at all clear that the motivation behind the actions of the legal profession are so blatantly aimed at the goals of wealth, status, and power. Lawyers may indeed have wealth, status, and power, however, it is by no means clear that these are the sole or dominant motives of individual lawyers. The actions of members may be quite differently motivated. Indeed many practitioners (and especially those active in the professional organisation) express a commitment to the altruistic aims of the profession and it is perhaps too cynical to suggest that such altruism is a Machiavellian cloak for self-interest. The second problem with the market approach is that it fails to explain recent changes in the profession such as the loss of the status of the profession, drop in incomes of lower earners, and erosion of the power of the profession. If the market model once did reflect professional reality (and it is suggested that to an extent it did) things have changed, and such a model needs to be adjusted to current realities.

1.4 The new profession of law

1.4.1 *Professional transformation*

A sociological analysis ideally supplies not only a descriptive framework by which to view social phenomena like the legal profession, but also is

42 See generally MRL Research Group *Polls of the Profession and the Public – Summary — The New Zealand Law Society* Wellington, 1997 for data on the perception of the profession.

43 T Dare, "Legal Ethics and Legal Education" [1997] NZLJ 311.

able to predict the development of the profession. In both respects the sociological theories discussed have had only limited success. The profession is currently undergoing a period of rapid change, much of which does not fit neatly into any particular sociological framework. There are real difficulties in maintaining either the functionalist or Weberian/market view of the profession in the current environment. The former is not persuasive, though the latter, while explaining some historical phenomena, misrepresents the current nature of the profession.

Some commentators take the view that the heyday of the professions is over. While the functions performed by lawyers, doctors and other professionals are still of central importance, the organised and collective power of professional organisations is at an end.[44] Many lawyers would agree that the profession has undergone such change over the past half-century that it is now radically different, with a changed place in society.[45] Much of the market power of lawyers has been diluted by a number of factors, including the increase in the number of practitioners, the consequent preparedness of lawyers to compete against each other, and pressure from the state and the public on lawyers to price competitively.[46] A number of trends in this regard can be observed which will now be discussed.[47]

1.4.2 *Growth of the profession*

There has been a considerable growth in the numbers of legal practitioners, and the number of people seeking to enter legal practice.[48] The possible reasons for this are numerous. The movement of the qualifying authority from the profession and Judges to the universities, and the acceptance of practitioners being admitted without practical experience has meant that qualification in law was not dependent on first

44 See, for example, E Krause *Death of the Guilds: Professions, States and the Advance of Capitalism* New Haven, Yale University Press, 1996, contradicting the views in H Perkin *The Third Revolution: Professional Elites in the Modern World* London, Routledge, 1996.

45 For an examination of change in the Australian Profession see D Weisbrot, "Competition, Cooperation and Legal Change" (1993) 4 Legal Educ Rev 1.

46 See E Freidson *Professional Powers: A Study of the Institutionalization of Formal Knowledge* Chicago, University of Chicago Press, 1986, 109-130.

47 See generally S Roach Anleu, "The Legal Profession in the United States and Australia — Deprofessionalisation or Reorganization" (1992) 19 Work and Occupations 184.

48 In 1979 3817 practising certificates were issued by the NZLS. In 1998 that number had risen to 7985. Similarly in 1979 there were 315 admissions to the bar. In 1998 there were 826 admissions: Law Society Annual Reports (older reports are cited in G Gatfield *Without Prejudice* Wellington, Brookers, 1996, tables A7 and A8).

securing a position within the profession.[49] This shift was enhanced by the growth and increased availability of university education, which might be seen as commencing in the 1960s. Growth may also be attributed to the increased participation of women in the profession. Female graduates equalled male graduates in law in New Zealand in 1989 for the first time and now frequently outnumber male graduates.[50] Women equalled men in new admissions to the bar in 1993, although notably they comprise only around 32 per cent of the profession in total.[51]

A consequence of the growth in the profession and greater ease of entry to the profession is a diversification of the profession. People from all backgrounds and walks of life become lawyers. The result is that lawyers hold diverse views in all areas and have divergent and often conflicting political views. No longer is there the degree of consensus that once existed in the profession. A recent phenomenon is the grouping together of lawyers into interest groups such as Maori or women to form a vehicle for the representation of the interests that are particular to that group.[52] Whether the professional organisation is robust enough to accommodate the views of its diverse members whilst retaining its strong position is yet to be seen.[53]

1.4.3 *Erosion of insulation from market forces*

The growth of numbers in the profession has led to the erosion of the cartel-like profession of some years ago.[54] Professional etiquette and

---

49 Although these developments predated the rapid growth in the profession. See B Coote, "Qualifications for Admission to the Legal Profession in New Zealand: A Brief History" (1996) 17 NZULR 140.

50 See G Gatfield *Without Prejudice* Wellington, Brookers, 1996, table A1 complied from various official statistics.

51 See G Gatfield *Without Prejudice* Wellington, Brookers, 1996, tables A7 and A8. The NZLS Annual Report for 1998 showed the gender split in the issue of practising certificates to be 68% male and 32% female. For a discussion of the possible reasons for the continued disparity see R Abel, "Between the Market and the State: The Legal Profession in Turmoil" (1989) 52 MLR 285 288-289 which though dated and from an English perspective contains useful insights.

52 There are numerous examples. Most districts have a group of women lawyers such as the Wellington Women Lawyers' Associations. There is also a Women's Consultative Group which is an ad hoc committee of the NZLS. Te Hunga Roia Maori O Aotearoa is a national group representing Maori lawyers. There is also an Auckland Gay and Lesbian Lawyers Group.

53 See J Van Hoy, "Intraprofessional Politics and Professional Regulations: A Case Study of the ABA Commission on Professionalism" (1993) 20 Work and Occupations 90, 107. For the experience of a senior Canadian woman practitioner see C Curtis, "Alternate Visions of the Legal Profession in Society: A Perspective on Ontario" (1995) 33 Alberta LR 787.

54 See generally W Reece Smith, "Professionalism and Commercialism in the Practice of Law" Proceedings of the 9th Commonwealth Law Conference 1990, 213.

regulation previously prevented competition between practitioners even to the extent of prohibiting the public offering of free work such as wills, prescribing the content of signage for premises, and entirely prohibiting advertising.[55] These restrictions have been steadily removed until the rules focus on proper conduct rather than limiting competition.[56] This has inevitably led to considerable competition between firms for market share in the respective markets.

This competition has perhaps contributed to the considerable changes in the way in which firms are organised and operate, from the mergers of large firms, association of medium-sized firms into alliances, and proliferation of suburban branch offices and small practices.[57] This has in turn meant that lawyers have had to spend time and energy on managing and marketing legal services to ensure that they retain old clients and attract sufficient new ones to stay in practice. There is a corresponding interest in the acquisition of skills in practice management and in larger firms the employment of specialist managers and chief executive officers is commonplace.

Lawyers are also increasingly having to compete with non-lawyer professionals who are offering services the same as or substitutable for services offered by lawyers. Accountants, for example, are willing providers of quality advice in taxation, corporate structures, issues of securities, and the like. Professional mediators and employment advocates have also taken over some of the role of dispute resolution that lawyers have traditionally occupied. Lawyers have responded in a number of ways including increasing their skills in areas such as mediation and dispute resolution, seeking to provide comprehensive quality services in areas that are open to outside competition, or specialising in areas in which competition is limited.

1.4.4 *State-funded assistance*

While legal aid is not a large source of income for the profession as a whole, there is a section of the profession whose income is comprised largely of fees paid for by legal aid. Fees paid under legal aid are generally lower than would be paid by a non-legally aided client. Consequently, those areas of practice in which clients are funded most frequently by

---

55 See generally NZLS, "Rules Governing the Conduct of Practitioners", 1969, part D.

56 Rule 4.01 provides: "Advertisements to or any other communications with any person relating to the services of a practitioner or of a firm of practitioners must be consistent with the maintenance of proper professional standards".

57 For recent trends in the New Zealand legal profession see D Arcus and R Arcus, "Professional Partnership Palpitations", paper delivered at the New Zealand Law Conference 1999. That paper showed a recent trend to sole practice fuelled by high achievers leaving firms, and low achievers being forced out.

legal aid, such as family and criminal work, are less lucrative.[58] This leads to a division in the profession between practitioners who work in such areas and those who concentrate on more profitable retainers.

1.4.5 *Declining autonomy*

While the profession in New Zealand still retains considerable autonomy over its own rules and processes, trends in other jurisdictions and pressures within New Zealand suggest that increased intervention in the regulation of the profession is likely.[59] The advent of the Legal Services Ombudsman in England and the Legal Services Commissioner in New South Wales are examples of the creation by legislation of offices to regulate the governance and discipline of the profession. Other government agencies such as the Commerce Commission are increasingly taking an interest in the conduct of the profession and dispelling any hope that the legal profession will not be touched by the regulation of anti-competitive practices.

1.4.6 *The learned profession*

While the foregoing demonstrates that there has been a shift in the nature of the practice of law it is premature to suggest that the profession is dead. The traditional indicators of a profession may no longer be apparent; however, the body of lawyers is still distinct and vibrant. While it may no longer seek to be thought of as the altruistic and independent body that it was previously regarded as, it is still accepted as a learned profession by society. This perhaps demonstrates the futility of attempting to pin down the defining features of an essentially fluid social institution.

1.5 A renegotiated professionalism

While something is to be learned from the functionalist and market views outlined above they may be criticised as over-simplistic. We may accept that lawyers are normal people and seek to lead lives that are rewarding and fulfilling to themselves, however, it is difficult to accept that this means that they are avaricious and overtly self-serving. Similarly, we reject the naive idealism of the functional model. Few people are wholly altruistic. It is, however, necessary to take into account the fact that the legal profession is only viable because individual lawyers

58 J Dixon, "Stratification in the Legal Profession: Sex Sector and Salary" (1995) 29 Law & Society Review 381. See also S Tomsen, "Professionalism and State Engagement: Lawyers and Legal Aid Policy in Australia in the 1970s and 1980s" (1992) 28 Australian and New Zealand Journal of Sociology 307.

59 Most recently there has been a suggestion that the rules made by the society would be supervised by the Minister of Justice. See Letter, President of the Law Society to all practitioners, 20 October 1999, and the attached paper.

are committed to the service of their clients as well as their own professional advancement. The motivations of any individual will be distorted if an attempt is made to reduce them to a single precept. It is necessary to look to both the short-term and long-term impacts of a practitioner's decision: the need to gain the cooperation of others; the desire to prefer oneself; the need to strengthen a beneficial framework of rules; and the impulse to break those rules when an advantage can be gained. In short, the motivations of a lawyer will be ridden with tensions which are continually being balanced.

Perhaps a more moderate view of the profession is appropriate. The fact that privileges are accorded to lawyers in terms of self-regulation and monopoly rights needs to be recognised. However, such privileges may be justified on a pragmatic basis. The legal profession generally changes with community expectations. It is widely accepted that some degree of protectionism is consistent with the continued health of the profession to ensure that there is a sufficient supply of legal services. There is no immediately apparent alternative to a responsibly regulated legal profession.

1.6 Social compact

One way of viewing the relationships between lawyers and the rest of society is as a kind of social compact or covenant. By and large, society is happy to relinquish control over the legal profession. This is done on the understanding that lawyers will act within a particular professional framework — one that approximates the functionalist ideology of altruism.[60] There are good reasons for lawyers to agree to enter into such an arrangement. If they accept the professional mantle, they are given not only a degree of status and autonomy which would be difficult to acquire elsewhere, but also a comfortable living:[61] It is only to be expected that the profession will tend to seek an arrangement that will favour the interests of its members, and will seek to perpetuate the power and systems upon which lawyers' privileged position depends.[62]

A contractual analogy is useful as it reflects an element of reciprocity that is central to the concessions given to lawyers.[63] Those concessions

60 C Menkel-Meadow in S Parker and S Sampford *Legal Ethics and Legal Practice: Contemporary Issues* Oxford, Clarendon Press, 1995, pp 39-40. Also Paterson in the same volume.

61 See the comments of A Smith *The Wealth of Nations* Book 5, ch 1, Part 3, art II.

62 R Granfield, "Lawyers and Power — Reproduction and Resistance in the Legal Profession" (1996) 30 Law & Society Review 205.

63 See C Parker, "Converting the Lawyers: The Dynamics of Competition and Accountability Reform" (1997) 33 Australian & New Zealand Journal of

of regulation, competition, and the like, are in consideration of lawyers acting in a manner which is in the interests of the system of justice and the community. Lawyers in general accept that there is a public interest element in what they do. This is apparent in the things that they see as of concern to the profession. In a recent survey some of the main issues lawyers saw as confronting the profession were delays in the Court system, dishonesty of some lawyers, and inadequate access to Courts or alternate dispute resolution for some members of the community.[64] The same survey also showed lawyers to be concerned about far more inward looking matters such as threats of competition, and the costs of fidelity fund levies.[65] Despite the perception of public attitudes, that survey showed an increased public belief that lawyers were concerned about meeting the community's needs for legal services.[66]

The relationship between the legal profession and society is one of continuing dialogue. The tacitly accepted framework of public service and professional responsibility is continually shifting. As the privileges and freedoms granted to the profession are revisited, then so must be the restrictions on the pursuit of self-interest by lawyers within the professional framework. Essential to the current model is the fact that the profession is left to organise itself in the best interests of the community. The actions of the profession need not be wholly altruistic, nor short-sighted. Some aspects of the profession, which are overtly advantageous to lawyers (such as high fees or the advocate's monopoly), may be justified in the larger picture These reasons might include the need to attract gifted people to the profession, and to enable control over the quality of the service provided.

While the terms of the compact between society and profession has changed over time, the legal profession is still accorded considerable

---

Sociology 39 for a discussion of change in the Australian profession and the role of dialogue in that change.

64 MRL Research Group *Polls of the Profession and the Public — Summary — The New Zealand Law Society* Wellington, 1997: 75% of lawyers surveyed thought this to be "a problem", 13% of lawyers surveyed thought delays in the Court system to be "one of the most important problems", 93% of lawyers surveyed thought dishonesty to be "a problem", 10% of lawyers surveyed thought dishonesty to be "one of the most important problems", 68% of lawyers surveyed thought access to the Courts to be "a problem", 10% of lawyers surveyed thought this to be "one of the most important problems".

65 72% of lawyers surveyed thought threats of competition to be "a problem", 16% of lawyers surveyed thought this to be "one of the most important problems". 62% of lawyers surveyed thought costs of fidelity fund levies to be "a problem", 13% of lawyers surveyed thought this to be "one of the most important problems".

66 The latest survey showed 54% of people thought this to be the case, compared with 47% of those surveyed in a 1987 report.

privileges. There is no challenge to the monopoly on the right to appear before the Courts, and regulation and discipline is still in the hands of the professional body. While it is almost certain that the changes in the profession will persist, the continued existence of the legal profession as a primarily self-regulated body is not in doubt. The challenge for lawyers, legislators, and scholarly commentators is to provide rules and rationales that accord with the modern environment, and at the same time be wary of both perpetuating old standards that are inappropriate to modern conditions or rejecting principles of continued relevance simply in the name of change.

Chapter 2

Perceptions of the Role of Lawyers

2.1 Introduction

This chapter gives an overview of the main ways in which the role of the lawyer is perceived, and the different problems lawyers face when dealing with clients. The moral role of the lawyer and the importance of the client's choice are observed in many contexts — from that of the hired gun approach, in which client autonomy is paramount, or the ethic of care and the virtue-ethics approaches, which reject a rule-based stance in favour of a more flexible outlook, to paternalism, in which the lawyer's judgment and moral point of view are paramount.

Sociological observations are of little use to lawyers who are questioning the nature of the rights and duties towards their clients or to the Court. A lawyer who asks the question, How ought I to act? is asking an ethical question. While much of this work is taken up with a discussion of the rules and ethics (and tensions between the two) and of particular problems, it is also useful to seek a framework within which such ethical questions can be considered.

Such an inquiry is also useful in considering the foundation of the rules imposed on lawyers. By exploring this base and the way in which lawyers' actions can be justified, a number of things are achieved. It soon becomes apparent that the rules are not wholly consistent with one another in their fundamental assumptions. Some promote individual rights and autonomy, whereas others promote a more consequentialist approach to duties. There is often no clear justification for a particular rule or duty. The rules have grown ad hoc from the practice of lawyers and the continual adjustment to meet modern conditions.

Some of the tensions in the life of a lawyer are readily apparent and widely discussed. Issues of whether lawyers should defend people that they strongly believe to be guilty, or should assist in defeating the principle of the law by recourse to technical and procedural points are raised frequently. Less frequently raised, and arguably running far deeper, are issues about what it means to be a lawyer. Entering into the legal profession, according to some views, is far more than merely assuming an occupation: it is a commitment to certain fundamental principles, and the adoption of a particular position. There are no obvious answers. There are a number of useful justifications for a lawyer's role; however, none is entirely persuasive. There is always a nagging suspicion that some of the things lawyers do are just not right. In some cases this suspicion may be correct.

2.1.1 *Different standards*

Lawyers act in ways which would be unacceptable were they not acting as lawyers; the ethical demands placed on lawyers are different from those placed on people in their everyday lives. If this is the case (as is widely believed) are the duties on lawyers of a lower or a higher standard? In some respects we place higher standards of fidelity, confidence, and diligence on lawyers than on other people. In other respects lawyers act in ways which we consider inappropriate. Lawyers will keep secrets where we would expect non-lawyers to disclose, and lawyers will advocate a case when a non-lawyer could not morally render assistance. These matters need to be explained.

An important distinction needs to be made at the outset of any discussion regarding the basis of the relationship between lawyers and clients. That is, the distinction between the way in which the relationship is, and how it ought to be. While the way in which lawyers actually view their relationship with clients is relevant, this does not assist us in answering the question of what conduct is ethical. Just because a certain state of affairs exists, does not mean that it ought to exist. Undoubtedly there are individual lawyers who act from mercenary motives, and others who act on altruistic grounds. These, however, are psychological observations and do not directly assist in the question of what is the appropriate way of viewing the ethical duties of a lawyer. That question must be answered by recourse to the nature of the legal and social system within which the relationship exists, the expectations of the parties to each other and to the wider community, and ultimately philosophical and ethical principles.

This discussion is made more complex because we are not discussing the ethical duties of ordinary citizens; rather, we are discussing the ethical duties of lawyers. If it is claimed that those duties are distinct, it must be shown how this is the case, and further, any differences which exist in the ethical duties imposed must be justified.

2.2 Is ethics relevant ?

Before embarking headlong into a discussion of the ethics of a lawyer's role it is necessary to justify such a discussion. After all, there are some who claim that ethics is not relevant to a discussion of the duties of lawyers. Some claim that ethics is irrelevant because it is an inappropriate arena for its application. The duties of lawyers is an area for regulation by rules rather than deliberation by recourse to ethical values. Such an approach sidesteps the entire issue of the content of the rules and takes a formal approach to the duties of lawyers. It is important to consider critically the content of the rules that do exist by recourse to the values which ought to be promoted. Such an enterprise requires discussion and dialogue in respect of what values are appropriate. The rules alone are inadequate to govern the conduct of lawyers. Lawyers are adept at subverting rules in both their own interests and the interests of their clients. A system of governance based wholly on rules will be ineffective. It is necessary to underpin any such system with a set of values to which, in cases of doubt, the parties can have recourse.

Some claim that there is no such thing as independent moral values. The claim that there is no such thing as ethical values is a difficult assertion to refute. The argument of a nihilist is often that ethics is no more than a front for the promotion of the interests of a particular group, or as a bond to ensure that the community does not fall apart. A nihilist does not necessarily deny that people believe strongly that right and wrong exist. However, it is asserted that there are no values of right and wrong in the moral sense which are independent of the mind. It may be that this is the case. However, human societies are ordered on the basis that such values do exist. Admittedly, those values may differ between societies, and the values change over time. But it is accepted that such values are a foundation upon which the norms governing the conduct of members is governed. Either the claim that moral values exist is true, or the existence of moral values is an indispensable fiction.[1] In either case, it is useful and indeed necessary to proceed on the assumption that moral values do exist. In a work of this nature it would be futile to attempt to decide between the two.

A further objection to embarking on a discussion of ethics is the claim that ethics is synonymous with self-interest — that it is morally right to seek to promote one's own interest regardless of the interests of others. Although apparently not nihilistic, such an approach asks why a lawyer should consider problems of conduct on any basis other than self-interest. The principles of this ethical egoism — that every individual is entitled (and in a sense ought) to pursue the course of action which will lead to the greatest satisfaction — are well established and widely followed, especially in the business environment. Proponents of free markets who place the utmost emphasis on rights to individual autonomy have advocated this view. While it is maintained that such an

1 See J Allan, "A Doubter's Guide to Law and Natural Rights" (1998) 28 VUWLR 243 for an analysis of the problem of moral scepticism, though Allan argues that the fiction of moral values should be dispelled.

approach will be for the greater good, the fundamental rationale is the right of the individual to pursue hedonistic ends rather than any utilitarian argument.[2]

Ethical egoism is often dismissed as unsophisticated and obviously wrong. However, this fails to recognise some of the subtleties of an egoistic approach. A person who is an egoist is unlikely to be the sociopath that some would paint.[3] Rather, egoists may act much as any other individual. If they gain pleasure from acts of charity they may appear to be a "better" person than most. They are probably law and rule abiding, and considerate and loving. After all, crime (almost) never pays, and all human relationships need nurturing. The fundamental difference is that the motivation for all of these acts is the long-term gain of the individual. And on the basis of ethical egoism, that long-term gain is the proper motive for all human acts.[4] It would appear that much regulation proceeds on the basis that individuals, including lawyers, act on an egoistic basis.[5] It might be argued that a lawyer ought to be egoistic out of a motive of self-preservation. A person who was altruistic might be regarded as simply foolish and more or less waiting to be taken advantage of. Rather, it can be argued, it is appropriate to change one's behaviour in accordance with what is convenient at the time.[6]

Such a Machiavellian lawyer is likely to appear as law and rule abiding as any other. However, the motivation for this rule adherence is that it is "the best policy". Indeed such a lawyer may spurn opportunities to break rules when there is a minute risk of discovery, but only on the basis that that minute risk is not worth running. Such lawyers may endorse and support the system of the altruistic profession, but only because it is the best deal for them. The privileges and protections of lawyers will be maintained only by cooperation with other lawyers in a professional framework. A situation where lawyers were not cooperating would lead to a state of continual tension and the expending of energy to

2 The approach is of considerable antiquity: Epicurus *Letter to Menoeceus* and *Principal Doctrines*.

3 J Rachels, "Egoism and Moral Skepticism" in A Minton *Philosophy: Paradox and Discovery* New York, McGraw Hill, 1976, 281.

4 This is the view of Ayn Rand. See *The Virtue of Selfishness: A New Concept of Egoism* New York, New American Library, 1964.

5 Indeed the tenor of the 1997 E-DEC *Report to the New Zealand Law Society on the Purposes, Functions and Structure of Law Societies in New Zealand* is premised on the economic basis that lawyers are wealth maximisers.

6 As Machiavelli observed: "For a man who wants to make a profession of good in all regards must come to ruin among so many who are not good. Hence it is necessary to a prince, if he wants to maintain himself, to learn to be able not to be good, and to use this and not use it according to necessity": N Machiavelli *The Prince* (H Mansfield trans) Chicago, University of Chicago Press, 1985, 61.

protect against the self-interest of others disadvantaging themselves.[7] Accordingly, self-interest is best served by the maintenance of a responsible profession of law. The profession regulates its members to ensure that the position of the profession is maintained. Members are not trusted, rather the rules and disciplinary measures exist as a disincentive to individuals to promote their own immediate self-interest at the expense of the profession. The profession, viewed in such a way, becomes a kind of contract amongst individually self-interested lawyers to ensure that all of their interests are satisfied as far as possible.

If lawyers ought to be egoistic, any such professional compact between them would be inherently unstable. Because lawyers are entitled to pursue ruthlessly their own self-interest, they would be acting ethically if they were to take advantage of everyone else's rule adherence, while breaking rules themselves. The risk of others taking advantage of a lawyer's rule-adherence would, if all lawyers were egoistic, lead all lawyers to break the rules.[8] An egoist would act in such a manner to avoid being taken advantage of by other rule breakers. This must ultimately lead to a collapse of the professional institution. While this does seem to show that ethical egoism is not applied in practice, it does not show conclusively why it is not a defensible moral approach.

Perhaps, the flaw in such an approach is that it claims to be a moral point of view when, in fact, it can only ever be a statement of personal belief. The ethical egoists, in stating that they ought to act only out of self-interest, are only making a statement about themselves. It would be at odds with the normal way in which we use words like "morals" or "ethics" to suggest that a claim that it is "right for me" to act in my self-interest could be said to be a moral principle. It is contradictory to suggest that two people should both pursue their own self-interest when those interests conflict. To say that a lawyer ought to charge a client as much as possible and a client ought to pay as little as possible (for example) is not giving any moral guidance. It is simply stating opposite and contradictory points of view.

In response to this it may be argued that the ethical egoist would endorse the principle for all parties: everyone ought to act in their own self-interest. This, however, is inconsistent with the egoist's own personal precept. A consistent egoist ought to maintain that egoists ought to act in their own self-interest and everyone else ought to act in

7 This view is Hobbesian. See T Hobbes *Leviathan* London, Dent, 1914, 290-291.

8 This is a version of the prisoner's dilemma, also known as the tragedy of the commons. See G MacKenzie, "Breaking the Dichotomy Habit: The Adversary System and the Ethics of Professionalism" (1996) 9 Canadian Journal of Law and Jurisprudence 33, 35.

the egoist's interest as well. If it is maintained that everyone ought to pursue their own self-interest this is not egoism at all, but a form of libertarianism which emphasises the right to autonomy and the pursuit of our own self-determined ends as fundamental.[9]

Lawyers do not follow an egoistic principle in organising their professional lives. Moreover, it is clear that egoism is not a coherent principle to advocate as a moral point of view for any person whether a lawyer or not. It is fundamental to our view of right and wrong that these concepts in some way transcend our own interests. When we consider the role of a lawyer and the duties which go with that role, we accept that there are ways to judge that behaviour as right or wrong outside of the lawyer's own interests. An egoistic approach fits ill with our understanding of the ethical expectations of both lawyers and non-lawyers. To view lawyers as Machiavellian egoists who have entered into a convenient professional compact is simplistic. It does not take account of the fact that any discussion of the moral position of lawyers seeks to make statements that transcend any individual lawyer. It is also counter-intuitive; it is widely accepted that lawyers, like anyone else, are subject to demands that prevail against their own self-interest in cases of conflict. These are moral demands.

A discussion of ethics is relevant to the regulation of the conduct of lawyers, and the way in which lawyers can approach difficult problems of conflicting duties and demands. This is only part of the task. More difficult is the issue of what is the appropriate attitude to such problems. There are a number of views of the best ethical framework from which to view the lawyer's role which conflict and overlap.

2.3 The hired gun — professional amoralism

It has been suggested that a lawyer is like a mercenary, for hire to anyone, regardless of the cause. That label, by its negative connotations, prejudges the appropriateness of such a view. Critics have used the term "hired gun"[10] to describe the position that lawyers need not (and possibly ought not to) question the moral foundation of instructions given by their clients. Moreover, that view suggests that lawyers ought to act entirely in the interests of their clients without regard for the moral justification of the case they are taking, the existence of moral duties to the Court, or respect for other counsel or parties to the litigation. To put it in more positive terms, the hired gun is entirely professionally

9 See R Nozick *The Nature of Rationality* New Jersey, Princeton University Press, 1993; *Anarchy, State and Utopia* New York, Basic Books, 1974.

10 Especially D Luban, "The Adversary System Excuse" in D Luban (ed) *The Good Lawyer: Lawyers' Roles and Lawyers' Ethics* Totowa, NJ, 1984, 83.

committed to the client's cause without any moral commitment. They are morally neutral.

On this view, the lawyer is more than a mere instrument to achieve a defined end. Rather, the lawyer is a specialist who will advise the client of the best course of action in the legal arena, thereby assisting in shaping the instructions he or she is to follow. While ultimately lawyers will follow instructions, they are more than a tool used to implement the wishes of the client, exercising no independent judgment. They are experts whose skill and judgment are vital to the protection and furtherance of the interests of the client. The distinctive features of the hired gun are the absolute commitment to the cause of the client for the time being, and the willingness to work for any cause regardless of its moral foundation. While they will counsel the client as to the best strategy to further the client's interest, they will not presume to counsel the client about the appropriateness of the wider ends sought.

The term "hired gun" is used as it plays on the combat analogy of litigation.[11] An equally appropriate term might be "champion" in the medieval sense of a person who does combat for another. A hired gun approach seems a particularly defensible approach in an adversarial system of litigation which demands that each litigant should put his or her case and try to undermine that of the opposition. If one does not recruit a zealous advocate to one's cause it seems likely that one will be the victim of the zeal of the opposition's lawyer. All of this seems to set aside the ideal that litigation seeks to resolve disputes in a just fashion by finding the truth of the matter. While some claim that the adversarial method is a superior method for truth finding, its detractors are many.

Implicit in the hired gun conception is the fact that lawyers are not morally responsible for their own conduct in furthering their client's case. Even if they engage in deception or bullying, they are absolved from any wrongdoing provided no rules are broken. The law, and litigation in particular, is seen as a special arena in which there are minimal rules. While hired guns will obey the rules of the Court and the profession, they will do no more.

A difficulty with the hired gun view of the lawyer is that it presumes that all or most of a lawyer's work is of an adversarial nature and, particularly, that the lawyer's work is mainly litigation. In fact, large parts of legal practice involve cooperative work, or counselling a client without any particular "other" whose interests are being affected. In such cases the

11 For an analysis of such analogies and metaphors see J Hamilton, "Metaphors of Lawyers' Professionalism" (1994) 33 Alberta LR 833.

concept of a hired gun falls flat. Where there is no opposition the role of the lawyer changes and so do the expectations of appropriate conduct.[12]

The hired gun approach is roundly criticised as creating an environment in which lawyers are given licence (and arguably are required) to act amorally. Some argue that it is wrong to view lawyers as simply a means by which clients can pursue their ends, whether those ends are legitimate or not. However, the defenders of a version of the hired gun approach suggest that this is simplistic and the arguments for the hired gun are somewhat more sophisticated.[13] A cornerstone of the defence is the apparent lack of a meaningful alternative. If lawyers are not governed simply by strict adherence to the rules of the Court and profession, then whose rules ought to apply? The lawyer's own moral beliefs may be worse, but in any event are not predictable. To suggest that "community values" or some such common morality should be applied creates significant problems of definition. At least we can predict the code of conduct for the hired gun, even if that code is minimal.

2.3.1 *Neutrality and partisanship*

The hired gun defence is founded on two principles: neutrality and partisanship. The claim that lawyers should be neutral emphasises the fact that lawyers serve a particular function in the legal system, and that function is legal helper rather than Judge. It is the lawyer's task to assist any citizen in gaining access to justice and the law, whether that is to the Courts, or simply assisting in a legal transaction. If a lawyer is not wholly neutral, instances will arise where such assistance is refused on some non-rule based grounds. This means that citizens, to gain legal assistance, will need to find lawyers who agree with their points of view or goals. This is particularly difficult when the client's aims are widely condemned or unpopular.

Neutrality also enables lawyers to distance themselves from their client's cause. In contrast, if lawyers were to choose to assist some clients and not others then those lawyers' views can rightly be equated with the views of their clients. In such cases it can at least be said that the lawyer does not find the client's case repugnant, whereas the hired gun is for hire — to anybody. There is no suggestion that such a lawyer has any personal allegiance to the cause advocated.

One reason why many find the hired gun approach unacceptable is because of the profile given to cases in which the advocacy or technical skill of a lawyer has led to consequences that they consider to be unjust.

---

12 M Schwartz, "Professionalism and Accountability of Lawyers" (1978) 66 California LR 669.

13 A defence of a hired gun approach is to be found in T Schneyer, "Some Sympathy for the Hired Gun" (1991) 41 Journal of Legal Education 11.

Stories of lawyers finding "loopholes" or relying on harsh contractual provisions abound. However, there is usually an inconsistency in such views. Most people expect their lawyers to accept their own judgments uncritically. While a purchaser may blame the vendor's lawyer for advising the vendor of a property that he or she is not obliged to disclose the unsoundness of the building, none would particularly appreciate it if in the reverse situation their own lawyer refused to proceed unless permission was given to make such a disclosure to the intending purchasers.

This is the essence of the concept of partisanship (sometimes also labelled zeal or loyalty). Arguably a lawyer is useful to a client only when the lawyer is unquestioningly on the client's side. Any model that divides the loyalty of lawyers between the client, the Court and the lawyers themselves faces considerable (and arguably insurmountable) difficulties in providing a framework for the resolution of the inevitable conflicts. Professional partisanship in no way entails a loss of neutrality. Neutrality refers to the stance of the lawyer to any prospective client. Partisanship is the lawyer's commitment to a client to promote that client's interest as far as possible within the bounds of the law.

2.3.2 *Client autonomy*

An associated argument for the hired gun approach is the importance of client autonomy based on libertarian principles.[14] If we accept that the appropriate moral framework is libertarian, then one way of viewing the lawyer's role is as an assistant to others who seek to pursue their own ends. If it is morally justifiable for persons to pursue their own self-serving aims without reference to others, then it is difficult to criticise lawyers who assist in this, thereby benefiting both themselves and their clients.

To say that there are instances where lawyers should not assist clients in effecting their wishes is to suggest that the lawyer is to decide whether the end sought by the client is one which is morally acceptable. In the sense that a lawyer is a necessary tool in effecting many legal consequences, the withdrawal of a lawyer's services on moral grounds amounts to preventing the client from exercising his or her autonomy. The advocates of the hired gun approach challenge others to justify why a limit on the client's autonomy should exist. This is especially so where the limit is an arbitrary one which depends on the view of a particular lawyer.

---

14 See S Pepper, "The Lawyer's Amoral Ethical Role: A Defense, A Problem, and some Possibilities" (1986) American Bar Foundation Research Journal 613, 617.

2.3.3 *Pragmatism*

Less esoterically, proponents of a hired gun approach often take such a position as a matter of pragmatism. While accepting that such an approach raises significant philosophical problems, it is advocated as a necessary evil in the real world. Even some proponents of a more morally interventionist stance by lawyers concede that there will be situations, usually where there is a massive imbalance of power, where a lawyer should be aggressively partisan.[15] There are significant pressures on lawyers to meet interests other than those of their clients. Judges may press for speedy trials, opposing counsel may take offence at hard tactics, the lawyers themselves may have a heavy workload which would benefit by the quick resolution of this client's particular matter. A commitment to a hired gun partisanship would act as a countermeasure to such pressures and ensure that the assistance rendered by the lawyer is rendered as zealously as possible.

2.3.4 *What is really wrong with the hired gun?*

The defence of the hired gun approach is troubling in many ways. Troubling because it makes some points which, while hard to refute, sit ill with our basic ideas of the role of lawyers. Although we accept that a lawyer is to be loyal to the client, we also think that a lawyer ought to aim for a just resolution of the matter in which he or she has been retained. Such an approach may be inconsistent. It is also deeply rooted. This contradictory approach may be attributable to the conflict between self-interest and objectivity. If we were to construct a Rawlsian veil by which we were ignorant of the position we held in society it is suggested that it is far more likely that we would advocate a morally responsible framework for lawyers rather than a hired gun approach.

To illustrate, consider a situation where two friends are involved in a significant dispute. They ask you to select two advocates to assist each of them in bringing the matter before a Court for resolution. Your motive in selecting advocates for each of your friends will be the interest of each of them. Presumably this will equate with a just resolution of the dispute. If you had the choice between selecting two equally skilled "hired guns" or two equally skilled morally responsible lawyers, which would you choose? It is suggested that almost all readers would choose the latter. If you choose the former you run a far higher risk of the dispute being resolved on the basis of some procedural matter, or without full disclosure of the facts, and, therefore, against the interest of your friends. If both disputants have morally responsible lawyers it is more likely that the matter will be resolved on the substantive merits of the case.

15 D Luban *Lawyers and Justice: An Ethical Study* Princeton University Press, Princeton, New Jersey, 1988, 61.

The problem is that the above situation is fanciful. More likely is the situation where one friend, involved in a dispute with a stranger, wants your advice as to a "good" lawyer. If you refer that friend to anyone other than a hired gun you run the risk of the friend falling a victim to the opponent's hired gun's arsenal of underhand tricks without giving him or her the opportunity to be armed with the necessary countermeasures. However, the vulnerability of the morally accountable lawyer to the arsenal of the hired gun can be overstated. If we accept that the hired gun adheres to the legal and professional rules, then these are considerable safeguards. Similarly, a morally accountable lawyer is not by definition a naive one. Our real concern is that our friend with the morally accountable lawyer will fail to obtain a legal, though morally dubious, advantage in a situation where his or her opponent would. Because clients cannot guarantee that all lawyers will be morally accountable, in order to fully protect their own interests, they require their own lawyers to be hired guns. The distinction then becomes one between what an effective utopian lawyer ought to be and what a practical lawyer, to be effective, must be.

One of the reasons that lawyers are sceptical of the hired gun approach is that it demands too much of lawyers. While some criticise the approach for allowing lawyers to act in an unfettered manner, this does not tell the whole story. What the approach does is demand that lawyers act without recourse to their own beliefs. Lawyers are prohibited from refusing assistance to a client whose cause they consider to be unworthy or reprehensible. While many would accept that a black person can choose to defend the Klu Klux Klan, or a Jew to represent neo-Nazis, only very few would suggest they should be compelled to do so.[16] Perhaps part of the poor perception of lawyers is due to the belief that many of them are hired guns. However, many lawyers are morally active. While they may not raise moral issues with their clients at every juncture, they will communicate their unease in troubling cases. To demand less of them is to require them to suppress a central part of their identity. Most lawyers reject the hired gun approach on essentially pragmatic grounds. Not only does it not reflect what lawyers are, it does not reflect what most lawyers find acceptable.

2.4 The problem of role differentiation

People find some attraction in the hired gun approach to the role of the lawyer. There is a degree of certainty to it, which would be lacking if the

16 See L Reaves, "It's Part of the Job: Black Lawyer Defends KKK", ABA Journal, 1984, 43. Also Goldberger, "The Right to Counsel in Political Cases: The Bar's Failure" 43 LCP 321 in which Goldberger (a Jew) explains why he defended the right of a group of Nazis to picket a Jewish community hall.

lawyer's own moral principles were accepted as a suitable guide for professional conduct. However, a hired gun approach seems to focus on the task of the lawyer in assisting the client in achieving his or her ends. The advocates of a morally active lawyer suggest that the focus should be on the acts of the lawyer and the lawyer's moral conduct. Another view is that the best way to view the role of lawyers is in the context of the social role that they fulfil. The focus by such a method is the broader ends of the community rather than the particular acts of the lawyer or the immediate ends of the client.

Such a view has a particularly utilitarian aspect. If it is accepted that some of the acts of lawyers are prima facie wrong, then this view looks to the wider aims of the legal profession in justifying those ends. On the role-differentiated model the fundamental aim is the wider end of justice in the community rather than justice being done in the particular case in hand. The lawyer who keeps the confidence of the client while recognising that disclosure would be proper in any normal situation, is doing so in the wider interests of justice, even though in the case in hand it may lead to injustice.

2.4.1 *Role differentiation and the liberal compact*

On a liberal analysis, lawyers are seen as vital intermediaries in a society composed of numerous, often conflicting, interests. Society has agreed on the distribution of rights and privileges between these disparate groups and encapsulated that distribution in law. The special role of a lawyer is to counsel parties who are in conflict over the distribution of such rights. In particular, they counsel the parties to the dispute as to exactly what their rights are in law, where areas of uncertainty exist, and the procedure to enforce rights and resolve conflict; and they act as an advocate in the dispute resolution process. On such an approach it is no part of a lawyer's role to advise as to the appropriateness of the conduct of the client.

At the heart of the role-differentiated model (and in common with the hired gun approach) is the liberal commitment to the maximum autonomy for citizens. Often this is linked to a contractarian approach, which sees the law as a compact between conflicting interests as to the extent of citizen's respective autonomy. On this analysis, the law is the arbiter of rights, and any disagreement about the appropriateness of the distribution of rights under law or the procedures it adopts should be raised using the accepted law-making procedures. In the sense that the law is the agreement of the community on these matters it has moral force. The lawyer in any particular case has no standing to question the moral content of the law, and, particularly, has no right to thwart clients' utilisation of the law to enforce their rights on the grounds that their aims are immoral. The law, the rules of procedure, and the professional rules of conduct, as public moral codes, are then the only appropriate guides for a lawyer's conduct in the relations with the client.

2.4.2 *The institutional morality and institutional excuses*

A number of ancillary reasons are put forward for the role-differentiated approach. If we accept the various rules as the only appropriate guides for a lawyer's conduct then there is a degree of certainty as to how the lawyer will react to certain given circumstances. The uncertainty that would flow if a lawyer were to approach each problem from his or her own view of the appropriate approach is circumvented. Moreover, the client can know what the basis for the conduct of a lawyer will be. Rather than being hidden and vague, it is transparent and publicly available. The client does not need to have knowledge of the lawyer's personal attitudes and beliefs but can rely on a public code of behaviour that is consistent across all lawyers. The claim is that:[17]

> [I]f clients do not know in advance when their lawyers will have a fit of courage and judge that this or that interest of the client should be sacrificed to the good of the law then the moral demands produced by the peculiar features of the professional-lay relationship will not be met.

The role-differentiated approach then relies not on the moral convictions of individual lawyers, but on the moral agreement of the institution of the profession of law and (perhaps) the community at large. We accept the existence of an institutional morality in many situations. We have special expectations of the duties of doctors, teachers, the clergy, and so on. However, in most cases those special duties place an expectation that the members of those groups will have higher standards. In this sense they are a supplement to "normal" morality. Lawyers, however, are frequently permitted, and occasionally required, to act in a manner that contradicts the normal expectations of ethical conduct. They are expected to assist people in evading criminal sanctions even when the client has confessed guilt, they are expected to assist in avoiding the onerous obligation imposed by the law by technical means, and must keep a client's confidence to the detriment of their parties in all but the most exceptional cases. The professional rules of lawyers demand that they act in a way which in normal life would be considered wrong. While such problems may arise in other areas (such as a doctor's duty of confidence) they arise most frequently for lawyers whose task as an advocate and adviser frequently places them in difficult situations. The role of a lawyer then is strongly differentiated in the sense that there is a strong divide between conduct expected of them as lawyers and conduct expected of them as ordinary citizens.[18]

---

17 T Dare, "Virtue Ethics and Legal Ethics" (1998) 28 VUWLR 141, 153.

18 A phrase used by A Goldman in *The Moral Foundations of Professional Ethics* Totowa, NJ, Rowman and Littlefield, 1980.

The idea of morality varying depending on the position of the subject is not new. Some scholars suggest that the concept of professionalism grew from the older idea of *noblesse oblige*[19] — the idea that those of the aristocratic class have a special paternalistic duty to protect the welfare of members of the lower classes, particularly those within their social or economic sphere. While role differentiation for lawyers has been used as an excuse for such paternal benevolence, the main concern in this discussion is its use as an excuse for a moral framework that contradicts our normal moral beliefs. The mere fact that a lawyer occupies a particular role cannot be sufficient. Many people occupy special roles, such as deans of law schools, debt collectors, and bankers. We accept that individuals occupying such roles may be faced with special ethical questions: should the dean admit disadvantaged students, should the debt collector use force to obtain repayment, should the banker foreclose on the farmer in a rural downturn? However, these problems are solved using normal ethical precepts. No one would suggest that there are special ethical rules that justify certain behaviour in those roles.[20] Lawyers, however, frequently make such a claim.

In some situations we consider that not only are the actions of a person immoral, but also that the role which the person occupies is inherently immoral — a person who seeks to hide the origins of money because he or she is a member of a criminal organisation, or a person who advocates apartheid because he or she is the leader of a neo-Nazi group. In these cases not only do we condemn the person's actions but we also condemn the role that the person occupies. However, there are many who claim that a lawyer who advises on the legality of money laundering transactions, and the barrister who advocates the right of neo-Nazis to promote racist laws are not only acting ethically, but would be acting unethically if they did not assist the furtherance of such admittedly unethical ends in such a way.

The excuse for such behaviour is that the institution of the legal profession is different from almost all other institutions. Unlike the neo-Nazis, or the criminal organisation, it is not inherently bad. In fact, the claim, which is necessary for the excuse to work, is that it is inherently good. The institutional defence of the role differentiation of lawyers is similar to that of the "just war" in that the acts, while perhaps bad in

---

19 D Luban, "The Noblesse Oblige Tradition in the Practice of Law" (1988) 41 Vanderbilt LR 717; N Tollemache, commentary on C Rickett, "Legal Ethics in General Practice" in *Legal Ethics* Auckland, Legal Research Foundation, 1994, 43.

20 See D Wueste, "Role Moralities and the Problem of Conflicting Obligations" in D Wueste (ed) *Professional Ethics and Social Responsibility* Boston, Rowman and Littlefield, 1994.

themselves, are justified by the greater end that they achieve.[21] If we are to accept role differentiation, we must justify the institution within which lawyers work. It is not sufficient to say that the institution exists, alone I cannot change it, and therefore I must work within it. This amounts to the kind of excuse that was made by the Nazi war criminals and rejected at Nuremberg.[22] It must be shown that the institution is good in such a way that outweighs the wrongs that are perpetrated within it.[23]

Some commentators seek to defend the adversarial system,[24] particularly in respect of the actions of criminal defence lawyers.[25] Indeed, lawyers are frequently stout defenders of such a system.[26] However, in most discussions of the conduct of lawyers the adversarial system is not questioned. Such a system is assumed as a natural starting point. While there may be some justification of a role morality on a purely pragmatic basis in exceptional cases (although such claims must be viewed with caution), any blanket acceptance of the adversarial system needs clear and cogent justification.[27] The institutional excuse only works if you accept a utilitarian principle, that is, that some harm or wrong is justifiable if it assists in the furtherance of some greater end. Such a view is not universally accepted in theory and is by no means widely accepted in practice. Few commentators on legal ethics have turned their minds to the possibility that the existence of some greater project may not be an

---

21 Even the doctrine of the just war was limited by jus ad bellum which laid down what kind of conduct was legitimate in pursing a just war and provided that the war must not, on balance, perpetrate a greater evil than the wrong it is punishing, and that it was not permissible to harm innocent onlookers.

22 International Military Tribunal *Judgment of the International Military Tribunal for the trial of German major war criminals (with the dissenting opinion of the Soviet member)* Nuremberg, 30 September and 1 October 1946, Cmd 6964, Great Britain, Foreign Office, no 12, London, HMSO.

23 See D Luban, "The Adversary System Excuse" in D Luban *The Good Lawyer: Lawyers' Roles and Lawyers' Ethics* Totowa, NJ, Rowman & Allanheld, 1983, 87.

24 The usual defences are that it is the best pragmatic way to the truth, and that it is the best protector of individual rights: G MacKenzie, "Breaking the Dichotomy Habit: The Adversary System and the Ethics of Professionalism" (1996) 9 Canadian Journal of Law and Jurisprudence 33, 41.

25 This is the view of D Luban in *The Good Lawyer. Lawyers' Roles and Lawyers' Ethics* Totowa, NJ, Rowman & Allanheld, 1983. See also D Luban "The Adversary System Excuse" in D Luban (ed) *The Ethics of Lawyers* Dartmouth, Aldershot, 1994. Luban has more recently accepted that such an adversarial approach is also justified in any case where the imbalance of power is great, such as tax cases, or civil actions between consumers and major corporates.

26 See the discussion D Rhode, "Ethical Perspectives on Legal Practice" (1985) 37 Stanford LR 589, 600.

27 For an analysis of the problems of the adversarial system and a proposed alternative see W Simon, "The Ideology of Advocacy: Procedural Justice and Professional Ethics" (1978) 29 Wisconsin LR 30.

excuse (or basis for compulsion) for engaging in morally questionable acts.

2.4.3 *The personal objection to the institutional answer*

The institutional excuse for the conduct of lawyers is based on a "macro" view of the world. That is to say, it looks to the sum total of the actions of the members of the community and is concerned only with the overall result. Individual wrongs are justified because in the larger scheme of things those wrongs are outweighed by the claimed attainment of some greater good. The personal objection to such a view is simple — the institutional view fails to recognise the fundamentally human nature of moral actors. The role-differentiated model requires lawyers to put their own values and projects to one side and act in a possibly amoral, or even immoral, way in furthering the ends of someone else. The role-differentiated model fails to take into account that lawyers are not themselves morally transparent. Lawyers will have their own values and moral commitments. The role-differentiated model requires that lawyers be prepared to put to one side their own firmly held beliefs and assist others in furthering projects which may be entirely counter to their own views.[28] The demands made of a lawyer in the role-differentiated situation are greater than many other special duties placed on professionals. When a doctor renders assistance to a criminal, the doctor is not actively assisting in the furtherance of that criminal's misdeeds. However, a lawyer who renders assistance to a tobacco company is retained solely for the purpose of assisting in the furtherance of an end that many consider immoral.

Role differentiation claims a degree of objectivity. It is claimed that there are goals, some of which are more important than others. These goals are the goals of a particular person or group. The role-differentiated model of lawyers' conduct requires lawyers to sacrifice their own moral point of view for that of some other person or group.

The role-differentiated model fails to take account of the personal identity of the lawyer. Lawyers are more than parts of a complex system of justice. They are individuals in their own right and any workable system of ethics needs to take account of this.[29] The utilitarian aspect of the role-differentiated model dehumanises the actors — lawyers — and expects them to behave only with reference to the wider goals of the system and without regard for their own beliefs. It is not enough to say that when a person becomes a lawyer he or she relinquishes the right to

28 This objection is fully explored in B Williams, "Consequentialism and Integrity" in S Scheffler (ed) *Consequentialism and its Critics* Oxford, Oxford University Press, 1991.

29 See J Rawls *A Theory of Justice* Cambridge, Mass, Harvard University Press, 1972, 26.

hold and preserve his or her own moral point of view. To expect this is to expect too much and reduce lawyers to a less than human state. It is necessary to recognise that lawyers have moral limitations. While it is not suggested that lawyers ought to act only for clients whose causes they agree with, lawyers should not be required, as part of being a lawyer, to engage in actions they find morally repugnant. This is more than mere moral squeamishness. It is recognition of the autonomy of lawyers and the limits that such autonomy imposes.

2.4.4 *The "technician" shortcoming*

The role-differentiated model has elements in common with the hired gun approach — there is no place in lawyers' tasks for the lawyers' own moral sentiment; only the professional rules and the law govern lawyers' conduct. If those regulatory frameworks do not prohibit the conduct in question, it is permitted, and if it furthers the client's project, it ought to be engaged in. Such an approach, however, wholly misses the nature of the task of a lawyer. It is an elementary lesson that both rules of law and rules of professional conduct are frequently unable to be answered in black and white terms. The occupation of a lawyer is referred to as a profession partly because it requires the application of considerable skill and personal judgment that may vary across practitioners. The suggestion that, given all of the law and all of the facts, every competent lawyer would come up with the same answer is rejected. Equally competent lawyers in such a situation could apply their respective judgments quite differently and reach different conclusions. It is for this reason that lawyers are quick to point out that they provide opinions and judgment on legal problems, not answers.

This is not to say that there are not areas of the law that are clear cut. Whether a recovery of a debt is statute-barred due to limitation is a question which requires a more or less mechanical application of a clear rule to facts of which there will rarely be much doubt. However, even a sophisticated commercial client will come to the lawyer to seek professional advice on the law and the best strategy to pursue legal rights and remedies. The client knows the lawyer will apply his or her personal judgment to those issues. In this sense the lawyer is entitled, and expected, to use his or her personal judgment in advising the client, and the client may either accept the advice proffered, or seek alternative counsel. It is not open to the client to instruct the lawyer how to act, and to use the lawyer as a mere tool in litigation. The point is illustrated by an anecdote concerning an eminent practitioner, G G G Watson, recounted by the Chief Justice, The Right Honourable Sir Thomas Eichelbaum, of his days in practice:[30]

30 T Eichelbaum, "Foreword" (1998) 28 VUWLR 1, 1.

> When the manager of a particular client declined to accept his advice Watson placed the client's entire tray of files in the manager's lap and showed him the door. The manager found himself in Brandon Street, somewhat bewildered, still carrying the tray.

The anecdote ends with the manager contritely returning and accepting the wisdom of Watson's advice. The Chief Justice noted that the story was an object of admiration, and hoped (perhaps forlornly) that it would be received in the same spirit in a modern partnership. The point is the importance of the primacy of the judgment of the lawyer in the relationship between lawyer and client. While the client's preservation or furtherance of the rights are given a central place in the relationship, the manner in which they are defined and methods by which they are furthered is the province of the lawyer.

The role-differentiated model fails to take account of this part of the lawyerly task. Central to the justification of the role-differentiated model is the claim that lawyers ought not to exercise personal judgment on their client's cases. In reality, professional and personal judgment are inseparably bound together. A decision on whether to cross-examine a witness ruthlessly or to stand on the letter rather than the spirit of a contract, is both a strategic and a moral question for a lawyer, and neither aspect of the question can be answered in isolation.

2.5 Lawyer as a friend

2.5.1 *The lawyer as a special purpose friend*

A particularly influential view of the lawyer-client relationship and the moral justification for the acts of the lawyer is that of a special purpose friend.[31] The view is metaphorical. However, it attempts to explain some of the misgivings that exist about the way in which the law and the legal profession operate. It is immediately problematic that lawyers devote their energies to the client who retains them regardless of the cause and the fact that if successful they may assist in an injustice. Also of difficulty is the fact that lawyers appear to do things as professionals which in ordinary citizens would be considered reprehensible. The point that the metaphor of friendship makes is that the relationship between lawyer and client is a very special one, one which warrants actions which would not be appropriate but for the existence of the special relationship. In the community we accept that friends and family will lend assistance to each other that would seem inappropriate but for the existence of the

31 The view is set out in C Fried, "The Lawyer as a Friend: The Moral Foundations of the Lawyer Client Relation" (1976) 85 Yale LJ 1060.

special relationship.[32] One is entitled to prefer the interests of those close to one over the interests of strangers. The lawyer, it is argued, in accepting a client, creates a close relationship that legitimates the preference of the interests of the client over those of others, and over the abstract interests of society and of justice.

One justification for such a preference of friends over strangers is the fact that we are far better at assisting in the specific needs of those close to us because we know exactly how to best use our resources to that end. In comparison, it is less efficient to use our resources for general or distant ends as our efforts are likely to be misguided and dissipated.[33] This is an essentially utilitarian justification. It is, however, generally rejected as being ultimately inaccurate. We tend to favour our friends even when charity to strangers would clearly do greater good than that to those close to us. An alternative justification is based on the concept of autonomy and person-hood. We have a natural tendency to recognise the needs of individuals and to respond to them. We recognise the needs of those close to us most acutely and therefore feel a stronger pull to respond.[34]

Different friends make different claims. The relationship between lawyer and client is a peculiar one and the quasi-friendship that exists is special. The relationship is formed for a particular purpose and in the unique legal environment. Because of the complexity of the law and the legal process, a friend or guide is needed to ensure that the client is able to act as an autonomous individual, rather than have rights trammelled by those more adept in the legal arena. The exact role of the lawyer is defined in terms of the institutionalisation of the role of lawyers and the expectations placed on lawyers by society.

It is argued that the existence of the special relationship between lawyer and client entitles the lawyer to take actions on behalf of the client that would otherwise be immoral. While the lawyer must still remain within the law, he or she may take advantage of the system or the law in a way that might be considered immoral. Fried, the main proponent of this view, argues that there is a distinction between personal wrongs and

32 See further E Loewy *Moral Strangers, Moral Acquaintance, and Moral Friends: Connectedness and its Conditions* New York, State University of New York Press, 1997.

33 This has been used as a defence to friendship in a utilitarian model of ethics: J Mill, "Utilitarianism" in M Cohen (ed) *The Philosophy of John Stuart Mill* 1961, 321, 342. Also H Sidgwick *The Methods of Ethics*.

34 There are objections to this latter approach such as the fact that it stretches the concept of autonomy and is essentially circular. See, for example, the response E Dauer and A Leff, "Lawyer as a Friend" (1977) 86 Yale LJ 573.

institutional wrongs.[35] If the law is such that certain moral wrongs are not legally prohibited (such as avoiding a statute-barred debt) then the lawyer may legitimately and ethically take advantage of the law on behalf of the client. However, where the immoral advantage is obtained by the lawyer acting improperly (such as lying in negotiations) then the lawyer must bear the moral responsibility for the act and cannot be shielded by the existence of a special relationship. It has been argued that the lawyer may assist the client in perpetrating a wrong — even to the extent of putting a client on the witness stand knowing he or she will lie. The defence is that the act of lying is that of the client not of the lawyer, and that the lawyer acts merely as a "letter carrier" rather than writer.

The lawyer as a "special purpose friend" approach rests ultimately on the value of client autonomy. The lawyer is regarded as having a special purpose, namely to act as a guide in matters of law. The fact that the client may wish to pursue ends that are immoral cannot, on this view, be visited on the lawyer. The lawyer is simply acting as an agent in enabling the client to implement his or her wishes, as permitted by law. The view is in reality a variation of the role-differentiated approach that distinguishes the actions of lawyers for clients from the actions outside of a professional capacity. It seeks to give some insight into why such differentiation is justifiable by drawing on the friend analogy and justifying actions of lawyers in promoting the rights of their clients over the interest of others and of the public.

2.5.2 *Inappropriate analogy*

A number of objections can be made to the "lawyer as a friend" analysis.[36] The first is that we tend to choose our friends, at least in part, by the kind of people they are and the values they espouse. It is true that we will act in their interests and assist our friends in pursuing their ends, but these are usually ends with which we broadly agree. Lawyers may not choose their clients.[37] The client selects the lawyer and except in rare cases the lawyer is obliged to accept the instructions.[38] The relationship is imbalanced. Unlike friendship, the parties do not owe obligations to each other. While the lawyer owes duties to the client, the client may disregard entirely the interest of the lawyer.

---

35 C Fried, "The Lawyer as a Friend: The Moral Foundations of the Lawyer Client Relation" (1976) 85 Yale LJ 1060, 1084.

36 See, for example, the respons in E Dauer and A Leff, "Lawyer as a Friend" (1977) 86 Yale LJ 573.

37 Although they are able to limit the likelihood of distasteful clients coming their way by tailoring their practice accordingly.

38 This differs from the US profession which was the context in which the original thesis was put forward by C Fried.

The relationship between lawyer and client is quite unfriendlike. It is artificial and constructed. The behaviour of the lawyer is largely dictated not by the nature of the relationship, but by social expectations and more specifically by contract, laws, and rules.[39] The narrow purpose of the relationship and the nature of that purpose make the friendship analogy strained. While friends may be called on to assist in times of need, that assistance is usually of a personal kind. A lawyer's assistance is impersonal. It is intentionally objective to the point of being standoffish. The kind of assistance one might expect from a lawyer one would never expect from a friend.

2.5.3 *The limits of friendship*

The "lawyer as a friend" analysis is based on the accepted phenomenon that we do not object to people favouring friends with their generosity and attention. If strangers need help (as in the case of famine relief in overseas countries) and friends need help (such as the urgent need for a small sum to travel to a family member's funeral) most people would usually give the funds to the friend before giving them to the stranger. Even if we accept this as appropriate it is quite distinct from the lawyer-client problem. We may do good for a friend even though it ignores the needs of others. However, the client often expects the lawyer to positively harm the interests of others in pursuing the client's cause.

Clients come to lawyers when they wish to press or defend their own interests. In some cases they wish to do this even though the moral foundation for their claim or defence is tenuous. They also require the lawyer's assistance in procedural matters and expect the lawyer to engage in tactics of concealment, bullying, confusion and deception. If such assistance were requested of a friend, the friend could rightly decline to render assistance on the grounds that both the ends and the means were repugnant. A lawyer, however, may not. While a friend who renders assistance accepts responsibility for the purpose in which he or she is assisting, a lawyer hides behind the autonomy of the client and considers his or her own acts to be morally neutral. Conversely, the client hides behind the law and the fact that the lawyer commits the acts himself or herself. A lawyer is expected to do acts and assist in causes in which a friend would be quite entitled to decline to assist. A friend who assisted might be considered to be acting immorally.

The "friend" analogy cannot justify the conduct of a lawyer who uses immoral means to pursue a client's interests. Perhaps it does provide some insight into the specialness of the relationship between lawyer and client, and the peculiar demand of loyalty that the client makes. The

39 On this point see the discussion of M Freedman, "Personal Responsibility in a Professional System" (1978) 27 Catholic University LR 191, 198.

lawyer must place the interests of the client first, and above others who, but for the relationship, deserve assistance. The kind of devotion required by a lawyer is found in few relationships other than those of a close personal nature. However, an assumed relation of friendship goes no way to solving the moral problem of how a lawyer can justify assisting in an immoral cause or acting in a way which would be immoral outside the professional sphere.

2.6 Ethic of care

2.6.1 *The nature of the ethic of care*

Perhaps what can be taken from the view of the lawyer as a special purpose friend is the pervasive feeling that the nature of the relationship between the lawyer and client is relevant to the ethical choices made. When a lawyer is faced with a decision as to which course of action to take there will be a number of considerations. Some will be pragmatic — such as the pressures of practice and financial constraints, others will be legal — such as the limits placed on acceptable conduct by the law and rules, others will be ethical — such as whether a particular course of action fits with the lawyer's conception of right action. This does not exhaust the possibilities. Other considerations will be personal. The lawyer (and indeed any person confronted with a difficult ethical problem) is unlikely to see the matter in a vacuum. The identity and relationships of the people involved in the problem will all be relevant. Such an approach has been labelled an ethic of care. It has been suggested that such an approach to moral reasoning is more prevalent in women than men. As such it can be used as a starting place for criticism of the, arguably gendered, approach to legal ethics that is usually taken.[40]

While the lawyer is in no way a friend of the client, they are in a particular relationship. The foundation of that relationship is an obligation of care. The lawyer is expected to take an interest in the plight of the client and to assist where possible. The lawyer is more than a detached and objective bureaucrat. He or she is (or ought to be) a sympathetic ally. On such an analysis a question of ethics becomes much more than a distillation of relevant facts and application of rule or principle. It is a reconciliation of the tensions between relationships. An ethic of care approach seeks to find an outcome which avoids harming any of the actors and results in a positive outcome. As such an application of a strict rule-based approach which might result in considerable harm to one of the parties in some cases is rejected. An ethic of care approach is particularist rather than universal. It seeks to

40 See the discussion and studies cited in C Menkel-Meadow, "Portia *Redux* Another Look at Gender, Feminism and Legal Ethics" in S Parker and S Sampford (eds) *Legal Ethics and Legal Practice* Oxford, Clarendon Press, 1995.

focus on the actual circumstances of the particular actors in the problem, rather than make the parties anonymous and purge the question of personal factors.[41] In this sense an ethic of care is not impartial. It specifically permits us to favour those with whom we have a special relationship.

Such an approach is explicitly contextual.[42] It focuses on the facts in hand rather than seeking to reduce them to material elements. Making a decision on such a basis enables the lawyer to base his or her action on the substance of the problem, rather than resorting to formalistic rules which may be a poor fit for the instant case Consider, for example, a case where a defendant's lawyer is negotiating with a plaintiff's lawyer as to the amount of a settlement (liability is admitted).[43] The lawyer for the plaintiff is clearly mistaken as to the law and as a result of that mistake is prepared to accept an inappropriately low settlement on behalf of the client. Should the lawyer for the defendant disclose the mistake? Under a traditional analysis we need go no further in our inquiry. We can answer the question by recourse to the established rules and principles. Those rules and principles state that we need not (and indeed may not) disclose the mistake to the other lawyer as it would be in breach of the duty of loyalty to our own client.[44] However, on a contextual approach, far more information will be relevant. For example, would full damages be a windfall to the plaintiff or only bare compensation? Is the defendant a modestly well-off individual or an insurance company? In overall terms would the lower amount of compensation offered be a fair settlement? In many cases the result of such an analysis would be that the plaintiff lawyer should disclose the mistake to the defence lawyer — a conclusion at odds with the usual rule-based approach. The fact remains that, outside the professional sphere, most people would find it inappropriate and almost nonsensical to make ordinary moral decisions without a full knowledge of the circumstances.

Such an approach provides no formula for solving problems. It simply endorses a particular approach and, perhaps, gives guidance as to relevant matters to take into account. Of itself the ethic of care does not

---

41 See, for example, N Noddings *Caring: A Feminine Approach to Ethics and Moral Education* Berkeley, University of California Press, 1984; A Baier, "Caring about Caring" in *Matters of the Mind* 53 Synthese 257-290 (1982).

42 See W Simon *The Practice of Justice — A Theory of Lawyer's Ethics* Cambridge, Mass, Harvard University Press, 1998, 138.

43 This example is taken from W Simon *The Practice of Justice — A Theory of Lawyer's Ethics* Cambridge, Mass, Harvard University Press, 1998, 141. Simon, however, talks of deciding such matters in context, but still, it seems, by reference to abstract principles of justice and proper procedure rather than in the context of an ethic of care.

44 We might, however discuss the matter with our client and seek to obtain the client's permission to disclose the matter, or raise the amount offered.

provide a system or theory which addresses how to resolve an ethical problem. Advocates of the approach claim it will assist in reaching a coherent and defensible decision. The lawyer's relationship with the client will give rise to expectations of sympathy, loyalty and trust. The role of the lawyer as a lawyer will give rise to a duties of justice and fairness. The identity and positions of the other parties to the situation may give rise to any number of values, for example, mercy or vengeance. Most importantly, the ethic of care requires lawyers to place themselves within the problem rather than to be indifferent to it.[45]

2.6.2 *Some objections to an ethic of care approach*

It might be objected that the ethic of care is not a moral theory. It provides no system of rules, and it is not impartial across actors. Indeed, the very basis of the approach is to reject the ability to deal with such issues in an abstract way. The foundation of the ethic of care is a rejection of the rule-based and principle-based approach to resolving ethical problems. Rather, it addresses and discusses such problems in a "different voice".[46] While an ethic of care is not a moral theory or system, it might be called a moral position. As such it is still possible to reason in a manner consistent with the ethic of care.[47] Rather than applying rules to the facts and discovering the appropriate course, the ethic of care requires the lawyer to deliberate in light of the relationships, obligations, responses, and expectations of the parties and to arrive at his or her own conclusion. Those considerations are not ranked in the way which ethical rules might be, rather they are balanced and reconciled. This is not to say that a lawyer must treat all people equally. There are reasons to treat some people preferentially. The reasons for doing so must be balanced against other considerations.

Such an approach has the difficulty of requiring lawyers to investigate in detail the often complex circumstances surrounding a problem. In practice a lawyer will have little time to engage in such detailed deliberation. The objection is that a thorough-going ethic of care approach is impracticable, however good it might appear in theory. Such

45 S Ellmann, "The Ethic of Care as an Ethic for Lawyers" (1993) 81 Georgetown LJ 2665. C Menkel-Meadow, "Portia *Redux* Another Look at Gender, Feminism and Legal Ethics" in S Parker and S Sampford (eds) *Legal Ethics and Legal Practice* Oxford, Clarendon Press, 1995.

46 This view of ethics was prompted by the psychological study of Carol Gilligan *In a Different Voice: Psychological Theory and Women's Development* Cambridge, Mass, Harvard University Press, 1982 which observed that a number of subjects in her study (predominantly female) addressed problems of ethics outside of the then accepted framework of moral development of L Kohlberg looking to the nature of the relationships between actors rather than the application of rules.

47 S Ellmann, "The Ethic of Care as an Ethic for Lawyers" (1993) 81 Georgetown LJ 2665, 2668.

an objection can be overstated. In making decisions in our everyday life we take, at least to some extent, an ethic of care approach. In most cases this does not consume large periods of time. It is not a particularly cogitative exercise. It is a recognition of competing interests and values, and the relevance of interconnected relationships. Most of us have a skill which enables us to make such decisions promptly and effectively on such a basis. The same kind of technique might be adopted in legal practice in all but the most complex of cases.

It might be argued that in most cases an application of established rules and principles will lead to a similar result and it is more efficient to simply apply those rules universally. Such an approach also has the advantage of consistency and certainty. The few cases where some unjust or inappropriate decision is made are warranted on the basis of the benefits of efficiency and certainty of a rule-based approach. However, proponents of an ethic of care approach object primarily to the process rather than the result of a rule-based approach. In failing to look to the context of the problem and apply the considerations relevant to the relationships, a rule-based approach alienates the lawyer from the decision that is being made. The lawyer is in fact a party to the problem rather than an impartial adjudicator.

Perhaps a more serious difficulty is the fact that the decision-making process is based on the lawyer's sympathy and an assumption of a responsibility of care for the client. There is danger that some clients will not engender any such sympathy. An ethic based on care is reliant to a large part on the feelings of the lawyer towards the other parties to the ethical problem. If the client fails to engender any feeling of sympathy, or even engenders feelings of disgust, any decision based on that relationship is unlikely to be favourable to the client.[48] Lawyers are expected to be able to put such personal feelings to one side and act in the interests of their clients regardless of their own feelings of abhorrence. In deciding matters of ethics on an ethic of care basis it is still possible to put values of loyalty and justice before those of personal dislike. However, it is of real concern that such personal feelings are of direct relevance in such decisions.

Probably the main objection to the ethic of care is that there is little predictability or consistency in the decisions reached. Lawyers would differ in the way in which situations are assessed and clients could never be sure how a lawyer faced with an ethical dilemma would act. Such a situation would run counter to everything we expect from our system of justice. We are by and large prepared to let people make personal moral

48 See for example the issues in M Ashe, "Bad Mothers, Good Lawyers and Legal Ethics" (1993) 81 Georgetown LJ 2533 considering the issue of acting for women who have injured or killed their own children.

choices based on such variable considerations. However, where the decision maker occupies an important social role such as lawyer, doctor, or even bureaucrat we expect decisions to be predictable and made on the basis of clear and transparent principle. It may be that when applying such rules and principles there will be grey areas which will ultimately be decided by personal factors. However, for the vast majority of cases publicly known rules are decisive and accepted.

2.7 Lawyer as a counsellor

2.7.1 *The role of counsellor*

A lawyer's conduct needs to be viewed as more than an extension of the conduct of the client. It cannot be denied that the task of the lawyer in assisting the client is central, and that the role of the lawyer is an important one in our societal framework. Any account of the lawyer's role needs to take notice of the fact that the lawyer is an independent moral actor. More attention also needs to be given to the fact that there is a personal as well as professional relationship between the lawyer and the client. The lawyer is not a mere robot that the client can demand anything of. The client recognises that the lawyer is also an individual with values and preferences, albeit an individual in a special role. The moral responsibilities of the lawyer are determined at least to some extent by the social relationships which exist and, in particular, by the relationship between lawyer and client which gives equal weight to each point of view.[49]

Notice also needs to be taken of the fact that the lawyer is an expert. Like doctors of medicine, they are employed because they have a skill that is required by the client. In general, clients and patients come to lawyers and doctors respectively with particular problems, need assistance in the diagnosis of those problems, and assistance with developing remedies. The client comes to that lawyer with the knowledge that the lawyer will exercise his or her own, independent judgment when giving advice. The lawyer is in a position ethically distinct from that of the doctor in a number of ways. Advice on the application of the law or enforcement of legal rights has an ethical dimension that diagnosis and therapy of a health condition does not. When a doctor diagnoses an infection and recommends a particular therapy, say a course of drugs, there is no immediately ethical dimension.[50] In contrast, a lawyer who ascertains that a tenant has

---

49 For a more developed relational view of ethical responsibility see T Floyd, "Realism, Responsibility and the Good Lawyer: Niebuhrian Perspectives on Legal Ethics" (1992) Notre Dame LR 587.

50 Though it is not denied that questions such as those of scarcity of medical resources or prolonging meaningless life lead to difficulty and special ethical questions in medical practice.

breached the terms of a lease and advises ejectment is engaged in moral matters. When a lawyer acts, he or she frequently acts in the capacity of the client. As the agent of the client the lawyer performs tasks which the client would perform if he or she were capable. In some cases those tasks may run against the moral grain of the lawyer.[51]

The role of the lawyer, therefore, will often have a moral element. The problem lies in determining what place that moral element has in the relationship between the lawyer and the client. At the extreme of the lawyer-technician it is relegated to a personal matter irrelevant to the professional activities of the lawyer. At the other extreme it is considered to be directly relevant to the client and a legitimate basis for withholding assistance from the client. Perhaps there is, and always has been, an intermediate place for the moral stance of the lawyer in his or her work.[52] Where a lawyer is faced with a tension between moral views and professional duties he or she may not be damned to breaching one of them. If the lawyer and client accept each other as moral actors within the somewhat artificial environment of the legal system there is room for the lawyer to voice his or her moral views without imposing them. The line between voicing moral concerns and imposing moral views is a fine but important one. The place of the moral view of the lawyer is perhaps best illustrated where the law being dealt with is complex or uncertain.

2.7.2 *Counselling at the boundaries*

Much of the lawyer's task does not raise difficult moral questions. It involves implementing transactions on the client's behalf. Even the criminal defence lawyer will spend much time defending charges and making pleas in mitigation and the like which may be quite routine. However, occasionally the lawyer is required to give advice about the limits of the law, and at the limits of the law. The role of the lawyer in such instances is more than mechanical and is not entirely legalistic. In some cases the legal rights of a party will be clear. A debt, though due and owing, may be time-barred and the debtor may be able to avoid payment with impunity. In such cases there is a division between the moral obligation to repay money owed and the (absence of a) legal obligation. Some might advocate that a lawyer should be morally active and not assist a client in avoiding such obligations. However, a lawyer can be a moral person and still assist in what is essentially an immoral act.

---

51 See G Postema, "Moral Responsibility in Professional Ethics" (1988) 55 New York University LR 61, 76-77.

52 A similar starting place is adopted in G Postema, "Moral Responsibility in Professional Ethics" (1988) 55 New York University LR 61, however, the conclusion reached is that the lawyer is justified in adopting a morally active approach. For a critique of a morally active approach see para 3.7 below.

In the case of a time-barred debt it may be appropriate for the lawyer to point out that the client is relying on a legal rule to avoid an obligation that is clearly owed, though not legally enforceable. In a sense, the lawyer's role requires that advice is given on all aspects of a proposed course of action, legal, economic and, if relevant, ethical. While lawyers are not ethicists, they ought to advise on the ethical as well as legal pitfalls of a client's proposed course of action. If a lawyer acts for the client in such matters the lawyer cannot be said to be acting in a personally unethical manner if the client proceeds to avoid the debt obligation. There are two reasons for this. The lawyer has made the ethical point of view clear and has advised the client of the implications of the possible courses of action.[53] It is not within the power or authority of the lawyer to bar a course of action that is within the law by refusing to assist the client, refusing to disclose the law, or browbeating the client into submission. A lawyer who refused to assist or who obstructed the client in availing himself or herself of legal rights or immunities would be acting as a barrier to access to the law. As Fried observed when considering the right of a citizen to publish pornographic material some would consider offensive and immoral: [54]

> There is no wrong if the venture fails through lack of talent or lack of money — no one's rights have been violated. But rights *are* violated if, through ignorance or misinformation about the law an individual refrains from pursuing a wholly lawful purpose.

Another commentator has observed that a lawyer who acts in this manner is hiding the law from the client and "the notion of 'secret law' is incompatible with the conception of citizens as free and equal and the government as the servant of the people".[55] Similarly, lawyers who acted paternalistically and imposed their moral point of view on their clients would be ignoring the clients' right to make their own choices about what course of action to take.

Where the law is clear, as in the case of a statute-barred debt, there is only limited room for the lawyer to shape the actions of the client in light of the lawyer's own moral point of view.[56] However, in some cases the law will not be clear at all. Consider for example the lawyer who is asked to arrange the affairs of a wealthy business person to avoid liability

53 See Greenwood, "Ethics and Avoidance Advice" (1991) 65 LIJ 724, 725.

54 C Fried, "The Lawyer as a Friend: The Moral Foundations of the Lawyer Client Relation" (1976) 85 Yale LJ 1060, 1075. Contrast, however W Simon "Ethical Discretion in Lawyering" (1988) 101 Harvard LR 1083.

55 See S Pepper, "Counselling at the Limits of the Law: An Exercise in the Jurisprudence of Lawyering" (1995) 104 Yale LJ 1545, 1599.

56 The classic example of a case where a technical defence was relied on to avoid a debt which was due but unenforceable is *Zabella v Pakel* (1957) 242 f 2d 452 (7th Cir).

for tax. If the client is unsophisticated in such matters the brief may be particularly wide. There will be a nearly infinite number of plans that the lawyer could put forward in such a case. They could take one of a number of possible stances to the existing tax regime ranging from a conservative approach which attempted to give the provisions of the legislation the meaning intended by the revenue, to an aggressive approach which presumed the interpretation most advantageous to the client. Some lawyers might even give advice on how a client might arrange affairs in such a manner as to be too complex, secret, or untraceable to enable the authorities to asses them for the purposes of taxation. Where along the continuum any particular proposal put to the lawyer lies will depend in part on the ethical beliefs of the lawyer.

Such an approach to the tasks of the lawyer has been labelled a realist approach because it recognises rather than disguises the active role that the lawyer plays in shaping the decisions of the client. On such a view lawyers are:[57]

> Creative constitutors who work the indeterminate relation between lawyers and clients to progressive effects. In doing this lawyers are entitled to retain their own sense of autonomy in their relations with clients and to exercise their own ethical judgment as to the best course to follow

To be effective and personally responsible, lawyers cannot avoid "making judgments in terms of their own values and influencing their clients to adopt those judgments".[58]

Many share the dim view of Viscount Simon LC when he said of schemes calculated to minimise taxation:[59]

> There is, of course, no doubt that they are within their legal rights, but that is no reason why their efforts, or those of the professional gentlemen who assist them in the matter, should be regarded as a commendable exercise of ingenuity or as a discharge of the duties of good citizenship.

---

57 A Hutchinson, "Calgary and Everything After: A Postmodern Re-vision of Lawyering" (1995) 33 Alberta LR 768, 776. Although in that article the author expands on this view to justify the questionable approach of a lawyer taking only clients, and adopting only strategies, which agree with the lawyer's own agenda.

58 W Simon, "The Dark Secret of Progressive Lawyering: A Comment on Poverty Law Scholarship in the Post-Modern, Post-Reagan Era" (1994) 48 University of Miami LR 1099, 1102. This is identified as a problem to an amoral model of the lawyer's role in S Pepper, 'The Lawyer's Amoral Ethical Role: A Defense, A Problem, and some Possibilities" (1986) American Bar Foundation Research Journal 613, 627.

59 *Latilla v Inland Revenue Commissioner* [1943] AC 377, 381.

Where there is a very high likelihood that if investigated, a scheme would be found to contravene the law (though perhaps only a slim chance that it will be investigated), it is at least arguable that the legal adviser who designed the scheme is acting unethically.[60] In such a case the lawyer is not able to cite client autonomy as a defence to a charge of unethical conduct. The reason for this is that the client is seeking advice as to where the boundaries of the law lie. In such a case it is up to the lawyer to give honest advice as to what kind of conduct is probably permitted by law, not to assist the client in thwarting the enforcement of the law by designing structures and transactions which are of tenuous legality and calculated to be difficult to investigate.[61]

Where the law is unclear and the lawyer counsels as to what the limits of the law are, he or she is exercising personal judgment and, therefore, is personally responsible for the ethical position taken. In such case, clients frequently rely on the judgment of the lawyer as to permissible and acceptable conduct. In this sense, the lawyer is the moral actor and must take responsibility for this. Where the real decision-making power of the client is largely removed by virtue of the complexity of the matter or the inability of the client to understand the issues, the lawyer becomes the effective decision maker for the client. As a result, the lawyer must accept moral responsibility for the decisions taken and may exercise moral judgment in the decisions they reach. While lawyers will inevitably assume such a role, it is important that lawyers give clients as much autonomy as possible. It is incumbent on lawyers to explain their role to their clients, and to assume an active role only where clients are incapable of doing so meaningfully.[62]

It is arguable that in many instances lawyers tend to make inappropriate moral judgments for their clients by default. Lawyers presume that if the client has instructed them then the client is committed to prevailing at all costs and that the moral choices have already been made. This is by no means clear. Clients come to lawyers for guidance in legal matters. One aspect of those matters is the costs, including moral cost, of pursuing a

---

60 On this point, and the related point of advising clients on the likelihood of prosecution see S Pepper, "Counselling at the Limits of the Law: An Exercise in the Jurisprudence of Lawyering" (1995) 104 Yale LJ 1545.

61 See the view of the Court in *In Re Moore* (1909) 6 GLR 678 where a lawyer arranged his client's assets to ensure he was divested of assets to enable him to claim the old age pension. It was held (at 680) that there is a distinction between arranging such a scheme reasonably believing it to be effective (even if it transpires it is not) and concocting such a scheme where it was known or ought to have been known to be ineffective.

62 J Heller, "Legal Counselling in the Administrative State: How to let the Client Decide" (1994) 103 Yale LJ 2503.

particular course of action.[63] In observing the tendency of the lawyers to preempt the moral judgments of clients it has been observed that:[64]

> Most commonly we [lawyers] assume that our function is to maximise the client's position — the client's material or tactical position that is — in every way that is legally permissible. ... [W]e tend to assume the worst regarding our client's desires. Much less frequently I believe a lawyer will decide that a particular course is morally preferable, even though not required legally, and will follow that course on the client's behalf. In either event the lawyer fails to maximise the client's autonomy.

It is the task of lawyers to ensure that they ascertain the client's goals, and the client's view on the acceptable means of achieving them rather than presuming the client seeks to maximise material wealth and seeks to be constrained only by law. In the words of one commentator:[65]

> The way to avoid such disrespectful assumptions is to talk to the client, to explore with the client his [or her] situation, desires and preferences, and discuss how the law impacts or interacts with all of these.

2.7.3 *The loyalty objection*

One objection to the argument that a lawyer should exercise his or her own discretion in dealing with clients is the duty of loyalty owed to the client. The client has retained the lawyer on the understanding that the lawyer will act in the client's interests. For a lawyer to moderate his or her advice or conduct and thereby lose some possible advantage for the client is, it is argued, to breach the duty of loyalty. A lawyer ought to zealously promote the interests of the client by all means that are within the law.

Such an objection, however, ignores the fact that a lawyer always draws the line somewhere regarding the steps to be taken in the client's interest. Research into the law will be limited by the resources of the client and time of the lawyer, as well as the utility of pursuing the issues beyond a certain level of detail. Procedural steps such as interrogatories will be taken only where the lawyer considers the costs and risks of seeking them will be offset by the information gained. Examination and cross-examination of witnesses will be steered by the lawyer's judgment

63 S Pepper, "Counselling at the Limits of the Law: An Exercise in the Jurisprudence of Lawyering" (1995) 104 Yale LJ 1545, 1563.

64 M Freedman, "Personal Responsibility in a Professional System" (1978) 27 Catholic University LR 191, 200. See also S Pepper, "Counselling at the Limits of the Law: An Exercise in the Jurisprudence of Lawyering" (1995) 104 Yale LJ 1545, 1600 where the author asserted "the lawyer ought not assume [the nature of] her client's goals or desires".

65 See S Pepper, "Counselling at the Limits of the Law: An Exercise in the Jurisprudence of Lawyering" (1995) 104 Yale LJ 1545, 1601.

on whether the evidence adduced or refuted warrants the risk of the witness being discredited. All such decisions are proper exercises of the lawyer's discretion in such matters which, while assisted by the client's views, will ultimately rest with the lawyer.

A similar discretion will lie in determining what conduct to enter into on the client's behalf in ethical terms. When a lawyer elects to issue interrogatories that are long and involved and contain questions that are unlikely to yield any significant evidence, it cannot be said that the lawyer was obliged to issue the interrogatories in the client's interest. While the lawyer may seek to justify the action by observing that the interrogatories might have produced evidence that was decisive and, therefore, it was in the interest of the client and a proper course of action, the real reason often lies elsewhere. The motivation may have been that the other party is of limited means and by requiring laborious interrogatories the funds to continue will be depleted making an advantageous settlement more likely, or that the interrogatories will buy time needed by the client. The fact is that if that other motivation did not exist the lawyer would not have taken the steps. This demonstrates that the claimed and legitimate basis of the so-called obligation is illusory. It cannot be suggested that engaging in tactics of trial by exhaustion or delay are required by the duty of loyalty to the client. A lawyer is entitled to refuse to undertake such tactics as inappropriate. The lawyer may be obliged to resist any pressure to engage in such tactics as an abuse of the procedure of the Court.

The duty of loyalty is not the only duty of the lawyer, nor is it the paramount one. The lawyer also owes a duty to the administration of justice. A client cannot expect unfettered loyalty, nor can a lawyer hide behind the duty of loyalty. A lawyer is required to exercise proper judgment in all actions for the client as to whether it is a legitimate step to take, or whether it is inappropriate conduct that thwarts the intent of the law, or the processes of the Courts. Not only is the lawyer not obliged to engage in conduct which might be an abuse, but the lawyer is also entitled to exercise his or her own judgment as to whether it is appropriate to take any particular action. Ethical rules are even more vague than legal rules. Lawyers are expected to use their own judgment in determining whether or not the contemplated action accords with the letter and spirit of the rules. A lawyer is personally responsible for the moral choices exercised when such decisions are made and cannot be said to be neglecting the duty of loyalty if a view is taken which limits unfettered zeal on behalf of the client.

2.7.4 *Inconsistency*

A further possible objection to the existence of discretion in the hands of lawyers might be the fact that there will be inevitable discrepancies between the decisions made by different lawyers. This is undoubtedly the case. Law more than any other profession relies on art and judgment rather than science and knowledge. In any given case two lawyers will differ in numerous respects in the way they consider best to approach the problem. Similarly, in ethical decisions regarding lawyers' conduct lawyers will differ in their views as to what is appropriate. The important matter, however, is not that lawyers will disagree about their own ethical decisions, but that the decisions that they take in respect of their conduct are their own. Regardless of the ethical stance taken by the lawyer the fact is that the lawyer cannot be shielded by the client and must take personal responsibility for professional actions decided upon by an exercise of personal judgment.

The defensibility of the judgments actually made is a separate issue from the question of whether the lawyer has responsibility for them. Whether the lawyer has acted ethically is a substantive question that is best dealt with in the context of specific kinds of conduct as considered in the rest of this work.

In some cases there will be little room for discretion. The law will be clear, or the Courts or authorities will have set out what kind of conduct is acceptable. In such cases the role of the lawyer is to inform the client of the law and the non-legal implications of the law, and to assist the client to arrange his or her affairs to take advantage of the legal rules that society has arrived at through an agreed process. The lawyer may be assisting the client in an end which is regarded as immoral, such as avoiding due debts or evading criminal conviction. However, where the rules are clear the lawyer cannot be criticised for following them. In many other cases lawyers will be required to use their judgment in advising as to the limits of the law and the best procedures to adopt.

In these latter cases lawyers make decisions of their own. While they make them with their client's interests in mind, the main motivation must be the moral values of the lawyer. Lawyers frequently counsel on what the law permits, what kind of conduct is wise, whether certain actions should be taken in the course of litigation, and whether the letter of the law is likely to be enforced. In such cases the lawyer is applying ethical standards in the advice that is given. The fact that it is given as a lawyer or at the request of a client does not change the fact that the values applied are those of the lawyer and, therefore, the lawyer is personally responsible for his or her professional acts.

2.7.5 *The paternalism objection*

It might be suggested that the lawyer who proposes a course of action, which is in part shaped by the lawyer's moral point of view, is acting paternalistically in the sense that the values of the client are being replaced by those of the lawyer in solving the problem. While it is true that the lawyer does apply his or her values to the problem in hand in most cases where latitude exists it does not follow that this is paternalistic.[66] Rather, the client has delegated the responsibility to the lawyer knowing and accepting that the lawyer will necessarily apply his or her own standards to the problem. Because ethical judgment is inseparable from other forms of judgment the client accepts that the lawyer will apply his or her own standards. The lawyer does not unilaterally impose his or her standards on the client; rather, inherent in the relationship is the client's acceptance of the inevitability of the relevance of the lawyer's standards. The appropriateness of a particular course of action is a matter of professional judgment, which is the very thing for which the lay person comes to the professional.

This is to be distinguished from situations in which no such latitude exists. If the client wishes to enforce a clear legal right and rejects any advice as to the morality of such a tactic the lawyer may not seek to thwart the client's intentions. Any refusal to act, lack of zeal in pursuing the client's interests, or obscuring of the law would amount to the lawyer substituting his or her judgment for that of the client in an unacceptable fashion. Fundamental to the counsellor view of the lawyer-client relationship is the mutual acknowledgment of both the lawyer's and the client's moral point of view, and the recognition that there is a place for both of them.[67]

2.8 Paternalism

2.8.1 *Moral activism and paternalism*

Paternalism is, in current discourse, a dirty word. It suggests interference, authority, compulsion, and a corresponding removal of autonomy from the actor. It also has its roots in the gendered concept of fatherhood.[68] The concept of paternalism is not necessarily a negative

---

66 See S Pepper, "Counselling at the Limits of the Law: An Exercise in the Jurisprudence of Lawyering" (1995) 104 Yale LJ 1545, 1557 where it is observed that many clients go to the lawyer for the very reason that they want the lawyer to assist them (or decide for them) these hard questions. Pepper concludes that there is a kind of paternalism in such an approach which is consistent with client autonomy.

67 See T Floyd, "Realism, Responsibility and the Good Lawyer: Niebuhrian Perspectives on Legal Ethics" (1992) Notre Dame LR 587, 606.

68 It has been suggested that because the profession of law has traditionally been dominated by middle-aged men (and white ones) that the attributes normally found in such a class of people have become identified with good lawyering: C Epstein *Women's Place: Options and Limits in Professional Careers* 1970, 87-88. Thus it may be that the fatherly view of a lawyer's role is similarly formed.

one.[69] If we use the concept of parenthood as a rough guide it can be seen that it emphasises the interests of the weaker (child/client) party over the interests of the stronger (parent/lawyer). There is recognition of a gap in wisdom and strength between the two parties, and a commitment of the stronger party to use its wisdom and strength for the benefit of the weaker party. It is more than simply a relationship of helping. It is also a relationship of care and responsibility. There is a concern for the welfare of the weaker party, and a desire to nurture the weaker party beyond a mere protection of its interests. The parent identifies with the child and by viewing the child's position with sympathy applies parental wisdom and strength to further the child's interest.

A further feature of a paternalistic approach is a responsibility for the other party by virtue of the position occupied. Because the lawyer is an office holder in the judicial system, and because the client retains the lawyer to provide legal services, the lawyer has a special responsibility to protect and promote the interest of the client. The responsibility flows not just from the relationship between lawyer and client, but also from the social position of the lawyer. The lawyer belongs to the professional class which justifies its position by virtue of the responsibility to act in the interests of others. The lawyer also has obligations to the administration of justice, and may balance the interests of the clients against the obligations to the system. In doing so the lawyer decides what interests can be legitimately pursued by the client.[70]

A paternalistic approach is usually justified only where the paternal party has access to knowledge or wisdom about the best course of action that the other party does not have. Paternalism often (though not always) is associated with a view of ethics that sees moral values as knowable. If one decision is, on an objective basis, better than another there is implicitly some objective value by which the two courses of action are judged. Paternalism is justified on the basis that the paternalistic party knows or is more likely to know what that objective moral standard is. The standard may be one of rationality, or perhaps religion.[71]

Central to a paternalistic approach is the recognition of the gap between lawyer and client in respect of power and knowledge. The client usually

69 See T Shaffer, "The Legal Ethics of Radical Individualism" (1987) 65 Texas LR 963, 986 for a defence of paternalism of this kind.

70 W Simon, "Ethical Discretion in Lawyering (1988) 101 Harvard LR 1083.

71 T Shaffer, "The Legal Ethics of Radical Individualism" (1987) 65 Texas LR 963; R Muise, "Professional Responsibility for Catholic Lawyers: The Judgment of Conscience" (1996) 71 Notre Dame LR 771.

needs the skills of the lawyer and without them they would be unable to effect the tasks required. In instances where the client is unsophisticated, the gap is large. In emphasising the gap between lawyer and client a paternalistic approach accepts the fact that the lawyer makes decisions for the client. This is not to say that the lawyer overrides the wishes and preferences of the client, or disregards instructions. The lawyer will pay close attention to the objectives the client seeks and to the instructions given. However, these are only of a general nature and in terms of the legal work required the client is generally ignorant of how it is best undertaken and how his or her preferences are best satisfied. On such a basis one eminent commentator claimed that the lawyer:[72]

> … serves his [or her] clients without being their servant. He [or she] serves to further the lawful and proper objective of the client, but the lawyer must never forget that he [or she] is the master. He [or she] is not there to do the client's bidding. It is for the lawyer to decide what is morally and legally right, and, as a professional, he [or she] cannot give in to a client's attempt to persuade him [or her] to take some other stand … the lawyer must serve the client's legal needs as he [or she] sees them, not as the client sees them.

Such an approach is at odds with approaches that consider client autonomy paramount. A paternalistic approach does not see client autonomy as wrong. Rather, it is simply impossible. While a client may have an idea of what he or she wants the lawyer to do, the client sees the issue in a limited sense only, from his or her own perspective. The lawyer sees the problem in detail, not only from the perspective of an expert in law and legal process, but also from an independent viewpoint. The lawyer is the only person able to make a truly informed choice which, within the constraints of the law and other interests which must be taken into account, accords with the client's wishes and interests.

2.8.2 *Moral responsibility*

Paternalism accepts that lawyers make decisions for clients. Those decisions are not purely legal. Many of the decisions reached will have a moral element. The lawyer must accept responsibility for those decisions as his or her own. A client who chooses to enforce a legal right in unethical circumstances does so with the advice and assistance of the lawyer. A paternalistic approach considers any such decision to be as much that of the lawyer as the client.[73] The lawyer is personally and morally responsible for all professional acts. Because the lawyer is

---

72 C Haysworth, former Chief Justice of the Court of Appeals for the Fourth Circuit (US), "Professionalism in Lawyering" (1976) 27 SCLQ 627, 628.

73 In W Simon *The Practice of Justice – A Theory of Lawyer's Ethics* Cambridge, Mass, Harvard University Press, 1998, 29-50 Simon argues that such an approach while legally permissible has no "legal merit" or is against the spirit of the law and therefore the lawyer is entitled to thwart the client's aim.

morally responsible for the decisions made, the lawyer may legitimately impose his or her own values and judgments on the issues at hand. The lawyer is, on the paternalistic approach, able to see the moral problems more clearly than the client is, or at least is entitled to reject the client's view. While the client might be quite happy to conduct the transaction or proceeding oppressively, or deceptively, this is coloured by the fact that the client naturally sees only his or her own interest. The lawyer, while sympathetic to the client, is removed from the problem and can put it in perspective. The lawyer is also an expert in matters of legal practice and proceedings, and is aware of the special circumstances and expectations which touch on legal practice. The lawyer is able to be a guide not only to appropriate legal action, but also to the proper moral conduct in legal matters. In respect of the conduct of legal practice a lawyer should aspire to be a moral as well as legal expert.

This view of the lawyer fits best with the functionalist view of the position of the lawyer in society as discussed in the preceding chapter.[74] The lawyer is seen as an altruist who has the public interest at heart in general, and the client's interest at heart in particular. The imposition of the lawyer's values on the client's presumes a legal profession and society which is in broad agreement in matters of morality, and perhaps with a view that there is a single defensible moral standpoint. There is a certain sense of elitism in the claim that lawyers are the best judges of what is in a client's best interest and what is the morally appropriate course to take. It sets professionals and, in particular, lawyers apart as a special class in society which is entitled (and expected) to protect the interests of ordinary citizens. Some trace this kind of approach to the traditional obligation of the nobility to the ordinary people who depended upon them.[75]

2.8.3 *Kronman's paternalism and the lawyer-statesman*

Perhaps the best expression of this conception of the lawyer as a special kind of modern day aristocrat is that of the "lawyer-statesman" in the well known book *The Lost Lawyer*.[76] The author, Kronman, bemoans the decline in the legal profession and claims that lawyers of today have

---

74 This relationship is demonstrated in A Kronman, "Living in the Law" (1987) 54 University of Chicago LR 835.

75 N Tollemache, commentary on C Rickett, "Legal Ethics in General Practice" in *Legal Ethics* Auckland, Legal Research Foundation, 1994, 43.

76 A Kronman *The Lost Lawyer* Cambridge, Mass, Belknap Press, 1993. This relationship is demonstrated in A Kronman, "Living in the Law" (1987) 54 University of Chicago LR 835. There are other conceptions of a morally active and paternalistic role of a lawyer. See G Postema, "Moral Responsibility in Professional Ethics" (1988) 55 New York University LR 61 although that author denies that refusing to assist a client on moral grounds amounts to paternalistic interference.

largely "lost their souls". While the book is primarily about the profession in the US, its observations are equally relevant to commonwealth jurisdictions like New Zealand.[77] The demise of the profession of law is argued to be based on the dominance of an interest-group based view of law and politics. This is the idea that a society is composed of groups that have different interests that may be largely irreconcilable. A political process by which each group will seek to have its view instilled as law resolves the differences between the groups. Under such a view the role of the lawyer is limited to assisting in the utilisation of the law by members of society. As such the traditional role of lawyers as wise counsellors and mediators between conflicting parties is gone. The task of lawyers is essentially technical and devoid of real meaning — thus, lawyers have lost their souls.

Kronman's view of how the role of a lawyer ought to be viewed is an idealistic one. He would be the first to acknowledge that lawyers in general do not adhere to the lawyer-statesman ideal. At the core of the concept is a different view of politics, one that claims that there is such a thing as the public good apart from merely private interests which groups of people happen to hold in common. This view of politics is implicitly translated into the sphere of private morality. There is a moral right and wrong (although at times it may be difficult to discern). Kronman is a moral absolutist. While answers to moral questions may change with circumstances, the moral values applicable do not change. Moral relativism or subjectivity, by which moral values depend on circumstances or the view of the individual respectively, is rejected.

2.8.4 *Practical wisdom*[78]

Because there is a moral point of view it is possible for a lawyer to judge whether the actions of a client are appropriate or not. Such judging is not an easy task and is one for which most lawyers today, it is argued, are ill-equipped. A person with the insight, intuition and wisdom required to discern the proper course of action in a difficult situation is said to have

77 The theme has been picked up by a number of commentators in the New Zealand profession. At the 1999 New Zealand Law Conference were presented Hon Justice Chisholm, "Disciplining the Lost Lawyer", Hon Justice Robertson, "The Lost Lawyer — Where have She and He Gone" and A Forbes QC "The Wandering if not yet Lost Lawyer".

78 Numerous discussions of the concept of practical wisdom exist. See G Postema, "Moral Responsibility in Professional Ethics" (1988) 55 New York University LR 61, 68; Nagel *The Fragmentation of Value in Moral Questions* 1979. Simon claims that it is the same as his contextual judgment in W Simon *The Practice of Justice — A Theory of Lawyer's Ethics* Cambridge, Mass, Harvard University Press, 1998, 23, 138.

practical wisdom. The term is drawn from Aristotle.[79] Like Aristotle, Kronman emphasises the fact that there is considerable variance between individuals in respect of their ability to discern and solve moral problems — they possess practical wisdom in varying degrees. Kronman abandons Aristotle's extreme elitism that disqualified women, slaves and others considered of inferior status from statesman-like tasks. Rather, the Kantian position that all people are autonomous and valuable in themselves is adopted. Every individual is entitled to determine his or her own ends and preferences. Importantly, however, Kronman considers that while any individual is entitled to govern and occupy important positions, only a few have the qualities which make them capable of doing so effectively: namely those with practical wisdom.

Practical wisdom is an elusive concept. Many commentators on the law have sought to identify that factor which distinguishes those with insight from those without. It has been named variously as prudence, craft, or even horse sense. Practical wisdom seems to be a sum of a number of factors. Certainly, a thorough knowledge of law and legal principle is required. Arguably, a general knowledge of society and the values associated with it is also required. It is a skill. Like eloquence, practical wisdom is an attribute that can only be said to exist by virtue of its being exercised. The exercise of practical wisdom is deliberation. The ability to deliberate effectively can be enhanced by practice and education. Similar to a difficult manual task like knitting, effective deliberation may at first be laborious and require concentration on every aspect. However, with practice and learning the exercise becomes more natural until finally the task may be completed smoothly and almost unconsciously. Important in learning the skill of deliberation is considered to be the case law method (by which students considered the alternative sides of a reported case) and the role of a lawyer as a counsellor.[80]

In deliberations a lawyer must have sympathy and detachment in considering the problem in hand. Sympathy in the sense that the lawyer must be able to put any point of view in its best light and accept the preferences which underpin it. Detachment in the sense that the lawyer must be able to stand back from the particular circumstances of the client and be able to view the matter unclouded by personal emotions or

---

79 And particularly from the *Nicomachean Ethics* as well as *The Politics*. A Kronman *The Lost Lawyer* Cambridge, Mass, Belknap Press, 1993, 41.

80 Kronman somewhat idealises the case law method claiming that "the result is ... an expanded capacity for sympathetic understanding coupled with the ability to see every claim with the coldest and most distant, most judicial, eye; ... coupled with an indefatigable willingness to enter the fray, hear the argument, render judgment and give reasons that support it ...": A Kronman *The Lost Lawyer* Cambridge, Mass, Belknap Press, 1993, 117, 118.

prejudices. The lawyer is cast as a benevolent but objective ally of the client.

A final element of practical wisdom is, perhaps, the most difficult — that of character. This appears to mean that the good lawyer is one of the right sort, or one with moral fibre. A person of the right character will have the right kind of dispositions (or habitual feelings and desires as Kronman puts it). These might be such things as calm, caution, sympathy, and prudence. This quality of character is not merely a part of practical wisdom, but rather a co-dependent attribute. A person of character will have practical wisdom and vice versa. A person with this practical wisdom is, therefore, a special person who stands above those without this ability to have insight into the proper resolution of conflicts. Lawyers ought to develop this practical wisdom. Lawyers ought to hone their moral skill and knowledge because lawyers particularly need the moral acumen to judge the problems of their clients and their clients' adversaries. Lawyers need these skills because of the special role of the lawyer.

2.8.5 *The role of the lawyer-statesman*

Kronman rejects the technician approach to the task of the lawyer. He describes this as the "narrow view" which sees the lawyer's role as simply informing the client on the law and then implementing the consequent instructions. On the narrow view the client is wholly responsible for the ends sought while the lawyer's task is to achieve those ends if it is possible within the law. The lawyer is simply the means to the client's ends. Such work requires only technical skill and the absence of moral judgment is probably an advantage. While this may be the way in which a number of lawyers actually conduct their practice it is, for Kronman, an inappropriate foundation for the role of a lawyer.

While there may be instances where the task of a lawyer is merely instrumental, there are many others where the client is in need of assistance in determining the appropriate legal end as well as implementing the means to that end. Few would disagree with the fact that lawyers are sometimes required to assist clients in clarifying the issues that face them and determining exactly what outcomes are desired. Kronman, however, goes further in claiming that the lawyer should in some cases advise the client on whether the ends sought are appropriate. The task of a lawyer includes "helping him [or her] to make a deliberatively wise choice".[81] The role of the lawyer-statesman, therefore, is far more active than that of the lawyer-technician. Because the lawyer has the attribute of practical wisdom, he or she is more capable than

81 A Kronman *The Lost Lawyer* Cambridge, Mass, Belknap Press, 1993, 129.

many clients of making wise choices. Kronman illustrates the point by the example of an:[82]

> Impetuous client — the client who, in the grip of some domineering passion like anger or erotic love, has made a quick decision to change his [or her] life in an important way, for example, by dissolving a long-standing partnership, or rewriting his will for a lover's benefit.

In such a case the lawyer should view the position with the sympathy and detachment which are essential components of practical wisdom. The lawyer ought to listen to the client and take note of the interests and values important to him or her, and then in light of those interests and values deliberate on the problem in hand. This special kind of deliberation where the lawyer assumes a benevolent but objective standpoint is central to the concept of the lawyer-statesman.

In the example given it is suggested that the lawyer should deliberate with the client. This will involve a discourse between lawyer and client in which the client may elaborate his or her position and justify his or her views. Similarly, the lawyer will seek to draw to the client's attention the pitfalls of the proposed approach and alternatives that may be open. The task of deliberation is a special and complex one. Kronman describes it thus:[83]

> It is from the perspective of the client's own interests that his judgment must be assessed. To do this, a lawyer needs to place himself [or herself] in the client's position by provisionally accepting his [or her] ends and then imaginatively considering the consequences of pursuing them, with the same combination of sympathy and detachment the lawyer would employ if he were deliberating on his own account. The kind of deliberation that is required might be termed "third personal" for it takes as its starting point not the ends of the person deliberating, but someone else's.

If all goes well the lawyer will persuade the client of the wise course of action. A problem arises, however, if the client steadfastly rejects the advice and reasons of the lawyer and insists on the lawyer implementing the original wishes. Here Kronman is somewhat vague. A lawyer faced with a client's insistent but unwise instructions "may" choose to do the client's bidding. While such a course will not breach any professional rules it is likely to give rise to considerable misgivings in the lawyer and the feeling that the lawyer has failed the client. The suggestion also seems to be that the lawyer may also choose not to do the client's bidding. Perhaps this is in light of the right of a US lawyer to terminate representation if "a client insists upon pursuing an objective that the

---

82 A Kronman *The Lost Lawyer* Cambridge, Mass, Belknap Press, 1993, 129.
83 A Kronman *The Lost Lawyer* Cambridge, Mass, Belknap Press, 1993, 130.

lawyer considers repugnant or imprudent",[84] a luxury not allowed their New Zealand counterparts.

The example given is an extreme one and is used simply to illustrate a situation where the disparity of wisdom between lawyer and client is marked. The suggestion is that much of a lawyer's work will involve deliberating on behalf of clients, and that the lawyer will be better than the client at doing so. Kronman's approach to the role of a lawyer is paternalistic. It sees the role of the lawyer as the wise protector of the interests of the client who is weaker and less able to see what might be in his or her own interests. The lawyer is expected to try to bring the client around to the better point of view. Certainly, the lawyer ought not to accept uncritically the client's own view of his or her interests. Kronman avoids the important question of whether the lawyer ought to override the client's own wishes if the lawyer is of the view that they are imprudent, however, this does seem to be the implicit suggestion in the role of the lawyer-statesman.

2.8.6 *Backward looking*

Kronman's view of the lawyer is self-confessedly retrospective. The lawyer-statesman is a concept that has been drawn largely from the way in which (it is claimed) lawyers were regarded in earlier times. In a sense lawyers in Kronman's vision are a kind of nobility who fill a special social place. Because lawyer-statesmen have attributes of wisdom superior to other people, they are expected to exercise them for the public good and for the good of their clients. Even if it is accepted that there was a time when the legal profession did fill such a role, the fact is that this is no longer the case. Any discussion of the proper role of a lawyer needs to address the question in the modern context. While Kronman argues persuasively that the lawyer-statesman was useful and appropriate in an earlier era, there is no compelling evidence that such a model is appropriate to current conditions.

2.8.7 *Paternalistic*

The distinction between lawyers and clients is at the heart of the justification for the more than technical role of lawyers. The lawyer-statesman is fundamentally paternalistic. By virtue of the position of the lawyer, the greater knowledge and wisdom, and the commitment to the client's best interests the lawyer is entitled (and perhaps obliged) to guide the client's conduct, where possible, in the client's interest. Where the lawyer and client cannot agree on an appropriate course of action the suggestion seems to be that the lawyer is entitled (and perhaps morally obliged) to cease to act. This is effectively a barrier between the client

84 Rule 1.16(3)(c) ABA Model Rules.

and his or her rights.[85] Such paternalism wholly overrides the autonomy of the client and somewhat arrogantly assumes that lawyers are better able to make decisions than clients. While the sentiment behind the paternalistic approach may be honourable, paternalism itself is an unjustified encroachment on the liberty of clients who are entitled to choose their own ends.

2.8.8 *Objectivity illusory*

A further problem with the approach is the assumption that the sympathetic detachment that is claimed exists. It is suggested that a lawyer is able to adopt the interests of the client and yet consider matters from some third place that is neither the perspective of the lawyer, nor that of the client. Rather, it is claimed to be a "third personal deliberation". This suggests not only that the lawyer is capable of putting his or her own social, cultural and personal perspective to one side, but also that he or she is able to understand (without assuming) the perspective of the client. The claim that there is an objective standpoint that can be assumed by any human being is a shaky one. What it amounts to is a claim that there can be a deliberation without any identifiable deliberator, a point of view without an identified viewer. The response to such a claim is that the very fact of deliberation, as well as the way in which a deliberation proceeds, is shaped by numerous factors unique to the actor such as gender, ethnicity, class and education.

To claim the ability to stand apart from such personal attributes and preferences amounts to a claim to assume a god-like perspective. While Kronman states that the lawyer will deliberate on the client's problems as if they were his (or her) own, this relates to the beneficence of the lawyer in protecting the client's interests as if they were his (or her) own. In considering the problem it is claimed that the lawyer is able to deliberate from above the personal perspective of lawyer or client. Such a claim is fatuous in that when a lawyer considers a client's problem the lawyer clearly applies his or her values and beliefs to the problem. To justify doing so it must be alleged that the values and beliefs of the lawyer are better than those of the client.

2.8.9 *Best decision maker not the lawyer*

The suggestion that a lawyer is a better judge of the client's interest is problematic. If we reject the ability of a lawyer (or anyone) to engage in the "third personal deliberations" claimed, the question is whether the deliberations of the lawyer or the deliberations of the client are to be preferred. In some situations the lawyer's view is clearly likely to be

85 C Fried, "The Lawyer as a Friend: The Moral Foundations of the Lawyer Client Relation" (1976) 85 Yale LJ 1060, 1075. In New Zealand it is also most probably in breach of r 1.02 of the rules which, with limits, obliges practitioners not to refuse to accept instructions.

better, namely in matters of law and legal procedure. Indeed, it is the lack of expertise in such areas that motivates a lay person to seek a lawyer's assistance. The lawyer's judgment may also be preferred over the client's in other circumstances, as where the client is a child, or labours under some particular disability. Few would disagree with the suggestion that in such cases the client requires guidance of some more capable person (but not necessarily a lawyer). However, where the client is a normal person who has reasons for his or her actions and preferences there seems no sound basis for preferring the lawyer's assessment of the best course of action to that of the client.

The example used of the client who is "in the grip of some domineering passion like anger or erotic love" is perhaps unfortunate because it suggests that there is some diminished responsibility on the part of the client. Most clients who seek assistance have carefully considered their instructions and have firmly held views about the ends that they want to achieve. Kronman's argument that the lawyer has an active role to play in deliberating for and with a client over a proposed course of action applies equally to such situations. Even where the client is angry, or in love, these may be legitimate reasons to the client for taking a particular course of action. The claim that a lawyer should persuade the client to abandon his or her point of view seems to be a claim that the basis for the client's decision is wrong whereas the basis for the lawyer's decision is right. The lawyer is seen as the better judge of the values that are appropriate foundations for action.

While it is accepted that the relationship between the lawyer and the client involves discourse and an exchange of views, it is questionable whether the persuasive role that is advocated is appropriate. A lawyer will frequently be required to discuss matters with a client in order to clarify the client's intentions and wishes, and to assist the client in formulating his or her intentions. The lawyer-statesman goes beyond this and seeks to exchange reasons with the client. The lawyer may gain more insight from the information given by the client and adjust his or her view accordingly; however, Kronman's suggestion is that the lawyer should seek to bring the client around to the lawyer's point of view. If the lawyer and client were equal parties in respect of knowledge power and forcefulness (as is indeed sometimes the case) this might be permissible. Such a dialogue between equal parties might lead to a distillation of reasons and an independent arrival by the client at a conclusion. However, in reality most clients will rely on the advice given by their lawyer whether legal or not. When a lawyer seeks to dissuade a client from a particular course of action only the most confident clients will be able to resist. A lawyer who acts thus is replacing the choice of the client with the choice of the lawyer for the client.

There is also a question of why lawyers are best equipped to guide others on the appropriate course of action. Clients approach lawyers to effect certain ends. The means to those ends probably requires the use of some legal process — thus, the use of the lawyer's skills. In a sense it is a mere coincidence if the task the client sets the lawyer also has a moral element. If a lawyer seeks to interfere (as opposed to simply draw the client's attention to such matters) the client might legitimately ask on what basis the lawyer claims the authority to dictate what course of conduct is the morally better one for the client. If that kind of advice were needed would someone more qualified not better deliver it? Why not priests, counsellors, or even psychotherapists?

2.8.10 *Practical wisdom a weak concept*

Perhaps most problematic is the problem of defining exactly what practical wisdom is. After all, if we cannot pin down exactly what it is, it is questionable whether it exists at all. Although there are plenty of synonyms offered, such as prudence or craft, these of themselves go no further in telling us what practical wisdom is. The problem is exacerbated when commentators import the term *phronesis* from Aristotelian philosophy.[86] Practical wisdom looks to the nature of the person who is considering the problem. If the person is of the right character, he or she will make the right judgments. Neither rules and principles, nor knowledge are a central part of practical wisdom.

The claim seems to be that those possessing practical wisdom arrive at their conclusions by a kind of informed intuition that defies any further analysis. If definition seems impossible attempts at description seem equally ill-fated. While it is possible to look back and point to examples of the statesman-like wisdom with the advantage of hindsight, there seems to be no way in which to determine whether a contemporary point of view is informed by such wisdom or not. The only persons capable of recognising that such wisdom exists are presumably those who posses the very wisdom they are judging. Ultimately, the concept of practical wisdom must be recognised as linked inextricably to the elitism that is at the centre of Aristotle's political and moral philosophy. On that approach certain people of the right sort are capable of making proper judgments and, therefore, holding important office. The rest are unable to make such judgments and, moreover, incapable of meaningfully questioning the acts of those superior persons who are able to make such judgments.

The concept of the lawyer-statesman seeks to justify lawyers interfering with the moral choices of their clients. In doing so it attempts to dispel the misgivings lawyers have regarding assisting clients with ends which

---

86 A term used particularly in the *Nicomachean Ethics* and adopted by Kronman and others.

they consider immoral. However, there is no firm foundation justifying lawyers substituting their own moral judgment for that of their clients. The suppression of the clients' autonomy rests ultimately on an unfounded and elitist claim that lawyers are better judges of moral choices and clients' interests than the clients themselves.

2.9 Virtue ethics

Most examinations of the ethics of lawyers ask the question, What is a right action in a given situation? Virtue ethics asks the question, What kind of person is a good lawyer? Kronman's ideal of the lawyer-statesman takes this approach. Rather than focusing on what rule or approach is necessary to ensure that a person will be correctly guided in his or her acts, virtue ethics asks what kinds of qualities should be fostered to promote a healthy and vigorous individual, profession, and society. Rather than judging whether people are good by reference to their actions, their actions are judged by reference to their character.[87] The ethical nature of an act is judged by recourse to the character of the actor rather the act in isolation.[88] Rather than focusing on keeping promises, virtue ethics focuses on being an honest person. Such a trait-based approach can have considerable advantages. It is very difficult on rule-based ethics to formulate rules regarding generosity, sympathy, or kindness. Rules tend towards prohibitions rather than exhortations. Virtue theory, however, is quite at ease with the idea that such virtues ought to be encouraged, and that people who are generous, sympathetic, and kind are of a better sort than those who are selfish, callous, and mean.

Virtue ethics emphasises the fact that a good lawyer is more than merely rule-abiding, technically proficient, or financially successful. Rather, a good lawyer is a particular kind of person who has admirable attributes. This is not to say that there is no place for rules. There will be some people who are not virtuous and the rules serve the purpose of ensuring that minimum standards are adhered to. Virtue is not an innate trait. It is acquired, and rules may form an important part of the process of learning to be a virtuous person.[89] Virtue (or moral skill as some have called it) is acquired over a long period of time. The role of legal education, professional training, and professional ethos will all play a part.[90] While at the outset we may base our actions on rules or deduce them from principles, over time, proponents of the virtue ethics school

87 G Watson, "The Primacy of Character" in Daniel Statman (ed) *Virtue Ethics-A Critical Reader* Washington, DC, Georgetown University Press, 1997.

88 See M Slote, "Law in Virtue Ethics" (1995) 14 Law and Philosphy 91.

89 See generally A Macintyre, "The Nature of the Virtues" from A Macintyre *After Virtue* London, Duckworth, 1985.

90 T D Eisele, "Must Virtue be Taught" (1987) 37 Jnl Legal Ed 495, A Gutmann, "Can Virtue be Taught to Lawyers" (1993) 45 Stanford LR 1759.

argue we will move from a mechanical process of determining the proper course of action to intuitively taking the proper course of action. This transition is the move from intellectual knowledge to moral skill. Some have suggested that this is akin to learning a craft. While our initial attempts will be awkward and based on the application of intellectual knowledge, as our aptitude increases we will be able to execute tasks naturally and without recourse to any constraining knowledge base.[91]

Such an approach (which underlies Kronman's view of the lawyer-statesman) fits well with the idealised conception of legal practice in earlier times. Lawyers were schooled in the profession to be good people who consequently had an acute sense of proper action. They were not constrained by strict rules which might not be appropriate to particular cases. They were people of excellent character who lived in accordance with the virtues of honesty, courage, loyalty, and so on. Some feel that lawyers ought still to live their professional lives by recourse to their moral virtues rather than professional rules. However, in reality this cannot be the case.

Virtue ethics is to a large part aspirational. It is concerned with the kind of people we should aspire to be. As such it is a poor foundation for the governance of a profession comprised of numerous individuals of varying virtue and for guidance in individual cases. If lawyers were universally, or even mainly, perfect moral beings virtue ethics might be a sufficient principle on which to regulate the profession. Few lawyers in fact fit into such a category. Most are fallible and if faced with a difficult ethical problem will not be able to resolve it by recourse to some acquired ethical intuition. In such cases rules are needed as a guide on which to base actions. Some lawyers are simply bad people and rules are needed to constrain their actions. It is simply not enough for lawyers to be told what kind of people they ought to aspire to be. They also need to be told that in certain circumstances they ought to act in a particular way.[92] Even the most virtuous person may find himself or herself in need of explicit guidance.

Perhaps more important in the practice of law is the fact that clients and prospective clients require certainty as to how their lawyers will act. Clients are ignorant of the character of their lawyers and, therefore, cannot be sure how their lawyer would act in any given situation. Will

91 See P Foot, "Virtues and Vices" in P Foot *Virtues and Vices and Other Essays in Moral Philosophy* Oxford, Blackwell, 1978, p 4 where she gives the example of a rescuer who instantaneously leaps to the rescue of a boy in a river as more virtuous than one who has to deliberate whether or not to take an action of such a nature.

92 R B Louden, "On Some Vices of Virtue Ethics" (1984) 23 American Philosophical Quarterly 227.

the lawyer consider the client's cause to be at odds with a virtuous life and refuse to assist or, worse, obstruct their purpose?[93] This might amount to frustrating the application of laws which have been agreed by a legitimate and democratic process. Even if there is an objection to the distribution of rights effected by the law at least it is transparent and arrived at by a legitimate process. A wholly virtue-ethics based approach to the profession would leave clients at the mercy of the vagaries of their lawyer's ethical tendencies.

Virtue ethics does, however, have a redeeming aspect. It highlights the fact that lawyers should aspire to be a better kind of person. Most other approaches to legal ethics focus on what kind of acts are permissible and which are reprehensible. Virtue ethics provides guidance as to what kind of people we should aspire to be. To be a good lawyer, it is not enough to do no harm, to not knowingly breach the rules. While a lawyer should act within the rules and the law, these are only minimum requirements. Lawyers should also be encouraged to be honest, charitable, courageous, sympathetic and loyal — in short, virtuous.

2.10 Conclusion

The role of the lawyer and the lawyer's duties have been viewed on a continuum, from the hired gun to paternalism. More recently philosophers and lawyers have questioned whether such an approach is helpful. Neither the ethic of care approach and the virtue-ethics approach fit well on any such continuum. This is because they reject the rule-based stance in favour of a more flexible outlook. While this raises difficulties, it also raises challenges to the established way in which we approach problems. The various approaches highlight different problems which face the lawyer when dealing with clients. An inherent tension exists between the lawyer's own moral stance and the right of the client to determine his or her own course of action unhindered by the lawyer's moral sensibilities. I have favoured an approach which recognises the importance of the client's choice, but also recognises that there are instances where a client is in fact unable to choose a course of action to take. Where a client has made a clear choice which is within the law, the lawyer must respect that choice. This is the case even when it cuts across the lawyer's own beliefs. There will also be instances where the client implicitly or expressly defers to the lawyer's moral judgment. In such cases the moral role of the lawyer must be recognised.

---

93 This is the argument of T Dare, "Virtue Ethics and Legal Ethics" (1998) 28 VUWLR 141.

Part Two

Professional Organisation and Control

Chapter 3

The Law Society and its Roles

3.1 The inevitability of a law society

A law society is inevitable for two reasons. The members of any closed profession will inevitably band together to promote and protect their own interests, and lawyers are no exception. Secondly, regulation of lawyers is necessary because of the fundamental importance of their role in assisting people in legal matters. Lawyers have moved to regulate themselves through the medium of the law society. While it is not a logical necessity that lawyers themselves fulfil these governance functions, it is a tradition of considerable antiquity which has been generally regarded as appropriate. Although the Courts and the legislature have periodically interfered (and will continue to interfere) in the rules governing the profession and the way that barristers and solicitors have governed themselves, it has usually been easier to leave actual governance to the profession itself. This was an approach followed in New Zealand from an early time.

Initially in New Zealand discipline of and admission to the profession lay in the hands of the Courts, largely because there was no clear professional organisation to whom such disciplinary matters could be entrusted.[1] Unlike the English situation, there were no Inns of Court or Society of Gentlemen Practitioners to select or discipline their members.[2] While there is evidence that informal and voluntary local associations of law practitioners existed in New Zealand as early as 1861, it was not until 1869 that a Bill was introduced to incorporate the New Zealand Law Society.[3] The law society that was thus created was not particularly active for the first years of its existence. A significant problem was the fact that the society was based in Wellington, whereas most lawyers practised in either Otago or Auckland. The main activity of the law society was the discipline of its members. The power to form

1 See R Cooke ed *Portrait of a Profession* Wellington, Reed, 1969, 138.

2 See Supreme Court Ordinances 1841, 1844; *In Re Justices of the Court of Common Pleas at Antigua* (1830) 1 Knapp 267, 268, 12 ER 321 per Lord Wynford.

3 The New Zealand Law Society's Act 1869.

branch law societies existed from 1877, however workable legislation did not exist until the passing of the District Law Societies Act 1878. Between 1879 and 1886 eight district law societies were constituted under the legislation. The district law societies assumed some of the responsibilities (particularly discipline) of the New Zealand Law Society. It is from their roots that the considerable organisation of the national and district societies grew.

3.2 The New Zealand Law Society

All lawyers who seek to practise law in New Zealand must be members of both the New Zealand Law Society and the district law society that covers the region in which they wish to practise. The existence of the New Zealand Society is confirmed by statute.[4] It acts as an umbrella organisation that unifies the district societies, provides an avenue of appeal against the proceedings of the district societies, and provides services and performs functions that are more effectively delivered at a national level.[5] These national services and functions include rule making, education, lobbying, law reform, practice supervision and investigation, public relations, and provision of a professional magazine.[6] Any lawyer who is a member of a district society and holds a current practising certificate is automatically a member of the New Zealand Society.[7] The council of the society, and the board conducts the business of the society.

The council of the society as its governing body is made up of members elected by the various district law societies.[8] From the council are elected the president, four vice-presidents, and a treasurer. In all the council comprise 23 members[9] making it a somewhat unwieldy body. The rules of the society provide for the election of a board by the council from its own members to act as the "executive body managing the affairs of the society".[10]

---

4 Section 3 Law Practitioners Act 1982. Section 18 affirms the existence of the district societies.

5 See the law society's web page "About the NZLS" at [http://www.nz-lawsoc.org.nz/about/intro.htm].

6 The powers of the council are found in ss 12-17 Law Practitioners Act 1982.

7 Section 3(2) Law Practitioners Act 1982.

8 Section 11 Law Practitioners Act 1982; rr 2.1 to 2.5 Rules of the New Zealand Law Society.

9 The district societies are represented by between one and four members depending on size as follows: Auckland (4) Canterbury (3) Gisborne (1) Hawkes Bay (1) Manawatu (1) Marlborough (1) Nelson (1) Otago (2) Southland (1) Taranaki (1) Waikato Bay of Plenty (2) Wanganui (1) Wellington (3) Westland (1).

10 Rules 10.1 and 10.15.1.

Committees that are comprised of members who give their time voluntarily carry out much of the work of the society in areas such as law reform, and education.[11] Some serve central roles such as reviewing the Rules of Professional Conduct (ethics committee), or overseeing the standards for admission of practitioners (admissions and credentials). Others act as a watchdog over different areas of the law, making submissions on legislation, and keeping members up to date on changing areas of the law and practice. The Women's Consultative Group is perhaps unique in its role relating to a specific demographic sector of the profession that includes the undertaking to "promote the advancement, retention and common interests of women studying, qualified in and employed in law". The Law Practitioners Act also created the New Zealand Disciplinary Tribunal to deal with matters of professional misconduct.[12] It is comprised of practitioners appointed by the council of the society and lay members appointed by the Governor-General.

The New Zealand Society also comprises a body of permanent paid staff housed in its Wellington offices. These people assist in providing administrative support to the council and board, as well as the committees. They also assist in numerous other activities of the society such as coordinating continuing legal education programmes, supervising the conduct of solicitors, producing *LawTalk* the profession's regular publication, and assisting in the administration of the complaints procedure.

3.3 The district law societies

The district societies are constituted under the Law Practitioners Act 1982.[13] While each society (there are 14) has the power to make its own rules, they operate on a similar basis.[14] Every practitioner who holds a practising certificate will be a member of the society in the district in

11 Although committees are frequently created for special purposes, at the time of writing there exist the following committees: Admissions and Credentials, Civil Litigation and Tribunals, Commercial and Business Law, Continuing Legal Education, Criminal Law, Dispute Resolution, Employment Law, Ethics, International, Law in Schools, Legal Executive, Legal Services, Legislation, Management Committee — Solicitors' Fidelity Guarantee Fund, Property Law and General Practice, Publicity Review, Resource Management, Taxation.

12 Section 108 Law Practitioners Act 1982.

13 Section 18, although some have been in existence since the 1870s they were first recognised by legislation in the District Law Societies Act 1878 although provisions passed in 1877 amending the Law Practitioners Act 1869 made such district societies technically possible. See R Cooke *Portrait of a Profession* Wellington, Reed, 1969, 145.

14 Section 27 Law Practitioners Act 1982. The rules must be consistent with the Act. This discussion is based on the Auckland District Law Society. The rules of that society are available at [http://www.adls.org.nz/rules.html].

which he or she practises.[15] A district society is governed by a council which is elected by its members from its members.[16] The council has substantively the same powers in relation to the district as the New Zealand Council.[17]

The functions of the district societies overlap with those of the New Zealand society in many respects, and are stated in the legislation to be the same.[18] However, district societies are a more direct route for involvement of practitioners in the profession by the election of members to the council, and the holding of general and special meetings which all practitioners may attend and at which they may vote. The district societies are also a point of focus both professionally and socially for practitioners with similar interests, either in a particular area of law, or by virtue of being recently admitted, or other commonality. The district societies have the function of maintaining law libraries for their respective districts that are used by both the practitioners and the Courts. They are also responsible in the first instance for the handling of complaints of practitioners' misconduct. Such complaints are heard either by a complaints committee comprising the council of the district society[19] or where more serious by a district disciplinary tribunal.[20] Where the alleged misconduct is of a nature that if proved a practitioner is likely to be struck off or suspended the matter will be referred to the New Zealand Disciplinary Tribunal.[21]

3.4 Reforms

At the time of writing reforms of the structure and functions of the law society are being contemplated. These reforms follow in many respects the recommendations made in the E-DEC Report in 1997.[22] The most recent statement of the proposed changes are to be found in a letter from the president of the society to its members and an attached paper of 20 October 1999.

The most fundamental change is the removal of compulsory membership of the law society. The New Zealand Law Society would

15 Section 23 Law Practitioners Act 1982. (There is provision for conscientious objection under s 24.)
16 Section 28 Law Practitioners Act 1982, r 9 ADLS Rules.
17 Section 29 Law Practitioners Act 1982 (excepting the power to levy and make rules).
18 Section 26 Law Practitioners Act 1982.
19 Section 100 Law Practitioners Act 1982.
20 Section 103 Law Practitioners Act 1982.
21 Section 106(2) Law Practitioners Act 1982.
22 *Purposes, Functions and Structure of Law Societies in New Zealand Final Report to the New Zealand Law Society* Wellington, E-DEC Ltd, 1 September 1997.

still have jurisdiction over such matters as discipline of all members, admission to the profession, the rules of conduct and financial assurance. However, societies offering services such as education, public relations, social and other such functions would be voluntary. There is no place for compulsory district law societies. Other functions would also be shed. The fidelity fund would no longer exist and costs revisions would be abolished. Similarly, there would be no compulsion on the district law societies to maintain law libraries.

Associated to these changes is a proposed liberalisation of the restrictions on lawyers as to the kind of business they may trade in. It is suggested that limited liability and multi-disciplinary partnerships would be permitted. Lawyers would also be permitted to sell real estate. These proposals have originated largely from government in consultation with the law society. Whether in the current uncertain political climate these reforms will proceed, or proceed in the form as they currently exist, is by no means clear.

The following discussion should, therefore, be read bearing in mind any reforms which have occurred since the publication of this work.

3.5 The roles of a law society

While the functions of discipline and admission to the profession are essential, law societies inevitably find themselves providing numerous other services. These include services for the benefit of individual members, the benefit of the profession generally, or for the public benefit. The following discussion is based on the roles that are fulfilled by the New Zealand Law Society and it is typical of the kinds of activities of most such organisations.

3.5.1 *Statutory functions*

The functions of the law society are set out in s 4 of the Law Practitioners Act 1982 as follows:

(a) To promote the interests of the legal profession and the interests of the public in relation to legal matters:
(b) To promote and encourage proper conduct among the members of the legal profession:
(c) To suppress illegal, dishonourable, or improper practices by members of the legal profession:
(d) To preserve and maintain the integrity and status of the legal profession:
(e) To promote opportunities for the acquisition and diffusion of legal knowledge [and skills relating to the practice of law]:
(f) To assist in and promote the reform of the law:
(g) To provide means for the amicable settlement of professional differences between members of the legal profession.

There is a tension in the functions of the society. The first role under the Act is to promote the interests of the legal profession and the interests of the public in relation to legal matters. This, arguably erroneously, presumes that the interests of the legal profession and the interests of the public will be in accord with each other.

3.5.2 *Protection of public*

(a) Admission and practice restrictions

A core role of any law society is the protection of the public from unscrupulous practitioners, and to ensure that all practitioners are trustworthy and competent. One way in which this is achieved is by ensuring that those admitted to practice are competent and trustworthy. Historically, the profession itself regulated the admission of new entrants. More recently, some of the functions of admission to the profession have been moved to other organisations,[23] however, the district law societies still play a role in determining that the candidates are of good character.

There are also restrictions that are administered by the district law societies as to when solicitors (but not barristers) may practise on their own account after admission. No practitioners may practise on their own account unless they have had three years' relevant experience, and have passed society exams concerning the management of trust accounts and client funds.[24] The society has recently been accorded the statutory power to require practitioners to take continuing education courses to ensure that they remain up to date with developments in the law and practice.[25] The extent to which this power will be exercised remains to be seen.

(b) Discipline

The competence and trustworthiness of lawyers is also ensured by the rather blunt instrument of discipline by which members who are found to have fallen short of the required standards may be punished: sanctions include suspension or disqualification from practising law. The discipline procedure protects the public from lesser wrongs as well, as complaints may be made in respect of minor wrongs such as excessive delay or discourtesy. In such cases the law society has the power to order

23 In particular education to the various law teaching universities, professional teaching to the Institute for Professional Legal Studies, and the oversight of the curriculum of those courses to the Council for Legal Education.

24 Section 55 Law Practitioners Act 1982.

25 Section 17(2)(fa) Law Practitioners Act 1982 inserted by the Law Practitioners Amendment Act 1999.

compensation and to fine or censure the practitioner. The discipline procedure is focused on discipline of the practitioner rather than compensation of the wronged client. While compensation may be ordered, this does not affect the right to bring an ordinary action in the Courts. The procedure before the law society disciplinary tribunals is more akin to a criminal procedure. The parties to the proceeding are the lawyer who is the subject of the complaint and the district or national law society. While the society may order some compensation to be paid, the appropriate forum for redress in respect of loss caused by the actions of a lawyer is the ordinary Courts.

(c) Rules

Associated with the role of discipline is that of rule making. Practitioner conduct is governed by the Rules of Professional Conduct for Barristers and Solicitors. These rules are not exhaustive and are supplemented by the general law and a broad interpretation of what will amount to misconduct. New rules or amendments for rules are drafted by the Ethics Committee and submitted through the board to the council for approval. The committee sometimes judges that consultation with other persons or bodies inside or outside the society is appropriate, depending on the subject. Occasionally, this will involve all society members. On other occasions the committee will judge that it is competent to act without consultation.[26] Most recently the practice has been adopted of publishing proposed new rules in *LawTalk* the magazine published by the society. The council of the New Zealand Law Society approves the rules or amendments to the rules. They cover matters of considerable importance such as conflicts of interest and confidentiality, and matters of less importance such as the name of a legal practice and the names included on a letterhead.

(d) Indemnity against loss by dishonesty

The existence of the solicitor's fidelity guarantee fund can also be seen as a measure to protect the public from lawyers' dishonesty. The fund is required under the Law Practitioners Act 1982 and funded by a levy on all solicitors practising on their own account or as partners in a firm.[27] Clients who have suffered loss through the dishonesty of their solicitor may claim against the fund in the last resort.[28] The fund acts as a kind of insurance against practitioner dishonesty (but not negligence or incompetence). It should, however, be noted that a client may not make a claim on the fund until all other avenues of relief by which the defrauded funds might be recovered have been exhausted.[29] In most

26 Correspondence with Eric Deane, Director of Standards, New Zealand Law Society, 28 April 1999.

27 Section 165 Law Practitioners Act 1982.

28 Section 171 Law Practitioners Act 1982.

29 Section 171(1) Law Practitioners Act 1982.

cases the fund will only pay out where the dishonest practitioner is bankrupt and unable to meet the claim.

(e) Costs review

The law society also has the power to review bills of costs of practitioners to protect against overcharging.[30] By the rules applicable to costs (which many lawyers regard as antiquated) practitioners are not free to charge whatever the client will pay. The bill must be "fair and reasonable".[31] While the way in which this has been applied has not prohibited high fees being charged by lawyers in some cases, it does enable clients who suspect that far too much was charged for routine work to have the bill examined by someone who is familiar with how long such tasks should take, and what kind of bill is considered reasonable in the circumstances.

(f) Supervision of practitioners

The law society also has the power to audit and inspect a solicitor's accounts to ensure that there is compliance with proper accounting practices and no financial irregularities.[32] The inspectorate[33] undertakes periodic reviews of all practitioners to ensure compliance with accounting procedures. While such inspections do not necessarily reveal frauds that have taken place they do ensure a degree of financial discipline which might not be present without such supervision.

The public protection role is essential to the effective functioning of the profession. While the public may be effectively protected without all of the measures outlined above (both the fidelity fund and the costs revision functions have been questioned), it is clear that some protection is needed. Whether it is appropriate or necessary that the very members of the organisation against whom protection is being provided fill this function will be examined shortly.

3.5.3 *Public service*

(a) Law reform

There are a number of other functions of the law society which are in the public interest generally (which often includes the interests of lawyers) and are aimed at improving either the law, or access to it. One such activity is the considerable energy devoted to law reform. Lawyers have a vested interest in some areas of law reform touching on their own

30 Section 143 Law Practitioners Act 1982. See further para 12.3.

31 Rule 3.01; *Gallagher v Dobson* [1993] 3 NZLR 611; *Property and Reversionary Investment Corporation Ltd v Secretary of State for the Environment* [1975] 2 All ER 436.

32 Section 85 Law Practitioners Act 1982.

33 Established under s 88A of the Law Practitioners Act 1982.

practice (such as the Conveyancers Bill 1998) and the submissions made on such areas must be regarded as partisan. In other areas lawyers have a particular interest in ensuring a continued role such as legal aid, or company law. However, in many other areas of law reform members of the law society give their views without any obvious self-interest and with a view to ensuring that any reform is effective and an improvement on the current position. Such input may be made prior to legislation being introduced into Parliament, or in the normal course of a Bill to select committee.

The law society will also act as a public watchdog on government action. When the government acts in a way that is considered unconstitutional, or infringing on personal liberty, the law society may, on rare occasions, speak out.

(b) Access to justice and public education

The law society also plays a role in improving access to justice in a number of ways. By doing such things as producing plain-English pamphlets in respect of some areas of the law or tribunals and making such information available to members of the public the general knowledge about legal rights is improved. A recent initiative is that of law-in-schools where the society has been collaborating with schools in the development of a general course in legal studies which will give a large number of young people an improved appreciation of the legal system. It is also usual for district societies to have a close relationship with community law centres, which often extends to making some resources available to them. Some district law societies also keep a register of specialisation of the members that they will pass on to members of the public in the event of inquiries. Registers of lawyers who are certified to act as duty solicitors, or on the legal aid list are also kept.

These activities can be seen as seeking to improve the lot of the public, or at least not see it worsen. They all cost money and/or time. Members of committees do much of the work undertaken in respect of law reform on a volunteer basis. While it is possible to attribute a selfish motive to such activities, such as the maintenance of prestige, much of this work is truly in the public's interest. There is no good economic rationale for the law society being involved in such activities, and suggestion has been made that such activities cease.[34]

3.5.4 *Profession's interest*

The original law society, the Society of Gentlemen Practitioners of London, was a strictly informal guild of solicitors who associated to

34 *Purposes, Functions and Structure of Law Societies in New Zealand Final Report to the New Zealand Law Society* E-DEC Ltd, 1 September 1997.

protect and further their own interests. The role of promotion of the interests of members of the profession still exists, and remains a large part of the activities of the law society. The numerous activities of the New Zealand and district societies which serve this role are too many to mention; however, some salient observations can be made.

(a) Market protection

An important role has been to protect the lawyer's market against incursion. One aspect of this is to ensure that unqualified practitioners do not provide services in the areas reserved for lawyers.[35] In the event that there has been an apparent breach of the prohibition on unqualified people acting as lawyers, the society will take the necessary action (including obtaining injunctions).[36] The law society has also been heard in cases where other professions claim that lawyers have been infringing on their monopolies. Lawyers selling houses for their clients is the best known example.[37] Similarly, where there is a threat to the lawyers' statutory monopoly, the law society will consider the matter in detail and provide a unified response to such proposals.[38] In the face of recent pressure by government to deregulate the professions generally, the law society has become more active in considering how to manage the inevitable change.[39]

A case in point is the recent initiative to enable licensed conveyancers to act in the sale and purchase of real estate, thereby removing an important part of the lawyer's monopoly.[40] The position of the law society is found in a well-crafted speech by the then president, Ian Haynes.[41] Although purportedly in favour of lower costs to consumers,

---

35 Sections 54, 64 & 65 Law Practitioners Act 1982.

36 *Auckland District Law Society v Dempster* [1995] 1 NZLR 210.

37 See for example *Lewis v Real Estate Institute of New Zealand* [1995] 3 NZLR 385; s 16, Real Estate Agents Act 1976.

38 See for example I Haynes, "Refocusing the conveyancing debate: Haynes challenges the real estate industry" *LawTalk* issue 482, 4 August 1997, p 6 where the then President of the NZLS opposes relaxing the conveyancing monopoly and seeks to refocus the debate on real estate agents, suggesting that lawyers should be granted wider powers in selling houses.

39 This is particularly apparent in a letters from the President of the New Zealand Law Society to all practitioners (15 September 1998 and 20 October 1999) making proposals for the reform of the structure and role of the law society which cite governmental pressure for reform and observed that "further indecision would see the profession losing control of its own destiny".

40 An initiative which looks set to succeed in some form under the wider reforms of the profession, see the letter from the President of the Law Society to all practitioners dated 20 October 1999 and the attached paper.

41 I Haynes, "Refocusing the conveyancing debate: Haynes challenges the real estate industry" speech to Auckland lawyers 23 July 1997 reproduced at

Haynes proceeded to argue that the creation of a second profession of conveyancers would increase costs. He also emphasised the professionalism and safeguards inherent in the current system that would not be guaranteed in the event of the emergence of a new profession of conveyancers. However, perhaps the most telling part of the speech is the observation that the largest cost of a property purchase is the real estate agent fees. From this observation it was argued that the statutory monopoly of real estate agents should be shared with lawyers. This would reduce the cost of purchasing a house. It would of course, coincidentally, be a further and possibly fruitful source of revenue for lawyers. While the speech is cloaked in the garb of public interest it is clear that the effect of the action advocated would be to protect and enhance the position of the profession.

(b) Marketing and public relations

The Law Society also acts as a central marketing and public relations organisation for the profession in general. One way it does this is by informing the public of the need for and availability of lawyers to perform certain tasks. Pamphlets on will making or de facto property agreements serve the dual purposes of informing the public about the law, and of the need to obtain legal assistance. The society also acts as a public relations organisation in promoting the image of lawyers. Where there is some misconduct or defalcation by a lawyer the society will serve as a media liaison point, informing of the steps taken against the lawyer in question and attempting to minimise the damage done to the profession as a whole by isolating the offending lawyer and demonstrating the effectiveness of the discipline procedures. The spokesperson role of the society will also extend to defending the stance of the society on its existing structure, and any proposed changes.

(c) Advocate with government

By acting as a representative to the government and its branches the society seeks to ensure that the privileges that lawyers enjoy are preserved or enhanced. Lawyers are interested in the way in which a number of government offices function, such as the Companies Office, the Land Registry, and certain securities registers. The law society will liaise with such offices as to the manner in which they will operate (such as the availability of computer-based information to practitioners). Similarly, the society acts as a representative of lawyers' interests generally with the Courts. When procedural rules are reviewed the society seeks to ensure that they remain workable and do not place over-onerous duties on lawyers.

[http://www.nz-lawsoc.org.nz/haynes.htm] and in *LawTalk* issue 482, 4 August 1997, p 6.

(d) Law libraries

Perhaps one of the most significant of the services provided by the district societies is the provision of libraries. All but the largest law practices are unable to afford to maintain comprehensive library resources and (depending on the nature of their practices) rely to a greater or lesser extent on the district law society libraries.

(e) Education

The New Zealand Law Society also seeks to enable practitioners to keep up to date on recent developments and changes in the law. It achieves this by organising numerous conferences and seminars, many of which travel to some of the smaller provincial centres.[42] Legal practice manuals and forms that are provided by the law society to practitioners also assist the provision of legal information. A national monthly magazine, *LawTalk*, which discusses current legal and professional issues, is also circulated to all practitioners. Recently, the society has been given the power to require practitioners to undertake education, though whether this will be used is yet to be seen.[43]

(f) Promotion of collegiality

An important part of professionalism from one view is the collegiality between members of the profession. The engenderment and fostering of such collegiality is an intangible aspect of the work of the law society that is very important. There are a number of activities the society engages in to foster such bonds. Practitioners are kept informed about the profession generally, and become included in professional activities by virtue of the society's monthly magazine *LawTalk*. Similarly, the organisation of many social events like dinners and sporting events establish and affirm relations between practitioners and assist in identifying them as belonging to a specific group. The district law societies (in particular) also act as a focus point for a number of interest-group lawyers such as women lawyers or Maori lawyers who form support groups which provide collegiality and support, and are able to address issues of particular importance to members of the group.[44]

---

42 More recently the Law Practitioners Act has been amended to enable the Council of the New Zealand Law Society to compel continuing education: s 17(2)(fa) Law Practitioners Act 1982.

43 Section 17(2)(fa) Law Practitioners Act 1982 inserted by the Law Practitioners Amendment Act 1999.

44 A number of groups such as the Wellington Woman Lawyers' Association, the Canterbury Women's Legal Association, Te Hunga Roia Maori o Aotearoa (The Maori Law Society of New Zealand) and Te Runanga Roia o Tamaki Makaurau (the Auckland Maori Lawyers' Group) exist.

(g) Practitioner support and benefits

There have been a number of efforts to provide advice to lawyers in respect of the management of their legal practice and problems that may arise. The society will offer advice on questions relating to the management of a practice and its financial affairs. Education is also provided by the Society in respect of business management by seminars at regular intervals. For more personal matters the society has provided an anonymous telephone line to seek the advice or support of another lawyer when problems arise. There have also been attempts to highlight the availability of counselling and psychological services to deal with personal problems that may affect the way in which lawyers conduct their practices. There are also a number of commercial benefits that the society obtains for its members. In some cases the society is able to negotiate advantageous prices on things like medical insurance and financial products for its members. In other cases providers approach the society seeking to use it as a route to a lucrative market for such products. This kind of activity is a considerable shift from the role of regulator that many regard the society as having.

3.6 Critique — conflict of roles and conflict of interest

It cannot be denied that the New Zealand and district law societies function effectively in numerous areas. Their tasks, however, require that a careful path be trod between protecting and promoting the interests of their members (lawyers) and protecting the interests of the public in general and clients in particular. The effective discharge of the duties of the law societies requires that it act with a degree of objectivity in balancing the interests of the profession and the public which is difficult to expect when the decision makers in the organisation are by definition lawyers.

No objection can be made to the fact that lawyers group together to promote and protect the interests of their members in a union-like manner. However, it is antithetical to expect the same organisation, which is committed to the interests of its members, to act in the interest of members of the public when regulating and disciplining its members. There are numerous occasions when the interests of lawyers and the interests of lay citizens will diverge. Consequently, the two roles are fundamentally inconsistent with each other. This has been well-expressed in the recent E-DEC report that was commissioned by the law society to advise on its structure and functions. The report notes:[45]

> At present, law societies endeavour simultaneously to benefit the public, assist and protect lawyers' clients, assist lawyers as producers and advance

45 *Purposes, Functions and Structure of Law Societies in New Zealand Final Report to the New Zealand Law Society* E-DEC Ltd, 1 September 1997.

> lawyers' personal interests. These all are legitimate objectives. However, there are inherent conflicts between public and client interests, on the one hand, and lawyers' interests, on the other. Public and client protection involves regulating lawyers' behaviour, forcing lawyers to do what they might not otherwise have done. This imposes burdens on lawyers. In contrast, promoting lawyers' interests involves supporting lawyers in what they want to do and creating benefits for lawyers. This situation of conflicting regulatory and member interest objectives is well recognised by lawyers who have even given it a name, saying that law societies are required to be both policeman and friend.

The protection of the public by the profession's self-regulation and peer discipline involves a conflict of interest with the interests of the members of the profession which is difficult to ignore. It is unreasonable to expect lawyers to devise rules other than those which are the most advantageous they can get away with. Obviously, the profession will not create ridiculously lax rules. If this were so a loss of confidence in the legal profession and consequent government intervention would be inevitable. However, this does not detract from the fact that, within these constraints, self-governance by lawyers can only be expected to be in the lawyers' own interest. This is unsatisfactory, as even an appearance of a conflict of interest in such matters should be avoided. In matters such as rule making and discipline it is not only actual justice, but also the appearance of justice which needs to be preserved. This raises the problem of whether it remains appropriate for the legal profession to regulate and discipline themselves.

3.7 The argument for self-governance by the profession

While the government and Parliament have stepped in from time to time to regulate aspects of lawyers' conduct, in the main, lawyers have been left to regulate themselves. Such regulation has been incremental. For much of the history of the profession its rules were unwritten. Members were expected to know what kind of conduct would fall foul of the standards expected of them. The rules or customs, such as they were, were passed on orally from senior to junior practitioner. Such a method may have worked when members of the profession were from similar backgrounds and had similar ideas about what kind of conduct was acceptable, and the profession was small. But as the profession has grown and diversified the rules have been written down.

While the need for regulation had been recognised by successive governments, the profession has always been seen to be doing a sufficiently good job to ensure that immediate intervention was not necessary. Reform in the area has generally been limited to providing the framework in, and powers by which, the profession regulated itself. Further, the profession has always responded to public and government pressure when its own methods were criticised.[46] There has perhaps historically been a greater tendency to accept that the legal profession was able to govern itself in an essentially paternalistic manner with the interests of the public at heart. Such a view is, however, no longer tenable. It is suggested that few non-lawyers would now accept that the rules governing the incidents of the relationship between themselves and their lawyers ought to be drafted exclusively by lawyers. Perhaps more importantly, they do not believe that lawyers have the necessary objectivity to make rules that do not lean towards self-interest.

(a) Autonomy and the rule of law

Lawyers argue that an autonomous legal profession is of fundamental importance. One of the central arguments raised in favour of self-regulation is the need for an independent legal profession to ensure the rule of law. It is argued that if there is to be true equality before the law, and the state is to be subject to the ordinary law of the land, the legal profession needs to be free from any state regulation. Advocates of self regulation suggest that if the state makes rules regarding professional conduct, it will not be possible to ensure the fearless advocacy and independent advice which is at the centre of the legal profession. This argument is, however, of questionable force. The legal profession is subject to many statute and common law rules as it is, and there is no suggestion that the existence of these rules realistically limits the independence of the practice and the loyalty of the advocacy. In fact, lawyers are dependent on the authority of the state which has granted and protects the privileged position of the profession. Lawyers are not the arbiters of justice, that is the role of the Courts. While lawyers undeniably play an important role in the judicial process they are simply assistants to the Court. Moreover, the argument overlooks the fact that the advocacy role is only a part of the role of the lawyer. The majority of the profession's work is in non-litigious matters such as conveyancing, business transactions, and wills and estate administration. In such matters there is no immediately apparent need for independence.

State governance of the legal profession would not lead to the downfall of the rule of law as we know it. It is clear that in the current environment the government would intervene if the profession abused its current privilege of self-governance. In reality, such self-governance under the shadow of intervention is not independent of government demands.

46 For example, the introduction of lay members and observers into the disciplinary process was the result of a *Report of the Public and Administrative Law Reform Committee on Discipline Within the Legal Profession* Wellington, 1977.

There are a number of jurisdictions where professional governance is closely overseen, or conducted by state bodies.[47] Such intervention seems to bear little relationship to whether the profession is able to discharge its functions effectively or not. Moreover, outside intervention in the governance of the legal profession need not come in the form of the imposition of government-drafted rules in a heavy-handed manner. The independence of the profession could be preserved by the implementation of an independent body or officer to oversee the rule-making process. Such a scheme would not be dissimilar in structure to the Legal Services Ombudsman and Legal Services Commissioner schemes that operate in England and New South Wales respectively (although the functions may be considerably wider).

(b) Honour code

A weaker version of the independence argument is that professional rules are really only the business of lawyers and there is no place for non lawyer involvement. The rules, on this view, are considered to be a voluntary code of conduct by which the members of the organisation set themselves higher professional standards than are required by the general law. No one would suggest that outside input is necessary into, say, a code of ethical conduct of mechanics. Such a code is a voluntary declaration of an intention to adopt certain standards by an autonomous group.

The claim is that rules of professional conduct amount to an "honour code" which is the province of members of the profession and outsiders have no interest in it. The problem with such an argument is that lawyers have a special role in society, which is considered of particular importance. The rules of conduct adopted for lawyers are of special importance. They are not mere customer service guidelines, but rules which ensure that anyone can have access to a lawyer, and determine that the lawyer will deal with the client's affairs with loyalty and in confidence. Further, the rules are more than a mere honour code. The rules created by the profession act as a substitute for the rules that would otherwise be made by government.

(c) Specialist area of regulation

Perhaps the most commonly cited reason for excluding non-lawyers from the governance and rule making of lawyers is that they could not possibly understand the complexities of the law and legal practice. Such an argument plays on the common perception of the way in which the public perceives lawyers and their role. One commentator claims that:[48]

---

47 See H W Arthur, "The Dead Parrot: Does Professional Regulation Exhibit Vital Signs (1995) 33 Alberta LR 800, 801.

48 G E Dal Pont, "Drafting Rules of Professional Conduct" [1996] NZLJ 313, 313.

> Even some of the basic tenets of professional responsibility are not understood by those lacking legal training. Consider the principle of partisanship. Judging by comments made in the media, and my own discussions with non-lawyers, many lay persons cannot understand, for example, how a lawyer can represent a person alleged to have committed an offensive crime, or a tobacco company defending a smoking suit.

It is suggested that this is a fallacy, equating media statements and off-the-cuff comments with considered opinion. Few members of the public would deny that the position of a lawyer in an adversarial system raises difficult ethical issues and lawyers require guidance in them. It may be that non-lawyers disagree with the way in which lawyers currently guide themselves in such matters, but this is not a reason for rejecting their opinions. Providing guidance by drafting rules applicable to the conduct of legal practice will require skill and consideration, however, lawyers do not have a monopoly on such skill. Lawyers need to accept that there is merit in non-lawyers' views about how such problems ought to be resolved. The fact that their views may differ from the views of lawyers suggests a division of interests between the two groups in such matters and a need for a greater diversity of views being taken into account. Any non-lawyer rule maker will obviously need to be skilled in such matters. There seems to be an unfounded fear that rule making would be left to lay people with no understanding or sympathy with the profession. More likely is the use of skilled people who would take a diversity of views into account in drafting such rules.

(d) Not stake holders

Associated with the claim that non-lawyers are not competent to assist in making rules for lawyers is the claim that because they do not have a stake in the rules they will not make rules that are fair and workable. The suggestion is that non-lawyers, given a free rein, would meddle with the status quo by imposing ridiculously high standards on lawyers, and imposing impossible regulatory requirements. This is unlikely for two reasons. First, the public has a large stake in the success of the legal profession. A legal profession that is unworkable would have far reaching repercussions for many sectors of the public. Further, it is not true to say that the people not directly interested in the content of the rules are incapable of making workable rules. The fact that a person does not have an immediate interest in the drafting of the rules and does not work in legal practice on a day-to-day basis is not a bar to having input into sensible and workable professional rules. Indeed, on most approaches, it is considered a positive benefit that a rule-maker's interest is not directly affected by the nature of the rule made.

(e) The argument from tradition

There is undoubtedly a great reluctance in the legal profession to accept that governance ought not be solely in the hands of members of the profession. After all, the profession has until recently been allowed free rein over its rules and internal procedures. While historical precedent is a poor argument for the maintenance of the status quo, it is frequently dressed up in various guises and presented as a reason for resisting change. The regulation of the profession by its members is touted as a venerable tradition that should be preserved. Alternatively, proponents of self-regulation claim that the current system works sufficiently well and it cannot be conclusively demonstrated that any replacement would improve matters. Such arguments amount to no more than the retention of the current state of affairs because that is how things are and have always been.

(f) Pragmatism

Other arguments in favour of self-regulation of the profession are based on pragmatism rather than principle. Some argue that the rules made by the profession to govern its members are more stringent than (or at least as stringent as) any rules that could reasonably be made by outsiders, or with outside input. One reason given for this is the knowledge lurking in the minds of the rule makers that if the profession makes lax rules the public (or government) would find this unacceptable and intervention would be inevitable.[49] Alternatively, it is argued that the better rules are made by self-regulation because of the ethos of the profession and its desire to preserve its own high standards. Such arguments do not, however, accord with the way in which professional rules have developed. For a considerable period of time the rules imposed by the profession were vague to say the least. The rules were unwritten, and even in their present form there remains considerable room for interpretation. It is at least arguable that the trend towards greater clarity and comprehensiveness in professional rules is due to public pressure rather than professional initiative.

Some lawyers also claim that where the rules are made and enforced by the profession they are more severe on their members than would be the case if non-lawyers were involved. The suggestion is that there is such a sense of collective professional responsibility that, when members break the rules, they are treated as having committed a wrong against the profession as well any other victim that may exist. Because the rule breaker has let the profession down the sanctions imposed are more stringent than would otherwise be the case. Such claims are, however, anecdotal and are contradicted by similar evidence the other way. This amounts to an argument that lawyers are effectively tough on themselves. An examination of the rules and the way in which they are enforced does not lend credence to such an argument.[50]

49 G E Dal Pont, "Drafting Rules of Professional Conduct" [1996] NZLJ 313.

50 Even if it were true it would be a matter of concern if lawyers were overly severe on their own members.

(g) Cost

Perhaps the best argument in favour of self-regulation of the legal profession is that it is cheap. If the profession is left to regulate itself the cost falls on the members of the profession, largely in the form of members' unpaid time. Indeed the law society and its many functions are largely run by members giving their time without fee, and any costs that are incurred are met by levies on lawyers. However, the costs of professional regulation are eventually passed on to the client through fees. Perhaps more important is the indirect cost of poor or inadequate regulation of the legal profession. It is a weak argument that self-regulation costs the public nothing if the regulation is inadequate. If the existing rules are vague or subject to evasion and abuse then the consequences of this will ultimately fall on individual clients. Moreover, it will fall on clients unevenly depending on the lawyer they retain.

3.8 The arguments for intervention

There are two main propositions at the heart of the argument that the legal profession should not be left to regulate itself. First, is the claim that the public has a legitimate interest in the professional rules that govern the profession. Secondly, is the claim that the interests of lawyers and the general public diverge. It has already been noted that the ordinary law governs the legal profession. Some of those laws are of general application (such as the law of contract or tort) whereas others are specific (such as the law of legal professional privilege). However, the Rules of Professional Conduct for Barristers and Solicitors relate exclusively to the conduct of lawyers and are in addition to the obligations of the ordinary law. While the professional rules are used as a guide as to the common law of the duties of lawyers, they are not determinative of them. Where there is deviation between the ordinary law and the rules, the rules generally impose a higher standard.

(a) Public interest in rules

The public has a legitimate interest in the creation and enforcement of professional rules because they are directly affected by the nature of the rules and the way in which they are enforced. The rules determine many aspects of the relationship between lawyer and client. The rules regarding the manner in which clients' money is to be dealt with under the professional rules are in considerably more detail than those of the ordinary law. These rules act as a kind of de facto contract between the lawyer and the client. Rather than having to negotiate the way in which lawyers will deal with clients and handle their funds and so on separately in every instance, the rules provide a set of default rules which the lawyer promises to abide by. However, the client plays no part in determining the nature of those rules. They are essentially bound by standard terms of which they have little knowledge and have had no part in negotiating.

Lawyers claim special privileges and duties (and to a degree rightly so) because of the special nature of the service they provide to clients. It is because of the special nature of this service that clients have an interest in the regulation of the profession. Because of the special role of lawyers a unique relationship is formed between lawyers and clients. Confidences are reposed, strategies discussed, dilemmas and legal obstacles confronted. Moreover, in the relationship there is a considerable imbalance of power. In the matters in hand the lawyer is an expert, this is the very reason for the relationship being formed. Further, the matters under consideration are almost certainly of considerable importance to the client and may concern the security of property or person. The client is particularly vulnerable, being unable to judge, except in the most simplistic way, the effectiveness of the legal adviser.[51]

Because of this unique and unusual relationship between lawyer and client, it is necessary to clearly articulate the way in which the lawyer will treat the client, keep confidences and pursue the client's cause. The public, as prospective and actual clients, has a considerable interest in the content of the code by which the lawyer-client relationship is governed.

(b) Balanced dialogue needed

The need for outside input into the governance of the legal profession is particularly needed because the interests of lawyers and clients diverge. It is difficult to deny that it is advantageous to a lawyer to have as few and as light duties as possible imposed on the lawyer-client relationship. Lawyers can be expected to seek to water down duties of confidence and advocate Chinese walls as an effective antidote to conflicts of interest. Additionally, in matters of regulation of the profession generally it is advantageous to exclude non-lawyers from competing with lawyers, and to restrict the degree of competition between lawyers. Conversely, it is in the clients' interest to seek more stringent duties on their lawyers, and to seek greater competition and openness in the profession generally.

If we accept that clients and the general public do have a legitimate interest in the rules and governance of the legal profession, and that the interests of the legal profession diverge from those of clients and the public generally, then continued self-governance by lawyers seems impossible to justify. It is necessary for both interested groups to exchange views and reach agreement on the regulation of the profession taking all perspectives into account.

51 See T Dare, "Virtue Ethics and Legal Ethics" (1998) 28 VUWLR 141, 153.

(c) Procedural unfairness

Self-governance also seems fundamentally unfair. If we accept that the public and clients have an interest in the rules and their enforcement, the fact that lawyers make the rules and enforce them against their members seems overly one-sided and procedurally unjust. The appearance of partisanship or bias is something that lawyers are quick to recognise, however, in the matter of self-regulation their own interest is claimed to be unobjectionable. The process of discipline also falls foul of the principle against bias. Admittedly, there are good arguments to use the expertise of practising lawyers when addressing the question of whether misconduct has occurred. However, the near exclusive decision-making power in the hands of lawyers under the current system means that discipline is being meted out by people with considerable commonalities with the offender.[52] This problem is particularly acute in smaller districts. The legal profession is renowned for the fact that it can be very close-knit, and in small centres this is particularly the case. Because discipline at the lowest level is a function of the district law societies[53] it is quite possible that members of the disciplinary tribunal will know, or know of, the practitioner being disciplined.[54] The central problem is the lack of independence of the disciplinary process. Some claim that the discipline process leads to harsher treatment of offenders, and others claim the opposite. Whatever the case, the fact is that when client complaints are being considered, and the property and livelihood of a practitioner is at stake, the necessary appearance of objectivity does not exist.

(d) Ineffective

The harshest criticism that can be made of self-governance of the profession is that it is ineffective. This can be shown most clearly by an examination of the rules that the profession creates for itself. It is of particular note while the drafting of clear, unequivocal and exhaustive documents is central to the trade of lawyers, these are not qualities that are found in the Rules of Professional Conduct for Barristers and Solicitors. The introduction to the rules admit as much when it is stated:

> Any attempt to compile an exhaustive code purporting to define exclusively the rules for a breach of which a person could be subject to the disciplinary processes of the Act would be self-defeating.

---

52 In District Law Society Disciplinary Tribunals there are two lay observers and between five and eight practitioners: s 103 Law Practitioners Act 1982. In the New Zealand Disciplinary Tribunal there are between five and twelve practitioners, and three lay observers: s 108 Law Practitioners Act 1982.

53 Section 103 Law Practitioners Act 1982.

54 There are provisions in the Law Practitioners Act to minimise such problems as appointing members from other districts to the tribunal (s 103), by having one tribunal for more than one district (s 105) or referring the matter to the national body: s 106(2).

Many of the rules, which are accompanied by an official commentary, are drafted in a general manner that leaves considerable room for interpretation (and evasion).

Rule 1.02 is a good example of the vagueness of the rules. It is the New Zealand articulation of the cab-rank rule and provides:

> A practitioner as a professional person must be available to the public and must not, without good cause, refuse to accept instructions for services within the practitioner's fields of practice from any particular client or prospective client.

Neither the rule nor the commentary which follows give much guidance as to what will amount to "good cause" to refuse to accept instructions. While the commentary states that insufficient time or expertise will be good cause, whereas race or gender of the client will not, there is no guidance as to the truly difficult problems. Must a lawyer accept instructions when the case has no prospect of success or where they find the cause of the client personally repugnant? This problem of vagueness pervades the rules and in many cases makes them ineffective as a guide for practitioners, and makes sanction for breach impossible. It is possible to punish a practitioner for unbecoming conduct notwithstanding that the conduct complained of is not expressly prohibited, though there is an understandable reluctance to do so. An examination of the records of disciplinary hearings demonstrates that the rules that are enforced are predominantly those that are regulatory in nature where the breaches are clear. In particular offences, such as failing to adhere to proper accounting practices or operating of nominee companies inappropriately, are far more regularly enforced than breaches of rules regarding conflicts of interest, duties to the administration of justice, and obligations of confidence.

A significant portion of the rules can also be criticised as largely to do with the protection of the profession and its interests. There are numerous examples: the prohibition on using a name of a legal practice that would bring the profession into disrepute (r 2.01); advertisements which are not "consistent with the maintenance of proper professional standards" (r 4.01); or the provision that approaches to prospective clients ought not bring the profession into disrepute: r 4.03. Such rules seem to limit the lengths to which lawyers may go in marketing themselves and restrict practitioners to conducting their marketing strategies in a seemly fashion. While these provisions have become more permissive over time (previously all advertising was prohibited), they are essentially aimed at limiting the competition between practitioners with the arguable effect that the costs to clients will be increased.

Other rules amount to broad statements of guidance that can not really be called rules at all. Rule 6.01 provides that a practitioner must promote and maintain proper standards of professionalism in relations with other practitioners. The commentary expands this by stating, amongst other matters, that practitioners should treat each other with courtesy and fairness, and should return telephone calls promptly. It is questionable whether the majority of practitioners adhere to either of these exhortations in practice. While there may be a place for such broad statements regarding how practitioners ought to conduct themselves, they do not function as rules which can guide conduct meaningfully, or act as a measure against which conduct can be measured in order to determine whether a breach has occurred.

In short, the rules which lawyers have created for themselves are far from ideal. While some of the rules serve important purposes, many are vague, self-serving and unenforceable. The fact that the current rules are defective is a good argument for changing the way in which they are created, and involving non-lawyers in the process.

(e)Balance

The flip-side of the objection that the current rules, created by lawyers, are unsatisfactory is the claim that non-lawyer input would improve matters. Rather than leading to unworkable or unduly stringent rules, it is suggested that, with an appropriate process, wider involvement would lead to more workable rules which achieve a better balance between the interests of lawyers, clients, public and state. Some have suggested that specialist assistance should be sought from the likes of sociologists and philosophers.[55] If this were the case then presumably economists, management consultants, and other experts would also be useful.[56] In any event, it is suggested the involvement of a diverse range of groups is important.

3.9 Alternatives

While it is beyond the scope of this work to propose a detailed consultative procedure, it is suggested that the benefits of wider involvement would be significant. One possibility would be to allow submissions by members of the public and interest groups to comment on proposed changes, or to propose changes themselves. The procedure might be similar to the select committee procedure adopted by Parliament. This would enable a wide range of opinions to be heard and

---

55 W Thompson, "Rules of Professional Conduct" [1995] NZLJ 128.

56 The views of such experts were not well received when the consultancy firm E-DEC Ltd submitted their *Report on the Purposes, Functions and Structure of Law Societies in New Zealand Final Report to the New Zealand Law Society* 1 September 1997.

avoid the criticism of any procedure under which representatives were selected. However, such a procedure would depend upon those considering the submissions to take them seriously and be prepared to change rules in accordance with suggestions and arguments received. If the rule-making group remained composed entirely of lawyers it may be that any such consultative procedure would be limited in its usefulness. There is also a danger in such a procedure of it being dominated by those interests that are most articulate, which is sometimes equated with those who have the most money to spend on such submissions.

An alternative would be to have a kind of rule-making commission, which would include members of the community who reflect a diversity of interests. It would be possible to reserve a number of places on such a commission for law society appointments. The problem with such a body will always be the manner of appointment, whether by some democratic process, or by selection (perhaps by the Attorney-General). However, there is a danger in letting such problems stand in the way of needed and beneficial reform.

There also exists a need for an independent scrutiny of the rules once made. Whatever system of rule making exists in the profession, it needs to be recognised that the Rules of Professional Conduct are a kind of delegated legislation.[57] They are made under an authority conferred by statute[58] and enable the disciplinary tribunals of the profession to punish practitioners. Such punishments may be significant and could include a fine, suspension or disbarment from practice. Like any law the rules are binding and so long as practitioners wish to practise law they are subject to the rules. However, unlike most delegated legislation the Rules of Professional Conduct are not subject to any general review procedure. A review procedure of the rules would be a significant step towards holding the profession accountable for the rules it makes. Whereas the smallest local authority is liable to have its bylaws disallowed, there is no such check on the rules by which significant aspects of the relationship between lawyers and clients, and the way lawyers run their practices, are governed. It seems that reform in this direction may be likely. In a letter to the profession the President of the Law Society disclosed that reforms proposed by the government would be subject to approval by the Minister of Justice.[59]

In England and Wales the Legal Services Ombudsman has a limited role in reviewing the rules by which barristers and solicitors are governed. The ombudsman's role under the scheme includes supervising the

---

57 W Thompson, "Rules of Professional Conduct" [1995] NZLJ 128.
58 Section 17 Law Practitioners Act 1982.
59 Letter, President of the Law Society to all practitioners, 20 October 1999, and the attached paper.

complaints and discipline procedure in individual cases, and making recommendations concerning the procedure in more general terms. This system has led to the law society improving procedures and areas of practice within the profession which require improvement. The criticisms that the Ombudsman has made of the profession have been severe, such as that the complaints bureau within the law society acted as "a defensive mechanism on behalf of the law society rather than a problem-solving mechanism for complainants".[60] Such criticism is the hallmark of an independent supervisory body and has led to meaningful improvements in the way complaints are handled.[61] This appears to be evidence that an independent body can have a significant beneficial effect on the way in which the disciplinary procedure operates. It may be that if the Ombudsman were given the wider power to criticise shortcomings in the rules as well as the procedure, further benefits would flow.

The argument for non-lawyer involvement in lawyer regulation is strong. The regulation of the profession and the relationship between lawyer and client cannot be left in the hands of lawyers on the basis that they can be trusted to act in an objective and even-handed manner. Even if this were the case it is no longer acceptable to exclude interested parties from a process of making rules which directly affect them. Moreover, regulation of the profession is delegated law making and as such needs to be supervised. The arguments put forward for self-regulation are weak. The fact that self-regulation has been a hallmark of the legal (and other) profession(s) is no reason for continuing such a tradition if it is fundamentally unsound. It is argued that an examination of the history of the rules, and their current content shows that the claim that when left to themselves lawyers make the best rules is unfounded. The sooner the governance of the legal profession includes all of those who hold a stake in it the better.

---

60 Legal Services Ombudsman *Annual Report* 1993, 8.

61 See generally R James and M Seneviratne, "The Legal Services Ombudsman: Form versus Function?" (1995) 58 MLR 187.

[illegible]

[illegible]

5 Legal Services Ombudsman Annual Report ([illegible]), 8.

6 See generally R James and M Seneviratne, 'The Legal Services Ombudsman: Form versus Function' ([illegible]) 58 MLR 187.

Chapter 4

Professional Standards

Introduction

A central part of the role of the profession is the promulgation and maintenance of professional standards. The creation and enforcement of the rules is left largely to members of the profession. This chapter examines the rules, their scope and purpose. It also examines the complaints and disciplinary procedure, and the concept of professional misconduct.

4.1 The Rules of Professional Conduct for Barristers and Solicitors

4.1.1 *How the rules are made*
The Council of the New Zealand Law Society[1] is empowered to make rules to govern its members under s 17 of the Law Practitioners Act 1982. That section confers wide powers to make rules in respect of numerous matters including the constitution and meetings of the council, discipline and professional practice of members, trust accounts, and insurance of members in respect of claims against them.[2] The power to make rules cannot be delegated to any other committee.[3] The council is relatively unwieldy having around 30 members. The task of examining the rules and drafting any new rules or amendments, therefore, falls to the ethics committee of the council. The ethics committee then reports recommendations back to the board that in turn reports to the council which then is able to examine them and amend, adopt or reject them.[4]

---

1 The council of the society comprises the president, vice-presidents, treasurer, members elected by the district societies and any president-elect: s 11 Law Practitioners Act 1982.

2 Amongst the rules and other publications made by the Rules of Professional Conduct for Barristers and Solicitors, are Rules of the New Zealand Law Society, Solicitors Trust Account Rules, Trust Account Guidelines, Nominee Company Rules, and Privacy Guidelines.

3 Section 15(4) Law Practitioners Act 1982.

4 Although consultation within the profession is commonplace: see Chapter 3.4.2.

In addition to the rules, the council is empowered to give rulings and opinions which interpret the various rules.[5] The rulings are binding on all practitioners. Opinions are less formal and technically non-binding (although practitioners would ignore them at their peril). The council has delegated the power to give rulings and opinions to the ethics committee of the society.[6] It is questionable whether the delegation of the power to make rulings that bind practitioners is within the power of the council. Such rulings have (and are intended to have) a precedent effect. They amount to a kind of rule making. The Law Practitioners Act expressly prohibits the delegation of rule making.[7] Both rulings and "significant" opinions are to be made available to practitioners. The former are published in the society's monthly periodical *LawTalk* and in the Rules of Professional Conduct.

4.1.2 *Scope of the rules*

The Rules of Professional Conduct are only one part of the law that governs the conduct of a lawyer. The general law is directly relevant to the rights and duties between lawyer and client, and if they are breached either party may litigate the matter before the Courts. Unlike the general law, the rules focus on what amounts to misconduct by a practitioner. This is in contrast to the general law which seeks to remedy wrongs committed and, therefore, protects the interests of the client. While the rules and the general law have many aspects in common they are not identical. For example, it is not considered misconduct if a practitioner is merely negligent whereas a remedy for such conduct will exist at law. Conversely, a failure of a practitioner to deal with a third party in a courteous manner is not a breach of a right under the ordinary law, but may amount to misconduct.[8]

Barristers and solicitors are regarded as officers of the Court and the Court has an inherent jurisdiction to govern their conduct.[9] The Court has the power to punish or reprimand those who appear before it where they are guilty of unacceptable conduct.[10] The stance of the Court in such matters will both affect and be affected by the profession's rules on conduct. The Court's view on such matters is, however, distinct from the professional rules.

---

5 Section 17(2)(h) of the Law Practitioners Act 1982.

6 Rule 13.5 Rules of the New Zealand Law Society.

7 Section 15(4).

8 Rule 7.01 Rules of Professional Conduct of Barristers and Solicitors.

9 The position is somewhat different in England where solicitors have historically been governed by the Courts, and the Courts have the power to discipline and strike names from the roll. Barristers, however, are governed by the various Inns of Court. The Judges of the Courts act as the final disciplinary authority as visitors to the Inns.

10 See further ch 14.

4.1.3 *Role of the rules*

The professional rules which govern practitioners and their relationships with clients serve several and diverse purposes. The nature of those purposes will affect both the contents of the rules and the way in which they are expressed. There are considerable differences of opinion as to what such rules ought to achieve. There are arguments as to what they should be called. Some claim that the label "rules" fails to encapsulate the ethical dimension of professional practice. Others object to the use of alternative terms such as ethical guidelines or canons and suggest that such matters ought to be relegated to philosophers and theologians. They argue that matters of personal values have no place in the relationships between lawyers and their clients. Some have advocated calling the governing text a "code", however this has been objected to on the grounds that such a code is never exhaustive and such a title would mislead. The fact that there is such disagreement over the (arguably) trifling matter of what the governing standards are named, illustrates the depth of the divide between the differing opinions.

An examination of the kinds of roles that rules of professional conduct can or might serve will act as a useful measure of exactly what the New Zealand Rules of Professional Conduct do achieve, and how they may be reformulated, improved, or added to, to achieve more or different ends.

(a) The statutory role

The Council of the New Zealand Law Society is authorised to make rules for the governance of the profession by virtue s 17 of the Law Practitioners Act 1982. That section grants a broad authority to make rules for the "regulation and good government of the Society and its members and its affairs" This includes achieving the statutory purposes of the society under s 4 of the Act which include proper conduct of the members of the profession, the suppression of illegal and dishonourable conduct, the preservation of the integrity of the profession, and the promotion of the interests of the profession. These statutory purposes, however, provide little guidance as to the numerous other less obvious purposes that the rules promulgated by the society do, or ought to, serve.

The New Zealand Law Society Rules of Professional Conduct for Barristers and Solicitors take the form of statements of a general rule followed by a commentary. The rules are not intended to be exhaustive, nor are they intended to be precise in application. For example, r 8.01 provides little real guidance as to how a practitioner ought to resolve the tension between the duties owed to the Court and the client when it states:

> In the interests of the administration of justice, the overriding duty of a practitioner acting in litigation is to the Court or the tribunal concerned. Subject to this, the practitioner has a duty to act in the best interests of the client.

While the commentary attached to the rule gives assistance in some specific matters such as contempt of Court, it does not substantially clarify the rule. This clarification is up to the individual practitioner and in the words of the introduction to the rules "their individual sense of professional responsibility". The fact that the rules are not exhaustive is iterated by the opening words of their introduction:

> The purpose of this publication is to provide guidance for practitioners in the practise of law in New Zealand. This is not to be considered an exhaustive code or treatise. It is rather a definition of the bounds within which a practitioner can practise the profession. Observance of those bounds, and managing all aspects of practice within them involves the acceptance of the basic principle of professional responsibility.

In the introduction to the rules and throughout the commentary practitioners are referred to numerous other sources including the ethical codes and rules of other jurisdictions, and numerous Court cases, legislation, scholarly articles and practice notes of the Courts. Where practitioners face a difficult ethical problem they may have to conduct considerable research before being able to form an opinion on the appropriate course of conduct.

Since 1997 a system has been implemented whereby the rules can be supplemented by rulings and opinions of the New Zealand Law Council.[11] Such a system enables practitioners to submit difficulties through their district law society to the New Zealand Law Council for consideration. The general issue raised will be considered and, in the case of a ruling, a statement that is binding in the instant case will be made. In the case of an opinion, the statement is not binding although the prudent approach is for a practitioner to adopt such an opinion. Rulings and opinions are published by the society and appended to the Rules of Professional Conduct.

(b) Guide to practitioners

A central function of any set of professional precepts is as a guide to members of the profession both as to the general conduct of their practice and, particularly, in cases of difficulty. The compendium of the rules promulgated by the Law Society of England and Wales, which

---

11 The power is delegated to the ethics committee of the society pursuant to r 13.5 of the New Zealand Law Society Rules.

governs the conduct of solicitors, is entitled *The Guide to Professional Conduct.* This emphasises the usefulness of such a publication to practitioners, as well as highlighting the fact that such a set of guidelines (as with any legislation) is never exhaustive and there will be occasions where the practitioner will have to apply the principles rather than rules of the *Guide* to novel situations, or cases where one or more rules unexpectedly conflict.

There are two quite distinct ways in which a set of rules can be an effective guide. One is to aim for exhaustiveness. Tax legislation, for example, takes this approach. This is also the direction in which the American Bar Association leans in its Model Rules of Professional Conduct. Like the New Zealand rules a rule-commentary approach is adopted, however, both the rules and the commentary are considerably more detailed than the New Zealand equivalent. A similar approach is taken in the Guide to Professional Conduct for Solicitors in England and Wales (which runs to more than 700 pages). Even with such detailed rules there are gaps and interpretation or extrapolation is necessary of even the most carefully worded commentary. While practitioners are invariably exhorted to interpret the rules applicable in the spirit in which they are intended,[12] there is always a danger of subversion by a technical reading, or minimal compliance.

An alternative to drafting comprehensive rules is to provide guiding principles which can be used to resolve ethical issues. Such governing documents issued by a professional body are used for assistance in resolving ethical problems in a manner which is more complex than the application of straightforward rules to clear-cut factual situations. To be useful in such cases the rules need to be more than regulatory. It is necessary to give principled guidance on matters such as the precedence of the various duties owed by practitioners, and the basis upon which gaps and vagueness in the rules may be resolved. The American Bar Association adopted such a method from 1908 when it adopted the "Canons of Professional Ethics" which stated the obligations of lawyers in a broad and principled manner. Those canons were supplemented with ethical considerations and disciplinary rules. This approach was, however, abandoned in 1983 in favour of a rule-based approach.[13]

Any standards set to govern human conduct are vulnerable to being read down by those who seek to avoid the inconvenient constraints imposed. Setting standards for lawyers is particularly difficult as lawyers are

12 See para 13 of the preamble to the ABA Model Rules of Professional Conduct.

13 An intermediate set of guidelines existed from 1969 until 1983 in the form of the Model Code of Professional Responsibility. It is of note that some states retain the Code-based approach, for example the New York State Bar Association.

experts at viewing rules in a light most favourable to the interest they seek to promote. Rules sufficiently detailed that anticipate every eventuality of legal practice are an impossibility. Lawyers will always be able to subvert the rules to their own advantage. In general, however, the rules will act as a boundary which, though not always clearly delineated, will show the limits of acceptable conduct.

(c) Education

The rules promulgated by the professional body serve an educative function. They act to educate practitioners in, not only the rules themselves, but also the standards and values that are expected of them. The rules are distributed widely, and copies are sent to every practitioner. Changes to the rules are publicised in the professional magazine and incorporated in later editions of the rules. An up-to-date version of the rules with all amendments consolidated is also published at the law society's website.[14] The rules act as a constant reference point to which practitioners may have recourse when considering matters of ethics and conduct.

The degree of direct knowledge that practitioners have of the rules is, however, open to question. It may rightly be pointed out by many practitioners that education in professional values is not achieved by laboriously reading rules which will be forgotten by a busy practitioner unless immediately relevant and useful. They are inculcated by working as a professional with (and against) other professionals. It was observed in one influential report that "lawyers do not know the rules of professional responsibility; they have never learnt them, or if they have they have forgotten them".[15] While the rules state what are the required standards, these are communicated informally (and perhaps inaccurately) within the profession rather than formally by practitioners reading the text of the rules.

There are obvious problems with the informal transmission of professional standards and values. Such a method of communication of the central precepts of the profession is unreliable. The way in which such principles are discussed and applied will vary between practitioners and firms. The duty to avoid a conflict of interest, for example, raises different problems for large firms from small ones. Some practitioners will apply strict standards, and others view them more liberally, and the way in which they are dealt with may differ accordingly. The danger is that the values that exist in different practising environments will vary depending on the differing demands of practice.

14 [http://www.nz-lawsoc.org.nz/about/profcom.htm].

15 *Cotter-Roper Report on Education and Training in Legal Ethics and Professional Responsibility* 1996.

The rules are also used as a primary source material from which to teach law students and prospective entrants into the profession the rules by which they will be governed, and the standards of conduct that will be expected of them.

(d) Public proclamation of standards

The rules also act as a statement of the standards of conduct that clients and members of the public can expect and demand from practitioners. Clients do not have a detailed knowledge of the Rules of Professional Conduct, or of their rights. However, by virtue of the public nature of the document the general tenor and implications of lawyers' obligations to their clients are generally known. Rather than relying on the moral judgment of any individual practitioner, clients and the public generally can look to the rules promulgated by the professional body as a kind of public code to which practitioners will adhere. The rules promulgated by the profession might, in this sense be regarded as a social compact or promise which the profession makes.

The need for a uniform and public set of guidelines is particularly important as it is no longer realistically possible for a prospective client to be personally acquainted with a practitioner nor can it be presumed that any particular set of values will be applied by the practitioner. Moreover, it is important that clients are aware that there is some degree of uniformity across the profession in respect of matters of professional conduct. The knowledge that lawyers bind themselves to precepts such as loyalty and confidentiality is of particular relevance in law for a number of reasons. Matters in which members of the public seek assistance from lawyers are necessarily of considerable importance to the client and may involve matters concerning the security of property, livelihood, or liberty. However, clients usually face the considerable difficulty that they are unable to police their lawyer's conduct. This is due to the lack of expertise in the area, the fact that the impact of a lawyer's performance on the outcome of a matter may not be immediately apparent, and the actions of the lawyer are executed outside the client's sphere of cognisance. It is because of this that the client needs to be sure of the basis on which the lawyer will conduct himself or herself.

Clients are generally aware of the precepts which govern the lawyer-client relationships, or the relationship would be unworkable. In particular, in the absence of the duty of loyalty to the client and of confidentiality, it is unlikely that a reasonable client would either trust a lawyer with his or her affairs or fully disclose the facts. While it might be possible in theory for lawyers and clients to agree such matters between them on a case-by-case basis, the existence of a public and workable set of rules is by far the most efficient way by which to regulate the lawyer-client relationship.

(e) Public relations

That the rules promulgated by the profession may also be seen to be a (largely effective) effort on the part of the profession to persuade the public that its members are trustworthy and that the professional organisation will protect client interests.[16] A central object of the rules is to reassure the public as to the professional integrity of the members of the profession. In this sense the rules amount to a code of consumer service to which members promise to adhere.

Professional rules are also intended to reassure the public that the profession is capable and trustworthy in governing itself. If the rules were lax or if damaging breaches went unpunished the public may not continue to tolerate the profession's self-governance. Commentators have also noted that the disciplinary bodies of professional organisations tend to sanction members mainly where the reputation of the profession demands it, for example, in the mishandling of client funds, or fraud, or in avoidance of the enforcement mechanism of the professional organisation (as in failing to respond to queries, or obstructing investigations).[17] The rules are a mechanism for protecting the reputation of the profession in the public eye.

(f) Aspirational values

Rules are generally drafted to demand, prohibit, or permit certain conduct. A lawyer must be honest to a Court, must not breach client confidentiality, and may advertise the practice within certain limitations. Pronouncements by the professional organisation that a lawyer ought to act in a particular way are rare. While members of the profession will point to altruistic aspects of professionalism, official statements or encouragement of such altruism are rare. One exception is the ABA Model Rules which in r 6.1 state: "A lawyer should aspire to render at least 50 hours of pro bono publico legal services per year". The rule is wholly unenforceable and in jurisdictions where it has been adopted adherence to it is inconsistent at best. While contained in the rules of the profession, it is itself not a rule at all, but a request or encouragement to practitioners to engage in pro bono work.[18]

---

16 See the arguments of H W Arthurs, "Why Canadian Law Schools do not Teach Legal Ethics" in K Economides *Ethical Challenges to Legal Education and Conduct* Oxford, Hart Publishing, 1998, 105, 112.

17 H W Arthurs, "Why Canadian Law Schools do not Teach Legal Ethics" in K Economides *Ethical Challenges to Legal Education and Conduct* Oxford, Hart Publishing, 1998, 105.

18 The New York State Bar Association Code of Professional Conduct also adopts such an approach in its canons. Canon One provides: "A Lawyer

A different vehicle for encouragement of ethical conduct of practitioners is to be found in the *Statement of Ethics* of the New South Wales Law Society. That document states:

> The law should protect the rights and freedoms of members of the community. The administration of the law should be just. The lawyer practises law as an officer of the Court. The lawyer's role is both to uphold the rule of law and serve the community in the administration of justice.
> In fulfilling this role, lawyers should:
> - Serve their client's interests competently;
> - Communicate clearly with their clients;
> - Treat people with respect;
> - Act fairly, honestly and diligently in all dealings;
> - Pursue an ideal of service that transcends self-interest;
> - Work with their colleagues to uphold the integrity of the profession and honourable standards and principles;
> - Develop and maintain excellent professional skills;
> - Act frankly and fairly in all dealings with the Courts;
> - Be trustworthy;
> - Keep the affairs of clients confidential, unless otherwise required by law;
> - Maintain and defend the rights and liberty of the individual;
> - Avoid any conflict of interest.
>
> In fulfilling this role, lawyers are not obliged to serve the client's interests alone if to do so would conflict with the duty which lawyers owe to the Court and to serving the ends of justice.

Such statements are admirable despite the fact that it is unlikely that many practitioners will achieve all of them. They do act as a signal to members of the profession, and a reminder of the claims of honour that the profession makes. They serve to ensure that there is at least formal agreement as to the function of the legal profession and the values to which it should aspire.

Aspirational guidelines do not exist in a vacuum. They are invariably linked to a substantial body of professional rules that give more practical guidance to practitioners. Such aspirational guidelines may, however, be of assistance in reading and interpreting such rules. A statement of the aspirations of the profession puts rules in a social context, and assists in determining their intended purpose which may assist in resolving vagueness, gaps, and ambiguities.

Should Assist in Maintaining the Integrity and Competence of the Legal Profession".

It might be argued that such aspirational codes introduce an inappropriate formalism into the core aspect of the profession and that attempting to write in a few broad statements the essence of professionalism is doomed to failure. A knowledge of the ethos of the profession is gained by being part of the profession and learning by practice. The difficulty with such an approach is that the modern legal profession is so large and diverse that it is difficult to accept that there really is a shared ethos. It is difficult to see how, in isolation, a small provincial firm that practises in criminal and family law would have the same fundamental values as a large commercial city firm which discourages such work. Without a central body through which members' voices could be heard any collective sense of what professionalism means would be absent. The values in such a statement are not held by all members of the profession. However, such a statement does represent agreement that the profession as a whole has reached as to the values they ought to aspire to.

(g) Promotion of professional unity

Members of the profession do not necessarily have a natural sense of collegiality. Professional guidelines or rules provide a useful point of commonality between members with essentially different interests. Previously, a number of factors may have assisted in the profession being more unified than it is today. Members were generally of the same gender, ethnicity, and social background. The current profession is considerably more diverse; within the profession are numerous groups and sub-groups with divergent interests and correspondingly divergent ideas about the role and function of lawyers. A set of rules or aspirational claims can serve as a consensus (or at least a majority view) regarding the place of lawyers. It can set out commonalities had by all members of the profession, and emphasise the uniting factors as well as the obvious differences.[19]

For rules to be an effective focus on which members can build a sense of collegiality it is important that the rules are made in a way which includes a diverse range of practitioners (putting aside the issue of non-lawyer involvement in rule making). It is important that the rules do not disadvantage one group of lawyers unreasonably.[20] While there is usually

---

19 The degree to which this purpose is achieved by rules or codes of professional conduct is unclear: L De Groot-Van Leeuen and W De Groot, "Studying Codes of Conduct: A Descriptive Framework for Comparative Research" (1998) 1 Legal Ethics 155, 164.

20 It has been claimed that the rules which prohibit fee splitting, finders' fees, limiting advertising, but implicitly permitting the forms of marketing such as sponsorships, membership of clubs and referrals from other professionals, favour large firms over the small. See T Schneyer, "Professionalism as Politics: The Making of a Modern Legal Ethics Code" in R L Nelson et al (eds)

consultation within the profession as to the drafting of the Rules of Professional Conduct in New Zealand, there is no clear procedure to permit this. The rules are drafted by the ethics committee of the New Zealand Law Society, referred to the board, and approved by the New Zealand Law Council (the governing body of the society). While the members of the council are elected from their representative district law societies, it is suggested that the current rules do not require any broad-based discussion about the rules or proposed changes by members of the profession (let alone non-lawyers). Because of this, the efficacy and legitimacy of the rules as a statement of a commonly held professional ethos, or goal, is questionable.

(h) Indicator to Court

The obligations imposed on lawyers by the general law are not determined by the professional obligations under the rules or guidelines promulgated by the professional organisation. The Court will not lightly disregard such rules in determining whether lawyers have breached their legal obligations to their client. The law regarding the obligations of lawyers has, in a large part grown from the customary practices of lawyers which have solidified into legal obligations. The Courts will look to the profession to determine the currently acceptable standards of conduct. The best and most authoritative source of such usages are the rules of conduct created by the profession to govern its members. The Court of Appeal has observed in respect of the rules that:[21]

> An ethical code of this kind expresses the profession's own collective judgment as to the standards to be expected of practitioners. While it does not impose legal obligations or have the force of law it is some indication of relevant public policy concerns.

The Court is, however, not bound to follow the rules of the profession. It may be that a lawyer has adhered to the professional rules of conduct, but still fallen foul of the law. The rules are generally drafted with the intention that they set standards as high or higher than the legal obligations imposed on practitioners. Instances of a lawyer complying with the rules but breaching the law will, therefore, be rare. One example where the Rules of Professional Conduct may be more lax than the law, is in relation to contingency fee arrangements. The rules expressly do not prohibit such arrangements.[22] Some commentators, however,

---

Lawyer's Ideals/Lawyer's Practises Ithaca and London, Cornell University Press, 1992, 95-144.

21 *Black v Taylor* [1993] 3 NZLR 403 at 409 per Richardson J (CA).

22 Rule 3.01 deals with fee arrangements and the commentary to that rule states that: "The rule is drafted in terms which contemplate the possibility of charging a contingency fee. The following points should, however, be noted in that regard:... It may be that, in some circumstances at least, the common law rules against maintenance and champerty may still apply, so as to

maintain that there is a clear legal prohibition on such arrangements.[23] In such cases the Court will not be bound by the professional standards. In other cases the professional standards will be directly relevant. For example, where the question is whether a practitioner has been guilty of a serious dereliction of duty and is liable for the costs of a proceeding bears a close relationship to the question of whether there has been incompetence or negligence sufficient to warrant disciplinary sanctions:[24]

> [T]he levels will often coincide and incompetence or negligence falling short of a disciplinary level … will not ordinarily amount to a serious dereliction of duty to the Court.

4.1.4 *The New Zealand position*

In practice, none of the codes, rules, or guides achieve all the above objectives completely. The degree to which the objectives are achieved will depend on numerous factors, including by whom and how they were drafted, the level of generality or specificity at which they are pitched, the comprehensiveness of the rules and the motives of the drafters, to name but a few. In New Zealand the Rules of Professional Conduct sit awkwardly, not amounting to a comprehensive code, and failing to guide practitioners in even a general way in some areas. While the rules set some bounds for the practice of law, the introduction to the rules themselves states:

> Within those bounds the prime responsibility of a practitioner is his or her own sense of professional responsibility. The preservation of the integrity and reputation of the profession is very much a matter for individual members.

The rules seem to aim for a degree of comprehensiveness. This is achieved with the statement of a general rule followed by a commentary that expands on and explains the rule. However the degree to which this is achieved varies considerably. Some matters lean towards more detail, such as the manner in which a lawyer may advertise, or the duty to honour an undertaking. Other arguably more important duties such as the duties of loyalty and confidentiality are harder to articulate in the form of rules, leading to gaps and vagueness in these central areas. For

---

invalidate an agreement for a contingency fee. In the absence of clear and current authority on the point, the Society draws the possibility of invalidity to the attention of practitioners."

23 See D Webb, "Contingency Fees: Riskier Than They Seem?" [1998] NZLJ 390. See also the Auckland District Law Society *Report on Contingency Fee Arrangements* 1998 (available on request from the society) found that in most cases such fee arrangements fell foul of the law. Contrast the paper of the NZLS Civil Litigation and Tribunals Committee (1999) which concluded that it was "seriously arguable" that such arrangements were not illegal.

24 *Harley v McDonald* [1999] 3 NZLR 545, 566 per Tipping J.

example, the rules state that there is a duty to divulge confidential information where "there is an overriding duty to a Court or tribunal" to do so,[25] however, no guidance is offered when such circumstances may arise.

The rules offer little or no guidance for significant areas of legal practice. For example, there is no specific guidance on the conduct of negotiations with other practitioners (or persons representing themselves). Is it appropriate to take advantage of another practitioner's mistake or oversight? Are false threats of groundless legal proceedings permissible? These are all problems which arise in practice, but for which guidance is lacking.

Some rules are stated in such general terms that they are unenforceable in all but the most clear-cut cases. Rule 1.01 is probably the most broadly stated rule, and is correspondingly difficult to pin down. It provides: "The relationship between practitioner and client is one of confidence and trust which must never be abused". The commentary to the rules is similarly broad. There is no guidance as to the actual circumstances when the relationship will be found to be abused save from statements such as those that there should be no self-advancement, and that there may be a breach where the lawyer enters a sexual relationship with the client. The rule provides no real guidance in concrete situations.

The New Zealand rules do not provide any aspirational guidance to practitioners. They are minimum standards. If a practitioner falls below them this will amount to misconduct and discipline may ensue. The rules are a guide for lawyers who want to stay out of trouble, rather than a guide for those who want to be excellent lawyers. Consequently, the guide to what makes excellent or admirable lawyers is often taken from peers or mentors with whom lawyers work. In some situations this works well and junior practitioners shape their conduct, and themselves, on worthy models. However, it is an unreliable way to provide guidance of what a practitioner ought to aspire to. In some environments, undue emphasis will be placed on winning at all costs, earning the greatest amount of fees possible, or pursuing a particular political end.

While there is no unanimity as to what lawyers ought to aspire to, provision of some guidance as to the values which underpin and objectives which ought to guide the practice of an excellent lawyer need to be provided in a consistent and clear manner. In this respect the current rules fail. It may be impossible to achieve a golden mean by which all of the many possible objectives of professional rules might be achieved, however, the current rules could be improved in numerous

25 Rule 1.08(x) of the Rules of Professional Conduct for Barristers and Solicitors.

respects. The first task must be to focus on what the rules are intended to achieve.

4.2 Grounds for disciplinary action

4.2.1 *Introduction*

Traditionally, the Court or the professional organisation has only invoked its disciplinary powers where the practitioner has been guilty of misconduct. "Misconduct" is a common law concept that has been adopted in legislation. It is defined by both judicial precedent and the rules and practices of the profession. With the regulation of the legal profession by statute the common law conception of misconduct has been added to and enlarged by statutory definitions.

4.2.2 *The statutory definition*

The standard of conduct required of practitioners is not directly referred to in the Law Practitioners Act, however, the grounds on which the District or New Zealand Disciplinary Tribunals may exercise their powers are set out in identical terms in ss 106(3) and 112(1) respectively. Those sections provide that misconduct for which a tribunal may make an order exists where the tribunal:

(a) Is of the opinion that the practitioner has been guilty of misconduct in his professional capacity; or
(b) Is of the opinion that the practitioner has been guilty of conduct unbecoming a barrister or a solicitor; or
(c) Is of the opinion that the practitioner has been guilty of negligence or incompetence in his professional capacity, and that the negligence or incompetence has been of such a degree or so frequent as to reflect on his fitness to practise as a barrister or solicitor or as to tend to bring the profession into disrepute; or
(d) Is satisfied that the practitioner has been convicted of an offence punishable by imprisonment, and is of the opinion that his conviction reflects on his fitness to practise as a barrister or solicitor, or tends to bring the profession into disrepute,

The statutory provision largely duplicates the common law rule by using the traditional term "professional misconduct" with three specific additions. Criminal conduct, which reflected upon a practitioner's ability to practise, has always been considered misconduct, however, the statute restricts the powers of the tribunal to cases where the offence of which the practitioner has been convicted is punishable by imprisonment (although this is in reality a low threshold). As with the common law rule negligence or incompetence alone will not be sufficient to prove a charge against a practitioner. It must be that such negligence or incompetence is so significant or frequent to suggest that the practitioner is not fit to practise law (or so as to bring the profession into disrepute). The widest ground is the catch-all phrase that the practitioner has been "guilty of conduct unbecoming a barrister or solicitor". Such a ground is, however, rarely invoked in isolation.

4.2.3 *Misconduct at common law*

Misconduct marks the threshold below which a practitioner's actions must not fall. It reflects actions that are not appropriate for a practitioner to engage in and would be disapproved of by other right-minded practitioners. This highlights a central feature of the common law concept of misconduct — it is based on the perception of other practitioners as to the acceptable standards of conduct.[26] While such an approach enables the self-regulation that is prevalent in the legal profession, it also means that lawyers become the standard setters for their own conduct.

While the Courts exercise a supervisory jurisdiction over the disciplinary process, they will intervene in matters of misconduct only rarely. Goddard CJ in *Re a Solicitor* expressed the basis for this view where it was observed:[27]

> This Court is always, and always has been, very loath to interfere with the findings of the Disciplinary Committee either on a matter of fact, because they understand these matters so well, or with regard to penalty. If a matter were one of professional misconduct, it would take a very strong case to induce this Court to interfere with the sentence passed by the Disciplinary Committee, because obviously the [members of the] Disciplinary Committee are the best possible people for weighing the seriousness of professional misconduct.

This stance has been adopted in New Zealand.[28] While it is true that practitioners are certainly the best judges of what kind of conduct is acceptable to the other members of the profession, it is questionable whether this is the appropriate standard. It is unlikely that the same benchmark would be reached if the test were what kind of conduct is acceptable to the client, or the community.

Although there exists a number of established incidents of misconduct it is an essentially vague term. It depends for its definition on the opinion of those members of the profession who are given the task of determining whether a breach has occurred. This problem of vagueness is further compounded by the fact that the rules promulgated by the profession will be of only limited assistance. While an action that is

26 *Allinson v General Council of Medical Education and Registration* [1984] 1 KB 750, 763.

27 [1956] 3 All ER 516, 517.

28 *Ellis v Auckland District Law Society* [1998] 1 NZLR 750, 758 .

permitted by the rules will not be misconduct,[29] the rules are not exhaustive. It is possible that a practitioner will act without breaching the rules, but be guilty of misconduct, nevertheless. The introduction to the rules provides:

> The proceedings of the New Zealand Law Practitioners Disciplinary Tribunal and the Disciplinary Committee that preceded it, have demonstrated clearly that a charge of misconduct in one's professional capacity need not be tied to any specific rule of ethics or to the Solicitors Trust Account Regulations or Rules. First the Committee, and later the Tribunal, have had the task of deciding whether any particular act or omission forming the basis of a charge of misconduct comes within the concepts of Part VII of the Act. In each case it is a question of fact having regard to the circumstances of that case.

That a practice is widespread among members of the profession is persuasive evidence that it is not misconduct, however, it is not conclusive. A practice may have grown which, though common, is incompatible with the role of a lawyer and may be found to be misconduct. Possible (but untested) examples are the use of Chinese walls to prevent the transmission of confidential information between firms, and the use of contingency fee arrangements in litigation. Both practices are widespread but have not received clear approval from either the professional body or the Courts.

The threshold for a finding of misconduct is high. It is generally conduct that reflects on the professional character of the practitioner and his or her adherence to the standards of loyalty, honesty, and fairness attaching to the profession. Conduct that shows the practitioner to be untrustworthy and not fit to be a lawyer will amount to misconduct.[30] Similarly, conduct which shows an inability to conduct the practice of law in a responsible manner by, for example, a failure to keep proper records and accounts may also be misconduct, though not of itself demonstrating dishonesty.[31] The fact that the conduct in question was understandable in light of the circumstances of the practitioner will not absolve him or her.[32]

A good guide to the concept of misconduct can be found in the words of Lord Wright in *Myers v Elman* where the Court was exercising its

29 As for example where a practitioner acts for two parties to a transaction in a potential conflict of interest situation but with the informed consent of both clients pursuant to r 1.04 of the Rules of Professional Conduct for Barristers and Solicitors.

30 *Re Bruges* (1907) 26 NZLR 541, 543.

31 *Re S* [1935] NZLR 908.

32 *Tan v ARCIC* (High Court, Wellington AP 65/98, 14 May 1999).

inherent jurisdiction to discipline a lawyer in the course of a trial for misconduct. It was there stated:[33]

> The matter complained of need not be criminal. It need not involve peculation [that is, embezzlement] or dishonesty. A mere mistake or error of judgement is not generally sufficient, but a gross neglect or inaccuracy in a matter which it is a solicitor's duty to ascertain with accuracy is sufficient. Thus a solicitor may be held bound in certain events to satisfy himself that he has a retainer to act, or as to the accuracy of an affidavit which his client swears. It is impossible to enumerate the various contingencies which may call into operation the exercise of this jurisdiction. It need not involve personal obliquity.

Conduct which amounts to mere negligence[34] or an error of judgment will not be misconduct.[35] The basis for such a view is that such negligence or errors do not reflect on the integrity of the practitioner, or the practitioner's ability to continue to practise law and, consequently, do not show that he or she is not conducting the practice in a proper manner. However, if negligence or oversights are gross or repeated, this may amount to misconduct.

There will also be instances where conduct outside the practice of a lawyer will amount to professional misconduct. While this will be rare, where the conduct of a practitioner in his or her non-professional life reflects on his or her appropriateness to practise law the disciplinary process may be invoked. An obvious example is where the practitioner has been convicted of some offence that reflects on his or her integrity. In *Re Shortland*[36] it was held that a practitioner who had been convicted of libelling a young woman by claiming that he had seduced her was found guilty of misconduct and struck from the roll. Values have changed and it is unlikely that conduct such as adultery would be of interest to the professional body, let alone grounds for striking off as it was at the beginning of the century.[37] More difficult are offences such recklessness or negligence which may be committed without a clear intent. In such cases the question will be whether the conduct brings the profession into disrepute. This may be so in some cases such as serious driving offences, or even manslaughter. In *Ziems v Prothonotary of the Supreme Court of New South Wales* Ziems was suspended following a conviction of involuntary manslaughter when he killed a motorcyclist whilst driving drunk.[38] While the conviction did not reflect on his

33 [1940] AC 282, 319.

34 See also *Myers v Elman* [1940] AC 282, 288, per Viscount Maugham; *In Re Four Solicitors* (1901) 7 TLR 672, applied in *Re Moore* (1909) 11 GLR 678.

35 *Y v M* [1994] 3 NZLR 581.

36 (1893) 12 NZLR 137 (CA).

37 *Re Baillie* (1915) 34 NZLR 705.

38 (1957) 97 CLR 297 (HC of Aust).

trustworthiness or competence as a lawyer it was considered that the matter was of such as serious nature that some action was required by the disciplinary body.

4.2.4 *Established classes of misconduct*

(a) Dishonesty

Actions that reflect on the integrity of the practitioner will usually amount to misconduct. While dishonestly taking or acquiring through fraud, theft or failing to account (even if not resulting in a criminal conviction) will clearly be misconduct, lesser instances of dishonesty may also amount to misconduct.[39] Lying to, or intentionally deceiving, a tribunal or another practitioner will, in most circumstances, amount to misconduct. Care must be taken to ensure that the dishonesty is not an honest mistake or erroneous recollection which would not usually be a disciplinary offence. Submitting documents to the Court that the practitioner knows are false, or making allegations that are without foundation will be misconduct. Examples of such conduct are initiating claims for which no cause of action exists,[40] seeking a summary judgment where it is clear that an arguable defence can be made, misrepresenting the progress or existence of proceedings to the client,[41] and seeking to wind up a company when it is clearly not insolvent.[42]

If it can be shown that a practitioner has intentionally misled another practitioner, a client, or a third party, this is likely to be misconduct.[43] Where a practitioner has made an undertaking, giving the practitioner's professional word to adhere to the terms of that undertaking, and if the practitioner fails to meet his or her obligations under such an undertaking without excuse, this will be misconduct.[44] Knowingly permitting a client to use a practitioner's services to further a fraudulent end will also amount to misconduct (as well as possibly being a criminal offence). Criminal conduct of a dishonest nature outside the professional life of a practitioner will also be likely to amount to misconduct.[45] The conduct in question must be such as to reflect upon

39 *In re Baillie (a solicitor)* (1915) 34 NZLR 705; *In re Bruges* (1907) 26 NZLR 541.

40 See D Webb, "Hopeless Cases: In Defence of Compensating Litigants at the Advocate's Expense" (1999) 29 VUWLR 295.

41 *Braithwaite v Law Society* [1998] PNLR 478.

42 See r 7.04 Rules of Professional Conduct for Barristers and Solicitors especially para (1) of the commentary.

43 See r 6.01 Rules of Professional Conduct for Barristers and Solicitors especially para (3) of the commentary.

44 See r 6.07 Rules of Professional Conduct for Barristers and Solicitors .

45 *Bolton v Law Society* [1994] 2 All ER 486, 491 per Bingham MR.

the integrity of the practitioner and his or her fitness to practise law. Such allegations of dishonesty must be provable and more than minor.

(b) Fiduciary breaches

Some fiduciary breaches will amount to dishonest conduct (such as misappropriation or misuse of client funds) and are clear instances of misconduct of the most serious kind for which striking from the roll is the inevitable sanction.[46] Arguments which seek to mitigate the misconduct by pointing out that no client money was actually lost, or the circumstances in which the conduct occurred were exceptional, are rarely entertained. The fact that client funds were meddled with without authority shows that the practitioner is not a fit person to practise law and should be struck off. Moreover, it is unlikely that an application for readmission will be successful unless there are some special circumstances to demonstrate that there is no risk of a recurrence. There will, however, be numerous less serious breaches of the fiduciary duty owed to the client which may amount to misconduct. Some fiduciary breaches in relation to the handling of money may be due to oversight or poor financial management, such as failing to deposit money, or overdrawing a trust account by drawing on uncleared funds. Such unintentional breaches may amount to misconduct, especially if they are repeated or serious.

Although not strictly breaches of a fiduciary duty of themselves, a breach of the rules or regulations in relation to the management of a trust account may be misconduct as well as a regulatory offence. The New Zealand Law Society *Solicitor's Trust Accounting Handbook* provides in its introduction:[47]

> Practitioners are warned that non-compliance with the Regulations may constitute the commission of an offence punishable in the ordinary Courts pursuant to Regulation 17 as well as professional misconduct under the Law Practitioners' Act.

Other obvious fiduciary breaches which would amount to misconduct are continuing to act in the face of a conflict of interest including failing to ensure that a client obtains adequate independent advice, breaching confidence, and obtaining a personal advantage through knowledge gained from a client. It may be that entering into a personal relationship with a client, or making sexual advances to a client will amount to misconduct as an abuse of the relationship of trust. Although the rules

46 See the Annual Report of the NZLS Disciplinary Committee reproduced in the Annual Report of the NZLS for illustrations of the penalties imposed for such offences.

47 See also r 5.01 Rules of Professional Conduct for Barristers and Solicitors.

give no meaningful guidance,[48] there have been instances in where such conduct has been the subject of discipline.[49] The American Bar Association has stated:[50]

> A sexual relationship between a lawyer and a client may involve unfair exploitation of the lawyer's fiduciary position and/or significantly impair a lawyer's ability to represent a client competently, and therefore may violate both the ABA Model Rules of Professional Conduct and the Model Code of Professional Responsibility.

(c) Billing and charging practices

Some cases of overcharging amount to dishonesty and are doubly subject to the disciplinary procedure. Where a practitioner claims for hours that were not worked, or tasks not performed, this amounts to a fraud on the client.[51] The same is the case where there are claims for disbursements that have not actually been incurred, or not incurred in the amount claimed.[52] It will also be misconduct to deduct from client funds costs that have not yet been billed.[53]

Entering into a fee arrangement that is manifestly unreasonable may also be misconduct.[54] To agree a flat fee that is wholly out of proportion with the time the work agreed might possibly consume will be misconduct.[55] On the rules and the law as it stands charging an hourly rate that is outrageously high may also amount to misconduct, although in practice the Courts have taken into account numerous factors to justify high rates such as complexity, urgency, the importance of the matter under consideration.[56] If, however, the bill is so disproportionate to the

48 Rule 5.01 Rules of Professional Conduct for Barristers and Solicitors especially para (3) of the commentary.

49 *Re E – A Barrister and Solicitor* (noted in NZLS *Annual Report* 1996); *Bar Association of Queensland v Lamb* [1972] ALR 285. Numerous authorities exist from the US jurisdictions where instances of inappropriate behaviour or entering a sexual relationship with a client have resulted in discipline: *People v Bergner* (1994) 873 P2d 726 (sexual conversation with client — attorney censured); *Re Lewis* (1992) 415 SE2d 87 (sexual relationship with client in matrimonial proceedings — attorney suspended for three years). See generally "Attorneys at Law" 7 *American Jurisprudence* 2nd ed, 1997, s 69 including cumulative supplement.

50 ABA Formal Opinion 92-364 (1992).

51 *Tan v ARCIC* (High Court, Wellington AP 65/98, 14 May 1999).

52 *Re McConnell* (1890) 8 NZLR 617.

53 *In re C (a solicitor)* [1963] NZLR 259.

54 Rule 3.01 Rules of Professional Conduct for Barristers and Solicitors states that a charge for legal work must be "fair and reasonable".

55 *In re Lundon* [1918] NZLR 193 but contrast *Re Moore* (1909) 11 GLR 678.

56 See *Gallagher v Dobson* [1993] 3 NZLR 611 following *Property and Reversionary Investment Corporation Ltd v Secretary of State for the Environment* [1975] 2 All ER 436.

amount of work done as to amount to a fraud on the client it will be misconduct of the most serious kind.[57]

There may also be instances where the method by which the fee is determined is inappropriate and amounts to misconduct. Although the law society has failed to give guidance on whether contingency fees are permitted[58] there will be instances where a contingent fee would be misconduct. Examples would be a contingent fee in a criminal case, matrimonial proceedings, or where the success of the claim was a moral certainty.[59]

(d) Inadequate supervision

There is a duty on practitioners to supervise any non-legal staff who work under them. This duty is particularly important with the growth in the use of unqualified people such as paralegals who undertake tasks like discoveries, and legal executives who conduct much of the routine conveyancing work. In the event that there is some error or omission by the employee the practitioner will be held liable for that misconduct. In *Myers v Elman*[60] a clerk had prepared a list of documents without fully explaining to the client the need for the list to be comprehensive. It was held that in such cases the practitioner is responsible if the list is ultimately deficient. In the words of Lord Atkin:[61]

> [Solicitors] cannot evade the consequences of a breach of duty by showing that the performance of the particular duty by which breach is alleged was delegated by them to a clerk. ... If a Court is deceived or the litigant is improperly delayed or put to unnecessary expense, the solicitor on the record will be held responsible and be admonished or visited with such pecuniary penalty as the Court thinks necessary in the circumstances of the case.

Principals of firms are also required to supervise the conduct of their junior practitioner employees. If a junior employee is guilty of misconduct through inexperience and insufficient supervision, the principal may be held partly responsible. The duty to supervise is particularly apparent with the growth of suburban branch offices of firms (focused on conveyancing work) often staffed by one practitioner and supported by a legal executive. In such cases the person in charge of

---

57 *Re McConnell* (1890) 8 NZLR 617.

58 See r 3.01 Rules of Professional Conduct for Barristers and Solicitors especially para (4) of the commentary Similarly inconclusive was the *Report of the Auckland District Law Society Working Group on Contingency Fees* Auckland, ADLS, 1998.

59 See K Tokeley, "Taking a Chance: A Proposal for Contingency Fees" (1998) 28 VUWLR 13.

60 [1940] AC 283. See also *Re a Solicitor* [1972] 2 All ER 811 (CA).

61 [1940] AC 283, 302.

the branch must be qualified to practise on their own account,[62] or the branch must be under the effective supervision of a person who is qualified.[63]

To a lesser extent a partner of a firm is required to supervise the conduct of fellow partners. While partners are not expected to have an intimate knowledge of every aspect of their fellow partners' practice, they are expected to be awake to any irregularities that may exist. Such a responsibility extends to actively involving themselves in the management of the firm's affairs and accounting matters. Under the Solicitors' Trust Account Rules 1996 of the New Zealand Law Society every firm must have one partner who is primarily responsible for the trust account.[64] However, those rules also explicitly state that all of the partners of a firm remain responsible for the financial matters of the firm.[65]

There is a general duty on all practitioners to report suspected defalcations or misconduct of other practitioners to the law society.[66] This is particularly apposite in respect of fellow partners who are more likely to be in a position to observe irregularities in the activities of their fellow partners. The commentary to the rule gives some guidelines as to what might amount to suspicious conduct such as extravagant living, inexplicable delays in settling transactions, and the dishonouring of cheques. A failure to make such a report in the face of such evidence may well amount to misconduct.

(e) Failing to cooperate with investigation

A failure to cooperate with a law society investigation into the operation of the trust account, or allegations of misconduct may themselves be misconduct. A failure to respond to a complaints committee inquiry, refusing to change accounting practices after a request by an auditor, or failing to produce books for inspection when required may also be sufficient for the professional body to invoke disciplinary proceedings. In some cases such refusals may also amount to a criminal offence.[67]

---

62 Section 55 Law Practitioners Act 1982 requires persons practising in partnership or on their own account to have had at least three years post-admission experience and have sat such exams as may be set.

63 Rule 2.04 Rules of Professional Conduct for Barristers and Solicitors, especially para (4) of the commentary.

64 Rule 16 Solicitors Trust Account Rules 1996.

65 Rule 17(4) Solicitors Trust Account Rules 1996.

66 Rule 6.03 Rules of Professional Conduct for Barristers and Solicitors.

67 Regulation 24 Solicitors Trust Account Regulations 1998. See also the statement to the same effect in the introduction to the *Solicitors Trust Accounting Handbook*.

(f) Incompetence

In most cases mistakes or omissions by practitioners will not amount to misconduct.[68] As with any profession or trade some errors are inevitable and while they may (though not necessarily) reflect on the skill of the practitioner, they do not usually reflect on the practitioner's professional conduct. The same can be said of incidents of delay or a failure to respond to telephone calls and the like.[69] However, in the event that the mistake shows a degree of recklessness, or where there are numerous instances of incompetence this may be a matter for disciplinary intervention.[70] This is especially the case where the recklessness or incompetence relates to the management of the funds of clients.[71] A breach of the duties attaching to the handling of client moneys will amount to misconduct even when no dishonest intent is shown.[72] Both recklessness and repeated mistakes reflect on the fitness of the lawyer to practise. The former suggests an inappropriate disregard for the affairs of the client while the latter suggests an inability to conduct the work desired to a required standard. Both require intervention to protect prospective clients against loss.

(g) Criminal offences

If a practitioner is guilty of a crime that relates to the conduct of the practice, this is obviously a matter for discipline. However, there will be instances where a practitioner has been found guilty of an offence outside professional life that does not reflect on his or her ability to practise. Mere regulatory offences such as minor traffic infringements would be an example. On the opposite side of the spectrum are serious offences that directly reflect on the integrity of the practitioner and his or her fitness to practise. Offences of dishonesty are the most obvious example.

More difficult are offences that are less serious or, though serious, do not reflect on the integrity of the practitioner. What, for example, of a practitioner who has repeatedly been convicted of driving with excess blood/alcohol offences, convicted of assault, or is guilty of offences against the revenue. In a case concerning a Canterbury practitioner the District Law Society Disciplinary Tribunal found that practitioner guilty

---

68 *Re Moore* (1909) 11 GLR 678; *Y v M* [1994] 3 NZLR 581.

69 The Rules of Professional Conduct for Barristers and Solicitors require a practitioner to be courteous in his or her dealings, which would suggest that failure to return calls, keep appointments and the like are matters of professional conduct: rr 6.01and 7.01.

70 Sections 106(3)(c) and 112(1)(c) Law Practitioners Act 1982.

71 *In re S a solicitor* [1935] NZLR 908.

72 See *Ellis v Auckland District Law Society* [1998] 1 NZLR 751.

of misconduct subsequent to convictions for failing to file GST and PAYE tax returns. In reaching the conclusion:[73]

> The tribunal decided that conduct "unbecoming" need not directly affect conduct of client's affairs. It did not consider any breach of revenue law would amount to conduct "unbecoming" but in this particular case, it was the number, extent and the protracted time period involved which brought the Tribunal to its view that the charge of conduct unbecoming had been established.

While it might be suggested that such practitioners have flaws of character which mean they are not fit to practise law, there can be no serious suggestion that clients' affairs or property are at risk. Similarly problematic are offences against morality.[74] Such practitioners are disciplined (or possibly struck off) because such conduct by a practitioner brings the profession into disrepute.[75] Such discipline protects the reputation of the profession as much as the interests of any particular client.

There have been instances of discipline were the offence has been one requiring minimal mens rea, namely, manslaughter by driving when drunk.[76] Some such offences are regarded as serious by society, as demonstrated by the significant penalties attaching to them. In some cases the disciplinary body of the profession will reflect this by disciplining its members for such offences even though it cannot be said that they were committed intentionally. It is not possible to categorise crimes as either amounting to misconduct or not. While the conviction of a crime is obviously relevant, it is the actions of the practitioner that the disciplinary authority will look at. The surrounding facts will be directly relevant to the question of whether the practitioner is guilty of misconduct, and each case will be dealt with on its own facts.

(h) Misconduct in litigation

A practitioner may also be guilty of misconduct if he or she has breached the duty to the Court, for example, if a practitioner is knowingly a party to an abuse of process. In *Gazley v Wellington District Law Society*[77] it was found that the practitioner was guilty of misconduct where he made allegations of malice and negligence which were wholly

73 *Report of the Tribunal in the Annual Report of the Canterbury District Law Society* 1996, p 11.

74 *Re H (a barrister)* [1981] 3 All ER 205; *Re a Solicitor* [1960] 2 All ER 621.

75 See *In re Shortland* (1893) 12 NZLR 137 where a practitioner was struck from the roll after being found guilty of criminal libel. Also *Weston v Law Society* (1998) Times, 15 July.

76 *Ziems v Prothonotary of the Supreme Court of New South Wales* (1957) 97 CLR 297 (HC of Aust) where the practitioner was suspended.

77 [1976] 1 NZLR 453.

without foundation. In such cases the Court before which such misconduct occurs has the option of taking disciplinary action itself under its inherent jurisdiction, or reporting the matter to the District Society for attention.

4.2.5 *Disciplinary sanctions: principles*

The primary role of the disciplinary process has been stated to be to protect the public from unscrupulous practitioners rather than to punish the practitioners.[78] A thorough exposition of the role of discipline in the profession is to be found in *Bolton v The Law Society*.[79] In that case Bolton had acted for the vendor, purchaser, and financier in a conveyancing transaction. Foolishly, he advanced funds from the financier to the vendor before the transaction was completed. The transaction was never completed. To complicate matters the vendor was his wife and the purchaser his brother-in-law. It was accepted that, although acting stupidly, the practitioner acted at all times without dishonest intent. The law society suspended him from practice. Bolton appealed.

In refusing the appeal it was observed that lawyers are expected to act with "integrity, probity, and complete trustworthiness". A breach of this requirement will invoke severe sanctions. While there is a punitive and deterrent element to the disciplinary procedure, these are not the dominant objectives. Rather the purposes of discipline are the protection of the public from repeat offences and:[80]

> To maintain the reputation of the solicitor's profession as one in which every member, of whatever standing, may be trusted to the ends of the earth. To maintain this reputation and sustain public confidence in the integrity of the profession it is often necessary that those guilty of serious offences are not only expelled but denied readmission. ... Otherwise the whole profession, and the public as a whole is injured. A profession's most valuable asset is its collective reputation and the confidence which that inspires.

Consequently, the sanctions imposed by the society on its members may appear harsh. Even where a lawyer has been punished in the criminal Courts for the acts which are the subject of the disciplinary proceeding, it may be appropriate to impose additional, heavy professional sanctions even though where there has been a criminal trial and sentence, the disciplinary proceeding has no significant punitive role.[81] For example, it

---

78 *L v Canterbury District Law Society* [1999] 1 NZLR 467, 473; *Bolton v The Law Society* [1994] 1 All ER 486, 492; *Sidney v Auckland District Law Society* [1996] 1 NZLR 431.

79 [1994] 1 All ER 486.1

80 *Bolton v The Law Society* [1994] 1 All ER 486, 492.

81 *Wellington District Law Society v Cummins* [1998] 3 NZLR 363. Although it is there noted that where there has been a criminal trial and sentence the disciplinary proceeding has no significant punitive role.

will be inappropriate for the tribunal to impose a fine if the matter has been or is also to be dealt with by the criminal Courts, especially if a fine or imprisonment is likely. Because a fine is solely punitive in nature, this would amount to a kind of double jeopardy.[82] Factors which might mitigate a sentence in primarily punitive proceedings will carry little weight before a disciplinary body, especially if the misconduct is serious. The most significant questions before a tribunal are: is this practitioner trustworthy, and does the profession's reputation require sanctions to be imposed? In *Bolton* the Court upheld the suspension of the practitioner even though the actions were not dishonest.

Misconduct will not be found simply because a lawyer chooses to act for unscrupulous clients, or engages in transactions at the boundary of the law. In the words of Denman J:[83]

> It is not, in my opinion sufficient that the party charged has been guilty of grave errors of judgement, nor that he has accepted a position which a highly sensitive and scrupulous solicitor would not accept, nor that he accepted an amount of remuneration enormously in excess of the professional services rendered; but that something has been established showing either that his conduct in the management of the professional business entrusted to him has been fraudulent, or that he has neglected some positive duty to his clients, or the conduct complained of be something *dehors* his professional behaviour.

In fixing an appropriate penalty in a disciplinary proceeding a number of factors which are secondary to the trustworthiness of the practitioner and reputation of the profession may be taken into account. One such matter is whether the practitioner has previously been found guilty of misconduct, in which case the sanction is likely to be heavier. Such repeat offending shows a propensity to act inappropriately and a failure to amend actions after the first offence. In *Sidney v Auckland District Law Society*[84] it was held that, even though the offences of themselves may not have warranted the three-year suspension imposed, the fact that the practitioner had previously been disciplined for similar charges meant that the suspension was appropriate (and on one view lenient).[85] In *L v Canterbury District Law Society*[86] an application for the lifting of practice

82 *Pickering v Auckland District Law Society* [1985] 1 NZLR 1.

83 *In Re Four Solicitors* (1901) 7 TLR 672, applied in *Re Moore* (1909) 6 GLR 678, 681.

84 [1996] 1 NZLR 431, 436.

85 See also *L v Canterbury District Law Society* [1999] 1 NZLR 467 where an application for the lifting of practice restrictions was refused in light of the fact that since the imposition of the restrictions there had been incidents of misconduct, and the practitioner showed a lack of understanding of the nature of his wrongdoing.

86 [1999] 1 NZLR 467.

restrictions was refused because since the imposition of the restrictions there had been incidents of misconduct, and the practitioner showed a lack of understanding of the nature of his wrongdoing. Alternatively, where a practitioner addresses the problem and acts to rectify any damage caused, this will be a mitigating factor.[87]

The fact that the conduct complained of is sustained and persistently inappropriate, will also compound the seriousness of the offence. In contrast, if the breach is isolated and out of character the tribunal will be more likely to find that it does not show a propensity to act inappropriately. Thus in *Wellington District Law Society v Cummins*[88] the fact that the conduct was "extended over a considerable period and … involved a sophisticated system which was designed to deceive" meant that striking off was warranted.

Delay in bringing the disciplinary proceedings may be relevant to the imposition of a sanction, especially where in the intervening period the practitioner has shown that he or she has rehabilitated.[89] However, where the misconduct was serious, even the effluxion of a long period of time may not mean that striking off is avoided, especially where the reputation of the profession is at stake.[90]

Where the misconduct is not most serious, the impact of the sanction on the practitioner may be relevant. While protection of the public and the reputation of the profession are paramount considerations, there will be situations where leniency can be shown while preserving those values. Where suspension would irretrievably damage a practice, only a finding of serious misconduct would warrant such an order.[91] Similarly, the financial burden imposed on the practitioner by the proposed order will be relevant.[92] Where the effects of the wrongdoing, or the disciplinary process have negatively impacted on the practitioner in other ways (such as publicity, loss of livelihood, or financial burdens) this may also be taken into account.[93] The mere fact that a criminal proceeding has been undertaken which the practitioner found arduous will not be relevant.[94]

---

87 *Ellis v Auckland District Law Society* [1998] 1 NZLR 750.

88 [1998] 3 NZLR 363, 369. See also *Complaints Committee of the Waikato and Bay of Plenty District Law Society v Osmond* (High Court, Wellington AP 100/97, 28 August 1998, Heron, Ellis & Gendall JJ).

89 *Ellis v Auckland District Law Society* [1998] 1 NZLR 750.

90 *Wellington District Law Society v Cummins* [1998] 3 NZLR 363

91 *H v Auckland District Law Society* [1985] 1 NZLR 8.

92 *Ellis v Auckland District Law Society* [1998] 1 NZLR 750.

93 *Ellis v Auckland District Law Society* [1998] 1 NZLR 750.

94 *Complaints Committee of the Waikato and Bay of Plenty District Law Society v Osmond* (High Court, Wellington AP 100/97, 28 August 1998, Heron, Ellis and Gendall JJ).

Disciplinary proceedings are unique in character. While they resemble criminal actions in some respects, such as the fact that charges are laid and sanctions imposed, they are quite different in other respects. In particular the obligation on the prosecuting body (the law society) to prove the charge is generally not as high as in criminal proceedings, though the burden will increase with the severity of the charge. Where the charge is one for which the likely sanction is striking off, the tribunal will have to be quite satisfied that the facts have been established.[95] Similarly, in any charge of professional misconduct involving an allegation of dishonesty or moral turpitude a high standard of proof is called for. While the articulations of the standard of proof have varied, it is clear that it is greater than a mere balance of probabilities.[96] In *Re a Solicitor*[97] it was held that the criminal standard of beyond reasonable doubt was applicable. If a prima facie case is established the practitioner will be required to answer it and it will not be a defence to claim that the charge has not been proved to the required standard.[98] The practitioner is required to assist the tribunal in investigating the charge and is not permitted (as would be the case in criminal proceedings) to withhold evidence or remain silent in the face of questioning.

4.2.6 *Disciplinary sanctions*

(a) Striking off

The most serious sanction that the professional body may impose on a practitioner is to strike the practitioner from the roll (also known as disbarment).[99] Many instances of misconduct will warrant a far less severe sanction which may range from mere censure to a period of suspension. The New Zealand Disciplinary Tribunal[100] will invoke the power to strike from the roll only where the misconduct shown is serious and demonstrates that the offender is not a fit and proper person to practise as a barrister or solicitor.[101] The test is the same as that applicable when considering whether a candidate for admission is a fit

95 *Cheape v New Zealand Law Society* [1955] NZLR 63. Numerous phrases are used such as "Comfortably and confidently satisfied" (*Re Hodgekiss* ((1959) 63 SR (NSW) 340, 356), and "very sure" (*Ziems v Prothonotary of the Supreme Court of New South Wales* (1957) 97 CLR 296, 297 (HC of Aust)).

96 *Bhandari v Advocates Committee* [1956] 3 All ER 742 (PC).

97 [1992] 2 All ER 335.

98 *In Re C* [1963] NZLR 259.

99 Striking from the roll refers to the roll which traditionally contains the names of all solicitors. Disbarment refers to removing from the "Bar", that is, the profession of barristers. In New Zealand there is no distinction between the two. The Law Practitioners Act 1982 uses the term "strike from the roll" and it will, therefore, be used in this discussion.

100 The district tribunals do not have the power to strike or suspend from the roll: s 106 Law Practitioners Act 1982.

101 Section 113 Law Practitioners Act 1982.

and proper person.[102] It has been recognised that such a standard is impossible to clearly define.[103] While misconduct involving dishonesty is usually required to warrant striking off, there may be cases where such an order is appropriate in the absence of dishonesty.[104] However, each case must be examined by itself. Both the facts surrounding the incident and the history and characteristics of the individual must be considered.

The question of whether someone is a fit and proper person to practise law is more than simply an inquiry into whether reoffending is likely. It is a question of whether, in light of the conduct complained of and to a lesser extent subsequent events, the circumstances are such to show that he or she is not fit to practise law or that the conduct was such that to allow him or her to continue to practise law would bring the profession into disrepute.[105] In *Wellington District Law Society v Cummins*[106] it was held that a practitioner should be struck off even though the offending had occurred some years previously and there had been an intervening period of some eight years of exemplary practice. Because of the seriousness of the misconduct it was held that the sentence of suspension imposed by the tribunal was inadequate and a sentence of striking off was imposed.

(b) Suspension

A practitioner may be suspended from practice by order of the New Zealand Disciplinary Tribunal. While less serious than striking off, suspension is still a grave step that will be exercised reluctantly. A suspended practitioner is prohibited from practising for a definite period. After the expiration of the suspension the practitioner is entitled to resume practice. In contrast, a practitioner who has been struck off may reapply for admission but has no guarantee of readmission.

Suspension will be used where the misconduct, though serious, does not show that the practitioner is irretrievably unfit to practise. It serves as a deterrent to further misconduct and punishment for the original offence. Where the misconduct does not reflect on the integrity of the practitioner but is still serious, an order of suspension may be made.[107] Similarly, where the dishonesty is explicable or significant mitigating

---

102 See s 46 Law Practitioners Act 1982; *Southern Law Society v Westbrook* (1910) 10 CLR 609, 620 per O'Conner J.

103 *Ziems v Prothonotary of the Supreme Court of New South Wales* (1957) 97 CLR 297, 297 per Kitto J (HC of Aust).

104 *In re S (a solicitor)* [1935] NZLR 908 (CA); *McDonald v Canterbury District Law Society* (High Court, Wellington M 215/87, 10 August 1989, Eichelbaum CJ, Heron & Ellis JJ); *Re Bruges* (1907) 26 NZLR 541.

105 *Wellington District Law Society v Cummins* [1998] 3 NZLR 363, 370.

106 [1998] 3 NZLR 363.

107 *Ziems v Prothonotary of the Supreme Court of New South Wales* (1957) 97 CLR 297 (HC of Aust); *Bolton v Law Society* [1994] 2 All ER 486.

factors exist, such an order may be appropriate.[108] However, where the misconduct is serious and involves dishonesty, in most cases striking off will be the proper sanction and a suspension will be inadequate.[109] If the breach is not serious and does not go to the integrity of the practitioner, and especially if there are additional mitigating factors, suspension should be avoided.[110]

Suspension may be appropriate where the misconduct is due to some temporary or remediable failure on the part of the practitioner. A practitioner whose actions were due to a temporary condition or mental illness may be suspended if it can be shown that there will be no significant risk of re-offending once the practitioner is restored to health. However, such arguments are not a defence to disciplinary charges and the tribunal and Court will be wary of excusing grave misconduct.[111]

(c) Fine

Where the misconduct is more than trifling but does not reflect on the ability of the practitioner to practise, an order to pay "a sum by way of penalty"[112] may be appropriate. A district tribunal may impose a fine of up to $2000 whereas the New Zealand Disciplinary Tribunal may fine up to $5000. Both sums are relatively small, and often the costs awarded against the practitioner are many times the amount of the maximum fine. A fine is quite separate from any order of compensation that may be made to the client. A fine is, however, still a serious matter and where the conduct is not serious and mitigating factors such as inexperience exist, a fine should be imposed with caution.[113]

(d) Censure

A censure (or reprimand) is the least serious penalty that may be imposed on a practitioner. Where misconduct is trifling or where the rule breached is regulatory, a censure may be appropriate.[114]

(e) Compensation

The disciplinary procedure as it currently exists is not a route by which a disgruntled client may seek effective redress for loss suffered at the hands of a lawyer. However, where the client has suffered loss a

108 *Ellis v Auckland District Law Society* [1988] 1 NZLR 751.
109 *Wellington District Law Society v Cummins* [1998] 3 NZLR 363.
110 *H (a law practitioner) v Auckland District Law Society* [1985] 1 NZLR 8.
111 *Goldberg v Law Society of New South Wales* (1991) 1 Legal Profession Disciplinary Reports 15, 28, per Hope J.
112 Sections 106(4)(a) and 112(2)(d).
113 *H (a law practitioner) v Auckland District Law Society* [1985] 1 NZLR 8, 24.
114 See *Kaye v Auckland District Law Society* [1998] 1 NZLR 151 where a barrister was found to have accepted clients without a referral from a solicitor in breach of r 11.03 of the Rules of Professional Conduct of Barristers and Solicitors.

compensatory order may be made.[115] For such an order it is necessary for the client to have suffered actual loss, therefore, a payment for humiliation or a payment for distress, seem beyond the jurisdiction of the tribunal. If an order for compensation is made against the practitioner it will not affect the right of the client to sue in the ordinary Courts. However, the Court must take the compensation paid into account in any award.[116]

(f) Limitations on practice and other orders

The Law Practitioners Act 1982 sets out a number of other orders that a tribunal may make against a practitioner who is guilty of misconduct. The New Zealand Tribunal may order that the practitioner may not practise on his or her own account or as a partner.[117] Such an order is serious and reflects a finding that the practitioner is not a proper person to practise unsupervised. Frequently, this will be the case where the conduct, though not dishonest, breached important rules governing the dealing with client funds. Such orders may also be used where the dishonesty is minor and does not warrant striking off or suspension.[118] Either tribunal may order a reduction in fees, or may order that the practitioner undertake or complete tasks without fee, order an inspection of the practice, order regular reports by the practitioner, and order the practitioner to take advice regarding the practice.[119]

(g) Costs

Where a practitioner has been found guilty of a charge of misconduct before a disciplinary tribunal, that tribunal may (and almost certainly will) make an order of costs against the practitioner.[120] The order will cover the costs incurred from the inception of the investigation including the costs of any complaints committee, any associated investigation, and the tribunal hearing itself. Such costs may run to many tens of thousands of dollars and frequently far outweigh any financial penalty imposed. A tribunal also has a discretion to award costs even where the practitioner has not been found guilty of the misconduct charged. The power to order costs in such cases is, however, limited to those where the charges proceeded to a defended hearing.[121] Such an order is most appropriate where it is clear that there have been actions by the practitioner which are dishonourable but fall short of misconduct, or cannot be established owing to some technicality.[122]

---

115 Sections 106(4)(e) and 112(2)(f).

116 Section 106(9) Law Practitioners Act 1982.

117 Section 112(2)(c) and see *L v Canterbury District Law Society* [1999] 1 NZLR 467.

118 *L v Canterbury District Law Society* [1999] 1 NZLR 467.

119 Sections 106(4)(d), (f)-(i), and 112(2)(f) Law Practitioners Act 1982.

120 Sections 106(4)(j), 112(2)(g), 129 Law Practitioners Act 1982.

121 *Kaye v Auckland District Law Society* [1998] 1 NZLR 151, 155.

122 *Kaye v Auckland District Law Society* [1998] 1 NZLR 151, 156.

Any order of costs by a tribunal must be supported by evidence showing how the costs were incurred. This gives the practitioner an opportunity to examine the costs and question them if necessary.[123] The ability of the practitioner to pay, including the current earning ability of the practitioner and other financial commitments, will be relevant in ordering costs. Costs may not be used to punish a practitioner.[124]

4.3 The complaints procedure

4.3.1 *Introduction*

Although clients often regard the complaints and discipline procedure of the New Zealand and district law societies as an avenue by which to vindicate their rights, this is not the intended purpose of the procedures. As the information sheet available to clients from the society states:[125]

> The complaints system is aimed at disciplining lawyers who are guilty of misconduct … the system is not primarily aimed at recovering any money you may have lost.

The procedures involve primarily the society and the practitioner and, while a client complaint may have initiated the action, the client is in fact only peripherally involved in it. While this lawyer-centred approach has been altered or replaced in some jurisdictions, it remains the blueprint in New Zealand.[126]

A major overhaul of the complaints and discipline procedure has been proposed.[127] The following discussion should, therefore, be read bearing in mind any reforms which have occurred since the publication of this work.

4.3.2 *Complaints and disciplinary procedures in New Zealand*

Most frequently, the disciplinary procedures are initiated by a complaint by a member of the public (usually the client of the practitioner

123 *H (a law practitioner) v Auckland District Law Society* [1985] 1 NZLR 8, 25; *Kaye v Auckland District Law Society* [1998] 1 NZLR151.

124 *Kaye v Auckland District Law Society* [1998] 1 NZLR 151, 156.

125 Available from the New Zealand Law Society or at [http://www.nz-lawsoc.org.nz/general/cmplnts.htm].

126 For example, in New South Wales the Legal Profession Reform Act 1993 amended the Legal Profession Act 1987 by creating an Office of Legal Services Commissioner which receives and oversees all complaints. In England the Legal Services Ombudsman oversees the operation of the Office for the Discipline of Solicitors under the Courts and Legal Services Act 1990.

127 Letter, President of the Law Society to all practitioners, 20 October 1999, and the attached paper.

concerned).[128] Alternatively, a complaint may be made by another practitioner who is concerned about the conduct of the practitioner in question (although this is not particularly common). Where a practitioner is aware of misconduct by another practitioner the Rules of Professional Conduct impose a duty to report the matter to the relevant district society.[129] A council of a district society may also investigate a practitioner without receiving a complaint where it has "cause to suspect" misconduct on the part of a practitioner.[130]

A complaint may be dealt with by the council of the district law society, or be referred to a complaints committee of the society. At this stage, information will be gathered to determine whether there is merit in the complaint. This will involve putting the complaint to the practitioner and seeking a response to the allegations.[131] If the complaint concerns a minor matter such as delay or poor service it is common for a resolution to be sought which is acceptable to all the parties. The remedy might be the practitioner immediately attending to the matter, or providing an apology. If the complaint is not resolved in this manner the council or committee will either dismiss the complaint or refer the complaint to a disciplinary tribunal. The council or committee has no power to make orders against a practitioner at this stage. The majority of complaints are resolved at this stage by agreement with the practitioner or dismissal as unwarranted. The results of the investigation of the council or committee into the complaint, and of any action to be taken as a result of the complaint must be relayed to the complainant.[132]

Where the complaint relates to a serious matter which warrants making a formal charge against the practitioner then the matter must be referred to a District Disciplinary Tribunal.[133] The tribunal is comprised of between five and eight practitioners and two lay members (non-practitioners). Such tribunals are free to determine their own procedure within the limited constraints of the Law Practitioners Act and the requirements of natural justice. In practice, such hearings are conducted relatively formally and the practitioner has a right to put his or her side

128 Section 98 Law Practitioners Act 1982.

129 Rule 6.03. The only exceptions mentioned in the commentary to the rules are where the knowledge is gained within the bounds of a lawyer-client relationship and a duty of confidentiality attaches, and where the disclosure is part of the "FRIEND' system run by some district societies whereby practitioners may anonymously discuss personal or professional problems with other members of the profession.

130 Section 99 Law Practitioners Act 1982.

131 Section 101(3)(a) Law Practitioners Act 1982; *H v Auckland District Law Society* [1985] 1 NZLR 8; *Wihapi v Hamilton District Law Society* [1992] 3 NZLR 367.

132 Section 101(5)(a) Law Practitioners Act 1982.

133 Section 103 Law Practitioners Act 1982.

of the case, and bring evidence in support.[134] In many cases, the practitioner will instruct another lawyer to act in such proceedings. There is no provision in the Act for the proceedings to be public.

The tribunal may make wide-ranging orders against the practitioner including censuring, limiting the areas of practice, ordering work to be undertaken without charge, imposing a fine or awarding compensation, reducing the fees of the practitioner, or taking steps to supervise the practice of the practitioner.[135] A district tribunal does not, however, have the power to strike a practitioner from the roll, may fine a practitioner no more than $2000, and may award only limited compensation. Where a charge is "of sufficient gravity" as to possibly require orders beyond the jurisdiction of the District Disciplinary Tribunal it must be referred to the New Zealand Law Practitioners Disciplinary Tribunal which is comprised of between five and twelve practitioners and three lay (non-practitioner) members.[136] There is a right of appeal from the decision of a district tribunal to the New Zealand tribunal. Either the practitioner concerned, or the district council or complaints committee that referred the complaint to the tribunal, may initiate the appeal.[137] Where the district council or complaints committee are a party to the proceedings (as, for example, where they are the appellant), they have a right to be heard by counsel.[138]

The hearings of the New Zealand tribunal are (unlike district hearings) in public, although the tribunal may make an order excluding the public if special circumstances exist.[139] As with district tribunals there is a right of the practitioner being charged to be heard, through counsel if desired. The hearings are conducted in a formal manner as is appropriate where serious charges are made, and the consequences to the practitioner may be catastrophic.[140] The hearing is ostensibly conducted as an inquiry rather than as an adversarial contest. Both the district and New Zealand tribunals have the power to require a person to appear before them to

---

134 Section 124 Law Practitioners Act 1982.

135 See s 106 Law Practitioners Act 1982 for a full list of the powers of a disciplinary tribunal.

136 Section 108 Law Practitioners Act 1982.

137 Section 107 Law Practitioners Act 1982.

138 Section 125 Law Practitioners Act 1982. That section gives a similar right to be heard in any proceeding to which the district council or committee is a party, as, for example, before the High Court in the event of an appeal from a decision of the New Zealand tribunal.

139 Or limit the publication of all or part of the hearing: s 111 Law Practitioners Act 1982.

140 Formal rules of procedure are made by the New Zealand Law Practitioners Disciplinary Tribunal pursuant to s 130 of the Act and are the New Zealand Law Practitioners Disciplinary Tribunal Rules 1984.

give evidence, and to produce documents.[141] In this way the tribunal acts as both the prosecution and the Judge, having the responsibility of making the case against the practitioner and deciding whether the charge has been effectively made.

If a charge of misconduct, unbecoming conduct, negligence, or incompetence is found to be proven against a practitioner by the New Zealand tribunal[142] wide powers exist to discipline the practitioner. The tribunal has all of the powers of a district tribunal,[143] as well as the power to suspend, limit the practice, or strike off the practitioner. The test for striking off or suspension is that the practitioner is not a fit and proper person to practise law. Additionally, at least five votes of the members of the tribunal must be cast in favour of striking off or suspension.[144] The New Zealand tribunal may also take the immediate step of suspending a practitioner from practice when a charge is yet to be heard under s 115 of the Act.

An appeal to the High Court (which will sit with three Judges in such matters) lies from the decision of the New Zealand tribunal.[145] Such an appeal may be made by the practitioner concerned or by the district council or committee that referred the complaint to the district or New Zealand tribunal. An appeal before the Court will be conducted according to the formal rules of the Court.

4.3.3 *The role of the lay observer*

Much of the disciplinary process excludes the complainant who will usually be a client of the practitioner, and who has probably suffered as the result of the alleged misconduct. The complainant is not a party to the proceedings before the district or New Zealand tribunal and has no right to be heard. Once the disciplinary proceedings are set in motion the complainant is treated in a way similar to that of a witness in a criminal trial. While their "story" may be of relevance to the finding, the Tribunal is not primarily concerned with vindicating the complainant's rights or effecting any compensation (although this may be a collateral result). The process is lawyer-centred and its objective is to maintain professional discipline and ensure that no person who is not fit to do so is permitted to practise law.

141 Section 126 Law Practitioners Act 1982.

142 Or if the practitioner has been convicted of an imprisonable offence and the nature of the offence reflects on the practitioner's fitness to practise, or brings the profession into disrepute: s 112(1) Law Practitioners Act 1982.

143 It may also impose a fine of up to $5000.

144 Section 113 Law Practitioners Act 1982.

145 Section 118 Law Practitioners Act 1982.

The lay observer system gives a complainant a limited ability to question the conduct of disciplinary proceedings, however, only at a district level.[146] A lay observer is a non-lawyer who is appointed to the position independently (by the Governor-General on the advice of the Minister of Justice).[147] There exist a number of lay observers who hear complaints from certain districts.[148] A complainant who is not satisfied with the manner in which the district society in question has dealt with the complaint may refer the matter to the lay observer. The lay observer is empowered to seek information on the complaint and the way in which it was handled from the district society and the practitioner concerned.

The lay observer will, after investigating the manner in which the original complaint was handled, write a report that will be given to both the district society and the complainant. Such a report may contain a recommendation of action to be taken by the district society, and the society is under an obligation to report back on any action taken as a consequence of the report. If the district society fails to take the actions recommended by the lay observer, or the lay observer is not satisfied with the actions taken, the lay observer may order that the report given to the district society be forwarded to the New Zealand Law Society.[149] The New Zealand society is then under an obligation to consider the report and if it agrees with the findings of the lay observer it will refer the matter back to the district society for further consideration.

Lay observers also have the power to make recommendations to a district society that it inquire into matters of legal practice, which the society is obliged to investigate. Observers also make annual reports to the Minister of Justice that may contain recommendations. That report is tabled in Parliament and is generally an overview of the work of the observers in the preceding year, with some comments on the nature and trends in the work.[150]

While the lay observer system does enable the complainant some avenue for redress where it is felt that the complaint has not been dealt with properly, this is only in a limited way. Unlike the practitioner and the district society the complainant is not directly involved in the proceedings and is not entitled to appeal against any of the decisions of

---

146 See s 97 of the Law Practitioners Act 1982 for the functions of the lay observers.

147 Section 96 Law Practitioners Act 1982.

148 135 complaints were forwarded to five lay observers nationally in the 1997/98 year: *Report of the Lay Observers*, 30 June 1998.

149 Section 97A Law Practitioners Act 1982 which was inserted into the Act in 1995.

150 See s 97(2),(7) and (10). The lay observer may also attend any proceeding of a District Disciplinary Tribunal under s 97(3).

the society. Moreover, the powers of the lay observer may only be invoked at a district level. If a complaint has been referred directly to the national disciplinary tribunal, or has been dealt with on appeal at that level, the complainant has no way in which to voice concerns at all. A further limitation is the fact that on the wording of s 97(1) of the Act the role of an observer is to examine allegations concerning the handling of complaints by district law societies. As such the observer will look to the handling of the complaint rather than the substantive merits of the case or the actual decision of the district society.

The matter is compounded by the fact that power of the lay observer is limited to making recommendations. While in most cases the district societies undoubtedly comply with such recommendations, they are no more than recommendations. If the recommendations are not complied with and the matter is referred to the New Zealand Law Society, it is only empowered to refer the report or recommendation back to the district society for "further consideration". It is difficult to consider that an office so bereft of real power can act as an effective check on the profession's handling of complaints against its members.

4.3.4 *Disciplinary procedures: critique*

The disciplinary procedures in New Zealand reflect a particular approach by the profession. They are entirely lawyer-focused. While lay members of the tribunals and the lay observers reduce the domination of the procedure by lawyers, they do not do away with it. The procedure is conducted primarily by lawyers, for lawyers. This may give an appearance of bias or cronyism to non-lawyer complainants.[151] While at the lowest level of the disciplinary procedure (at the district council or complaints committee level) there is a duty to inform the complainant of the outcome of the initial inquiry, there is no corresponding duty on either the District or New Zealand Disciplinary Tribunals.[152] The complainant is not a party to any of the disciplinary proceedings and has no right to be heard, or to appeal against a decision of a tribunal. Indeed in the case of a district tribunal there is no right to be present at the hearing. The complainant is not formally included in the proceedings once the complaint is made. The rationale for the exclusion appears to be that discipline is an internal matter in which the profession does not recognise that the client has an interest or a right to be included.

Such a view sees the profession as standing apart from the society in which it operates, and as being wholly autonomous. It presumes that it is in the best interests of society if the profession is left to deal with

151 See the comments of G Faulds in *Report of the Law Observers*, 30 June 1998, p 9.

152 This is presumably because the results of these tribunals are public. This places the burden of getting the information on the client.

complaints against its members internally, and clients are left to seek redress through the usual Court system. It also presumes that fellow lawyers are appropriate judges of what kind of conduct of legal practice and relations with clients is acceptable.[153] Such a system is not demonstrably objective, nor is it accountable to the public whom it claims to protect.

Such a position is no longer tenable. While there may be cases where it is appropriate for a client to seek redress through the Courts (as in the case of mere negligence by a practitioner), in matters of professional conduct the client ought to be able to seek redress through an easily accessible forum which is focused on the rights of the client as well as the conduct of members of the legal profession. Clients have a real interest in any proceeding which concerns the conduct of their lawyer towards them. Even if, in the main, the current system results in correct decisions, this is not the perception of clients who are largely excluded from the process. For those on the outside of the disciplinary process it appears that their interests are secondary to the interests of the profession in the proceeding. From this perspective a fair result may seem unlikely to the wronged client.[154]

This view is compounded by the weakness of the lay observer system. The lay observer is involved only after a district body has made a decision, and has only the power to make recommendations (not binding orders) in respect of what action ought to be taken in the event that the proceedings are considered deficient. If proceedings before the New Zealand Disciplinary Tribunal are considered defective by the client the client has no avenue for complaint whatsoever.

4.3.5 *Alternatives*

(a) Client inclusion

There is a need to include the complainant in the proceedings of any disciplinary body. While the client/complainant is not equivalent to a plaintiff or prosecution, he or she is a party who has a direct interest in the proceedings. Such an interest ought to be reflected in a right to be present at the hearing and be heard by the disciplinary body, and a right to question the outcome of the body's decision by appeal.

---

153 For a justification see *Re S (A Barrister)* [1982] 2 All ER 952.

154 This is evident in the fact that in a recent poll a number of clients commented on the failings of the complaints process including an appearance of bias and an absence of assistance to complainants: *Polls of the Profession and the Public "Summary" — The New Zealand Law Society* Wellington, MRL Research Group, 1997, p 51.

(b) Ombudsman supervision

There has been a move away from a wholly lawyer-centred approach to the way in which complaints against lawyers are dealt with in a number of jurisdictions. In England and Wales a Legal Services Ombudsman system has been established which oversees the way in which complaints are handled by the Office for the Supervision of Solicitors, the general Council of the Bar, and the Council for Licensed Conveyancers.[155] This scheme replaced an earlier lay observer scheme.

An ombudsman scheme has a number of significant advantages. A central office will ensure that consistent standards are applied. The creation of a central ombudsman's office rather than the ad hoc appointment of lay observers gives a signal of authority and status that is currently absent from the lay observer system. The creation of an ombudsman also enables a degree of public relations to be undertaken, giving a high profile to the supervisory function of such an office which makes its recommendations harder to ignore.[156] Such a scheme requires greater resources than are currently devoted to the lay observer scheme to ensure that it can operate effectively and not become a hindrance rather than assistance to clients in ensuring effective resolution of their complaints.

Perhaps the most important aspect of an ombudsman scheme is that they are non-lawyers who act outside the professional organisation. The fact that an ombudsman is a separate office demonstrates the ability to investigate a complaint independently and accords sufficient status to the office to lend weight to its views and opinions.

(c) Independent Commissioner

In New South Wales the Legal Profession Reform Act 1993 created the Office of Legal Services Commissioner.[157] This office differs from its English counterpart in that it is the initial point of contact for complainants. This is a significant improvement as the complaint is being made to an organisation which is wholly independent from the individual being complained against.[158] The office of the Commissioner may refer the complaint to the professional organisation to be dealt with,

---

155 Pursuant to ss 21-26 of the Courts and Legal Services Act 1990 (UK). The system does suffer from the problem that the ombudsman may only make non-binding recommendations. Although, if recommendations are not followed, there is a power to publicise the name of the person or organisation who failed to follow the recommendation. A similar system exists in Manitoba under the title of the Complaints Commissioner.

156 This seems to be the case under the English scheme. See "The Legal Services Ombudsman: Form versus Function" (1995) 58 MLR 187.

157 See generally ss 131-155 Legal Profession Act 1987 (NSW).

158 See S Ross *Ethics in Law: Lawyers' Accountability and Responsibility in Australia* 2nd ed, Sydney, Butterworths, 1998, 164.

or investigate it itself. If the complaint is investigated by the professional organisation the Commissioner will supervise the conduct of the investigation and may give directions to the organisation. However, if the organisation dismisses the complaint the client has a right of appeal to the Commissioner. The Commissioner is not only given the power to supervise the complaints procedure of the profession, but also is an independent body which will hear and determine an appeal. The focus in this procedure has shifted to the client who may initiate an appeal if the professional body does not deal with the matter satisfactorily.

(d) Mediation

A number of jurisdictions have provided for mediation between lawyer and client where the complaint is not a serious one.[159] Under the New South Wales Act complaints may be referred to mediation where the matter is a consumer dispute — one which may not involve professional misconduct.[160] The mediation is confidential and any disclosures made may not be used if further proceedings ensue. Such a process involves the client directly in the process and recognises the complainant as an important part of the discipline and complaints procedure. One lay observer has noted:[161]

> Many of the matters should be much more easily sorted out if both sides were forced to confront one another face to face in front of an independent arbitrator.

(e) Consumer protection

Traditionally, professional organisations have been reluctant to deal with disputes about the quality of service provided by their members.[162] It has been considered that this is not a matter of discipline, and is best left to the individual members to deal with, or for the client to pursue through other avenues (such as the Courts). Such a distinction is often understandably difficult for the client to appreciate. The failure of a lawyer to call certain evidence in a trial, or an oversight in the conveyance of a property might be a source of far more concern (and actual loss) to a client than minor breaches of confidences, or the existence of an undisclosed conflict. However, mere negligence or errors

---

159 In a sense this is what happens if a complaint is dealt with by a complaints committee and does not proceed to a tribunal in New Zealand, though the process in unclear and the parties usually communicate only by correspondence through the committee.

160 See s 144 Legal Profession Act 1987 (NSW). A system of mediation also exists in Manitoba.

161 *Report of the Lay Observers for the year ended 30 June 1998*, comments of the observer for Auckland, Waikato and Bay of Plenty, and Taranaki District Law Societies, p 3.

162 Although such matters are often resolved in practice by the complaints committee at the district level.

of judgment are not matters with which the professional organisation usually concerns itself; even less so, poor practice management such as failure to keep clients informed, late billing, or a failure to promptly attend to a client's affairs.

More recently, there has been a welcome acceptance in some jurisdictions that it is in the interests of both the profession and the public for such complaints to be dealt with. In England and Wales the Office for the Supervision of Solicitors divides complaints between the Office for Client Relations (dealing with inadequate service or minor misconduct) and the Office for Professional Regulation (dealing with serious breaches).[163] The mediation process in New South Wales (mentioned above) is designed to deal primarily with consumer disputes.

(f) Client care and complaints procedures

Many complaints reach the professional organisation due to a simple failure to explain to the client the nature of the work to be undertaken, how long it will take, or how much it will cost. The practitioner's failure to attend to the client's concerns when first raised frequently compounds the problem. While there are some serious complaints that will necessarily be referred directly to the governing authority, much is to be gained by encouraging a clear understanding of the nature of the lawyer's task and resolution between the client and the practitioner where possible.

This has been taken a step further in some jurisdictions where practitioners are required to inform clients at the outset of the lawyer-client relationship, the nature of the obligations of the lawyer, the basis upon which costs will be charged, and the manner in which a complaint made by the client will be handled by the firm.[164] Such a rule exists in England and Wales under which practitioners are obliged to have a complaint procedure and inform the client of how to make a complaint and how it will be dealt with.[165]

(g) Client advocate

A client advocate may alleviate some of the significant hurdles facing complainants. A significant problem for any client who has a complaint about the lawyer is that they are entering into a potential conflict with a professional negotiator/advocate. It is unlikely that the client has had any dealings with the law society, or any knowledge of the complaint process. In many cases the clients are unfamiliar with the steps open to

163 Section 93 Courts and Legal Services Act 1990 (UK).

164 See for example the *Queensland Solicitors Handbook* para 4.09.

165 Rule 15 of the English *Guide to the Professional Conduct of Solicitors*.

them when a complaint is contemplated. It has been observed in respect of the current system:[166]

> The general public really have little knowledge of the procedures relating to the laying of complaints and even less of the existence or functions of a Lay Observer.

Conversely, the practitioner is a member of the society, and is likely to be aware of the general nature of the complaint process. The parties are unevenly matched. It is important that the client is able to bring a complaint against a lawyer, understand how it is resolved, and feel that the complaint has been properly heard. To do this, at least in some cases, assistance may be needed. The provision of assistance in advising whether grounds for a complaint exist, and with whom it ought to be raised in the first instance, would assist in both the client, and the governing body getting complaints resolved quickly and effectively. It would also be likely to reduce the number of unfounded complaints, or complaints that would be better resolved directly with practitioners.

Such a system of consumer advocacy has been created in respect of the delivery of health services by virtue of Part III of the Health and Disability Commissioner Act 1994. The roles of advocates under that Act includes the provision of assistance to people who wish to make a complaint to a professional body[167] as well as the broader functions of ensuring consumers are aware of the Code of Health and Disability Services, and promoting awareness of procedures for resolving complaints. A similar role would be appropriate in the legal arena. If a matter was unable to be resolved informally the advocate would be able to assist in the complaints procedure, or in obtaining redress through other forums. The role would not be that of counsel or a substitute lawyer, but rather a method to ensure that clients were aware of their rights and how to exercise them.

166 *Report of the Lay Observers for the year ended 30 June 1998*, comments of the observer for Canterbury and Westland District Law Societies , p 8.

167 Section 30(i).

Part Three

Lawyer and Client

Chapter 5

Lawyer and Client

5.1 Introduction

Few contracts of service, other than between lawyer and client, owe such strict duties of loyalty, frankness, and confidence to the client. These duties exist by virtue of not only the fiduciary nature of the relationship, but also because the professional organisation imposes further stringent duties on lawyers. The duties of lawyers are, therefore, both professional and legal.

The duties of lawyers ought to be viewed critically. There are significant tensions between a lawyer's duty to clients and wider duties both as a lawyer and as a citizen. Just because a duty is onerous, or has always existed, is no reason to accept it without question. Some duties may be too stringent for modern conditions, or have the effect of stifling deserving claims. The duties of confidentiality and restrictions on conditional fee arrangements, respectively, have been subject to such criticism. Clear and powerful justifications are required to place such extraordinary duties on lawyers, and to grant such privileges to clients.

Claims that the duties placed on lawyers are entirely for the clients' benefit need to be examined with caution. There may be a number of advantages for lawyers. One such advantage is the fact that clients will be far more likely to use the services of a lawyer if they can be sure of the loyalty and confidence of the lawyer. The law and the rules have relieved lawyers of moral duties which would make their profession difficult if not impossible were they imposed. The existence of such rules provides a welcome compulsion to lawyers rather than leaving them in a moral and practical quagmire. In most cases a lawyer is not called upon to decide whether confidential information may be disclosed, or whether the client's cause is worthy. The rules provide guidance, relieving them of a difficult decision.

Other rules appear more obviously to favour lawyers. The restrictions on advertising have had the effect of reducing competition amongst lawyers, though with the relaxation of the rules competition is increasing. Rules still seem to be aimed at the preservation of the reputation of the profession. Such rules deal with names of firms, business activities outside the practice of law, maintaining decorum in advertising, and limiting the manner in which direct approaches to prospective clients may be made.[1] Rules of courtesy between practitioners, and the corresponding duties to honour undertakings and promises, also make the practice of law considerably easier for practitioners.

The duties in their current form should not be accepted uncritically and it can be questioned whether they are appropriate to the environment in which legal services are delivered today. Many of the duties place constraints on the way in which a lawyer or law firm can act which may ultimately increase the cost of legal services and/or limit access to such services. One effect of the strict application of the rules of confidence is to preclude a lawyer from acting for a later client who might benefit from information held about a former client of the lawyer.[2] One practical result is that clients may be forced to change lawyers when such problems arise increasing their legal costs and depriving them of their first choice of lawyer. Such costs may be justified by the values being protected. However, such questions need to be examined carefully rather than unquestioningly accepting the law as it stands.

5.2 The professional relationship

5.2.1 *The traditional analysis*

The rationale for these special and strict duties owed by lawyers to their clients is based on the perception of the lawyer-client relationship as a special one. On a traditional view, the client reveals sensitive and personal information to the lawyer with the utmost frankness. The client is quite possibly unaware of the legal complexities surrounding the task that they have given the lawyer. The matter brought to the lawyer for assistance will be one of considerable importance concerning perhaps protection of property, or liberty. Accordingly, the lawyer has strict duties of loyalty to ensure that all actions taken are in the best interests of the client. The lawyer has a duty not to act in a situation where the client's interests conflict with those of the lawyer or another client. This view is premised on clients being weak, uninformed, and vulnerable, whereas lawyers are seen as powerful, informed, and in a position of advantage. In many cases this may be so, particularly where the client is an individual with no direct knowledge of the law or legal system, and little experience in dealing with members of the legal profession.

1 Rules 2.01, 2.03, 4.01, and 4.03 respectively.
2 See more particularly ch 9.

On such a view, the tasks performed by the lawyer require an application of more than mere technical skill. They require in addition the exercise of judgment that will depend on the experience and professional values of the lawyer. In most cases, the lawyer will not be known personally to the client, therefore, the rules of conduct exist as an external standard below which the conduct of the lawyer must not fall.

5.2.2 *Diversity of relationships*

This archetypal picture of the lawyer-client relationship may be misleading. While many relationships do roughly answer such a description, there are many others which are quite different. Numerous commercial clients are very familiar with the law and legal profession, and will often have their own in-house lawyers to deal with the law firms they retain. Such commercial clients will spread different aspects of their work between different firms, or seek price competitive bids from firms to ensure that they are getting the best deal. They cannot be regarded as vulnerable or unsophisticated, and it might be claimed that, if there is any power imbalance, it is the lawyers who are the weaker party.

Some clients are regular users of the Court system and are not naïve in the processes of the Court, or the obligations of their counsel. Some clients may use their knowledge of the law and legal process to thwart the lawyer in the lawyer's duty to the Court by concealing documents, and making dubious claims. The ignorance of everyday citizens and business people can also be overstated. Many know with some clarity why they are retaining their lawyer and what outcome they expect. They are also able to determine whether the service is delivered in a timely and professional manner, even if the acuteness of the professional judgment of the lawyer may not be entirely clear.

The kinds of lawyers and clients and the relationships between them vary infinitely. The rules might be criticised as contemplating only one kind of lawyer-client relationship. The duties of lawyers on which the rules are based were formed when there was a fixed view of the paternalistic role of the lawyer in relation to the client. The rapid and recent changes in the nature of the legal profession and the society in which it exists means that the rules are, in many cases, not entirely appropriate. The expectations of clients and the way in which legal services are delivered is sometimes at odds with the orthodox conception of the lawyer-client relationship and attached duties.

5.3 Sources of duties

5.3.1 *General law*

When a lawyer is retained by a client, a number of legal consequences result. The parties have formed a contract with express and implied terms that will bind them. It is on this basis that a lawyer charges fees, and sues for them if they remain unpaid. It may also give rise to claims in damages where the work is performed below standard or negligently, and the client suffers loss. The existence of a contract for the supply of professional services will also mean that legislative provisions will apply to the relationship. The provisions of the Consumer Guarantees Act 1993 will apply provided that the client satisfies the test of "consumer" pursuant to s 2 of the Act. Section 28 provides that services provided to a consumer must be carried out with reasonable care and skill. Similarly, the provisions of the Fair Trading Act 1986 will operate to prohibit any misleading or deceptive conduct in trade.[3]

Notwithstanding the fact that lawyers owe duties to their clients in contract, the Courts have frequently affirmed the fact that concurrent duties are also owed in tort.[4] A lawyer will have a duty of care to the client whether a contract between them exists or not.[5] Where a lawyer fails to carry out the work with a reasonable degree of care and skill the client will have a tort claim in damages for any loss suffered.[6] The tort duty on a lawyer to take care may also be owed to third parties if they can establish sufficient proximity. It has been found that where a client had given instructions to draft a will, but the lawyer failed to do so before the client died, the intended beneficiaries were able to claim against the lawyer.[7]

5.3.2 *Fiduciary duties*

The relationship between lawyer and client automatically gives rise to a fiduciary relationship The existence of such a relationship imposes onerous duties on a lawyer. This reflects an assumption that the features giving rise to a fiduciary relationship will almost invariably exist between lawyer and client.[8] Those features include an imbalance of power, vulnerability of one party, a relationship of trust and confidence, and an assumption by one party of a duty to act in the other's interests.[9] The

---

3 Sections 9 and 11.

4 *White v Jones* [1995] 1 All ER 691, 698, 704 per Lord Goff; *Asteley v Austrust Ltd* [1999] HCA 6, (1999) 161 ALR 155.

5 Where a lawyer acts pro bono (ie without fee) there would be no contract for lack of consideration.

6 *Bannerman Brydone Folster & Co v Murray* [1972] NZLR 411, 429 per Woodhouse J.

7 *Gartside v Sheffield Young and Ellis* [1983] NZLR 37; *White v Jones* [1995] 1 All ER 691 although in the latter case Lord Goff expressed a reluctance to dilute the lawyers' duty to their clients with a duty to third parties.

8 *Sims v Craig Bell and Bond* [1991] 3 NZLR 535.

9 See generally *Hospital Products Ltd v United States Surgical Corporation* (1984) 156 CLR 41; *Watson v Dolmark Industries* [1992] 3 NZLR 311.

obligations imposed by the fiduciary relationship are heavy and have been stated as duties to:[10]

- Avoid conflicts of interest between client and self, former clients or existing clients;
- Not make a personal gain (other than fees) from the relationship;
- Disclose all matters that are material to the client to the client;
- Maintain all information disclosed or gained in the course of the relationship as confidential;
- Account for all moneys held on behalf of the client.

5.3.3 *Professional rules*

As well as the duties imposed by the general law are the duties imposed by the law society. Unlike rules imposed by the general law many of the Rules of Professional Conduct are stated in broad terms and act as a guide rather than rule. A breach of professional rules may give rise to a complaint to the law society, but will not, of itself, give rise to any claim for damages before the Courts.

Most of the professional rules concerning duties to clients have a counterpart in the general law. There are, however, instances where duties which are owed to clients under the professional rules do not exist under the general law. For example, the prohibition contained in r 6.09 on spouses acting for different clients whose interests conflict, has no direct counterpart in the general law. Conversely, there are instances where the general law prohibits certain conduct but there is no corresponding prohibition in the professional rules. For example, the law prohibits contingency fees, but there is no such prohibition in the rules.[11]

It is arguable that the duties owed by practitioners to clients under the Rules of Professional Conduct are part of the terms of the contract between them. The rules are universal across the profession in New Zealand, known to all practitioners, not excluded by the terms of any contract, and reasonable. They meet all the requirements of being customary terms of a contract and will be incorporated on this basis.[12] The rules are also used as a guide to the standard of practitioners' conduct. When the Courts consider whether the conduct of a practitioner has fallen below the reasonable standard of skill and care required in both tort and contract, they will look to the standards imposed by the professional rules for assistance. While the Court is not

10 See G E Dal Pont *Lawyers Professional Responsibility in Australia and New Zealand* North Ryde, NSW, Law Book Co, 1996,115.

11 *Mills v Rogers* (1899) 18 NZLR 291.

12 *Woods v Ellingham & Co Ltd* [1977] 1 NZLR 218.

bound to adopt the rules as the standard of acceptable conduct, if the rules have been breached this will be an indication that the conduct of a practitioner was not that of a reasonable practitioner taking care and skill.

5.3.4 *The Court's inherent jurisdiction*

A further source of duties owed by lawyers to their clients and to the Court is the inherent jurisdiction of the Court over lawyers. The ability of the Court to supervise and control the conduct of lawyers as its officers exists concurrently with the disciplinary jurisdiction of the law society. This supervisory jurisdiction will extend to enforcing duties owed to clients and is apparent in the Court's power to enforce practitioners' undertakings,[13] and the power to discipline counsel who misconduct themselves in the course of litigation.[14] Further, they have the power to prohibit counsel from acting in a case where there is a risk that a former client's confidence would be breached.[15]

The focus of the Court's inherent jurisdiction over lawyers is the efficacy of its own proceeding and the efficient administration of justice. To ensure this, it needs to have the ability to intervene in a proceeding, and ensure the proper conduct of a barrister or solicitor. The existence of the power to prevent its process being used for a collateral purpose or as an instrument of injustice has long been recognised.[16] The power is one that is derived "from the very nature of the Court as a superior Court of law"[17] to ensure that they are indeed instruments of justice rather than oppression.

5.4 Conclusion

The following chapters examine in more detail the duties placed on lawyers by the law, the profession, and the Courts. The duties have long been accepted as appropriate without examining closely the justificatory rationale. This will assist in exploring the nature and extent of those duties in greater detail.

---

13 See *Re Grey* [1892] 2 QB 440, 443, per Lord Esher MR; *Gill and McAsey v Wainui Timber Co Ltd* [1992] 1 NZLR 1, 4 per Richardson J (CA).

14 *McDonald v FAI (NZ) General Insurance Co Ltd* [1999] 1 NZLR 583, affirmed on appeal in *Harley v McDonald* [1999] 3 NZLR 545.

15 *Black v Taylor* [1993] 3 NZLR 403.

16 *Metropolitan Bank v Pooley* (1885) 10 App cas 210, 220 (HL). The power has similarly long been recognised in respect of the power to stay frivolous or vexatious proceedings: *McHenry v Lewis* (1882) 21 Ch D 202 (HC).

17 J Jacob, "The Inherent Jurisdiction of the Court" [1970] CLP 23, reprinted in J Jacob *The Reform of Civil Procedural Law* 1982, 224. See *New Zealand Social Credit Political League v O'Brien* [1984] 1 NZLR 84 (CA) for the leading New Zealand authority.

Chapter 6

Lawyer-Client Relationship — Formation, Termination and Abuse

6.1 Duty to be available — the cab rank rule

One of the most challenging, yet fundamental, duties of a lawyer is the duty to accept clients. Because in our current legal system lawyers are essential to enable access to justice, it is important that lawyers do not turn away people who seek their assistance. In most cases, few problems arise, the lawyer is happy to work for clients seeking a lawyer's services. However, there will be cases where a lawyer would rather not assist a client. The lawyer's reluctance to assist may be due to a number of factors.

Commonly cited are cases where the lawyer is being asked to represent a reprehensible cause, as where the retainer is to defend the perpetrator of a heinous crime, or to defend the rights of free speech of neo-Nazis or other extremist groups. Other, more mundane, problems are more difficult, for example, when a prospective client seeks to retain a lawyer to evade clear duties through the use of legal technicalities, or where a litigant seeks to press a claim that has little prospect of success in order to delay or frustrate the other side. There are also situations where the client is known to be difficult and may have terminated a retainer with a previous lawyer, or even be seeking to bring an action against the former adviser.

The New Zealand rules place particularly high demands on lawyers. This contrasts with England where the duty applies only to barristers.[1] In New Zealand both barristers and solicitors are obliged to accept any client requiring assistance they are able to render. This also contrasts

---

1 The English rule is contained in the Code of Conduct for the Bar of England and Wales. That rule states in para 2.09: "A barrister in independent practice is in general bound to accept any brief to appear before a Court in the field in which he professes to practise, having regard to his experience and seniority, at the proper professional fee having regard to the length and difficulty of the case and his availability". See also *Rondel v Worsley* [1969] 1 AC 191, 274 per Lord Pearce (HL).

with the US position exemplified by the ABA Model Rules which do not require a lawyer to undertake any particular retainer,[2] and r 1.16(b)(3) expressly permits withdrawal from a case where the lawyer considers the client's objectives "repugnant or imprudent".

6.1.1 *The rule*

The articulation of the cab rank rule in New Zealand is found in r 1.02 of the rules of professional conduct that provides:

> A practitioner as a professional person must be available to the public and must not, without good cause, refuse to accept instructions for services within the practitioner's fields of practice from any particular client or prospective client.

The rule is superficially clear, however, as there is no real guidance as to what will amount to "good cause" to refuse to accept instructions. The commentary to the rule provides a limited degree of guidance in stating that practitioners are not obliged to accept clients where the work is outside their expertise, or they are too busy. It is also stated that a refusal to accept instructions may not be based on the "race colour ethnic or national origins, sex or creed of the prospective client". This partially reproduces some of the prohibited grounds of discrimination in respect of the supply of services under the Human Rights Act 1993.[3] The commentary also notes that practitioners must notify clients if they are eligible for legal aid, and must not distinguish the service given between legal aided and non-legally aided clients.[4] The Courts have affirmed the fact that the source of funds for an action should not alter the behaviour of a lawyer.[5]

2 Rule 1.16 of the ABA Model Rules which deals with declining or terminating retainers is phrased in terms of when a client is prohibited from further acting for a client. Although r 1.2 states in general terms that "Legal representation should not be denied to people ... whose cause is controversial or the subject of popular disapproval".

3 Sections 21 and 44. It would also be illegal for lawyers to refuse their services on the grounds of the marital status, disability, age, political belief, employment status, sexual orientation or family status of the prospective client under that Act. See also the *Equality Code* of the English Bar which deals in detail with the prohibition on discriminatory practices.

4 Although a new r 3.05 proposed at the time of writing provides in para 5 of the commentary that a legally aided client should receive the practitioner's best efforts "having regard to the time and funding available".

5 *Ridehalgh v Horsefield* [1994] Ch 205, 235 (CA).

6.1.2 *The rationale*[6]

The most obvious reason underpinning the cab rank rule is the value placed on access to justice. The ideal that every citizen has a right to bring his or her grievances before the Court runs deep in the common law tradition. The cab rank rule brings this closer to reality by ensuring that the assistance of a legal adviser is not denied.[7] This is especially so in respect of cases which concern facts or causes that may be repugnant to individual lawyers, or of society in general. The rule removes the opportunity for the lawyer's decision to accept the case from being affected by his or her own attitudes, or by pressure from peers or the wider community. It is, therefore, more likely that any litigant, regardless of the popularity of the cause, will be able to bring the matter before the Courts.

The concept that a lawyer is obliged to assist anyone who requires such assistance regardless of the person's identity or the nature of the cause also fits well with the traditional ideal of the legal profession being altruistic and service-oriented. Because of the special privileges and immunities given to lawyers (such as the monopoly on advocacy immunity from claims in negligence for the conduct of litigation) lawyers have special responsibilities placed on them. One such responsibility is to put to one side personal squeamishness and concern over societal disapproval and accept any client regardless of identity or cause.

Allied to the access to justice rationale is the value placed on individual autonomy, in particular, the right of clients to pursue their interests without any moralistic or paternalistic interference. If a client wishes to enter into a transaction or bring litigation it is not up to the lawyer to prevent this on other than legal grounds. The fact that the intended action of the client appears immoral, unwise, or even unlikely to succeed cannot be a reason for declining to act; though it might be a reason for remonstrating with the client. There is a hint of the technician or "hired gun" approach in the rule in so far as it places little importance on the moral views of the lawyer.

The amoral position of the lawyer is also argued to be important in enabling the lawyer to be objective and neutral in the advice. By providing that the personal views of a lawyer ought not be a consideration in accepting a client the rules make it clear that lawyers' personal views and actions are quite separate from their professional views and actions. It is claimed that lawyers are more likely to be able to give effective advice and assistance where they are dispassionate and

6 See D Wikins, "Race Ethics and the First Amendment — Should a Black Lawyer Defend the Klu Klux Klan?" (1995) 63 Geo Wash LR , also "Do You Act for Rapists?" (1990) NLJ 392.

7 See *Giannarelli v Wraith* (1988) 165 CLR 543, 580.

unaffected by their personal views. This is in considerable distinction to the position in the US where many lawyers publicise their political leanings and invite retainers from clients with similar views. There are also numerous public interest firms in the US actively seeking retainers touching on particular political causes such as tenancy rights, racial equality, or gender issues.[8]

An additional advantage of the cab rank rule is that it absolves (at least to some extent) lawyers from culpability for assisting in repugnant causes.[9] If lawyers had a choice of whether to assist a client or not, they may be blamed in the event that they chose to assist in defending the perpetrator of an abhorrent crime, or assist in the furtherance of distasteful political objectives. However, because lawyers have no choice they cannot be tainted by the views and beliefs of the people they act for. If this argument is accepted, the lawyer becomes a morally neutral assistant who cannot be accused of acting in a morally reprehensible way by assisting someone with a repugnant cause.

6.1.3 *Refusing clients*

A lawyer may legitimately turn away a client. In some cases, the lawyer is clearly prohibited from taking on the new retainer. Where the lawyer is already working for a client whose interests are in conflict (or potentially may be in conflict) with those of the new client the lawyer is prohibited from taking on the new client unless both parties consent.[10] In matters of litigation the rules place a blanket prohibition on one lawyer acting for opposing parties.[11] Lawyers are also obliged to refuse a retainer where their own interests conflict with those of the client.[12] Similarly, where a lawyer is in possession of confidential information of a former client which would be of use to the prospective client, the lawyer must ensure the security of that information; this will usually entail refusing the new retainer.[13]

As well as such reasons of principle that require a lawyer to refuse to act for a prospective client, there are numerous more pragmatic grounds on which a lawyer may decline a retainer. The commentary to r 1.02 actively encourages practitioners to recognise that they are not competent in all

---

8 See the discussion in David Luban *Lawyers and Justice: An Ethical Study* Princeton, New Jersey, Princeton University Press, 1988, 293.

9 See the comments in the *First Report on the Legal Profession* Sydney, New South Wales Law Reform Commission, 1982, para 6.78.

10 Rule 1.04.

11 Rule 8.07.

12 Rule 1.03.

13 *Prince Jefri Bolkiah v KPMG (a firm)* [1999] 2 WLR 215; *Russell McVeagh v Tower Corporation* [1998] 3 NZLR 641; *Wells v Wellington District Law Society* [1997] 1 NZLR 660.

fields of practice and should be ready to inform a client of this and ensure that the matter is dealt with by another practitioner with the requisite degree of skill and experience. A lawyer may, and ought to, decline to take a case where the lawyer does not have the time to deal with it expeditiously due to other commitments.

There may be cases where a lawyer will work for a reduced fee, for nothing, or take fees only from the fruits of litigation.[14] However, if a client is unable to pay for the professional services required a lawyer is entitled to decline to act. The rules at the time of writing are unclear as to whether a lawyer might properly refuse a case simply because it was legally aided (and therefore less lucrative than a non-legally aided case). The commentary to r 1.02 states that a practitioner should bring the availability of legal aid to a client's attention where appropriate, though they do not go so far as to say that it is inappropriate to decline to act on legal aid. A new r 3.06[15] is under consideration that provides:

> A practitioner may decline to act where a client will be legally aided if the practitioner believes that:
>
> 1. the legal aid rate or the likely legal aid rate is not fair remuneration;
> 2. the grant of legal aid in the particular case has been capped at an unacceptably low figure.
>
> In declining to act the practitioner must, however, at that time advise that there are other competent practitioners who are likely to be willing and able to do the work on a legal aid basis.

The proposed rule comes at a time of considerable negative media attention regarding the allegedly high level of fees earned by lawyers through legal aid and a consequent move to reduce the level of remuneration available to lawyers working for legally-aided clients. If adopted (as is expected) this will operate as an exception to the duty to accept clients under the cab rank rule.

Lawyers will also be required to refuse to act if the client seeks assistance in perpetrating a fraud or other wrong. If lawyers assist in such an endeavour they are not only acting unprofessionally but may also find themselves liable for their actions under the criminal or civil law. More difficult is the prohibition on lawyers assisting in a case which amounts to an abuse of the process of the Court. Where lawyers know or ought to know that they are assisting in bringing a case, or raising a defence that is not bona fide and is brought for a purpose other than the vindication of legal rights, they will be guilty of misconduct and may be

---

14 Within the limits imposed by law: see *Thai Trading v Taylor* [1998] 3 All ER 65.

15 A proposed new r 3.05 also clarifies the duty of the lawyer in advising of the availability of legal aid, as well as advising of the shortcomings of funding a case by legal aid.

disciplined by the Court or the professional body.[16] While the Courts will only find that a case is an abuse of process in clear cases, the spectre of disciplinary proceedings may make some lawyers wary of assisting in cases which are of doubtful merit.[17]

Other than these few specific instances there is little guidance as to when a lawyer may decline to act. The rule is expressed in broad terms and what may amount to a "good cause" to refuse a client is not defined. However, the equivalent rule in the English Code of Conduct of the Bar[18] seems to suggest that only matters of legal practice and not personal belief are relevant considerations. The New Zealand rule and professional jurisprudence is closely based on the English stance and it is likely that a similar approach would be taken. Such an approach emphasises, perhaps fictitiously, the detachment of the lawyer and the ability to advocate a cause with which the lawyer personally considers ill-founded or immoral. In New South Wales a provision in the Bar Rules permitting a retainer to be refused by a barrister where the barrister objected on conscientious grounds from accepting the brief was recently removed,[19] thus making it clear that such personal beliefs are not a ground for refusing a retainer.

6.1.4 *Critique*

(a) Practical shortcomings

The cab rank rule has considerable advantages. It provides assistance to those who might otherwise be left without legal counsel, and it provides a defence to lawyers who are accused of acting unethically when acting as an advocate for morally repugnant causes. However, there are a number of shortcomings. One real shortcoming is that the rule is easily avoided in practice, and breaches are rarely, if ever, discovered or punished. Lawyers make it quite clear what kinds of clients are acceptable. Some practices actively discourage certain, usually less lucrative, areas of work such as criminal and family matters. By choosing a particular firm to work for, or specialisation, lawyers are effectively limiting the kinds of cases that they are available to take and making it

16 *Chua v ANZ* (1997) 11 PRNZ 523 (HC); *McDonald v FAI* [1999] 1 NZLR 583 (HC) (affirmed by the Court of Appeal as *Harley v McDonald* [1999] 3 NZLR 545.

17 See D Webb, "Hopeless Cases: In Defence of Compensating Litigants at the Advocate's Expense" (1999) 29 VUWLR 295, 297.

18 Code of Conduct of the Bar of England and Wales paras 501-503 which state that a barrister must not accept instructions if to do so would be to lead to "*professional* embarrassment".

19 The exception, r 2(o), was removed in 1994.

less likely that a case that is distasteful to them will come their way.[20] Because lawyers do choose whether to take criminal cases, or cases for large corporates, the claim that they are "forced" to defend perpetrators of heinous crimes, or holders of repugnant views holds little water.

Numerous lawyers seek to gain work by making it clear that they take a particular political stance in such matters as the Bill of Rights, Treaty of Waitangi, consumer actions, and equal opportunities cases. This is a recent development in New Zealand and demonstrates a move away from the neutrality which is traditionally expected. A number of lawyers seek retainers which ally with their own political views. Lawyers are after all, human, and to expect them to suspend their own firmly held beliefs in representing a cause to which they fiercely object is asking the nearly impossible. At a more day-to-day level if a case arises which a lawyer does not want to take there are innumerable devices to avoid doing so. Most lawyers are busy, and it would be hard to show that a refusal to take a case was not justified on the ground that there was insufficient time to deal with it expeditiously. However, where a case is an attractive one there are few lawyers who will not reshuffle their commitments to take on the extra work. Similar claims may be made about expertise and the degree of complexity that the work requires to avoid inconvenient briefs.

Even if such devices are not used to avoid work, and a more straightforward approach is used, there are few clients who would insist on retaining a lawyer who bluntly stated that he or she did not condone the client's actions or intentions. It is certainly open to a lawyer to express such reservations to a client, especially if there is a belief that personal views will interfere with the lawyer's professional judgment.[21] However, in the unlikely event that the client still wishes to retain the lawyer in the face of such an admission, the rules seem to require the lawyer to continue with the retainer.

Cases where litigants have been unable to retain legal counsel are not unknown even in the face of the rule. Such instances are not restricted to abhorrent causes such as defending terrorists or child abusers. In the case of *McKaskell v Benseman*[22] the plaintiff represented himself. It was reported that this was due to the fact that "the legal profession had closed ranks against him and he could not get a lawyer to act for him".[23] The case was one where the plaintiff was claiming against numerous

20 See A Hutchison, "Taking it Personally: Legal Ethics and Client Selection" (1998) Legal Ethics 168.

21 See N Wilson *Lectures on Advocacy and Ethics in the High Court* Auckland, Legal Research Foundation, 1982, p 36.

22 [1989] 3 NZLR 75.

23 *The Press*, Christchurch, 14 February 1989, p 14.

legal practitioners who had had varying degrees of involvement in his affairs previously. This demonstrates that there are difficult or distasteful clients who have difficulty in obtaining legal assistance.

(b) Objections of principle

Even if the cab rank rule worked in practice there remain some serious misgivings about its foundations. The rule has also been criticised as reducing lawyers to mercenaries and subverting their own personal autonomy.[24] Some commentators suggest that lawyers ought to hold themselves personally responsible for the actions of their clients.[25] It is unrealistic to expect lawyers to put aside their own beliefs and become morally transparent in the representation of their client's cause. If a lawyer is required to assist in the furtherance of a cause that is repugnant, this will be at considerable cost to the lawyer's own sense of personal integrity. It is certainly arguable that requiring lawyers to ignore their own moral views in the assistance of their clients does not make for morally better lawyers.

At a more practical level is the observation that for a lawyer to most effectively represent a cause they must have a belief that the arguments mounted are justifiable. In most of the work of a lawyer,[26] the lawyer will believe that the actions of the client are reasonably defensible at law. Lawyers may "persuade themselves" that their client's cause is a good one.[27] Lawyers who consider the client's case ill-founded and unlikely to succeed will use considerable skill in persuading the client that the course of action originally proposed is ill-advised. An advocate who wholly disagrees with the client's course of action is unlikely to be effective regardless of protestations of independence and neutrality. The American approach rejects the need for disinterested assistance by lawyers and accepts that lawyers will tend to seek clients with whose causes they agree, and that lawyers are likely to be more zealous and therefore effective in pursing such causes.[28]

---

24 M Quinlivan, "The Cab Rank Rule: A Reappraisal of the Duty to Accept Clients" (1998) 28 VUWLR 113.

25 D Kennedy, "The Responsibility of the Lawyer for the Justice of Their Causes" (1987) 18 Texas Tech LR 1157.

26 With the exception of criminal law in which counsel frequently are required to suspend their own belief of the innocence or guilt of the accused. An important distinction is the fact that defendants are compelled to come before the criminal Courts whereas in civil matters a litigant has a choice to settle or abandon an ill founded claim or defence.

27 See R Eli Rosen, "Devils, Lawyers and Salvation Lie in the Details: Deontological Legal Ethics, Issue Conflicts of interest and Civic Education in Law Schools" in K Economides *Ethical Challenges to Legal Education and Conduct* Oxford, Hart Publishing 1998, 61.

28 See M Mayer & S Linowitz *The Betrayed Profession: Lawyering at the End of the Twentieth Century* New York, C Scribner & Sons, 1994, 25.

It is imperative that all citizens have access to competent legal advice and assistance regardless of the abhorrence of their cause. However, it is not clear that the cab rank rule is the best way to achieve this. Not only is it illusory in practice, but also if strictly applied it would place unreasonable demands on lawyers. Under the current rule a lay person may be unable to obtain the chosen legal assistance. If the cab rank rule were done away with the incidence of such cases would not increase perceptibly. Those cases where a client would be left without assistance because no lawyer was willing to adopt the cause could be solved by a less blunt instrument than the cab rank rule.

The ethical rule which requires lawyers to act against their own beliefs may contravene fundamental human rights as enshrined in some of our foundational laws. For example s 13 of the New Zealand Bill of Rights Act 1990 provides:

> Everyone has the right to freedom of thought, conscience, religion, and belief, including the right to adopt and to hold opinions without interference.

This right, along with the right to observe or practise beliefs enshrined in s 15 of the Act seems to run counter to the demand of the cab rank rule that such personal views be suspended.[29] Unfavourable treatment on the grounds of ethical or religious belief is a prohibited ground of discrimination under the Human Rights Act 1993.[30] The fact that the law society might discipline a lawyer who contravenes the cab rank rule by refusing a client based on the lawyer's own ethical beliefs would seem to amount to discrimination based on those beliefs. A challenge to the cab rank rule on these grounds might well succeed.

6.2 Terminating the relationship

6.2.1 *Duty to continue retainer*

A natural extension of the cab rank rule is the rule that a lawyer may not cease to act for a client who has retained him or her unless the lawyer has good cause. In general, when a retainer is accepted, it is presumed that the lawyer will complete the whole task and not just part of it although the presumption may be varied by contract.[31] Like the cab rank

---

29 The New Zealand Bill of Rights applies to "any person or body in the performance of any public function, power, or duty conferred or imposed on that person or body by or pursuant to law" (s 3) which certainly would cover the rule-making activities of the New Zealand Law Society.

30 Under s 21(1)(c) and (d). The Act specifically applies to professional organisations under s 37 of the Act.

31 *Re Romer and Haslam* [1893] 2 QB 285, 298 per Bowen LJ; *Warmingtons v McMurray* [1936] 2 All ER 745.

principle this rule, known as the "whole retainer" principle, ensures that individuals are not deprived of legal advice and assistance because their lawyer does not agree with their course of action, or finds them difficult or distasteful. The need for the rule is particularly apparent in litigation where it could be disastrous for a client to be abandoned by the lawyer immediately prior to a hearing.

6.2.2 *Justifications for terminating the retainer*

Where a lawyer seeks to terminate the lawyer-client relationship there must be good reason for doing so. Moreover, if the termination of the retainer would cause considerable prejudice to the client, termination will not be permitted. The fact that the lawyer has undertaken too much work will not be a justification for terminating the retainer once accepted though it would have been a ground for declining it in the first place. Similarly, the fact that a client is difficult to communicate with, obtuse, and even obnoxious is regarded as a normal incident of professional practice and not grounds for ceasing to act.[32] There may be cases where the client has disappeared, or refuses to reply to the lawyer's inquiries to such an extent that it can be implied that the client has himself or herself terminated the retainer.

The most common basis upon which a lawyer will seek to withdraw services from a client is where the client is unable to pay the lawyer's costs. Under the whole retainer principle, a practitioner is not entitled to render a bill of costs until the work is completed. However, in most instances the parties will have expressly or impliedly contracted out of this presumption. The practice in most law firms is to bill clients either periodically or when the work completed amounts to a sum to warrant billing. This is particularly the case in large matters that take a considerable period of time.[33] Accordingly, if a client fails to pay a bill of costs which is properly rendered, a lawyer will be justified in terminating the retainer.

There will be limited circumstances in which a lawyer is compelled to terminate a retainer. For example, a lawyer "must not act or *continue to act* for any person where there is a conflict of interest".[34] While such

---

32 *McDonald v FAI* [1999] 1 NZLR 583 (affirmed by the Court of Appeal as *Harley v McDonald* [1999] 3 NZLR 545) although, as that case shows, a lawyer may not proceed without clear instructions no matter how hard they are to obtain.

33 Indeed the practice is endorsed by the rules as between barristers and their instructing solicitors in r 11.08. Where the work is general in nature, rather than relating to a specific case or transaction, the Courts have been reluctant to apply the whole retainer principle: *Caldwell v Treloar* (1982) 30 SASR 202, 210.

34 Rule 1.03.

conflicts should usually be detected before a retainer is accepted there may be instances where this is impossible, such as where the identity of a prospective defendant is not known. Where a lawyer discovers that he or she has conducted the client's affairs negligently or in such a manner as to give rise to a possible claim by the client against the lawyer there is a conflict of interest between the lawyer and client; the lawyer should immediately cease acting and advise the client to retain a new lawyer.[35]

Where the retainer involves Court appearances it may sometimes be impossible for the lawyer instructed to appear — perhaps where two hearings are set down for the same time. In practice, if the appearance is in respect of an interlocutory matter the lawyer may arrange for a colleague to appear, although this should be done only with the client's consent. Where the matter is important and efforts to adjourn the matter to another date are impossible it may be necessary to return the brief and give the client the opportunity to choose a new lawyer. In general, where two hearings are irreconcilably in conflict the brief which was received later should be returned, to avoid the advocate deciding which brief to retain on the basis of the more attractive or lucrative case.[36] However, there is an argument that where one matter is civil and the other a serious criminal matter the criminal matter should prevail because of the primary importance of liberty over property.[37]

In other instances, continuing to act for the client would require the lawyer to breach the Rules of Professional Conduct. If, for example, a practitioner is likely to be called to give evidence either in person or by affidavit in litigation in which he or she is acting, the practitioner is under an obligation to withdraw.[38]

It will also be permissible, though not mandatory, for a lawyer to terminate the retainer if the client has been deceptive in dealing with the lawyer, or has failed to adhere to an undertaking upon which the retainer depended. If the client insists that the lawyer act in a manner inconsistent with the law or professional rules the lawyer ought to terminate the relationship. A lawyer should also terminate the retainer if the client is using the lawyer's services to perpetrate some crime or civil wrong. Lawyers can never be compelled to be party to something that is

35 Rule 6.06. That rule permits the lawyer to continue to act if the client, having been independently advised, requests the lawyer to continue to act.

36 See r 16.4 of the South Australian Professional Conduct Rules.

37 This is the approach taken by r 20 of the Australian Bar Association's Advocacy Rules.

38 Rule 8.06.

a wrong in law, and they have an overriding duty to the administration of justice.[39]

There will also be personal situations where a lawyer is entitled to terminate a retainer. If a lawyer is rendered incapable of fulfilling the client's instructions through sickness or mental incapacity he or she will be entitled to terminate the lawyer-client relationship.[40]

More problematic is the situation where a client refuses to accept the advice of the lawyer, for example, where the lawyer severely doubts that the defence that the client wants to raise to a claim is likely to succeed. In the absence of the defence being wholly fatuous (and, therefore, an abuse of process) there seems no defensible ground for the lawyer refusing to act. If this were not the case it would mean that the lawyer was effectively the Judge of the matter and the client was denied the right to put that particular defence before the Court. While it may offend a lawyer's pride for his or her advice to be rejected, it cannot justify terminating a retainer.[41] This contrasts with the position in the US where a lawyer is entitled to terminate a retainer where a client's proposed course of action is repugnant or imprudent.[42]

6.2.3 *Repugnant instructions*

More difficult is the situation where the client gives instructions which, while within the bounds of the law, the lawyer finds repugnant. None of the subtle devices such as pleading overwork or lack of expertise which might be used in declining a retainer can be used to terminate it. Such problems might arise where the client's claim is defensible (and, therefore, the retainer was accepted by the lawyer) but the means by which the client seeks to pursue it are questionable. Similar problems may emerge where the client was not entirely forthright regarding the true nature of the action to the lawyer when the retainer was accepted, as is occasionally the case. In such instances, it may later become apparent

---

39 Rule 8.01. See also Justice Ipp, "Lawyers' Duties to the Court" (1998) 114 LQR 63.

40 Explicit provision for such an eventuality is r 17.3(b) Western Australian Professional Conduct Rules. See also r 1.16(a)(2) ABA Model Rules.

41 See the words of Giles J in *McDonald v FAI* [1999] I NZLR 583 (HC) (affirmed by the Court of Appeal as *Harley v McDonald* [1999] 3 NZLR 545 where it is suggested that it is appropriate for a barrister to assist in a hopeless case if the client insists on such a course being taken. Compare r 1.16(b)(3) ABA Model Rules which allows withdrawal if the client insists on pursuing a course of action that the lawyer considers imprudent. See also *R v Frawley* (1993) 69 A Crim R 208 which suggests a right to withdraw in such circumstances, also *R v McLoughlin* [1985] 1 NZLR 106, 108 per Hardie Boys J for a similar view.

42 Rule 1.16(b)(3) ABA Model Rules.

to the lawyer that the case is one he or she might not have undertaken had they been fully informed of its weaknesses.

While the US approach to declining or terminating a retainer would allow a lawyer to cease acting for the client in such circumstances,[43] there is no such latitude under the New Zealand approach. Although, regrettably, there is no specific guidance in the Rules of Professional Conduct in respect of terminating retainers, it can be drawn from r 1.02 that, if a practitioner may not refuse to accept a retainer on the grounds of repugnance, the practitioner certainly cannot terminate for the same reasons. The commentary to r 11.09 provides that a barrister should not accept a brief transferred from another barrister until it is ascertained that there is a satisfactory reason for the change of barristers.

6.2.4 *Minimising the prejudice to the client*

Where the lawyer has discretion to terminate the retainer he or she is required to take into account the prejudice that will flow from the termination. If the client would be unable to obtain legal assistance prior to a hearing, or other important event (such as a scheduled meeting) where assistance was required, the lawyer should refrain from terminating the relationship. The prejudice may be minimised where the lawyer assists the client by contacting and meeting with another lawyer and handing over and explaining documentation.[44] In any event, reasonable notice of the intention to terminate should be given to enable the client to make alternative arrangements for legal assistance.

Even where the lawyer is compelled to terminate the retainer, as in cases of conflict of interest, the lawyer should use his or her best endeavours to ensure that the client is prejudiced as little as possible. Such a duty is explicitly stated in the ABA Model Rules which provide in r 1.16(d):[45]

> Upon termination of representation, a lawyer shall take steps to the extent reasonably practicable to protect a client's interests, such as giving reasonable notice to the client, allowing time for employment of other counsel, surrendering papers and property to which the client is entitled and

---

43 See r 1.16(b)(3) ABA Model Rules which allows withdrawal where the client insists on pursuing an objective that the lawyer considers repugnant or imprudent.

44 The lawyer is not compelled to hand over documents to the new solicitor over which a lien is held. However, the efficacy of the lien in respect of private individuals has been eroded by the provisions of the Privacy Act 1993, and in particular Principle 6 of s 6, which entitles individual access to information. See *Privacy Act 1993 Guidelines for Practitioners* issued by the New Zealand Law Society.

45 See also the similar provisions of r 17.3 of the Western Australian Professional Conduct Rules.

refunding any advance payment of fee that has not been earned. The lawyer may retain papers relating to the client to the extent permitted by other law.

It is proper for a lawyer who terminates a retainer in New Zealand to follow a similar procedure.[46]

6.2.5 *Court's discretion to give leave to counsel to withdraw*

Where a lawyer is representing a client in an action before the Court there is not an unfettered right to withdraw, even where justification exists. The practitioner must apply to the Court for leave to withdraw and that withdrawal will only be effective when the application is granted.[47] The Court has a discretion whether to grant such leave,[48] although, in most cases, the Court will grant such leave without much inquiry, relying on the practitioner that good reason exists for such an application. However, in an exceptional case where the withdrawal of the lawyer would leave the client in a predicament, the Court might treat the matter more seriously and even insist that the lawyer continue acting. Where the lawyer does seek leave to withdraw the lawyer "should consider carefully what they may disclose to the Court, in conformity with their professional obligations to the client, and then give as much information as possible".[49]

6.3 Unfettered right of client to change practitioners

Although the ability of a practitioner to refuse or terminate a retainer is greatly limited, there is no such limitation on the right of a client to terminate the relationship with the lawyer and retain a new adviser. Rule 6.05 provides: " A client has an unequivocal right to change from one practitioner to another". Moreover, the commentary to the rule states that the practitioner should not seek to exert influence on the client not to change solicitors. The rule is justified not only on principles of freedom of contract[50] but also due to the special nature of the relationship between lawyer and client. If a client loses confidence in the lawyer, the relationship is undermined and is no longer workable.

46 See the commentary to r 6.05, which states that when a client chooses to change practitioners the practitioner should facilitate the transfer. Similar requirements exist when it is the practitioner who has precipitated the change. See also *R v Shaw* [1992] 1 NZLR 652.

47 *Re Salaman* [1923] NZLR 50; *Entrican v Clark* (1910) 12 GLR 699. See also the comments of Barker J in *Foodstuffs (Auckland) Ltd v R W Schweiger* (1986) 1 PRNZ 173, 174. Rule 45A High Court Rules.

48 *R v White* (1995) 77 A Crim R 531.

49 *Colonial Mutual Life Assurance Society v Welsh* (1992) 5 PRNZ 354, 358 (HC). Appealed at (1995) 5 PRNZ 550.

50 Indeed in a sense it is a limitation on the freedom of contract as it would prohibit any contract of retainer which limited the client's right to change practitioners.

Accordingly, the client may dismiss the lawyer without needing to justify his or her actions.

In legal practice, it is inevitable that clients will wish to change solicitors from time to time. The respective practitioners should seek to make the transition as smooth as possible, should transfer documents as soon as possible, and attend to matters such as billing expeditiously. There may even be instances of urgency where it would be inappropriate for a lawyer to stand on strict legal rights as regards a lien or retention of documents for billing purposes.

The right of the client to terminate a retainer will extend to the right to appear as a litigant in person in both civil and criminal matters. No litigant can be forced to retain the services of a legal adviser when he or she does not wish to do so.[51] This will extend to serious criminal cases, notwithstanding the fact that the litigant will almost certainly do himself or herself a disservice by appearing on his or her own behalf.[52]

6.4 Abuse of relationship

6.4.1 *Personal relationships with clients*

The relationship between lawyer and client is usually a close one. Feelings of genuine friendship may emerge from what began as a wholly professional relationship. In the commercial arena it is common to seek to socialise with clients and prospective clients specifically to build such a relationship. In many relationships the client will repose considerable trust in the lawyer, disclose personal matters, and feel a degree of dependence, trust, and associated affection for the legal adviser. It is understandable that lawyers may develop a degree of empathy with their clients. The converse situation should not be discounted. There may be instances where lawyers feel pressured by their clients to enter into a relationship with which they are not comfortable. In some situations there may be considerable pressure on the lawyer not to offend clients in such circumstances. Evidence exists to suggest that women lawyers occasionally receive unwanted sexual advances from male clients.[53]

Close relationships with clients are normal and even useful. However, it cannot be denied that the relationship may become inappropriate and will amount to professional misconduct. The professional independence

51 *R v Woodward* [1944] KB 118.

52 For a full discussion of the problems of litigants in person in criminal cases see the US Supreme Court decision in *Farretta v California* (1975) 95 S Ct 2525, 422 US 806.

53 Heylen Research Centre *Women in the Legal Profession* vol 3, 1987, 211 stated that 8% of women practitioners had received such advances cited in G Gatfield *Without Prejudice* Wellington, Brookers 1996, 233.

of the lawyer is impugned and efficacy of the relationship is in doubt.[54] The New Zealand Law Society gives little guidance as to the kind of relationships that might be inappropriate, or how a lawyer might avoid such pitfalls. Rule 1.01 provides: "The relationships between a practitioner and a client is one of trust and confidence which must never be abused". The commentary to that rule notes: "The relationship of trust and confidence may be breached where a practitioner and a client enter into a sexual relationship". In the 1996 edition of the rules it was noted in the commentary that at that time no complaints of misconduct of such a kind had come to the notice of the society.[55] This reference has since been omitted.[56]

It is important that the issue of lawyers entering into improper relationships is not dismissed as unimportant or rare in practice. While perhaps not widespread, the fact is that such relationships do occur.[57] Incidents of improper conduct of this nature by lawyers may also be under-reported. The possibility that complaints against the lawyers in such cases are not made, is readily explicable. In the majority of cases the client's matters will have been concluded effectively by the lawyer and there will be no motivation for complaint. The client may not realise or care that the relationship is inappropriate. Where matters have not turned out so well there is a strong disincentive for such a complaint. The client has already had one disastrous brush with the legal profession, and is unlikely to relish a second. The prospect of making and sustaining personal allegations against a lawyer to the law society is likely to be especially daunting. This is especially the case where the trust and vulnerability of the client has been abused. Further, it is possible that the client feels ashamed or partly to blame for the relationship.

---

54 While most commentators discuss the problem in the context of lawyers having sexual relationships with their clients, it is important to recognise that an inappropriate relationship could exist in which no sexual element is present.

55 In September 1995 such a complaint was heard by the New Zealand Law Society Disciplinary Tribunal: *Re R* noted in the NZLS *Annual Report* 1995. The practitioner was censured, fined and ordered to pay costs demonstrating that without aggravating factors such conduct will not warrant striking off or suspension. See also *Re E — A Barrister and Solicitor* (noted in NZLS *Annual Report* 1996); *Bar Association of Queensland v Lamb* [1972] ALR 285.

56 There were several such cases prior to the insertion of the rule. See G Gatfield *Without Prejudice* Wellington, Brookers, 1996, 235. It is of note that Right 2 of the Code of Health and Disability Services Consumer' Rights provides: "Every consumer had the right to be free from discrimination, coercion, harassment and sexual, financial or other exploitation".

57 G Gatfield *Without Prejudice* Wellington, Brookers, 1996, 234. See also *Witten-Hannah v Davis* [1995] 2 NZLR 141.

To date the law society had not taken a firm stand in cases concerning such conduct. In *Re R*[58] a barrister was censured for entering into an inappropriate relationship. Similarly, in *Re E*[59] where a practitioner "entered into a personal intimate relationship with [the client] in circumstances where he was in breach of her confidence and trust", he was censured and fined $3000. By way of comparison *Director of Proceedings v Nealie*[60] recounts proceedings before the Medical Council in which a doctor was struck from the roll of medical practioners and fined $10,000, even though the relationship was wholly consensual and appeared to be at least in part initiated by the patient.[61] This seems to demonstrate a considerable disparity in the way in which such matters are dealt with by the respective professional bodies.

The US profession has given considerably more guidance in the matter.[62] Some states have expressly adopted rules which prohibit sexual relationships with clients.[63] The American Bar Association has also issued a Formal Opinion part of which states:[64]

> In the opinion of the Committee, such a relationship may involve unfair exploitation of the lawyer's fiduciary position and presents a significant danger that the lawyer's ability to represent the client adequately may be impaired, and that as a consequence the lawyer may violate both the Model Rules and the Model Code. The roles of lover and lawyer are potentially conflicting ones as the emotional involvement that is fostered by a sexual relationship has the potential to undercut the objective detachment that is often demanded for adequate representation.

---

58 Noted in the NZLS *Annual Report* 1995.

59 Noted in the NZLS *Annual Report* 1996.

60 [1999] 3 NZLR 603.

61 See also *Brake v Medical Council* [1997] 1 NZLR 71 (reported only as regards name suppression) (High Court, Auckland HC 169/95, 8 August 1996, Tompkins, Cartwright & Williams JJ) where a psychiatrist entered into a consensual relationship with a patient, his name was removed from the register of medical practitioners, although the condition of his client and callous conduct on his part were exacerbating factors.

62 US scholarship abounds. For a selection see C Fleishman, "Sexual Relations Between Lawyers and Clients" (1998) 34 Trial, 46, "The Profession Hits the Skids: Lawyer Client Sex. Why Should We Ban It" (1993) 47 Wash St Bar J 17; L Langford, "Criminalising Attorney-Client Relations — Toward Substantive Enforcement" (1995) 73 Texas LR 1223. Numerous US authorities exist on the disciplinary measures taken for inappropriate sexual conduct. See 7 *American Jurisprudence* 2nd ed, 1997, s 69 including cumulative supplement.

63 See, for example, Disciplinary Rule 1.1c2(7) New York State Bar Association Code of Professional Responsibility, and r 3-120 California Rules of Professional Conduct.

64 American Bar Association Formal Opinion 92-364 Sexual Relations with Clients.

There is a temptation to presume that a close personal relationship between lawyer and client are only inappropriate in certain circumstances. In particular, much criticism is directed at lawyers who form relationships with their clients in matrimonial proceedings.[65] However, the pitfalls consequent on entering into a personal relationship with a client may be just as severe in respect of clients in matters other than domestic proceedings. As the American Bar Association observed:[66]

> While it may be argued that such a conflict only arises in the special situations presented, for example, by divorce proceedings, the fact is that these conflicting interests can arise even in seemingly benign settings. For instance, although it is generally thought that the ethical concerns raised by a sexual relationship are not present in the commercial corporate setting, a sexual relationship with a corporate client's representative can be just as problematic as in other contexts.

While some of the problems inherent in relationships between lawyers and their clients (such as the abuse of the relationship) may not be applicable in the corporate setting, other risks may be equally or more apparent in such a setting. The following examines the kinds of problems that may emerge.

6.4.2 *Abuse of relationship*

As r 1.01 provides: "The relationship between practitioner and client is one of confidence and trust which must never be abused". While the entering into of a close relationship may not be an abuse in every instance, there are frequently cases where a client is in a particularly vulnerable position. This vulnerability is particularly acute as regards the lawyer to whom they have had to disclose the most personal details. In such cases, clients rely on their lawyer for guidance and assistance. There is, in short, a considerable imbalance of power.

It is possible for a practitioner to become involved with the client's problems at a personal level, and for this to lead on to an inappropriate relationship. It is also possible that a client might be active in seeking to extend dependency on the lawyer to more than merely professional matters, or to take what was intended as a professional interest in the client's personal matters to be an invitation to take the relationship to a more personal level. In a situation where there is an imbalance of power

65 The prohibition contained in Disciplinary Rule 1.102(7) New York State Bar Association Code of Professional Responsibility is aimed specifically at such cases. See also Dubin, "Sex and the Divorce Lawyer: Is the Client Off Limits?" (1988) 3 Geo J Leg Eth 585; Lyon, "Sexual Exploitation of Divorce Clients: The Lawyer's Prerogative" (1987) 10 Harv Women's LJ 159.

66 American Bar Association Formal Opinion 92-364 Sexual Relations with Clients.

between lawyer and client it will be inappropriate for the lawyer to enter into a close personal relationship with a client. It is difficult to escape the conclusion that, but for the special nature of the relationship between the lawyer and client, the client would not have entered into the relationship. If this is so there does appear to be an element of advantage-taking. There is also the possibility that the lawyer took advantage of the influence over the client to initiate the relationship. Even if in fact this was not the case there is an appearance of impropriety. In such cases the presumption must be that the lawyer acted improperly, and allegations by the client to that effect will be nearly impossible to refute.

A claim that the relationship was entered into with the full consent of the client will not alter the fact that the relationship is inappropriate. The fact that the client was vulnerable to the lawyer means that the lawyer is the person to whom such consent is least likely to be genuine. If the imbalance of power between the lawyer and client is such that the relationship is an abuse of the lawyer's position, then any consent will be vitiated by that very fact. It was noted in *Re R* that even where the relationship was consensual it needed to be placed in the context of the kind of issues with which the practitioner was dealing and the vulnerability of the client.[67]

6.4.3 *Loss of independence*

Even where the lawyer cannot be said to be abusing his or her position in entering into a relationship with the client, it is likely to affect the lawyer's ability to maintain a professional and objective viewpoint. A lawyer who continues to act for someone with whom there is a close personal relationship is likely to be empathetic towards the client's position. Moreover, success for the client (whether in a transaction or litigation) is a kind of personal as well as professional success for the lawyer. It is possible that a lawyer would find it difficult to fulfil the stringent duties to the Court and the profession in such circumstances. It would, for example, be easy to omit bringing authorities to the Court's attention if they weakened the client's case, and the duty to disclose damning evidence may be overlooked.[68] An additional danger is that the personal relationship might sour while the lawyer is acting for the client, resulting in a real conflict between the lawyer's personal feelings and professional obligations.[69]

---

67 Decision of the NZLS Disciplinary Tribunal 199, noted in the NZLS *Annual Report* 1995.

68 See Justice Ipp, "Lawyers Duties to the Court" (1998) 114 LQR 63 for a survey of a lawyer's duties to the Court.

69 See *Witten-Hannah v Davis* [1995] 2 NZLR 141.

6.4.4 *Conflicts of interest*

Where the lawyer and client are engaged in a personal relationship there may be a conflict of interest between the interests of the client and those of the lawyer. It is conceivable that if the lawyer were to act in the best interests of the client this would be prejudicial to the lawyer's own interests and possibly to the continuance of the relationship. This might take the form of prolonging litigation to ensure continued dependence on the services of the lawyer. However, far less obvious conflicts might arise. For example, the lawyer might not be eager for their lover-client to gain custody of children in matrimonial proceedings, or be reconciled with the former partner. The conflict between the interests of lawyer and client may not be glaringly obvious even to the lawyer. It is possible that the lawyer will alter the advice given to the client and action taken on behalf of the client unintentionally.

6.4.5 *Confidences at risk*

Where a lawyer and a client enter into a personal relationship there is likely to be a confusion of boundaries between the personal and professional aspects of the relationship. The law and the professional rules protect confidences in the lawyer-client relationship. However, where the information is imparted in the context of a personal relationship, the information will not be confidential notwithstanding the fact that the person to whom it was imparted also happens to be the confider's lawyer.[70] This distinction may lead to confusion and an unfounded expectation on the part of the client that all personal information imparted to the lawyer, whether in the context of the personal or professional relationship, is confidential.

6.4.6 *Are any lawyer-client relationships permissible?*

There may be instances where a relationship between lawyer and client will give rise to none of the problems mentioned above. In some situations the client will not be in a vulnerable position (perhaps an employee of a large corporation) and the issue will be one concerning non-contentious work (say a lease negotiation). In many such situations where relationships between lawyer and client do exist no difficulties emerge. Indeed, it may be hard for the lawyer or client to envisage how the entering into of a relationship in such circumstances could cause problems. However, such problems are not inconceivable. The possibility of the lawyer being pressured by the client to enter into an unwanted relationship should not be ignored. Alternatively, negotiations in transactional work may break down, litigation may ensue, and the lawyer may be called as a witness to elements of the negotiation process,

70 Rule 1.08 provides: "A practitioner has a duty to hold in strict confidence all information concerning the business and affairs of the client acquired *in the course of the professional relationship*, and should not divulge such information...". (Emphasis added.)

and the impartiality and objectivity of the lawyer is thrown into question. While some professions, notably doctors, impose a blanket ban on such relationships, the legal profession in New Zealand has not done so. Such a relationship is plagued by professional as well as the inevitable personal pitfalls and is to be advised against.

Chapter 7

Loyalty

7.1 Introduction

The concept of loyalty is superficially simple. Once a client retains a lawyer the lawyer's loyalty must be undivided. Lawyers are committed to acting in the interests of the client to the exclusion of their own interests, or the interests of any third party. The duty is not merely negative in proscribing conflicts of interests. It also positively requires lawyers to act in the interests of the client. This covers not only the duty to do the work, for which they were retained, but a number of other duties such as to keep the client fully informed, and to disclose all material information.[1] The need for loyalty is obvious in light of the classical model of the role of the lawyer. Lawyers are employed by clients because of the clients' lack of expertise. Clients want the lawyers to do a specific job which the clients are inadequately skilled to do themselves. This is particularly the case in transaction work such as administering wills, conveyancing, and complex business arrangements. Similarly, in adversarial situations clients avail themselves of the special skills of the advocate because they do not have the skills themselves. Because of this gap in skill and knowledge the clients need to be assured that the motivation behind the actions of the lawyer is the promotion of the clients' interest rather than any collateral or conflicting purpose.

7.2 Rationale

There are a number of ways in which the duty of loyalty might be justified. Each way leads to different conclusions about the extent to which the duty to the client ought to override duties to others. Some clients see their lawyer as an agent of themselves and wish the lawyer to complete the work as they would, if they had the needed skill. On a pure "agency" view of the relationship, the role of the lawyer is to act solely in the interests of the client and that loyalty should be undivided. The lawyer is really no more than a hired gun.[2] Where judgments are to be made the role of the lawyer is to fully inform the client of the

---

1 See the discussion in ch 10.

2 See para 2.3 for a more detailed discussion of the hired gun view of a lawyer.

circumstances and repercussions of the problem, so that the client can make the decision informed of all the relevant circumstances.

An agency view sees the lawyer as little more than an extension of the client and devoid of any significant decision-making role. It emphasises the role of the lawyer as a functionary to ensure that the client's autonomy is preserved and that lack of skill or knowledge does not thwart the implementation of the client's intentions. On a strict application of such an analysis the loyalty of the lawyer to the client will be absolute. As a mere tool the lawyer ought to exercise no personal or professional judgment. It is clear, however that a lawyer is not merely an extension of the client. Lawyers have a moral view of their own and in many cases it may not agree with that of their clients. In complex legal matters lawyers inevitably exercise a degree of judgment in matters of considerable importance. In so doing they are drawing on their own system of values which may well differ from that of the client. A lawyer is not obliged to assist in a breach of law, however more difficult are those cases where the actions proposed by the client, though in the client's interest, are ethically questionable. There will on occasion be a conflict between the values of the lawyer and the interests of the client that is not easy to resolve. In practice, an agency view is not applied in an unmitigated fashion. There will always be conflicting duties and demands which will mean that there are some things a lawyer will not do.

An alternative justification for the duty of loyalty looks to the system in which the law and citizens' rights are administered. On this analysis, lawyers fulfil a particular role which is defined by the structure in which they operate and the applicable rules. On this view, lawyers moderate their actions by reference to the legal and professional obligations imposed, in particular, by reference to the duty of loyalty imposed by virtue of the fiduciary nature of the relationship, and the rules dealing with conflicts of interest in the Rules of Professional Conduct. A justification of loyalty based on the way in which the role of the lawyer is defined only by law fails to justify the assumptions upon which the system of law is based.[3]

Like the hired gun approach the role-differentiated approach sees the lawyer as essentially morally neutral. Rather than applying moral judgment lawyers simply apply the law in determining the extent of the duty of loyalty to the client. This approach is justified because it is inappropriate to apply personal judgment when the outcome would vary between lawyers. Publicly made and acknowledged rules ought to be applied to ensure consistency and to ensure that the agreement between

---

3 See para 2.4 for a discussion of the nature of and problems with role-differentiated ethics.

members of society as to the distribution of rights and duties (including those concerning the duty of loyalty) is not subverted. However, such an approach fails to take into account the fact that the lawyer is a moral actor and not a mere automaton who will blindly follow rules. Moreover, the rules will sometimes be inadequate to resolve the conflict or issue facing the lawyer, and more than a mere rule-based and role-based approach will be required.

Loyalty may also be justified as integral to the efficacy of the relationship between lawyer and client without going so far as to require unfettered zeal on behalf of the client or slavish rule adherence. Perhaps the best way to view the duty of loyalty is as part of a reciprocal relationship in which the lawyer accepts the duty of loyalty impòsed and the client recognises that there are limits of both a personal and legal nature that may restrict the extent of that duty. On such a view, lawyers remain bound by the legal and professional rules requiring loyalty and setting its limits but may also, in cases of doubt or vagueness, exercise their own judgment as to the proper course of action.[4]

The duty of loyalty might also be justified by reference to the paternalistic view of the role of the lawyer. On such an analysis the lawyer is not bound to follow the instructions of the client in every regard. Rather the lawyer has an active part to play in determining what ends are most appropriate and what are the best means for achieving those ends. The duty of loyalty is then seen as a commitment to the best interests of the client, though those interests are as determined by the view of the lawyer. The rules and law are seen as reflecting as well as determining the duties of loyalty and, therefore, are consistent with them. A paternalistic approach, however, does not see the duty of loyalty as necessarily a duty to obey the client's instructions or achieve the client's objectives. Rather, it is a duty to consider the client's circumstances and to pursue what is, in the lawyer's judgment, in that client's best interests. Such an approach views the client's choices as not paramount but merely one factor in the decision of the best course of action. Such a view suffers from the fact that there is no cogent reason why a lawyer should be trusted with such control over a client's affairs.[5]

7.3 Practical problems

In practice, the application of the principle of loyalty is not simple. There are a number of reasons why total and undivided loyalty is not always rendered by a lawyer to his or her client. At a practical level, many clients do not require the degree of absolute loyalty which is needed for truly adversarial situations. In some transactions, particularly simple ones

---

4 See para 2.6 discussing the role of the lawyer as a counsellor.

5 See further para 2.7 discussing paternalism and its problems.

where the interests of the two parties are more or less in accord, it is far more efficient for one lawyer to do the job for both clients rather than for each party to retain separate advisers. The cost of absolute loyalty is, in some cases, not justified in light of the small value of the transaction or the minimal risk of any adverse consequences to either party. In some situations it is positively beneficial for one lawyer to act for both parties and to facilitate the transaction or even the resolution of a dispute in a cooperative environment.[6]

The structure of the profession also means that problems of loyalty are likely to arise — for instance, in the market for specialised commercial services to large corporations.[7] A few large and specialised firms have emerged which dominate the market for this type of work. Additionally, the movement of clients between these few firms, in search of the best lawyers and most competitive pricing, has meant that instances of firms acting for two parties whose interests conflict are relatively frequent. Another situation in which the duty of loyalty strictly applied can cause practical difficulties, is where there are few lawyers readily available in the immediate vicinity. This can occur in isolated rural areas. Some small towns have only one or two firms of solicitors or even one office that is staffed intermittently, and members of the community may regard a particular person as "their" lawyer. When a dispute arises or parties are negotiating in the community, they will seek to retain the same lawyer and possibly be offended if the lawyer refuses to act for them against the other party. It may be onerous to send one or both parties to lawyers in other towns.

Under the duty of loyalty lawyers are required to put to one side entirely their own interests in pursuing their client's ends. However, this must be viewed in a realistic light. That the client will usually be paying for the lawyer's services on an hourly basis is a potential source of conflict, but must be accepted.[8] It must also be recognised that lawyers' actions will be modified by their natural tendency to protect themselves against claims. Lawyers are aware of the possibility of a claim being made against them by their clients in the event that the clients perceive that some loss has been incurred through their lawyers' act or omission.

---

6 In R Tur, "Family Lawyering and Legal Ethics" in S Parker and S Sampford (eds) *Legal Ethics and Legal Practice* Oxford, Clarendon Press, 1995, 145 the author argues that matrimonial disputes should be able to be resolved with both parties using one lawyer to avoid spiralling costs and acrimonious proceedings.

7 E Nosworthy, "Ethics and Large Law Firms" in S Parker and S Sampford (eds) *Legal Ethics and Legal Practice* Oxford, Clarendon Press, 1995, 57.

8 Though it is regulated by the rules which require that a fair and reasonable fee only be charged (r 3.01) and the availability of costs revision to the client under Part VIII of the Law Practitioners Act 1982. See more particularly ch 12.

Lawyers will seek to minimise (or in current parlance "manage") the risk of such a claim being made, and in this sense are aware of their own interest when acting for their clients.

In practice the duty of loyalty is not absolute. There are competing interests in many situations that must coexist with the interests of the client. Some have suggested that lawyers (and particularly advocates) owe duties not only to the client but also to the Court, the opponent, the state and themselves.[9] The duty to the Court (also sometimes stated as a duty to the administration of justice) is well established. Certainly, a lawyer may not intentionally mislead a Court in furthering the interest of the client. Similarly, a lawyer is required to act honourably toward the other party and the other party's lawyer, as well as zealously for the client.

The existence of a number of demands on the loyalty of the lawyer creates complex questions regarding the kinds of demands that can be made and the priority of those demands in cases of conflict. The result is the development of a large and frequently confusing body of case law and professional rules that seek to provide principled guidance to practitioners while making allowances for the pragmatic demands of practice. As the cases demonstrate it has proved impossible to anticipate the developments in practice and provide guidance for every situation which might arise. The Courts have been thrown back on a few, not particularly clear, principles with the result that in borderline cases the view of the Courts is impossible to predict.

7.4 Conflicts of interest between clients

A central aspect of the duty of loyalty is the obligation of a lawyer not to act for two clients whose interests conflict. In such circumstances it will be impossible for the lawyer to discharge the duty of loyalty, as to promote the interests of one client would be to damage the interests of the other.[10] Such difficulties are obvious in matters such as litigation where the idea of an advocate representing a plaintiff and defendant in the same action is patently absurd. There are other situations in which it is by no means clear whether a conflict of interest exists or not. It is impossible to draw a clear line between situations where a conflict exists and those where it does not, as the discussion that follows will show. In general, the law has taken a prophylactic approach and prohibits not only actual conflicts of interest, but also potential conflicts. Where the

9 *Meek v Fleming* [1961] 2 QB 366, 379 per McMillan J.

10 See generally F Reynolds, "Solicitors and Conflict of Duties" 107 LQR (1991) 536.

parties' interests currently coincide but at a later date may diverge, a lawyer should be cautious in acting for both of them simultaneously.

The position of the law society is set out in various parts of the rules,[11] in particular, r 1.04 provides:[12]

> A practitioner shall not act for more than one party in the same transaction or matter without the prior informed consent of both or all parties.

The rule duplicates more or less the substance of Richardson J's statement in *Farrington v Rowe McBride and Partners*:[13]

> A solicitor's loyalty to his client must be undivided. He cannot properly discharge his duties to one whose interests are in opposition to those of another client. If there is a conflict in his responsibilities to one or both he must ensure that he fully discloses the material facts to both clients and obtains their informed consent to his so acting.

Situations in which lawyers act for more than one party to a transaction are commonplace both in small firms, in matters such as conveyancing and family law, and in large firms, in corporate and business matters. Indeed, in domestic conveyancing it is standard practice for the lawyer for a purchaser to act also as the lawyer for the lending institution from whom finance is being obtained to effect the purchase. Where the transaction is unusual in some way, this can raise real problems of conflicting duties.[14] Rule 1.04 expressly permits lawyers to act for more than one party to a transaction where there is informed consent, thereby signalling that a conflict of interest is at least to some degree tolerable. Members within one firm of lawyers are considered to be bound by the identical obligations of loyalty and confidence. It will not be possible to avoid a conflict of interest simply by using different members of the same firm to act for the different clients.[15]

The English position seems considerably more strict. Rule 15 of the *Guide to the Professional Conduct of Solicitors* provides:

> A solicitor or a firm of solicitors should not accept instructions to act for two or more clients where there is a conflict or a significant risk of a conflict between the interests of those clients.

---

11 Rules 1.03. 1.04, 1.05, and 8.07.

12 Somewhat contradictorily r 8.07 provides: "In litigation matters, as in the course of other aspects of practice, a practitioner must avoid a conflict of interest", which seems to suggest that conflicts should be wholly avoided.

13 [1985] 1 NZLR 83, 90.

14 *Haira v Burbery Mortgage Finance and Savings Ltd* [1995] 3 NZLR 396.

15 Rule 1.07 (2).

Further, under the English rules, if a conflict arises between two clients the lawyer should cease acting for both clients.[16] However, the prohibition is not as broad as it may first appear. The ban on acting for two clients in the same matter only applies where there is an actual conflict, or a significant risk of a conflict. In many cases concerning non-contentious work, no such conflict will exist. There are also guidelines given in respect of the circumstances in which a practitioner may act for both parties to a conveyancing transaction.[17] The circumstances in which an English practitioner may work in the face of a conflict of interest appear more limited than those of the New Zealand counterpart.

7.4.1 *Non-contentious matters*

While no clear line can be drawn between situations in which a conflict exists and situations in which they do not, a division is made between contentious and non-contentious matters. In the latter it may be possible to act for both parties to a transaction, whereas in the former it is impossible. In many transactions there is a concurrence rather than conflict of interest between the parties: the commentary to r 1.04 notes: "a conflict of interest does not exist between parties simply because a practitioner is acting for more than one of them". In a straightforward advance of funds with security the parties have substantially similar objectives. Similarly, where spouses arrange their taxation and estate matters they will usually have common interests, and there is no actual conflict of interest. The lawyer is able to comply with the requirements of the duty of loyalty in respect of both clients. This will include the ability to disclose all matters relevant to the affairs of the client to that client, as well as the ability to keep confidential all information imparted by a client to the lawyer in the course of the relationship.

More problematic are cases in which the interests of the parties do not coincide. Where the question is a matter in which the parties are negotiating, such as a lease agreement, or a sale of a business, it would be difficult for a lawyer to act for both parties. The reason is that in such cases the terms of the agreement are not finally settled and the lawyer's task is to negotiate the final terms of the contract on the client's behalf. In such circumstances, an advantage acquired by one client will often result in a detriment to the other client. The work is more than merely transactional and there is a divergence of interests. A further possibility is a situation where the lawyer has been requested to complete the formalities to a transaction that is clearly not in the interests of one party. An example might be where a gift is being given, or a guarantee or surety undertaken between family members. In such cases there is a real conflict between the interests of the donor/guarantor and that of the donee/debtor.

---

16 Rule 15.03 of the English *Guide*. Compare r 1.07 of the New Zealand rules.

17 Rule 25.01 of the English *Guide*.

In any situation where two or more parties are represented by one legal adviser the risk of problems arising increases. The risk of a breach of duty or fraud on the client is greater than it would be if all parties had separate representation.[18] However, in many cases this is a risk that both clients and lawyers are prepared to run in return for the advantages, mainly financial, gained by using one lawyer to handle both sides of a transaction.

7.4.2 Clark Boyce v Mouat

The difficulties inherent in a lawyer acting for two parties to a transaction are well illustrated by *Clark Boyce v Mouat*[19] which was ultimately heard by three Courts and the decision of the Court below overturned on two occasions. In that case Mrs Mouat and her son had attended on the offices of the law firm Clark Boyce and instructed Boyce to complete the formalities of a mortgage and guarantee transaction. Under the transaction Mrs Mouat mortgaged her house to a financial institution and her son received a $110,000 loan from the institution. The son guaranteed the loan and was primarily responsible for the repayments. The transaction was patently not in the interests of Mrs Mouat and was beneficial only to the son. The dilemma for Boyce in acting for both parties is clear. If he were acting for Mrs Mouat alone he would advise her of the imprudence of the transaction. However, to do so would be palpably against the interests of the son and in breach of the lawyer's obligations to him. Boyce was clearly aware of this problem and sought to refer Mrs Mouat to another solicitor for independent advice.[20] Mrs Mouat firmly rejected repeated suggestions that she retain another solicitor and acknowledged this in writing, along with the fact that she consented to the lawyer acting for both parties.

It transpired that the son, who was the recipient of the funds advanced under the mortgage, was unable to repay the advance, the mortgage fell into arrears and Mrs Mouat was required to pay the amounts owed. She sued Clark Boyce in tort for negligence, in contract for a breach of the contractual duty of care, and in equity for a breach of the duties under the fiduciary relationship between lawyer and client. The claim was unsuccessful in the High Court, however the Court of Appeal reversed the High Court in finding for Mrs Mouat. The matter then went to the Privy Council where the High Court judgment in favour of the lawyer was restored. The reasons for that final decision demonstrate that the

18 See *United Overseas Finance Ltd v Victor Sakayamary* [1997] 3 SLR 211.

19 [1993] 3 NZLR 641 (PC).

20 As a practical point it is commonplace in such situations for one lawyer to undertake the transactional part of the work and to send one party to a second solicitor for advice on the implications and wisdom of the transaction.

duty on a lawyer to avoid a conflict of interest is by no means absolute. The Privy Council took the view that the duty to avoid a conflict of interest is for the benefit of the client, accordingly, the client is entitled to waive the benefit of such a rule if desired. The duty of loyalty and corresponding obligation to avoid a conflict of interest is not only a duty of the lawyer, but also a right of the client and as such the client can surrender that right. It is not incumbent on the lawyer to insist that the client be represented by an independent lawyer where the client has refused that right.

(a) Consent

In *Clark Boyce* Mrs Mouat had given her consent to the lawyer acting for both herself and her son. This was evidenced by a letter of instruction that was prepared by the lawyers and signed by Mrs Mouat. Moreover, Mrs Mouat was advised on three further occasions that independent advice was recommended. In the Court of Appeal the Court had found that this consent was not adequate to relieve the lawyers of their duty of loyalty.[21] The basis for the decision was that the conflict was so great that it was impossible to act adequately for both clients. This view had been suggested by Richardson J in an earlier case when he stated:[22]

> There will be some circumstances in which it is impossible notwithstanding such disclosure, for any solicitor to act fairly and adequately for both parties.

While the Privy Council accepted that there will be cases where it is not possible to act for both clients, they seemed to limit those cases to situations where the retainer could not be carried out without disclosing information to one party which was detrimental to the interests of the other.[23] In the present case it was found that the steps taken in advising of the need for independent advice, and fully explaining the implications of the transaction were sufficient. In the words of Lord Jauncey: "One might well ask what more he could reasonably have done".[24] The Privy Council concluded that the consent of Mrs Mouat to the existence of the conflict relieved the lawyers of their duty of undivided loyalty.

Any consent to a lawyer continuing to act in the face of a conflict of interest must be given freely and the client must be made fully aware of the consequences of such consent. It must be more than a mere giving of an opportunity to seek independent advice. It will be necessary to

---

21 *Mouat v Clark Boyce* (1991) 1 NZ ConvC 190,917 (CA).

22 *Farrington v Rowe McBride and Partners* [1985] 1 NZLR 83, 90.

23 *Mouat v Clark Boyce* [1993] 3 NZLR 641, 647 per Lord Jauncey of Tullichettle (PC).

24 *Mouat v Clark Boyce* [1993] 3 NZLR 641, 648 per Lord Jauncey of Tullichettle (PC).

positively advise the parties to seek independent advice.[25] The person giving the consent must be of full capacity and capable of understanding the problems of a conflict of interest. In particular, it is important that the client understand that this may mean that the lawyer will not be able to fully disclose all information relevant to the matter in hand to the client, or unable to advise effectively on matters which affect the interests of the other client. It was held in the Privy Council that Mrs Mouat met this test and was fully informed and had firmly declined the offer of independent advice.

(b) Kind of retainer

Also of relevance in *Clark Boyce* was the nature of the work that the lawyer was asked to do. Part of the claim of Mrs Mouat was based on the alleged failure of the lawyer to make certain disclosures. The facts not disclosed included that earlier solicitors had refused to act, that there was no information on the ability of the son to service the mortgage, and the failure to advise that the transaction was not in her interest. The Privy Council upheld the original finding in the High Court that the lawyer was required only to carry out the necessary conveyancing, and explain the legal implications of the transaction. This did not extend to the more general advice that Mrs Mouat claimed ought to have been given. This may be an appropriate stance where the client is sophisticated, the transaction is routine, and the instructions clear as may be the case in many conveyancing matters.[26] However, where there is some unusual or unique aspect to the transaction, the parties are unfamiliar with the nature of the transaction, or the instructions are not entirely clear, the lawyer ought to ensure that the clients' intentions are fully understood and their interests being protected.

(c) Critique

The decision in *Clark Boyce* raises some difficult problems. The position taken by the Privy Council sends strong signals about the limits of the responsibility that lawyers have for the actions of their clients. That case indicates that it will only be in the rarest of cases that a lawyer is bound to refuse to act notwithstanding the acceptance of the client of the existence of a conflict.

If the concept of loyalty is seen as a right of the client as much as a duty of the lawyer then there seem to be few situations in which a client may not relinquish the right and accept a conflict of interest. It is at least arguable that on the reasoning of the Privy Council that two clients in aggressive negotiations over the sale of property could accept the limitations of both using the same lawyer. Possibly more problematic is the situation where the parties are less sophisticated as appeared to be

25 *Taylor v Schofield Peterson* [1999] 3 NZLR 434.
26 See *National Home Loans Corp plc v Gitten Couch* [1997] 3 All ER 808.

the case in *Clark Boyce*. In some cases, clients are clearly not astute business people and are being taken advantage of. This author suggests that it is inadequate for a lawyer simply to do the paperwork as a mere technician and absolve himself or herself of any responsibility in protecting the client from the oppressive conduct of others.

When a lawyer accepts a retainer he or she is required to complete the work competently. While there may be circumstances such as urgency which mean that the job may not be as thoroughly completed as otherwise would be the case, the job must be adequate. In some cases the retainer cannot be fulfilled competently in the face of a conflict of interest. It may require frank advice or disclosure that would injure the interests of the other party. If the constraints of working in a position of conflict mean that only half of the job, or an inadequate job, can be done the retainer should be declined or terminated. Where a fiduciary is acting for two different parties to a transaction he or she may only continue to act as long as it is not necessary to put the interests of one client above the other.

As soon as a potential conflict of interest becomes an actual conflict the lawyer-client relationship should be brought to an end. In *Armitage v Paynter Construction Ltd*[27] a lawyer was acting for two companies to a joint venture agreement. It became clear that one party was in financial difficulty, however, the lawyer continued to pay joint venture funds to that party. It was held:

> Mr Walker, as the solicitor for the joint venture parties, was placed in a position of actual conflict. The interest of the joint venture parties diverged and he could not properly discharge his duty to one without breaching his duty to the other. It is for this reason Mr Walker, in the Judge's view has to cease paying out the proceeds or acting for the joint venture.

There is a responsibility on a lawyer to protect and promote the interests of the client that is owed as a professional. The duty is not only a right of a client but an independent professional duty owed by the lawyer. A client is always free to terminate the retainer, or decline legal advice. However if a client's instructions require a lawyer to breach the duties owed to another client the retainer should be terminated. It is not appropriate for the lawyer to gain the client's consent to the existence of an actual conflict of interest.

The role that the consent of Mrs Mouat played in *Clark Boyce* was pivotal. In the absence of such consent the actions of the lawyer would have been in breach of the legal and professional duties imposed. It is

---

27 Court of Appeal, CA 183/97, 18 December 1998, Thomas J. See also *Bristol and West Building Society v Mothew* [1996] 4 All ER 698, 713 per Millett J.

important to understand why the consent of the client is perceived as changing matters. Consent, to be effective, must always be informed. This suggests that the client will understand the problems which working in a conflict of interest situation brings, and the possible shortcomings of the advice and assistance that the lawyer will be able to render. This is perceived as redressing an imbalance of power by ensuring that the client is informed of the consequences of the decision to accept the conflict.

Consent, however, rarely plays such a role. In some cases it is impossible for clients to fully understand the position because they are simply insufficiently sophisticated. No matter how much information is given to the clients, and how well it is explained, the depth of the problem will not be understood. In other cases, the circumstances will be such that it is impossible to inform the clients of the dangers of a conflict of interest, as they will only be known once the work in question has been undertaken. In *Clark Boyce* it became apparent that the son who was responsible for the mortgage payments did not have, and never had had, any means of meeting the obligations. Had the lawyer not been in a conflict of interest situation it is at least possible that inquiry would have revealed this. Because a conflict of interest existed, it was inappropriate for the lawyer to initiate such an investigation that might have injured the interests of one client.

Consent really focuses on the conduct of the lawyer and does no more than show that the lawyer has used his or her best efforts in an attempt to ensure that the client is aware of the problems in a conflict of interest situation.[28] By ensuring that the client is aware as far as possible of the consequences of consenting to the existence of a conflict of interest, the lawyer is showing that he or she has acted properly and has done everything possible to ensure that the relationship is a proper one. This reasoning is borne out by the words of Lord Jauncey when he absolved the lawyer in saying:[29]

> Mr Boyce did all that was required of him in before accepting her instructions when he advised her to obtain, and offered to arrange, independent legal advice .... Indeed not only did Mr Boyce in carrying out these instructions repeat on two further occasions his advice that Mrs Mouat should obtain independent legal advice but he told her in no uncertain terms that she would lose her house if [her son] defaulted. One might well ask what more he could reasonably have done.

28 See the discussion of consent in D Webb, "A Proposed Decision Making Process for Oppressive Credit Contracts" (1997) NZ Law Rev 394, 416.

29 *Mouat v Clark Boyce* [1993] 3 NZLR 641, 648, 649 per Lord Jauncey of Tullichettle (PC).

While such an approach, that demonstrates that there was no advantage-taking by one party, is appropriate to contractual situations, it is not necessarily appropriate to the fiduciary relationship that exists between lawyer and client. Such an approach in the lawyer-client relationship dilutes the obligations of the lawyer to such an extent as to make them almost meaningless. Moreover, it fails to protect clients who are unable to anticipate the problems which, had they retained their own adviser, would have become clear to them.

The Privy Council in *Mouat* relied on the fact that the retainer in that case was a limited one. The lawyer was instructed only to attend to the technical details of the transaction and no more. Such an approach must be treated with caution. It will only be appropriate where the transaction is of a kind that is straightforward, and the parties to it clearly understand its implications. Consider the approach of the Court of Appeal in *Haira v Burbery Mortgage Finance and Savings Ltd.*[30] There the lawyer had assisted in the arrangement of a dubious scheme involving the investment of money in foreign exchange transactions at the suggestion of the brother of the client. It was claimed that the scheme would double the initial sum invested. To finance the scheme the client's home was mortgaged. The lawyer acted for both mortgagee and mortgagor. It was held that not only had inadequate consent been obtained to the existence of the conflict but also that, because of the highly unusual nature of the transaction, the lawyer was under a duty to advise the lender that the repayment of the funds was to come from such a scheme. It was also held that the lawyer should have advised the client to obtain independent advice on the soundness of the scheme. The *Haira* case concerned an unusual transaction. Unlike *Mouat* the client did not come to the solicitor for technical assistance only, but for help with the entire transaction. Accordingly more was expected of the lawyer than simply completing the paperwork.

In *Dornbusch v Dobson*[31] a lawyer acted for both parties to a loan transaction. It was held that once the lawyer had raised the issue of security it was necessary to investigate whether the security offered was adequate. It was held that lawyers are not to restrict their endeavours only to the letter of the instructions given by the client but ought to use their own initiative to follow up issues where appropriate. There will be instances where the lawyer is obliged to inform one of the clients of the facts giving rise to unusual risks in a transaction.[32] If the duty of loyalty to the other client precludes this the lawyer should cease to act and ensure that both clients receive independent advice. In cases where the

30 [1995] 3 NZLR 396, 406.

31 High Court, Napier AP 65/98, 18 May 1999, Heron J.

32 *Black v Shakespeare* (Court of Appeal, CA 37/99, 22 March 1999, Blanchard J).

client's instructions are unclear the lawyer should presume that the wider duty to advise on all aspects of the transaction exists, or obtain clarifying instructions.[33]

7.4.3 *Action when conflict becomes apparent*

There will be instances where a lawyer will agree to undertake work for two parties whose interests appear to converge. However events or the receipt of further information may lead to the conclusion that there exists a conflict or potential conflict of interest which renders it inappropriate to continue to act. In such cases the lawyer is required to take immediate steps. Rule 1.07 provides:

> 1. In the event of a conflict or likely conflict of interest among clients, a practitioner shall forthwith take the following steps:
>   (i) Advise all clients involved of the areas of conflict or potential conflict;
>   (ii) Advise the clients involved that they should take independent advice, and arrange such advice if required;
>   (iii) Decline to act further for any party in the matter where so acting would or would be likely to disadvantage any of the clients involved.

Where it is impossible to represent a client adequately due to the conflict it will be necessary to terminate the retainer with both clients and to assist with finding a replacement adviser. Where no party would be disadvantaged by the lawyer continuing to act, no termination will be necessary under r 1.07(1)(iii).

Where a lawyer has obtained the client's consent to continue to act in a conflict of interest situation, the ability of the lawyer to act is limited. In consenting to the conflict, the client is consenting to the lawyer not fully disclosing all information available in relation to the matter in hand, and in particular not disclosing any information confidential to the other side. While the duties of skill and care are the same, the duty of loyalty is necessarily diluted.[34] The danger in such a situation is that the lawyer will fail to take action or give advice to one client because it would damage the interests of, or upset the relationship with, the other client. This can be particularly problematic even in relatively straightforward matters such as conveyancing. In such cases there may be a temptation to overlook minor defects in title, or other deficiencies to ensure that the settlement is completed. This is especially so if more than one transaction hangs on the outcome, as where the proceeds of the sale are to be used for a subsequent purchase, as is frequently the case.[35]

---

33 *Ismail bin Ibrahim v Lim Lim & Oon* [1998] 1 AMR 339.

34 *Mouat v Clark Boyce* [1993] 3 NZLR 641, 646 per Lord Jauncey of Tullichettle (PC).

35 See *Stewart v Layton* (1992) 111 ALR 687.

7.4.4 *Prohibited conflicts — contentious matters*

There will be cases where the nature of the conflict of interest between two clients will be so great that it will not be possible to serve the interests of both clients adequately.[36] The most obvious kind of situation where this would arise is in litigation. Clearly, it is impossible to be a zealous advocate for two sides in the same action. It is for this reason that r 8.07 provides: "In litigation matters, as in the course of other aspects of practice, a practitioner must avoid a conflict of interest". The commentary to the rule explicitly states in paragraph one that parties with different interests should be represented by different practitioners.

Even where the parties to litigation have identical interests r 1.03 will apply so that for one lawyer to act for both clients their informed consent must be obtained. In advising the clients, the lawyer must be alert to the possibility that the interests of the two clients will diverge and it will become impossible to continue to act. This is particularly problematic in the case of co-defendants in criminal matters. There are significant advantages in co-accused being represented by the same lawyer. Their defence will be consistent, and it will be more difficult for the police to obtain admissions from one accused to use against the other. However, while it is possible that they will have identical interests (and are mounting an identical defence) it is also possible that one of the accused will seek to absolve himself or herself by laying blame on the other — the cut-throat defence.[37] In such cases, counsel should withdraw and both defendants should be represented by new and separate counsel. The onus is on the lawyer to ensure as far as possible prior to trial that the defences of the respective co-accused do not give rise to such a conflict of interest. The duty is a continuing one. If at any point prior to trial it becomes apparent that there is a conflict of interest between the two accused then new counsel should be obtained. If the conflict emerges after trial has commenced it may be necessary to break off the trial and conduct a retrial with new and separate counsel.[38]

Irreconcilable conflicts of interests between clients will exist outside litigation proper. Many commentators use the phrase "contentious" to describe the kind of work where it will not be possible, even with consent, to act for two clients. Clearly, where the reason for seeking legal assistance is the existence of a dispute, one lawyer cannot act as an adviser, negotiator, or advocate for both parties. This will be the case whatever method is adopted to resolve the difference, whether it be negotiation, mediation, arbitration or litigation. However, where a lawyer

---

36 That is where "acting would or would be likely to disadvantage any of the clients involved" in terms of r 1.07(1)(iii).

37 Rule 8.07, para 3. See also *Saminadhen v Khan* [1992] 1 All ER 963 (CA).

38 *Mills v R* [1995] 3 All ER 865 (PC).

has been retained to act in the capacity as an independent referee of some kind there will be no conflict of interest. Many lawyers are retained as arbitrators or mediators in disputes. In such a case they are the lawyers of neither party and consequently no conflict of interest arises.

There will be work that is contentious even though it cannot be said that the problem is one requiring a dispute resolution mechanism like arbitration or litigation. For example, in transactional matters such as company takeovers,[39] or competitive bidding for government or private tenders it is difficult to see how one lawyer could act for both parties. Similarly, where a lawyer is asked to assist with lobbying the government or making submissions to select committees, it is clear that the lawyer would face grave difficulties if representing opposing views for different clients in such circumstances.

There are inherent difficulties facing a lawyer who must decide whether a matter is contentious and, therefore, involves a prohibited conflict, in particular, where it is not feasible to discuss the matter with both clients. This problem is well illustrated by *Russell McVeagh McKenzie Bartleet & Co v Tower Corporation*.[40] In that case Tower Corporation had instructed Russell McVeagh in respect of a tax dispute concerning some $40m which was finally concluded in April 1997. However, some eleven months prior to the tax matter being settled, an agent of Guinness Peat Group approached Russell McVeagh seeking legal assistance in respect of a proposal to aggressively take over Tower Corporation. When the instructions were received the tax partner advised that there was no conflict of interest and, therefore, no reason why Russell McVeagh should not accept the instructions to assist in the takeover. This was notwithstanding the fact that it was almost certain at the time that the takeover was likely to be strongly opposed by Tower Corporation.

Russell McVeagh did not disclose to Tower the fact that they were considering taking instructions in respect of such a takeover.[41] Accordingly, the decision to proceed to act for Guiness Peat Group (initially through its agent) was made by Russell McVeagh, and ultimately by the partner who would be conducting the takeover work. The first indication that Tower Corporation had that Russell McVeagh was acting for Guinness Peat Group in respect of the takeover was at a meeting in September 1997 when Guinness Peat Group put the takeover proposal to Tower. Tower was surprised to find members of their own firm of lawyers, Russell McVeagh, representing Guinness Peat Group. Tower

39 As in *Russell McVeagh McKenzie Bartleet & Co v Tower Corporation* [1998] 3 NZLR 641.

40 [1998] 3 NZLR 641.

41 In respect of the duties of disclosure generally, and a discussion of this aspect of the case see ch 10.

objected by letter on 7 November to the existence of the conflict and shortly thereafter filed proceedings to disbar Russell McVeagh from representing Guinness Peat Group further. On Tower objecting to the Guinness Peat retainer, Russell McVeagh put in place restrictions to limit the likelihood of the flow of confidential information between the solicitors concerned — the so-called "Chinese wall".[42]

A major problem in the above case is that the decision whether or not to act against Tower was made by Russell McVeagh. While it is arguable that the matter should have been disclosed to Tower, action was not taken because the partner involved decided that there was no conflict of interest. If that had been the case then there was no reason to tell Tower because in the absence of a conflict of interest the decision to act could not be said to be a matter material to Tower. It was argued by Russell McVeagh that the Tower retainer was narrow and concerned only taxation matters and, therefore, was entirely separate from the Guinness Peat retainer which concerned the takeover which was clearly contrary to the interests of Tower. There are, however, powerful objections to a firm acting both for and against a client simultaneously regardless of how separate the matters might be. The duty of loyalty is not owed only by the lawyer who is acting but by all members of the firm and for the firm, to act for and against a client cuts irreconcilably across this duty and, without the express consent of the client, is inexcusable.

There is also a ready inference that information will move between members of a firm.[43] Even where the matters are apparently disconnected it is difficult to discount the possibility that it would be damaging for the confidential information of one party to fall into the hands of the other. This might easily happen accidentally where a solicitor is unaware of the source of the information that is being utilised for a client's benefit. This is clearly a risk that a client should not have to take involuntarily.[44]

7.4.5 *Different solicitors within a firm: Chinese walls*

It is often attempted to circumvent problems of conflict by using different lawyers within the firm to act for the different sides. In very large firms it is possible that the lawyers concerned will not know each other particularly well. Where the firm has offices in different cities they may not even have met. Even where it is permitted to act for two parties to a single transaction the practice of having different lawyers in one

42 See 7.5.3 below for discussion of the efficacy of Chinese walls in such situations.

43 *Russell McVeagh McKenzie Bartleet & Co v Tower Corporation* [1998] 3 NZLR 641, 652 per Henry J.

44 *Prince Jefri Bolkiah v KPMG (a firm)* [1999] 2 WLR 215, 226.

firm acting is frequently adopted to ensure that there is as great a degree of independence and loyalty as possible. Even in simple conveyancing transactions it is common for different solicitors to act for purchaser and vendor.

Because of the likelihood that within a firm confidences of clients are shared, a conflict of interest cannot be avoided simply by using different solicitors within the same firm. The House of Lords has stated: "The starting point must be that unless special measures are taken, information moves within a firm",[45] and the Australian Federal Court has observed:[46]

> A firm is in no better position than a sole practitioner if it purports to act for separate clients whose interests are in contention. If it purports to continue to act for both clients by imposing a qualification on the duties of partnership it thereby denies the respective clients the services the clients have sought from the firm, namely the delivery of such professional skill and advice as the partnership is able to provide. In such a circumstance the appearance provided to the public is that the interests of the solicitors as partners are in conflict with, and may be preferred to, the interests of one or both clients.

Lawyers will seek to overcome this problem by constructing physical and procedural barriers between the lawyers who are acting for the opposing interests. In erecting such barriers the lawyers seek to displace the presumption that confidential information will pass between them. However, the rules take a dim view of the efficacy of such Chinese walls. Rule 1.07(1) requires a practitioner to decline to act further for any party once it is apparent that a conflict of interest has arisen or will arise and if to continue to act would be disadvantageous to any client. The rule also requires the lawyer to advise the client of the nature of the conflict and the need to obtain independent advice. It proceeds in r 1.07(2) to state:

> Once a situation [where it is clear that to continue to act would be disadvantageous to any client] arises, it is not acceptable for practitioners in the same firm to continue to act for more than one client in a transaction, even though a notional barrier known as a Chinese wall may be or may have been constructed. Such a device does not overcome a conflict situation.

Notwithstanding this apparently unequivocal bar on the use of Chinese walls, they are commonplace in many, particularly larger, firms. Their use is, presumably, justified on the basis that the continued conflict of interest does not disadvantage any of the clients concerned. It is argued by proponents of Chinese walls that quite the reverse is the case and their use is directly beneficial to clients in such cases. This is premised

45 *Prince Jefri Bolkiah v KPMG* [1999] 2 WLR 215, 227.

46 *Blackwell v Barroile Pty Ltd* (1994) 123 ALR 81, (1994) 51 FCR 347 para 52 per Davies and Lee JJ.

on the claims that clients obtain their lawyers of first choice and are not put to the bother or expense of instructing a new lawyer from scratch. Such an argument gains strength when the clients are business people who are used to protecting their own interests.

There is, however, a danger of lawyers viewing such conflicts with a jaundiced eye. It is understandably difficult for a lawyer to accept that he or she (and his or her colleagues) are not to be trusted to zealously protect the interests of the respective clients, and that he or she may not be entirely even-handed when promoting the interests of respective clients. Lawyers might also be accused of overestimating their irreplaceability. In some cases there are many lawyers in other firms who could take over the work with little difficulty and the prejudice of a client not being able to retain the lawyer of first choice is small. The other significant factor which may cloud a lawyer's judgment in such matters is the fact that if the conflict is recognised it will mean that two retainers will have to be terminated which will result in the loss of the fees that would otherwise have been generated. This can be compounded where the clients are frequent users of legal services, as the rule requires the lawyer to assist in finding alternative legal advice. Areas of business can exist where one is required to send a valuable client to a competitor and run the risk that they will never return. It is therefore understandable that lawyers frequently adopt an interpretation of the conflict rules which is favourable to them, rather than being cautious in avoiding such possible conflicts and referring work to other lawyers.

The use of Chinese walls has been cautiously accepted by the House of Lords in *Prince Jefri Bolkiah v KPMG*[47] although as a method by which the risk of disclosure of confidential information might be removed. While it is assumed that information will move between members of a firm, if sufficient steps are taken, it may be that the Court will accept that the relevant information has been isolated. The House of Lords considered that such a Chinese wall must be robust indeed. It will not be sufficient that all reasonable measures have been taken to ensure that no disclosure will occur.[48] Rather, such measures must be effective. It was suggested that an effective Chinese wall will be an established part of the firm and not a device of convenience erected ad hoc to circumvent individual problems.

The New Zealand Court of Appeal cautiously approved the use of Chinese walls, at least to protect confidential information, though on less

---

47 [1999] 2 WLR 215. That was, however, a case concerning the successive retainer of forensic accountants, although the principles applicable were stated to be identical to those concerning solicitors.

48 The Canadian test set out in *MacDonald Estate v Martin* (1990) 77 DLR (4th) 249.

stringent terms than the House of Lords. In *Russell McVeagh McKenzie Bartleet & Co v Tower Corporation*[49] Henry J stated that the Court will consider the likelihood of confidential information being disclosed, and if there is no real risk of disclosure, there will be no bar to the firm acting for the new client. His Honour put the matter thus:[50]

> Although the concepts of Chinese walls and cones of silence leave much to be desired, and cannot be allowed to obscure the realities of life and the ordinary behaviour and incidents of relationships where individuals practise together in a firm, internal control measures may nevertheless in some circumstances be both appropriate and sufficient to ensure protection.

This is supported in the concurring judgment of Blanchard J who took the view that a Chinese wall will be evidence to assist the Court finding that a breach of confidence has not occurred and that there is no likelihood that it will occur.[51] Thomas J, in his dissent, also accepted the possibility of the use of Chinese walls, although only in "exceptional circumstances where there is an overriding and compelling need".[52] The Court was, however, reluctant to give any real guidance as to the features of a Chinese wall, or the associated measure of a cone of silence,[53] which would lead the Court to accept it as effective. All of the members of the Court were cautious and it appears that they do not wish to provide a checklist or formula that would possibly be viewed as minimum acceptable standards by which the profession will operate.[54]

There are real difficulties in accepting that Chinese walls are effective, especially where there is a current conflict between existing clients. There will always be a possibility that the firm will prefer the interests of one client over another, particularly where one client is longstanding or likely to provide considerable work to the firm. There is also a danger that the lawyer will not act as zealously against a client represented by a lawyer in the same firm as for a client represented by a lawyer who is a stranger. For example, a member of staff might be reluctant to take advantage (on behalf of his or her client) of failures of a partner.[55] There may also be a tendency to conduct the matter less formally (perhaps by a

---

49 [1998] 3 NZLR 641.

50 [1998] 3 NZLR 641, 654-655.

51 [1998] 3 NZLR 641, 678.

52 [1998] 3 NZLR 641, 670.

53 That is a system of protocols designed to isolate one (usually new) member of a firm who possesses confidential information.

54 See further D Webb, "Clients' Secrets and Secret Clients: Conflicts Confidentiality and Disclosure in the Court of Appeal" [1999] 5 NZBLQ 91 from where much of this discussions was drawn.

55 See evidence of this in the research in D Lamb, "Ethical Dilemmas: What Australian Lawyers Say About Them" in S Parker and S Sampford (eds) *Legal Ethics and Legal Practice* Oxford, Clarendon Press, 1995, 217, 223.

discussion at the coffee machine) than would be the case where the lawyers were in different firms. It will also be impossible for the client to determine whether the Chinese wall is working effectively. Such an arrangement requires the client to trust the lawyer to respect what are often notional rather than real boundaries.[56]

7.4.6 *Government lawyers*

Problems face lawyers who work in the state sector. Numerous lawyers advise and assist the government in carrying out its daily work, and in protecting the interests of the government in Court. In most cases the identity of the client will be clear as an identified minister or department of government. However, situations may arise where one lawyer is required to act simultaneously for more than one government body, or a government body and a non-government body. Such a situation may raise considerable difficulties. The introduction to the rules observes that many lawyers will be employed in the state sector and elsewhere and observes:

> No matter which branch of legal work the salaried practitioner engages in, and whether or not private practice is combined with the salaried occupation, the contents of this publication apply to every practitioner.

Such a situation arose in *Pasini v Vanstone*[57] which concerned an application by Mexico to extradite an accused for trial. The government lawyers were acting for both the Attorney-General's Department and the government of Mexico in pursuing the application. It was observed:

> There well may be good reason for not translating in an unmodified form to the public sector the common law's objection to a person serving "two masters" in the same or related matters — an objection affecting lawyers in the private sector with increasing stringency .... Nonetheless the public still is entitled to appropriate reassurance that the integrity of the advisory function in the public sector does not appear to be compromised through an adviser in a given instance being in a position of conflicting responsibilities.

While the words of Finn J to seem to suggest that there will be cases where the duty of loyalty might be diluted when acting for the government, His Honour is clear that the duty of loyalty is still important. An important consideration is the appearance of propriety in the conduct of the public sector. There is an argument that a public body, and its legal advisers, should be held to higher standards. Because

---

56 See further para 9.5.3.

57 [1999] FCA 1271, para 50 per Finn J (Fed Ct of Aust). See also *Hughes Aircraft Systems International Ltd v Airservices Australia* (1997) 146 ALR 1 where the Australian Government Solicitor was accused of acting in the face of a conflict of interest in respect of the negotiation of the tender for air traffic control systems.

government deals on behalf of the citizens it is at least arguable that there should be a special reluctance to allow the government to agree to its advisers diluting their loyalty in favour of the interest of another party.

7.5 Finance transactions between clients

Lawyers are in a singularly good position to facilitate the lending of money. In many cases their clients will approach them for advice on the investment of funds, while other clients will seek advice on where to obtain finance. In addition to this, lawyers have the legal expertise to effect a transaction between the two parties which is mutually beneficial and efficient. Transactions where a lawyer acts as an intermediary in facilitating one client lending to another, or a client lending to a third party are relatively commonplace. Lawyers have developed a method to effect this which uses the vehicle of a "nominee company". By this device the client lender advances the funds to the company which then in turn lends it to the client borrower. In many cases the funds of several clients are advanced to one borrower. The company acts as a bare trustee for the lenders.[58] Such a system has considerable advantages. It enables lawyers to consolidate funds from several clients in one advance; it makes management of the funds easier; and it means that contracts and actions can be taken in the name of one entity. There are also regulatory benefits, as the scheme has been given dispensation by the Securities Commission from certain regulatory requirements.[59]

This system of lending through a lawyer is closely regulated by the Solicitors' Nominee Company Rules which ensure that strict procedures are followed when dealing with client money. The firm (whose partners will be directors of the company) may not charge for the services of the company, however, they will charge their normal fees in respect of the legal work involved in effecting such transactions. Such a structure can be particularly beneficial to firms who can attract lucrative retainers by the possibility of the availability of such funds for clients.

Firms who employ the nominee company system are not exempted from the stringent professional rules. In particular, a lawyer must be wary of advising clients to invest in or borrow from the nominee system when it may be more advantageous for them to use or acquire their money elsewhere. Rule 1.06 provides:

> Where a practitioner advises a client on either an appropriate investment of the client's moneys or the borrowing of moneys by a client, the practitioner must act as an independent adviser and where appropriate advise the client

58 Rule 5.2(a) Solicitors' Nominee Company Rules 1996.

59 Securities Act (Contributory Mortgage) Regulations 1988.

on a representative range of investments or sources of loan moneys as the case may be.

The commentary to the rule expressly extends it to transactions made under the auspices of a nominee company. Some law firms have significant sums of money which clients wish to invest, and the work generated from the nominee company can be considerable. However, lawyers must be wary of over-emphasising the lending role. Rule 4.06 provides that lawyers must not give the impression that they are running a financing or banking business, and it must always be clear that the funds are those of clients, and the nominee company is merely acting as a trustee.[60]

It is also possible that a client may wish to lend money and another client wish to borrow that money outside the nominee company framework. Such transactions are more risky for the lawyer, and it is harder to ensure that the fiduciary obligations of the lawyer (or lawyers in the firm) are discharged. The reason for this is that under the Solicitors' Nominee Company Rules there are clearly prescribed guidelines as to the manner in which funds may be lent. These include the kind of security that is appropriate; the proportion of the value of the security that may be lent, and steps to be taken on default. Where the transaction is directly between two clients of one firm no such constraints exist and there is a danger that the final terms negotiated may later be found to be too onerous by one party. If this is the case the disgruntled client may seek redress from the lawyer for any loss suffered. If the lawyer chooses to act for both parties, it will be important to obtain the informed consent to continuing to act in accordance with the principles enunciated by the Privy Council in *Clark Boyce v Mouat*.[61] Where the transaction is unusual or there is a clear and irremediable conflict between the parties, even such consent might not suffice to absolve the lawyer from the responsibilities imposed by the duty of loyalty.[62]

7.6 Acting for insurer and insured

One situation in which legal advisers must be particularly careful is when they are acting for both an insurance company and the insured party in respect of a claim. There are a number of instances where an insurer is

60 It should also be noted that the lawyer has a duty to advise clients that money invested in a nominee company does not receive the protection of the Solicitors' Fidelity Guarantee Fund: r 5.03 and s 196A Law Practitioners Act 1982.

61 *Mouat v Clark Boyce* [1993] 3 NZLR 641, 647 (PC) as applied in *Taylor v Schofield Peterson* [1999] 3 NZLR 434.

62 *Haira v Burbery Mortgage Finance and Savings Ltd* [1995] 3 NZLR 396.

entitled to bring and conduct litigation in the name of the insured. First, where the insurer has paid out under a policy by loss caused to the insured by a third party, the insurer is entitled to pursue the third party for the amount of the loss. Secondly, where the insured causes loss to some third party and seeks to be indemnified under a policy of insurance, the insurer is invariably entitled under the policy to elect to defend the claim and manage the conduct of that defence. While in the majority of cases the interests of the two parties will coincide and there will be no objection to joint representation by one lawyer, there will be isolated cases where the interests of insurer and insured will diverge.[63]

Such a situation arose in *Nicholson v Icepak Coolstores Ltd*.[64] In that case Icepak was storing a quantity of nashi pears in its coolstores. The pears were inadvertently frozen and consequently ruined. Icepak informed its insurer of the incident and the possible liability to the various owners of the fruit, claiming an indemnity for any such liability under the policy. In accordance with the terms of the policy, the insurer appointed a lawyer to defend the claims. In the conduct of the case the lawyer was given information by agents of Icepak that gave grounds for the insurer to decline cover (in particular, that false statements had been made and that admissions to the plaintiffs had been made). This gave rise to an immediate conflict of interest between the insurer and the insured.

In such cases the lawyer is acting for both parties. Although the lawyer will invariably be appointed and paid for by the insurer, both the insurer and insured are considered clients.[65] The insured party will be named as a party to the litigation and is clearly being represented by the lawyer. Although the insurer will manage the proceedings, the lawyer is under an obligation to act in the interests of both parties. The lawyer may not take a step that is to the detriment of one client.[66]

In *Icepak* the lawyer was in a conflict situation due to conflicting duties of confidence and disclosure to the two clients. As lawyer for the insured there was an obligation to keep confidential the information disclosed, especially in light of the fact that disclosure would be severely

63 See further C Chapman and J Mallon, "Conflicts of Interest Faced by Solicitors Instructed by Insurers to Conduct Litigation on Behalf of Insureds" (1996) 26 VUWLR 679.

64 [1999] 3 NZLR 475. See also *State Government Insurance Commission (SA) v Paneros* (1988) 5 ANZ Insurance Cases 60-857, (1989) 5 ANZ Insurance Cases 60-940.

65 *Groom v Crocker* [1938] 2 All ER 394 (CA).

66 Although it is permissible to forward an argument which would establish a defence, even under the facts of the argument the insured would not be covered by the policy: *Kabadanis v Panagiotou* (1980) ANZ Insurance Cases 60-409.

detrimental.[67] Conversely there was a duty to disclose the information to the insurer as it was of direct relevance to the insurer's liability to pay out under the policy.[68] In the event, the lawyer did disclose the information to the insurer. The insurer was now trying to produce the statements made to the lawyer in proceedings in which Icepak was claiming under the policy.[69] Icepak claimed that the statements were privileged, that the lawyer had breached the duty of confidence, and had acted in a conflict of interest and therefore the statements were inadmissible as evidence.

It was decided that the statements were privileged and could not be produced in evidence; it was found that the statements had been made in confidence to the lawyer who was required to keep them secret. Even though the insured was obliged under the contract to disclose all relevant facts to the insurer this did not relieve the lawyer of the obligation of confidence. Once it became apparent to the lawyer that a conflict of interest had arisen (as it should have been as soon as the disclosure occurred) the lawyer ought to have informed both parties that a conflict had arisen and declined to have acted further for either party.[70]

Such problems may arise in any situation where a lawyer is acting for parties jointly in litigation.[71] The lawyer must always tread carefully when representing two or more parties where their interests are not identical. While the parties' interest may accord at the outset the lawyer must be sensitive to situations where the interests diverge. If this does occur the lawyer must immediately cease to act for both parties.

7.7 Lawyer-client conflicts

As with any fiduciary, lawyers may not act in a situation where their own interests conflict with that of their client. In such a case the loyalty they owe to their client is seriously at risk, and there is a real danger that the lawyers will take steps in their own interest that will be prejudicial to the

67 Rule 1.08.

68 Rule 1.09.

69 The insurer was named as a third party. The claim was one by the owners of the fruit against Icepak, Icepak was defending the claim, but arguing that if they were liable the insurer was bound to indemnify them. The insurer was therefore joined as a third party. The case itself is a judgment on an interlocutory matter concerning whether the statements made to the lawyer were privileged.

70 Rule 1.07.

71 For example a lawyer might act for both debtor and guarantor in a claim by a creditor, several mortgagees against a mortgagor, or for company and directors in claims by creditors or shareholders.

client, and therefore not disclosed to them.[72] It is for this reason that any such conflicts are prohibited. The rules provide:[73]

> A practitioner must not act or continue to act for any person where there is a conflict of interest between the practitioner on the one hand, and an existing or prospective client on the other hand.

As with many commercial situations, there is an inherent divergence of interests between lawyer and client in any situation. The fact that the lawyer is receiving a fee for the professional services rendered is one source of potential conflict. It is not uncommon for a client to feel that a lawyer has taken longer than necessary to complete work, or that a matter has been unnecessarily strung out. Such claims are occasionally well founded. Moreover, lawyers are well aware of the possibility of claims being made against them in the event that something goes wrong. They conduct their practices carefully, maintaining close records of their actions and their clients' instructions, not only out of good practice, but also to ensure that there is a trail to follow in the event that they are accused of wrongdoing. These conflicts or potential conflicts are normal incidents of legal practice. As such they are accepted incidents of the lawyer-client relationship.

Within these unavoidable constraints the relationship between lawyer and client requires that lawyers will act exclusively in the interest of the client without regard for their own interests, except where required by law. Lawyers are expected to avoid not only an actual conflict with their own interests, but also the appearance of any conflict. There is no allowance in the rules for a practitioner to continue to act for a client where a conflict of interest between lawyer and client exists.

The rules lack an express statement to the effect that in a lawyer-client conflict of interest situation a lawyer is prohibited from acting even with the consent of the client. Some commentators suggest it may be presumed that lawyers are permitted to act in the face of a conflict with their own interests providing informed consent is obtained.[74] However, such an interpretation seems inconsistent with r 1.04, which deals with client-client conflicts. That rule specifically states that where consent exists lawyers may continue to act in the face of client-client conflicts. This would suggest that if it were intended that the lawyer could act in the face of a conflict, the rules would provide accordingly. However, no dispensation to act where consent is obtained is given in r 1.03 that prohibits lawyer-client conflicts. The difficulty is that this interpretation

---

72 *Nocton v Lord Ashburton* [1914] AC 392.

73 Rule 1.03.

74 G Dal Pont in *Lawyers' Professional Responsibility in Australia and New Zealand* North Ryde, LBC Information Services, 1996, 128.

conflicts with the well-established practice in the profession of acting in the face of a lawyer-client conflict provided that fully informed consent is obtained. It may be that the drafters of the rules lapsed in this regard and the long-standing practice of acting with the consent of the client where a lawyer-client conflict exists demonstrates that such conduct is not unethical.

The legal, as opposed to professional, position in respect of such conflicts is clear. The legal obligations of the lawyer as a fiduciary permit such conduct in some cases. In *Official Assignee of Collier v Creighton*[75] Crighton accepted instructions to act on a purchase of a house which he had himself put an offer on, and had indicated to the seller a continuing interest in. In observing that this resulted in a conflict of interest between lawyer and client the Court of Appeal observed that the lawyer was free to act in the conflict situation only with the fully informed consent of the client.

Where the lawyer seeks to continue to act, the obligation to disclose fully the interest held is an onerous one. It is necessary to explain fully the extent of the interest and the implications of it. This means more than merely recommending independent advice, or encouraging clients to make their own inquiries. In *Day v Mead*[76] it was found that Mead, the lawyer, was in breach of his fiduciary obligations to his client when he advised Day to invest in the company. While Day knew of the interest of his lawyer in the business, he was ignorant of certain difficulties the business was suffering and Mead failed to advise him of the problems. The best solution in such a situation is to procure independent advice from another lawyer for the client in respect of the transaction. However, that alone may not be sufficient. It will be necessary to ensure that the advising lawyer is in possession of all the relevant facts, and not merely the paperwork, with which to advise the client.[77] The onus on the lawyer to show that the transaction was at arms' length and the client was fully informed is a high one.

Where the lawyer is found to be in breach of fiduciary obligations, and the client has suffered loss, it will be presumed that the loss was caused by the fiduciary's breach. It will not be necessary to show that the breach was causative of the loss suffered. It will be sufficient to show that the breach was a material element in the series of facts that led to the loss.[78]

---

75 [1993] 2 NZLR 534.

76 [1987] 2 NZLR 443.

77 *Re Beard* (1917) GLR 228.

78 *Everist v McEvedy* [1996] 3 NZLR 348; *Brickenden v London Loan and Savings Co* [1934] 3 DLR 465. To avoid liability the defendant must show that the loss would have been suffered even if the breach had not occurred.

7.7.1 *Claims against the lawyer*

There are, inevitably, instances where lawyers make mistakes. In some cases this will give rise to a possible claim by the client against the lawyer for damage suffered. Frequently, lawyers will be aware of the existence of such a possible claim well before the client. This may be because they have a better grasp of their duties, and the legal implications of their breach, or because they are the first to discover the existence of their lapse and the effects of it. When such a possible claim arises there is an immediate conflict of interest between lawyer and client. A common impulse by lawyers in such a situation is to seek to put things right, often without troubling the client with the details. Or in a case where the consequences of the breach are unclear, to let the matter proceed until it is certain that the client will suffer some detriment through the lawyer's breach. However, such a course of action is depriving the client of the choice of proceeding against the lawyer, and throws into question the ability of the lawyer to act independently in the client's sole interest.

The only appropriate course of action in such a case is to advise the client that a conflict has arisen and that it is in the client's interest to retain new advisers. Rule 6.06 provides:

> Where a practitioner becomes aware of a potential claim for negligence, the practitioner must advise the client to seek independent advice in connection with the matter, and must inform the client that the practitioner can no longer act in the matter unless the client, having been independently advised, requests it.

While the lawyers are not required to assist the client in making a claim by detailing the minutiae of the wrongs committed, they must ensure that the client is able to retain new lawyers who can competently advise as to the nature of the claim.

Such a situation arose in *Kooky Garments v Charlton*[79] where a tenant was suing the landlord claiming that a letter written by the landlord's lawyers amounted to an acceptance of an offer. The lawyers who had written the letter in question represented the landlord throughout the Court hearing. The case noted that it was arguable that the letter was written negligently and a claim existed by the landlord against her lawyers. In criticising the law firm (and ordering it to pay all of the costs) Thomas J stated:

> Where the acts or omissions of the law firm, including situations where the actions of the client are based on advice given by the solicitors are at the heart of the question in issue, the firm is, in a real sense, "defending" its actions or advice. There is, in such circumstances, a danger that the client will not be represented with the objectivity and independence which the

79 (1993) 7 PRNZ 253.

> client is entitled to and which the Court demands. There is no sound reason to presume or accept the solicitors must first have the opportunity to clarify whether their client is liable as a result of their actions or of acting on their advice before confronting the conflict.

The lawyer who had written the letter in question did not appear for the landlord. Another member of the firm conducted the proceedings on her behalf. It was held that the conflict precluded any members of the firm from continuing to act. The reason for this is that in such cases the loyalty of all members of the firm will be to the firm at the possible expense of the duty of loyalty to the client. This is particularly so in the case of partners who will be personally liable if the breach leads to an award of compensation in favour of the client.

Perhaps more problematic is the situation where a lawyer or firm has given advice on a particular course of action to a client and the client is being sued for action taken in reliance on that advice. While the lawyer has not been negligent, the correctness of the advice is being tested by the litigation. In England, lawyers have been prohibited from acting where "they have been responsible for deciding on a course of action and that course of action is in dispute in the proceeding".[80] That provision has been interpreted not to extend to mere advice that a course of action is legal, as opposed to the lawyer actually taking the action in question.[81]

7.7.2 *Lawyer as a witness*

A lawyer should never act as both a witness and counsel in the same matter. Such a situation might give rise to numerous problems. A lawyer whose loyalty is to the client may have a temptation not to be entirely frank where the client's interests are at risk. Additionally, where the lawyer's actions are called into question there is a direct conflict between the interests of lawyer and client. It is also likely that in such cases the objectivity of the lawyer would be affected by the need to balance the interests of the client knowing the nature of the evidence to be given in Court.[82] The prohibition on a lawyer acting as a witness is contained in r 8.06 which provides simply: "A practitioner must not act as both counsel and witness in the same matter".[83] The prohibition extends not only to oral, but also to written evidence.[84] While the rules do not expressly prohibit a lawyer acting as a solicitor only in litigation in which

80 Rule 4.1(e) Law Society's Code for Advocacy 1993.

81 *Christie v Wilson* [1999] 1 All ER 545 (CA).

82 See the American Bar Association Model Rule 3.7 and commentary for the rationale underlying the prohibition; also V Shirvington, "A Current Favourite Problem: The Solicitor Witness" (1998) 36 (1) LSJ 32.

83 *Barrott v Barrott* [1964] NZLR 988; *R v Jukich* (District Court, Auckland T 46/94, 30 March 1994, Judge Moore).

84 See also *R v Lui* [1989] 1 NZLR 497.

they are a witness (and, therefore, never appear before the Court as counsel) the principles seem equally applicable to such practitioners. The Courts have consistently found that:[85]

> For the reason that it is desirable to avoid any suggestion of real or apparent conflict between the duty to the Court and the obligation to the client, I consider that it is generally unwise for a solicitor, who is not himself appearing as advocate or as instructing solicitor in Court but who is aware that it is likely that he will be called as a material witness (other than in relation to formal or non-contentious issues), to continue, either personally or through his firm, to represent the client if this can be reasonably avoided.

The prohibition is expressly stated to apply where the lawyer acts as both solicitor and counsel in the matter.[86]

Difficulties can also arise where a member of the same firm as the counsel is called as a witness.[87] This might occur when a transaction that the firm was instrumental in effecting is the subject of litigation. The lawyer who assisted in the transaction may be called to explain the events leading up to the transaction, put the contractual terms into context, and confirm the existence of any unwritten understandings that may have been reached. While the rules do not expressly prohibit a member of the firm acting as counsel in such a matter, it is fraught with danger. The rules do not provide clear guidance on this matter. Rather providing in the commentary to r 8.06 that:

> Where a practitioner, having already accepted instructions as counsel, becomes aware that a partner or employee of the practitioner might be called as a witness for the client, the practitioner must exercise care and professional judgment in deciding whether or not to continue as counsel in the matter.

Even if the actions of the firm are not in question (as they were in the *Kooky Garments* discussed above) there is still going to be a desire on the part of both lawyers to paint the actions of their firm in the best light. More difficult would be a situation where the counsel thought that the lawyer-witness was lying. It would be an invidious situation for the counsel who has a duty to reveal such deception to the Court. It is suggested that, in any cases where the evidence to be tendered by the

---

85 *Chapman v Rogers: ex parte Chapman* [1984] 1 Qd R 542, 545 per Campbell CJ. The English *Guide to the Professional Conduct of Solicitors* similarly provides that solicitors are only precluded from acting as advocates (that is, counsel) where they are called as a witness in a matter.

86 Rule 8.06(6) provides: "The constraints expressed above apply to the same extent where a practitioner acts as both solicitor and counsel".

87 *Barrott v Barrott* [1964] NZLR 988.

lawyer is more than formal, it is inadvisable for a lawyer from the same firm to act as counsel.

7.7.3 *Secret profits and referral fees*

Lawyers are frequently in a position to refer business to other professionals. Lawyers will often be involved in selling houses for clients (or deceased estates), obtaining finance, and retaining accountants or other forensic experts. Often cordial relations are built up between different professional businesses and a very beneficial relationship is established.[88] It is important to ensure that the relationships with such other professionals do not adversely affect the duty of loyalty to the client. In particular, when advising on the retention of the services of another professional there should be no hidden financial reward for the lawyer.[89]

In some industries it is common to pay to a referring business a referral fee. Such a fee encourages subsequent referrals. However, such an inducement is considered inappropriate in the legal profession as it may induce the lawyer to use the services of certain professionals over other, more competent, candidates. It is for this reason that such fees are prohibited by the terms of r 4.04 which provides:

> A practitioner must not directly or indirectly offer to, or receive from, a third party, a reward or inducement, whether financial or otherwise, in respect of services rendered or to be rendered to the client.

Lawyers are prohibited from receiving any remuneration or benefit other than that expressly authorised by the client.[90] This will extend to a prohibition on referring clients to a business in which the lawyer has a financial interest.[91]

The prohibition extends to any kind of profit or benefit flowing from the lawyer-client relationship other than the agreed fees.[92] A lawyer will not be permitted to purchase a house after a client's attempt at such a purchase has failed,[93] or to implement a decision to purchase shares

---

88 It is noted in the commentary to r 4.04 which notes that such associations are not to be discouraged and the usual trivial gifts of calendars, pens etc are acceptable.

89 V Shirvington, "Making a sideline profit out of a client?" (1996) 34 (7) LSJ 24.

90 In the event that the lawyer receives an undisclosed benefit corruptly (that is, with a wrongful intent: *R v Smith* [1960] 2 QB 423, 428) the lawyer will be criminally liable under the Secret Commissions Act 1910.

91 *Law Society of ACT v Lardner* (1996) 72 FLR, [1998] SCACT 24.

92 Rule 3.02 provides: "A practitioner must not receive a reward, whether financial or otherwise, of which a client is unaware, in respect of services rendered to the client".

93 *Official Assignee of Collier v Creighton* [1993] 2 NZLR 534.

based on information gained as a fiduciary.[94] The lawyer is prohibited from taking advantage of any situation where, but for the lawyer client relationship, the opportunity would not exist or the lawyer would not be aware of it. The reason for such a prohibition is largely prophylactic. While in many instances the seizing of such opportunities would be of no detriment to the client, there is a danger of blurring the line between professional and private lives. It also serves to ensure that the legal profession is seen to apply the highest professional standards to its members.

The terms of r 4.04 also prohibit lawyers giving or receiving referral fees in referring work to another lawyer.[95] Where for one reason or another a client requires legal assistance which the lawyer they are using is unable to give, the lawyer is required to assist them in obtaining competent advice. Such assistance must be rendered wholly to the benefit of the client untrammelled by any possible benefit from the lawyer to whom the clients are referred.

The only situation when a sum of money may be paid for the referral of clients is where a legal practice is sold.[96] The sum of money paid for goodwill (which will be a significant part of the purchase price) is effectively a payment for the likelihood that the existing clients of the selling practitioner will now become the clients of the buying practitioner. This sits awkwardly with the precept that practitioners have no proprietary interest in clients.[97] While there is no obligation on the clients of the practice to bring their work to the new practitioner, there is a high likelihood that they will do so, and this is what the payment of goodwill was for. It may be that the payment is defensible on the basis that as no payment was made for any particular client, no particular client could be said to have been taken advantage of. In fact, the tacit allowance of goodwill payments is motivated by business reality. The practice that a lawyer has built up over years of loyal service to clients is a valuable asset. To deprive a retiring lawyer of the ability to capitalise that asset by giving another practitioner the opportunity to take over the practice would serve little purpose.

7.7.4 *Business transactions with clients*

There are numerous reasons why lawyers and clients might want to enter into business transactions with each other. Lawyers may supplement

---

94 *Boardman v Phipps* [1967] 2 AC 46.

95 Compare r 7.2(c) of the ABA Model Rules. In England any such fee splitting is prohibited: see r 7 of the Solicitors Practice Rules 1990, applied in *Mohamed v Alaga & Co (a firm)* [1999] 3 All ER 699.

96 Detailed guidance on the sale of a law practice can be found in r 1.17 of the ABA Model Rules. No express guidance exists in the New Zealand Rules.

97 See para 1 of the commentary to r 6.04.

their professional income with business enterprises,[98] or become aware of opportunities through the course of their work that they are in a position to take advantage of. In all such situations, lawyers must be careful to ensure that their own interests are fully disclosed to their clients, and that the clients consent. It is a fundamental precept of the obligations of a fiduciary that in the absence of clear permission they are not entitled to profit from their position.[99] This prohibits not only secret profits such as referral fees,[100] but also prohibits taking advantage of information gained in the relationship of lawyer and client. It is inconsistent with the duty of loyalty to a client to enter into a business transaction in which the lawyer's interests are at odds with those of the client. Such a transaction is likely to affect the objectivity and loyalty of the lawyer adversely.

A lawyer in commercial practice will often gain considerable information of business opportunities in the course of practice. They may well also choose to invest their own earnings into ventures that require active management such as property and business ownership, or financing the ventures of others. It is advisable for lawyers engaged in private business, to keep professional and business matters quite separate. It is not possible to act in respect of a client in two different capacities, that is, as lawyer and as businessperson. The lawyer will continue to be the lawyer of the client, even if they choose to enter into business arrangements with them:[101]

> It would be disruptive of the solicitor-client relation, undermining of the principles underlying that fiduciary relationship and contrary to the public interest to allow the solicitor to opt out of that professional duty by pleading that acting in a different capacity he had discharged the different responsibilities attaching to that other relationship. There is every reason to require the solicitor who has two roles to play to discharge the fiduciary responsibilities attaching to each.

---

98 Note that r 2.03 provides: 1. A practitioner shall not, while the holder of a practising certificate as a barrister or solicitor or as both, engage in a business or professional activity other than the practice of law unless the business or professional activity: (i) Will not detract or have the potential to detract from the standards of independence and professionalism a client is entitled to expect from a practitioner; (ii) Does not have nor has the potential to have a harmful effect on the privilege or confidentiality attaching to communications between a practitioner and a client; (iii) Would not of itself have the potential to create a conflict of interest on the part of a practitioner.

99 *Boardman v Phipps* [1967] 2 AC 46.

100 Such secret profits are expressly prohibited by r 3.02 which provides: "A practitioner must not receive a reward whether financial or otherwise, of which a client is unaware, in respect of services rendered to the client".

101 *Sims v Craig Bell & Bond* [1991] 3 NZLR 535, 545 per Richardson J.

Where a lawyer does enter into a transaction with a client the onus will be on the lawyer to establish that the client consented to this modification of the fiduciary obligations of the lawyer, and was fully informed as to the nature of the transaction. The disclosure by the lawyer must be complete. In the words of Street CJ:[102]

> There cannot be any doubt that the duty of the solicitor to his client is paramount, and that he must not prefer his or the interest of another to that of his client ... where there is any conflict between the interest of the client and that of the solicitor, the duty of the solicitor is to act in perfect good faith and to make full disclosure of his interest. It must be a conscientious disclosure of all material circumstances, and everything known to him relating to the proposed transaction which might influence the conduct of the client or anybody from whom he might seek advice. To disclose less than all that is material, may positively mislead. Thus, for a solicitor merely to disclose that he has an interest, without identifying the interest, may serve only to mislead the client into an enhanced confidence that the solicitor will be in a position better to protect the client's interest.

There may be cases where it is not realistically possible for a lawyer to discharge this burden himself or herself and the client will need to obtain independent advice.[103] The commentary to r 1.03 provides:

> A practitioner may not enter any financial, business or property transaction with a client if there is a possibility of the fiduciary relationship between practitioner and client being open to abuse. This applies even if the practitioner does not propose to act for the client in the particular transaction.

A wide range of interests might give rise to a breach of the duty of loyalty. Not only must lawyers be aware that indirect interests such as share holdings, directorships, the relationship of debtor or creditor or the like, might give rise to a conflict of interest between themselves and their client, but also the interests of the members of their immediate family must be taken into account.[104]

---

102 *Law Society of New South Wales v Harvey* [1976] 2 NSWLR 154.

103 See the words of Hardie Boys J in *Sims v Craig Bell & Bond* [1991] 3 NZLR 535, 546: "It may be very difficult indeed for the solicitor to avoid such a conflict without requiring the client to take independent advice"; also *Re Beard* [1917] GLR 228 (CA).

104 See r 1.03(6): The rule will usually apply to any interest or dealing through the practitioner's family or relatives or any company, trust, partnership, or other body in which the practitioner has or exerts a material measure of control or influence. It will also include interests that are not personal in the strict sense but representative in character such as directorships and trusteeships. See also *Day v Mead* [1987] 2 NZLR 443.

One example (of many)[105] is the case of *Farrington v Rowe McBride & Partners*.[106] The client had a sum of money to invest which was the proceeds of a successful legal claim. The lawyers suggested investing in a certain company. Not only was the company a client of the firm (creating a potential conflict between clients) but also four of the partners of the firm were shareholders and two partners were directors of related companies. This created a conflict between the interests of the lawyers and the client. The client invested a large portion of his wealth in the company which, some two years later, collapsed. The client sued on the basis of the breach of the fiduciary duty. It was held that, due to the conflict (primarily with the other client), there had been a breach of duty. In such cases it is presumed that the failure to disclose led to the loss suffered.[107] Similar problems arose in *Sims v Craig Bell & Bond*[108] where a solicitor employed by the firm was also a business partner of a client. When the firm arranged mortgage finance for the client the solicitor paid the funds to himself and used them to repay a personal debt, claiming that the client had authorised this action. The transaction (which the High Court found had been agreed to) would be unimpeachable had it not been for the fact that one of the parties to it was the solicitor of the other party. Because of this the relationship could not be viewed as a normal business transaction. Rather the firm had to show that the client was fully informed of the nature and consequences of the arrangement. For the lawyer who was the recipient of the funds to do this would require a level of objectivity that could not be realistically attained in the face of such an obvious interest.

More complex were the facts in *Witten-Hannah v Davis*.[109] The motivation for the lawyer entering into a business transaction with a former client was the fact that they had become lovers (though now estranged) and the lawyer sought to ensure that the former lover/client had a home suitable to accommodate her and the children she had had to him. In that case the transaction, though unusual, was not patently unfair. However, it was noted that it "should not have been made between a solicitor and a client who were in the close relationship of the present parties without the client being independently advised".[110]

105 See *Apatu v Peach Prescott & Jamieson* [1985] 1 NZLR 50.
106 [1985] 1 NZLR 83.
107 *Brickenden v London Loan & Savings Co* [1934] 3 DLR 465.
108 [1991] 3 NZLR 535.
109 [1995] 1 NZLR 141.
110 [1995] 1 NZLR 141, 153 per McKay J.

It is almost inevitable in the practice of law that the professional and business affairs of lawyers will occasionally overlap.[111] In such cases the prudent course is to withdraw from acting. However, the lure of the retainer and its accompanying fees means that practitioners will attempt to satisfy their professional obligations as well as protecting and promoting other business interests. Such a course is often difficult and sometimes impossible. There is a presumption that any such transaction between lawyer and client is inappropriate, and the onus is on the lawyer to displace that presumption. If it is found that the lawyer has breached professional obligations, the lawyer will be held liable for any damage or loss suffered by the client which will be presumed to have resulted from the lawyer's breach.

7.7.5 *Gifts by clients*

There will be cases where a client wishes to gift property to the lawyer, or to bequeath property to the lawyer by will. A lawyer should be very wary of accepting such gifts.[112] While not prohibited, it is important that a lawyer is not seen as inappropriately benefiting from the professional relationship. As stated in r 1.01: "The relationship between practitioner and client is one of confidence and trust which must never be abused". If the lawyer proposes to accept the gift, and it is a significant one, it is advisable that the client obtain independent advice to ensure that he or she understands the purport of the actions and there is no suggestion of illegitimate pressure. In the absence of the lawyer recommending such advice, the gift is not only likely to be void, but the lawyer may also be guilty of misconduct.[113]

7.7.6 *Lending and borrowing*

Entering into a relationship of debtor or creditor with a client is problematic as it is often inconsistent with the fiduciary obligations owed by the lawyer. The lawyer himself or herself may be in need of finance, and a client may be prepared to act as lender. However, for the lawyer to borrow money directly from clients is difficult. It places the interests of lawyer and client in quite opposed positions.[114] It is for this reason that the commentary to r 1.03 provides:[115]

---

111 See *Official Assignee of Collier v Creighton* [1993] 2 NZLR 534 where a solicitor was asked to complete a conveyancing transaction in respect of a house on which he had himself made an offer to purchase.

112 See generally Virginia Shirvington, "Gifts from clients — manna from heaven?" (1997) 35 (5) LSJ 31.

113 *Re a Solicitor* [1974] 3 All ER 853; *Wintle v Nye* [1959] 1 All ER 552 (HL).

114 See the useful discussion in *Law Society of New South Wales v Harvey* [1976] 2 NSWLR 154.

115 The rule may be dictated by r 6 of the Solicitors' Trust Account Regulations 1998 which prohibit absolutely the lending of money by a client to the client's lawyer, members of the lawyer's family, the lawyer's firm, or any interest connected with the lawyer.

> ... where a practitioner borrows money from a client other than a client whose normal business is lending money. It is not then enough to offer independent advice to the client. The solicitor must sever the relationship of solicitor and client in that matter and ensure that the person concerned receives independent and competent advice. If the client refuses to take independent advice, the transaction should not proceed.

This blanket prohibition on lending transactions contrasts with the rather vague approach taken by the rules in respect of other transactions between lawyer and client. It reflects the fact that a client will often trust the lawyer to a greater degree than they would others, even when the lawyer is clearly negotiating for personal advantage. Because the client will have a possibly unfounded expectation of fair dealing, the rules state that if such a transaction is to proceed the lawyer-client relationship must be severed. Not only must the relationship be severed, but it is also incumbent on the lawyer to ensure that the client receives independent advice on the transaction, without which the transaction must not proceed.[116]

7.7.7 *Pillow talk*

An increasingly frequent problem is the possible conflict between lawyer and client when the lawyer's spouse has been retained to act for the other party. The dangers of such a situation are obvious. There is a risk that confidential information will inadvertently be disclosed to the other lawyer in a domestic setting (often referred to as "pillow talk"). There is also a possibility that the lawyers will not act as zealously in the interests of their clients as they might have, had the other lawyer not been their spouse. Such problems may arise in situations other than where the parties are married or defacto partners. There will be situations where lawyers will live as flatmates together, or where there will be other family relationships (siblings, parent-child etc) between practitioners. In these situations the dangers of inadvertent disclosure or preferential treatment are reduced, however, they still undeniably exist.[117]

Two lawyers who are related may well be able to act in a manner unaffected by that relationship. However, there is a danger that a disappointed client who discovers such a previously undisclosed relationship would feel that his or her lack of success was attributable to

---

116 The New Zealand approach is particularly stringent. The English *Guide* provides in the commentary to r 15.04 only that the lawyer must ensure that in such a situation the client must receive independent advice. For the similar positions in the Australian jurisdictions see G Dal Pont *Lawyers' Professional Responsibility in Australia and New Zealand* North Ryde, LBC Information Services, 1996, 135, 136.

117 See further D Buchanan, "Strange Bedfellows? Married Lawyers and Conflicts of Interest" (1998) 11 Georgetown Journal of Legal Ethics 753-766.

some failing of the lawyer motivated by the existence of the relationship. Such an allegation would be hard to disprove and, if it could be shown that there was a conflict of interest between professional and personal loyalties, a good foundation for a claim would exist.

The rules were amended in 1998 to address this problem by the addition of r 6.09 which states:

> A practitioner (practitioner A) closely related[118] to another practitioner (practitioner B) shall not act for a client in a matter directly adverse to a person who practitioner A knows is represented by practitioner B, except upon consent by the client after consultation regarding the relationship.

The rule states that the rule is not breached where a member of the firm is acting against a close relation. Such a conflict may be avoided by the work being handed by one of the lawyers to another member of the firm, and the original lawyer having no further involvement in the case. The practitioner who was retained later in time will be expected to hand the matter to another lawyer. It is observed in the commentary to the rule that there may be other relationships between lawyers which "render it unwise" to continue to act. Where two lawyers have a relationship but do not cohabit or where they are separated spouses, it may be advisable for the lawyer retained later in time to disqualify himself or herself from acting.

A new rule has been proposed which would deal with the similar problem that arises where a legal practitioner is closely related to a judicial officer. The proposed new r 8.10 provides that in the absence of exceptional circumstances a person who is closely related[119] to a judicial officer may not appear as counsel before the officer. The exceptions include where all parties consent, where the matter is urgent, and where the matter is merely a formal interlocutory application.

7.7.8 *Acting for family*

An area in which there is little formal guidance is where a lawyer acts as legal adviser to family or friends. It is common for lawyers to be approached for assistance both formally and informally by such people. Not only do they already trust the lawyer, but also they are probably hoping for favourable treatment in respect of fees. In many cases such an arrangement will give rise to little difficulty. In purely transactional

---

118 "Closely related" is defined in r 6.09(2)(l): "Two practitioners are closely related if one is to the other the parent or sibling or if they are married or living as partners on a domestic basis."

119 Defined as a parent, spouse (including de facto), sibling, child, parent in law, or child in law, but with the observation that other relationships may "render it unwise" to appear.

matters such as conveyancing and the like there is little likelihood of problems arising. However, where matters are complicated, contentious, or have considerable significance there are good practical reasons for a lawyer to avoid acting for family or close friends.

It could not strictly be said that there is a conflict of interest between the lawyer and his or her clients in such cases. If anything the lawyer will work more diligently than is really required, as both personal and professional motivations exist. However, the objections to such retainers are several. The first is the possibility of a lack of objectivity. There is danger that when appraising the chances of success of a possible claim or defence, weaknesses will be overlooked and strengths over-emphasised. Not only is it sometimes difficult to admit that those close to one are in the wrong, it is also hard to accept the possibility that they may be distorting the truth, or not be credible witnesses.

The second problem is that of over-zealousness. Most lawyers have a desire for their clients to succeed whether in litigation, business transactions, or personal affairs. Such a desire is a natural professional inclination to do well in one's work and see positive results for those one is assisting. When the client has a close relationship with the lawyer the desire may be strengthened considerably. In a normal professional relationship if the endeavour of the client is unsuccessful there may be some disappointment, but nothing other than some professional pride hangs on the matter. The situation may be quite different when the endeavour is for a close member of the family. Failure becomes much more like a personal failure, and the lawyer will have a strong incentive to avoid the prospect of the responsibility for such failure being placed on the lawyer by the client.

The existence of such pressure may lead the lawyer to make errors of judgment. There is also a risk that extreme loyalty to the client's cause may result in the dilution of loyalty to others and, in particular, to the Court. It would be difficult to adhere to the obligations of ensuring full discovery and revealing even disadvantageous authorities to the Court if it was likely to jeopardise success for the family member. This would be compounded if the family member were to put pressure on the lawyer to breach the ethical obligations. While such pressure by an ordinary client might be resisted, where the client is a family member, insisting on strict compliance with the rules might be more difficult.

A further problem is that the professionalism with which lawyers are expected to conduct their business may be missing when they act for people they are close to.[120] Understandably, one may feel awkward in setting out matters in writing, or laboriously explaining transactions to

120 *Walsh v Law Society of NSW* (1999) 164 ALR 405.

such people and may be tempted to take short cuts. Clients may well encourage this tendency. Rather than trouble the lawyer with the task of setting matters out in writing, or require documents to be fully explained, family members may be happier to trust the lawyer and rely on the lawyer's judgment. Such a trusting approach and consequent short cuts can lead to problems. Such an approach may have led to the action in *Everist v McEvedy*[121] where a junior lawyer was acting on a mortgage transaction between his brother and the brother's mother in law (the case also concerned a conflict of interest between these two clients). By failing to advise properly on the effect of discharging a mortgage to the mother-in-law the firm was held liable for the losses suffered when the funds which had been secured were lost.

7.8 Duration of duty of loyalty

The duty of loyalty will last for as long as the client retains the lawyer. However, once the retainer has been terminated the lawyer is no longer under a duty to act in the best interests of the clients, to disclose information to them, or to advise them. This more or less goes without saying. It would not be feasible for the duties attaching to the lawyer-client relationship to last forever.

A lawyer may act against the interests of a former client after the retainer has been terminated.[122] Questions may arise when a lawyer is retained by one client to act against a person who was previously the lawyer's client. Previous clients may be understandably disgruntled to discover that their former adviser is now furthering the interests of their nemesis. There is no conflict of interest for the lawyer — the lawyer owes no loyalty to the former client, and is free to act for the new client. The only situation where a lawyer will be prohibited from acting for the later client is where the lawyer is in possession of confidential information of the former client that might be turned to the advantage of the new client.[123] If this is the case then the lawyer will be unable to act. Such a prohibition is based on the duty of confidentiality that arises from the fiduciary relationship rather than the duty of loyalty. Problems arising in such successive retainers by clients with opposing interests are considered in detail in ch 9. Where the matter in which the lawyer now acts against the former client is unconnected to the earlier retainer there is no prohibition on the lawyer acting for the new client.

121 [1997] 3 NZLR 349.

122 *BOC NZ Ltd v Trans Tasman Properties Ltd* (1996) 10 PRNZ 199.

123 This is set out in r 1.05. The law is in a state of flux: see *Russell McVeagh McKenzie Bartleet & Co v Tower Corporation* [1998] 3 NZLR 641 and compare *Prince Jefri Bolkiah v KPMG (a firm)* [1999] 2 WLR 215.

Chapter 8

Confidence

8.1 Introduction

The knowledge lawyers gain of clients and their affairs through the professional relationship is secret. The lawyer is under an obligation to keep such information confidential indefinitely and in most cases absolutely. The rules provide:[1]

> A practitioner has a duty to hold in strict confidence all information concerning the business and affairs of the client acquired in the course of the professional relationship, and should not divulge such information.

The duty is a strict one and extends to all information regarding the client, and even the fact that the client has retained the lawyer. Not only is a lawyer under a duty to keep the affairs of the client secret, but they must also ensure that all reasonable steps are taken to protect against inadvertent disclosure. This will include keeping information secure, as well as not accepting retainers from other clients who might profit from the use of the information. The House of Lords has said a lawyer should not take any steps in respect of the confidential affairs of a client which "exposes him to a potential and avoidable risk to which he has not consented, and fails to give him a sufficient assurance that his confidence will be respected".[2]

8.2 Rationale and objections

8.2.1 *Practical reasons*

The duty of confidence is seen as a natural incident of the closeness of the lawyer-client relationship. The work required of the lawyer involves the disclosure by the client of information which is of a sensitive or personal nature. For the lawyer to be able to effectively advise and represent the client it is necessary for the lawyer to know all the relevant facts. Without the protection of confidentiality clients may withhold relevant information for fear of disclosure to third parties. It is claimed

1 Rule 1.08.

2 *Prince Jefri Bolkiah v KPMG (a firm)* [1999] 2 WLR 215, 226.

that the duty of confidence is necessary to make the lawyer-client relationship work.

The duty of confidentiality is superficially simple; however, at its heart it reveals the tensions that underlie the role of the lawyer.[3] Most secrets that the lawyer is required to keep will be innocuous and concern matters that are only of private interest. However, there will be cases where by virtue of the special position held, a lawyer will come into information where, but for the relationship of lawyer and client, there would be a moral duty to disclose. The examples are numerous: when it is revealed that a client has AIDS but has not disclosed the fact to the client's sexual partner, where a lawyer's advice is sought on a fraudulent transaction, or — the classic problem — when a client that the lawyer is defending confesses guilt to a crime.

In such cases, considerable harm to identified individuals or a real injustice may result from a failure to disclose the information revealed. Where a lawyer defends a case knowing that facts exist which show that the client is guilty, the object of the trial (to discover and punish the perpetrator) is defeated. The claim that the onus to prove guilt is on the prosecution and unless the prosecution prove all elements of an offence, a not guilty verdict is appropriate, rarely satisfies informed and reasonable lay people.[4] The Court seeks to find out whether the accused committed the offence charged. It is undeniable that a lawyer who withholds compelling evidence is instrumental in defeating the object of the trial. Keeping confidences is irreconcilable with honesty and truth telling. By remaining silent in the face of such misapprehensions a lawyer is an accessory to the concealment of the truth. How is it then that the duty of a lawyer to keep confidences can be defended? The issue then is whether the rules which compel the lawyer to act in this way are justifiable in some wider sense. There are several possible arguments supporting the duty of confidence. They rely either on a consequentialist view of the duties of the lawyer or a rights-based approach which seeks to protect the freedoms of the client.

8.2.2 *The consequentialist justification*

A consequentialist approach looks to the ultimate and wider consequences of a course of action rather than the act itself or its immediate affects. Rather than focusing on the rightness or wrongness of the specific acts of the lawyer in their own right, one is required to consider the aims of the rule which requires the lawyer to keep confidences and its intended affects. Legal assistance is considered

---

3 A useful discussion of the duty, along with similar duties of other professionals is to be found in P Finn, "Professionals and Confidentiality" (1992) 14 Syd LR 317.

4 This is the stance taken by the rules in rr 10.03 and 10.04.

crucial in the protection of the rights of the individual. Accordingly, it is important that the impediments to effective legal assistance be minimised. One defence of the duty of confidentiality argues that if such a duty did not exist the ability of citizens to avail themselves of the best legal advice would be greatly impeded.[5] Were it permissible (or obligatory) for lawyers to disclose damning information on their clients to the authorities, clients would be less likely to fully and frankly disclose all of their affairs to the lawyer. In such cases the advice given by a lawyer may be inadequate and quite possibly harmful. Moreover, in the absence of legal expertise it is possible that exculpatory information would be withheld in the mistaken belief that it was irrelevant, or possibly even damning. This is the argument most frequently cited in the cases as exemplified by the words of Lord Brougham as long ago as 1836:[6]

> The interests of justice cannot be upholden, and the administration of justice cannot go on, without the aid of men skilled in jurisprudence, in the practice of the Courts, and in those matters affecting the rights and obligations which form the subject matter of all judicial proceedings. If the privilege did not exist at all, everyone would be thrown upon his own legal resources; deprived of all professional assistance, a man would not venture to consult any skilful person, or would only dare to tell his counsellor half his case.

If it were common for clients to keep secrets from their lawyers this would greatly hinder the Court process. When lawyers have full information they are able to streamline litigation by identifying central issues and the strengths and weaknesses of the evidence. If this is not the case, central facts may come out only late in the proceeding, or possibly not at all. If information were withheld because of the absence of a duty of confidentiality trials may be delayed, and would certainly be more drawn out. Moreover, clients may well be sabotaging their own cases by preventing their lawyers from preparing the case based on all the facts.

The duty of confidentiality in the criminal context (where it is most criticised) has further been defended on the basis of the significant imbalance of power between the prosecution and the defence. The defendant is an individual, commonly of meagre means, whereas the prosecution has the resources of the state behind it. It is defensible for the scales to be tipped back in the defendant's favour by providing that he or she may instruct an advocate secure in the knowledge that any disclosure to the advocate will be protected.[7] This argument has been

5 M Freedman *Lawyer's Ethics in an Adversary System* Indianapolis, Bobs-Merril, 1975, 4-5.

6 *Greenough v Gaskell* (1836) 1 My & K 98, 103.

7 This is the approach taken by D Luban in *Lawyers and Justice: An Ethical Study* Princeton, New Jersey, Princeton University Press, 1988, 202-205.

extended to other cases where there is a significant imbalance of power between litigants, such as those between consumers and giant corporations.

The consequentialist justification of the duty of confidence claims that for the system to work effectively and fairly in most cases the duty is necessary. It is not denied that in some situations injustice will result as where a criminal is not convicted even though the lawyer is in possession of damning evidence. However it is suggested that in the long run a more just system results when confidences are respected.

8.2.3 *The rights-based justification*

A rights-based approach is based on the value of personal autonomy, and views the right to effective legal assistance as essential to that autonomy. The right to effective assistance is considered inviolable and the duty of confidentiality is justified accordingly. The rights-based approach is based on the rights of the individual concerned rather than the wider benefits of the duty of confidence. This analysis works best where the lawyer is considered to be a mere agent of the client. Clearly, if clients were to act on their own behalf (as they are entitled) no problem of confidentiality would arise. Why therefore should the information they hold be placed at risk simply because they choose to avail themselves of the right to legal representation? If a legal adviser were allowed or required to breach confidence, clients may be worse off (at least in this respect) in instructing a lawyer than if they had acted for themselves.

This approach can be seen in the words of Jessel MR in *Anderson v Bank of British Columbia*:[8]

> It is absolutely necessary that a man, in order to prosecute his rights or defend himself from an improper claim, should have recourse to the assistance of professional lawyers, and it being so absolutely necessary, to use a vulgar phrase, that he should be able to make a clean breast of it to the gentleman whom he consults..... that he should be enabled properly to conduct his litigation.

The right to frankly and freely consult a legal adviser in the prosecution of a case is seen as central to the ability to get justice before the Courts — a right which is rooted in our earliest laws.[9] Such a view is premised on the indispensability of lawyers, a fact that the adversarial system compounds. In the absence of an advocate the inequalities of ability between litigants would be more likely to influence the outcome of a

---

8 (1876) 2 Ch D 644, 649.

9 Magna Carta 1297, 25 Edw I Cl 29, Statute of Westminster the First 3 Edw I cl 1, Observance of Due Process of Law Statute 1368, 42 Edw 3 cl 3.

case. Where one litigant is stupid, inarticulate, or uneducated, a lawyer is required to ensure that the litigant does not lose the case owing to the superiority of the other litigant. It is argued that without the duty of confidence such a system would be worthless.[10]

8.2.4 *Objections*

As with any consequentialist justification for action, there is a real and problematic tension between the act and the ends achieved (or at least aimed at). It is easy in the abstract to identify the merit in an approach that accepts minor short term injustices in achieving a longer-term goal. However, this wider perspective is of little assistance in considering individual cases. For example, in a case where a criminal defence lawyer knows of damning facts regarding his or her client's conduct, but remains silent, the wider goal of justice is of no comfort to the victim of the crime or possible later victims, when a dangerous defendant goes free. The value we tend to place on individuals means that there is an aversion to treating their misfortunes as necessary to effect some greater purpose — the equivalent of the Kantian imperative that persons are ends in themselves and should never be treated as mere means to other ends.

The duty of confidentiality which requires a lawyer to remain silent even when in possession of relevant information also seems inconsistent with the wider demands placed on lawyers. Lawyers are expected to uphold professional standards by acting with probity and integrity. In most cases a person of integrity, knowing of facts that would assist a Court, or protect a third party, would disclose those facts. It is, however, incumbent on lawyers to keep such revelations by their client secret. While in some cases, such as commercial disputes, this may raise few qualms and be regarded as a normal incident of litigation or business, there are other more troubling situations. Consider the situation where the lawyer has assisted an estranged spouse to negotiate a matrimonial settlement, but subsequent to execution the client reveals that numerous assets have been concealed in tenuously legal (though not clearly fraudulent) trusts and other entities. Such conduct almost certainly deprives one spouse of the just share of the matrimonial property, and without the information that such assets and entities exist they will be unable to challenge the wrongly obtained settlement.

Such an action requires the lawyer to subjugate his or her own moral judgment to that of the client. It is this kind of action that leads to the popular perception that lawyers are dishonest or amoral. Such an

---

10 This rights-based approach is particularly prevalent in the American approach, see the ABA Model Rules r 1.6 and the discussion of those rules in D Luban in *Lawyers and Justice: An Ethical Study* Princeton, New Jersey, Princeton University Press, 1988, 177-184.

allegation is hard to dismiss, as it is clear that the personal integrity of a lawyer is suspended by such silence. The response that the silence of the lawyer is compelled by a professional morality does little to allay the fears that such actions perpetuate injustice rather than justice.

The duty of confidentiality is often stated to be at the heart of the adversarial system of justice which prevails in the Anglo-American legal tradition. It is argued that without such a duty the adversary system would be unworkable. Such an argument, however, presumes that with the duty of confidence the adversary system is workable. Such a fundamental discussion is beyond the scope of this work, however, it is observed that serious criticisms can be directed at the adversarial system of which the duty of confidentiality is an integral part. This amounts to rejecting the claimed utility of the consequentialist end. It can be questioned whether the end achieved by small injustices caused by the duty of confidentiality does in fact achieve any greater good. It can be cogently argued that the duty causes more harm than good as it simply serves to conceal injustice.[11]

Even if it is accepted that the duty of confidence does have the effect of encouraging frankness between lawyer and client, in many cases it can also be argued that there are other consequences which are equally detrimental to the administration of justice. One such detrimental consequence is the fact that the duty can be used as a shield behind which unscrupulous practitioners can hide when they and their clients are engaged in questionable or even fraudulent conduct. Many of the massive frauds that occur could not be effected were it not for the complicity of the legal advisers. If the duty of confidentiality did not exist such assistance would be much more difficult to lend.[12] The duty also results in a reduced confidence of the public in the integrity of the profession. If the rules devised by lawyers to govern their conduct require them to remain silent in the face of harm to others the public may rightly question whether the profession truly upholds the values of justice and integrity that it claims.

8.3 The practical context

The situation is perhaps saved by virtue of the fact that in practice such acute problems arise rarely. Most of the secrets that lawyers are required

---

11 This was the essence of the argument of J Bentham who maintained that the duty only served to protect the guilty as the innocent had nothing to fear from the truth. See Bentham J *The Handbook of Political Fallacies* New York, Harper Torchbooks, 1952, 34-38; J Bowring (ed) *The Works of Jeremy Bentham* New York, Russell & Russell, 1962, vii, 474-475.

12 For a full exposition of this argument see R Tur, "Confidentiality and Accountability" (1992) 1 Griffith LR 73.

to keep are mundane, or where they are of importance the maintaining of confidence accords with most people's belief of the moral course of action. Despite the need for frankness between lawyer and client it is suggested that many clients keep some information from their lawyers. Indeed, a skilled and cynical lawyer will be able to assist the client in determining what information is relevant and should be disclosed and on what information the client should remain silent. Lawyers in criminal cases may well discourage their clients from making any kind of confession to the lawyer, as it may put the lawyer in an awkward position if the client seeks to defend the charge.

Lawyers are not mere technicians and, if they come into information where there is a compelling argument that it ought to be disclosed, such matters will often be discussed with the client. Where a defendant discloses facts which lead the lawyer to a conclusion that if the Court were apprised of those facts a guilty verdict would be certain, the lawyer may counsel a plea to that effect to be entered.[13] The relationship between lawyer and client in such situations is not one of mere agency; it is a cooperative relationship in which a course of action is agreed rather than dictated. There will be cases where agreement cannot be reached and the client will instruct the lawyer on how to act. In such cases the lawyer is bound to follow those instructions in so far as they are within the law and the professional rules.[14]

The duty of confidence is not absolute. There are a number of important exceptions to the duty, and a number of statutory incursions. Such exceptions are based on grounds including public interest, the safety of third parties, and the detection of crimes. Although there are instances where important information must be withheld by the lawyer, increasingly, the protection afforded to secrets disclosed to lawyers is being eroded by the need to balance the interests of the client and the ends of justice against the safety of others and the public interest.

8.4 Legal foundation[15]

The duty of confidentiality is an implied term of any contract of retainer, and as such is a normal incident of the contract between lawyer and client.[16] The obligation is also founded in equitable principles, and will

13 Rule 10.04(2).

14 Rule 1.02.

15 For a judicial examination of the complexities of the jurisprudential foundations of the duty of confidence see *General Mediterranean Holdings SA v Patel* [1999] 3 All ER 673.

16 *Parry Jones v Law Society* [1969] 1 Ch 1. See also *Tournier v National Provincial and Union Bank of England* [1924] 1 KB 461 for a discussion of the

exist even where there is no contractual arrangement (as in the case of pro bono work). The position of the lawyer as a fiduciary imposes a duty of confidence, along with a duty not to use the information for the lawyer's own benefit[17] or the benefit of another client.[18] Equity will also act to protect information in any situation where it was communicated in circumstances that made it clear that it was to be kept in confidence. On top of these legal duties is the clear professional duty to keep all information disclosed by the client confidential unless a clear justification to disclose exists. The rules provide:[19]

> A practitioner has a duty to hold in strict confidence all information concerning the business and affairs of the client acquired in the course of the professional relationship, and should not divulge such information…

The duty of non-disclosure is imposed by Principle 11 of the Privacy Act 1993.[20] When applied to lawyers, that principle provides that personal information[21] may only be disclosed to the individual to whom it relates unless one of a number of stated exceptions apply. Those exceptions include public interest such as detection of crime or the protection of public health or private safety. It seems that the legal duty of confidence is more stringent than that imposed by Principle 11, and therefore the principle has no appreciable impact on the duties owed.

8.5 Scope and duration of the duty

All information disclosed to a lawyer by the client must be kept confidential. The duty is imposed from the moment that the lawyer is retained. There is a good argument that the duty of confidence should apply to information imparted prior to the creation of a retainer, as long as it is imparted in the context of a lawyer and potential client relationship. Consider an example where a prospective client meets a lawyer to discuss the possibility of undertaking legal work, but it transpires that work is beyond the expertise of the lawyer, or the lawyer is unable to accept the retainer because of a possible conflict of interest. In such a case a lawyer-client relationship has not been created. However, it is clear that the information imparted to the lawyer was imparted in confidence, and it would not be permissible for the lawyer to reveal the information, or even the nature of the transaction, to a third party. The discussion clearly took place with the lawyer in the

---

contractual duty of confidence in the context of the banker-customer relationship.

17 *Boardman v Phipps* [1967] 2 AC 46.

18 *Prince Jefri Bolkiah v KPMG (a firm)* [1999] 2 WLR 215.

19 Rule 1.08.

20 Section 6 Privacy Act 1993.

21 The Act does not protect the information of corporate entities.

capacity of a lawyer, and even though no contract of retainer or lawyer-client relationship has been created, the disclosures made are confidential.[22]

The duty of confidence will continue after the lawyer-client relationship has been terminated,[23] and indeed after the death of the client. The duty of confidence continues indefinitely, along with the fact that the lawyer is prohibited from running any risk that the information of the client might inadvertently be disclosed. This places considerable constraints on the conduct of a lawyer's practice. In particular, the duty to protect confidential information means that a lawyer will usually be prohibited from accepting a retainer for a subsequent client against the interests of a former client in a related matter.

Where a client dies, the right to confidentiality passes to the personal representatives.[24] Similarly, when a company is wound up the right of confidentiality passes to the liquidator. As long as the information imparted remains secret, and not in the public domain, the duty to keep it confidential will remain. The duty to refrain from disclosure will last only as long as the information remains secret. If the information falls into the hands of parties who are not bound by a duty of confidence or it becomes widely known or available, the information can no longer be regarded as confidential and there will be no breach of the duty if the information is disclosed.[25]

The duty of confidence will only apply to information divulged to the lawyer in his or her capacity as a lawyer.[26] This is a simple proposition, and clearly secrets divulged in a social setting, or in a different capacity will not be protected by this duty. Problems, however, arise where a lawyer attempts to act in more than one capacity. Where friends, family, business associates, or lovers are also clients it can be very difficult to distinguish where the obligations of the lawyer-client relationship start and stop. In cases where lawyers have attempted to mix their roles the Courts have tended to construe the relationship against the lawyer.[27]

---

22 This rule certainly applies in respect of the related doctrine of privilege: *Minter v Priest* [1929] 1 KB 655, 666 per Lord Hanworth MR.

23 *Earl of Cholmondeley v Lord Clinton* (1815) 19 Ves 261, 34 ER 1231.

24 *Gartside v Sheffield Young & Ellis* [1983] NZLR 37, 49 per Richardson J.

25 *Re a Firm of Solicitors* [1995] 3 All ER 482, 489 per Lightman J; r 1.08(v) of the rules.

26 See *Rosenberg v Jaine* [1983] NZLR 1, 8 per Davison CJ where this principle is applied in respect of privilege; also *Minter v Priest* [1930] AC 558, 568 per Lord Buckmaster.

27 *Sims v Craig Bell & Bond* [1991] 3 NZLR 535.

A wide variety of information will be protected. Not only will all of the details of the dealings between the lawyer and client be protected, but also any information that the lawyer acquires in the course of the relationship. The law will step in to protect against the leakage of general insights into the strengths and weaknesses of a client. In *Black v Taylor*[28] the Court intervened to prevent a solicitor who had acted for several members of a family from acting against them because of the possibility of misuse of information of the clients' "weaknesses, fears and reactions" which had been gained in the former relationship.

The duty of confidentiality is not only a duty not to disclose the information held (although this is its focus). It is also incumbent on the lawyer not to use the information gained for a purpose other than that for which it was acquired, and most importantly not to use it against the interests of the client.[29] The lawyer is also required to take steps to prevent the information from inadvertent disclosure. A lawyer must ensure that information is stored securely.[30] A new r 1.08A is proposed which states: "A practitioner has a duty to do his or her best to ensure that a valid claim for legal professional privilege is not inadvertently waived or waived without the client's consent". Where information is privileged (and therefore confidential) the lawyer must be careful not to take any steps which might lead to the loss of the legal protection afforded the privileged information.[31]

It will not be a breach of confidentiality to discuss a client's affairs in a manner that will not reveal the identity of the client. Such discussions are common between spouses, and in social settings. One of the ways in which practitioners learn is by exchanging information and anecdotes about their own practices, often in a social setting. Precisely this kind of situation arose in *McKaskell v Benseman*[32] where a young lawyer was faced with a difficult problem when another lawyer had sent him a letter containing insulting comments about his clients. In deciding to invite the other solicitor to rewrite the letter he had recourse to a group of legal

---

28 [1992] 3 NZLR 403.

29 *Black v Taylor* [1993] 3 NZLR 403.

30 *Nationwide Building Society v Various Solicitors (No 2)* (1998) Times, 1 May (finding that this duty did not extend to taking Court action against third parties). Compare the *Report of the Canterbury District Law Society Disciplinary Tribunal 1996* which records the censure and fine of a practitioner who on changing offices allowed files to fall into the hands of a third party and took inadequate steps to recover them.

31 Privilege may be lost, for example, by a party referring to or relying on a document but refusing to disclose the contents of it in a manner that is unfair: *Tau v Durie* (1995) 9 PRNZ 7; *Chandris Lines Ltd v Wilson & Horton Ltd* [1981] 2 NZLR 600; *Equiticorp Industries Group Ltd v Hawkins* [1990] 2 NZLR 175.

32 [1989] 3 NZLR 75.

practitioners who met socially on a Friday night in a local bar. The clients discovered this and claimed that such actions were a breach of the duty of confidence. Because in those circumstances there was no possibility of linking the information to the clients discussed and the offending letter itself was not shown, it was held that there was no breach of confidence.[33] It is, however, clear that caution must be exercised when discussing legal work in a social setting. In many instances the identity of a client may be inferred from the tenor of the discussion, or where the information is commercially sensitive (for example, the existence of a proposed takeover of a named company) there may be a breach of confidence even where the identity of the client is not revealed.

8.6 Distinct from privilege

Closely associated with the duty of confidentiality is the doctrine of lawyer-client privilege. Both concern restricting the dissemination of information that is confidential to the client. Many of the principles applicable to privilege are applicable to the duty of confidence. However, there are important differences.

Though the doctrine of privilege is a rule of the general law, it is primarily concerned with evidence. It protects communications from disclosure to a body which would otherwise be able to demand that it be produced such as a Court, the police, or the Revenue.[34] As a consequence of this, it also protects information from disclosure to any other third party. It is in essence the right of a person to refuse to deliver up evidence in limited circumstances. The duty of confidence on the other hand is a duty owed by the lawyer to the client founded in the professional duties of the lawyer as well as obligations in contract and equity. The information protected by the doctrine of lawyer-client privilege is also considerably narrower than that protected by the duty of confidence. Information will only be privileged when, in addition to being confidential,[35] it came into existence for the dominant purpose of obtaining legal advice or in respect of contemplated or actual litigation.[36] There are numerous communications between a lawyer and client which,

---

33 Although it is arguable that even where the identity of the client is not disclosed the use of information itself is a breach of confidence. This was the view of the Court in *R v Department of Health* [1999] 4 All ER 185. Compare *Duncan v Medical Practitioners Disciplinary Committee* [1986] 1 NZLR 513, 520 and *W v Egdell* [1990] 1 All ER 835, 848, [1990] Ch 359, 419.

34 *CIR v West-Walker* [1954] NZLR 191.

35 *Re Golightly* [1974] 2 NZLR 297; *Ritz Hotel Ltd v Charles of the Ritz Ltd [No 2]* (1988) 14 NSWLR 132, 133, per McLelland J.

36 *Konia v Morley* [1976] 1 NZLR 455; *Carlton Cranes Ltd v Consolidated Hotels Ltd* [1988] 2 NZLR 555.

though confidential, will not be covered by privilege. Matters where the lawyer is a mere functionary assisting in implementing a transaction, or facts such as billing costs and the like, while confidential will not be covered by privilege.

Privilege, once established, is unqualified and absolute. In contrast, there are numerous exceptions to the duty of confidentiality. Once it is established that privilege attaches to a document there are no grounds on which it may be disclosed against the client's wishes.[37] While privilege is of fundamental importance to legal practice, as a principle that is primarily applied in the area of evidence, it is best left to specialised texts.[38] This chapter will focus particularly on the duty of confidence owed by a lawyer to the client.

8.7 Justifications for breach of the confidence

8.7.1 *Introduction*

The public policy reasons for the existence of the duty of confidentiality and the underlying rationale have been discussed above. Those reasons purport to justify a rule that requires a lawyer to keep secret information disclosed by the client, or gathered in the course of the lawyer-client relationship. There will be countervailing reasons, usually similarly policy based, for excusing the lawyer for breach in the case of disclosure. In most instances the justifications permit disclosure. It is only in the rarest cases that a lawyer is compelled to break the confidence and inform a third party of some aspect of his or her client's affairs. Given the special position of lawyers and the fact that they are officers of the Court, it is worth considering when discussing the following justification whether or not a positive duty to speak out should be imposed more frequently.

8.7.2 *Consent*

The duty of confidence is owed to the client and the client has a corresponding right to insist that confidences be kept. A natural corollary of this is that the client is free to consent to disclosure of information and waive the right to confidentiality. The ability of a client to consent to disclosure is expressly referred to in r 1.08(i) of the rules which provides that information may be divulged where "a client expressly or impliedly authorises the disclosure". A lawyer must be wary of claiming that disclosure had been impliedly authorised, and it is obviously better to obtain express consent where possible. It follows also that where a lawyer seeks to act against the interests of a former

---

37 *R v Uljee* [1982] 1 NZLR 561, 577 per McMullin J; *R v Derby Magistrates' Court* [1995] 4 All ER 526.

38 See *Cross on Evidence* 6th NZ ed, 1997 (consulting editor, Donald L Mathieson, editorial board, John Black, Christopher Chapman, Simon France) Wellington, Butterworths, especially ch 10.

client in which the confidences reposed in the course of the earlier retainer are put at risk, the client may consent to the risk of inadvertent disclosure without consenting to any actual disclosure.[39] Such consent amounts to a permission to the lawyers to relax the precautions which they would otherwise be required to take in protecting the information.

8.7.3 *Public interest*[40]

There will be occasions where the keeping of confidences will be against the immediate public interest. However, it will only be in rare cases that the public interest will be a justification for a breach of confidence. It will be necessary to show that the public interest promoted in disclosing the information clearly outweighs that promoted by protecting the confidence. There are surprisingly few instances of such a disclosure occurring in respect of lawyer-client relationships. It has long been accepted in respect of confidential information generally that (unlike privilege) it is a matter of balancing interests. As Lord Goff has observed:[41]

> Although the basis of the law's protection of confidence is that there is a public interest that confidences should be preserved and protected by the law, nevertheless that public interest may be outweighed by some other countervailing public interest which favours disclosure.

One case where it was found that a breach of confidence was justified was *W v Egdell*.[42] In that case a psychiatrist released a report on a patient that was covered by doctor-client confidentiality. It was there held that the disclosure was justified because the report contained a medical opinion that the patient was a danger to the public. The duty of confidence imposed on lawyers is generally considered to be more stringent than that imposed on doctors.[43]

There may be circumstances where, although no crime is contemplated by the client and no immediate harm is intended to be inflicted on another, the lawyer is permitted to disclose information divulged. There is little guidance as to when the threshold justifying disclosure is met. It is inevitable that reasonable people will disagree over whether in any

39 *Prince Jefri Bolkiah v KPMG (a firm)* [1999] 2 WLR 215; *Russell McVeagh McKenzie Bartleet & Co v Tower Corporation* [1998] 3 NZLR 641.

40 See generally Y Cripps *The Legal Implications of Disclosure in the Public Interest* London, Sweet & Maxwell, 1994.

41 *Attorney-General v Guardian Newspapers (No 2)* [1990] AC 109,182.

42 [1990] 1 All ER 835. Also *Woolgar v Chief Constable of Sussex Police* [1999] 3 All ER 604 (CA) where it was held that the police could release confidential information (an interview transcript) to a professional body in the interests of public health or safety.

43 See K Wheat, "Lawyers, Confidentiality and Private and Public Interests" (1998) 1 Legal Ethics 184, 190-191.

particular instance the public interest justifies disclosure of confidential information. Consider, for example, a lawyer who becomes aware that the client, a building contractor, has constructed a building that is defective and inherently dangerous, or a situation where it becomes apparent that a client chemical manufacturer has concealed to authorities the devastating effects on endangered native wildlife of a herbicide.[44] There is a distinction between the two hypotheticals, in one there is a threat to human life and welfare, in the other there is not. This demonstrates the fact that the matter concerns a balancing of interests and views which will vary as to whether a breach of the duty is justified across different circumstances.

Precedents that concern confidences other than those between lawyer and client must also be treated with caution. The Courts have held that some breaches of confidence were justified, for example, by an employee of a defective breathalyser device,[45] and by a doctor that a patient is dangerous.[46] However, because the exercise is one of balancing, one must take into account not only the public interest protected or promoted by the disclosure, but also the public interest protected by the duty of confidence. It appears from that case that the public interest protected by the duty of a lawyer is considered to be particularly great and, therefore, the public interest promoted by disclosing confidential information will have to be correspondingly greater.[47]

The existence of such uncertainty is a considerable disincentive to disclosure for a lawyer who is considering whether to break a confidence or not. The bona fides of the lawyer may not be in doubt, however, if after balancing the interests, the Court finds that disclosure was not justified sanction will follow. The cautious approach in such cases is, therefore, not to disclose.

8.7.4 *Client's interest*

There will be limited instances where disclosure will be justified because it is in the client's own interest. In most cases the client's own judgment of what is in his or her interest should be respected. There will, however, be occasions where it is clear that the client's judgment is impaired and a

---

44 See M Brindle and G Dehn, "Confidence, Public Interest, and the Lawyer" in R Cranston *Legal Ethics and Professional Responsibility* Oxford, Clarendon Press, 1995, 122 where the example of a fairground owner running dangerous rides is used. Also I Russell, "Cries and Whispers: Environmental Hazards, Model Rule 1.6 and the Attorney's Conflicting Loyalties to Clients and Others" (1997) 2 Wash LR 409.

45 *Lion Laboratories v Evans* [1985] QB 526.

46 *W v Egdell* [1990] 1 All ER 835.

47 *Rakusen v Ellis Munday & Clark* [1912] 1 Ch 1 831, 840 per Fletcher Moulton LJ.

degree of paternalism is justified. Rule 1.08(ix) states that the duty of confidentiality may be breached where there is a "serious and imminent risk to the health or safety of the client". In *Howell Smith v Official Solicitor*[48] it was held that a solicitor acting for a mentally ill patient was justified in breaching confidence when he suspected the client's doctor of dealing inappropriately with the client's funds and so reported the doctor to the hospital administration.

Consider a situation where a client seeks advice from a lawyer as to how a friend might assist in ending the client's life without breaking the law. The client is clearly contemplating suicide, but may be doing so after careful consideration and acting wholly rationally.[49] For a lawyer to breach the duty of confidence and inform others of the client's intentions, is to substitute the judgment of the client for that of the lawyer and is paternalistic in an unacceptable way. It is suggested that in the absence of some clear incapacity such as an illness of the mind the mere fact that there is a "serious and imminent risk to the health or safety of the client" ought not to justify breaching confidence.

A similar problem exists when the lawyer becomes aware that the client has been a victim of a crime, or even is a continuing victim of a crime. Where a woman is the victim of continuing spousal abuse it may be that the woman is reluctant to report the abuse to the authorities, or indeed anyone. Such a wish must be respected. While the lawyer may counsel the client to seek assistance in the matter from support groups, professionals, or authorities, there are no grounds for unilaterally involving a third party and thereby breaching the duty of confidence.[50] The situation is, however, different where the victim labours under some disability, or is a child. In such circumstances, the client's judgment may be flawed, and it may be inappropriate to seek guidance from parents or guardians. In such cases the client relies on the judgment of the lawyer as well as the lawyer's expertise, and if the lawyer perceives it to be in the client's interests the confidence should be breached.[51]

---

48 QB ENF 95/0325/C, 26 April 1996, Pill LJ (CA).

49 See G Oddie, "The Moral Case for the Legalisation of Voluntary Euthanasia" (1998) 28 VUWLR 207.

50 See *Guidance — Confidentiality and Privilege — Child Abuse and Abduction* from the Standards and Guidance Committee of the Law Society of England and Wales.

51 See *Guidance — Confidentiality and Privilege — Child Abuse and Abduction* from the Standards and Guidance Committee of the Law Society of England and Wales. Also R Tur, "Confidentiality and Accountability" (1992) 1 Griffith LR 73, and r 16.02(4) of the English *Guide*.

8.7.5 *Fraud*

A lawyer will never be compelled to be a party to a wrong. It is established that a lawyer is permitted to disclose an "iniquity".[52] Where the client is engaged in some wrongdoing,[53] and particularly where the client is using the services of the lawyer to effect the wrong[54] the lawyer may disclose it to the relevant authorities, or to the victim of the wrong. Lord Denning stated that the liberty to disclose:[55]

> … should extend to crimes, frauds, and misdeeds, both those actually committed as well as those in contemplation, provided always — and this is essential — that the disclosure is justified in the public interest.

It is not necessary to establish that the wrong intended or committed is criminal. It must simply be shown that the interest in disclosure outweighs that of the protection of the confidence. The disclosure of a past crime revealed to a lawyer is not justified. The very reason for the existence of the lawyer-client confidence is often the need for assistance in the defence or mitigation of such actions against the authorities. For example, where a practitioner reveals to another practitioner as his or her lawyer (as opposed to a colleague) that he or she has taken funds from the trust account the lawyer may not report the existence of the defalcation to the law society.[56] In such cases the disclosures will be privileged as well as confidential.

8.7.6 *Disclosure within firm or incidental to retainer*

A lawyer may discuss a client's affairs with other members of the firm unless there is an express or implied prohibition on doing so.[57] In cases where one member of a firm is acting against the interests of a former client of another member of a firm, restrictions on the flow of information, that is, a Chinese wall, will commonly be set up. It is

---

52 *Gartside v Outram* (1856) 26 LJ Ch 113; *Annesley v Earl of Anglesea* (1743) 17 State Tr 11339, LR 5 QB 317N; *Kupe Group Ltd v Seamar Holdings Ltd* [1993] 3 NZLR 209; *Finers v Miro* [1991] 1 All ER 183 (CA).

53 Though it is not necessary for the lawyer to be implicated in the fraud or wrongdoing for the confidence or privilege to be lost: *Dubal Aluminium Co Ltd v Al Alawai* [1999] 1 All ER 703. See also commentary 1(b)(2) to the proposed r 8.01A.

54 See *Re Golightly* [1974] 2 NZLR 297, 304 per Mahon J and *Kupe Group Ltd v Seamar Holdings* [1993] 3 NZLR 209 (both of which relate to privilege, but applying identical principles) and the English *Guide* 16.02(1).

55 *Initial Services Ltd v Putterill* [1968] 1 QB 396, 405. See also *British Steel Corporation v Granada Television* [1981] 1 All ER 417, 455 per Lord Wilberforce, 480 per Lord Fraser.

56 Rule 6.03.

57 Rule 1.08 para 7 of the commentary.

presumed or readily inferred that in the absence of such steps lawyers in a firm will share confidential information.[58]

Where a lawyer is an employee rather than a partner of a firm, he or she is always permitted to disclose the nature of all the work undertaken to a partner. Because the partners of a firm are ultimately responsible for the conduct of their employees it is necessary that all matters conducted by an employee are able to be supervised by a partner. If a partner fails to take notice adequately of the work undertaken by a junior member of staff the partner may be breaching the duty to adequately supervise the conduct of the practice. As provided in the commentary to r 1.08:[59]

> A practitioner who is employed by a practitioner practising on his or her own account or by a firm of practitioners may always disclose the client's affairs to his or her employer. Such a practitioner may not agree to accept instructions or directions from the client on any other basis. [60]

Where disclosure is necessary to conduct the work required by the client disclosure will be permitted. Such disclosure can be presumed to be consented to by implication.[61] In many cases the use of the services of others is inevitable. Such third parties will, of course, also be bound by the duty of confidence, and in many cases where they produce further information (such as reports prepared by forensic accountants for litigation) that information will be privileged as well as confidential.

8.7.7 *Ethical or professional adviser*

There will be times when a lawyer will need to seek guidance on matters of professional conduct or practice. It may be impossible or inappropriate to obtain that advice from within the firm and, in such circumstances, it will be permissible to disclose matters to a third party lawyer. This occurred in *McKaskell v Benseman*[62] where a young practitioner received a letter from another lawyer that contained insulting remarks about his clients. He sought guidance from a partner in another firm (where he had been previously employed) as to whether the

---

58 *Prince Jefri Bolkiah v KPMG (a firm)* [1999] 2 WLR 215; *Russell McVeagh McKenzie Bartleet & Co v Tower Corporation* [1998] 3 NZLR 641.

59 Para 8.

60 This position is reinforced by r 2.04 which requires that every practice must be under effective and competent management, and notes in the commentary that the management of a practice by a non-partner "cannot derogate from the ultimate responsibility of the practitioner who is a principal of a firm or sole practitioner for the acts or defaults of the employee". See *Everist v McEvedy* [1996] 3 NZLR 348 for a cautionary tale where an employer was held liable for the defaults of an employee.

61 Rule 1.08(i).

62 [1989] 3 NZLR 75.

letter should be disclosed to his clients or not. The Court dismissed a claim that this had amounted to a breach of confidence, noting that:[63]

> ... to find [the ethical consultant] liable in law in the circumstances revealed by the evidence would be wrong in that it would result in a damaging chill to the benefits to society that flow from the type of consultation he was involved in.

The public interest in enabling limited disclosure to facilitate consultation on the appropriate and ethical course of action in any particular circumstance was held to justify the breach.

8.7.8 *Defence of allegation or prosecution of claim*

Where the lawyer and client are in dispute, and the subject-matter of the dispute is bound up in the very information that is confidential, the lawyer will be permitted to break the confidence in defence of his or her own interests.[64] This right to disclose is, however, limited to those disclosures deemed reasonably necessary to defend an allegation or establish a claim. A common example is where a lawyer sues for costs.[65] In such a case it will be necessary to produce the bill rendered as evidence. If the client denies that the work was done, or that the fee is excessive, the lawyer will be justified in disclosing the contents of the client's file and the corresponding time spent on the work in justifying the fee.

Similarly, where the client claims compensation for an alleged breach of duty, the lawyer may adduce evidence that would otherwise be confidential in defence of the claim.[66] Such disclosure is justified, as without disclosure, it would be impossible for a lawyer to defend such allegations effectively.[67] In such cases the client, in making the claim is seen to waive the right to confidentiality. Where a complaint is made to the law society, or where criminal charges concerning the dealing in client's affairs are laid, the lawyer is entitled to reveal the information in defending the allegations.[68] In the absence of such a right, there would

---

63 [1989] 3 NZLR 75, 90.

64 Rule 8.01(ii) and (iii).

65 Rule 1.08(ii). In *Tournier v National Provincial and Union Bank of England* [1924] 1 KB 461 this is one of the accepted grounds for disclosure in the context of the banker-customer relationship.

66 Rule 1.08 (iii).

67 *Nederlandse Reassurantie Groep Holding NV v Bacon and Woodrow (a firm)* [1995] 1 All ER 976, 978, 986 Coleman J; *Kershaw v Whelan* [1996] 2 All ER 404, 412-415 per Ebsworth J; *Lillicrap v Nalder & Son (a firm)* [1993] 1 WLR 94.

68 *Nederlandse Reassurantie Groep Holding NV v Bacon and Woodrow (a firm)* [1995] 1 All ER 976, 978, 986 Coleman J; *Kershaw v Whelan* [1996] 2 All ER

be a breach of natural justice in rendering it impossible for a lawyer so charged to effectively mount a defence based on the facts.

More difficult, perhaps, are a number of other situations that have been known to arise where either the claim is not made by the client, or the dispute exists outside any formal forum. Consider the case of *Gartside v Sheffield Young and Ellis*[69] where an intended beneficiary was suing the lawyer for failing to execute the instructions diligently and within a reasonable time. The result was that the testatrix died before the will was executed, and the intended beneficiary was bequeathed nothing under the original will. The intended beneficiary sued the lawyers in negligence. To establish such a claim it was necessary to gain access to the files of the deceased. It is equally conceivable that the lawyers in similar circumstances would seek to disclose the files to establish a defence. The problem, of course, was that the information was confidential to the estate of the deceased.

Cooke J considered this issue and observed:[70]

> Any Court will be slow to impute to the client an intention that, to the prejudice of the plaintiff, instructions in favour of the plaintiff should be treated as confidential. And in the converse case, where evidence of the instructions would tell against the plaintiff's claim it may well be equally difficult to persuade a Court that the client's interests require the instructions to be kept secret.

Without deciding the matter His Honour seemed to suggest that, at least in respect of deceased clients, consent to the disclosure of information regarding a claim against the lawyer by a third party should be assumed.[71] There is also a case for permitting disclosure where the client is alive, even against the client's consent. Without such information it may be impossible for a litigant to press, or a lawyer to defend, a claim, and the existence of the confidence would have the effect of enabling justice to be thwarted.[72]

404, 412-415 per Ebsworth J; *Lillicrap v Nalder & Son (a firm)* [1993] 1 WLR 94.

69 [1983] NZLR 37. The more well known case on similar facts is *White v Jones* [1995] 1 All ER 691. See also the comments of Cooke J in *Allied Finance v Hadlow & Co* [1983] NZLR 23, 25.

70 [1983] NZLR 37, 44.

71 This contrasts sharply with *R v Derby Magistrates' Court* [1995] 4 All ER 526 where privilege (rather than confidence) attaching to information was considered to be absolute, even to the extent of facts that would absolve an accused of a murder charge.

72 It would be possible for the Court to make orders ensuring that such information disclosed in Court be kept confidential.

Similarly problematic are cases where the Court as part of its inherent jurisdiction to discipline its officers makes allegations of misconduct against counsel regarding the conduct of a proceeding. In *Tolstoy-Miloslavsky v Aldington*[73] counsel was accused of misconduct in bringing a case that was an abuse of the process of the Court and doomed to fail from the outset. There was no suggestion that in defending the allegation the affairs of the client could be disclosed. In fact, the Court proceeded on the basis that such matters must be kept confidential. The Court took care to point out, when making the order against the legal advisers to pay the costs of the other side, that they had taken into account the fact that they were not permitted to disclose privileged documents or confidential information in mounting their own defence. While the Court must always be aware that the advocate may be unable to "tell the whole story" there does not appear to be any authority for disclosing the information. In such cases the onus to show misconduct is high and in cases of doubt the lawyer is entitled to the benefit of that doubt.[74]

Similarly difficult is the case where a client makes allegations in the media against the former lawyers. If the claims are unfounded the duty of confidence will preclude the lawyers defending their reputation by disclosing the truth if to do so would require a disclosure of confidential information. There is some authority that if a lawyer were to pursue a case in defamation against the former client disclosure would be permitted.[75] However, in the absence of such proceedings it seems that the lawyer must maintain a dignified silence.[76]

8.8 Mandatory disclosure

8.8.1 *Introduction*

In all of the above instances the lawyer is permitted, or to put it another way, is at liberty, to disclose information confidential to the client. In many of the cases where such a liberty exists there are strong reasons why such information should be disclosed, particularly where disclosure is in the public interest. The tendency of lawyers is to act conservatively and refrain from disclosure. In keeping with the tradition of the common law, there are relatively few instances where a positive duty to

73 [1996] 1 WLR 736 (CA).

74 See also *Ridehalgh v Horsefield* [1994] Ch 205, 236 (CA).

75 First, by analogy with the liberty of a practitioner to disclose to enforce legal rights to costs, and secondly, by analogy with the opinion of Cooke J in *Gartside v Sheffield Young and Ellis* [1983] NZLR 37, 44.

76 See r 6.3 Professional Conduct Rules (WA) and *Solicitors Handbook* (Qld), para 4.02.1

disclose exists and many of those are recent incursions into the duty imposed by statute.[77]

8.8.2 *Statutory disclosures*

Any duty of confidentiality is subject to the express requirements of the law to disclose.[78] While there are numerous statutory provisions, which require the disclosure of information to authorities, the instances in which a lawyer is actually required to disclose confidential information are relatively few. The provisions of the Financial Transactions Reporting Act 1996 require "financial institutions" (which includes lawyers[79]) to take certain steps in respect of the financial transactions of their clients. This includes verifying the identity of their clients and, most importantly reporting transactions where: [80]

(a) Any person conducts or seeks to conduct any transaction through a financial institution (whether or not the transaction or proposed transaction involves cash); and

(b) The financial institution has reasonable grounds to suspect
 (i) That the transaction or proposed transaction is or may be relevant to the investigation or prosecution of any person for a money laundering offence; or
 (ii) That the transaction or proposed transaction is or may be relevant to the enforcement of the Proceeds of Crime Act 1991.

Privileged communications are protected under s 19 of the Act.

There are also numerous search and seizure powers of various authorities.[81] Where a search is conducted under such an authority the lawyer will be obliged to allow the authorised officers access to confidential information. The same does not apply to privileged

---

77 Where the lawyer is at liberty to disclose information and fails to do so where harm is caused to some third party who is in a relationship of proximity to the lawyer, it is possible that a tort claim would exist for negligent non-disclosure. This argument is made in K Wheat, "Lawyers, Confidentiality and Public and Private Interests" (1998) 1 Legal Ethics 184, 187 and is founded in normal tort principles: *White v Jones* [1995] 1 All ER 691; *Caparo Industries v Dickman* [1990] 2 AC 605.

78 *Tournier v National Provincial and Union Bank of England* [1924] 1 KB 461.

79 Section 3(1)(l) provides that a financial institution includes:

> A lawyer, but only to the extent that the lawyer receives funds in the course of that person's business
> (i) For the purposes of deposit or investment; or
> (ii) For the purpose of settling real estate transactions:

80 Section 15.

81 For example, s 198 Summary Proceedings Act 1957, s 25(1) Indecent Publications Act 1963, s 7(1)(d) Continental Shelf Act 1964, s 18 Misuse of Drugs Act 1975. s 117 Gaming and Lotteries Act 1977, ss 36 and 37 Massage Parlours Act 1978, s 217 Customs Act 1966.

information which, once privilege is established, is absolutely protected from disclosure.[82] Where a warrant is issued it must be clear that it excludes privileged documents. Unless the legislature makes it absolutely clear that the privilege of the client is extinguished the Court will presume it to continue.[83]

Similar powers and limitations in respect of privileged documents will exist in respect of the powers under s 17 of the Tax Administration Act 1994 which gives wide powers to the Commissioner of Inland Revenue to inspect and copy records and require information to be furnished.

8.8.3 *Law society inspections*

Lawyers are subject to rigorous supervision by the law society. To ensure that such supervision is effective the society has the power to inspect and investigate the affairs of lawyers.[84] Such inspections necessarily require the disclosure of the affairs of clients, but are justified on the basis that such inspections are in the client's best interests to protect against dishonest or incompetent advisers. Further, the harm from the disclosure is minimal as the information disclosed will remain confidential and in most circumstances go no further than the inspecting officers.[85] In such cases the disclosure is effectively required by law and, therefore, displaces the duty of confidence usually owed by a lawyer.[86]

8.8.4 *Whistle blowing*

Where one member of a firm becomes aware that another member is guilty of serious misconduct there is an obligation to report the matter to the law society.[87] This may involve disclosing the affairs of clients, which are otherwise confidential, to the society. The disclosure is a limited one and the society will be expected to preserve client confidences as far as possible.[88] If a lawyer who is guilty of misconduct in respect of a client's affairs seeks professional advice from another lawyer then those disclosures are confidential and privileged. The second lawyer will be required to keep secret the details of the first lawyer's wrongdoing.

---

82 *Rosenberg v Jaine* [1983] NZLR 1.

83 *Rosenberg v Jaine* [1983] NZLR 1, 8 per Davison CJ; *CIR v West-Walker* [1954] NZLR 191.

84 Regulations 10-14 Solicitors Trust Account Regulations 1998. See also s 35A Evidence Amendment Act (No) 1980

85 Regulation 14 Solicitors Trust Account Regulations 1998. Disclosure is permitted where required by law for the purposes of an investigation by the Council of the District Society or other limited circumstances.

86 *Parry Jones v Law Society* [1969] 1 Ch 1.

87 Rule 6.03.

88 See also *Woolgar v Chief Constable of Sussex Police* [1999] 3 All ER 604 (CA) in respect of the public policy justifications for reporting member misconduct to professional bodies in breach of confidences.

8.8.5 *Proposed commission of crime*

Disclosure of confidential information is not compulsory in all situations where a client has disclosed the intention to commit a crime (or it is clear to the lawyer that such an intention exists). However, where the "anticipated crime is one involving the possibility of physical injury to another person, disclosure is mandatory".[89] The commentary to the rule suggests that in such cases disclosure should be made to the police or in cases of extreme urgency to the intended victim of the crime.

The rule creates some inconsistency. It creates a distinction between crimes involving personal injury and those involving wrongs of another kind. A seriously intended declaration by a client that the client is going to punch someone in the face must be disclosed, but there is no such compulsion if the client intends to commit an arguably more serious wrong and burn down somebody's house. It is suggested that the rule should also be read liberally so that crimes of kidnapping or other violations of the person, although they involve no injury, should be considered as those which a lawyer is compelled to disclose.

It is also arguable that wherever the course of action disclosed to the lawyer is likely to result in harm to persons a mandatory duty of disclosure ought to exist. It is possible that actions (or omissions) which are not criminal could lead to real harm. Take the famous case of the Ford Motor Company's Pinto cars. The company chose not to recall defective Pinto cars in the knowledge that the defect would cause considerable loss of life. That decision was made on the basis that it would cost the company less to pay damages to the victims of the inevitable accidents than to modify the numerous cars already sold. If in such a case a lawyer was aware that by their dubiously legal tactics life would be lost there is a strong argument that an obligation to speak out should exist.[90] Similar difficulties exist in some family situations. Problems may arise where a parent seeks advice on how to thwart Court orders by illegally removing a child from a parent who has been granted custody. In such a case, there is a strong argument that the client's

---

89 Rule 1.08(iv). Compare r 1.6(b)(1) ABA Model Rules which provides that disclosure is only permitted where the proposed crime is one "likely to result in imminent death or substantial bodily harm" — and even then disclosure is discretionary rather than mandatory.

90 In that case Ford was acquitted of reckless homicide (manslaughter). See D Luban in *Lawyers and Justice: An Ethical Study* Princeton, New Jersey, Princeton University Press, 1988, 207-209; F Cullen, W Maakestad, G Cavendar *Corporate Crime Under Attack: The Ford Pinto Case and Beyond* Cincinnati, Anderson, 1987. See also the example of the fairground owner who is running dangerous rides in M Brindle and G Dehn, "Confidence, Public Interest, and the Lawyer" in R Cranston *Legal Ethics and Professional Responsibility* Oxford, Clarendon Press, 1995, 122.

wishes and interests should be overridden to protect the interest of the children, and prevent a breach of the law.

8.9 Advocates' dilemmas: client untruths

The difficulties in keeping client confidences are particularly acute for the advocate. Decisions which may be made after consideration and reflection in a lawyer's office may have to be made immediately in the Courtroom. Much will rest on the decision of the advocate. Disclosure by the advocate of confidential information may cause considerable procedural difficulties, as it may be necessary to retain alternative counsel. Alternatively, remaining silent in the face of a client untruth will amount to assisting the client in the perpetration of an injustice.

To remain silent in Court when the client is lying (and, therefore, committing perjury), distorting the truth, or concealing facts, is to mislead the Court, and a breach of the most fundamental duty of the advocate.[91] To continue the case where the client is actively misleading the Court would amount to assisting the client in such an endeavour and is anathema to all that the legal profession stands for. The alternative of the advocate withdrawing services from the client seems equally problematic. Not only does this leave the client without assistance at the most difficult of times, but it also sends to the Court and the opposing litigant a message that something significant is awry.

A problem of this kind arose in *Vernon v Bosley (No 2)*.[92] The plaintiff was suing for nervous shock and psychiatric injury following the witnessing of a motor accident and unsuccessful rescue attempts involving his two daughters and their nanny. The evidence of certain experts was that the plaintiff's mental health had deteriorated significantly as a result of the accident and there was no immediate sign of improvement. The trial concluded and the Court found in favour of the plaintiff. The plaintiff was also taking certain family proceedings regarding the care of the children. In those proceedings expert medical evidence was given that the plaintiff's mental health had dramatically improved. This latter information was known to counsel prior to the judgment (but after the close of trial) in the civil matter, but it was not disclosed to the Judge, nor was it disclosed to the Court in a subsequent appeal.

The case discusses two important matters: the duty of an advocate to ensure that the Court is not misled by the evidence of the client, and the steps to be taken in the event that the client refuses to correct a misapprehension of the Court when later evidence shows a former claim to have been unfounded. The difficulty of the problem is reflected in the

91 Rule 8.01.
92 [1997] 1 All ER 614, [1999] QB 18.

fact that of the three Judges one dissented[93] and the other two, while finding a breach to have occurred, disagreed on what steps counsel in the case ought to have taken. The problem is particularly acute in light of the adversarial system of litigation. At the heart of that system is an assumption that it is not incumbent on a litigant to disclose evidence that weakens the case. The respective sides are expected to present the best case possible and attempt to adduce evidence to weaken that of their opponent.[94] It is clear that there can be no duty of absolute candour to the Court. In this matter, at least, all three of the Judges in *Vernon v Bosley* agreed.

The common law has a long history of distinguishing between act and omission. It is not surprising that the Courts have consistently upheld the silence of advocates where the Courts are labouring under some misapprehension or mistake known to the advocate:[95]

> A barrister must not wilfully mislead the Court as to the law nor may he actively mislead the Court as to the facts; although consistently with the rule that the prosecution must prove its case, he may passively stand by and watch the Court being misled by reason of its failure to ascertain facts that are within the barrister's knowledge.

While some philosophers may have difficulty with the distinction between idly standing by while the Court makes a mistaken assumption as to facts, and actively misleading the Court, lawyers are adept at discriminating between the two.

Both Stuart-Smith and Thorpe LJJ agreed in *Vernon v Bosley* that where it becomes apparent to counsel that evidence adduced on behalf of the party they represent is inaccurate they should seek to undeceive the Court. Ideally, on seeking an adjournment and advising the client of the situation, the client's consent to the disclosure to the Court would be obtained, and the trial could proceed normally. However, problems arise where the client refuses to consent to the disclosure of such information to the Court. Smith LJ was of the view that where the client refuses to accept the advice to disclose the lawyer remains bound by the duty of confidence. Being stranded between a duty to the Court and a duty to the client the only option left is to withdraw from the case completely.[96] It was observed that this would amount to a kind of de facto disclosure

93 Evans LJ concluded that on the evidence the Court had not been misled, and therefore there had been no duty to disclose any changed facts to the Courts: [1997] 1 All ER 614, 642, [1999] QB 18, 54.

94 *Tombling v Universal Bulb Co* [1951] 2 TLR 289, 297 per Denning LJ.

95 *Saif Ali v Sydney Mitchell & Co (a firm)* [1980] AC 198, 220 per Diplock LJ.

96 [1997] 1 All ER 614, 631, [1999] QB 18, 39.

as it was almost inevitable that the other side or the Court would have "smelt a rat", in the words of Stuart Smith LJ.

On the basis that such withdrawal is tantamount to disclosure the approach of Thorpe LJ seems more sensible. His Honour held that:[97]

> In such circumstances counsel has a duty to disclose the relevant material to his opponent and, unless there be agreement between the parties otherwise, to the Judge.

Such an approach avoids speculation as to the motivation behind counsel's decision to withdraw, and enforces the obligation on the client to refrain from misleading the Court. The mere withdrawing from a case is an ineffectual compromise that only serves the purpose of extricating the advocate from a difficult ethical problem. There is a risk that when the client retains a new advocate the client will simply conceal the truth from the new advocate thereby perpetuating the untruth that the Court labours under. If the ends of justice are to be achieved, and the client refuses to cooperate, it is justifiable to require an advocate to disclose the true state of affairs to the tribunal which has been misled.

8.9.1 *Duty to inform the client of disclosures of confidences*[98]
The fact that the duty of confidence to the client is to be breached is a matter that is material to the client and in most cases ought to be disclosed to the client.[99] In the facts of *Vernon v Bosley* discussed above, the lawyer is expected to encourage the client to disclose the information before any breach of confidence should be contemplated by the lawyer. It is but a small step to inform the client that in the absence of the client's consent, the lawyer feels compelled to breach confidence. Similarly, where there is an order or warrant to deliver information to an authority, the lawyer ought to inform the client of the order and the lawyer's intention to comply.

Such disclosure is also appropriate on procedural grounds. Informing the client prior to the actual breach, gives the client an opportunity to object and seek the intervention of the Court. The lawyer's judgment may be ill-founded, and on hearing of the matter a Court will injunct the lawyer from breaching the confidence. If the confidence is breached first, there is frequently no meaningful remedy that can be granted if it is later shown that the breach was wrongful.[100]

---

97 [1997] 1 All ER 614, 654, [1999] QB 18, 64.
98 On the duty to disclose generally see ch 10.
99 Rule 1.09.
100 *Russell McVeagh McKenzie Bartleet & Co v Tower Corporation* [1998] 3 NZLR 641.

There are exceptions to this. Some disclosures are mundane, such as those incident on the routine inspections of the law society, or made in the course of completing the work with other members of the firm or agents. Where the client has consented to the disclosure in general terms there is no breach of the duty and no disclosure need be made. In other cases the very purpose of the breach of confidence would be defeated if the client was informed of it. For example, s 20 of the Financial Transactions Reporting Act 1996 prohibits disclosure of the fact that a report has been made of a suspicious transaction under that Act. The report is required to assist in the detection of crime, and to inform the client of the report would simply be to alert them to the likelihood of an investigation. By analogy, where the breach is a report of a continuing fraud by the client, or similar criminal activity, it would be inappropriate to disclose the breach to the client.

Where the disclosure of the breach of confidence would exacerbate the very problem that the breach sought to alleviate, disclosure will be excused. Where the lawyer reports violent intentions of a client to the police, to disclose this to the client may well have the effect of endangering both the intended victim and the lawyer. Similarly, where suspicions of child abuse have been reported it may well be in the child client's best interests not to disclose the report, at least until the suspicions have been confirmed or allayed.

Chapter 9

Protecting Confidences of Former Clients

9.1 The problem of subsequent retainers

9.1.1 *Introduction*

In practice, honouring the duty of confidence raises few problems throughout the period of the retainer. It is not common for clients to confess crime outright or to be the perpetrators of frauds, or for any of the other situations to arise where breach of confidence is justified. Lawyers most frequently find the duty of confidence problematic when the retainer has come to an end but the duty to keep confidences (and the consequent duty not to inadvertently use or to take risks with confidential information) continues. Problems arise, in particular, where later in time a different client seeks the services of a lawyer, but the affairs of a former client are of relevance to the affairs of the later client.

Perhaps the smallest risk in such a situation is that the lawyer will intentionally use the information that is confidential to the former client for the benefit of the later client. Such an action would be a flagrant breach of the duties owed to the former client. While the possibility of such actions by unscrupulous lawyers must not be discounted, actual incidence appears rare. More likely is the possibility that the lawyer will use the knowledge of the affairs of the former client unwittingly or subconsciously in assisting the later client. A further risk exists where the later client is using the same firm as the former client, but a different lawyer. In such cases there is a chance that the lawyers will have exchanged information about their respective clients, possibly on an informal basis, and the second lawyer will use the confidential information so gained for the benefit of the second client. A final possible situation where a client's information appears at risk is where a lawyer who acted for one client moves to a firm which is acting for a second client to whom the information regarding the affairs of the first client would be of relevance.[1] In such a case the transferring lawyer takes

1 Or when entire firms merge. See R Ramage, "Conflicts of Interest on the Merger of Two Firms of Solicitors" (1997) NLJ 147, also *Supasave Retail Ltd v Coward Chance* [1991] 1 All ER 668; *Re a Firm of Solicitors* [1995] 3 All ER 482.

with him or her the confidential information of the previous firm. There is a danger that the new lawyer will reveal confidential information to his or her new colleagues who may use it for the benefit of the second client. However, probably the greatest risk in all such situations is that the original client will perceive the situation as being improper. While there may be no actual use or disclosure of the original client's confidential information, that client may well view the situation with scepticism. Such an appearance of impropriety should be avoided, if at all possible.

9.1.2 *Ethical prohibition on risking client confidences*

The lawyer's obligation goes beyond simply refraining from telling client's secrets, and extends to avoiding any risk that the information will be inadvertently disclosed, and refraining from using the information other than for the purpose for which it was revealed or acquired. Where one of the situations described above gives rise to such a risk the lawyer or firm must refuse to act for the new client. This is set out in r 1.05:

> A practitioner must not act for a client against a former client of the practitioner when through prior knowledge of the former client or of his or her affairs which may be relevant to the matter, to so act would be or would have the potential to be to the detriment of the former client or could reasonably be expected to be objectionable to the former client.

A lawyer who holds confidential information of one client is absolutely prohibited from acting for a second client where that information would be relevant. In particular, if detriment would flow to the former client if the information were disclosed to the second client the lawyer may not act. Any suggestion that a lawyer could compartmentalise information within his or her mind and not subconsciously use it for, or disclose it to, a later client is to be rejected.[2] The lawyer is disqualified from acting for the new client where there is a real possibility of the misuse of the confidential information of the former client or in circumstances to which the client "could be reasonably expected to object in terms of the rule".[3] The test is not whether the client does in fact object, as there will be instances where the client objects without grounds. The test is that of a reasonable client and, therefore, an objective one.[4] The rule has generally been considered absolute. It was justified by reference to the

---

2 *Black v Taylor* [1993] 3 NZLR 403, 408 per Richardson J, 417 per McKay J.

3 *Equiticorp Holdings Ltd v Hawkins* [1993] 3 NZLR 737; *MacDonald Estate v Martin* (1990) 77 DLR (4th) 249, 257, 266. *Mallesons Stephen Jaques v KPMG Peat Marwick* (1990) WAR 357; *Carindale Country Club Pty v Astill* (1993) 115 ALR 112.

4 *Black v NZ Disciplinary Tribunal* (CA 201/98, 14 May 1999); *Equiticorp Holdings Ltd v Hawkins* [1993] 2 NZLR 737.

need to protect both the confidential information and ensure that the reputation of the profession was upheld in the eyes of the public.[5]

The same principles will be applicable where a different lawyer in the same firm seeks to act for the second client. There is a ready inference that confidential information is shared by all of the members of a firm. Therefore, in most cases all of the members of the firm are prohibited from acting where the confidential information of a former client of one member of the firm is relevant to the affairs of a subsequent client. The only exception to this is where there are circumstances that show that information is not shared between members of the firm and there is no risk of the confidential information being leaked (that is, an effective Chinese wall). In the event that a former client gives his or her informed consent to the former adviser acting for the adversary no issue arises. It is always open to a client to consent to the disclosure of confidential information. It is also possible for the former client to agree that a risk of inadvertent disclosure be taken. Where a litigant is aware that his or her former adviser is representing the adversary any objection is expected to be made at an early opportunity if it is to be made at all. In the absence of such an early objection, it may be assumed that there is either an implied consent, or that the objection is being inappropriately "held in reserve".[6]

This approach has far-reaching consequences for the practice of law. Many small communities have few lawyers. It is more common in such communities for clients to develop close ties with professional advisers and regard a particular lawyer as "theirs". When a dispute arises in such communities it is frequently the case that both clients have the same lawyer. The duty to protect the confidences of both clients will usually mean that the lawyer is precluded from acting for either client who must look further afield for assistance. At the opposite end of the spectrum are large corporate clients who utilise specialised commercial services. Relatively few firms undertake international and large corporate work. The paucity of firms that have the resources and infrastructure to mount very large litigation cases, or assist on large company floats and the like means that most of such work is spread across five or six firms. The difficulties of protecting confidences in such situations is compounded by the fact that such clients are more frequently changing their legal advisers, or going to different advisers simultaneously for different services.

---

5 See J Midgeley, "Confidentiality, Conflicts of Interest and Chinese Walls" (1992) MLR 822.

6 *In the Marriage of B J McGillivray and P K Mitchell* (1990) 23 FLR 238.

9.2 The legal protection of professional confidences in New Zealand

In most areas of professional conduct the law and the ethical rules governing the conduct of lawyers mirror each other closely. However, there has recently been a divergence in respect of the rules governing the protection of client confidences. In *Russell McVeagh McKenzie Bartleet & Co v Tower Corporation*[7] the Court of Appeal adopted a test which appears to make it more difficult to show that confidential information is unacceptably being put at risk. The test has moved away from looking to potential detriment and the perceptions of a reasonable client, to a balancing of interests.

9.2.1 Russell McVeagh McKenzie Bartleet & Co v Tower Corporation

In the *Tower* case Tower Corporation, the large investment, insurance, and superannuation company, had retained Russell McVeagh in respect of a tax dispute concerning some $40m. That dispute was finally concluded in April 1997. Prior to that matter being settled, a merchant bank (acting for the then undisclosed Guinness Peat Group) sought to retain Russell McVeagh in respect of a proposal to aggressively takeover Tower Corporation. Members of Russell McVeagh formed the view that there was no reason why they should not accept the instructions. This was notwithstanding the fact that it was almost certain at the time (and transpired to be the case) that the takeover was likely to be strongly opposed by Tower Corporation.

Russell McVeagh did not disclose to Tower the fact that they were considering taking instructions in respect of such a takeover (and thereby almost certainly breaching their professional and fiduciary duty to disclose all relevant matters).[8] The decision to proceed to act for Guinness Peat Group was made by Russell McVeagh, and ultimately by a partner who was to be conducting the takeover work. Tower Corporation discovered the conflicting instructions at a meeting in September 1997 (after the conclusion of the taxation matter) when Guinness Peat Group put the takeover proposal to Tower. Tower was surprised to find members of Russell McVeagh representing Guinness Peat Group. Tower objected by letter to the existence of the conflict and filed proceedings seeking to disbar Russell McVeagh from representing Guinness Peat Group further. On Tower objecting to the Guinness Peat

7 [1998] 3 NZLR 641. For further discussion see D Webb, "Clients' Secrets and Secret Clients: Conflicts Confidentiality and Disclosure in the Court of Appeal" (1998) 5 NZBLQ 91; also R Tobin, "Former Clients and Chinese Walls: *Russell McVeagh v Tower* and *Prince Jefri Bolkiah v KPMG*" [1999] NZ Law Rev 305.

8 Rule 1.09.

retainer, Russell McVeagh put in place restrictions to limit the likelihood of the flow of confidential information between the solicitors concerned — the so called "Chinese wall".

Initially the problem was one of conflict of interest as Russell McVeagh was acting simultaneously for two parties with divergent interests. However, by the time Tower brought an application to prevent Russell McVeagh from acting further, the Tower taxation retainer was at an end and the sole question was whether it was necessary to disqualify Russell McVeagh from acting further for Guinness Peat to protect the information confidential to Tower.

This case is illustrative of a number of issues. One is that the question of whether it was appropriate to act was not referred to the firm's ethics committee, and that no formal barriers were set up at the outset suggests that the firm did not regard the acceptance of the later instructions as particularly problematic. Additionally, where there are facts that prevent disclosure to the former client of the existence of the subsequent retainer (as there were here) the decision whether or not to accept the later retainer will be made by the very people who will benefit most if it is accepted — the lawyers. In many cases it will ultimately be the lawyer who is to do the work who will decide whether or not to accept the retainer. In the context of modern law firms, particularly large ones, there is considerable pressure to generate a high level of fees, and such pressures may outweigh the more abstract professional considerations in a lawyer's decision.

9.2.2 *The* Russell McVeagh *approach*

In delivering the leading judgment Henry J set out a number stages of inquiry when addressing the issue of whether a firm ought to be disqualified from acting where a former client's confidences are at risk. It does not provide an absolute rule. It is essentially a balancing exercise by which competing interests are satisfied according to the Court's discretion. The Court will disqualify where:

- The lawyer or a member of the firm holds confidential information; and
- The information is sensitive, that is to say, of a nature such that its disclosure would adversely affect the client; and
- The lawyer or a member of the firm continues to act for the client with whom a conflict exists and there is a real or appreciable risk that the information would be disclosed.

- In considering whether to disqualify the Court should take into account relevant considerations which will include:
  - The value of litigants being able to avail themselves of their counsel of first choice; and
  - The "right of the solicitor to offer his or her services to the public generally"; and
  - The ability of lawyers holding confidential information to move between firms; and
  - The value of competition within the profession and access to specialist advice.

It was held that on this test Russell McVeagh were not disqualified from continuing to act. While confidential information was held, the Court did not consider it to be of a sufficiently sensitive nature. Of relevance to the majority was the fact that the information related to a purportedly narrow area of taxation advice. It was considered that in light of the nature of the information, the risk of disclosure did not warrant disqualification. In assessing the risk of disclosure, the Court took notice of the existence of the Chinese wall erected by Russell McVeagh, the division of the firm itself into distinct teams, the existence of separate offices in Wellington and Auckland, and the fact that the documentary material had been lodged with the High Court. In light of these findings, and the values of the availability of expertise to clients and competition within the profession, it was concluded that disqualification was not appropriate.

9.2.3 *Relevance of nature of information*

The Court made a fundamental distinction between confidential information the disclosure of which would adversely affect the client, and confidential information that, if disclosed, would have no adverse affect on the client. This does seem to reflect the approach in the rules which state that a lawyer should not act where, because of the existence of confidential information, "to so act would be or would have the potential to be to the detriment of the former client or could reasonably be expected to be objectionable to the former client".[9] The approach focuses on the detriment to the former client and largely ignores the fact that disclosure may be objectionable to the client without being detrimental. If such an approach is taken it appears that an intermediate class of information is created: information which is confidential, but does not warrant protection by the Court. As Thomas J noted, this requires an inquiry by the Court into the area of commercial sensitivity of information in which they are not expert. In this case the Court decided that certain information was not commercially useful and therefore if disclosed could not cause detriment to the client — Tower.

---

9 Rule 1.05.

This appears to mean that the Court will not intervene to protect information which, while confidential, is not sensitive. Such an approach seems to tacitly condone the actions of lawyers who risk disclosure of such non-sensitive information. In its inquiry the Court looked for specific information that might be harmful to Tower if released. The argument by Tower that general information about the policies of the company and propensities of senior staff were sensitive was rejected. In doing so the Court distinguished its own approach in *Black v Taylor*[10] where it was held that the knowledge of a client's "weaknesses, fears, and reactions" deserved protection.

9.2.4 *Relevance of professional structure*

The Court of Appeal considered as highly relevant constrictions created by the structure of the profession in New Zealand. The "right to counsel" (which is probably better labelled the value of making counsel of first choice available) is frequently recognised. Representation by counsel of choice is seen as a central value in the operation of the adversarial system of justice. Henry J also mentions access to specialist services, and competition within the profession as matters relevant to the public interest. It may also be rephrased as the ability of firms to offer specialised services in an unfettered market — a matter of as much interest to lawyers as the public generally. Mobility within the profession (that is, the freedom of lawyers to change firms) is clearly beneficial to lawyers, but of only secondary interest to clients. Perhaps the clearest indication of the shift in favour of promoting the interests of lawyers is the statement that the Court should take into account the "right of the solicitor to offer his or her services to the public generally".[11] This represents a departure from the traditional approach that the licence to practise law is a privilege to be exercised subject to the constraints imposed by the Court and the profession.

The claim that such an approach will encourage competition within the profession appears ill-founded. Admittedly, the rule does enable clients to choose more freely which of the few sufficiently specialised lawyers to retain. In the longer term, relaxation of the disqualification rules enables those firms to maintain and strengthen their dominance of the market for such specialised legal services. If lawyers were disqualified from acting in circumstances such as those of the *Russell McVeagh* case, clients would have to look further afield for such services, either to overseas lawyers or to slightly smaller firms. Such an environment would result in the development of more lawyers with sufficient expertise to engage in specialised work.

---

10 [1993] 3 NZLR 403, 406. See also *Owen v Macalpine Industries Ltd* (Employment Court, Auckland AC 51/99, 13 July 1999, Judge Shaw).

11 [1998] 3 NZLR 641 at 658. See most recently *Craddock v Registered Securities Ltd* (CA 11/99, 19 May 1999).

9.2.5 *Narrow retainer*

The majority of the Court considered the fact that the Tower retainer concerned a tax dispute weighed against disqualifying the firm from acting further. The reason was that because the subject-matter of the dispute was narrow the information was less likely to be relevant to the affairs of Guinness Peat. If the information could be of no use whatsoever to the new client clearly disqualification would be inappropriate. The Court of Appeal seemed to distinguish between different kinds of retainer and suggest that the duty of confidence attaching will vary accordingly. There is also a danger of placing too much emphasis on the fact that the subject-matter of a retainer has no substantive commonality with the new instructions. As Thomas J noted, taxation matters (and arguably any significant legal issue) "can rarely be resolved in isolation".[12]

9.2.6 *The movement of information within a firm*

There are very few cases where one lawyer will seek to act for a client whose interests are directly opposed to those of his or her own former client. More frequent will be the case where a different lawyer in the same firm will seek to act for a client who might benefit from a breach of confidence. While it cannot be said that each lawyer knows all the information of every other lawyer in a firm, it is clear that there is a relatively free flow of information about clients' affairs between members of a firm. In many of the earlier authorities the Court has presumed (either rebuttably or irrebuttably) that information will flow between members of a law firm.[13] In *Russell McVeagh* Henry J rejected this approach stating that where confidential information exists there is no presumption of any kind that the confidence will be shared with other members of the firm. Rather, where there is possession of relevant information, in the absence of negating evidence of protection the Court will "readily infer there is a risk of disclosure".[14] This seems to come very close to stating that once it is shown that confidential information is held by one member of the firm, in the absence of evidence showing that the information will not be shared, the Court will order disqualification.[15]

12 [1998] 3 NZLR 641, 658, 658.

13 *Equiticorp Holdings Ltd v Hawkins* [1993] 2 NZLR 737; *MacDonald Estate v Martin* (1991) DLR (4th) 249; *Carindale Country Club Pty Ltd v Astill* (1993) 115 ALR; *In Re a Firm of Solicitors* [1997] Ch 1, [1995] 3 All ER 482

14 [1998] 3 NZLR 642, 652.

15 Blanchard J makes a similar analysis at p 677 of his judgment where he states that the Court will tend to favour the view of the client and view the situation "objectively but cautiously".

The House of Lords in *Prince Jefri Bolkiah v KPMG (a firm)*[16] took a similar approach. There the suggestion that there was a presumption that confidences would be disclosed to subsequent clients or to other members of a firm was firmly rejected. Whether information will move between members of a firm was considered to be a matter of fact, although once it can be shown that relevant information exists in the hands of the adviser "the starting point must be that, unless special measures are taken, information moves within a firm".[17] The consequence of this approach is that where one member of a firm holds confidential information of a sensitive nature about the affairs of a former client then, in the absence of evidence which shows that the information will not move (and has not moved) within the firm, all the members of the firm will be disqualified from acting for a later client who might benefit from that information.

9.2.7 *Appearance of propriety*

One of the central reasons for disqualifying lawyers who have access to confidential information has been not only to protect the information, but also to ensure that such information was seen to be protected.[18] This ensures that the public can be sure that the confidences they reposed in their lawyers are safe. However in *Russell McVeagh* Henry J rejected as a relevant factor the client's perceptions of the lawyer's actions, or the perception of the public of the legal profession generally. Indeed at one point he stated that "possible difficulties perceived by the public" is not an acceptable standard.[19] Internationally, the jurisprudence concerning the incidents of the fiduciary relationship between lawyer and client, and the nature of the duty of confidentiality have stressed the confidence of the public in the relationship between lawyer and client, and the appearance of the due administration of justice, to be of central importance.[20]

There are obvious reasons why the integrity of confidences between lawyer and client must not only be protected but also be perceived by members of the public as one in which confidences are kept. Without both the protection of such confidences, and the appreciation by the public that such confidences are protected, clients will be unable to instruct their lawyers in an environment in which full and frank

16 [1999] 2 WLR 215.

17 [1999] 2 WLR 215, 227.

18 *Black v Taylor* [1993] 3 NZLR 403.

19 [1998] 3 NZLR 642 at 651. Compare *R v Dam* [1997] Crim LR 46.

20 *MacDonald Estate v Martin* (1990) 77 DLR (4th) 249 at 254 per Sopinka J; *Carindale Country Club Pty v Astill* (1993) 115 ALR 112 per Drummond J. See also the approach of the New Zealand Court of Appeal in *Black v Taylor* [1993] 3 NZLR 403; also *Owen v Macalpine Industries Ltd* (Employment Court, Auckland AC 51/99, 13 July 1999, Judge Shaw).

disclosure is possible. The need for clients to be sure that their confidences are kept and are not put at risk is obvious. If the only reassurance that the client has is the lawyer's undertaking to adhere to certain protocols, it is unlikely that that client will be persuaded that the confidence has been kept. A feeling of betrayal is particularly likely where the client is the unsuccessful party to an action in which the former lawyer now represents the adversary.

9.3 English criticism of the New Zealand approach: the *Bolkiah* case

The House of Lords considered the question of the protection of confidences in *Prince Jefri Bolkiah v KPMG (a firm)*[21] shortly after the decision in the *Tower* case. *Bolkiah* contains an express disapproval of the approach of the New Zealand Court of Appeal: [22]

> I would also reject the approach taken by the New Zealand Court of Appeal in *Russell McVeagh McKenzie Bartleet v Tower Corporation* and adopted by the Court of Appeal in the present case. In my opinion the balancing exercise which was undertaken was inappropriate.

This demonstrated a refusal to balance the interests of solicitors against those of their clients. Lord Millett emphasised the importance of the absolute protection of confidential information, as well as the proper administration of justice, and the appearance of propriety within the legal profession.

9.3.1 *The facts*

The *Bolkiah* case arose from the fact that Prince Bolkiah (brother to the Sultan of Brunei), was the Minister of Finance for Brunei and managed the funds of the Brunei government through the Brunei Investment Agency (BIA). The Prince fell under suspicion of defalcations from those funds which resulted in the Brunei Government deciding to investigate. Since the fund's establishment, KPMG had been the auditors for BIA, as well as undertaking associated tasks. While he was Minister of Finance a company controlled by the Prince retained the services of KPMG in respect of a major piece of personal litigation which involved the forensic accounting department of the firm.[23] This resulted in KPMG acquiring considerable sensitive information in relation to the affairs of the Prince. Difficulties, however, arose when the

21 [1999] 2 WLR 215.
22 [1999] 2 WLR 215, 227 per Lord Millett.
23 Although the case concerned the work of accountants the House of Lords was clear in stating that the principles of confidence applicable were identical to those applicable to lawyers.

Prince fell from favour and the affairs of BIA were investigated by KPMG on the instructions of the Sultan. That investigation was clearly opposed to the interests of Prince Bolkiah. Moreover, the information given to and obtained by KPMG's forensic team when they were working for the Prince's interests was now of direct relevance to the investigation of BIA by KPMG.

9.3.2 *The House of Lords' strict approach*

In deciding that an injunction should be granted to prevent KPMG from acting further for the Sultan of Brunei the House of Lords not only rejected the New Zealand approach (which the English Court of Appeal had adopted) but also rejected earlier authorities of the English Courts[24] in imposing a strict test. In the House of Lords, Lord Millett emphasised the importance of the absolute protection of confidential information, as well as the publicly evident proper administration of justice and the appearance of propriety within the legal profession. The Court's intervention was predicated on the possession of confidential information by the former adviser, and the need for the Court to take steps to protect that information. This approach is based on the fact that in the case of successive retainers the fiduciary relationship which had subsisted between the parties is at an end and the solicitor has no continuing duty of loyalty to the former client. The only duty which survives is the duty to hold in confidence all information imparted during the subsistence of the relationship. It was on this basis that Lord Millett stated:[25]

> [I]t is incumbent on a plaintiff who seeks to restrain his former solicitor from acting in a matter for another client to establish (i) that the solicitor is in possession of information which is confidential to him and to the disclosure of which he has not consented and (ii) that the information is or may be relevant to the new matter in which the interest of the other client is or may be adverse to his own. Although the burden of proof is on the plaintiff, it is not a heavy one. The former may readily be inferred; the latter will often be obvious.

Lord Millett rejected the formulations which seek to identify a level of risk of disclosure as "real", "appreciable", "possible", or "probable". His Lordship preferred to say:[26]

> The Court should intervene unless it is satisfied that there is no risk of disclosure. It goes without saying that the risk must be a real one, and not merely fanciful or theoretical. But it need not be substantial.

24 In particular the foundation authority of *Rakusen v Ellis, Munday and Clarke* [1912] 1 Ch 831 was overruled.

25 [1999] 2 WLR 215, 225.

26 [1999] 2 WLR 215, 226.

The test set out in *Bolkiah* is that:[27]

> No solicitor should, without the consent of his former client, accept instructions unless, viewed objectively, his doing so will not increase the risk that information which is confidential to the former client may come into the possession of a party with an adverse interest.

In basing the decision firmly on the protection of client confidences the House of Lords rejected other approaches which entitled a lawyer to take risks with the client's information. Any such approach was rejected because:[28]

> It imposes an unfair burden on the former client, exposes him to a potential and avoidable risk to which he has not consented, and fails to give him a sufficient assurance that his confidence will be respected. It also exposes the solicitor to a degree of uncertainty that could inhibit him in his dealings with the second client when he cannot be sure that he has correctly identified the source of his information. It is in any case difficult to discern any justification in principle for a rule which exposes a former client without his consent to any avoidable risk, however slight, that information which he has imparted in confidence in the course of a fiduciary relationship may come into the possession of a third party and be used to his disadvantage.

The division of opinion between the House of Lords and the New Zealand Court of Appeal does cause a degree of uncertainty. While the *Russell McVeagh* approach must be regarded as the law in New Zealand it is quite possible that if a case on similar facts were to be taken to the Privy Council the *Bolkiah* approach would be preferred.

9.4 Lawyers changing firms

Conceptually identical problems arise when lawyers move between firms, either where lawyers seek to change from one firm to another or where entire firms merge. It is readily inferred that the lawyers will take with them all of the confidential information held by the firm they leave and bring it to the firm they join. Similarly, when two firms amalgamate it will be readily inferred that all members of the new firm are possessed of all of the confidential information of both of the former firms.[29] This can raise considerable problems, particularly as it will not always be immediately apparent to any of the parties exactly what information the transferring lawyer will be presumed to have. Lawyers who move between firms have been said to "infect" firms with the information they

---

27 [1999] 2 WLR 215, 227.

28 [1999] 2 WLR 215, 226.

29 *Equiticorp Holdings Ltd v Hawkins* [1993] 3 NZLR 737.

bring and have been dubbed "typhoid Marys".[30] Even where the new lawyer is relatively junior they may disqualify the new firm from acting against the interests of one of the clients of the former firm.[31]

9.5 Chinese walls

Whatever test is adopted to determine whether a lawyer should be disqualified from acting due to the risk that confidential information might be disclosed, a central aspect of the test is the degree of risk to which the information is exposed. While the English approach tolerates no risk, the New Zealand approach balances the level of risk against a number of other interests. If a system can be set up within a firm which eliminates (on the strict approach) or reduces (on the balancing approach) the risk of the information being disclosed, this will be relevant to whether a lawyer in the firm can act against the interests of the former client. If the risk that information might be disclosed can be reduced or eliminated, it will be possible to act despite the fact that another member of the firm is in possession of information which if disclosed would be damaging to a former client. Methods by which the risk of disclosure might be minimised have been dubbed Chinese walls.[32]

9.5.1 *Nature of Chinese walls*

An exhaustive definition or description of a Chinese wall is impossible. It is a term used to label any steps taken in an effort to minimise or eliminate the flow of information within a firm, particularly to protect against disclosure of confidential information.[33] It will usually involve procedural barriers to the flow of information such as prohibiting staff from entering certain offices, and implementing rules regarding discussion of the work involved. Physical barriers such as locking files away, securing offices, or even working in separate buildings may also be put in place.[34]

A particularly rigorous Chinese wall (though ultimately not accepted as effective) was implemented in *Prince Jefri Bolkiah v KPMG (a firm)*.[35] The

30 See D Coull, "Typhoid Marys: The Ethical Dilemma of Lawyers Who Switch Firms" (1998) 28 VUWLR 41.

31 *MacDonald Estate v Martin* (1990) 77 DLR (4th) 249, 257, 266.

32 "Cone of silence" is also a term sometimes used where the intended effect is the isolation of information held by one member of a firm rather than the separation of large parts of the firm.

33 See further R Tobin, "Former Clients and Chinese Walls: *Russell McVeagh v Tower* and *Prince Jefri Bolkiah v KPMG*" [1999] NZ Law Rev 305.

34 R Tobin, "Former Clients and Chinese Walls: *Russell McVeagh v Tower* and *Prince Jefri Bolkiah v KPMG*" [1999] NZ Law Rev 305, 306.

35 [1999] 2 WLR 215.

steps taken by KPMG to ensure that there was no leakage of information included:

- The firm's solicitors interviewing all prospective members of the project team and requiring affidavits to be sworn deposing that no confidential information was held;
- The establishment of a separate and secure room for work on the project in a building separate from the rest of the forensic accounting department team;
- Depositing records of and documents relating to the relevant earlier project with the firm's solicitors rendering them inaccessible to the later project team; and
- Removing all earlier electronic records from the computing system and a setting up of a separate computer server for the later project.

That wall was considered ineffective because of the size of the firm involved and the fact that the wall had been erected within the firm out of convenience. It was suggested that an effective wall would be part of the institution of the firm rather than erected on an ad hoc basis. A Chinese wall was also used in the *Russell McVeagh* case, however, the fact that it was put in place well after the later retainer had been accepted meant that it was ineffective as there had already been a considerable period of time in which information was at risk.

9.5.2 *Judicial reaction to the use of Chinese walls*

The New Zealand Court of Appeal in *Russell McVeagh v Tower*, though rejecting the Chinese wall in that case as ineffective, cautiously approved their use in some cases. Because the New Zealand test is a balancing exercise which considers the likelihood of confidential information being disclosed it must take into account any system or structure put in place which reduces that risk.[36] If there is no real risk of disclosure there will be no bar to the firm acting for the new client. Henry J stated:[37]

> Although Chinese walls and cones of silence leave much to be desired, and cannot be allowed to obscure the realities of life and the ordinary behaviour and incidents of relationships where individuals practise together in a firm, internal control measures may nevertheless in some circumstances be both appropriate and sufficient to ensure protection.

This is supported in the concurring judgment of Blanchard J who took the view that a Chinese wall will be evidence to assist the Court finding that a breach of confidence has not occurred and that there is no

---

36 R Tomasic, "Chinese Walls, Legal Principle and Commercial Reality in Multi Service Professional Firms" (1991) UNSWLJ 46.

37 [1998] 3 NZLR 642, 655, 655.

likelihood that it will occur.[38] Thomas J, in his dissent, also accepted the possibility of the use of Chinese walls, although only in "exceptional circumstances where there is an overriding and compelling need".[39]

In *Bolkiah* before the English Court of Appeal there was a comparatively ready acceptance of Chinese walls. Lord Justice Woolf stated: "Conflicts between clients cannot be avoided, but they must be managed",[40] suggesting that it was an inevitability that loyalties of a firm to clients would conflict. It was further observed that Chinese walls were appropriate particularly to large firms where it was claimed that teams could be isolated effectively. In taking this approach the Court of Appeal declined to follow the stricter approach taken in the older authorities. In this respect the Court emphasised (perhaps unduly) the professional environment and "the effect of exhortation and a culture where the importance of the preservation of confidence is given a high priority".

The approach of the Court of Appeal was not accepted by the House of Lords in *Bolkiah* which was more cautious in accepting such devices as a method by which the risk of disclosure of confidential information might be removed. While it is assumed that information will move between members of a firm, if sufficient steps are taken it may be that the Court will accept that the relevant information has been isolated. In the view of the House of Lords such a Chinese wall must be robust indeed. It will not be sufficient that all reasonable measures have been taken to ensure that no disclosure will occur.[41] Such measures must be effective. A significant criticism of the Chinese wall relied on by KPMG in *Bolkiah* was the fact that it was constructed ad hoc. It was suggested that an effective Chinese wall will be an established part of the firm and not a device of convenience to circumvent individual problems. Lord Millett stated:[42]

> Even in the financial services industry, good practice requires there to be established institutional arrangements designed to prevent the flow of information between separate departments.

More recently it has been held on similar facts that a Chinese wall will not be effective unless there is an actual physical separation of staff members who are in possession of confidential information.[43]

---

38 [1998] 3 NZLR 642, 678.

39 [1998] 3 NZLR 642, 670.

40 (1998) 148 NLJ 1602; *The Independent*, 22 October 1998, *The Times*, 22 October 1998.

41 The test in *MacDonald Estate v Martin* (1990) 77 DLR (4th) 249.

42 [1999] 2 WLR 215, 228.

43 *Young v Robinson Rhodes* [1999] 3 All ER 524.

9.5.3 *Shortcomings of Chinese walls*

Many law firms use Chinese walls, and solicitors in those firms invariably defend them as effective and required by the exigencies of modern practice. There are, however, issues at both a practical and theoretical level, which suggest that Chinese walls cannot act as an effective antidote to a risk of disclosure, and the appearance to the public that such a risk exists.

Never impermeable

A serious practical objection to the use of Chinese walls can be drawn from the words of Parker LJ when he doubted "whether an impregnable wall can ever be created and I consider that it is only in very special cases that any attempt should be made to do so".[44] Similarly in *Re David Lee & Co*[45] Sir Nicholas Browne-Wilkinson V-C seemed to suggest that lawyers could not always be trusted to maintain their own protocols. He stated:

> Experience in this Court demonstrates that the maintenance of security on either sides of Chinese walls in the context of the City does not always prove to be very easy. I think it is a very difficult task.

In actual practice no measure taken to secure confidential information will be impregnable. There will always be a possibility of breach of confidence.

Protection illusory

It is obvious that any Chinese wall is susceptible to breach either by accident, or intentionally. The protection of the confidence is not guaranteed. As Tompkins J stated:[46]

> Once a potential conflict of interest situation has arisen or an allegation of a breach of fiduciary duty is made, the protection thought to be given by a "Chinese wall" will almost always prove to be illusory.

This is aptly demonstrated in the *Russell McVeagh* case. In the first place the Chinese wall was not erected until after the period of concurrent instructions (and, therefore, after the period of the greatest risk of disclosure) had ceased. Moreover, it appears that notwithstanding the existence of this notional barrier, an affidavit which Tower claimed contained sensitive information was inadvertently sent to the wrong person in Russell McVeagh. That person was, unfortunately, a partner concerned with the Guinness Peat retainer. Although the Court did not

44 *Re A Firm of Solicitors* [1992] QB 959, 971.
45 [1992] Ch 259, 268.
46 *McNaughten v Tauranga City Council (No 2)* (1987) NZTPA 429, 431.

consider the information disclosed to be material, this is the very kind of breach that a Chinese wall, if effective, ought to protect against.

The wall erected in *Bolkiah* was considerably more elaborate, however, it failed to meet the stringent test imposed by the House of Lords. It was found that despite the steps taken there was still a risk of information leakage. The objections to the arrangements were that it was constructed ad hoc rather than as part of a standing arrangement, and the size and fluid membership of the teams engaged on the various projects meant that there was a possibility of unwitting disclosure of information. It was also of relevance that the wall erected attempted to separate members of the same department.

Secret breaches are undetectable

Moreover, if we accept that the appearance of the proper administration of justice including the protection of confidences is a value to be preserved, Chinese walls are of questionable merit. The usefulness of Chinese walls are premised on their constructors being trusted to honour them. There is, however, no way for the former client to ascertain whether or not they have been honoured. In such situations the lawyer is in possession of confidential information which, if released would damage the former client and, furthermore, there are considerable pressures to disclose or use that information in the interests of the current client. If such a breach were to occur it is extremely unlikely to be discovered. To endorse such a state of affairs seems to be naively trusting. A Chinese wall or cone of silence will never be effective protection against a deliberate breach of confidence. As Thomas J noted in *Russell McVeagh* the construction of any notional barriers to the flow of confidential information within a firm amounts to no more than the firm insisting that the client simply trust each and every member of the firm. The client may legitimately ask why such trust is warranted, and certainly such trust should not be unilaterally demanded of the client as it was in that case.

Dilution of obligation of confidence

Perhaps more compelling still is the fact that an acceptance of Chinese walls indicates a significant dilution of the incidents of the fiduciary relationship of confidence between lawyer and client. The construction of a Chinese wall is an acknowledgment that the firm has placed itself in a situation where the confidence is at risk. The existence of such a risk without the informed consent of the client is itself a breach of the obligations of the fiduciary. The construction of a Chinese wall does not remove the risk; it lessens the likelihood that the existence of the risk will be causative of loss to the former client. If the use of Chinese walls is endorsed this tacitly recognises that the obligations of a fiduciary are no longer absolute. A fiduciary may, at least in some circumstances, act in a position where there is a risk of disclosure of confidential information, provided that there is no real or appreciable risk that that confidence will be breached, or cause loss to the former client. This is the case with or without the consent of the former client. This reflects a view that the Courts must accommodate the business practices of the modern commercial environment rather than lawyers adopting the practices to accord with the high professional obligations that have been placed on them.

Chapter 10

Duties to Disclose and Keep Informed

10.1 Introduction

As a fiduciary, any information that the lawyer has or comes into the possession of in the course of the lawyer-client relationship is to be used for the benefit of the client. As the agent of the client the lawyer is required to disclose all relevant information regarding the client's affairs to the client. This will include matters detrimental as well as beneficial to the client. The duty is set out in r 1.09:

> In most circumstances, a practitioner is bound to disclose to the client all information received by the practitioner that relates to the client's affairs.

The duty is not only a duty to disclose facts relevant to the case, but also a duty to keep clients informed of progress and to inform clients to enable them to have meaningful control of the proceedings. Lawyers are not at liberty to take unilateral decisions for clients on the best course of action. Lawyers must ensure that as far as possible clients are knowledgeable of the facts and legal implications so that they may give effective instructions to the practitioner.

There will be exceptions to the duty of disclosure. Information that is trifling or irrelevant need not be disclosed. If there is a legal duty to keep information from a client, this will obviously be an excuse for non-disclosure. More difficult are those situations where some competing third interest requires that the information be kept secret, or where disclosure of the information would be traumatic to the client.

While the duty to disclose is not new, it has risen in prominence recently. Not only has society generally become more aware of citizen's rights to information concerning their own affairs, but also there has been a corresponding rejection of the paternalistic approach that was previously dominant. The practice of a professional adviser collating the pieces of information regarding the case and unilaterally exercising professional judgment on the matter is no longer acceptable. It is now expected that the client will be kept fully informed of all developments and actively involved in any decisions that are made.

10.2 Impact of the Privacy Act 1993

This change in the way in which personal information is viewed is exemplified by the passing of the Privacy Act 1993.[1] Under that Act lawyers are deemed "agencies", bound by the strict rules governing disclosure where individuals request information, as well as equally demanding rules concerning the collection, storage, and use of personal information. Principle 6 in s 6 of that Act provides that an individual is entitled to access to any personal information held by an agency. The law society has issued a set of guidelines for practitioners concerning the collection and disclosure of information under the Privacy Act.

In adverting to the situations in which disclosure is not required of a lawyer the provisions of the Privacy Act have been adopted by r 1.09:

> There are certain exceptions [to the duty to disclose] which include cases where one of the reasons set out in ss 27-29 of the Privacy Act 1993 provides good reason to refuse a request from the client for access.

In claiming that some of the reasons not to disclose are included in ss 27 to 29, the law society appears to have adopted those sections of the Privacy Act as merely a guide to the reasons for refusing to disclose information to clients. If information is requested under the Act, unless one of the grounds in ss 27 to 29 excuses lawyers from producing the information they are compelled to do so and no other grounds for non-disclosure are recognised.[2]

The Privacy Act only places a duty on lawyers to provide information when requested.[3] The duty of disclosure on lawyers is wider in that it requires lawyers to disclose information of relevance to their client that comes into their hands even in the absence of any request for such disclosure. It may be that those other grounds justifying non-disclosure alluded to in r 1.09 refer only to those cases where the client has not actually requested the information and, therefore, the Privacy Act does not apply.

---

1 Some detailed discussions of the Privacy Act are Longworth and McBride *The Privacy Act: A Guide*; Wellington, GP Publications, 1994; *Privacy Law and Practice* Wellington, Butterworths, 1995; *The Privacy Act NZLS Seminar Series* presented by Bruce Slane and Elizabeth Longworth, 1997.

2 Section 30 Privacy Act 1993. The only situation where this is not the case is where the client is not an individual and therefore the provisions of the Privacy Act do not apply.

3 Section 33 Privacy Act 1993. For a detailed guide on the procedural steps to be taken when such a request is made see the Law Society's *Privacy Act 1993: Guidelines for Practitioners.*

The scope of the Privacy Act is also limited in that its provisions relate only to personal information, and not to the information of incorporated bodies. Incorporated companies, provident societies, and the like may not avail themselves of the rights to information under the Act. The professional and legal obligations of disclosure by lawyers in respect of such bodies are unaffected by the Act, except in so far as it has been incorporated into the rules. There may be grounds for refusing to disclose information to such bodies which would not be available were the clients individuals. However, such an approach would introduce an inappropriate disparity in the way clients are treated. It is suggested that a better approach would be to apply the higher standards of the Privacy Act to all clients regardless of whether they are natural persons or not, even though such a step is not required by law.

10.3 Duty to obtain informed instructions

Clients rarely abdicate all control of their affairs into the hands of their lawyer. Clients look to the lawyer for special skills and knowledge while seeking to maintain control over their affairs. To ensure that this is possible it is necessary for a lawyer to take time to explain to clients their affairs and the relevant aspects of the legal environment. This enables clear instructions which accord with the actual wishes of the client to be obtained. It was stated in *Groom v Crocker*:[4]

> It is an incident of that duty that the solicitor shall consult with his client on all questions of doubt which do not fall within the express or implied discretion left by him, and shall keep the client informed to such an extent as may be reasonably necessary.

This recognises that at the outset of the relationship clients will either expressly or impliedly consent to their lawyer conducting most of the normal incidents of the work required without further instructions.[5] This is not an instruction to act without recourse to the client. In the event that situations arise outside of the express or implied instructions, the lawyer must inform the client and obtain clear instructions before proceeding.

There is a mountain of information in the hands of a legal adviser and it is neither necessary nor possible to disclose all of it to the client. It is always difficult to decide where to draw the line between inadequate information and over-simplification, and an overload of information and

4 [1938] 2 All ER 384, 413 per Scott LJ.

5 Note that it is an implied term of the retainer that a lawyer will provide the service rather than some unqualified executive or assistant: *Pilbrow v Peerless De Rougemont* [1999] 3 All ER 355 (CA).

losing the client in complexity. Rule 1.4(b) of the ABA Model Rules (entitled "communication") accepts this in stating: "A lawyer shall explain a matter to the extent reasonably necessary to permit the client to make informed decisions regarding the representation."[6] The commentary to that rule emphasises the motivation for such disclosure in ensuring that the client has sufficient information to intelligently participate in the decisions being made. Obviously, the way in which the information is presented, and the amount of information will need to be tailored to suit the identity of the client. Some people can be expected to understand relatively sophisticated documents, and grasp legal concepts and strategies. Other clients may not be able understand some of the complexities of the matter and in such cases the lawyer has a duty to simplify things as far as possible and put matters at a level that is understandable to the client. This is particularly so where the client is a child, or suffers from some mental disability.

One of the tasks of a lawyer is to discover the wishes of the client, and to assist the client in deciding how to achieve them. While the lawyer must act in the best interests of the clients, it is important that the lawyer find out from the clients what is the clients' perception of their own best interest. Such a task involves explaining the legal and factual context in which the problem exists. This element of the duty to communicate is particularly difficult and not dissimilar to the duty of a doctor when obtaining a patient's consent to a procedure. To fully explain the circumstances and reasons behind the professional's judgment is not only inefficient but also usually impossible. There are important decisions that have to be made without client involvement, particularly, in pressing circumstances such as in Court (such as whether to pursue a particular line of questioning), or in the midst of lawyer-to-lawyer negotiations (such as whether to propose less advantageous terms of settlement). While such decisions may not contravene the instructions of the client, and a client should be kept informed of the strategic decisions, there will be cases where important decisions are made unilaterally by the lawyer.

A lawyer may not act in contravention of the instructions of a client. It may be appropriate for the lawyer to counsel against a particular course of action where it is considered not to be in the best interests of the client. But where clients are firm in their instructions the lawyer may not substitute the lawyer's own judgment for that of the clients. In R *v*

6 The English equivalent is to be found in r 13.01(2)(c) of the *Guide to the Professional Conduct of Solicitors* which provides that solicitors must "ensure that clients are at all relevant times given appropriate information as to the issues raised and the progress of the matter": r 15 Solicitors Practice Rules 1990.

McLoughlin[7] a barrister chose not to call the alibi evidence of the defendant to a rape charge against the defendant's instructions. The Court of Appeal observed:

> The reason, it appears, was that counsel thought the proposed evidence unreliable and thought that it would be improper for him and detrimental to the client appellant for it to be called. It is not for this Court to question counsel's judgment about that, or to comment upon the evidence ourselves. But the plain unvarnished fact is that counsel most certainly had no right to disregard his [the appellant's] instructions. Following any advice he thought it proper to give his client, his duty was either to act on the instructions he received or to withdraw from the case.

Where the client's instructions are unclear it is incumbent on the lawyer to obtain clarification of those instructions. The lawyer may not proceed on the assumption that the client agrees to a certain course of action.[8]

It is important that lawyers discuss with clients any decisions of importance or decisions that may be contentious, such as whether allegations of fraud or misconduct should be put to a witness or whether failures of another party to negotiations should be exploited. The lawyer may have good reasons for preferring a particular course of action which, along with the relevant facts, should be put to the client. The lawyer should not assume that the client is happy to defer to the lawyer's judgment in such matters.

10.4 Disclosure to client

10.4.1 *Client conflicts*

It goes without saying that conflicts of interest are matters that ought to be disclosed to the client. Rule 1.07 provides that in the event of a conflict of interest or likely conflict of interest the practitioner must advise all clients involved of the situation.[9] The application of this rule relies, however, on the judgment of the lawyer as to whether a conflict or possible conflict has arisen. As can be seen from the case of *Russell McVeagh McKenzie Bartleet & Co v Tower Corporation*,[10] there are considerable difficulties in such an approach. The work in that case being conducted for the other side was sensitive, and disclosure would have involved breaching the duty of confidence owed to the other client. If such circumstances exist, this should alert the practitioner to the fact that the interests of the two clients are potentially in conflict, and the

7 [1985] 1 NZLR 106, 107 per Hardie Boys J. See also *Thompson v Howley* [1977] 1 NZLR 17 in respect of the prohibition on a lawyer settling a dispute in the face of contrary instructions.

8 *Ismail bin Ibrahim v Lim Lim & Oon* [1998] 1 AMR 339.

9 See also *Farrington v Rowe McBride & Partners* [1985] 1 NZLR 83.

10 [1998] 3 NZLR 641.

mere fact that the situation is unable to be disclosed suggests a difficulty which precludes the firm from acting further for the parties. There are also compelling commercial reasons for the lawyer (or firm) to decide that there is no conflict which needs to be disclosed to the client. To disclose the matter to the client would be to give the client the reason and the opportunity to terminate the retainer. When that client is likely to be a regular user of legal services (as was the case in *Russell McVeagh v Tower*) it is poor business sense to give the client a reason to find another lawyer. This is especially the case in the environment of the modern law firm where there is considerable pressure on individual lawyers within a firm to generate a high level of fees. To ask lawyers under such pressure to invite clients to find another lawyer is difficult indeed.

Lawyers are not at all used to erring on the side of caution when complying with rules. They are trained in and experts at assisting clients to conduct their business to their advantage at the limits of the law. In doing so they frequently put matters in the best light for the side of the case they are acting for, and understate objections to their stance. Such a position is wholly inconsistent with the role that a lawyer is expected to adopt when considering the ethical duties owed to the client. As a fiduciary, and in light of the special relationship of trust between the lawyer and client, the lawyer should always decide such matters from the perspective of a concerned client, rather than in the lawyer's own interest. Where there is the slightest doubt in such matters any erring should be in favour of the client. It must be presumed that the client would want to know and has a right to know of any possible conflict.

When disclosure of the existence of a potential conflict of interest is made it must be thorough. It will not be sufficient to simply note that another client is concerned in the transaction. The possible risks involved where such a potential conflict exists and the exact nature of the conflict must be explained to the client. As with all disclosure, the lengths to which the lawyer must go to ensure that the client is fully informed will differ. In some cases the client will be sophisticated and readily grasp the problems involved. In others such disclosure will require more care, and it may be necessary to insist that the advice of a third party be obtained.[11]

10.4.2 *Disclosure of lawyer-client conflicts*

Any personal interest of the lawyer which might possibly touch on the affairs of the client should also be disclosed. This will be the case even if the interest does not create a conflict in the eyes of the lawyer. The commentary to r 1.03 provides:

---

11 *Farrington v Rowe McBride & Partners* [1985] 1 NZLR 83, 90 per Richardson J.

> The existence of a personal interest of a practitioner should be disclosed to the client or prospective client irrespective of a perceived lack of conflict. The practitioner should consider carefully whether a personal interest is directly or indirectly in conflict with the interests of the client, and refuse to act if there is any such direct or indirect conflict. … The rule will usually apply to any interest or dealing through the practitioner's family or relatives or any company, trust, partnership, or other body in which the practitioner has or exerts a material measure of control or influence. It will also include interests which are not personal in the strict sense but representative in character such as directorships and trusteeships.

Similarly r 6.06 provides that where there is a potential claim against the practitioner the lawyer must "advise the client to seek independent advice on the matter" which presumably involves also disclosing the existence of a possible claim.

The duty on a lawyer to fully disclose all details of the conflict is absolute. It will not be sufficient simply to note that the lawyer has an interest of a certain nature. For a client to make an informed decision on whether or not to continue the lawyer-client relationship it is necessary to understand the full implications of the conflict. If the relationship does continue the lawyer will be obliged to inform the client of any changes in the interests held which affect the conflict.

This is illustrated in *Day v Mead*.[12] In that case a client was looking to invest a considerable sum of money. It was held that it was not sufficient for the lawyer to explain to the client that he was a director and shareholder of a company in which it was suggested an investment be made. It was necessary that disclosure be made of any special circumstances which would be material to the decision to invest in the company. The company was suffering significant financial difficulties and went into receivership some four months after one sum was invested. It was held that even though the client was an experienced businessperson the lawyer still had an ongoing duty to disclose all material facts at his disposal which would have been relevant to the investment decisions. This ought to have included details of the troubles being suffered by the company.

10.4.3 *Content of disclosure*

One of the most difficult problems with the duty of disclosure is that lawyers may have a different perception of what ought to be disclosed from that of their clients, and indeed lawyers may differ amongst themselves on this question. The standard set by the rules is not very helpful. There will be an area of doubt as to what information "relates to the client's affairs" in terms of r 1.09. This formula seems more stringent

12 [1987] 2 NZLR 443.

than the duty of the common law which requires a fiduciary to disclose all material facts.[13] The test has been stated:[14]

> A primary obligation of the fiduciary is to reveal all material information that comes into his possession concerned with his client's affairs. The emphasis is on what is material or essential. That is a matter of judgment by the solicitor on the facts of each case, for certainly he is not obliged to pass on trifling and insignificant detail.

This suggests that matters which relate to the affairs of a client but are not material or are of only trivial significance need not be disclosed.

The application of such a standard is difficult as was demonstrated by the facts of *McKaskell v Benseman*.[15] In that case a young lawyer was dealing with an acrimonious dispute between two neighbours. He received from the lawyer acting for the other side a letter that contained the following passage: "Are your clients considering moving? Their behaviour is more suited to that of persons living in a state housing area". The words were clearly intended as a slight on the clients of the young practitioner. The remark was observed by the Judge to be "capable of producing snide and foolishly snobby reactions … offensive and insulting about the McKaskells".

The lawyer who received this letter was troubled by it because it would clearly be distressing to the clients if they were to read it, and embarrassing to the writer if the letter were to come before the Court. After seeking advice from colleagues and a senior practitioner from another firm it was resolved that the writer should be invited to rewrite the letter expunging the offensive parts, after which all copies of it would be destroyed. This was done. Some time later the clients discovered the earlier existence of the letter quite by accident in a meeting with their barrister. They then commenced proceedings against their solicitors, and several other parties, for failing to disclose the existence of the letter and contents.

The Court found in favour of the clients on this point deciding that their lawyers had breached their fiduciary obligation of disclosure in failing to reveal the existence and contents of the letter. This decision is premised on the basis that the contents of the letter were material rather than trifling matters. While they were not material to the determination of the fencing dispute of the client, they were clearly matters that the clients wished to be informed about. It appears that the lawyer must approach

13 *Brickenden v London Loan and Savings Co* [1934] 3 DLR 465, 469 per Lord Thankerton.

14 *McKaskell v Benseman* [1989] 3 NZLR 75, 87.

15 [1989] 3 NZLR 75.

the question of materiality not from a legalistic or lawyerly point of view, but rather they must consider whether the client would wish to be apprehended of the particular facts. The duty to disclose is not restricted to information relevant to the particular legal or business matter which the lawyer is handling but will extend to all information which comes into the hands of the lawyer which is relevant to the client's wider affairs.

The issue is whether the information is material in the eyes of the client, rather then in the eyes of the lawyer. The fact that the lawyer considers in good faith that the information is not relevant and need not be disclosed will not relieve him or her of that obligation. In *McKaskell* it was obvious (at least in retrospect) that the clients would have wanted to be told of the offending letter. It was not open to the lawyer to decide that it was better not to disclose it to them. If on all the facts, and knowing the client, it is clear to the lawyer that the client would wish to be informed of the relevant information then the information must be considered as material and disclosed to the client. As the agent of the client it is incumbent on the lawyer to apply the standards of his or her clients to the question of whether the information was material, rather than paternalistically applying the lawyer's own standards.

10.4.4 *Accounting for trust funds and billing*

Much of a lawyer's work involves dealing with funds that belong to the client. As well as holding such funds, lawyers will frequently spend them on effecting the work required, and, of course, bill the client for work that they complete themselves. It is incumbent on the lawyer to ensure that any dealing with, or expenditure of, client funds is fully disclosed and explained. Bills rendered ought to fully describe the work completed and how the figure stated was arrived at.[16] When a lawyer holds the funds of a client they are held in the capacity of trustee.[17] There is a fiduciary duty to account for all dealings in the funds. There is also a statutory duty to account to clients for the funds held and to ensure that accurate and clear records are kept to enable this.[18] There are comprehensive rules and guidelines concerning exactly how this is to be achieved.[19]

---

16 In the absence of itemisation the practitioner may be required to itemise the bill fully on costs revision under s 152(1) Law Practitioners Act 1982. Lawyers are obliged to charge only an amount which is "fair and reasonable" under r 3.01. See further ch 12.

17 Section 89 Law Practitioners Act 1982.

18 Regulation 3 Solicitors' Trust Account Regulations 1998; r 5 Solicitors Trust Account Rules 1996.

19 Solicitors Trust Account Regulations 1998; Solicitors Trust Account Rules 1996; Solicitors Trust Account Guidelines.

10.4.5 *Exceptions to the duty to disclose*

There will be circumstances in which the lawyer may hold information that may legitimately be withheld from the client. Such instances will be rare, and clear justification will be required. One effect of the Privacy Act 1993 has been to remove the efficacy of the solicitors' lien in respect of individual (as opposed to corporate) clients. A lawyer can no longer refuse to disclose the contents of the client's file (and render copies of all important documents) on the basis that fees are outstanding.[20]

Consent

There will be cases where a client will consent to less than full disclosure of the information that comes into the hands of the lawyer or other members of the lawyer's firm. Where a lawyer is acting for two clients who are parties to the same transaction with their consent, there will be instances where information of one party may not be passed on to the other. Occasionally, former clients will consent to a firm acting against their interests. It is common to set up information barriers to ensure that information held by one lawyer confidential to the former client is not passed on to the lawyer acting for the current client. The current client consents to the firm not disclosing information regarding the affairs of the former client.

Obtaining the consent of the client may be used as a method to obviate the difficulties that attach to other information which ought to be disclosed, but good reasons exist for not disclosing it. For example, a lawyer may know the address of a client's spouse where the client has a history of harassment. It may be possible to get the client's consent to the lawyer not disclosing the address to the client.[21] Similarly, in cases on facts similar to *McKaskell* a better approach would have been to seek the client's consent to the return of the letter unread by the client (although on those particular facts the clients would have been unlikely to give such consent).

There are instances where, even with the consent of the client not to disclose, the lawyer ought to be under a duty to disclose. Where clients consent to non-disclosure of material information, they do not know the details of the information that they are consenting to be kept in the dark about. They will have given a general waiver of the duty of disclosure in respect of any of a particular class of matters. However, the information which the lawyer is in possession of may be of such a nature as to make the discharge of the other duties to the client very difficult. If, for example, a lawyer becomes aware that the security offered by one client to another to secure a loan advance is worthless, or that the client has no means of repaying the loan, there is an irreconcilable conflict between

20 Rule 1.09 para 6 of the commentary.

21 See para 4 of the commentary to r 1.09.

the interests of the two clients. Notwithstanding the consent to non-disclosure, and corresponding waiver of the strict fiduciary duties, the lawyer can no longer render any meaningful assistance to the client without alerting the client to these facts. Such disclosure would breach duties of confidence owed to the other party. In such an invidious position the lawyer should cease acting for either party as soon as the conflict is apparent and ensure that both parties receive competent independent advice.

Received in error

There are inevitably instances where confidential information of one party is inadvertently sent to the lawyer acting for the other party. The most common situation where this happens is in the process of discovery — the exchange of parties' documents prior to a Court hearing. In litigation certain documents are privileged and need not be disclosed to the other side. For example, correspondence between a lawyer and the client in contemplation of the litigation falls into the class of privileged documents. Occasionally, such documents are sent in error to the other side along with other non-privileged documents. If a pure agency approach toward the role of the lawyer were adopted, once such documents are received by the lawyer they ought to be disclosed by the lawyer to the client.

However, this is not the case. If this were so, the interests of one client would be defeated by the inadvertence of the lawyer, and the policy behind legal professional privilege would be defeated. When lawyers become aware that they have received documents in error they should return the privileged documents to the sender.[22] The commentary to r 16.06 of the English *Guide* states:

> [W]here it is obvious that privileged documents have been mistakenly disclosed to a solicitor on discovery, or otherwise, the solicitor should immediately cease to read the documents, inform the other side and return the documents. The solicitor may tell the client what has happened.

Where the documents are privileged there is an established public policy against the disclosure of the documents, namely, the protection of the confidence of the lawyer-client relationship in litigation. More difficult is where the inadvertent disclosure does not concern privileged information. Consider, for example, a situation where the lawyer for a vendor of property inadvertently sends a building report detailing defects in the property to the lawyer for the purchaser. Such an error

22 See *National Insurance Co Ltd v Whirlybird Holdings Ltd* [1994] 2 NZLR 513; *Spicers Paper (NZ) Ltd v Whitcoulls Group Ltd* [1996] 1 NZLR 72; *Roundtree v Complaints Committee of the Canterbury District Law Society* (High Court, Christchurch M 450/96, 26 May 1997, Fraser J).

probably breaches the lawyer's duty to the client, and there is doubtlessly a strong urge to return the information without disclosing it to the client, especially if the lawyer for the vendor has noticed the mistake and sought the return.

There appears to be no legal duty to return such information to the other lawyer, and the desire to save the other lawyer from professional embarrassment or claims is clearly no excuse for non-disclosure.[23] The best course in such a situation would appear to be to discuss the existence of the inadvertent disclosure with the client and seek instructions on the matter. In most cases clients will want to know the contents of the inadvertent disclosure, and the lawyer has a legal duty to facilitate this unless one of the other exceptions discussed provides an excuse for non-disclosure.

Procured by fraud or misconduct

The situation may be different where the information comes into the hands of the lawyer by some fraud of a third party. If an agent of the lawyer exceeds the authority and tricks the other party into disclosure, or steals information, it is suggested that the lawyer is obliged to decline to be an accessory to such a wrong. The lawyer ought to treat the action as a nullity by returning or destroying any record of such information, and refusing to disclose it to the client. Such a view is supported by the cases that observe that the Court has a discretion based on its equitable jurisdiction to protect confidential information by injuncting against its dissemination or use.[24] Where the possession of the information has come about by fraud the Court will be ready to exercise that jurisdiction.

Client's interest

There may be grounds for withholding information from a client, at least temporarily,[25] in the client's interest. This may be the case in respect of clients who are particularly vulnerable due to their heath, age, or mental condition.[26] For example, where the client is a child and one parent makes allegations of abuse, it may be in the best interests of the child to withhold the existence of such allegations until it has been established that there is some foundation to them.[27] Information of this kind may be

---

23 *McKaskell v Benseman* [1989] 3 NZLR 75.

24 *Corporate Group Holdings Ltd v Corporate Resources Group Ltd* [1991] 1 NZLR 115, 120 per Hillyer J; also *National Insurance Co Ltd v Whirlybird Holdings Ltd* [1994] 2 NZLR 513.

25 The corresponding ABA Model Rule, r 1.4 contemplates, in the commentary, the possibility of delaying the transmission of information until a more appropriate time to tell the client.

26 See further s 29(1)(c) Privacy Act 1993.

27 Section 28(1)(d) Privacy Act 1993 allows a more paternalistic approach to be taken by permitting non-disclosure to children when it would be "contrary to that individual's interests".

better disclosed by a professional person such as a social worker or counsellor who is trained in dealing with such delicate matters.[28]

An earlier version of the rules permitted non-disclosure on humanitarian grounds.[29] However, in most instances where information that the client will find hurtful or traumatic comes into the hands of a lawyer such information ought to be disclosed. While non-disclosure may be justified on the basis of the mental or physical health of the client, it will not be justified because it will be merely hurtful or upsetting to them. It appears that the humanitarian ground for non-disclosure no longer exists. In the words of Jeffries J:[30]

> Lawyers, as well as other professional men, as part of their practice, have to convey not infrequently to clients unwelcome, bad, and even at times, devastating information. The greatest care should always be taken on the occasion of such communication, but, nevertheless, it must be done.

Court orders

There will be instances where the Court makes orders that information should not be disclosed to clients. Instances may include keeping the identity of witnesses secret, concealing the residence or workplace of an estranged spouse, or protecting confidential information that has inappropriately come into the hands of the lawyer. In such instances the lawyer is obviously bound by the order of the Court.[31]

Statutory prohibitions and exceptions

There are statutory provisions that require a lawyer not to disclose certain information. In the event that a lawyer has made a report (or is contemplating making such a report) under the provisions of the Financial Transactions Reporting Act 1993 which aims to prevent money laundering, s 20 of that Act prohibits the disclosure that such a report has been made (or contemplated) to the client or any other person (with limited exceptions).[32] The law society has also adopted ss 27 to 32 of the Privacy Act 1993 as a non-exhaustive guide to the grounds on which lawyers are entitled (rather than compelled) to refrain from disclosing information to their clients.[33] Those grounds include the protection of national security, defence and international relations, the protection of government confidences, the protection of law and order, the protection of the safety of third parties, the protection of trade

28 See further para 4 of the commentary to r 16.06 of the English *Guide*.

29 Rule 1.09 was revised in 1997 and now adopts the grounds for non-disclosure in ss 27-29 Privacy Act 1993.

30 *McKaskell v Benseman* [1989] 3 NZLR 75, 87.

31 See para 4 of the commentary to ABA Model Rule, r 1.4.

32 Detailed guidance on the similar English provisions is contained in r 16.07 to the English *Guide* and the accompanying commentary.

33 Rule 1.09.

secrets, the protection of other confidences or agreements, and the avoidance of frivolous or vexatious requests.

Public or national interest

A lawyer may be in possession of information which it would be in the interests of the client to be aware of, however, it may be in the interests of the public, or some law enforcement agency, that the client should remain ignorant. For example, a lawyer may become aware that a client is under police surveillance, or that the client's financial affairs are being investigated on suspicion of laundering drug-related funds. In such a case, to disclose the information to the client would be likely to defeat the object of the endeavours of the enforcement agency. Section 27 of the Privacy Act expressly permits the lawyer to refuse to disclose information in such cases.

Third party interest

The duty of loyalty requires the lawyer to pursue zealously the interest of the client to the exclusion of others in most situations. There will, however, be extraordinary cases where the lawyer's conduct should be altered in consideration for the interests of third parties. If, for example, a lawyer can be reasonably sure that a client would use the information to perpetrate an offence against a third party (such as intimidating a witness) then non-disclosure will be justified.[34]

Paragraph 4 of the commentary to r 1.09 of the rules alludes to the difficulty that may arise where the lawyer is apprised of certain information that the client would use to harass or otherwise make life difficult for some third party. The acts contemplated by the client may not be criminal or even in breach of civil law duties, and may not cause serious harm. However, there is often a strong paternalistic urge to refrain from passing the information on due to the fact that the conduct contemplated by the client is improper in a wider sense. Such a stance is paternalistic and substitutes the judgment of the lawyer for that of the client. In the absence of disclosure facilitating some likely criminal wrong by the client, the withholding of information from a client would almost certainly be in breach of the professional and fiduciary duty to disclose.

That there are instances where third party interests justify non-disclosure demonstrates that the rights of the client cannot be regarded as absolute and that the lawyer is not a mere agent of the client. There will be limited cases where lawyers are expected to (or at least be permitted to) take the interests of a third party into account and to modify their conduct to protect the interests of the third party. However, such steps should not

34 See also s 27(1)(d) Privacy Act 1993.

be taken lightly and more than a mere suspicion is needed before information is withheld from a client.

Information received in confidence

One lawyer may seek to impart information in confidence to another lawyer in respect of a client's affairs.[35] Any invitation to receive information from another lawyer in confidence ought to be treated with the utmost caution as creating an irreconcilable conflict between the duty of disclosure owed to a client and the duty to honour the undertaking to another member of the profession.[36] Unless the information so imparted is excused from disclosure on one of the grounds discussed above it is suggested that the fact that it was imparted in confidence will be no grounds for failing to disclose it to a client.[37] In the event that such a conflict does arise between a duty of confidentiality to a third party and a duty of disclosure to the client the normal rules of conflict of interest will apply and it may be incumbent on the lawyer to withdraw from acting completely.[38]

Where such a revelation is prefaced by a request that it not be disclosed to the client, the lawyer receiving the information will have an opportunity to refuse to accept it. More difficult is the situation where information is foisted on a lawyer with such a caveat, as, for example, where one solicitor writes a "personal" note to another with a request that its contents not be disclosed. If the contents of such correspondence are material to the client it is suggested that they should be disclosed. The lawyer who received the information at no time consented to any duty of confidentiality to the lawyer who sent the note. Accordingly, no such duty is owed. This is reinforced by the English position where the guide states: "If a confidential letter is written [by one solicitor] to the solicitor for the other side, the writer cannot insist on the letter not being shown to the client." For a lawyer to seek to bind another lawyer to keep information material to the client in confidence is inappropriate. To do so is to encourage the lawyer to breach a duty to the client and ought to be discouraged.

The unusual case of *D v Hall*[39] provides a limited exception to this. The case concerned the adopting out of a child of the client. Some time after

35 Substantially identical problems will arise where a third party seeks to impart information to a lawyer in confidence creating conflicting duties of disclosure and confidence.

36 See para 2 of the commentary to r 1.09 of the rules.

37 Although s 29(1)(b) Privacy Act provides a limited exception where the information supplied by the third party in confidence is "evaluative material".

38 Rule 1.07 and para 2 of the commentary to r 1.09 of the rules.

39 [1984] 1 NZLR 727. Such a case is now unlikely since the passing of the Adult Adoption Information Act 1985.

the adoption the client sought information from the lawyer's file as to the identity of the adoptive parents. The lawyer refused to disclose the information. The Court upheld this refusal on the basis that the duty of confidence owed to the parents was justifiable on public policy grounds.[40] Such a stance is also justifiable on the basis that the client in accepting the non-disclosure of the identity of the adoptive parents at the outset had consented to the non-disclosure of the information irrevocably.

40 Such non-disclosure is warranted by the terms of s 28(1)(a) Privacy Act 1993 which permits non-disclosure where it would involve an unwarranted disclosure of the affairs of another individual (in this case those of the child and adoptive parents).

Chapter 11

Competence and Advocates' Immunity

11.1 Introduction

The duty to carry out the instructions of a client competently is the most fundamental of a lawyer's duties. Without such a duty of competence the work of a lawyer may be more hindrance than help. The need to ensure a lawyer's competence is due to the fact that, because of the complexity of the matter, it may be difficult for a client to assess whether the service was rendered competently. In arguing for greater attention to lawyer competence it has been observed:[1]

> By ensuring that legal practitioners meet stipulated minimum standards, those clients who are unable to assess or control quality nonetheless can be confident that any lawyer they choose will provide at least a reasonable quality of service.

Little emphasis is placed on the need for competence in the regulation of the New Zealand profession.[2] Except in extreme cases practitioner incompetence is not a matter of ethics or professional conduct and intervention of the law society is not warranted. In contrast to the New Zealand approach, the duty of competence is given prominence in other jurisdictions. In the US the first sentence of the first rule of the ABA Model Rules provides: "A lawyer shall provide competent representation to a client".[3] There is no such clear statement in the New Zealand Rules. The nearest the New Zealand Rules get to such an exhortation is in the commentary to r 1.02 (the duty to accept clients) which observes as an exception to that rule:

> It would be improper for a practitioner to accept instructions unless the matter could be handled promptly with due competence and without undue

1 E-DEC Report para 3.3.

2 This may be changing. The Law Practitioners Amendment Act 1999 inserted a new s 17(2)(fa) which stated that the New Zealand Law Council may make rules "Requiring that holders of practising certificates, or any class of holders of practising certificates, undertake ongoing legal education relating to the law or the practice of law".

3 ABA Model Rules, r 1.1. See also r 12.02 of the English *Guide*.

> interference by the pressure of other work or other obligations. Instructions for work which is outside the field of competence of a practitioner should be either declined or, with the consent of the client, referred to another practitioner.

A duty of care exists by virtue of the contract between the parties as well as the tort duties owed by a lawyer. The existence of the fiduciary duty imposes a duty to take care, although this is usually eclipsed by the more demanding duty of loyalty. While the relationship of lawyer and client is a special one, the principles under which duties in tort, contract, or equity are applied are principles of the ordinary law.[4] It is to these duties that clients must look, where they have suffered loss through the incompetence of their legal adviser rather than to intervention by the professional body.[5]

11.2 The New Zealand position

The professional body has not been primarily concerned with complaints against its members that do not involve dishonesty or some other moral turpitude. It is increasingly being recognised that as a service profession it is incumbent on the profession to ensure that its members provide their services competently as well as honestly. Under the current law in New Zealand incompetence of a minor and occasional sort will not amount to misconduct. However, the District Disciplinary Tribunals or New Zealand Disciplinary Tribunal may exercise their powers where the tribunal:[6]

> Is of the opinion that the practitioner has been guilty of negligence or incompetence in his professional capacity, and that the negligence or incompetence has been of such a degree or so frequent as to reflect on his fitness to practise as a barrister or solicitor or as to tend to bring the profession into disrepute.

Where a lawyer's incompetence is isolated and due to mere negligence there will be no professional implications and clients are left to look to the ordinary law and Courts for redress if they have suffered loss. It is only where the incidents of incompetence are repeated, or where isolated, gross, that it will be considered a breach of professional

4 Discussion is best left to works specialising in those areas. The fiduciary duty will not extend beyond the scope of the contractual or tortious duties of the lawyer even where those duties have been expressly or impliedly limited: *Clark Boyce v Mouat* [1993] 3 NZLR 641, 648 per Lord Jauncey of Tullichettle.

5 See *Jackson & Powell on Professional Negligence* 4th ed, London, Sweet & Maxwell, 1997.

6 Sections 106(3)(c) and 112(1) Law Practitioners Act 1982.

obligations.[7] Only infrequently will such a charge be established without the added presence of more serious wrongdoing entailing an element of dishonesty.

Once a lawyer has completed the requirements to qualify for admission as a barrister and solicitor, the society is not required to take any further action in ensuring competence.[8] A person who has completed the required degree in law and the 13-week course run by the Institute of Professional Legal Studies may, on admission, commence practice as a barrister sole accepting any work that may come his or her way. To suggest that a newly qualified lawyer is competent to act in all or even many areas of law is palpably incorrect. As any recent graduate will attest, after admission there remains a lot to be learned about legal practice and it is only after a considerable amount of supervised practice that any real competence is attained. The New Zealand position contrasts starkly with that in other jurisdictions such as England where extended periods as pupils or trainees in barristers' chambers or law firms are required before a graduate is considered properly qualified.

There are good arguments for the law society to assume the responsibility for ensuring continued competence of its members. All of the professional duties will amount to naught if the lawyer retained by a client fails to conduct the work required in a competent manner. It is a stated purpose of the law society to "promote … the interests of the public in relation to legal matters".[9] At the heart of the interests of the public in legal matters is an assurance that when the clients go to a lawyer for assistance they can be as certain as possible that the lawyer will complete the work in a competent and timely manner. This difficulty has been observed by a lay observer (who supervises the complaints and disciplinary procedures): [10]

> In my view the whole complaints procedure is too narrowly focused in that the Law Society can only act in cases of fraud or gross negligence. Nearly all cases fall outside these criteria and are simply complaints against poor quality work. I believe the Society should be able to state clearly that the work was

---

7 See *L v Canterbury District Law Society* [1999] 1 NZLR 467 for an example of conduct which fell into this category.

8 The only limitation seems to be the prohibition contained in s 55 Law Practitioners Act 1982 on a lawyer commencing private practice as a solicitor on his or her own account until he or she has had at least three years' legal experience. Most recently the society has acquired the power to require practitioners to undertake continuing education, though at the time of writing no steps have been taken to implement any such education programmes: s 17(2)(fa) Law Practitioners Act 1982.

9 Section 4(1)(a) Law Practitioners Act 1982.

10 Correspondence with the lay observer for Auckland, Waikato, Bay of Plenty and Taranaki, 24 September 1999.

> not up to standard and at least ensure the lawyer concerned writes a letter of apology to the complainant. I also think that they should be able to suggest that the lawyer refund fees where applicable.

The need for the law society to take a greater interest in the competence of its members is reflected by the E-DEC study commissioned by the law society to report on its structure and functions. It was observed that there was a need to ensure that the quality of service provided by lawyers was more consistently of a high standard. It also noted that at present lawyers are permitted to practise in all areas of law immediately on admission, before they are equipped for such practice. The suggestion was made that the three-year period of supervised practice similar to a pupillage be required before a lawyer is considered fully qualified. It is also suggested in the E-DEC report that there be a greater focus on client service in the regulation of the profession, and less emphasis on the maintenance of the public perception of the profession. In considering the current grounds of discipline it was noted: "These criteria appear to relate more to lawyers' image than to client service or the rule of law".[11] The report further observed that the main objective of state-sanctioned regulation of the legal profession should be:[12]

> ... to ensure that legal services are of an acceptable quality. Input standards, enforced through the practising certificate system, provide the basis for this but they are not sufficient. There is also need for redress for clients in those instances in which the legal service provided is of inadequate quality.

11.3 What competence means

It is impossible for a lawyer to be an expert in all areas of legal practice. To be a competent lawyer it is not necessary to be able to accept any work that is offered. The concept of lawyer competence is focused on being competent in the areas in which the lawyer practises.[13] Competence does not necessarily require an exhaustive knowledge of the law or procedure in any particular area. It entails an ability to complete the work required by finding the relevant law and applying the relevant skills.

The standard of competence is an objective one. The question is whether the lawyer under scrutiny applied the care or skill that any reasonable lawyer in the same position would have done. In establishing that the conduct was reasonable it will be of assistance if the lawyer can show that normal legal practice was adopted. For example, where the

11 E-DEC Report, para 4.4.

12 E-DEC Report, para 4.6.

13 See the test of competence proposed by the Final Report of the Ontario Law Society Competence Task Force, 28 November 1997.

issue is whether a mistake of law amounts to negligence it will be of assistance if the lawyer can show that a sufficient amount of time was spent researching the problem[14]

Errors of judgment

Being competent does not, in professional practice, preclude the making of mistakes. Because law is not a science there will be instances where practitioners have demonstrably erred in their judgment. Lawyers do not guarantee the outcome of their work.[15] It is conceivable that in hindsight it can be shown that the course of action proposed by lawyers or their interpretation of the law was demonstrably wrong. However, where the error is in the exercise of judgment or the interpretation of an uncertain, unclear, or complex provision a lawyer cannot be said to be incompetent.[16]

Guidance as to the level of competence required from lawyers can be drawn from cases where the Courts have been asked to exercise their inherent jurisdiction to control and discipline those who appear before them by an order of costs against lawyers personally. The Courts have been slow to discipline practitioners for poor quality work, intervening only where a serious dereliction of duty is found.[17] In *Y v M*[18] a practitioner filed an affidavit in the Family Court which contained allegations of sexual abuse by a father of his child which transpired to be quite unfounded. The father sought an order that the mother's lawyer pay his legal costs on the ground that the actions of the lawyer amounted to gross incompetence and, therefore, misconduct. The Court took the view that the filing of the affidavit was inappropriate. This was due to errors of judgment in using an insufficient degree of caution, unquestioningly accepting the word of the mother, and the advocate's lack of a degree of scepticism of her client's version of events. There was also a degree of urgency to the case that meant that a full investigation was not possible. It was held that this was more an error of judgment than incompetence or misconduct and costs would not be awarded against the lawyer.[19]

---

14 *Antonelli v Wade Gery Farr* in *Ridehalgh v Horsefield* [1994] Ch 205, 264.

15 See the words of Lord Denning in *Greaves & Co (Contractors) Ltd v Baynham Meikle & Partners* [1975] 1 WLR 1095, 1100D.

16 See *Ridehalgh v Horsefield* [1994] Ch 205, 206, 244(CA).

17 *Harley v McDonald* [1999] 3 NZLR 545. 564.

18 *Y v M* [1994] 3 NZLR 581 (HC). The duty not to admit evidence of serious allegations unless the advocate is satisfied that the making of such an allegation is justified on the facts of the case is also found in r 8.05 of the Rules of Professional Conduct of Barristers and Solicitors. See also *Gazley v Wellington District Law Society* [1976] 1 NZLR 452, 454.

19 Following *R & T Thew Ltd v Reeves (No 2)* [1982] QB 1283, 1286 (CA).

Error of law

Where the law is clear and yet the lawyer counsels an untenable interpretation may amount to incompetence for which a professional sanction will lie. In *DaSousa v Minister of Immigration*[20] it was found that an application for entry permits, and the application for review subsequent on the refusal of entry, were doomed to fail: "to a legal practitioner familiar with the provisions of the Act and Regulations there should have been no doubt that ... Mrs DaSousa did not qualify for the grant of such permits".[21] In *DaSousa* French J noted that it was not the fact that the claim failed which led to an order of costs being made against the advocate, but the fact that the bringing of the action amounted to a serious dereliction of duty. The application amounted to such a dereliction because it reflected "a serious failure to give reasonable attention to the relevant law and the facts".[22]

DaSousa was relied on in New Zealand by Giles J in *McDonald v FAI (NZ) General Insurance Company Ltd*.[23] In that case the lawyer brought a case against another lawyer's insurer in respect of losses suffered by the fraud of the other lawyer. The action against the insurer failed on a number of counts. In light of these failures the Court found that "there never really was any prospect whatsoever of success against FAI".[24] It was decided there that the conduct of the lawyer in bringing the case was inappropriate and the costs of the insurer were ordered to be paid by the incompetent counsel. In reaching this conclusion the following test was applied:[25]

> The [jurisdiction to award costs against lawyers] does not require serious professional misconduct. Mistake or error of judgment will not justify an order, but misconduct, default or even negligence is enough if that negligence is serious or gross. Neither will the fact that the case was lost be enough. All the circumstances have to be looked at. The jurisdiction is compensatory not punitive, but if the facts cry out for a remedy (as they do here) then the jurisdiction exists.

---

20 (1993) 114 ALR 708 (Federal Court of Australia).

21 *DaSousa v Minister of Immigration* (1993) 114 ALR 708, 710.

22 *DaSousa v Minister of Immigration* (1993) 114 ALR 708, 713.

23 *McDonald v FAI* [1999] 1 NZLR 583 affirmed by the Court of Appeal as *Harley v McDonald* [1999] 3 NZLR 545.

24 *McDonald v FAI* [1999] 1 NZLR 583, 587.

25 *McDonald v FAI* [1999] 1 NZLR 583, 592 although the Court of Appeal stated that the threshold for such an order is serious dereliction of duty rather than mere incompetence or negligence. See *Harley v McDonald* [1999] 3 NZLR 545, 559.

In contrast is the case of *Ridehalgh v Horsefield*.[26] There the solicitor-advocate made a fundamental error of law, however, the error was not considered serious enough to invoke the wasted costs jurisdiction of the Court. This was because the law involved was complex, the authoritative works in the area gave no clear answer to the issue, the matter was a minor one and they were not specialists in the area, a Judge in a lower Court made the same mistake, counsel for the opposing party acceded to a consent order based on the mistaken point of law, and the final judgment on the point was reached only after two days' argument and a reserved judgment. Even though the point taken was clearly and demonstrably wrong after thorough investigation, the level of complexity involved showed that the argument was not frivolous, and that a competent solicitor could reasonably make such an argument.

It is proper for a lawyer to make any reasonable legal argument possible for the client and the mere fact that the Court disagrees with the argument, or finds it untenable, will not mean that it was incompetent for the lawyer to make it. Change in the common law is only achieved by lawyers' challenging established precedents and arguing for new interpretations of the law. In *Abraham v Jutsun* Denning MR noted that it is an advocate's "duty to take any point which he believed to be fairly arguable on behalf of his client. The advocate is not to usurp the province of the Judge".[27]

Urgency

Advice or representation may be needed urgently. A lawyer who is an expert in the area may not be available immediately. It is acceptable for another lawyer to give what assistance he or she can even though in other circumstances the assistance would not be considered of a high enough standard. In such cases of legal "first aid" it may be proper to ensure that the client's position is not worsened, and advise the client to retain more competent advice.

Where assistance is needed urgently it may not be possible to delay matters and seek more experienced counsel, particularly in respect of litigation where litigants find themselves without counsel immediately prior to a trial. In *Antonelli v Wade Gery Farr*[28] a barrister accepted instructions to appear six days before trial. The brief itself was not delivered at all, and only meagre papers were ever in the hands of the barrister. The finding of the trial Judge that it was improper to accept a

---

26 Reported as part of *Ridehalgh v Horsefield* [1994] Ch 205, 244. For a US equivalent where the research was inadequate see *Crookham v Crookham* (1990) 914 F 2d 1027 (Illinois Court of Appeals)

27 *Abraham v Jutsun* [1963] 1 WLR 658, 663 (CA) followed in *Utah Construction and Mining Co v Watson* [1969] NZLR 1062, 1065 (CA).

28 Reported as part of *Ridehalgh v Horsefield* [1994] Ch 205, 264.

brief at such short notice was overturned on appeal. It was noted that under the cab rank rule the barrister was obliged to accept any instructions that were within her area of expertise and for which she was available. Her action in taking the case at such short notice could not be said to amount to misconduct. In cases where for one reason or another a client is without a legal representative at the last moment the Court should not make it more difficult for such litigants to gain assistance.

Cut price and free advice

Related problems arise where a lawyer gives advice or assistance for a reduced fee, or for no fee at all. In theory, the duties of a lawyer in such cases are the same as they would be where a full fee was paid. However, it has been observed that where the lawyer is under pressure it is most likely that the quality of the low fee or no fee client will suffer.[29] In such instances a lawyer will undertake to spend only limited time on work that, if done thoroughly, would take much longer. The fact that the quality of the work rendered by a lawyer will vary with the amount paid is recognised in a new rule which has been proposed in respect of the duty of a lawyer acting for a legally-aided client. The commentary to that proposed rule provides:[30] "A client should always receive the benefit of the practitioner's best efforts, having regard to the time and funding available".

It is incumbent on lawyers to fulfil their duties to all their clients competently, regardless of whether they are fee paying or not. Clients who do not pay, or pay a reduced fee, may get worse service than those who do pay, however, both clients have a right to be served competently. It would, therefore, be permissible for a lawyer to attend to a paying client's affairs before those of a pro bono client, all other things being equal. However, it is not acceptable to offer a less than competent standard of service to any client.

Relying on others

A lawyer will be expected to rely on the expertise of others. In gathering evidence it will be necessary to rely on experts' interpretations of the facts. If those interpretations prove unfounded, and even outlandish, this will not indicate incompetence on the part of the lawyer providing they were relied on in good faith.[31] However, the lawyer may not rely on subordinates such as para-legals to discharge duties such as proper discovery for which ultimate responsibility lies with the lawyer.[32]

---

29 Gilbert and Gorenfeld, "The Constitution Should Protect Everyone — Even Lawyers" (1984) 12 Pepp LR 75; D Webb, "Why Should Poor People get Free Lawyers" (1998) 28 VUWLR 65, 83.

30 Proposed r 3.05, para 5 of the commentary.

31 *Orchard v South Eastern Electricity Board* [1987] QB 565 (CA).

32 *Myers v Elman* [1940] AC 282 (HL).

In matters of law it is common for solicitors to seek the advice of barristers or occasionally other solicitors who are more specialised in the area. Such reliance is to be encouraged and even where the advice proves quite wrong the solicitor will not be considered incompetent for having relied on it.[33] Where the matter is one in which a solicitor should be expected to be competent such reliance will not absolve the solicitor of responsibility.[34] A solicitor should not accept the advice of a barrister uncritically:[35]

> A solicitor does not abdicate his professional responsibility when he seeks the advice of counsel. Rather he must apply his mind to the advice received. But the more specialist that nature of the advice, the more reasonable it is likely to be for a solicitor to accept it and act on it.

11.4 The emerging duty of client care

While there is a professional duty of competence in New Zealand, albeit one which is particularly focused, there is no duty to provide a high level of service to clients. The duty of competence is, in reality, a duty not to be really incompetent and is aimed at ensuring minimum standards of service. The duty of competence is also focused on the outcome of lawyers' work rather than the way in which they deal with clients. Other jurisdictions have moved towards setting clear quality standards in the way they deal with clients, as well as purely legal matters.[36] While the manner in which lawyers deal with clients may not impact on the effectiveness of the work they complete, it may have a negative effect on the clients' perception of the work, and can alienate clients from the legal process. The E-DEC report noted:[37]

> Some lawyers are not good managers but we do not regard management failings as a problem for the regulator, as long as the consequences affect only the lawyers themselves. However, consequences that take the form of unreasonable quality of service to clients are the regulator's problem. We have found several types of problem that do affect clients, in particular problems in (i) timeliness of service, (ii) not providing cost (pricing) information to clients, (iii) not responding to client requests, (iv) not

33 *Kemp v Burt* (1833) 4 B & Ad 424; *Francis v Francis & Dickerson* [1956] P 87, 96.

34 *Davy-Chiesman v Davy-Chiesman* [1984] Fam 48, 64 per May LJ.

35 *Ridehalgh v Horsefield* [1994] Ch 205, 237.

36 See r 15 Solicitors' Practice Rules 1990 reproduced as para 13.01 of the English *Guide* discussed in C Christensen, S Day and J Worthington, "Learned Profession? — The Stuff of Sherry Talk: The Response to Practice Rule 15" (1999) 6 International Journal of the Legal Profession 27; also *Queensland Solicitor's Handbook* r 4.09.

37 E-DEC Report, para 4.6.

properly informing the client as to what to expect, what is happening or what is not happening, and (v) patronising behaviour or other poor attitudes to clients. Such problems may have nothing to do with the inherent quality of the legal transaction but they have much to do with satisfying the client's need.

The codes concerning client care, including that proposed by E-DEC in its report deal with the above matters. Also central to the client care approach is the need for a clear complaints-handling system within the firm that the client is aware of. The Code of Client Service proposed by E-DEC is as follows.[38]

Engagement

1. The lawyer must agree with the client, at the commencement of an engagement, the objective and the intended output of the engagement (i e the service to be provided).
2. The lawyer will discuss with the client what is involved in an engagement of this kind, the events likely to occur, the processes to be gone through, and the actions to be taken. The lawyer will give the client the lawyer's best estimate of the likely outcome of the engagement.
3. The lawyer will define for the client, at the commencement of the engagement, the basis for charging and the procedures which will be followed in charging for the engagement. If requested by the client, the lawyer will provide the client with an estimate of the likely cost of the engagement although such an estimate will not be binding unless agreed to by both the lawyer and the client. The lawyer will inform the client of the client's entitlement to this cost estimate.
4. The lawyer will provide the client, at the commencement of the engagement, with an estimate of the time required to carry out the engagement and an estimate of the probable time schedule for the main components within the engagement.

Performance

1. The lawyer will inform the client when the main components of the transaction are completed and if major changes occur. The lawyer will respond in a timely manner to all client questions. The lawyer will inform the client if the engagement develops so that the likely achievements, time or costs start to diverge significantly from the estimates initially provided.
2. The lawyer will provide a reasonable quality of legal service to the client. Charges to the client will not be unreasonably high.

Complaints

1. Each law firm must have a documented complaints receipt and handling system and must use this system to handle all complaints. This documentation must be made available to the client on request and in the event of the client expressing a complaint. The current

38 The adoption of such a code of client service is also advocated in NZLC SP1 *Women's Access to Justice* Wellington, 1998.

documentation also must be provided to the New Zealand Law Council.

2. Each lawyer in private practice is subject to the oversight of the New Zealand Law Council in matters concerning client service. This oversight will take place within the framework defined by this Code of Client Service. This oversight will include also investigative and resolution procedures as adopted and as executed by the New Zealand Law Council.

The E-Dec report suggests that the code ought to be enforced by a separate part of the law society entitled the Office of Client Service concerned with standards rather than discipline. This is similar to the position in England where matters of quality are dealt with by the Office for the Supervision of Solicitors[39] and it is only when misconduct is involved that Solicitors' Disciplinary Tribunal will become involved.[40]

This author advocates the adoption of such a code of client care on the lines proposed by E-DEC. While such values, like that of competence, cannot be said to be ethical in nature, they are central to the effective working of the lawyer-client relationship. While many lawyers pride themselves on the way in which they treat their clients and exceed the standards imposed by such a code, others do treat clients poorly. In consequence, clients are confused about their legal position and alienated from the legal process. This is the opposite of the benefits that the legal profession is expected to bestow on the public. The legal profession has a duty to make the law and its procedures less daunting and more accessible. It is necessary to ensure not only that legal work is completed competently, but also that the client understands how this is achieved, and why it cost what it did, and that any query or complaint will be dealt with properly. Reforms have been proposed which would see client care rules introduced into the rules.[41] The preceding discussion should be read bearing in mind any reforms which have occurred since the publication of this work.

39 See also the provisions of the Legal Profession Act 1987 (NSW) which deals with incompetence as "unsatisfactory professional conduct" and therefore of a less serious nature than "professional misconduct".

40 A similar split between the supervisory and disciplinary functions of the law society was suggested in the E-DEC Report which advocates District Standards Committees which would enforce the client care rules as well as disciplining matters of minor misconduct, and a Lawyers' Complaints Office to deal with matters of serious misconduct.

41 Letter, President of the Law Society to all practitioners, 20 October 1999, and the attached paper.

11.5 Litigation immunity from legal actions

11.5.1 *Introduction*

Lawyers who appear in Court are subject to the same professional discipline and control as when they are acting outside the Court. When a lawyer appears before the Court his or her conduct is subject to the scrutiny of the Judge who may exercise the Court's inherent power of supervision to summarily discipline the lawyer in the event of misconduct. Unlike work that is not connected to litigation, where an advocate is incompetent in the conduct of a trial the ability of a client to sue for redress for loss suffered is limited.[42] When lawyers act as counsel in the conduct of litigation the law provides that they are immune from claims by their clients for breach of a duty of care. Consider then a situation where a lawyer incompetently conducts a case, and the client suffers loss through failing in a claim or defence and thereby losing, or becoming liable for, the value of the judgment. The lawyer may have failed to call vital witnesses, omitted to plead a central claim, or conceded a point which should have been argued. Through such act or omission the client suffers loss, but the client is barred from recovering that loss at all.

It is common for professionals not to warrant the result of their work. Doctors do not guarantee cures, and lawyers do not guarantee that litigants will win. All that is expected of them is that they will bring to bear a reasonable level of skill and care and exercise their professional judgment in the matter. Where it transpires that judgments were flawed, this cannot be visited upon the professional. It is recognised that matters such as medicine and law are partly an art and it is not possible to make decisions with arithmetical accuracy. Where the loss is due not to an error of judgment but to a failure to exercise the required degree of skill and care a right of action will usually exist against the professional. In the case of lawyers who appear in Court no such right of action will lie. It has long been established that a client cannot impeach the actions of counsel in the conduct of the case in Court by claims of professional negligence. It was stated in 1860:[43]

> An advocate is not responsible for ignorance of the law or any mistake of fact, or being less eloquent than he was expected to be… if he is acting with

42 See T Dugdale, "Advocates Immunity Under Scrutiny" (1998) 14 Professional Negligence 75 for a more detailed discussion of the scope and history of the immunity; M Oldham, "The Advocate's Common Law Immunity" (1996) 3 Deakin LR 55; Osborne [1986] NZLJ 17; A Grant, "The Negligent Advocate" [1980] NZLJ 260; S Todd *The Law of Torts in New Zealand* 2nd ed Wellington, Brookers, 1997, 362-369. For a recent judicial discussion see *Arthur J S Hall & Co v Simons* [1999] 1 Lloyd's LR PN 47.

43 *Swifen v Lord Chelmsford* (1860) 5 H & N 890. This view was affirmed by the House of Lords in *Rondel v Worsley* [1969] 1 AC 191.

> perfect good faith with a single view to the interests of his client, he is not responsible for any mistake or indiscretion or error of judgment of any sort.

This means an advocate's decisions in the course of proceedings to call or not to call evidence, to press or abandon a legal argument, or to make an application to the Court or not are not impeachable by the client. This is the case even if the decision made is clearly negligent and leads to loss being suffered by the client.

11.5.2 *Scope of the immunity*

Any conduct of counsel that occurs in Court will be covered by the immunity. The protection also extends to actions taken that, though not in Court, are intimately connected with the conduct of litigation.[44] Where counsel is drafting pleadings, briefing juniors, or doing any similar work which is effectively part of the hearing, he or she will be immune from any claim of a breach of a duty of care. For the immunity to attach it is necessary to show that the lawyer is involved in the conduct of litigation. In jurisdictions with a split profession this raises few problems, as the immunity is granted to barristers, but not to solicitors (except in those limited cases where they are acting as advocates).[45] In New Zealand it is common for one lawyer to act as both barrister and solicitor in the one matter, and it is necessary to distinguish between those acts undertaken as solicitor and those as undertaken in the role of counsel.

In *Feldman v A Practitioner*[46] the Court analysed the actions of the practitioner as if the tasks were undertaken by two quite different people. The Court described a practitioner as "advising him or her self as a solicitor" and "as a solicitor he failed to obtain material ... to put before himself as counsel". Such an analysis brings a considerable degree of artificiality into the consideration of the immunity and perhaps exposes the tenuous grounds on which it is imposed. The better approach is that of McCarthy P in *Rees v Sinclair*: [47]

> What of the practitioner who practises both as a barrister and solicitor? Should a different result be arrived at in that case? I think not. The considerations which I have mentioned seem to apply with equal force to such a practitioner...It may be argued that on this reasoning the protection

---

44 *Rees v Sinclair* [1974] 1 NZLR 180, 187, adopted in *Saif Ali v Sydney Mitchell & Co* [1980] AC 198.

45 Although this can lead to inconsistency as in *Somansundarum v M Julius Melchior & Co* [1989] 1 All ER 129 where it was held that a solicitor could be liable for negligently drafting pleadings, even though if the task had been conducted by a barrister the immunity would apply. Compare however *Landall v Dennis Faulkner & Alsop* [1994] 5 Med LR 268.

46 (1978) SASR 238 (a case from South Australia where the profession, like that of New Zealand, is fused).

47 *Rees v Sinclair* [1974] 1 NZLR 180, 186.

> should be extended to solicitors when they are appearing in Court or performing duties incidental to such appearances.

The better approach, and one adopted in New Zealand gives the immunity to a lawyer who is doing work which, if it were performed by a barrister, would be covered. This approach avoids the possibility of a practitioner acting as both a barrister and solicitor being liable for conduct from which, if practising as a barrister alone, he or she would have been immune.

It has been held that the immunity extends to cover some settlement discussions and agreements when made in the context of litigation that is actually in progress. There is, however, no blanket protection to protect advocates who advise as to the wisdom or otherwise of such settlements.[48] Each matter will have to be addressed on its own merits and the question of whether the actions in advising the settlement were "intimately connected" with the trial. In *Biggar v McLeod*[49] a party claimed that a settlement effected at the conclusion of the oral evidence in a case was not reflected in the consent order of the Court. The claim against the legal adviser failed as the conduct was held to be the subject of the immunity because it was inextricably bound up in the trial itself. The immunity is more likely to exist where the settlement arrived at is included in a consent order of the Court. It has been held that any attack on the order would amount to an inquiry into the conduct of the Court which would be inappropriate.[50] More difficult questions arise, such as whether the conduct in negotiating a settlement prior to litigation coming to trial, or a settlement reached which is not reflected in a consent order of the Court, would be covered by the immunity. The decisions in both *Biggar v McLeod* and *Rees v Sinclair* make it clear that the immunity should not be extended further than is absolutely necessary. If it were extended to the conduct of negotiation of proceedings prior to trial there is a danger of a slippery slope. Would it also be extended to situations where litigation had not been commenced but was contemplated? And what of the situation where, though not actually contemplated, litigation might ensue if no settlement were forthcoming. Clearly these latter cases do not warrant the protection of barristerial immunity, though the actual dividing line is unclear.[51] Any conduct must

48 *Arthur J S Hall & Co v Simons* [1999] 1 Lloyd's LR PN 47, 64.

49 [1977] 1 NZLR 321. See also *Donellan v Watson* (1990) 21 NSWLR 335; *Kelly v Corston* [1997] 4 All ER 466 (CA).

50 *Kelly v Corston* [1997] 4 All ER 466. Though there may be cases where a claim in respect of a consent order will not involve any inquiry into the conduct of the Court, as where the barrister mistakenly represents the nature of the settlement, or acts outside the authority granted by the client.

51 For a discussion of where the line does and ought to lie see S Williams, "Immunity in Retreat?" (1999) 15 Professional Negligence 75. Most recently see *Arthur J S Hall & Co v Simons* [1999] 1 Lloyd's LR PN 47.

be measured against the test in *Rees v Sinclair* as to whether the action is intimately connected with the conduct of the trial. Settlement negotiations prior to trial are doubtlessly affected by the impending litigation, but it is suggested that they are quite separate from it and practitioners engaged in such negotiations ought not benefit from the immunity.

A suggested distinction between strategic decisions as opposed to tactical decisions has been made in *Atwell v Perry & Co.*[52] In that case a dispute over a boundary was being litigated. Counsel for one party failed to take note of documentary evidence (official survey plans) which would have settled the matter. The counsel quite incorrectly conceded in Court that the plans were of no help. The unsuccessful party sought to recover due to his counsel's negligent failure to amend documents prior to the trial to take note of the obvious defence. In finding the counsel immune in this case a distinction was made between initial strategic thinking about how to frame and plead a claim or defence, and the more detailed work intimately connected with the trial such as deliberations immediately prior to trial (as in this case). It seems that where the actions of the advocate are close to the time of trial, and concern matters of detail rather than generality the immunity will apply.

Clients may sue their lawyer where the lawyer has negligently failed to pursue an appeal.[53] Further, if an appeal has been successful, an action against a lawyer who through his or her negligence was responsible for the loss at first instance will not be an abuse as it does not seek to impugn a final decision of the Court.[54]

Not all the work of a barrister will be protected by the immunity.[55] In some cases a barrister will undertake work that is not connected with litigation at all, as where an opinion is requested on a legal point of significance.[56] Further, not all litigation-related work of a barrister is intimately connected with the conduct of a trial. In *Saif Ali v Sydney Mitchell & Co*[57] it was held that a barrister whose advice led to the commencement of proceedings against the wrong party and the inability to proceed against the correct defendants was not immune from action. It was considered that the wrong decision to proceed against the inappropriate defendants was not itself intimately connected with the way in which the litigation was to be conducted. On this analysis any

---

52 [1998] 4 All ER 65.

53 *Walpole v Partridge and Wilson* [1994] QB 106, [1996] 2 All ER 353 (CA).

54 *Acton v Graham Pearce & Co* [1997] 3 All ER 909.

55 For a discussion of the boundaries of the immunity see T Bullimore, "Liability for Negligent Settlement Advice" (1997) Solicitors' Journal 1078.

56 *NRMA Limited v Morgan* [1999] NSWSC 407.

57 [1980] AC 198.

decision to proceed or not to proceed is not subject to the immunity. If a barrister advises an action to be taken which has no prospect of success, or that an action not be taken which would in fact almost certainly have succeeded, it would seem that the litigant would be able to sue for the loss caused by the negligent advice. A failure to plead a particular cause of action or head of damages will similarly not fall under the immunity.[58]

Where a practitioner acts in the role of a solicitor only and does not appear in Court he or she will only be able to claim immunity in relation to matters closely connected to the trial.[59] This differs from the English approach under which a solicitor who instructs a barrister may under no circumstances claim the immunity.[60] If a barrister is instructed, the solicitor will be liable for any negligent acts or omissions which occur in assisting the barrister. Where a practitioner acts as both barrister and solicitor thereby completing all of the work connected with the litigation, he or she is in one sense instructing himself or herself. The alternative is to seek the assistance of a more specialised or experienced practitioner to act as counsel. In most cases this will mean instructing a practitioner who holds a practising certificate as a barrister only. If a practitioner is careless in instructing a barrister, and instructs a barrister who is clearly inexperienced and not up to the rigours of the task, there may be a claim against the solicitor for negligently delegating the work. Similarly, where the lawyer fails to delegate the work and is clearly incapable of conducting the litigation himself or herself there will be a claim in negligence for failing to brief a barrister in the matter.

The English Court of Appeal has recently attempted to recast the immunity of advocates in terms of the public policy arguments against allowing collateral attacks on final decisions of the Court. In *Arthur J S Hall & Co v Simons*[61] Lord Bingham CJ suggested that the question of whether an immunity exists in any particular case must be resolved as a matter of public policy. This is to be determined by a balancing exercise. On one side of the equation are the interests of finality in litigation and

58 *Yates Property Corporation v Boland* (1998) 157 ALR 30. See further B Hocking, "An Immunity Built on Shifting Sands: The Barrister, the Expert and the Judge" (1999) 15 PN 185.

59 *Rees v Sinclair* [1974] 1 NZLR 180, 186, though the words of MacArthur J in that case were obiter. It is suggested that because of the fused profession in New Zealand (which has become more fused since that case was decided) every solicitor is also a barrister and therefore it is impossible to meaningfully distinguish between barristers and solicitors in the same way as is the case in England.

60 *Acton v Graham Pearce & Co* [1997] 3 All ER 909. Though a solicitor who acts as a solicitor-advocate may claim the immunity in the same way as a barrister.

61 [1999] 1 Lloyd's LR PN 47.

protecting final decisions of the Court against attack. On the other side is the fundamental principle of law that citizens should not be denied redress for wrongs against them. Relevant to such an analysis will be the nature of the decision which is sought to be questioned, the basis of the claim made against the advocate, and the grounds upon which such a claim is made.[62] It is well established that a claim against an advocate will not be permitted where it amounts to a collateral attack on a Court's decision and is an abuse of process.[63] *Arthur J S Hall & Co v Simons* places the question of abuse as the first and foundational question of any issue concerning immunity.[64] On such an approach the advocate's immunity rule is an aspect of the wider prohibition on abusing the procedure of the Court.[65] It was also held in that case, that the nature of the judgment that is sought to be impugned will be relevant to the wider question of whether the action amounted to an abuse. A Court will be more reluctant to inquire into a criminal conviction than a finding of a civil trial, and more reluctant to inquire into a considered decision of a Court than an interlocutory or consent order.[66] The Court in *Arthur J S Hall & Co v Simons* decided that there will be cases where a collateral attack on a decision of the Court will be justified in light of the nature of the earlier judgment, the nature of the claim against the advocate, and the grounds relied on in that claim. This does seem to run counter to the prior authorities of the House of Lords which proceed on the basis that, once it is established that the acts or omissions complained of occurred within or were intimately connected to legal proceedings, the immunity is absolute.[67] On that analysis the core of the immunity is the protection afforded against claims made in respect of actions of advocates in Court.

In all the recent cases where the Court has considered whether the acts of a lawyer are protected by the immunity, the need to construe strictly the scope of the immunity has been stressed. The effect of the existence of the immunity is to leave a wronged litigant without a cause of action. This is clearly a serious injustice to visit on an individual for the greater good. It has been observed:[68]

62 [1999] 1 Lloyd's LR PN 47, 64.

63 *Hunter v Chief Constable of West Midlands* [1981] 3 All ER 727 733 per Diplock LJ.

64 *Arthur J S Hall & Co v Simons* [1999] 1 Lloyd's LR PN 47, 63, 64 per Lord Bingham CJ.

65 Though see the approach of T Dugdale, "Advocates' Immunity Under Scrutiny" (1998) 14 Professional Negligence 75, 79.

66 [1999] 1 Lloyd's LR PN 47, 65 per Lord Bingham CJ.

67 *Rondel v Worsley* [1969] 1 AC 191; *Saif Ali v Sydney Mitchell & Co* [1980] AC 198.

68 *Arthur J S Hall & Co v Simons* [1999] 1 Lloyd's LR PN 47, 65 per Lord Bingham CJ.

> Any doubt must be resolved against the grant of forensic immunity, since the immunity derogates from what we have described as a fundamental principle and the law should be slow to grant its own practitioners a protection denied to members of other professions.

The trend until recently appears to have been to incrementally extend the immunity from conduct in Court only, to conduct intimately connected with the trial including tactical pre-trial work and settlement discussions. Only in the past few years, and in *Arthur J S Hall & Co v Simons* in particular, have the Courts been more ready to recognise that there may be cases where there is no good policy reason for protecting a barrister from liability for loss caused to lay clients.

11.5.3 *The policy arguments*

It is axiomatic to the law that where the actions of one person can be shown to have caused loss to another in circumstances of close proximity the law should ensure that the wrongdoer is liable to compensate the victim. How is it then that this anomaly of barristerial immunity means that lawyers can, in the conduct of litigation, act negligently with impunity? There is a wrong without a remedy. The arguments upon which the immunity was originally based were founded on old principles of liability whereby, because the client had no contractual relationship with the barrister (that relationship was between client and solicitor), no claim could be made. The emergence of the modern law of negligence has done away with such arguments.[69]

The existence of the immunity has since been justified on grounds of public policy which are said to outweigh the public policy interest of granting to litigants who suffer loss at the hands of incompetent counsel the right to recover damage. It was noted in *Saif Ali v Sydney Mitchell & Co*[70] that the parties concerned in the issue in that case (and in many such cases) were a barrister and a solicitor respectively.[71] Any argument put before the Court will invariably be put by a barrister who is enjoying the very immunity he or she is arguing for or against. Even the Judges listening to the matter will have been lawyers and at one time enjoyed such an immunity. It is wise to view the reasons given for the immunity in the cases with a healthy scepticism.

---

69 This was accepted in *Rondel v Worsley* [1969] 1 AC 191, 216 per Lord Diplock who saw *Hedley Byrne & Co Ltd v Heller & Partners Ltd* [1964] AC 465 as "casting doubt on this facile explanation which had been current for 100 years".

70 [1980] AC 198, 223 per Lord Diplock.

71 The argument essentially revolved around the issue of whether the barrister could be joined to proceedings brought against the solicitor.

Ultimate duty to the Court

There will be instances where counsel is required to act in a manner that is against the interest of the client because a higher duty is owed to the Court. If a client insists on presenting evidence to the Court which is untrue counsel may withdraw. It is argued that if the litigant had a right to sue the counsel, such decisions would be tainted by the prospect of a claim by the litigant. Throughout the proceedings the lawyer would have to have an eye not only to the duties owed to the Court, but also to the duty owed to the client. One such duty to the Court is to conduct trials and pre-trial matters expeditiously. This duty might be compromised if counsel engaged in "defensive advocacy" as some have suggested might occur.[72] Counsel might conduct a case in a manner which was affected by the possibility of a claim being made against them and rather than fearlessly pursuing the interests of their client, they would be overly cautious in the conduct of the proceeding. For example, a lawyer is to refrain from unnecessarily prolonging proceedings, or obscuring issues. Even if there exist many witnesses who could attest to a particular matter a lawyer is not expected to call all of them. It will be sufficient to call those considered most reliable and sufficient to persuasively corroborate each other. An attempt to call all witnesses would meet with disapproval from the Court and may result in an adverse order of costs against counsel for unnecessarily prolonging proceedings. It has been claimed that if the lawyer were liable to be sued by the client there would be a tendency to be cautious in such matters and a likelihood that more witnesses than necessary would be called.[73] The same point can be made in a proliferation of legal arguments, documentary evidence, and pre-trial applications, out of an excess of caution.

Such an argument is speculative. It is open to doubt that the duty to conduct a trial expeditiously is a real consideration in the way a lawyer presents a case. The fact is that advocacy that is clear, to the point, and not obscured by repetition and unnecessary detail, is usually most effective. Where a client's cause is best served by obscuring facts and confusion of issues, lawyers will not refrain from engaging in such practices. It seems that the existence of the immunity plays little part in the decision processes relating to trial tactics. In conducting a trial, a lawyer may decide not to call a witness (or take any other decision in the litigation) for a good reason based on a professional judgment. The witness may be unreliable, or there may be disagreement with portions of another witness's evidence, or it may be duplicative. In such cases the decision not to call the witness may be flawed in hindsight, as when other evidence is not accepted by the Court. However, where the error is one of judgment no claim will lie in any event. Certainly, in the example

72 *Giannarelli v Wraith* (1988) 165 CLR 543, 573 per Wilson J, 594 per Dawson J.

73 *Saif Ali v Sydney Mitchell & Co* [1980] AC 198, 233 per Lord Russell of Killowen.

above there is no breach of a duty of care and no action would lie. However the immunity goes further and protects a lawyer who forgets to ask a vital question out of pure carelessness, or omits to call a witness to establish a vital fact, and thereby loses a case.

Lawyers will be expected to disclose precedents and legislation that are adverse to their client's cause (although they may argue that they can be distinguished, overruled or ignored). It is argued that the existence of the immunity encourages such fearlessness and impartiality when observing the duty to the Court. Without such immunity, it is asserted, there would be a reluctance to assist the Court at the expense of the client's cause as is sometimes required.[74] Such an argument presumes that lawyers, unless protected from claims by their clients, will (or are more likely to) breach their obligations owed to the Court. Such an argument advocates sacrificing a client's right to redress for wrong committed against him or her to ensure that lawyers behave as required. The argument is essentially one of policy, but can be phrased in terms rather unflattering to lawyers — as lawyers would be likely to breach their duty to the Court if there was a threat of action for negligent handling of a case, a remedy for negligence by lawyers in Court should be refused.

Lawyers are required to be fearless and independent in their presentation of a case to the Court. It has been argued that lawyers, as officers of the Court, should be immune from actions taken in Court as a natural corollary of the immunity of Judges and witnesses.[75] The claim is that as independent actors in the trial process they should not be liable for any action taken in Court proceedings in the absence of malice.[76] Such protection is needed in respect of witnesses to ensure that they tell frankly what they consider to be the truth of the matter without fear of a claim against them in the event of a mistake. It is required in respect of Judges to ensure that they may discharge their duties and give decisions in good faith without fear of an action if errors are made. The position of a witness or Judge is different from that of a lawyer. A Judge is required, almost by definition, to be impartial and the decision is to be made with reference only to the issues in the case. Witnesses are required to tell the truth no matter how damaging it might be, or what the consequences are if their memory is faulty. In their capacity of witness or Judge there is no suggestion that there is any third party to whom they owe special duties. Lawyers are in quite a different position. They have undertaken to act, within the bounds of their other duties, in the interests of the client. They are in all other situations under

74 *Rees v Sinclair* [1974] 1 NZLR 180, 182.

75 *Rees v Sinclair* [1974] 1 NZLR 180, 185; *Rondel v Worsley* [1969] 1 AC 191, 273 per Lord Pearce.

76 *Saif Ali v Sydney Mitchell & Co* [1980] AC 198, 222 per Lord Diplock, 230 per Lord Salmon.

contractual and tortious duties to practise their profession with due care and skill. They accept a healthy fee for rendering the professional services in which they claim to have special skill. If they fail to exercise the promised and expected degree of skill and care it is difficult to see how the administration of justice would be damaged by granting the injured client the right to sue.

Collateral attack on final decision of the Court

The second kind of policy argument that has been relied on by the Courts in defending the continued existence of the immunity is the need to ensure that litigation eventually comes to an absolute conclusion, and to prevent the undermining of the judicial process by collateral attacks on the decision of a Court. While complex litigation with its numerous pre-trial applications and appeals may stretch over many years, after the final avenue of appeal is exhausted the parties must accept the decision of the Court. Under the principles of res judicata and issue estoppel it is not permissible to bring the same dispute before the Court again, no matter how it is disguised. It is argued that if it were permissible to sue lawyers for their conduct of a case this would open the door to an effective retrial of the trial itself.[77] The whole of the proceedings of the Court would be brought into question and would amount to a collateral attack on the decision of the Court. The appropriate avenue for redress if it is considered that the decision of the Court was wrong is an appeal.[78] If all appeals are exhausted the matter is at an end.

There are two aspects of such questioning of a Court's decision which proponents of the immunity consider troublesome. The first is that it appears "to require a Court of coordinate jurisdiction to try the question whether another Court reached a wrong decision and, if so, to inquire into its causes for doing so".[79] It is considered to be inappropriate for a Court to undertake such a task as it may involve a Judge in an inquiry as to whether a fellow Judge of coordinate jurisdiction had decided the case rightly or wrongly. Secondly, and related to the first point, is the suggestion that such second guessing of the decision in the first trial would bring the administration of justice into disrepute.

The problem is that if lawyers were able to be blamed by their clients for the loss of a case the lawyers would in defence seek to shift the blame to the Judge who decided the matter. If it were demonstrated in an action

---

77 *Rondel v Worsley* [1969] 1 AC 191, 249 per Lord Morris of Borth-y-Gest; *Rees v Sinclair* [1974] 1 NZLR 180, 183.

78 *Saif Ali v Sydney Mitchell & Co* [1980] AC 198, 222, 223 per Lord Diplock. Where a claim amounts to a collateral attack on a final decision of the Court this will be a defence to any defendant, not just a barrister: *Smith v Linskills* [1996] 2 All ER 353 (CA).

79 *Saif Ali v Sydney Mitchell & Co* [1980] AC 198, ,223 per Lord Diplock.

for negligence against a lawyer that the cause of the loss was not some act by the lawyer but due to the fact that the Judge made an error, then the lawyer would not be liable. Understandably the Courts have been reluctant to do away with the immunity where the results might be that their own conduct is questioned in other equal Courts.

This fear is scant reason to deny redress to a client who has suffered at the hands of a negligent lawyer. We do not doubt that if an engineer designed a building or bridge poorly he or she would be liable for any losses flowing from the defect. Similarly, there is no question that a lawyer who is negligent in some non-litigious piece of work will have to compensate the client for any losses suffered as a consequence. It is only due to the fact that the negligent act occurs in the course of litigation that the client is denied redress. This seems a particularly fickle basis on which to decide the matter.

The argument is one of public policy — that the administration of justice would be brought into disrepute by the questioning of what goes on in Court. This very argument can, however, be turned on its head. The public is far more likely to view the judicial process with contempt if they realise that the law precludes inquiry into the incompetence of the conduct of lawyers' actions in Court. There may indeed be a perception that:[80]

> … barristers, with the connivance of the Judges, [have] built for themselves an ivory tower and have lived in it ever since at the expense of their clients.

More respect would be gained if the Courts accepted that all of the actions of a lawyer are open to scrutiny, even if this requires the scrutiny of the conduct of the judiciary at the same time.

This objection could also be simply avoided by procedural safeguards. There are several instances where a Court will sit with more than the usual number of Judges.[81] In actions concerning the conduct of a trial it could be required that a Court be informed when the conduct of another member of the judiciary was to be called into question and a more authoritative forum convened. Alternatively, a higher Court in such cases could hear the matter.

80 *Rondel v Worsley* [1967] 1 QB 443, 468, cited in *Giannarelli v Wraith* (1988) 165 CLR 543, 575 per Wilson J.

81 For example where the High Court is considering an appeal from the New Zealand Law Society Disciplinary Tribunal (s 118(2) Law Practitioners Act 1982) or where the Court of Appeal is being asked to consider overruling one of its own precedents.

Even if the objection is accepted it really only justifies the immunity in a small number of cases. There will be numerous cases where a claim against an advocate could be taken without questioning the competence of the Court which decided the question. Where there has been an obvious procedural failure such as failing to plead a cause of action, or error of law such as pleading a palpably untenable claim, there will be no need to inquire into the deliberations of the Court. This was the view of the English Court of Appeal in *Arthur J S Hall & Co v Simons*[82] which decided that where the claim does not entail a collateral attack on a decision of the Court it will not be barred by the immunity. It was held that even where the claim does involve such an attack it may still be permitted where it can be shown that the alleged breach deprived the plaintiff of a reasonable opportunity of appreciating that better terms of settlement were available than were obtained, or otherwise placed the plaintiff in a position of having to accept a settlement less advantageous than he or she should have obtained.[83]

Cab rank principle

It is a central duty of a lawyer who is sufficiently competent and available to accept any client who seeks assistance.[84] In defending the existence of the immunity Lord Pearce observed in *Rondel v Worsley*:[85]

> It is easier, pleasanter, and more advantageous professionally for barristers to advise, represent or defend those who are decent and reasonable and likely to succeed in their action or their defence than those who are unpleasant, unreasonable, disreputable and have an apparently hopeless case. Yet it would be tragic if our legal system came to provide no reputable defenders, representatives, or advisers for the latter.

From this observation it was argued that because lawyers cannot choose whom they represent they cannot refuse to act for cantankerous and litigious clients who are more likely to sue them in the event of a failure. Accordingly, the barrister is granted immunity. The House of Lords doubted such an argument where Lord Diplock sceptically stated:[86]

> I doubt whether in reality, in the field of civil litigation at any rate, [the cab rank rule] results often in counsel having to accept work which he [or she]

82 [1999] 1 Lloyd's LR PN 47.

83 *Arthur J S Hall & Co v Simons* [1999] 1 Lloyd's LR PN 47, 64, 66.

84 In jurisdictions where the profession is split the duty usually only applies to barristers.

85 *Rondel v Worsley* [1967] 1 AC 19, 275 (CA). In that case the barrister had been retained on a "dock brief" that is to say the barrister being in Court and not immediately occupied, and the litigant being without counsel, the barrister was required to act for the litigant for a fixed fee. See also *Rees v Sinclair* [1974] 1 NZLR 180, 184.

86 *Saif Ali v Sydney Mitchell & Co* [1980] AC 198, 221 per Lord Diplock.

> would not otherwise be willing to undertake. But even if there are rare cases where it does, this does not seem to affect the character of the decisions that the barrister has to make in carrying out instructions that he receives thorough the client's solicitor.

The weakness of the argument that the cab rank principle is relevant is compounded in New Zealand where solicitors involved in non-litigious work are equally bound, yet still susceptible to claims in negligence. By way of analogy we can also observe that doctors are expected to render services to those who need them regardless of their identity. In jurisdictions where suing for personal injury is possible such a duty to render medical assistance has not been suggested as a ground for granting any kind of immunity to a doctor.

Lawyer-centred approach

Underneath the formal arguments made for the retention of the immunity is a sense that the position of lawyers who conduct litigation is special. They are required to make decisions of fine judgment on matters of great importance. Often these decisions must be made in the middle of a trial, perhaps in the middle of a question in cross-examination. The crucible in which this all occurs is seen to be particularly unique. The Courtroom is an environment that is not reproduced elsewhere and where special pressures and conflicts are brought to bear on the lawyer. The effective functioning of the process in Court is seen as of paramount importance. If the administration of justice were to be rendered less effective the effects would be far reaching.

Much of this is true, though it reflects a very lawyer-centred perspective. The need for the effective administration of medicine, building of bridges, or designing of houses are all important to the effective functioning of society, and all require the discharge of special skills, often in a demanding and unique environment. There is no suggestion that doctors, engineers, or architects should be granted any kind of immunity from claims in negligence.[87] The fact that one professional works on a building site, or in an operating theatre and the other works in the Courtroom seem a frail basis upon which to grant an immunity from actions to one and not the other.

Assumptions: floodgates and causation

Central to all of the arguments in favour of the immunity is the assumption that if the immunity did not exist there would be a large number of claims against lawyers for negligence in the conduct of legal

87 Some such immunities did in fact exist but have been progressively done away with: architects — *Chambers v Goldthorpe* [1901] 1 QB 624 overruled in *Sutcliffe v Thackrah* [1974] AC 727; accountants — *Finnegan v Allen* [1943] KB 425 overruled by *Arenson v Arenson* [1977] AC 405.

proceedings, and that these claims would have the negative effects feared. There is no evidence that there would be a flood of claims against lawyers if the immunity were removed. There is no reason for there to be proportionately more claims than there are against any other group of professionals who will inevitably make occasional mistakes. There is evidence against such a flood. There is no such immunity in Ontario[88] and there is no evidence from that jurisdiction to show that the fears of the English and New Zealand Courts would come to fruition if the immunity were done away with.

The predictions that the task of lawyers would be made unmanageable, that there would be a flood of litigation, and that the administration of justice would be thrown into disrepute, are merely predictions. There is no evidence that this would come about in the absence of the immunity. They are empirically baseless and a shaky foundation on which to build an impregnable barrier to claims against lawyers for wrongs committed in the conduct of litigation.

Immunity is a blunt device

Granting a blanket immunity to lawyers for any wrong committed in the conduct of proceedings is a clumsy method by which to protect the administration of justice. Even if we accept that in the absence of controls the removal of the immunity would lead to some harm, this does not mean that the immunity should be retained. There are numerous controls already in place to ensure that groundless actions are not brought against lawyers. Such actions may be struck out as vexatious, without foundation, or an abuse of the process. Litigants who believe the lawyer has acted negligently in conducting their litigation will almost always seek advice on whether or not a claim exists. Very few clients would proceed to sue their lawyer after receiving advice that there was little foundation for a claim.

The instances when a lawyer will be found to have been negligent in the course of the conduct of proceedings will not be vast. While lawyers who make obvious blunders will be held liable to those who suffered loss by those blunders, no liability has ever attached to a professional for errors of judgment or an opinion of the law that reasonably differed from that of the Court.

The dilemma of a lawyer faced with a hard problem where the duties to Court and client lie can also be avoided. It is not necessary for a lawyer to run the risk of either breaching the duty to Court or client. It would not be negligent for a lawyer, exercising reasonable care and acting in

88 *Demarco v Jungaro* (1979) 95 DLR 3d 385; *Leslie v Ball* (1863) 22 UCQB 512, 517. See also *Chang Yeo & Partners v Guano Min Hardware and Engineering Pte Ltd* [1997] 2 SLR 729 (CA).

good faith, to err in favour of the duty to the Court.[89] It is within the power of the Courts to frame a defence to such a claim where lawyers took an action in the honest, even if negligently mistaken, belief that the action was required by the lawyer's professional duties.

Countervailing private and public interest

Almost all of the judicial discussions regarding the immunity focus on the possible harm that might flow to the administration of justice if the immunity did not exist. Little attention is paid to the considerable private and public interest that is harmed by the existence of the immunity. Confidence in the legal profession is not increased by the knowledge that in one of its most important activities the profession claims the benefit of a legal immunity. The confidence in the judicial system must also be harmed by the knowledge that there is a class of actions, that is, those against officers of the Court, which may not be brought before the Courts. Litigants are effectively denied justice ostensibly to protect the very system from which they seek assistance.[90]

Perhaps most telling, however, are the numerous individual wrongs that are done to each and every litigant who is refused redress because their negligent lawyer claims the benefit of the immunity. Such a denial of redress sacrifices the right of that individual to the essentially abstract interest of the administration of justice. The subjection of all citizens to the law is a central tenet of the existing system. Where the rights of a litigant are denied and the liability of the lawyer is excused, the wronged litigant might legitimately wonder whether redress outside the Court system is the only alternative left.[91] Perhaps most ironic in this is the exhortation in the rules that lawyers should not seek to evade liability for their acts. Rule 1.12(1) provides:

> A practitioner must accept legal responsibility for his or her actions. Subject to the following provisions, a practitioner must be prepared to meet any liability arising out of any act, error or omission in the course of the practitioner's professional duties or business.

It does seem somewhat against the spirit of this that the litigation immunity has exactly the effect of relieving lawyers of legal responsibility for their actions.[92]

---

89 *Giannarelli v Wraith* (1988) 165 CLR 543, 573 per Wilson J.

90 In S Williams, "Immunity in Retreat?" (1999) 15 Professional Negligence 75 it is observed that the rule contravenes the right to have grievances tried by a Court, a right enshrined in art 6 of the European Convention on Human Rights 1950.

91 See J Lock *Second Treatise of Government* 3rd ed (JW Gouge ed) Oxford, Blackwell, 1976, ch XX, p 322.

92 In light of the immunity, as there is no legal responsibility the fact that a lawyer avails him or herself of the immunity will not breach the rule.

Chapter 12

Fees

12.1 Introduction

The fees payable by the client for the services rendered by the lawyer are an important aspect of the relationship between lawyer and client. The level (or existence) of the fees will often be determinative of whether clients will be able to avail themselves of the services of a lawyer. The lawyer will act only on the understanding that the client will pay for the services rendered. The comparatively high income of lawyers generated by fees is a strong incentive to enter the profession of law. A significant portion of the public consider that lawyers' services are excessively expensive and that lawyers benefit in an inappropriate way from the need of the public for legal services.[1]

The fees charged by a lawyer raise a number of ethical issues. The existence of a fee is, at least on the face of it, a source of conflict between lawyer and client. It is in the lawyer's interest to maximise the fee, whereas the opposite is true for the client. The existence of such a conflict of interest is an accepted incident of the everyday practice of a lawyer, and lawyers are generally regarded as able to be trusted not to generate work needlessly to increase their own fees. The position of lawyers is unusual in that as a professional the lawyer is notionally motivated by an ethic of service in rendering legal assistance. This is in contrast to the commercial motivation of other business enterprises. This service ethic leads to a number of matters with an ethical dimension which require consideration. Unlike other businesses lawyers are not permitted to price their services on the basis of what the prospective customers are prepared to pay, rather they are required to charge only a reasonable fee.[2] To overcharge a client may be considered misconduct in

---

1 In a recent poll 81% of the sample considered that lawyers were expensive to use, 34% of the sample thought that lawyers did not give good value for money. *Polls of the Profession and the Public*: Wellington, MRL Research Group, 1997.

2 Rule 3.01.

some circumstances.[3] There are strong arguments that in some circumstances lawyers should act for no fee, or a reduced fee. The professional rules and general law not only supervise the amount of the fee charged, but also regulate the terms of the fee agreement between the lawyer and client. In particular, where the lawyer and client agree that the amount or existence of the fee will be dependent on the outcome of the case (that is, a contingency fee), the arrangement may be in breach of the law and possibly the rules.

The fee aspect of the retainer between lawyer and client is of ethical significance. Whether the rules are meaningful or appropriate (or indeed consistently enforced) in the commercial climate in which law is currently practised is open to argument. However, it is clear that for the present the law and the profession will continue to supervise both the level of fees and the manner in which they are calculated.

12.2 The duty to charge only a reasonable fee

12.2.1 *Overview*

Lawyers are constrained in the fee they charge. Unlike a businessperson who may charge whatever price the customer is prepared to pay, the rules provide that: "a practitioner shall charge a client no more than a fee which is fair and reasonable for the work done having regard to the interests of both client and practitioner".[4] A lawyer, in contracting with a client, is expected to exercise good faith and honesty. He or she should be open about the nature and difficulty of the work proposed.[5] While the liability of a client for fees is based on the contract of retainer between lawyer and client, the terms of the contract are strictly regulated. This even extends to a requirement that, where a lawyer makes an estimate of the fee, he or she may not depart radically from it.[6] In light of the commercial environment in which most lawyers work, this is a difficult requirement. While it goes almost without saying that a lawyer may not impose a fee in circumstances that are unconscionable or otherwise improper, the requirement that the fee be reasonable is a quite distinct obligation. The imposition of the duty to charge a fee that is reasonable is a limit on the pursuit of self-interest of the lawyer. While a lawyer is entitled to charge a fee that reflects the degree of expertise required and the professional nature of the task, a lawyer may not extract the highest fee possible from the client where this exceeds a reasonable fee.

---

3 For an explicit example of such a rule see r 14.13 of the English *Guide*. See also *Re Lundon* [1918] NZLR 193 where improper charging practices resulted in the practitioner being struck off.

4 Rule 3.01.

5 Also *Re Lundon* [1918] NZLR 193.

6 *Wong v Vizards* [1997] 2 Costs LR 46 see also para 13.07 of the English *Guide*.

12.2.2 *Rationale*

The reasoning behind the rule is that, as professionals, lawyers are distinct from entrepreneurs who simply seek to maximise profits. Lawyers are interested in rendering a service to the public and to the maintenance of the justice system. While they are entitled to a reasonable degree of recompense for their efforts, and certainly should be able to live comfortably on their professional fees, they should not be motivated primarily by profit.[7] The public service motivation is traditionally considered to be a hallmark of a professional. Such reasoning is at odds with the actual practice of law where the profit motive is of central importance in many firms. Pricing of work, whether it is on an hourly rate or a fixed fee, is often done on the basis of purely commercial considerations. In many cases this leads to a fee which is reasonable, as the market for legal services is a competitive one. However, there are dangers that fees determined on solely economic grounds will be excessive.

A possibly more defensible justification for the supervision of lawyers' charging practices is the disparity of knowledge between lawyer and client. Legal services are a complex commodity. At the outset of a matter it will often not be entirely clear to the client how much assistance is required. At the conclusion of a matter it may not be obvious to the client how well the lawyer completed the work, whether all of the work undertaken was necessary to the result, how long the work undertaken should have taken to complete, or whether the result was the best that could be achieved. It is impossible for the client to assess whether the fees charged were commensurate with the work completed. To overcome this lack of knowledge a degree of supervision is required.

A complicating factor is the nature of the service provided by lawyers. Like medical assistance, it is often not practicable to economise on the quality of the service provided. Low quality legal assistance could leave a client worse off. Lawyers will not usually give a guarantee that the work will be able to be completed for a fixed sum, except in the case of the most straightforward of transactions. Lawyers will not be able to give any assurance as to the outcome of the work. The result is a degree of uncertainty as to the amount of the fee at the outset, and an inability of the client to assess whether the anticipated fee is worth the risk that the assistance of the lawyer will bear no fruit.

Supervision is required to ensure that lawyers do not take an illegitimate advantage of the gap in knowledge between lawyer and client by

7 See the comments of A Forbes in "The Wandering if not yet Lost Lawyer" a paper delivered at the New Zealand Law Conference 1999.

undertaking work that is not required, or by overcharging for work that is completed.

12.2.3 *What is a reasonable fee?*

The concept of a reasonable fee is a difficult one. Rule 3.01, which deals with fees, refers to the Costs and Conveyancing Practice Manual which sets out some considerations and observes that the fees are expected to give a fair and reasonable return for the services rendered. There is no external guide or benchmark as to what will be a reasonable amount for a lawyer to charge.[8] Any determination of whether or not a fee is reasonable is dependent on what fees other practitioners charge for similar work.

The test of "reasonableness" appears to be what is reasonable in the eyes of fellow practitioners. Although such a test is not explicitly stated in the rules, the procedure by which a client may question the amount of a bill of costs requires consideration of the bill by the District Council which will, in practice, delegate the matter to costs revisers who will be practitioners.[9] This reflects:[10]

> … the view that fellow practitioners are probably the persons best qualified to consider solicitors' bills of cost. They should be familiar with the overheads, fair charge out, and what is a proper amount of time to charge for a particular job.

This differs from the approach in other jurisdictions where the question of what is reasonable is generally dealt with by a registrar or master of the Court who is quite separate from the profession.[11] It is certainly arguable that the question of what costs are reasonable should not be left to be decided by members of the profession alone. Lawyers will naturally value the services they provide highly, and be reluctant to find that practices that may be widespread in the profession are inappropriate or excessive. There is a strong argument that representatives of clients' interests should be involved in examining the fees charged and work undertaken from a perspective untainted by professional allegiances.

The process of setting a fee ought not to be merely arithmetical. It is an exercise of judgment as to what an appropriate fee is for the work

8 Compare the detailed guidance given by the New South Wales Law Society in its *Costs Guidebook* 1999 which may be of assistance to New Zealand practitioners.

9 See ss 15, 29, 143, and 145 Law Practitioners Act 1982 and *Gallagher v Dobson* [1993] 3 NZLR 611, 613 per Barker J.

10 *Gallagher v Dobson* [1993] 3 NZLR 611, 615 per Barker J.

11 For a discussion of the position in the Australian jurisdictions see G Dal Pont *Lawyers' Professional Responsibility in Australia and New Zealand* North Ryde NSW, LBC Information Services, 1996, ch 17.

done.[12] This leaves room for differences of opinion between practitioners as to what the appropriate fee will be. In order to minimise such variations the rules provide a list of factors that will be relevant in determining the fee.[13] While none of these alone is conclusive, and they do not provide any kind of formula by which to calculate a fee, they certainly bear consideration.[14]

Skill

The degree of "skill, specialised knowledge and responsibility" required to complete the task will be relevant. Where the task is routine and does not need an experienced or specialised practitioner the costs can be expected to be lower than where cases are novel, complex, or require particular expertise. In such cases, there is an expectation that the work will be able to be completed quickly by a competent practitioner. There ought to be no need for arduous research or the applications of specialised skills for which a premium might be expected. Most clients seek the services of the principals of a firm, and accordingly the fees charged by a principal who will bear ultimate responsibility for the work, will be correspondingly higher. In a similar vein, the charges made by a non-lawyer ought to be less that those charged by a qualified lawyer.[15]

Time

The amount of time spent on the work will be directly relevant to the bill of costs. It is common practice in modern firms to record carefully the amount of time spent by any member of the firm on a particular matter and use those individuals' "charge out rate" multiplied by the time they spent on the matter as a starting place for the bill of costs. Such calculations should not be given too much weight. There will be instances where the time spent is disproportionate to the nature of the task, suggesting that the lawyer undertook unnecessary work, or is not competent in the area. Barker ACJ observed that it is inappropriate to place undue reliance on time-costing alone:

> Whilst the reality of life in the modern law office requires the keeping of time records, these records must only be used as a guide to ascertaining the proper fee; otherwise a premium is placed on inefficiency; experience and skill may not receive a proper reward.

---

12 See *Property and Reversionary Investment Corp v Secretary of State for the Environment* [1975] 1 WLR 1504, [1975] 2 All ER 436.

13 See the commentary to r 3.02 and the *Costs and Conveyancing Manual.*

14 These considerations were judicially examined in *Property and Reversionary Investment Corp v Secretary of State for the Environment* [1975] 1 WLR 1504, [1975] 2 All ER 436.

15 *Gallagher v Dobson* [1993] 3 NZLR 611, 619.

Value of the subject-matter

While the profession has long discarded the practice of charging a percentage of the value of the transaction according to a set scale, it is still common to charge more where the value of the subject-matter of the transaction is high. This is approved by the rules which provide: "value or amounts of any property or money involved" are a relevant consideration in determining the level of fees. There is some justification where the magnitude of the matter requires special care to be taken, and extra checks to be carried out. That a particular transaction concerns a large sum of money or valuable property does not, of itself, seem to justify a higher fee any more than a mechanic working on an expensive car can claim a higher hourly rate for the same work. There may be a temptation where lawyers are dealing with transactions worth millions of dollars to inflate the bill. The reasons for such a move might be that the bill will be a minute fraction of the value of the transaction and unlikely to be objected to. Or the client may be ignorant of the fact that work to that value was not necessary to the transaction. There may also be a tendency to see a "cut" of the transaction as a legitimate basis for fees.

Lawyers are not commission agents and in the absence of express agreement there seems to be no justification for an increase in the fees charged merely because the work concerns an issue of particular importance, or asset of considerable value. Obviously, an increase in fees will be appropriate where extra prudence is required because of the importance of the matter. In such cases, it may be appropriate for a small premium to be added to reflect the increased risk that the lawyer assumes if the task is performed negligently. The test ought to be based on whether the work completed was reasonably necessary in light of the nature and value of the matters at stake.[16] This writer is of the view that the provision of an increase in fees merely because the matter is one that the client considers important is premised on the outdated (and inappropriate) method of calculating costs as a proportion of the value of a transaction.

Importance to client

A related consideration is the "importance of the matter to the client". Unlike value, importance concerns how clients perceive the matter. Like the monetary value of the matter, the importance to the client ought to increase the costs only in a secondary manner. Where clients stress the importance of a matter, it may be appropriate for the lawyer to take extra precautionary steps beyond what might be done by a normally prudent lawyer. Research may be undertaken in greater depth, staff involved may be of greater seniority, documents may be perused by more people, and so on. Such increased costs may be passed on to the client in the bill. It

---

16 *Re Chapman Feenstra Cartwright and Gendall* [1977] 2 NZLR 196.

will not be appropriate to increase costs simply because the matter is of importance to the client.[17]

Results

The rules also provide that the "result achieved" will be relevant. This will be particularly relevant in respect of litigation where a negative result will be of no benefit to a client and may well mean additional liabilities are imposed by the Court. In such circumstances, it may be appropriate to reduce the fee, although it cannot be said that there is an obligation to do so. The implicit suggestion that the normal rate of a lawyer might be increased or a premium added to the bill of costs where a case is successful is inappropriate. There are strong arguments to permit contingency fees where the lawyer and client expressly agree that the fee will be calculated in light of the outcome. However, in the absence of such an express agreement the law society guidance amounts to a suggestion that where a lawyer effectively carries out the client's instructions and achieves the desired result it is acceptable to charge more than would otherwise be allowed. There appears no rational justification for charging a premium for achieving the objective sought at the outset by the client.

Complexity

Where the work is difficult and requires the application of special skill the costs will be correspondingly higher: "The complexity of the matter and the novelty of the questions involved" will also be relevant when fixing fees. Greater time will be spent than where the issues are straightforward. Where a matter is complex more skill and expertise will be required and a client can be expected to pay a premium for this. Where an issue is novel it will require fresh research and a corresponding degree of skill which will justify an increased fee.

Documents

Also of relevance will be the "number and importance of the documents prepared or perused". This seems to be simply a particular instance of the complexity of the matter. Where documents are prepared which are longer than necessary or where they could have been dispensed with altogether there will be no grounds for increasing the fee. It is far more demanding to draft concise and clear documents than rambling and lengthy ones.[18]

---

17 This seems to have been the approach of Donaldson J in *Property and Reversionary Investment Corp v Secretary of State for the Environment* [1975] 1 WLR 1504, [1975] 2 All ER 436, 443.

18 *Gallagher v Dobson* [1993] 3 NZLR 611, 618 per Barker J.

Urgency
In some cases a client will need the immediate assistance of a lawyer. Examples might be on arrest, or where an injunction is required to preserve property or evidence. Commercial transactions will sometimes need to be undertaken with considerable urgency. A lawyer will often have to put to one side other commitments and give precedence to the urgent matter. The rules provide that the "urgency of the circumstances in which the business is transacted" will be a relevant consideration in determining the level of fees.

Overheads
Some law firms are well known for their plush offices, and disparaging comments have been made about the money spent on such things as original art works with which they are decorated. It has been observed that the cost of such trappings must be drawn from the fees charged to clients. The rules note that the "reasonable costs of running a practice" are to be taken into account when setting the fees. There are huge variations between the overheads of different practices, from small suburban sole practitioners without support, to large city-based national firms complete with a comprehensive support system. The nature of the firm will be taken into account when assessing costs. To an extent, by choosing the firm the client chooses the kind of overheads he or she will be contributing to. The nature of the work will be more suited to a particular kind of practitioner or firm. When determining whether a bill is reasonable it will be appropriate to take into account the fact that the bill represents more than just the time spent by the lawyer, but from it must also be drawn the costs of premises, support staff and so on.

Many law firms have adopted the practice of charging separately for expenses that previously have been absorbed as overheads. This includes such items as postage, telephone charges, and the time of non-legal staff. If such items are charged, the allowance for overheads should be correspondingly decreased.

12.3 Costs revision

One of the peculiar features of the relationship between lawyer and client is the fact that the client is not usually in a position to determine whether the fees charges are reasonable. This difficulty is recognised, and to a limited extent met, by the fact that the Law Practitioners Act sets out a comprehensive procedure by which a client may seek to revise a bill of costs rendered by the lawyer.[19] The core feature of the procedure is that, in the first instance, it is a peer review. The individuals

19 The costs revision procedure may also be invoked by the District Council, or by the Court: s 143 Law Practitioners Act 1982.

reviewing the bill of costs will be lawyers who practise in the same district as the lawyer whose bill is under examination. While the Act provides for a review of the bill by the district committee, in practice, this task is delegated to nominated "revisers" under the powers of delegation provided in the Act.[20]

There is suggestion that the statutory costs revision procedure be abolished.[21] The following discussion should, therefore, be read bearing in mind any reforms which have occurred since the publication of this work.

12.3.1 *Procedure*

A client[22] may seek a revision of the bill of costs by applying in writing (no special formalities are required) to the district law society.[23] When such a request has been made the practitioner will be asked to submit an itemised bill of costs showing a full breakdown of how the bill was calculated.[24] The Act gives no guidance or principles as to the basis upon which the revision should proceed, implicitly leaving such matters to the Rules of the profession, and the discretion of the revisers. In practice, this means that the principles in r 3.01 and the commentary will be applied.

In the event that either party disagrees with the decision of the revisers as to the appropriateness of the bill, they may appeal to the registrar of the High Court of the district. The registrar may conduct the appeal as a fresh revision if desired.[25] If either party is not satisfied with the decision of the registrar there is a right to apply to the High Court for a review of the registrar's decision.[26] The right to seek revision of a bill of costs is in

---

20 See ss 15, 29, 143, and 145 Law Practitioners Act 1982 and *Gallagher v Dobson* [1993] 3 NZLR 611, 613 per Barker J.

21 Letter, President of the Law Society to all practitioners, 20 October 1999, and the attached paper.

22 Or "party chargeable" in the language of s 145 of the Act. Where a person other than the client is paying the bill he or she will therefore be entitled to seek revision.

23 There are a number of procedural restrictions such as a six-month limitation from the date of the delivery of the bill (s 145(2)) or where the bill is paid by deduction or set off the limitation is one year from the date of the deduction or set off (s 150).

24 Section 152 of the Act.

25 *MA v Brookfields* [1998] NZAR 433.

26 The application is for review rather than a rehearing by way of appeal: *Hollamby v Timpany Walton* (1995) 8 PRNZ 656. The Court will examine the registrar's decision and overturn it only if founded on wrong principle. See also *Brons v Buddle Findlay* (High Court, Auckland M 1048/90, 1 October 1991).

addition to any other contractual rights to dispute the bill.[27] Where the amount charged is excessive it may also be grounds for a complaint that the overcharging amounts to misconduct.

12.3.2 *Critique of the revision procedure*

There is a strong argument that the standard of the appropriateness of a bill of costs should not be set by the peers of the practitioner whose bill is under review. While there is value in the views of experienced practitioners as to what normal practices and billing rates are, there needs also to be an objective assessment as to whether those practices and rates are acceptable. It may be that billing practices that are widely accepted and practised in the profession are inappropriate from the perspective of the general community. While the registrar is a non-lawyer who has some power to determine whether a bill is fair and reasonable on appeal, the registrar's input will be limited to determining whether the bill is reasonable according to the standards prevalent in the profession.

Both parties have a right of appeal in the event that they do not agree with the decision of the revisers of the district committee. Such a right of appeal is obviously appropriate where there has been a breach of procedural justice in the way in which the revision was conducted. However, it is open to question whether it is appropriate for a lawyer to have a right of appeal on the grounds that he or she disagrees with the amount of the bill that has been assessed as reasonable. There is a strong argument that in such a consumer protection measure the lawyer should be compelled to accept the revision and bring finality to the proceedings. The alternative is to allow some lawyers who are unwilling to accept that they have charged too much to put the client to considerable trouble (and probably expense) in bringing further appeal and review proceedings.[28] There may be instances where the costs revision would be overturned in favour of lawyers on appeal. It is suggested that no real benefit is to be gained from allowing lawyers to pursue their rights on appeal, and the minimal loss incurred by individual lawyers in such instances is justifiable on public policy grounds.

It is important that clients are made aware of their right to question the amount charged by their lawyer. Some provision is made for this in the rules. If a client expresses dissatisfaction about the amount of the fee charged "and continues to do so after having the matter explained [he or she] must be advised of the clients' rights [of costs revision] under Part

27 When a bill is under revision the practitioner is prevented from pursuing payment by an action in the Courts: s 155.

28 By way of comparison, under the Rules of the Banking Ombudsman where the banking ombudsman makes a decision on a complaint, that decision is binding on the bank, however, the customer is free to reject the decision and pursue remedies in the normal way.

VIII of the Act".[29] Before the right to seek revision must be expressly made known to the client, the client must express the view that the bill is too high and must maintain that view in the face of justification by the lawyer of the bill. There will be few instances where this will occur. In some cases the client will not voice misgivings about the amount of the bill, especially where the client is not an assertive person. In other cases clients will be unlikely to press the point once their lawyers have justified their views. It is suggested that a greater incidence of client dissatisfaction with the level of fees would be apparent if all clients were advised of their right to seek revision when they were billed, or at least as soon as any query in relation to the bill was raised. In several other jurisdictions a lawyer is prohibited from seeking to recover fees unless the client has been advised of the right to have the bill assessed by a third party under the applicable rules.[30]

12.4 Transparency in fees

It is increasingly recognised that one of the main contributors to client dissatisfaction with the bill rendered by the lawyer is the fact that the clients were not prepared for it, and/or were unaware of how it was calculated. It is good practice for a lawyer to explain at the outset of the relationship how costs will be calculated, how much they are likely to amount to, and to agree on when they will be billed.

In England and Wales this has been taken one step further by requiring lawyers to give prospective clients accurate information on costs at the outset of a matter and of keeping the client informed of the position on costs regularly.[31] These are moves that are reflected in other jurisdictions.[32] The English rules recognise that it is not possible to give an accurate estimate in all cases but aim at ensuring that the best information possible is given to the client at the outset. This may mean simply an explanation of the method of calculating the fees along with regular information on the current level of fees incurred. English practitioners are also required to inform clients of various matters in respect of costs such as the client's right to set a limit on costs, the possibility of the costs being covered by insurance or legal aid, and the implications of an adverse order of costs in litigation. Perhaps most

---

29 Rule 3.01 para 3 of the commentary.

30 See r 14.09 of the English *Guide*, also s 175(2)(d) Legal Profession Act 1987 (NSW).

31 "Solicitors' Costs Information and Client Care Code", para 13.02 of the English *Guide*.

32 See the discussion of the duty to advise of an estimate of costs and keep the client informed in the various Australian jurisdictions in G Dal Pont *Lawyers' Professional Responsibility in Australia and New Zealand* North Ryde NSW, LBC Information Services, 1996, 276-279.

interestingly, the lawyer is required in all matters to consider with clients whether the likely outcome will justify the expense or risk involved.[33]

There are no such similar requirements in the New Zealand context. While there is passing reference to the obligation of a practitioner to draw the possible availability of legal aid to a client's attention[34] there is no other obligation to discuss costs at any time. There is no obligation to give a detailed breakdown of costs and many bills simply describe the tasks completed and the amount due.[35] A duty to disclose costs cannot be said to be an ethical duty in the same way as other duties, such as the duty to the Court. However, the trend to impose such obligations on lawyers reflects the fact that ensuring that clients are informed of costs and their rights of redress against lawyers are important factors in ensuring access to justice for citizens, and the maintenance of a healthy, client-focused profession.

12.5 Contingency fee arrangements

12.5.1 *Introduction*

Lawyers and their clients are generally allowed to enter into any arrangement in respect of fees that they desire within the normal constraints of the law.[36] One arrangement that has obvious advantages is where the client pays no fees unless the lawyer is successful in the client's action. An arrangement in which the payment or level of a fee is contingent on the outcome of the case has the advantage for the client of minimising the fruitless outlay of money on unsuccessful actions. It also enables litigants who have no funds to pay for an action to bring cases concerning wrongs that would otherwise go unremedied.

---

33 "Written Professional Standards, standard (f)", in the English *Guide*, para 13.11.

34 Rule 1.02 para 5 of the commentary.

35 On costs revision the district committee may require an itemised bill to be rendered: s 152(1) Law Practitioners Act 1982.

36 The Courts will, however, view such agreements with caution and be wary of lawyers taking an illegitimate advantage of their clients: *Clare v Joseph* [1907] 2 KB 369. Such agreements may be revised under the costs revisions procedure described above: s 142 Law Practitioners Act 1982. It has been suggested that the statutory recognition of fee arrangements extends to a legislative acceptance of contingency fees. However, the reference in the Act to fees calculated by commission or percentage almost certainly can be explained as a reference to the now defunct scale of charges which calculated fees by reference to the value of the transaction. It is not a statutory recognition of the legitimacy of contingency fee arrangements. That argument is found in R Harrison, "Civil Litigation and Tribunals Committee Paper on Contingency Fees", 26 December 1998, a paper submitted to the Auckland District Law Society.

There are numerous variations of the manner in which a contingency fee might be calculated.[37] Examples are:

- Speculative fee — the normal fee only is payable in the event that the action is successful;
- Bare percentage — lawyer takes a fixed percentage of the winnings;
- Sliding percentage — lawyer takes a percentage if the case is settled, a higher percentage if trial is necessary, and a higher percentage again if the matter is appealed;
- Fee premium (uplift) — the lawyer calculates the hours spent and charges the normal rate plus a premium where the case is successful.

The English position takes a bare percentage approach with the limitation that the percentage may not be more that 25 per cent of the proceeds of the case, and the total fees cannot exceed a 100 per cent premium on a fee premium basis. A number of similar limits or combinations are possible. The following discussion is generally applicable to any such arrangement, but uses the simplest bare percentage arrangement as a model.

There is a general prohibition on contingency fees in New Zealand, although increasingly there are calls for liberalisation of this area of the law. It is well known that some jurisdictions (notably the US) have embraced contingency fees for some time, and a number of ills of the justice system and the profession have been attributed to this. There are dangers in drawing comparisons from the US system which is lightly regulated and where the absence of costs awards against unsuccessful litigants in most cases removes a disincentive to bringing litigation which is present in New Zealand. The absence of a right of action for personal injury in New Zealand is also a fundmental difference. It is by no means clear that the evils of the American legal system are able to be attributed to contingency fees at all.[38]

12.5.2 *The legal prohibition*[39]

The law in New Zealand is relatively clear. The torts of maintenance and champerty that emerged from the common law of England still exist and have not been altered by case law or statutory intervention.[40]

37 For a discussion see K Tokeley, "Taking a Chance: A Proposal for Contingency Fees" (1998) 28 VUWLR 13, 28-32; also S Zindel, "The Case for Contingency Fees" [1996] NZLJ 295, 296.

38 D Luban, "Speculating on Justice: The Ethics and Jurisprudence of Contingency Fees" in S Parker & S Sampford *Legal Ethics and Legal Practice: Contemporary Issues* Oxford, Clarendon Press, 1995.

39 This is discussed in more detail in D Webb, "Contingency Fees: Riskier than they Seem" [1998] NZLJ 390.

40 *Brothers Inn Limited v Southland Regional Council* (1998) 12 PRNZ 303, *Rawlinson v Purnell Jenkinson & Roscoe* (CA 128/97, 21 October 1997). For

Maintenance "arises when a person, without lawful justification, assists a party to a civil action to bring the action, thereby causing damage to the other party".[41] The rule prohibiting maintenance developed to combat the mischief of persons maliciously assisting in the pursuit of litigation against personal enemies. Champerty is a particular form of maintenance whereby the funder (maintainer) of the action supports the action in return for a promise of a share in the proceeds of any action.[42] A lawyer who agrees to bring a case on the condition that fees are to be paid only from a share of the proceeds if the action is successful is committing the tort of champerty.

The champerty is a tort committed against the other party to the litigation. In the event that the action is successfully defended by the other party the defendant may seek compensation for the costs incurred by the wrongfully maintained action from the champertous lawyer. In addition, champertous contingency fee arrangements will also be illegal as against public policy and, therefore, void and unenforceable.

The law on champerty was affirmed in New Zealand in *Mills v Rogers*.[43] In that case the Supreme Court (later affirmed by the Court of Appeal) held that an arrangement whereby a lawyer was to fund actions in defamation on behalf of the litigant, and the litigant would receive a third of the fruits of the action, was maintenance. It was held that: [44]

> It is maintenance because it is an agreement to supply legal assistance and money by persons not interested legally or morally in the litigation; it is champerty because it is in effect and agreement to be repaid in the event of success by a part of the subject matter of the litigation. It is therefore void.

The decision was affirmed on appeal where it was considered:[45]

> An arrangement more calculated to foster and encourage improper litigation and unscrupulous professional conduct can hardly be conceived. The agreement being thus illegal, it is incapable of being enforced in an action.

---

the English position see *Camdex International v Bank of Zambia* [1996] 3 All ER 451; *Bevan Ashford v Geoff Yeandle Contractors Ltd* [1999] Ch 239.

41 *Rawlinson v Purnell Jenkinson & Roscoe* (CA 128/97, 21 October 1997) p 8. Note also that "a solicitor who is acting in his or her professional capacity cannot be liable in the tort of maintenance. He or she possesses a legitimate interest in the proceeding which removes them from the scope of that tort". See also *Giles v Thompson* [1994] 1 AC 142 (HL).

42 *Laws NZ*, Law Practitioners para 270.

43 (1899) 18 NZLR 291.

44 (1899) 18 NZLR 291, 296 per Denniston J.

45 (1899) 18 NZLR 291, 310 per Williams J.

In New Zealand it has long been accepted that there is one circumstance in which a lawyer may bring an action on the basis that payment of fees will be forthcoming only in the event that the action is successful. That is where the lawyer charges only the normal professional fee for the work done but discounts or forgives the fee in the event that the action fails. The effect of such an arrangement is that the lawyer bears the risk that the action will be unsuccessful but does not assume any corresponding benefit of an increase in the fees payable in the event of success. It amounts to a kind of pro bono work in that the lawyer is (over a number of cases) giving free or reduced fee legal work. Not only is such an arrangement not illegal or tortious, but also "consistent with the highest professional honour".[46] It amounts to a waiving of the lawyer's fees, which should always be permitted.[47]

12.5.3 *The case for contingency fees*[48]

It has often been observed that the prohibitions on maintenance and champerty are founded in historical circumstance that is of little relevance in the modern environment.[49] Litigation is no longer considered to be an evil of itself, and there is recognition that it may be appropriate for one person to assist another in the bringing of an action. The justification for prohibition against champerty has been recast in terms of placing an unacceptable temptation before a lawyer to engage in unprofessional conduct to secure the victory in litigation and thereby collect a fee.[50] Whether such arguments accurately predict the impact of such a fee arrangement is a moot point. Even if the risk is a real one, it is worth considering whether it is one worth running in light of some of the benefits that would flow from allowing contingent fee arrangements. There is an increasing dissatisfaction with the limits placed on the contractual freedom of lawyers and clients by the law of champerty.

---

46 *Sievwright v Ward* [1935] NZLR 43, 48 per Ostler J. More recently this position was adopted in the English Court of Appeal in *Thai Trading v Taylor* [1998] 3 All ER 65 overruling *Aratra Potato Co Ltd v Taylor Joynson Garret* [1995] 4 All ER 695. See also *Sears Tooth v Payne Hicks Beach* [1997] 2 FLR 116.

47 See r 3.01(2).

48 There are numerous discussions of the pros and cons of contingency fees. A good recent overview is K Tokeley, "Taking a Chance: A Proposal for Contingency Fees" (1998) 28 VUWLR 13; A Paterson, "Contingent Fees and their Rivals" (1989) Scots Law Times, 10 February, 81; T Swanson, "The Importance of Contingency Fee Agreements" (1991) Oxford Journal of Legal Studies 193; M Trebilcock, "The Case For Contingent Fees: The Ontario Legal Profession Rethinks its Position" (1989) 15 Canadian Business LJ 360.

49 See especially J McDermott, "Contingency Fees and the Law of Champerty" [1993] NZLJ 253.

50 See *Re Trepca Mines (No 2)* [1963] 1 Ch 199, 219-220 per Denning MR.

Access to justice

At the centre of the drive to liberalise the law on contingency fees is the claim that such arrangements would provide access to justice for litigants who currently are precluded from taking an action due to their lack of funds. While there is a system of legal aid in New Zealand it is generally available only to people who have very few disposable assets and limited disposable income.[51] The result is that there is a broad band of people who could pay to litigate an action, but for whom the costs would be crippling and the hardship not commensurate with the possible benefits. Under the contingency fee system such litigants would not be risking funds other than those which might be gained under the action proposed. The litigant, to bring an action, need not have the funds in hand to finance it; he or she need only have a cause that is likely to succeed. This enables a large part of the risk of losing a case to be shifted to the lawyer.

One area in which contingency fees may be particularly useful is that of class actions.[52] Because in such cases the loss of each member of the class is small in comparison with the total loss caused, such wrongs often go unremedied. Contingency fees overcome one of the hurdles for such actions by obviating the need to find a number of litigants who are prepared to underwrite the costs of the action. They enable all members of the class to be "free riders" in the sense that if the action is successful they will receive a benefit without having to take the risk of being liable for the fees of an unsuccessful case.

The willingness of lawyers to take cases on a contingency basis would overcome the problem of an imbalance in the wealth of litigants leading to abuses of the procedural rules calculated to disadvantage the poorer litigant. Not only is lack of funds a barrier to commencing litigation, but even if the decision to litigate has been taken there is the possibility that the other side will intentionally protract the proceedings and increase the cost. This is done in the knowledge that the poorer litigant does not have an inexhaustible supply of funds and may be forced to accept a less advantageous settlement offer, or abandon the proceedings altogether. If the action were being taken on a contingency basis such a tactic would be less effective as the pool of funds available for litigation would not be limited in the same way.

Not all cases that are deserving will be appropriate for contingency fee arrangements. Some litigant's claims will be too small to enable sufficient fees to be taken from the proceeds. The subject-matter of other cases

---

51 See the Legal Services Regulations 1990, rr 38 and 39.

52 See K Tokeley, "Taking a Chance: A Proposal for Contingency Fees" (1998) 28 VUWLR 13, 17-18; V Morabito, "Federal Class Actions, Contingency Fees, and the Rules governing Litigation Costs" (1995) 21 Monash LR 233, 242.

may not have financial benefits, as in the case of human rights claims. It is clear that contingency fees are not a panacea for the problem of the current limitations on access to justice.[53]

Concurrence of interest

An additional benefit of contingency fees is that the lawyer and client have a concurrence of interest. Where the lawyer is to be paid only if successful the incentive to be committed to the client's cause is increased. Such a situation will ensure that a client's case is not neglected and it is pursued zealously. While the interests may concur they are not identical. The interest of the client is full compensation for the wrong suffered. The lawyer's interest is a maximisation of the fee in relation to the time spent on the case which may not be identical to full compensation for the client.

Efficiency

The existence of a contingency fee will also lead to more efficient practice by lawyers. Where a lawyer is employed on an hourly rate there is no external pressure to conduct matters efficiently, to reduce the length of pleadings, and to bring an early conclusion to the proceedings. This problem is sometimes compounded where the matter is taken on legal aid. The client is not paying the fees directly (although they may be taken from the proceeds of the action), therefore, there may be less concern with the level of fees and the time taken by the lawyer to complete various tasks. The funder of the action is less able to closely supervise the conduct of the case. However, where a case is conducted on a contingency basis there is a strong motivation for the lawyer to maximise productivity by expediting the proceedings and obtaining the best result in the shortest time possible.

Freedom of contract

The current prohibition on contingency fees amounts to a limitation on the freedom of parties to enter into a particular type of contract. There need to be compelling reasons to restrict the freedom to contract in such a way. Provided that the parties both understand the nature of the transaction, and there is no material inequality, there seems to be little reason to prevent them from entering into an agreement whereby the lawyer's fees are not payable in the event that the action is unsuccessful.

53 See D Owles, "'No Win No Fee': Confusing Change with Reform" (1989) NLJ February 10, 196.

12.5.4 *Dangers*[54]

The dangers that have been voiced in respect of the adoption of contingency fees are generally well known. Many commentators draw on the US position as a model of a system in which such fees are permitted. There are perils in this. It is important to be wary of presuming that the problems with one system of contingency fee arrangements will arise in any such system regardless of the manner of implementation and regulation. It is also not at all clear that the problems that do exist in the US system are attributable in whole or in part to the contingency fee litigation.[55] There is also a danger of inflating the shortcomings of the system and ignoring the advantages and improvements due to the focus of popular media and literature on the evils of the system (and the lawyers who work in it).

There has been a liberalisation of the rules applying to contingency fees in the United Kingdom over the last decade, and it is perhaps more instructive to look at the developments there. Not only does the English legal system more closely resemble that of New Zealand, but the incremental and regulated liberalisation of the rules is more likely than a wholesale abolition of the prohibition on contingency fees.

Litigation explosion

There is a fear that if contingency fees were permitted there would be a sharp rise in the number of cases brought before the Courts. The central argument in favour of allowing contingency fees is that it would enable more people to bring deserving cases. This of itself is not objectionable. While litigation is not encouraged where there are other avenues to resolve a dispute, it is to be encouraged where there is a genuine dispute, the parties are at a stalemate and cannot settle their differences without intervention. That recourse to the Courts might increase if such actions were put within financial reach of less wealthy citizens simply means that redress will not be denied (and no windfall will rest in the hands of wrongdoers simply because the wronged party cannot afford to go to Court). Such an increase in litigation may burden the judicial system, but is not to be discouraged.

Of more concern is the bringing of cases that have only a tenuous chance of success, or are wholly hopeless. Controls exist on the bringing of cases with no prospect of success. The Courts are reluctant to expect lawyers to be a pre-trial screen of the merits of a case and in any event there is no bar to bringing a case which is arguable, though unlikely to

---

54 For arguments of an American scholar bemoaning the introduction of contingency fees in the United Kingdom see C Graffy, "Conditional fees: Key to the Courthouse of the Casino?" (1998) 1 Legal Ethics 70.

55 For an overview of the US position see D Bedingfield, "The Contingency Fee System in America" (1991) NLJ 1670.

succeed.[56] It is not at all clear that there would be a proliferation of such cases were contingency fees permitted. If a case were doomed to fail, no competent lawyer would take it on a contingency basis, as there is no chance of a payment from which the fees could be drawn. If a case were tenuous, the chance of success would make most lawyers reluctant to take it on. Lawyers who are unable to find much work may be tempted to take a chance on tenuous cases in the hope of a windfall, and perhaps making a reputation for themselves. The risk of this happening appears small, and the harm negligible.

Excessive awards

Periodically, reports are heard from the US of awards of millions of dollars by juries in favour of plaintiffs. There is a tendency to think that such awards are made in the knowledge that a large proportion of the award will find its way into the purse of the lawyers who assisted rather than to the litigants themselves, and that in reaching the sum a generous allowance is made for the costs component. This is, however, supposition. Even if true it is unlikely to occur in New Zealand for a number of reasons. First, in all but a few cases, Judges and not juries make awards of damages. This is due to the abolition of cases for damages for personal injuries and their replacement by the universal accident compensation regime. The removal of personal injury cases removes a large proportion of those cases where the level of damages to be awarded is uncertain and largely impressionistic. The ability of New Zealand Courts to award costs against unsuccessful litigants means that some compensation for the fees incurred can be enforced. The level of damages awarded to litigants in New Zealand is unlikely to be greatly influenced by the fact that the plaintiff has agreed to fund the case from a share of the proceeds of the litigation.

Ethical hazards

The central objection to contingency fees is that they are unethical. In particular, there are circumstances in which such an arrangement will create a conflict of interest between the lawyer and the client. Consider the following example:

A lawyer has agreed to take a complex case on a contingency fee basis, taking 20 per cent of the proceeds of the claim. It is anticipated that from first instruction to the delivery of judgment will take two years and if charged normally the fees would amount to \$100,000. The claimed damages are \$1m. In the first month proceedings are issued. The defendant indicates that it will defend the claim, but intimates that it would be prepared to settle for \$200,000.

56 See D Webb, "Hopeless Cases: Compensating Litigants at the Advocate's Expense" (1999) 30 VUWLR 295.

If accepted, the lawyer would receive $40,000 for very little work, perhaps as little as $2000 or $3000 on a time-costed basis. On the other hand, the claimant would receive only a fraction of the claimed amount.[57] At this point the interests of the lawyer and the client have diverged.[58] There is a strong financial incentive for the lawyer to advise that the offer be accepted so that he or she can take the fees and move on to other work. Assuming that the claim is a good one this is clearly not in the interests of the client.[59]

The dangers associated with such conflicts may, however, be overstated. An historical analogy may be helpful. When the system of charging a fixed fee depending on the task completed and its value was under scrutiny strong objections were raised to its replacement. Of particular concern was the fact that where a lawyer can fix his or her own fee on a time-cost basis a conflict of interest arises. It is in the client's interest that the lawyer work as efficiently as possible. In contrast, it is in the lawyer's interest to extend the proceedings by arguing every point, labouring the facts, extending interlocutories, and so on (that is, over-servicing the client). This conflict is a real one. However, in practice it leads to few difficulties. Lawyers are sufficiently busy not to need to drag out proceedings in order to inflate their fees, and such conduct would amount to misconduct. Most lawyers adhere to the ethical requirements of the profession and are committed to the interests of their clients. In the event that fees are needlessly incurred the client may also bring the matter to the law society either as a matter of misconduct, or costs revision.

The liberalisation of the rules prohibiting contingency fees is likely to have a similar absence of catastrophic effects. Any system of fees has its shortcomings and susceptibility to abuse. It is, however, necessary to rely on the integrity of the majority of the members of the profession, the regulation of the profession, and the pragmatic observation that the harm caused by incidents of abuse does not justify limiting the freedoms of clients and lawyers who use the system properly.

---

57 Although allowance must be made for the fact that the payment is certain rather than having to rely on the fact that the if the matter goes to trial the Court may refuse the claim, or award an amount less than that claimed.

58 There have been suggestions that such problems be addressed by regulation in the US. See M Horowitz, "Making Ethics Real, Making Ethics Work: A Proposal for Contingency Fee Reform" (1995) 44 Emory LJ 173.

59 Similar conflicts between lawyer and client might arise in many other situations such as where there is a modest offer immediately prior to trial (and therefore the lawyer may be reluctant to risk all in proceeding). See S Zindel, "The Case for Contingency Fees" [1996] NZLJ 295, 297.

Excessive zeal

Even where the interests of the lawyer and client accord there is a temptation for the lawyer to engage in unethical conduct. Because the collection of the fee rests on the success of the case it is often argued that there is a greater temptation for a lawyer to engage in unscrupulous and unprofessional tactics to ensure success. Critics of contingency fees often cite the words of Denning MR:[60]

> The reason the common law condemns champerty is because of the abuses to which it may give rise. The common law fears that the champertous maintainer might be tempted, for his own personal gain, to inflame the damages, to suppress evidence, or even to suborn witnesses.

Less cited is the following observation:

> These fears may be exaggerated; but be that so or not, the law for centuries has declared champerty to be unlawful, and we cannot do otherwise than enforce the law.

It cannot be denied that the risk of unethical conduct is greater in cases in which a contingency fee exists than where traditional fee arrangements exist. However, one must be careful not to overstate the problem. It is not likely that there will be a wholesale disregard for the ethical and legal precepts governing the conduct of litigation. While a few isolated lawyers may not honour their ethical obligations, the vast majority will deal with contingency fee litigation on exactly the same basis as any other litigation they have been retained to pursue.

There are pressures for lawyers to ignore their duties to the Court and breach their ethical obligations where the fee arrangement is an ordinary one. There will often be pressure from clients to use obstructive tactics, to suppress disadvantageous evidence, and to obfuscate issues. There is also frequently a desire to win that may stem from a desire for prestige amongst professional peers that may lead to the ignoring of the rules or spirit of the obligation to the Court. It cannot be said that under the current system counsel universally act in accordance with the ethical precepts by which lawyers are bound. It is suggested that lawyers who honour their obligations to the Court will continue to do so under contingency fee arrangements. For those who do not, little will change, and it can only be hoped that the disciplinary powers of the Court and the law society will be invoked at some stage.

Excessive fees

In the example given above, where the defendant made an early settlement offer, it was observed that, if the offer were accepted, the

60 *Re Trepca Mines (No 2)* [1963] 1 Ch 199, 219-220 per Denning MR.

lawyer obtained a windfall of a fee which was several times that which would be due if the fee was calculated on a charge-per-hour-worked basis. The same may well be the case if the litigation is pursued to judgment. It is central to the concept of a contingency fee that there is a premium paid if the action is successful to allow for the possibility that there is little or no recovery in some other cases. The fact that the lawyer takes a percentage share of the proceeds of the fruits of litigation means that in many cases it will be impossible to predict how large (or small) the final fee will be. In some cases the fee will be extremely large in comparison to the amount of time spent on the case. The question is whether this can be justified.

The appropriateness of the level of the fees needs to be judged as at the time that they are agreed, not with the benefit of hindsight. If the case is unsuccessful there is an injustice in that the lawyer gets no fee for the many hundreds of hours that may have been worked. Implicit in contingency fees is the fact that sometimes the action will be unsuccessful and the lawyer will get no fee — the phrase "no win no fee" has been given to such arrangements in the United Kingdom. If in the long run, lawyers' fees from contingency arrangements are not significantly greater than those from normal fee work, then there is little ground for complaint. The concern is that such arrangements will be a source of an overall increase in lawyers' fees.

One risk is that lawyers will conservatively estimate the chances of success and demand an inappropriately high proportion of the fruits of the action as the fee. The liability of the defendant may not be in question, only the quantum of damages is in issue. This certainly seems to be a problem in the US where there has been a steady rise in the proportion of the winnings that the lawyer takes as costs.[61] In some cases high fees may be justified by the risk of failure. However, the trend appears to be towards a standardised fee structure that does not take account of the level of the risk. This is possibly due to the difficulty of meaningfully assessing risk. In the United Kingdom this problem has been limited by guidance from the law society which provides that the fee should not exceed 25 per cent of the award, nor should it exceed

61 In A Paterson, "Contingent Fees and their Rivals" (1989) Scots Law Times, 10 February, 81, a figure of up to 40% of the award is cited. K Tokeley, "Taking a Chance: A Proposal for Contingency Fees" (1998) 28 VUWLR 13, 17 cites up to 50%. See also L Brickman, "Contingency Fee Abuses, Ethical Mandates and the Disciplinary System: The Case against Case-by-Case Enforcement" (1996) 53 Wash & Lee LR 1339, 1340.

twice the fee which would be payable on a normal charging basis.[62] It has been observed that in the United Kingdom:[63]

> Nearly all agreements follow the Law Society model agreement. In a recent study three quarters of the cases studied had success fees [ie premium on the normal fee] of 50% or less, with the average uplift for all cases being only 43%. In 90% of cases the voluntary cap of 25% [of the award] was applied. This evidence does not suggest that rapacious lawyers are seeking to take in fees large parts of the client's damages. It shows that they can balance their duty to their client with the need to ensure that their firm can make a profit on the work it undertakes.

Litigants ultimately bear burden

It has also been observed that the effect of the contingency fee system is to make litigants effective insurers of each other's costs. Looking at an individual contingency fee arrangement it appears that the lawyer bears the risk that the action will be unsuccessful and that he or she will have to forgo fees. However, the costs of unsuccessful actions are not borne by the lawyers in the long run. Those costs are recouped from the premium taken from successful clients. Ultimately, successful clients pay the fees of unsuccessful clients. It can be appreciated that such a situation is not ideal. The objection is that this is an inappropriate transfer of wealth from the compensation awarded to one client to another unsuccessful client. Why should the client with a successful action contribute to the costs of a client without a good claim? The objection would be a good one but for the brutal fact that neither litigant would have had the opportunity to bring the action in the absence of the contingency fee arrangement. In pragmatic terms, it is far better that a successful litigant's award is reduced by an increased lawyer's fee and the second litigant pay nothing where the case is lost, than the alternative: neither litigant gets the opportunity to bring either matter before the Courts and the wrongdoer fortuitously gets off scot-free.

Other costs

The fees charged by a litigant's lawyer will be a large part of the costs that a litigant will have to bear. They will by no means be all of the costs. Additional expenses may include filing fees, witness expenses, expert opinions and various other disbursements incidental to the conduct of the proceeding. In complex cases these may well exceed the lawyer's fees. There is always the possibility that the action will be unsuccessful and the litigant will be liable for a portion of the costs of the other

62 See para 14.05 of the English *Guide*; Conditional Fee Arrangement Regulations 1995 (UK); order 4 Conditional Fee Agreements Order 1998 (UK).

63 "Access to Justice with Conditional Fees", a Lord Chancellor's Department Consultation Paper, March 1998, para 2.10.

party.[64] Where the plaintiff is not wealthy it is also always open to the defendant to apply for an order that the plaintiff demonstrate that he or she is sufficiently wealthy to meet a possible order for costs.[65] The result is that contingency fee arrangements overcome only one of the financial hurdles facing a prospective litigant.

One way around this is to insure against the possibility of losing. In England insurance against costs of possible Court actions is readily available from commercial insurers. In addition, the law society has provided an insurance scheme to protect against an adverse order of costs in respect of cases that are actually in contemplation. One problem with the latter kind of insurance is that it is frequently taken out only by those who need it most (that is, are likely to lose) and therefore is not commercially viable.[66]

12.5.5 *Regulation*

In the United Kingdom and a number of Australian states there has been a recent liberalisation of the law to permit contingency fees. The liberalisation has come with regulation of the kinds of cases in which such fees are permitted, of the kinds of arrangements which may be entered into, and the manner in which they may be arrived at. Few advocates of contingency fees suggest that the content and procedure of entering into such arrangement should be left entirely in the hands of the parties. In the absence of regulation there is room for clients to be taken advantage of, to be confused as to the nature of the arrangement, and for lawyers to inappropriately increase their fees. By appropriate regulation clients may avail themselves of the advantages of contingency fees while the risks and dangers may be minimised.

The applicable rules impose a cap on the amount of fees that may be recovered, either as a proportion of the award, or an increase in normal fees, or a combination of both.[67] Such rules are considered necessary to combat the steady upward creep in fees which has been prevalent in the US where no formal cap exists. It also reduces the likelihood of lawyers taking cases that are highly tenuous for a large proportion of the possible

64 Contingency fees are particularly successful in the US because in almost all cases an unsuccessful plaintiff will not be required to pay the costs of the successful defendant.

65 High Court Rules, R 60. The Court does have a discretion in making such an order and may take into account the merits of the claim: *Meates v Taylor* (1992) 5 PRNZ 524.

66 See A Dekany, "'No Win, No Fee' – Impact on Companies" [1998] NZLJ 103.

67 For an overview of the Australian position see G Dal Pont *Lawyers' Professional Responsibility in Australia and New Zealand* North Ryde NSW, LBC Information Services, 1996, 310-313. The US rules are found in r 1.5 ABA Model Rules. The ABA has considered the position more fully in formal opinion 94-389 on contingent fees, 5 December 1994.

winnings. Such limits go some way to overcoming the objection that lawyers might abuse such agreements to take excessive fees.

It is also common to require that such agreements be recorded in writing and signed by the client. The South Australian rules require that a conditional fee agreement not only be in writing and signed by the client, but also that it must be in plain English, contain certain prescribed terms and must provide the client with a period of five days in which they may cancel the agreement.[68] Such stringent requirements concerning the formation of the contract seek to ensure that the client is fully informed of the nature and impact of the agreement.

In some areas, contingency fees are not appropriate. Family and criminal matters are universally excluded from contingency fee arrangements.[69] Such prohibitions are justified on public policy grounds. Contingent fees are not permitted in criminal cases.[70] The reason for such a prohibition is that the duty of the lawyer to the Court should be protected from any risk of dilution by other pressures. The consequences of a lawyer acting improperly in a criminal trial may be considerable, therefore, no increase in the risk of such conduct should be contemplated.[71] A similarly policy-based argument applies to family and matrimonial matters. It is considered inappropriate that issues such as care of children should be decided under contingent fee arrangements. The same argument is extended to matters such as matrimonial property, although the argument does seem weaker. The liberalisation of contingency fee arrangements in the United Kingdom has been effected by allowing such fees only in certain types of litigation, in particular, personal injury and insolvency matters, although there are currently moves to allow contingent fees arrangements in all but very few cases.[72]

The requirement that fees charged be reasonable is as applicable to contingency fees as to any other fee arrangement. Where a client is dissatisfied with the final fee charged under a contingency arrangement

---

68 Rule 8.10 South Australian *Professional Conduct Rules*.

69 See, for example, s 58A Courts and Legal Services Act 1990 (UK) as amended by the Access to Justice Act 1999.

70 The prohibition was most recently applied in *Hughes v Kingston upon Hull City Council* [1999] 2 All ER 49.

71 For a thorough analysis and argument for contingent fees in criminal cases see P Lushing, "The Fall and Rise of the Criminal Contingent Fee" (1991) 82 Journal of Criminal Law and Criminology 498.

72 See "Access to Justice with Conditional Fees", a Lord Chancellor's Department Consultation Paper, March 1998, para 2.8, confirmed in "Conditional Fees Consultation — Summary of Responses", a Lord Chancellor's Department Consultation Paper, July 1998, para 1. This liberalisation has been implemented with the passing of the Conditional Fee Agreements Order 1998.

the client may apply for a revision of the costs under Part VIII of the Law Practitioners Act 1982.[73] Indeed the rules adopt r 18 of the International Code of Ethics of the International Bar Association which provides:

> A contract for a contingent fee, where sanctioned by the law or by professional rules and practice, should be reasonable under all the circumstances of the case, including the risk and uncertainty of the compensation, and subject to supervision of a Court as to its reasonableness.

12.5.6 *Possible reform*

While the case for contingency fees is strong, there appears to be little progress in official channels to change the law in New Zealand. In this respect New Zealand seems to be falling behind its Commonwealth neighbours. The law society seems to take an equivocal attitude to such arrangements observing on the one hand that "The rule [3.01] is drafted in terms which contemplate the possibility of charging a contingency fee"[74] and immediately thereafter noting:[75]

> It may be that, in some circumstances at least, the common law rules against maintenance and champerty may still apply, so as to invalidate an agreement for a contingency fee. In the absence of clear and current authority on the point, the Society draws the possibility of invalidity to the attention of practitioners.

A committee of the Auckland District Law Society examined the issue in 1998.[76] While the report analyses the law in the area and traverses the arguments for reform and regulation it is clear that no consensus could be reached on the appropriate kind of regulation, or whether regulation was appropriate at all.

In any event there is a growing use of contingency fees in New Zealand. More and more lawyers are aware that clients are unable to afford to fund litigation from existing resources. The limited availability of legal aid means that in such cases a "no win no fee" arrangement is the only way clients will have the ability to seek vindication of their rights. This trend is also illustrated by the number of cases where the fact that the

---

73 See r 3.01 para 4(ii) of the commentary.

74 Rule 3.01 para 4 of the commentary.

75 Rule 3.01 para 4(i) of the commentary.

76 *Report of the Auckland District Law Society Working Group on Contingency Fees.* In the introduction to that report it is noted that the New Zealand Law Commission has expressed an interest in examining the matter, but no formal steps in that direction have been taken. See also the later report of R Harrison, "Civil Litigation and Tribunals Committee Paper on Contingency Fees", 26 December 1998, a paper submitted to the Auckland District Law Society.

costs of litigation were being funded on a contingency basis has been commented on by the judiciary.[77]

12.6 Pro bono work[78]

The charging of any fee, even on a contingency basis would sometimes render the pursuing of an action impossible. The subject-matter of the action may not be financial (as in the case of human rights cases, for example) or the amount claimed may be so small that any reasonable fee would devour the entire proceeds. To what extent does the legal profession and, at a more personal level, each and every practitioner have an obligation to ensure access to justice where impecuniosity would be an otherwise insurmountable barrier? Ought a lawyer, in some circumstances, work for nothing? It is argued that a lawyer, or firm, has an ethical duty to provide pro bono work as part of the duty to foster a healthy profession. This is argued from the premise that in practising law, lawyers are part of a system that they have a duty to uphold and promote.

It is clear that an amount of pro bono work is carried on in New Zealand, though the amount is unclear. The E-Dec Report claimed that "there is a considerable amount of pro bono work carried out voluntarily by lawyers",[79] however, this appears to be an unsupported assertion, presumably based on anecdotal evidence of lawyers. In a 1997 survey one per cent of lawyers surveyed stated that they engaged in pro bono work.[80]

12.6.1 *What is pro bono work?*

It is important to be clear what is meant when we talk about pro bono work. The phrase pro bono publico (invariably abbreviated to pro bono) indicates that the service is tendered "in the public good". One of the most compelling reasons for a practitioner to provide free work is not the conferral of a benefit on any particular person, but rather the conferral of the benefit of legal services on members of a class of persons, in particular on those to whom access to justice would otherwise be denied — and consequently on society as a whole.

---

77 See *Nikau Holdings Ltd v BNZ* (1992) 5 PRNZ 430, (1992) 6 NZCLC 67, 939; *Gosper v Re Licensing (NZ) Ltd* (1997) 11 PRNZ 34.

78 The following arguments are traversed in D Webb, "Why Should Poor People get Free Lawyers?" (1998) 28 VUWLR 65. See also A Boon and J Levin *The Ethics and Conduct of Lawyers in England and Wales* Oxford, Hart, 1999, 231.

79 Para 3.12.

80 *Polls of the Profession and the Public —Summary — The New Zealand Law Society* Wellington, MRL Research Group, 1997, 58. Though 35% spent an average of two hours per week on "other voluntary legal activities".

The motives of a lawyer in providing free assistance may be mixed. The lawyer may undertake work either because of the nature of the issue involved or because the work gives profile to the lawyer or the firm (or both). If a lawyer takes a case for no fee for self-promotion,[81] or to advance the interests of a particular group, the work cannot really be said to be pro bono work. Similarly, work undertaken on a contingency fee basis cannot be regarded as pro bono work when the case is unsuccessful, because in a contingency situation a client promises to pay a fee provided that the case is successful. In other respects, we need to have a broad, though not unlimited, conception of what amounts to pro bono work. It is not just the traditional kind of legal advice and advocacy that will amount to pro bono work. There are numerous ways in which members of the profession can give their time to assist in access to justice for poorer members of the community. Activities such as community education, or self-help legal clinics amount to pro bono work. However, one must be careful not to go too far. Work can only properly be considered pro bono if it is both in the public good and the work requires the exercise of skill as a lawyer. Being a committee member of the symphony orchestra or on the board of trustees of the local school, are not of themselves pro bono activities.

12.6.2 *Professional guidance*

The Rules of Professional Conduct of the New Zealand Law Society provide little guidance on matters such as pro bono work. They set out minimum standards of conduct to which lawyers are to adhere if they are to avoid a disciplinary hearing. Those rules state in their introduction:

> It is reiterated therefore that this publication, to the extent possible defines the bounds within which a practitioner may practise the profession. Within those bounds the prime responsibility of a practitioner is his or her own sense of professional responsibility. The preservation of the integrity and reputation of the profession is very much a matter for individual members.

This does not appear to fulfil the statutory functions which the law society is obliged to meet under s 4 of the Law Practitioners Act 1982 which provides: "The general functions of the Society shall be … To promote and encourage proper conduct among the members of the legal profession...". No formal assistance is offered by the law society to those seeking legal assistance for no fee or reduced fees. [82]

---

81 See the promotional material of Russell McVeagh and Phillips Fox (two prominent law firms) which refer to their pro bono work at [www.rmmb.co.nz/recruit/Welcome.html] and [www.phillipsfox.co.nz/publications/pbd96007.htm] respectively.

82 While no Australian jurisdictions provide for pro bono work in their professional rules, some professional organisations do assist in coordinating and promoting such work, for example, the New South Wales Bar Association

The New Zealand Law Society provides little or no guidance on what kind of lawyer one ought to aspire to be. The predominant focus of ethics, both within and without the professional sphere has been, What am I prohibited from doing?" rather than, How ought I conduct myself? The American Bar Association Model Rules of Professional Conduct takes a different approach. In respect of the pro bono obligation it gives detailed guidance by providing:[83]

> A lawyer should aspire to render at least (50) hours of pro bono publico legal services per year. In fulfilling this responsibility, the lawyer should:
> (a) provide a substantial majority of the (50) hours of legal services without fee or expectation of fee to:
> (1) persons of limited means or
> (2) charitable, religious, civic, community, governmental and educational organisations in matters which are designed primarily to address the needs of persons of limited means; and
> (b) provide any additional services through:
> (1) delivery of legal services at no fee or substantially reduced fee to individuals, groups or organisations seeking to secure or protect civil rights, civil liberties or public rights, or charitable, religious, civic, community, governmental and educational organisations in matters in furtherance of their organisational purposes, where the payment of standard legal fees would significantly deplete the organisation's economic resources or would be otherwise inappropriate;
> (2) delivery of legal services at a substantially reduced fee to persons of limited means; or
> (3) participation in activities for improving the law, the legal system or the legal profession.
> In addition, a lawyer should voluntarily contribute financial support to organisations that provide legal services to persons of limited means.

12.6.3 *Objections to a pro bono duty*

A lawyer might agree with the claim that it is good to provide free legal assistance to impecunious people, and that all should have access to justice, but consider that it really is not his or her concern. After all, the comparison might be made that a builder may consider it a good thing if

legal assistance scheme and the New South Wales Law Society Community Assistance Service Pro Bono Scheme. The Auckland District Law Society offers a prize to a lawyer engaged in pro bono work.

83 Rule 6.1 ABA Model Rules. The ABA Model Code of Professional Responsibility, which was replaced by the Model Rules, takes an even more aspirational code by framing nine canons upon which ethical rules and considerations are based. Canon 2 provides: "A Lawyer Should Assist the Legal Profession in Fulfilling Its Duty to Make Legal Counsel Available". Ethical Consideration 2-25 provides: "A lawyer has an obligation to render public interest and pro bono legal service". Some states (such as New York) still use the Model Code.

everyone has adequate housing — however, that does not place an obligation on the builder to seek out those with inadequate housing and redress the inadequacy. It could be argued that it is not a lawyer's job to provide free legal advice no matter how essential to those who cannot afford it. Linked to this objection is the argument that the provision of access to justice is a task that falls to government. To provide those services where government fails is to tacitly endorse that failure. Understandably, when a disadvantaged person comes to a lawyer and clearly cannot afford the cost of the work that is needed the first question is whether or not that person qualifies for legal aid. While legal aid goes some way to solving the problem of access to justice there are numerous reasons why it is not adequate by itself, or a substitute for pro bono work. Legal aid is payable only in respect of litigation, not the numerous other kinds of advice needed for disadvantaged people to take full advantage of the law[84] and is subject to numerous other limitations.[85] Further, civil litigants who receive legal aid will generally be required to make a contribution to the costs of litigation.[86]

A further objection that has been made to legal assistance for the disadvantaged is that it encourages inappropriate litigation on an already overburdened Court system. Such an argument is easily dismissed. There is no suggestion that lawyers should take unmeritorious cases, and certainly should not take abusive or vexatious cases or cases predicated on blackmail. However, the mere fact that it will cost the defendant more to defend the claim than the amount claimed is no reason for not pursuing it. It simply indicates that our system is flawed if rights exist which cannot be economically enforced. In reality those rights are illusory. Further, the fact that the Courts are busy is absolutely no reason to discourage poor litigants. Commercial interests pursuing complex claims take up much Court time. To suggest that the system is too cluttered for disadvantaged people is to give the claims of the wealthy priority over those of the disadvantaged — a gross breach of the principle of equality before the law.

A further danger of pro bono work is that the legal assistance available to disadvantaged people is of an inferior quality.[87] It is sometimes argued

---

84 See ss 4 and 19 Legal Services Act 1991.

85 Further, no grant will be made to groups of people (such as incorporated associations, unincorporated associations or charitable trusts). Legal aid will not be granted where the fruits of the litigation do not justify the costs incurred. Although provision is made for the non-financial fruits of litigation, such as, perhaps, the protection of civil rights: ss 27 and 34(3)(e)(ii) Legal Services Act 1991.

86 Section 37 Legal Services Act 1991.

87 Gilbert and Gorenfeld, "The Constitution Should Protect Everyone — Even Lawyers" (1984) 12 Pepp LR 75.

that there is no incentive or benefit for a lawyer to do anything more than a satisfactory job if the client is not paying. Where sophisticated clients are paying, they are more likely to be critical of the performance of the lawyer. If it appears unsatisfactory they may, in extreme cases, change lawyers prior to trial, or in less extreme circumstances, not retain them again. Clients who are not paying for the work in the current environment, however, have little or no power to take their work elsewhere. However, there are a number of incentives other than the payment of a fee and return business for lawyers to perform well. These are: the esteem of their colleagues and members of the judiciary, word of mouth amongst other prospective clients, and a personal pride in their profession. The profession of law is distinguished from other non-professional occupations by the strong sense of collegiality that includes scrutiny of the conduct of other members of the profession. A further incentive is, of course, the Rules of Professional Conduct for Barristers and Solicitors, which sets minimum standards of conduct in legal practice. A further protection in litigation against substandard advocacy is the duty of the barrister to the Court. If advocates are incompetent in the presentation or defence of a case they wrong not only their client but also the Court to which they owe their primary duty to serve.[88] Lastly, a lawyer who provides service to a client which falls below the standard of care and skill expected of a reasonable lawyer will be liable in tort for any loss caused. This will be the case whether or not the client is fee paying or pro bono.

Even if it is accepted that the service provided on a pro bono basis will be "Morris Minor" rather than "Rolls Royce" service, this is a significant improvement on treading the treacherous legal path alone and on foot. Put less metaphorically, even a lawyer who meets only the bare requirement of competence will increase an impecunious client's chance of enforcing his or her rights immeasurably. The fact that this kind of legal service is not of the highest quality to which we aspire is not a sufficient reason to deprive the disadvantaged person of it.

If pro bono work were coordinated properly it may be that some of the problems may be avoided. One of the main difficulties is the fact that, no matter how bad the service, there is no real ability for pro bono clients to "fire" their lawyer.[89] Such a situation is, however, a vast improvement on the alternative — having no access to legal assistance at all. Moreover the incidence of incompetence, or the need to dismiss the lawyer would be small and is no real objection to the offering of free legal assistance.

---

88 Rule 8.01.

89 And, therefore, there is a dilution of the right to change from one practitioner to another under r 6.05 of the rules.

A further, and in one sense more fundamental, objection may also be based on the claim that there is no moral duty to provide that free advice. It may even be argued that there is a moral duty not to provide that advice. This may come in a number of forms. One might reject any suggestion that there is any meaningful moral duty other than to promote one's own interest — and giving free representation to others does not do that. Secondly, it could be argued that it is bad policy to provide free advice and representation to disadvantaged people. This ground is usually based on the objection that such a duty is impossible to administer. This may be due to the illusory nature of the concept of "poverty", the fact that this places those who fall just outside the "poverty" category at a significant disadvantage, and that it encourages litigation over relatively minor sums. It may also be argued that to expect a lawyer to provide free work for poor people is a breach of fundamental rights of property and liberty. To require free work, on this argument, is a kind of enslavement, or at least enforced servility. Alternatively, if the lawyer's time is "money" then it is an involuntary transfer of wealth from the lawyer to the disadvantaged person. The problem with these kinds of objections is the mistaken assumption that the role of pro bono work is the relief of the disadvantaged. While this is an incidental and beneficial effect, pro bono work is underpinned by a need to protect and promote the legal system.

12.6.4 *Rationale for the pro bono obligation*[90]

While there is no duty on a lawyer greater than that owed by any other member of society to assist a disadvantaged person per se, there is a significantly greater, and different duty to promote and protect the legal system. This duty exists because a lawyer accepts the responsibilities of the system by participating in it and becoming an officer of the Court and member of a profession that claims public service as a core value. Becoming a lawyer is not like a grant of monopoly rights to profit from the practice of law. It is entry into the institution of the Courts and law with a licence to gain from that institution, but with corresponding responsibilities. If one accepts that a lawyer does have a duty to maintain the integrity and workability of the legal system, and that the maximum possible access to the law is needed to maintain the system's workability, one must then accept that a lawyer has a duty to provide that access to those who cannot afford to pay.

One of the central aspects of the legal profession is its integrated character. The judicial system is comprised of not just the judiciary, but also counsel who appear before the Courts and their instructing solicitors. By becoming a member of the profession, lawyers obtain a number of privileges, one of the most important being the exclusive

90 See D Rhode, "Cultures of Commitment: Pro Bono for Lawyers and Law Students" (1999) 67 Fordham LR 2415, 2418.

right to act as an advocate for others before the Court. Historically, senior members of the bar undertook, by oath, to pursue the causes of clients without delay due to coveting money or profit. While some view the role of the lawyer as little more than that of an artisan others view the lawyer as an integral part of a system with a corresponding duty to maintain and uphold that system. Further, lawyers have, by their learning and their position, a monopoly on the provision of legal advice and services. Chief Justice Burger expressed it thus:[91]

> As a profession with a monopoly over the provision of certain services, we have special obligations to be energetic and imaginative in producing the best quality justice at the lowest possible costs for those who use it with a minimum delay.

12.6.5 *Deserving cases*

Obviously a lawyer cannot be expected to take every case that is worthwhile without fee Such a lawyer would have not time left to earn a living. Some guidance is needed as to what kind of cases are most deserving. It comes as no surprise to find that many if not most clients consider that they have a right to the law or the justice system, and a similar belief that that right ought not be impeded by the imposition of legal fees.

To most efficiently use this limited resource it should be used where the demand is greatest. Pro bono work ought to be bestowed on those to whom access to justice would be denied without it, not upon those who decline to retain a lawyer because, although they could afford it they have made a decision that the amount/likelihood of a benefit from such a move would outweigh the cost. The difficulty, however, is that this distinction is by no means clear. One of the main objections to assistance directed to disadvantaged people is the imposition of a test as to what amounts to poverty. Where a single line is drawn between the deserving and the undeserving the effect is to cause an injustice to those who only just cross the threshold into the "wealthy" class. By providing assistance to those defined as "poor" the barely wealthy are disadvantaged. This difficulty is reflected in the fact that many government assistance schemes (such as income supplements) are applied on a graduated scale. There is no poverty line, above which there is no need, and below which there is an absolute inability to obtain the necessaries of life. There are varying degrees of need.

This ought to be reflected in the approach to pro bono work. There will be cases where the client is clearly unable to afford any part of the legal fees incurred. In terms of whether that person is sufficiently

---

91 Hon W Burger, "The Role of the Law School in the Teaching of Legal Ethics and Professional Responsibility" (1980) 29 Cleveland State LR 377, 378.

impecunious, there will be no question. It is more difficult where to bring the action or retain the lawyer while not entirely beyond the means of the disadvantaged, will cause considerable hardship. In such a case it is suggested that an answer may be partially free legal work — that is, the matching of the fee to the client's means. The proportions of assistance and contribution will be able to be matched to ensure that there is not an accidental disadvantaging of those in less than abject poverty.

A deserving case is not necessarily one on which there is consensus as to the merits being argued. When our mind is turned to what is a deserving case it usually leaps to consider whether the right claimed is one which is deserving of protection. Consider a situation where a journalist is being sued in defamation for roundly criticising a political figure and claiming that the politician has questionable morals. If one agrees with the opinions expressed and considers them justifiable, this appears to be a good reason for assisting the impoverished journalist by providing free services in the defence. Compare this with the neo-Nazi who is arrested on a pretence for a distasteful but peaceful demonstration that was airing views that most find repugnant. Many lawyers would find representing the members of such a group an unattractive proposition for full fees — and a ridiculous proposition to provide such services for free. There is a strong feeling that pro bono work is a kind of charity and may be conferred on the causes one considers the most deserving.

There are a number of problems with the above approach. First, if the main motivation behind providing free legal services is access to justice then a political view of the case ought not to be a relevant factor when deciding if the case is deserving. It is trite to say that people we disagree with, and even disdain, have as much right to representation as those we endorse and admire. Secondly, it is inaccurate to think that it is a matter of beneficence to provide free work. The provision of pro bono work is not like bestowing honours on those who meet with our approval. It is more akin to the duty to act that one would have when we see people in immediate distress — drowning is the traditional example. We have no excuse to decline to assist because if they had worn a life jacket they would not be in this trouble, or their predicament is only due to ignoring clear navigation signs. We have a moral (though not legal) duty to rescue simply because they have a pressing need, and we have the ability to alleviate that need. The duty on lawyers to provide pro bono work regardless of whether we agree with the person of low income is even greater than in the example given. Lawyers are not idle bystanders who happen across the distressed individual. They are more akin to the harbour-masters whose reason for being is to ensure the safe passage of people through their waters.

The fact that the matter is minor or mundane does not necessarily mean that it is not deserving. Many cases in which assistance is most needed are common matters such as consumer complaints, or disputes with bureaucracies. People of low income generally feel alienated in any situation where they come in contact with the law, and are often ignorant as to the benefits of the law. While it is unlikely that disadvantaged people would set up companies, or create family trusts, there are still a number of aspects of the law that they could take advantage of but often do not either through ignorance of the law, or fear of the process. Things as common as making a will, or jotting down the basic terms of a contract are too difficult and foreign for many people to undertake. Some of these kinds of tasks may be considered by lawyers as too trifling to concern them, and certainly were they to charge a reasonable fee for them the client would be losing money. This is no good reason for not providing such a service. From the perspective of indigent clients the arranging of their meagre assets will be of immense importance to them.

The disputes where pro bono assistance is most required are also generally mundane, at least to most lawyers. They will rarely be defamation suits of public figures, or civil rights claims. More frequently, they will be claims against welfare agencies for underpayment, family disputes in respect of custody of or access to children, complaints in respect of public health or education, consumer claims for defective goods or services, or perhaps landlord-tenant disputes. These are not the files that lawyers relish working on. They are often tedious, and to the lawyer the benefits of success are negligible. However, if these files are not undertaken for that reason it is tantamount to saying that only rights that have a significant value in our eyes are worth enforcing. From the perspective of the low income person, the interests which are being protected or pursued often relate to fundamental matters such as housing, education, health, and family etc which most take for granted.

12.6.6 *Excuses*

No lawyer is exempt from the pro bono duty. When addressing the question of which lawyers ought to undertake pro bono work, it is usual to think of a lawyer who is, in some way, quite different from oneself. There are a number of common reasons why it would be thought inappropriate to undertake pro bono work — such as that the nature of the work is outside of one's area of expertise, one's practice is far too busy to engage in further unpaid work, or the practice makes little enough money as it is without diverting valuable time to non-paying clients. Few of these excuses are persuasive.

A claim of lack of skill or expertise is not a persuasive excuse for a refusal to engage in pro bono work. Much of the work is quite mundane and, to a moderately skilled lawyer, simple. The fact that there is a degree of learning involved in acquiring the necessary skills to undertake these tasks is not an insurmountable barrier. Even the basic grounding in legal principles and the ability of the lawyer to communicate effectively and from a position of power will place the client in a far more advantageous position. Pro bono work is not restricted to taking on cases or advising clients. Other tasks might include advising charitable bodies or other legal agencies such as community law centres, or undertaking an educative role informing low income people of the law and how to take advantage of it. When one considers the gross inadequacy of legal knowledge of many disadvantaged people, it is a weak reply indeed to say that one is not possessed of the precise kind of legal expertise required. It is possible to seek out the places in which one's expertise is best utilised, or if necessary engage in the lawyerly task of researching to extend one's expertise.

Legal practitioners are busy individuals. It is not surprising that a common counter to the claim that more pro bono work ought to be undertaken is that the practitioner in question simply does not have the time. Such a response is premised on the assertion that those things that the practitioner does have time for are more important than doing pro bono work. Invariably, important (and paying) clients consume the time in question. It must be squarely admitted that the provision of pro bono work costs practitioners. The fact that if pro bono work were taken on, paying clients would have to be turned away is no excuse for not undertaking pro bono work. Such work is not like giving small change to a charity street collector — to be handed over if you have some lying around. It is a fundamental tenet of participation in the legal system. One other alternative for the busy practitioner is to fund another, less busy practitioner, to fulfil the pro bono obligations. While this may not be an ideal solution, it is a pragmatic response to the immediate problem.[92]

A different response to the exhortation to undertake pro bono work is the complaint that, unlike many big city practitioners, many lawyers do not make a "fortune". Rather they need to devote all their energies to eking a living out of their practice, and/or need to charge every client that comes in the door to cover basic overheads. The main fallacy in this objection is that doing pro bono work is charity. Undertaking legal work at low or no cost is not some extra special duty that confers some kind of saintly quality on those who undertake it. It is an obligation that is concomitant with the privilege of practising law and being part of the institution of the justice system. A lawyer who is struggling does not expect relief from the obligation to contribute to the fidelity fund, and

92 And is endorsed by the ABA Model Rules in the commentary to r 6.1.

should not expect relief from the professional obligation to provide pro bono work.

It is also necessary to be cautious about the validity of the claim that engaging in pro bono work would cause real hardship to the lawyer concerned. It is undeniable that undertaking pro bono work may well reduce the possible income of a lawyer. If the lawyer is truly indigent and cannot afford the basics of life, there is no real ability to bestow a benefit on others and pro bono work cannot be expected. However, it is suggested that there are very few lawyers in such a situation. While claims that lawyers are universally rich are untrue, they are well off compared to those in need of pro bono work. This is particularly the case when one compares the means of most lawyers with those of the clients who most need the assistance of pro bono work. In such cases there is usually such a disparity that the claim that the lawyer cannot afford to undertake pro bono work is not sustainable.

12.6.7 *Conclusion*

The basic premise is uncontroversial — that people ought not to be denied the benefits of the legal system and law because of low incomes. The fact is that in New Zealand today there are many people who would avail themselves of the law and legal system and thereby improve their lot, but for the fact that they cannot afford a lawyer. The duty to alleviate this problem falls at the feet of the profession. This is a distasteful conclusion. It runs counter to many prevalent views such as the right to the fruits of one's labour, and the freedom to sell one's labour in the open market. It also meets the objection that it is the task of government to supply the funds to meet such a need.

Arguments against the existence of such a duty are rejected on the basis that lawyering is distinct from other occupations. The profession of law holds a monopoly on a fundamental element in the social ordering of a society subject to the rule of law — the ability to utilise and enforce the law. This privilege has associated costs. If one is to become part of the legal system, one must also be committed to the preservation and promotion of its values including access to the law.

There are also a number of more practical problems regarding the provision of pro bono work. How is one to distinguish between a deserving and undeserving case? How is one to best utilise one's skill to assist disadvantaged people? And how is one to avoid the problem of habitual litigants availing themselves of free services? These problems can be largely dealt with by the central administration of the provision of pro bono work. The central regulation of the provision of pro bono work is necessary to deliver such services most efficiently. Organisations, such as Community Law Centres, already exist which are capable of undertaking such a task.

Pro bono work is not charity. It is a natural incidence of being a member of the legal profession. While failing to undertake such work may not be grounds for removal from the roll, it does show a lack of commitment or loyalty to the very system upon which the lawyer relies for livelihood.

Part Four

Duties to the Administration of Justice

Chapter 13

The Administration of Justice

13.1 Introduction

The position of lawyers is central to the administration of justice. Clients depend on them to advise them and represent their cause with skill and judgment. Less obvious, but equally important, is the reliance that Courts place on lawyers when bringing matters before them. The words of Lord Reid in *Rondel v Worsley* illustrate this balance:[1]

> Every Counsel has a duty to his client fearlessly to raise every issue, advance every argument, and ask every question, however distasteful, which he thinks will help his client's case. But, as an officer of the Court concerned in the administration of justice, he has an overriding duty to the Court, to the standards of his profession, and to the public, which may and often does lead to a conflict with his client's wishes or with what the client thinks are his personal interests. Counsel must not mislead the Court, he must not lend himself to casting aspersions on the other party or witnesses for which there is no sufficient basis in the information… The same public duty applies when drawing pleading or conducting subsequent stages in a case as applies to counsel's conduct during the trial.

There is an important public interest aspect to the services lawyers render to their clients. Clients rely on lawyers to understand the law and to advise them how to arrange their affairs most advantageously. When negotiating with other parties a lawyer brings specialist skills in framing obligations in clear language and anticipating all eventualities. As litigant, the client relies on the lawyer as advocate to prepare the case skilfully, to exercise judgment in presenting the facts to the Court, and be articulate in presenting the litigant's arguments. Without such assistance the ability of individuals to avail themselves of the benefits of the law would be greatly diminished, and the utility of the law in arranging affairs or resolving disputes would be reduced.

In a wider sense, lawyers are relied on to enhance the effectiveness of the legal system. While individuals may occasionally bring cases without the assistance of a lawyer, a lawyer is used in the majority of cases that

---

1 [1969] 1 AC 191, 231. See also *Gazley v Wellington District Law Society* [1976] 1 NZLR 452; *NZ Social Credit Political League v O'Brien* [1984] 1 NZLR 84.

come before the Courts. The Courts depend heavily on lawyers who appear before them in a number of respects. The lawyer may be more knowledgeable in the specific area of law at issue than the Judge. Lawyers are able to specialise, whereas Judges are usually generalists, with the exception of some specialist Courts. Lawyers are able to reduce a case to the core issues for presentation and are knowledgeable about what information is admissible in evidence. Without such assistance the Court would be inundated with information much of which would be inadmissible or irrelevant to the issue in hand, and would have to spend considerable time determining the real issues.

Lawyers also act as a screen in cases that are brought to Court and the facts presented. Where a case has little or no hope of success it is incumbent on a lawyer to inform the client accordingly. Where the possibility of success is truly remote the lawyer will usually try to discourage the client from bringing hopeless litigation. Similarly, a lawyer has a duty to ensure that false information is not knowingly laid before the Court, and that witnesses tell the truth. This will include adherence to the rules of the Court regarding the disclosure of information to the opposing side. Lawyers are also depended upon to manage a case efficiently, not to delay unduly, and not to use the proceedings for a purpose collateral to the obtaining of the actual relief sought. Were lawyers to refuse to adhere to such duties the administration of justice would be thrown into disorder. The adversarial nature of proceedings would render the conduct of litigation to an unrestrained competition for personal advantage rather than the strictly controlled proceeding which it currently is. Lawyers are central to ensuring that the rules of litigation are adhered to in both letter and spirit.

13.2 The adversarial paradox

The adversarial system depends on a lawyer having a loyalty to both the client and to the administration of justice. The duty to the administration of justice is more than merely a duty to serve one's client within the bounds of the law. Ideally, it requires a commitment to the effective and efficient disposal of proceedings and adherence to the spirit of the rules as well as the letter. Frequently, this will run counter to the interest and wishes of the client.

This can result in a conflict of duties of the highest kind. There may be cases where the loyalty to the client will be overridden by the duties of the lawyer to the administration of justice, which require assistance to be rendered to the Court against the interests of the client. That the duty to the administration of justice is to prevail is made clear by r 8.01 which provides:

> In the interests of the administration of justice, the overriding duty of a practitioner acting in litigation is to the Court or the tribunal concerned. Subject to this, the practitioner has a duty to act in the best interests of the client.

While the duty to ensure that the ends of justice prevail over the aims of the client in the event of conflict is clear, its implementation is not so straightforward. Where rules exist and their application is clear, the duties of the lawyer will be easily discharged. However, where there is an element of discretion or judgment in the hands of the lawyer as, for example, in the drafting of pleadings or advising on how evidence might be presented, the impact of the duty to the administration of justice is questionable. The more immediate demands of the client, the pressures of practice, and the desire to obtain a beneficial outcome for the client will frequently mean that the more esoteric duties will not be in the forefront of a lawyer's mind.

The dilution of the loyalty to the client in favour of the duty to the administration of justice may have significant and immediate effects. A client who considers his or her lawyer to be less than committed to the case is unlikely to retain the lawyer again, and may change lawyers immediately. The fact that a lawyer will not do the client's bidding where a duty to the administration of justice is perceived to be in conflict with the request, is unlikely to attract further clients. In contrast, where a lawyer does breach the duty to the administration of justice, the incidents of sanction are rare. The breach will often go undetected. There is a strong motivation for lawyers to adhere only to the clear rules which dictate the course of their conduct, and where discretion exists, to exercise it in their client's favour. Any lawyer who does not follow such a course is likely to be placing the client at a disadvantage in respect of other clients represented by a more pragmatically minded lawyer.

13.3 Independence

Essential to the discharge of the duty to the administration of justice is the independence of the lawyer from both the Court and the client. There are some obvious advantages in such independence. When clients seek out lawyers they want to be told frankly their legal position. To ensure that this is achieved it is important that lawyers maintain a clear division between the clients' cause and their own perspective. In assessing the position of clients, lawyers will have to assess the law, the evidence, and the procedural and practical hurdles facing the client. Where a lawyer is not wholly independent from the client there is a danger that there will be a tendency to overrate a client's chance of success, or be insufficiently sceptical of the client's version of events.

The need for independence is illustrated by the Code of Conduct of the Bar of England and Wales which states:[2]

> A practising barrister must not:
> (a) permit his [or her] absolute independence integrity and freedom from external pressures to be compromised;
> (b) do anything (for example accept a present) in such circumstance as may lead to any inference that his [or her] independence may be compromised;
> (c) compromise his [or her] professional standards in order to please the client, the Court or a third party.

Independence is also required to ensure that the rules of procedure are adhered to in the conduct of litigation. Lawyers are expected to determine impartially matters such as which documents are privileged and protected from disclosure to the other side on discovery. Lawyers are expected to discourage clients from taking a course of action which is illegal, and certainly are expected not to appear to assist or condone any such activities. Lawyers must have a purely professional relationship with clients to enable this task to be effectively discharged. There is, it is considered, a risk that the lawyer's judgment will be skewed if the relationship with the client or the cause is a personal one, or the lawyer assumes the interests of the client as his or her own.

This need for independence is more than the absence of a conflict of interest with the lawyer or another client of the lawyer, though in the rules independence is discussed primarily in the context of conflicts of interest. The commentary to r 1.10 does however provide that:[3]

> The professional judgment of a practitioner should at all times be exercised within the bounds of the law solely for the benefit of the client and free of compromising influences and loyalties.

The requirement of independence demands a degree of objectivity that is unaffected by personal beliefs as well as conflicting interests. It is this objectivity which is sometimes said to be a hallmark of lawyers as professionals. This is not to say that lawyers may not have personal views on their clients' affairs, but rather that they must be wholly put to one side in furthering the clients' interests.

The demand that a lawyer be independent is, however, not viewed without some scepticism. There are strong arguments against lawyers representing those with whom they are intimately connected such as

2 Para 205.

3 Compare r 2.1 ABA Model Rules which provides: "In representing a client, a lawyer shall exercise independent professional judgment and render candid advice".

family or spouses, or in cases of obvious conflicts of interest. It does not follow that lawyers should not be personally committed to the causes they represent, and be able to bring that personal commitment to their work.

Clients would prefer to retain lawyers who believe that their case has merit rather than those who do not. The reason for this is that clients can be confident that lawyers will labour more diligently for a cause they believe to be worthy, or at least just, than one they consider to be inappropriate or doomed to fail. Such a view has considerable force. Despite best intentions it is doubtful that lawyers could be as devoted to a cause with which they disagreed as to one which accorded with their own views. True independence requires that lawyers accept a retainer from any client regardless of the lawyers' view of the cause they are being asked to further.[4] This requires lawyers to become moral chameleons and, in their professional guise, forward the views of their client sometimes against their own beliefs. This requires a suspension of personal morality which few lawyers are really comfortable with. It is far easier for lawyers to be at ease with their profession if they believe that the cause they represent is a good one.[5]

The suggestion that absolute independence is required presumes that lawyers are incapable of forming a clear judgment if they agree with the cause. This assertion is open to two criticisms. First, it seems to ignore the fact that all lawyers' training and practice equip them to put aside personal prejudice or belief in assessing the strengths or weaknesses of a particular case. Secondly, it is inevitable that lawyers will gravitate towards accepting cases with which they are more likely to agree. A socialist lawyer is more likely to work in the area of immigration than banking law. A civil libertarian is more likely to encourage retainers from individuals taking action against the state than the other way around. Lawyers do act for clients whose causes they agree with, and there is no suggestion that in such cases their judgment is distorted.

The requirement that a lawyer be independent from the interests he or she represents also places an obstacle in the way of two possible developments in the way in which lawyers deliver legal services. First, it is a fundamental objection to any contingency fee arrangement. A lawyer who conducts litigation on the basis of a contingency fee arrangement

4 See the discussion of the cab rank principle in ch 6.

5 The position of a criminal advocate is an exception to this. Such advocates frequently do not affirmatively believe in the innocence of their clients, or necessarily sympathise with their clients' position. However their position is justified on abstract grounds, perhaps that every client has a right to be represented or that, even if guilty, accused go free, which is better than innocent accused being convicted.

has a direct and personal interest in the case. If the case is not successful the lawyer will not be paid. A common argument raised against any moves to allow such fees (which are currently prohibited by law) is the danger of a lawyer's judgment being clouded by personal interest. Secondly, it stymies the growth of public interest law practices in which lawyers associate themselves with a particular cause and hold themselves out as available to litigants in that cause at a reduced or low fee. Such lawyers are quasi-charitable and offer their services due to their strong personal convictions. Such lawyers frequently seek out cases to use as a political platform to further their policy objectives. Such legal practices, which are widespread in US jurisdictions, offer legal services to clients who would otherwise go without help. Such an arrangement would run counter to the need for independence required of lawyers in New Zealand which follows the English model.

The need for independence can be overstated. Even its most ardent supporters would not suggest that lawyers should refuse to act for clients simply because they wholeheartedly agreed with their point of view. The requirement of independence accepts that a lawyer can exercise independent judgment even on matters in which strong personal views are held, but requires a lawyer to eschew any appearance of personal as opposed to professional partisanship. The position is one that has considerable internal tension, if not inconsistency.

13.4 The duty to honour the law

The duties to the administration of justice flow from the recognition that lawyers are not merely agents for their clients, but also officers of the Court. A lawyer, therefore, is considered to be part of the machinery of justice, as such a lawyer is expected to adhere to the rules and principles of the system of which he or she is a part. This will include not only refraining from breaking the law, but also acting in a manner that is consistent with the principles of the law. There may be conduct that, while not illegal, will amount to misconduct. The duty to honour the law extends beyond the merely professional activities of the lawyer.

This is expressed in canon 1 of the New York State Bar Association's Code of Professional Conduct:[6]

> A lawyer should be temperate and dignified, and should refrain from all illegal and morally reprehensible conduct. Because of the lawyer's position in society, even minor violations of law by a lawyer may tend to lessen public confidence in the legal profession. Obedience to law exemplifies respect for

6 The Code is based on; the Model Code of the ABA, which was a predecessor to the ABA Model Rules of Professional Conduct that replaced it in 1983. The Code, is still the basis of standards in a small number of states.

law. To lawyers especially, respect for the law should be more than a platitude.

This canon has since been replaced in most US jurisdictions by a more rule-based approach that provides that it will be misconduct for a lawyer to:[7]

…

(b) commit a criminal act that reflects adversely on the lawyer's honesty, trustworthiness or fitness as a lawyer in other respects;

(c) engage in conduct involving dishonesty, fraud, deceit or misrepresentation;

(d) engage in conduct that is prejudicial to the administration of justice.

13.4.1 *Criminal offences*

Not every criminal offence will amount to misconduct, or be a breach of the duty of a lawyer to honour the law. There may be merely regulatory offences that have been committed by oversight or mistake. Such offences cannot be said to undermine the esteem in which the legal system is held. Where the offence is serious, or shows a disregard for the law in its commission, it may amount to misconduct.[8] In general if a lawyer commits an offence which has an element of moral turpitude to it then there will be a breach of the duty to uphold the law.

13.4.2 *Criticism of the law and legal process*

Although lawyers are expected to uphold the law, this does not preclude them from criticising particular aspects of it.[9] One of the purposes of the law society is to: "Assist in and promote the reform of the law".[10] Such a function requires the shortcomings and flaws in the present law to be pointed out. Some criticisms of the law made by lawyers (or of the legal profession) go to the very root of the system and call for a radical overhaul of fundamental parts of the system. Such criticisms (whether ultimately well-founded or not) are to be encouraged and are consistent with the lawyers' duty to honour the law. Such criticism is expected to be made in a proper manner. Criticism that is offensive or contemptuous may amount, in extreme cases, to misconduct.[11]

---

7 Rule 8.4 ABA Model Rules.

8 Sections 106(3) and 112(1) provide that a practitioner will be guilty of misconduct where either there has been a commission of a crime punishable by imprisonment which reflects on the practitioner's fitness to practise, or the practitioner has been guilty of unbecoming conduct.

9 *Ambarde v Attorney-General of Trinidad and Tobago* [1936] AC 322, 325 per Lord Atkin.

10 Section 4(1)(f) Law Practitioners Act 1982.

11 *Hilborne v Law Society of Singapore* [1978] 2 All ER 757 (PC).

The question is more problematic where a lawyer considers the entire system to be fundamentally unjust, arguing that it is simply not a legitimate system of law. Some lawyers do take such a view from a radical perspective. If so they are committed not so much to the reform of the law as to the destruction and replacement of the existing system. Such a view means that the lawyer does not in fact honour the law or the legal system. In the liberal environment, radical views are tolerated, including such views within the profession. It is arguable that lawyers who espouse such views are in fact in breach of their duty to honour the law.

This problem is well demonstrated by the problem of civil disobedience. There may be instances where an individual who is a lawyer wilfully breaks the law to make a political point. A lawyer might be involved in demonstrations that involve trespass or illegal assembly. Such lawbreaking respects the rule of law, as the existence of the law and the consequences of breaking it are central to the act of civil disobedience. In contrast, a lawyer who seeks to subvert the law would be in breach of the duty to honour the law. If a lawyer advocated that particular laws (or all law) be simply ignored as unjust, this would be in breach of the duty to honour the law.

13.4.3 *Avoiding and subverting the law*

A lawyer is frequently retained to give advice on whether a proposed activity contravenes the law, or how to arrange a transaction to ensure that it is conducted within the law while remaining advantageous to the client. In business there are numerous examples where the manner in which a transaction is effected will affect the obligations of the parties to each other, to third parties, and to the state. This has led to the proliferation of certain kinds of arrangements to avoid the need for regulatory compliance.

Most obvious is the role of the taxation lawyer. Clients frequently seek to arrange their affairs to minimise their obligation to pay tax. This can be done in numerous legitimate ways. Schemes are designed to take advantage of aspects of the rules which would have been drafted differently had the legislators known of the loophole. It is for this reason that there is a steady flow of legislation repealing, creating, and amending taxation law. To many, the taking advantage of such loopholes resulting in the minimisation of tax seems fundamentally wrong. By one taxpayer avoiding the obligations, a proportionally higher burden is placed on other taxpayers. However, as long as the lawyer is proffering advice, and devising schemes under which the client pays the taxes required by law, the conduct of the lawyer cannot be impeached. It is the very task of the lawyer to assist clients in taking full advantage of the law. To do otherwise would be to remove the choice from the clients and for the lawyers to substitute their own judgment.

It is quite inappropriate for a lawyer to assist a client in breaking the law or in evading detection after having broken a law. Assisting in devising schemes that hide funds or the creation of fictitious transactions to avoid tax otherwise payable will amount to misconduct. The problem is that the line between simply arranging one's affairs in a manner as advantageous as possible and assisting a client in evading liability can be a fine one. When such schemes are devised there will often be a "risk" that if tested by the Court it will be found to be illegitimate and ineffective in minimising tax. In euphemistic terms an arrangement with a high degree of risk is said to be "aggressive". There will be cases where the advice given by the lawyer does not have any foundation in an opinion held in good faith that the law permits the structure, and the lawyer will be in breach of the duty to uphold and honour the law.

A client may seek advice in order to further an illegal purpose. A client may seek assistance in concealing money illegally obtained,[12] or seek advice on the best way to thwart anticipated surveillance of illegal operations by officers of the law. If the client refuses to be persuaded against such a course of action a lawyer is required to cease acting for the client. The commentary to r 1.01 qualifies the duty of the lawyer by noting that "the professional judgment of a practitioner should always be exercised within the bounds of the law". If the lawyer considers the client is seeking assistance for an improper purpose, the lawyer is entitled to make inquiries as to the bona fides of the client.[13] Where the lawyer fails to make such inquiries in the face of suspicious circumstances he or she may be liable in law for losses suffered by a third party due to the client's acts and made possible by the assistance.[14]

13.5 Duty to use the law for a proper purpose

Legal processes can be used for numerous purposes other than those for which they were designed. Companies and trusts can be used to achieve avoidance of creditors or disguising the ownership of assets. The devices are usually legal, however, in some cases they are used to thwart the enforcement and objects of the law. Laws intended to protect against dishonest actions may be used to stymie legitimate claims. For example, the limitation on claims prevents actions for wrongs after the limitation period has expired.[15] Its original purpose was to prevent bogus claims

12 Duties to disclose would also exist under the Financial Transactions Reporting Act 1996.

13 Rule 3.03.

14 Under the restitutionary doctrine of knowing assistance. See for example *Brunei Airlines v Tan* [1995] 3 All ER 97, [1995] 2 AC 378, [1995] 3 WLR 64 (PC).

15 Sections 4 and 5 Limitation Act 1950.

being made which were so old that it was impossible to marshal evidence to refute them. While such a rule has a legitimate purpose — to discourage unfounded or fraudulent claims — it can also be used to avoid meeting legitimate liabilities. Equally problematic it the fact that legal processes may be used to embarrass, distress, or inconvenience others, quite apart from their intended objective.

If a lawyer assists in using the law for a purpose which is quite contrary to that for which it was intended, the lawyer will be guilty of using the law for an improper purpose. The rules provide:[16]

> A practitioner must make all reasonable efforts to ensure that legal processes are used for their proper purposes only and that their use is not likely to cause unnecessary embarrassment, distress or inconvenience to another person's reputation, interests or occupation.

The lawyer must be cautious of uncritically implementing the instructions of a client, and ought not necessarily to accept all that the client says at face value. It is as important to establish the purpose of the work requested as the nature of the work itself.

It is obvious that a lawyer should not assist in an illegal purpose. More difficult, however, is the assertion that lawyers should not assist with an improper purpose. It is not immediately apparent what makes a purpose improper where it is not illegal. One extreme approach is to suggest that where an action is immoral a lawyer should not assist in its furtherance. Examples are manifold. Should a lawyer assist in the eviction of a tenant who has fallen on hard times and will have no other home to go to? Should a lawyer assist in effecting the repossession of goods that were sold on onerous hire purchase terms where the seller should have known that payments would not be maintained? Should a lawyer inform a recalcitrant debtor of the availability of the limitation defence even though the debt is clearly owed?

Some commentators suggest that where a client seeks to avoid a legitimate debt through the provisions of the Limitation Act 1950[17] a lawyer should refuse to assist.[18] The client clearly seeks to gain an illegitimate advantage (avoidance of obligations) by misusing the law. The difficulty with such an approach is that, by refusing to assist, the lawyer becomes a defacto legislator who rules that clients may not avail

---

16 Rule 7.04.

17 Section 4 of which provides that actions founded on simple contract or on tort shall not be brought after the expiration of six years from the date on which the cause of action accrued.

18 This seems to be the position of D Luban in *Lawyers and Justice: An Ethical Study* Princeton, New Jersey, Princeton University Press, 1988.

themselves of the benefit of the law in these circumstances. If the lawyer decides that to assist in such an endeavour would not be using the law for a proper purpose the lawyer is, arguably, usurping the role of the Judge. The problem of lawyers impressing their own views of what is right and wrong on their clients, and withholding their services accordingly has been identified by others. Dare argues that the lawyer should simply apply the law on a client's instructions. Lawyers may point out the moral dimension of the course of conduct proposed but, Dare argues, they should not restrict actions that are within the law by withholding their services.[19] He argues that the law represents a kind of social agreement on acceptable conduct — a public moral code — and for a lawyer to overrule this is to upset the balance of rights agreed by the citizens and accorded by the law.

Clearly, a lawyer who acted for a client who was immorally avoiding debts by shielding behind the provisions of the Limitation Act would not be in breach of any of the professional rules, nor would a Court consider the conduct improper. There is a clear distinction between such conduct and conduct in which a lawyer assists in a breach of the law.

A middle ground exists between that of a lawyer assisting in an outright fraud, and that of a lawyer assisting in immoral but legal acts. There will be cases where clients wish to avail themselves of some legitimate legal machinery, but where the motive for employing the law is at odds with the purpose of the law. This is best illustrated by example. Imagine a company that has sold on retention of title terms building materials to a builder who has built a house, but failed to pay for the materials. The materials have become part of the land so no claim of ownership can be made. The company might be tempted to place a caveat on title to the land claiming (falsely) that it has an interest in the land. Such a caveat would be doomed to fail. The purpose of putting a caveat on the title to the land is not to register a legitimate interest, but to obstruct a proposed sale of the property as leverage to obtain payment.[20]

For a lawyer to assist in such an enterprise would be in breach of the duty to act for a proper purpose.[21] Where it is clear that the action taken is not intended to affect any legal rights, but to achieve some collateral purpose the action is inappropriate and an abuse of legal process. A lawyer should never be a party to such an abuse. The Court will always exercise its jurisdiction to ensure that the ends of justice are not

19 Tim Dare, "Virtue Ethics and Legal Ethics" (1998) 28 VUWLR 141, 150.

20 See the discussion in D A Ipp, "Lawyers' Duties to the Court" (1998) 114 LQR 63, 81.

21 The commentary to r 7.04 gives similar examples such as serving a statutory demand on a company when it is known that a debt is disputed, and placing a caveat on land when it is known that there is no caveatable interest.

thwarted by those who use its procedure for improper ends. Lord Diplock stated this policy in *Hunter v Chief Constable for the Western Midlands* when observing that the case concerned: [22]

> … the inherent power which any Court of justice must possess to prevent misuse of its procedure in a way which, although not inconsistent with the literal application of its procedural rules, would nevertheless be manifestly unfair to a party to litigation before it, or would otherwise bring the administration of justice into disrepute among right-thinking people.

It is often difficult to show that an action has been taken or a proceeding brought for an improper purpose. To find that an action is an abuse of process will result in the barring of the action and the denying of the litigant the right to make the claim. This is a serious step and the Court will generally be slow to make such a finding. It has been suggested that some claims made to disqualify lawyers from acting on successive retainers against former clients are motivated by such a purpose. Such applications may be motivated by a desire to undermine or destroy the relationship between the lawyer and the other client, rather than any genuine concern about a breach of professional duty. Not only is the cost of retaining new advisers enormous, but the advice of lawyers who have been involved throughout, had an intimate understanding of all of the issues, and were selected as (in the judgment of the client) the most able advisers, would be lost.[23]

The dividing line between using a legal process to one's advantage, and abusing a legal process to gain an illegitimate advantage, is difficult to detect objectively. A key ingredient is the motivation of the client in taking the action complained of. In all but the most obvious of cases this will not be readily apparent. The onus lies on the lawyer to determine the intentions and objectives of the client and to ascertain whether they amount to the use of legal processes for an improper purpose or not. If the purpose is improper the lawyer should refuse to assist.

22 [1982] AC 529, 536 (HL), applied in *Christensen v Peat Marwick* [1994] 3 NZLR 745 (HC). Some commentators have referred to the power as one of a "superior Court", however, the current view is that any Court has the power to prevent an abuse of its own procedure by making orders against advocates.

23 If the bringing of a disqualification application is an abuse of process it will also amount to improper conduct on the part of counsel. See *Black v Taylor* [1993] 3 NZLR 403, 420 per McKay J. See also comments of Blanchard J in *Russell McVeagh v Tower Corp* [1998] 3 NZLR 641, 676.

13.6 Improving access to justice

In accepting the privilege of being able to practise law, a lawyer, must also accept certain responsibilities. One such responsibility is the duty to promote access to justice. This duty exists because a lawyer accepts the responsibilities of the system by participating in it and becoming an officer of the Court. Becoming a lawyer is not like a grant of monopoly rights to profit from the practice of law. It is entry into the institution of the Courts with a licence to gain from that institution, but with corresponding responsibilities. A lawyer has a duty to maintain the integrity and workability of the legal system. The maximum possible access to the law is needed to maintain the system's workability. One must accept that a lawyer has a duty to provide that access in a manner that is consistent with his or her other duties.[24] This is recognised in the profession in the US in the Model Rules which state:[25]

> As a member of a learned profession, a lawyer should cultivate knowledge of the law beyond its use for clients, employ that knowledge in reform of the law and work to strengthen legal education. A lawyer should be mindful of deficiencies in the administration of justice and of the fact that the poor, and sometimes persons who are not poor, cannot afford adequate legal assistance and should therefore devote professional time and civic influence in their behalf. A lawyer should aid the legal profession in pursuing these objectives and should help the bar regulate itself in the public interest.

The right of citizens to have unencumbered access to justice and the Courts is a fundamental tenet of our society.[26] Innovations such as the Disputes Tribunal and the legal aid scheme which operate in New Zealand demonstrate that we consider ourselves committed to improving access to justice wherever possible. However, they are not sufficient to meet the need. It is part of the profession's wider responsibility to ensure that this need for access to justice is met. It is tempting to point out that any citizen can file a claim in Court and have the dispute considered by the Courts. This is obviously simplistic. It is tantamount to saying that even impecunious people have the right to eat at the Ritz. The fact is that many people, and especially the under privileged, simply do not have the means to bring their complaints before the Courts. They almost universally do not have the knowledge, expertise, confidence, and emotional fortitude to pursue a claim to conclusion.

It is also simplistic to claim that access to the Courts means access to justice. Access to justice includes access to the rules that form the law. If

24 See also the discussion of pro bono work in ch 12.

25 Preamble.

26 B Harris, "Equal Access to Justice: A Constitutional Principle in Need of a Higher Profile" [1995] NZ Law Rev 282.

it is practically impossible for people to determine what their rights and obligations according to the law are, then those rights may as well not exist. It is not simply the availability of Court-based dispute resolution procedures which are important as access to justice, but it is also important that advice on the law in a non-litigious context be available.

The aspects of the duty to provide access to justice are unlike many of the other duties that are imposed on lawyers. Most of the duties, while having a moral content, are given some force by the rules, or by the general law, or frequently both. However, many aspects of the duty to promote access to justice have moral force alone. Lawyers who conduct their practice in a self-centred way which ignores the needs of society, will not generally be disciplined. However, by such conduct they cannot be said to be fulfilling their part of the implicit compact between the profession and society. Nor can they be said to be upholding the standards of integrity and service to which the profession claims to aspire. Such duties are essentially a personal matter for each lawyer to consider and fulfil, as he or she deems appropriate. While guidance can be given by governing bodies (and in some jurisdictions is) the duties are not susceptible to regulation.

A need to use clear language

Lawyers are (perhaps a little unjustly) notorious for using language that is incomprehensible to many lay people. This criticism can also be aimed at the judiciary and rulemakers who adopt and expect language of a particular kind. This is attributable to a number of quite explicable factors, often of an historical nature. The use of a mixture of Latin, old French and old English terms throughout the language of the law, as well as some hard-to-shake habits of verbosity and complexity can result in the law being nearly incomprehensible to non-lawyers.[27]

The problem is a difficult one as in many cases the law is complex, and the phrases which are criticised are a helpful shorthand for complex concepts which make communication between lawyers more efficient and accurate. The existence of a language of law has the effect of excluding non-lawyers. While this may not have given rise to objections a century ago, it is now accepted that all citizens ought to be able to understand their legal rights, and if necessary to take action to protect and enforce them. The duty to ensure that this is the case rests not only with rulemakers and Judges, but also with the legal profession. The New

27 This problem has recently been directly addressed in England and Wales where the Woolf Reforms (a package of reforms resulting from a report chaired by Lord Woolf) have resulted in massive changes in the regulation of the profession and the rules of civil procedure, including the replacement of much archaic and obscure language. See the government white paper *Modernising Justice*, Cm 4155.

York Bar Association identifies the need for access to the law and the role of a lawyer in achieving it when it observes:[28]

> Rules of law are deficient if they are not just, understandable, and responsive to the needs of society If a lawyer believes that the existence or absence of a rule of law, substantive or procedural, causes or contributes to an unjust result, the lawyer should endeavour by lawful means to obtain appropriate changes in the law. The lawyer should encourage the simplification of laws and the repeal or amendment of laws that are outmoded. Likewise, legal procedures should be improved whenever experience indicates a change is needed.

Because there is a duty to promote access to justice, there is a consequent duty to communicate in a manner that is accessible to non-lawyers. The most obvious situations where this duty will arise are in communications with a client. A client has a right to be informed clearly and regularly on the progress of the work.[29] There is also a public dimension to the duty to give advice in a clear and comprehensible manner. If a lawyer does so, he or she is making the law accessible to clients generally, not just one client in particular. The importance of clear advice is identified in the ABA Model Rules:[30]

> A client is entitled to straightforward advice expressing the lawyer's honest assessment. Legal advice often involves unpleasant facts and alternatives that a client may be disinclined to confront.... Advice couched in narrowly legal terms may be of little value to a client, especially where practical considerations, such as cost or effects on other people, are predominant. Purely technical legal advice, therefore, can sometimes be inadequate.

The duty to avoid unnecessary complexity and to communicate in plain English extends beyond communications with the client. Because the duty is not only a duty to the client, but also a duty to the administration of justice it pervades all aspects of a lawyer's work. It is part of the duty to be efficient in the presentation of a case to the Court, and part of the duty to be courteous to other practitioners. A duty not to confuse matters, and to communicate in a manner that is not intended to obscure or deceive is central to the proper and effective functioning of the legal system.

The elimination of archaisms and unnecessary jargon is a first step in making the justice system understandable and accessible to non-lawyers. While the perpetuation of a learned aura around the law and the legal

28 Ethical Consideration 8.2 of the New York State Bar Association Code of Professional Responsibility (which is based on the largely superseded ABA Model Code of Professional Responsibility).

29 See ch 11.

30 In the comment to r 2.1.

profession may enhance the prestige of lawyers (and the profession of law) it has the effect of obstructing ordinary people from understanding their legal rights and how to protect them. Demystifying the law may have the effect of demonstrating that some law is not as difficult and obscure as it currently appears, and of making the justice system more approachable and therefore more effective in resolving differences and determining rights of citizens.

Professional obligation to be available and to provide assistance

Equally important for citizens to have access to justice is the need for effective legal advice to be readily available. One aspect of this is the duty not to refuse to act for a prospective client who seeks assistance (the cab rank rule).[31] The duty to ensure that legal assistance is at hand goes beyond merely not refusing services to a client who seeks them and is prepared to pay. A lawyer is expected to contribute to the availability of legal advice to those who are unable to pay. The most obvious avenue for doing this is by the provision of assistance to clients for free (pro bono work).[32] The appropriateness of providing assistance for free is reflected in r 6.1 of the ABA Model Rules which states: "A lawyer should aspire to render at least (50) hours of pro bono publico legal services per year".[33]

Another way in which a lawyer is able to render assistance to those who need it is though established legal assistance organisations such as community law centres[34] or other organisations offering assistance to members of the public. Assistance may be given to organisations which have as an aim the helping of people in need of assistance, including legal assistance, such as agencies rendering assistance to battered women, prisoners, tenants, and the like. The lawyer is improving the legal system by acting as an intermediary for people who would not otherwise have access to the law and the legal system. A distinction between this kind of work and other charity and voluntary work needs to be made. Acting for a local arts society, sports team, or school may be admirable work, and the lawyer may render assistance, however, it cannot be said that the people or organisations concerned need special assistance to effect their legal rights and achieve access to the law.

31 The cab rank rule is discussed in more detail in ch 6.

32 Pro bono work is discussed in more detail in ch 12.

33 The commentary to that rule observes that there will be cases where a lawyer is unable to fulfil it, and that the rule is not enforceable by the disciplinary process.

34 Which may be funded by the interest on lawyers' trust accounts pursuant to s 91F(5) Law Practitioners Act 1982.

Need for education

At the root of the problem of access to justice is a widespread ignorance of the law along with formidable barriers to overcoming that ignorance. Lawyers are ideally placed to assist with the tasks of dispelling the myth of the impenetrability of the legal system, and providing education in relevant areas of the law. The New York State Bar Association Code of Professional Responsibility provides:[35]

> The legal profession should help the public to recognise legal problems because such problems may not be self-revealing and often are not timely noticed. Therefore, lawyers should encourage and participate in educational and public relations programs concerning our legal system with particular reference to legal problems that frequently arise.

Such work may seem mundane, but it is important. While talking to community and school groups, and simplifying the law to its essentials may not be cutting-edge legal work it is a fundamental step in redressing the problem of access. Education acts in a preventative manner. Citizens who are aware of their legal rights are far less likely to need to have recourse to the Courts to enforce them as they are less likely to place themselves in problematic situations or in situations where advantage is likely to be taken of their ignorance.

Contribution to legal developments

Social need frequently moves faster than legal developments, and lawyers dealing in the law on a daily basis are frequently made aware of the shortcomings of the law. As officers of the Court there is an expectation that lawyers will take an interest in the improvement of the law. One way in which this is effected is through the efforts of the law society that spends a considerable amount of time through the voluntary efforts of its members on law reform. It is a function of the law society to "assist in and promote the reform of the law".[36]

Improvement of the profession

The legal profession occupies an important place in the legal system. An honest, effective, and efficient legal profession is essential to a society in which people are treated fairly and according to law. In the absence of a healthy profession citizens will in many cases be left without recourse to the Courts and will be left to resort to self-help remedies, and to settle disputes based on power rather than rights. It is in the public interest

35 Ethical Consideration 2.2 of the New York State Bar Association Code of Professional Responsibility (which is based on the largely superseded ABA Model Code of Professional Responsibility). It also bears noting that in s 4(1)(e) Law Practitioners Act 1982 it is stated to be a function of the Law Society to "Promote opportunities for the acquisition and diffusion of legal knowledge and skills relating to the legal profession".

36 Section 4(1)(f).

that the legal profession be maintained and improved constantly. The law reflects this need by stating that the functions of the law society include maintaining the integrity of the legal profession and promoting proper conduct among its members.[37] The position is also reflected in the ABA Model Rules, which provide:[38]

> A lawyer ... should help the bar regulate itself in the public interest.... A lawyer should strive to attain the highest level of skill to improve the law and the legal profession and to exemplify the legal profession's ideals of public service.

Such a role is contradictory as it presumes that a lawyer will be willing to advocate change to the profession that may be detrimental to the profession, but beneficial to the public. It has been observed that a similar inconsistent role is expected of the law society:[39]

> Public and client protection involves regulating lawyers' behaviour, forcing lawyers to do what they might not otherwise have done. This imposes burdens on lawyers. In contrast, promoting lawyers' interests involves supporting lawyers in what they want to do and creating benefits for lawyers.

It may be unrealistic to expect lawyers to regulate themselves in every respect wholly in the public interest. This observation is at the heart of a strong argument for closer outside involvement in the legal profession. However, there are many areas in which lawyers are able to observe ways in which the practice of law can be improved without acting against their own interests. It is in such areas that the expectation that a lawyer will promote a healthy legal system by ensuring a healthy profession will be fulfilled.

37 Section 4(1)(b) and (d) Law Practitioners Act 1982.
38 Preamble paras 5 and 6.
39 E-DEC Report, para 3.4.

Chapter 14

Duties in the Conduct of Litigation

14.1 Introduction

The incidents of the duty to the administration of justice are highlighted in the conduct of litigation. Litigation is the most visible of the services rendered by lawyers and is effected under the scrutiny of the Courts. It is only one aspect of the duties of the lawyer to the administration of justice, and many of the principles applicable to the conduct of litigation are equally applicable to other aspects of a lawyer's practice. The duties of a lawyer when bringing litigation to Court are often phrased in terms of a duty to the Court; indeed this phraseology is adopted by the New Zealand rules which provide: "In the interests of the administration of justice, the overriding duty of a practitioner acting in litigation is to the Court or the tribunal concerned".[1] In some ways this is misleading, as the duty is one to the administration of justice which may entail disagreeing with and seeking to overturn the decision of any particular Court. The lawyer is a "helper in the administration of justice"[2] and therefore his or her aims ought to be the same as those of the Court, even though the lawyer's role in the process is quite different. It is important to distinguish the duty to assist the Court in its proper purpose from a duty to follow all of the demands and directions of the judicial officer presiding. The lawyer may be requested (or indeed ordered) to take steps which he or she considers inappropriate, such as breaching confidence, or desisting in pressing a point of fact or law. While ultimately the lawyer will have to comply with the demands of the Judge, the lawyer should be prepared, in appropriate cases, to press his or her client's case forcefully, even against the insistence of the Judge. If the Judge persists in his or her demands the lawyer must of course comply, but may have to resort to appeal procedures, and possibly urgent proceedings to protect the position of the client.

1 In r 8.01.

2 *Beevis v Dawson* [1956] 3 All ER 837, 839 per Singleton J (CA).

14.2 Core value of integrity

At the heart of the duties to the Court is the fact that the Courts rely heavily on the lawyers who appear before them to act with integrity. It is incumbent upon lawyers to be frank with the Court and not to mislead or obstruct a tribunal. This integrity must coexist with the duty to the client and there is an uneasy tension in some of the conduct of lawyers in Court. For example, a lawyer has a duty of candour to the Court, but is constrained from disclosing information confidential to the client. In presenting evidence the lawyer must not lead evidence known to be false, but need not intervene when it is clear that the Court is labouring under a misapprehension. The principle of integrity underlies the many and diverse duties of lawyers who appear in Court, however, it has been interpreted narrowly and in some cases somewhat artificially. In particular, a clear distinction arises between the acts of an advocate in Court, and his or her omissions. There are very few instances where a lawyer is compelled to act in the Court's interest to the detriment of the client.[3] The duty is mainly prohibitive: a lawyer may never act in a way that is calculated to obstruct or deceive the Court.

14.3 The inherent and disciplinary jurisdictions

The duties of a lawyer in respect of litigation are both legal and professional. The legal duties are found in the general law, rules of procedure, and the inherent jurisdiction of the Court to regulate its proceedings. The professional and ethical obligations of the lawyer are found not only in the Rules of Professional Conduct, but also in statements of the Court in cases where it exercises its supervisory jurisdiction over lawyers who appear before it. The Court is also entitled to determine its own procedure and make demands on the lawyers who appear before it (where consistent with the law) as part of its inherent jurisdiction to manage its own proceedings. Where a lawyer is guilty of misconduct, or breaches the rules of procedure, the Court is entitled to act summarily to discipline the lawyer in the lawyer's capacity as an officer of the Court. [4]

---

3 One exception appears to be the disclosure of authorities adverse to a client's legal argument.

4 In New Zealand both barristers and solicitors are officers of the Court. The position is somewhat different in England where solicitors have historically been governed by the Courts, and the Courts have the power to discipline and strike names from the roll. The various Inns of Court, however, govern barristers. The Judges of the Courts act as the final disciplinary authority as Visitors to the Inns. This supervisory jurisdiction is also apparent in the Court's power to enforce practitioner's undertakings. See *Re Grey* [1892] 2 QB 440, 443 per Lord Esher MR; *Gill and McAsey v Wainui Timber Co Ltd* [1992] 1 NZLR 1, 4 per Richardson J (CA).

The existence of the power to prevent its process being used as an instrument of injustice has long been recognised.[5] This is part of the inherent jurisdiction of the Court.[6] The power is one that is derived "from the very nature of the Court as a superior Court of law"[7] to ensure that the Courts are indeed instruments of justice rather than oppression. As long ago as 1885 Lord Blackburn stated that from early times:[8]

> [T]he Court had inherently the right to see that its process was not abused by a proceeding without reasonable grounds, so as to be vexatious and harassing — the Court had the right to protect itself against such abuse.

These powers to protect against abuse, and the related duty to supervise its own officers, are the foundation for the Courts' power to make orders and declarations. The Courts' jurisdiction over lawyers is doubly justified in regulating its own procedures and in supervising its officers. As Lord Wright said in *Myers v Elman*:[9]

> The Court has a right and duty to supervise the conduct of those appearing before it, and to visit with penalties any conduct of a lawyer which is of such a nature as to defeat justice in the very cause in which he is engaged professionally.

The existence of such a jurisdiction was reiterated by the Court of Appeal in *Gazley v Lord Cooke of Thorndon*[10] where it was observed that the jurisdiction to impose duties on lawyers has existed since time immemorial, and that the jurisdiction is grounded in the Court's role in fostering the interests of justice.

Courts exist as tribunals to which citizens may turn when they find themselves at an impasse in a dispute. However, the process of the Court also lends itself to other uses such as delaying inevitable liabilities by mounting hopeless defences, making exaggerated allegations in the hope of a windfall payment, and employment as a platform on which to

---

5 *Metropolitan Bank v Pooley* (1885) 10 App Cas 210, 220 (HL). The power has similarly long been recognised in respect of the power to stay frivolous or vexatious proceedings: *McHenry v Lewis* (1882) 21 Ch D 202 (HC). Most recently see *Ebert v Birch* (1999) Times, 28 April, 34 (CA).

6 See M S Dockray, "The Inherent Jurisdiction to Regulate Civil Proceedings" (1997) 113 LQR 120.

7 J Jacob, "The Inherent Jurisdiction of the Court" [1970] CLP 23, reprinted in J Jacob *The Reform of Civil Procedural Law* 1982, 224. See *New Zealand Social Credit Political League v O'Brien* [1984] 1 NZLR 84 (CA) for the leading New Zealand authority.

8 *Metropolitan Bank v Pooley* (1885) 10 App Cas 210, 220 (HL).

9 [1940] AC 282, 319.

10 [1999] 2 NZLR 668.

air grievances for which no legal remedy exists. Such tactics are abuses of the procedure of the Court. If the objectives of the Court are to be achieved rather than thwarted by such abuses, it is necessary for the Court to be able to act immediately against lawyers who assist in perpetrating such abuses. The ability of the Court to sanction lawyers' acts is an important signal to the profession as to what standards of conduct are acceptable, and as a considerable deterrent against breaching those standards. Such a disincentive is particularly necessary in light of the considerable pressures from the client or from the financial realities of legal practice, to accept a case or take certain dubious procedural steps at a client's behest. The ability to sanction lawyers ensures that the Courts are equipped to be instruments of justice rather than injustice.

Although misconduct in the conduct of litigation by a lawyer falls within the disciplinary jurisdiction of the law society, it is still necessary for the Court to act against such lawyers within the course of the offending proceeding. In some cases of professional misconduct the Court may also see fit to refer the matter to the district law society to take further action.[11] While the two jurisdictions are obviously related they are quite distinct and both remain important. The focus of the Court's jurisdiction is the efficacy of its own proceeding. To ensure this it requires the ability to intervene in the proceeding itself rather than to defer to a separate and later disciplinary hearing of the professional body.

The inherent power of the Court to discipline a lawyer for misconduct in litigation is not an isolated power. It exists as part of the overall jurisdiction of the Court to ensure that its officers act at all times properly, and that its procedures are not abused. The Court will summarily discipline lawyers wherever misconduct is apparent. Examples are where a lawyer's later retainer places the confidential information of a former client at risk, where a lawyer refuses to honour an undertaking, and where reckless or unfounded allegations are made from the bar.[12] Such a jurisdiction assists in the speedy and efficient delivery of justice, and demands the highest standards of conduct from lawyers. Where the actions of its officers are in error, the Court will move swiftly to rectify the situation.

---

11 This course was adopted by Hammond J in *Chua v ANZ* (1997) 11 PRNZ 523, 529 (HC). Similarly in *McDonald v FAI* [1999] 1 NZLR 583 the matter was referred to the district law society by Giles J for revision of the offending lawyer's bill of costs to her client.

12 *Black v Taylor* [1993] 3 NZLR 403 (CA); *Re McDougall's Application* [1982] NZLR 141, 142 (HC); *Gazley v Wellington District Law Society* [1996] 1 NZLR 452, 454.

14.4 Specific duties

The duties of a lawyer when conducting litigation are difficult to enumerate and any attempt is sure to have some omissions. The following discussion concentrates on the duties of the lawyer to the administration of justice and, accordingly, duties to other parties are dealt with only in passing or not at all. In particular, the duty of loyalty (which includes avoiding conflicts of interests) is not dealt with.[13] The following discussion has been divided roughly chronologically from the decision whether to litigate or settle, through pre-trial matters, to the conduct of the trial itself.

14.5 Duty to encourage settlement

It is in all of the parties' interests to avoid recourse to litigation in resolving a dispute. To bring a claim to Court is an expensive and exhausting procedure. From the first instruction of the lawyer to the conclusion of the final step, litigation may take several years. Over that time claimants will not have received any of the compensation claimed, and defendants will have the contingent liability of an award against them hanging over them. The time, money, and energy expended by the litigants in preparing for a trial can be immense and will often detract from their efficiency or enjoyment of other parts of their lives. In addition to these hardships to the litigants, is the fact that most Courts have a heavy workload and are hard pressed to deal with all the claims made by litigants in a timely fashion.

Numerous statutory provisions encourage the resolution of differences outside the adjudicative function of the Court.[14] Although there is no statutory compulsion, lawyers should seek to resolve disputes out of Court where possible. This is dictated by the International Code of Ethics,[15] which in r 11 provides:

> Lawyers shall, when in the client's interest, endeavour to reach a solution by settlement out of Court rather than start legal proceedings. A lawyer should never stir up litigation.

---

13 The duty of loyalty is dealt with in ch 7, confidence is considered in chs 8 and 9.

14 Examples include s 8 Matrimonial Proceedings Act 1980, s 78 Employment Contracts Act 1991, s 88 Residential Tenancies Act 1986, s 80 Human Rights Act 1993, s 170 Children Young Persons and their Families Act 1989. See further C Baylis, "Reviewing Statutory Models of Mediation/Conciliation in New Zealand: Three Conclusions" (1999) 30 VUWLR 279.

15 Promulgated by the International Bar Association and appended to the New Zealand Rules as app III.

It is improper for a lawyer to encourage or incite parties to litigate unnecessarily. This is one of the justifications on limitations of the manner in which lawyers may advertise their service, or approach prospective clients,[16] and why the law of champerty prohibits lawyers taking a share in the fruits of any litigation.[17] A natural corollary to the duty not to clutter the Courts with unnecessary, frivolous, or vexatious litigation is a duty to ensure that all other reasonable avenues by which the dispute might be resolved have been or are being pursued.

Such a duty is not entirely straightforward in application. The ability to have recourse to the power of the Courts in resolving a dispute is often needed to encourage parties to settle their differences. It may be necessary to commence proceedings, and indeed to prosecute them energetically to persuade the other side that the claimant is serious about seeking redress for the wrong claimed. The volume of settlements which occur only when the hearing is imminent, or has commenced, bears witness to the persuasive force of the immediate threat of an adverse decision of the Court. The willingness to seek a settlement out of Court may also be frustrated by the stance of the other side or, of course, by a genuine irreconcilable difference of views as to where liability ought to fall.

As many lawyers would testify, pre-trial procedures can also be a real assistance in achieving a settlement. Diligent discovery, skilful pleading, and careful use of procedures such as interrogatories, whereby specific questions can be asked of the other side, can result in a clarification of the factual and legal issues and the removal of much of the guesswork as to where the evidence leads. Once in possession of such information both clients and lawyers are better equipped to gauge the chances of success at trial and reach a settlement that accords with their assessment of their risks.

The content of the duty to seek a non-litigious settlement is obviously not a duty not to litigate, nor is it an attempt to limit the amount of legitimate claims that need the Court's assistance to be resolved. It is an instruction to the profession to ensure that non-litigious solutions are pursued. It is important that lawyers raise the possibility of a settlement with their clients, and broach the matter with the other side. Some argue that there is an advantage to be gained from stonewalling suggestions of a negotiated settlement, or of refusing to be the first to raise the possibility. Such claims are rarely well-founded and there is a danger that clients will lose out through escalating costs and personal brinkmanship on the part of their lawyers if such a stance is taken.

---

16 Rules 4.03 and 7.03 of the ABA Model Rules.

17 *Mills v Rogers* (1899) 18 NZLR 291, 309-310 per Williams J (CA).

Lawyers should not bow to the pressures exerted by the opposition (and sometimes by the Court) to settle where, in the lawyers' professional judgment, it is not in the clients' interest to do so. The duty to act in the clients' interest accords with the duty to seek a settlement, but requires the lawyers to exercise independent judgment as to whether or not they should advise that a settlement offer ought to be made or accepted. That judgment should not be affected by any interests other than those of the clients. Facts such as that the case contains an interesting point, or that the lawyers' fees will be greater if a particular course of actions is taken, are irrelevant to such a decision and ought to be studiously put to one side.

14.6 Duty not to be a party to an abuse

A practitioner is required to make all reasonable efforts to ensure that legal processes are used for their proper purposes only.[18] In terms of litigation this will translate to a duty to ensure that an action that is brought is not an abuse of the procedure of the Court. A litigant may legitimately take an action for the purpose of getting the facts of a matter put right rather than any financial gain. It is not appropriate for an action to be brought solely for the purpose of airing claims or making allegations against another that cannot be proved in evidence, or for which no legal remedy exists.[19] In *R v Weisz*[20] it was held to be an abuse when an action was instituted against a bookmaker notwithstanding the fact that the law clearly stated that gambling contracts were unenforceable before the Courts.[21] The sole purpose of the action was to embarrass the bookmaker and was, therefore, an abuse of the Court's process. Wherever a litigant is motivated in the action not by the aim of obtaining a Court order in his or her favour but by some collateral purpose the action will be an abuse.

The tendency to misuse the procedures of the Court is particularly prominent in the defence of claims. In *Chua v ANZ*[22] the advocate sought to frustrate a mortgagee sale by raising unfounded defences and in the course of making an application for an ex parte injunction he knowingly misled the Court.[23] Such actions are an abuse because the

18 Rule 7.04.

19 *Flower and Hart (a firm) v White Industries (Qld) Pty Ltd* (1999) 87 FLR 134.

20 [1951] 2 KB 611, discussed in D A Ipp, "Lawyers' Duties to the Court" (1998) 114 LQR 63, 80.

21 The same rule applies in New Zealand under s 128 Gaming and Lotteries Act 1977.

22 (1997) 11 PRNZ 523 (HC).

23 See also *Flower and Hart (a firm) v White Industries (Qld) Pty Ltd* (1999) 87 FLR 134 where costs were ordered against a solicitor who assisted in bringing a claim simply to delay the recovery of money owed to the respondent.

Court procedure was being used as a device to delay the inevitable mortgagee sale. It is particularly easy to multiply defences to an action by claiming that some or all of the numerous common law or statutory defences exist. Judges are often seen to complain that although unconscionability, deceptive conduct, mistake, and oppression were argued there was no hope of any (or most) of them being established. Frequently, such defences are abandoned at the hearing after having put the opposing counsel to the trouble of researching the facts and law in respect of each defence. Where claims or defences are made which have absolutely no prospect of success there is a high likelihood that they will amount to an abuse of the process of the Court.[24] Where a case is obviously hopeless, it is not brought with a view to a favourable decision of the Court. It must be being brought for a collateral purpose and, therefore, is an abuse of the Court's process.

In *Tolstoy-Miloslavsky v Aldington*[25] the plaintiff had formerly been successfully sued by the defendant for libel and a significant order for damages and costs had been made against him. In this action (which was brought some four years after the initial case) the plaintiff sought to have the earlier judgment set aside on the ground of fraud. The Court held that none of the evidence presented to the Court was capable of establishing the fraud relied on, and that the action was brought solely for the collateral purpose of impugning the findings in the earlier case. It was found that the proceeding was "utterly hopeless" and an abuse of the process of the Court.[26]

The commentary to r 7.04 gives some examples of conduct that would amount to using legal processes for improper purposes. They include issuing a statutory demand on a company as leverage only, knowing that the debt is in dispute, registering a caveat which prevents dealing in land knowing that there is not (or failing to inquire whether there is) any registerable interest held in the land. The list could go on almost indefinitely. A lawyer should never be involved in an action where the Courts are used unfairly, for a purpose which is not connected with the outcome of the case, or as a collateral attack on an earlier decision of the Court.

24 See more particularly D Webb, "Hopeless Cases: In Defence of Compensating Litigants at the Advocate's Expense" (1999) 29 VUWLR 295; also *Harley v McDonald* [1999] 3 NZLR 545.

25 [1996] 1 WLR 736 (CA). The consequence was an order of costs against the lawyers involved. Compare *Ridehalgh v Horsefield* [1994] Ch 205, 206 (CA) where six cases concerning wasted costs in hopeless cases were considered together, none of which resulted in an adverse finding against the advocate.

26 *Tolstoy-Miloslavsky v Aldington* [1996] 1 WLR 736, 747(CA).

It will not be an absolute defence to a claim of abuse for a solicitor to claim that he or she relied on the expertise of a barrister. Such reliance may be warranted where the material is technical or the facts complex, but in most cases solicitors are expected to exercise independent judgment in light of their own skill as to whether the claim is well-founded.[27] In matters of law and legal practice legal representatives may not, by relying on the advice of another, divest themselves of their responsibility to conduct litigation responsibly.

14.7 Duty to expedite proceedings

Not only is a lawyer prohibited from assisting in a proceeding that is an abuse, but even where the claim or defence is well-founded the lawyer must ensure that the proceeding is brought to trial without undue delay. This position is reflected in the approach of the ABA Model Rules, which in r 3.2 provides: "A lawyer shall make reasonable efforts to expedite litigation consistent with the interest of the client". Where it is clear that the lawyer does not have adequate time to handle a matter properly the case should not be taken. The Code of Conduct of the Bar of England and Wales provides:[28]

> A barrister must in all his professional activities act promptly, conscientiously, diligently and with reasonable competence and must take all reasonable and practicable steps to ensure that professional engagements are fulfilled. He [or she] must not undertake any tasks which...he [or she] does not have adequate time and opportunity to prepare and perform; or he [or she] cannot discharge within a reasonable time having regard to the pressure of other work.

The duty to expedite proceedings is more than a duty to act diligently in the interests of the client. It is also a duty to assist the Court and not to obstruct the proper progress of litigation. Delay could be in the interests of the client, as where a client needs time to raise funds to stave off creditors, or where one litigant seeks to wear down the other side by the costs and time consumed by the proceedings. However, to seek to lengthen proceedings for such a motive is inappropriate and is thwarting the effective working of the Court.

It is not uncommon for the judiciary to become impatient and even frustrated with litigants who appear to be reluctant to bring a matter to trial. Such reluctance frequently results in a generation of further work for the Court, and the cluttering of the Court's calendar. Lawyers should

27 *Flower and Hart (a firm) v White Industries (Qld) Pty Ltd* (1999) 87 FLR 134; *Tolstoy-Miloslavsky v Aldington* [1996] 1 WLR 736, 747(CA).

28 Rule 5.4(b) Written Standards for the Conduct of Professional Work: General Standards of the Code of Conduct of the Bar of England and Wales.

be wary of bringing a matter to trial before all important pre-trial matters have been disposed of. There are numerous situations where good reasons exist for delaying proceedings and in such cases seeking such a delay by the appropriate methods is proper. It may be that further evidence is required, witnesses are unavailable, time is needed to consider settlements, or even counsel of choice is unavailable to act in a matter for some time. It is appropriate for a lawyer to resist pressure to come to trial before the case is ready. Not only will such a delay be in the interests of the client, but it will also be in the interests of the administration of justice as leading to either a settlement, or a more just resolution of the issues when they do come before the Court.

The duty to expedite proceedings is more than a duty to act in good faith. The Court will not take action against a lawyer merely because the lawyer's judgment differs from that of the Court or is poor.[29] Where the lawyer is guilty of a serious dereliction of his or her duty to the Court in the conduct of the case the Court may step in. A Court will not usually take such a step where the error is minor. Giles J stated in *McDonald v FAI* when considering whether to award costs against a barrister:[30]

> Mistake or error of judgment will not justify an order, but misconduct, default or even negligence is enough if the negligence is serious or gross. Neither will the fact that the case was lost be enough. All the circumstances have to be looked at.

Frequently, there are calls for lawyers to act more cooperatively in the conduct of litigation and thereby dispose of proceedings more quickly and effectively.[31] Such calls rightly point out that a rigorously adversarial approach increases the time and cost of proceedings and makes the task of the Court more difficult. Such calls require lawyers to lessen their zeal for their client's cause, and refuse to take advantages when available in order to assist the Court. This is anathema to the adversarial process. While it is clear that a lawyer should not obstruct the Court, and should act only within the rules for a legitimate purpose, it is unreasonable in the adversarial system to expect a lawyer to act in any more extensive way as an agent of the Court.

---

29 *Y v M* [1994] 3 NZLR 581, following *R & T Thew Ltd v Reeves (No 2)* [1982] QB 1283, 1286 (CA).

30 [1999] 1 NZLR 583, 592 affirmed by the Court of Appeal in *Harley v McDonald* [1999] 3 NZLR 545, 564 per Tipping J where the test of serious dereliction of duty was adopted.

31 See D A Ipp, "Lawyers' Duties to the Court" (1998) 114 LQR 63, 96 and the numerous cases cited there.

14.8 Truth and simplicity in pleadings

Allied to the duty to expedite proceedings is the duty to draft Court documents in an accurate and clear manner. It is common when making claims or defences for lawyers to use what have become known as "shotgun" pleadings, that is, pleadings that state numerous claims or defences in the hope that at least one will hit the mark and be able to be established. Such an action can cause considerable work for the Court and the parties. It may be necessary to make application to the Court to compel a party to clarify pleadings, or to strike out unfounded claims prior to trial. It will also be necessary to prepare for trial on the basis of the pleadings, large parts of which are frequently not pursued in Court. In the event that tenuous claims or defences are argued in Court considerable time can be taken up with points which are peripheral to the main issue and doomed to fail.

There are collateral advantages to be gained by such pleadings. By including certain claims (such as of fraud or malice) evidence may be put before the Court that will gain the sympathy of the Judge, even though that part of the claim is doomed to fail. Or, by asserting a certain defence, the plaintiff will be put to further expense of refuting it, thereby making an advantageous settlement more likely. A claim may be filed or damages claimed which are simply not supportable on the law or facts. The Courts have been firm in admonishing such actions stating that lawyers should not be associated with claims that are without foundation and brought in terrorem.[32] There is a duty on lawyers drafting pleadings to ensure that they are supported by facts that they reasonably believe to be true, and are reasonably arguable in law.[33] This will exclude many of the frivolous claims that might be made. It does not exclude the tactical use of claims that while arguable, will not be pursued.

More fundamental than the duty to plead clearly is the duty to plead honestly. Whenever a claim or defence is lodged with the Court the lawyer of the record signs it. In signing a pleading lawyers are certifying that the case is not a mere fiction.[34] The Court presumes that the lawyers have investigated the evidence and believe, in their judgment, that there is at least a prima facie case to be answered in respect of the claims made.[35] While lawyers are advocates for their clients, they are expected

---

32 *Ellison v L* [1998] 1 NZLR 416, 419.

33 Rule 5.8(a) and (b) Written Standards for the Conduct of Professional Work: General Standards of the Code of Conduct of the Bar of England and Wales. See also *H v H* [1997] NZFLR 869.

34 *Great Australian Gold Mining Co v Martin* (1877) 5 Ch D 1, 10.

35 *Re a Company (no 006798 of 1995)* [1996] 2 All ER 417 where a solicitor was held to have acted improperly and was liable for costs where a winding-up petition was filed without foundation.

to exercise independent judgment in accepting the assertions made.[36] And where there is some doubt as to the veracity of a client's allegations lawyers are entitled to seek corroboration from independent investigation.[37]

At the outset the claim may have appeared well-founded but subsequently it becomes apparent that there is no prospect of success. If it becomes clear that the pleadings are unfounded and there is no real likelihood of success of a claim or defence when new evidence comes to hand (for instance, by discovery) the lawyer may be obliged to amend the pleadings accordingly, or possibly to discontinue a claim. In *Edwards v Edwards*[38] it was held by the Court that the continued prosecution of a claim that a husband was wilfully neglecting his wife was unreasonably continued once the documents discovered by the husband made it clear that the claim was unsustainable. Sachs J stated that it was the duty of legal advisers to:[39]

> Examine closely whatever is disclosed on his opponent's affidavit of documents to see whether the relative prospects of success or failure have been altered thereby.

The duty is not merely one to use good faith, or best endeavours. The decision to proceed after discovery must be tested against the judgment of a reasonable adviser who investigated the facts with proper care.[40] This amounts to a duty not to pursue a case which is revealed to be hopeless.

The onus on a lawyer to ensure the truth of pleadings is particularly high where serious allegations are made. The commentary to r 8.04 provides:

> A practitioner should not be a party to the filing of a pleading or other Court document containing an allegation of fraud, dishonesty, undue influence, duress or other reprehensible conduct, unless the practitioner has first satisfied himself or herself that such allegation can be properly justified on the facts of the case. … If necessary, a practitioner must test the instructions which have been given, by independent inquiry, before making such allegations.

---

36 *Y v M* [1994] 3 NZLR 581.
37 Rule 3.03.
38 [1958] P 258 (HC). In this case the Court also noted that the solicitors for the wife had needlessly required voluminous amounts of information which caused considerable wasted expenditure.
39 [1958] P 258, 252, 253.
40 [1958] P 258, 255.

If allegations of such a kind are made without foundation it may amount to misconduct.[41] It is common practice when replying to allegations of facts made in a statement of claim to put the other party to proof on the matters stated. A common formula used in statements of defence when replying to particular statements is to observe that "the defendant has no knowledge of, and therefore denies, the allegations contained in paragraph *x* of the statement of claim". Alternatively, the lawyer may be instructed (or may advise his or her client) to flatly deny the truth of the allegations. Where the lawyer is aware that an allegation made by the other side cannot be refuted on any interpretation of the evidence it is inappropriate to deny that this is the case or to insist that evidence supporting the facts be laboriously adduced. This is quite distinct from putting the other side to proof on matters which are in doubt or of which one's client is unaware.

14.9 Duties in pre-trial matters

An important part of most civil proceedings occurs prior to trial. Interlocutory proceedings serve to ensure that the parties are in possession of all the available documentary evidence, and the issues to be put before the Court have been clarified as far as possible, and in many cases the evidence to be presented by witnesses has been outlined to the other side. The duties owed by a lawyer to the Court attach to these pre-trial matters as much as to conduct in the trial itself.

Of particular importance is discovery. By this device all parties are required to list the documents relevant to the case in their possession (or the possession of their agents) and make all documents which are not privileged available for inspection to the other side. There is a strong temptation for clients to withhold or even destroy documents that damage their cause. Lawyers are required to ensure as far as possible that their clients do not engage in such activities, and secure compliance with the obligations.[42] New rules have been proposed which provide that it is a breach of the practitioner's duty to the Court and abuse of process for a lawyer to claim or to allow a client to claim privilege without reasonable grounds, or to knowingly fail to discover a discoverable document.[43]

While a lawyer will not be liable for a client's failure where the lawyer has taken all the proper steps and could not reasonably be expected to have

41 *Gazley v Wellington District Law Society* [1976] 1 NZLR 452. As regards allegations of witness perjury by opposing counsel see *Re Harawira* [1989] 2 NZLR 714, 726; also *Thatcher v Douglas* (1996) Times, 8 January, Nourse LJ (CA).

42 *Rockwell Machine Tool Co Ltd v E P Borrus (Concessionaires) Ltd* [1968] 2 All ER 98.

43 Proposed rr 8.01A and 8.01B.

been aware of the breach, the Court places a heavy responsibility on the lawyer. In the leading case of *Myers v Elman*[44] the solicitors of the defendant had failed to advise the defendant carefully of the scope of the discovery which was necessary. The Court held that the extra costs incurred ought to be borne by the solicitor in question. Although the affidavit in question was completed by a managing clerk of the office, the solicitor was held responsible for the clerk's misconduct demonstrating that the duties owed by a lawyer may not be delegated to others. The duty to discover is an ongoing one. Where new discoverable documents are found or come into existence subsequent to the initial discovery they must be disclosed to the other side. Such a duty may extend up until the moment of final judgment.[45]

The duty of a lawyer to ensure proper discovery might be considered an aspect of the duty not to mislead the Court. It is a positive duty. In *Vernon v Bosley (No 2)*[46] the plaintiff claimed for nervous shock and psychiatric damage consequent on witnessing an accident where the car in which his children were travelling plunged into a river and the children drowned. The plaintiff was successful at first instance. The defendant appealed. After the hearing of the appeal, but before the judgment was delivered, the defendant's counsel received documentary evidence[47] (anonymously) that the damage sustained by the plaintiff was significantly less than claimed and accepted by the Court. That information was known to the lawyers for the plaintiff. The defendant applied for a rehearing claiming that the information should have been disclosed. It was held, allowing the application, that up until the time that the judgment was delivered the plaintiff had an obligation to disclose the documents and, in failing to do so, this obligation had been breached. The plaintiff's legal advisers had breached their duty by wrongly advising the plaintiff that the documents need not be produced. The members of the Court differed on the exact nature of the obligation of a lawyer where a client refused to disclose a discoverable document. At the very least the lawyer should withdraw from acting further.[48] However Thorpe LJ was of the view that the lawyer had a duty to disclose the material to the other side and the Court.[49]

---

44 [1940] AC 282 (HL).

45 *Vernon v Bosley (No 2)* [1999] QB 18, [1997] 1 All ER 614. See also P Matthews, "Ongoing Discovery in English Law" (1994) 44 NLJ 327. See also the commentary to the proposed new r 8.01B.

46 [1999] QB 18, [1997] 1 All ER 614.

47 Copies of judgments from family proceedings in the County Court where the plaintiff was seeking custody of his children showed that expert medical evidence had been given that the plaintiff's condition had improved dramatically and had an excellent prognosis.

48 Per Smith LJ at 39 , 631, and thereby protect the client's confidence.

49 At 54, 654.

The schedule for the progress of a case is determined by pre-trial conferences to ensure timely compliance and speedy progress to either trial or settlement. Where such directions are not complied with without a good excuse and, in particular, where the blame lies with the lawyer rather than the client, the Court will consider this to be misconduct and may take action against the lawyer. In *Kamo Sports & Dive Ltd v Harrison Sports (Kamo) Ltd*[50] counsel for the plaintiffs sought to introduce new expert evidence at the trial when timetable orders allowing for the exchange of briefs of evidence had not been complied with. The default was solely the fault of counsel. In ordering the lawyer to pay the increase in the costs of the defendant which had been caused by the non-compliance Fisher J stated: "[T]he time has come to blow the whistle on non-observance of pre-trial directions".[51] Inexcusable delay which puts the other side to expense will warrant action against the lawyer possibly giving rise to a pecuniary remedy.[52]

14.10 Evidence

14.10.1 *Presenting facts to the Court*

The advocate is not a fact-finder. The primary task of an advocate in our judicial system is to present the client's case in the best light possible. They are not to usurp the Court's role in determining the credibility of witnesses, or the inferences that may be drawn from the evidence. A lawyer should never knowingly mislead the Court.[53] Thus in presenting the evidence to the Court the lawyer should never allow evidence to be put before the Court knowing that it is false. Rule 10.02 provides:[54]

> Counsel must not in the course of making submissions or cross-examining a witness say or lead a witness to say anything that might mislead the Court. In particular, counsel must not make any statement to the Court or put any proposition to a witness that is not supported by reasonable instructions, or that lacks factual foundation by reference to the information available to the Court.

The duty to ensure as far as possible that witnesses tell what they believe to be the truth extends beyond conduct in Court. It is not appropriate for a lawyer to seek to dissuade witnesses from telling their version of events if it is clear that the witnesses believe it to be true, even if the

50 (1993) 7 PRNZ 321 (HC).

51 *Kamo Sports & Dive Ltd v Harrison Sports (Kamo) Ltd* (1993) 7 PRNZ 321, 324 (HC).

52 *Sinclair-Jones v Kay* [1989] 1 WLR 114 (CA) where a delay in applying to set aside a default judgment of liability meant that the plaintiff needlessly prepared submissions as to quantum.

53 *R v Visitors to the Inns of Court, ex parte Calder* [1994] QB 1.

54 Although ch 10 of the rules is entitled "Advocate for the Defence" the rule applies across all advocacy.

lawyer is convinced that it is false.[55] This extends to evidence given by experts. A lawyer should never suggest that an expert's report be altered or modified to remove unfavourable aspects.[56] Such conduct is usurping the fact-finding responsibilities of the Judge or jury. A lawyer must be especially careful not to be seen as intimidating witnesses or placing pressure on them to change their evidence. Such actions are not only misconduct, but also quite possibly criminal as an attempt to obstruct, pervert, or defeat the course of justice.[57] In *R v Taffs*[58] a practitioner was found guilty of that offence when he contacted the mother of a prospective witness (who was a schoolboy) and claimed that there were inconsistencies in his evidence that would lead to his being "humiliated as a liar and a homosexual". It was held that the conduct of the practitioner was criminal and amounted to misconduct even though he believed the witness's evidence to be false.

14.10.2 *Advising witness of obligation of honesty*

Lawyers frequently discuss giving evidence in Court with their clients prior to the trial, and with the advent of the exchange of prepared witness briefs in many civil cases it is common to go through much or all of the evidence a witness will give prior to trial. When witnesses are prepared for trial lawyers must emphasise the need for absolute honesty in giving evidence. It is imperative that a lawyer should never suggest or even insinuate that because certain evidence is damaging to the case it should be withheld, distorted, or forgotten, or that the client should be evasive in answering.[59] If a lawyer is aware that the evidence a witness proposes to give is knowingly at variance with the truth the lawyer ought not to call that witness.[60]

14.10.3 *Witness coaching*

There has been a wariness of allowing lawyers to prepare witnesses too thoroughly for trial. In England and Wales, where the profession is divided, it is regarded as the solicitor's task to gather evidence and the barrister's task to present the case. The witnesses did not discuss the evidence they were to present with the barrister. This stringent approach has been relaxed.[61] There is still a prohibition on "witness coaching".[62]

---

55 See G Williams, "Evading Justice" [1975] Crim LR 430, 611.
56 *Kelly v London Transport Executive* [1982] 2 All ER 842, 851 per Lord Denning (CA); *Whitehouse v Jordan* [1981] 1 All ER 276.
57 Section 117(d) Crimes Act 1961.
58 [1991] 1 NZLR 69.
59 *R v Sweezey* [1987] 39 CCC 3d 182 (Newfoundland Court of Appeal).
60 *Brand v College of Surgeons* (1990) 83 Sask rep 218.
61 See r 6.2 of the Written Standards for the Conduct of Professional Work: General Standards of the Code of Conduct of the Bar of England and Wales.
62 See Sheppard, "Communications with Witnesses Before and During their Evidence" (1987) 3 Aust Bar Rev 28; R Wydick, "The Ethics of Witness Coaching" 23 IALS Bull (1996) 8.

The expression itself is unhelpful as it simply refers to conduct overstepping the proper degree of preparation of a witness. Certainly it is considered good practice to meet with and discuss the evidence to be presented by a prospective witness. The commentary to r 8.05 of the New Zealand Rules confirms this in providing:

> [I]t is permissible for a practitioner acting for one party to interview a witness or prospective witness at any stage prior to the hearing whether or not that witness has been interviewed by the practitioner acting for the other party or called as a witness.

While a witness should not be told what to say and what not to say, it is acceptable to prepare a witness for the ordeal of giving evidence. It would be irresponsible to fail to prepare an unsuspecting witness for the difficult circumstances which may be encountered. It is acceptable to suggest questions that might be asked in cross-examination, to clarify what the client means if answers are unclear, to point out internal inconsistencies, and to advise on matters such as dress and demeanour. As the Bar Code of England and Wales points out lawyers should be aware of the danger that witnesses may misconstrue such comments of the lawyer as an insinuation that certain evidence be presented or withheld.[63]

The problems are even more acute once the trial has been commenced and some witnesses have given evidence. It is usual to exclude from the hearing witnesses yet to give evidence, to ensure that they do not tailor their evidence to fit that of the previous witnesses. It is incumbent on the lawyer ensure that a witness who has given evidence does not confer with one who is yet to do so. It is also important that the lawyer does not seek to influence the nature of the evidence given by witnesses in light of the evidence that has already been given. Where a witness is aware of evidence that has been given the lawyer should advise witnesses not to alter their evidence as a consequence:[64]

> Great care must always be exercised by legal practitioners when conferring with witnesses yet to be called in circumstances where they know the evidence, particularly the cross-examination, of witnesses already called, especially witnesses on their own side of the record. It is important for the due administration of justice that such practitioners, should not make known to witnesses yet to be called what was the evidence given by prior witnesses. It is a well known fact in the legal profession that it is both possible and essential in obtaining instructions during the running of a case, not to make known to the witness from whom these instructions are being sought, the

---

63 See r 6.2.4 of the Written Standards for the Conduct of Professional Work: General Standards of the Code of Conduct of the Bar of England and Wales.

64 *Re Bankers Trust Australia Ltd* (NSW G30/1989 Federal Court of Australia, FED 63, Foster J).

evidence which has been given in Court and which requires the obtaining of those instructions. Considerable care is required, but the operation is successfully performed every day by skilled and conscientious lawyers.

If a lawyer is using an expert witness it is important that the opinion of the expert is independent and informed. It would be improper to attempt to influence the conclusions reached by the witness, or to suggest that an initial or preliminary finding be changed. It is permissible for a lawyer to discuss the contents of the evidence presented with a view to ascertaining whether it addresses the issues raised by the trial. The lawyer must also ensure that the expert is apprised of all of the relevant facts and must not be selective in the information proffered on which the final report is based.[65]

14.10.4 *Multiple witnesses*

It is usually inadvisable to disclose the evidence to be given by one witness to another witness as it may be construed as an invitation to recast the evidence in a more consistent fashion.[66] Similar risks will exist where matters of evidence are discussed in the presence of more than one witness: there is a risk of collusion between the witnesses, and a contamination of the evidence. This leaves a lawyer in a dilemma where the evidence of two witnesses conflicts. While it is sensible to put the conflict to the witnesses prior to trial (as it will certainly be put to them in cross-examination) the lawyer must avoid any appearance of encouraging witnesses to depart from their belief of the truth of the matter in seeking consistency. Where a lawyer does ensure consistency between witnesses it may detract from their persuasiveness because the Court will be suspicious that the evidence is concocted and not genuine.

Where a lawyer is representing several clients jointly, it may be appropriate and necessary to meet with them together to discuss matters concerning the conduct of the proceeding and to keep them informed of the progress of the case. In the event that the evidence of the clients diverges in such a way as to create a conflict of interest between the clients[67] there will be an irreconcilable conflict of interest. The lawyer will be compelled to withdraw from acting for either client.[68]

---

65 *R v Ellis* (Court of Appeal, CA 120/98, paras 24 and 25, 14 October 1999).

66 *Smith New Court Securities Ltd v Scrimgeour Vickers (Asset Management) Ltd* [1994] 1 WLR 1271.

67 As where one co-defendant alleges another co-defendant is guilty of the crime charged, or where co-defendants in civil proceedings may dispute the apportionment of any damages.

68 Rule 8.07.

14.10.5 *Cross-examination*

The veracity of the evidence given by a witness is often determined by how it fares under cross-examination when the opposition lawyer has the opportunity to ask questions of the witness. Such questions usually seek to show weaknesses or inconsistencies in the evidence. Cross-examination of a witness may span several hours or even days. In such cases there is a near absolute ban on communication between the lawyer who led the evidence of the witness and the witness.[69] The commentary to r 8.04 provides:

> A practitioner who calls a witness at a hearing may discuss matters with the witness at any stage up to the commencement of cross-examination. If discussion with the witness is sought during the course of cross-examination or re-examination, this can only be permitted with the consent (for good reason) of the Judge and opposing counsel. This applies even during adjournments of the hearing.

The reasons for such a ban are obvious. If the cross-examination is successful, the witness may be confused and in doubt as to the accuracy of some of his or her previous statements. The witness may desire reassurance or advice as to how to proceed. The lawyer may consider that the guidance given in the preparation of the witness has been ignored, and a refresher would be helpful. Such contacts are prohibited for the obvious reason that the opportunity of the cross-examining lawyer to rigorously test the evidence of witnesses under cross-examination unassisted is central to the adversarial process. Where the trial is adjourned in the middle of a cross-examination, even when it is adjourned overnight or for a period of days, any contact between the lawyer and the witness is prohibited.

Abrogation of this rule prohibiting contact with a witness under cross-examination is only permitted in exceptional circumstances and with the consent of the Judge and the opposing counsel. An example of a good reason for such contact might be where the witness is also the client and the cross-examination has shown a fatal weakness in the case. In such circumstances the lawyer may wish to confer with the client-witness to advise immediate settlement of the claim, and to discuss possible terms of the settlement.

14.10.6 *Interviewing opposing witnesses*

No party has the sole right to confer with, or indeed call, a witness. Rule 8.05 makes this clear when it provides:

> No practitioner engaged in a proceeding, criminal or civil, has the sole right to call or discuss the case with a witness.

---

69 *Kelly v ARCIC* (Employment Court, Wellington, WEC 20/97, 31 July 1997).

While no witness is compelled to cooperate with a lawyer, or meet with the lawyer prior to trial, there is no bar to a lawyer seeking that cooperation from the witness.[70] While a lawyer may advise witnesses that they are not compelled to cooperate with the other lawyer, they should never encourage them to refuse to assist. Allied to the fact that a lawyer may not preclude a person from cooperating with the other side, or insist that the person cooperate with him or her, is the prohibition on lawyers using overbearing conduct to coerce prospective witnesses to cooperate. Witnesses may be unfamiliar with legal procedure and intimidated by the position a lawyer occupies. A lawyer should be careful in ensuring that a prospective witness is aware of the fact that they are not obliged to cooperate, but may be required to give evidence in any event. Whatever the case, a lawyer should never use overbearing conduct to obtain cooperation. The commentary to r 10.08 provides:[71]

> It should be remembered that while a practitioner has the "right" to interview anyone, so also has the person the "right" to refuse to be interviewed. No one is obliged to make a statement, if he or she does not wish to do so, when interviewed by a solicitor, counsel or anyone else.

Wherever a lawyer chooses to interview a witness who is being, or is likely to be, called by the other side the utmost caution must be exercised. Because the evidence of such a witness is likely to be adverse to the interests of the lawyer's client there may be a perception that the lawyer is attempting to change the evidence to be given.[72] To avoid such an appearance it is advisable to inform the other party of the intention to interview the witness, and in some cases to arrange the interview through the other lawyer (as, for example, where the witness is closely related to the other litigant).[73] It may also be advisable to conduct any interview in the presence of an independent third party to ensure there is no appearance of improper conduct. The rules provide:[74]

> Counsel should bear in mind the possibility of subsequent accusations of tampering with the evidence to be given by that witness. Depending on the

70 With the obvious exception of a lawyer seeking to contact the opposing client directly. See r 6.02.

71 While ch 10 of the rules is entitled "Advocate for the Defence" this rule is applicable to all practitioners.

72 See the comments in *Transamerica Life Insurance Co of Canada v Seward* (1997) 33 OR (3d) 604 at 608-609 per Brennan J.

73 See the commentary to r 10.08 which also suggests that in criminal matters it is advisable to inform the prosecution if the defence proposes to interview a complainant especially in sexual offence cases, and also in cases where depositions evidence has already been given.

74 In the commentary to r 10.8 which although entitled "Advocate for the Defence" is applicable to all practitioners.

> circumstances of the matter, including the nature of the offence and the importance of the witness in the case, consideration should be given to carrying out the interview in the presence of an independent and reputable person.

Practitioners should also exercise care when interviewing children, especially when the child may have been the subject of abuse. The rules state that in such cases the interview should be "conducted in the presence of an independent and reputable person who is able to ensure that the child is not pressured or unreasonably distressed by the event".[75]

14.10.7 *Evidence in ex parte applications*

The duty of candour to the Court is especially important in ex parte applications. Because the other party does not have an opportunity to respond, and the order sought may have far-reaching consequences, it is incumbent on the lawyer to ensure that all of the relevant information is put before the Court. It is not sufficient for the lawyer to state only the facts advantageous to his or her client's case, as might be acceptable in other circumstances. In *Chua v ANZ*[76] a lawyer successfully obtained an injunction on an ex parte application to prevent a mortgagee sale. The defences raised and allegations made in the course of that application were unfounded defences and the lawyer knowingly misled the Court. In the words of Hammond J:[77]

> This appears to me to be a case in which Mr Middleton has put his zeal for his client's interests ahead of his plain duty of candour to the Court. On the evidence before me I have to say that he actively misled the Court on 24 October.

As well as ordering the lawyer to pay costs the Judge took the step of drawing the conduct of counsel in this case to the attention of the district law society.

14.10.8 *Client confessions and witness perjury*

One of the dilemmas most often posed hypothetically to lawyers is that of what to do if it is clear that one's witness is lying. The first observation to be made is that a lawyer should be careful before assuming that a witness is lying, or intends to lie. Even though the witness's story may stretch the credulity of the Court, it is up to the Court to decide whether the truth is being told. There may be good

75 In the commentary to r 10.8 which although entitled "Advocate for the Defence" is applicable to all practitioners, for example where the child is being interviewed in respect of family or care and protection proceedings.

76 (1997) 11 PRNZ 523 (HC).

77 *Chua v ANZ* (1997) 11 PRNZ 523, 529.

tactical or strategic reasons for not putting witnesses who are unlikely to be persuasive on the stand, however, this is not an ethical prohibition.

There will be instances where it is obvious to the lawyer that the evidence of a witness (who is also frequently a client) is false. A witness may intimate or infer as much to the lawyer, or there may be such compelling evidence contradicting the truth of the evidence that such a conclusion is inevitable. A lawyer should never allow a witness to take the stand and to commit perjury. A lawyer should not conduct the case in a manner which presumes that the false claims of the witness are in fact true, even if the claims are not put before the Court in evidence. To do so would amount to misleading the Court and seeking to pursue a cause that is without foundation.

In the event that a witness gives evidence that the lawyer knows to be false, or a client insists on taking such a course of action the lawyer must refuse to continue to act. To do otherwise would not only be in breach of the duty to the Court, but also quite possibly a criminal offence. This course of action is to be taken even where the trial is in progress.[78] Where the opportunity exists the lawyer should strongly counsel against the presentation of such evidence and advise the client of the consequences of such evidence being put before the Court.[79] The lawyer is not at liberty to ignore the client's instructions and conduct the case in accordance with the lawyer's ethical obligations. If the client insists that the false evidence be given the only option open to the lawyer is to withdraw.[80]

Where a lawyer is compelled to withdraw it should be done in a manner which is least prejudicial to the interests of the client. Indications of the reasons for the withdrawal should not be made in open Court and an adjournment should be sought to enable new counsel to be instructed. The Court of Appeal has stated:[81]

> It does happen from time to time that a barrister will find himself unable or unwilling to act in accordance with his client's wishes. They may, for example, be incompatible with his duty to the Court or with his professional obligations; or he may consider that compliance would be prejudicial to his client's best interests. Should such a circumstance arise, then he must inform the client that unless the instructions are changed he will be unable to act further. If the difficulty arises during a trial he should immediately inform the Judge and seek leave to withdraw. It will then be the Judge's responsibility to determine what should be done, whether in terms of

78 *R v Lyons* (1978) 68 Cr App R 104.

79 *Sankar v Trinidad and Tobago* [1995] 1 WLR 194.

80 *R v McLoughlin* [1985] NZLR 106; *Sankar v Trinidad and Tobago* [1995] 1 WLR 194.

81 *R v McLoughlin* [1985] 1 NZLR 106, 108 per Hardie Boys J.

> arranging for an adjournment or otherwise. But certainly counsel may not take it upon himself to disregard his instructions and to then conduct the case as he himself thinks best.

This problem is particularly acute in criminal proceedings. The burden of proof is on the prosecution who must prove the offence beyond reasonable doubt. Until this burden is discharged the accused is presumed innocent. Even where a lawyer knows that the client is guilty of the offence charged, for example, where the client confesses, the rules permit a lawyer to conduct a defence. A mere belief, however strong, that the client is guilty will not be relevant. The lawyer will have a duty to take the case and, if instructed, defend the charge.[82] Even if there is a confession of guilt, or there is no possibility that the client is innocent, the lawyer must still conduct the defence in accordance with the client's instructions. Such a defence must proceed under the constraint that at no time may the lawyer adduce evidence inconsistent with the client's confession, nor may the lawyer in cross-examination suggest to a witness a version of the facts inconsistent with the confession. This amounts to requiring the prosecution to prove the case beyond reasonable doubt, and testing all the evidence put forward. The position is stated in r 10.04:[83]

> 1. Where counsel has been instructed to defend a criminal charge and before or after the proceedings have started the client makes a confession of guilt to counsel, counsel must bear in mind:
>
> (i) a trial is for the purpose of finding whether the accused person is guilty or not guilty, and not whether the accused is innocent;
>
> (ii) it is for the prosecution to call evidence to justify a verdict of guilty;
>
> (iii) a "crime" is a defined offence committed by a person of sound mind and understanding.[84]

---

82 Rules 10.03 and 10.05. The rules generally deal only with confessions. However, r 13.6 of the Written Standards for the Conduct of Professional Work: General Standards of the Code of Conduct of the Bar of England and Wales mentions the problem where an irresistible conclusion of guilt is arrived at, but unhelpfully states that such problems "can only be answered after careful consideration of the actual circumstances of the particular case".

83 The rule deals only with outright confessions, which are rare. Where there is a belief of guilt but no confession the commentary to the rule unhelpfully states: "No rule can deal with doubts raised in counsel's mind after he or she has been instructed to act on a not guilty plea, by inconsistent statements by the client which might suggest to counsel that the client is guilty. Counsel can deal with such a situation only in the light of all the circumstances and pursuant to counsel's professional judgment and duty as an officer of the Court". It is suggested that the guidelines in the rule ought to be applied in any case where there are no grounds upon which the client's innocence can be argued in good faith, however that conclusion is arrived at.

84 These precepts are drawn almost verbatim from guidance given by the Council of the English Bar to the Shanghai Bar Committee at the beginning of

> 2. In such circumstances, counsel may continue to act only if the plea is changed to one of guilty or if not, within very strict limitations. Counsel must not put forward a case inconsistent with the confession.
> 3. If the plea is to remain one of not guilty, counsel may conduct the defence by putting the prosecution to the proof, and if appropriate, assert that the prosecution evidence is inadequate to justify a verdict of guilty; but must not raise any matter which suggests that the client has an affirmative defence, for example an alibi. Counsel may, however, proceed with a defence based on a special plea such as insanity, if such a plea appears in counsel's professional opinion to be available.

The rule, while justifiable if one accepts certain premises (such as the value of the presumption of innocence and the amoral role of the lawyer), is rarely satisfactory to lay people. The prospect of defending a criminal client who has confessed a crime is unlikely to appeal to many lawyers. There is certainly a compelling argument that in rendering such assistance lawyers are perverting the very system they are supposed to uphold. Where there are no grounds on which a lawyer can mount a good faith argument for the acquittal of a criminal client (including any technical grounds) the entering of a not guilty plea on behalf of the client seems to be a prime example of pursuing a case which has absolutely no prospect of success.

The difficulties of this position are illustrated by the absurd course that a lawyer is forced to take in such circumstances:[85]

> Take a case where the client has confessed to his counsel that he has committed the offence, and the Crown calls a witness to testify that he saw the accused assaulting the victim. It would be open to counsel to suggest to the witness that he *might* be mistaken, but he could not put to the witness that he *was* mistaken.

The distinction between the two lines of questioning relies on a medieval logic that only a lawyer could accept. It turns on the semantic distinction between being actually mistaken and being possibly mistaken. Inherent in a question that a witness might be mistaken is the possibility that he could be mistaken. The lawyer whose client has confessed knows full well that there is no possibility whatsoever that the witness who identifies the client could be mistaken. Therefore, to ask a witness "Might you be mistaken?" is to say, "Since it is possible that my client is innocent it is also possible that you are mistaken — might you be mistaken?" Such a statement is untrue where a lawyer's client has confessed.

---

the century and quoted in Lord McMillan *Law and Other Things* Cambridge, Cambridge University Press, 1937, 189.

85 D A Ipp, "Lawyers' Duties to the Court" (1998) 114 LQR 63, 88.

The dilemma is that the alternatives to the rule are unattractive. Some maintain that where no defence can be raised the lawyer should continue to act only where the client agrees to plead guilty — in which case the lawyer may seek to mitigate the sentence imposed. Such an approach means that the lawyer has effectively decided the issue. Such an approach would appear to penalise those defendants who naively confess to their lawyers whilst advantaging the more wily defendant who keeps the lawyer in the dark.

It is suggested that the better approach is to entitle the lawyer only to conduct the defence in a manner that is wholly consistent with the client's confession. To fail to continue owing to personal squeamishness is to let the client down. In *Tuckiar v R* a lawyer was reprimanded when, in the face of a client confession, he admitted in open Court he was in a difficult predicament. The Court complained:[86]

> Why he should have conceived himself to have been in so great a predicament, it is not easy to understand. He had a plain duty both to his client and to the Court, to press such rational considerations as the evidence fairly gave rise to in favour of a complete acquittal or a conviction of manslaughter only.

Any testing of evidence which is palpably true would be prohibited (including the question above of whether the witness might be mistaken). The defence would then be left to argue technical defences (such as the exclusion of evidence) and that the evidence adduced by the prosecution is insufficient grounds upon which to convict. Such a defence would usually fail and would be unlikely to convince a Judge or jury, but would be consistent with the lawyer's duty of candour to the Court.

Such an approach seems to be taken by the Bar Council of England and Wales when it states that when a client has confessed:[87]

> [I]t would be right to take any objections to the competency of the Court, to the form of the indictment, to the admissibility of any evidence or to the evidence admitted, it would be wrong to suggest that some other person had committed the offence charged, or to call any evidence which the barrister must know to be false having regard to the confession, such, for instance, as evidence in support of an alibi. In other words a barrister must not (whether by calling the defendant or otherwise) set up an affirmative case inconsistent with the confession made to him [or her]:[88]

86 (1934) 52 CLR 335, 346.

87 See r 13.4 of the Written Standards for the Conduct of Professional Work: General Standards of the Code of Conduct of the Bar of England and Wales.

88 However, r 13.5 of the Written Standards for the Conduct of Professional Work: General Standards of the Code of Conduct of the Bar of England and

Where a lawyer does continue in the face of compelling evidence that the client is guilty it is important that he or she conducts the trial in a way which is as beneficial to the client as possible in the circumstances. No allusion to the reasons why the client is not giving evidence should be made.[89] Counsel must take care that where a confession occurs mid-trial the inevitable change in the tactics of the defence is as inconspicuous as possible.[90]

14.10.9 *Lawyer not a pre-trial screen*

While a lawyer should never knowingly allow a witness to give evidence that is false, it is necessary to be wary of pre-judging a matter because of a scepticism of the client's version of events. In *Orchard v South Eastern Electricity Board*[91] Donaldson MR stated the balance that an advocate must achieve in respect of the veracity of the client's assertions:[92]

> [I]t must never be forgotten that it is not for solicitors or counsel to impose a pre-trial screen through which a litigant must pass before he can put his complaint or defence before the Court. On the other hand no solicitor or counsel should lend his assistance to a litigant if he is satisfied that the initiation or further prosecution of a claim is mala fide or for an ulterior purpose or, to put it more broadly, if the proceedings would be, or have become, an abuse of the process of the Court or unjustifiably oppressive.

Where clients make allegations that, it transpires, are unfounded, the Court will be slow to punish an advocate for taking the clients at their word. While advocates should not bring a case if they are certain that it is ill-founded, they are entitled to make their own judgment as to their client's veracity. If the advocate in question suffers a failure of judgment this does not amount to improper conduct or incompetence and intervention by the Court is inappropriate. In *Y v M*[93] a practitioner filed

---

Wales does seem to open the door to the "might you be mistaken" question when it proceeds to say in respect of mounting a defence in respect of a client that has confessed.

88 No clearer rule can be laid down than this, that he [or she] is entitled to test the evidence given by each individual witness, and to argue that the evidence taken as a whole is insufficient to amount to proof that the defendant is guilty of the offence charged. Further than this he [or she] ought not to go.

89 *Tuckiar v the King* (1934) 52 CLR 335.

90 *Sankar v Trinidad and Tobago* [1995] 1 WLR 194.

91 [1987] QB 565 (CA).

92 *Orchard v South Eastern Electricity Board* [1987] QB 565, 572.

93 [1994] 3 NZLR 581. The duty not to admit evidence of serious allegations unless the advocate is satisfied that the making of such an allegation is justified on the facts of the case is also found in r 8.05 of the Rules of Professional Conduct of Barristers and Solicitors. See also *Gazley v Wellington District Law Society* [1996] 1 NZLR 452, 454 (High Court sitting with a full panel of three Judges).

an affidavit in the Family Court which contained allegations of sexual abuse of a child by its father which were quite unfounded. The Court took the view that the filing of the affidavit was inappropriate. However, it was held that it was due to a lack of the proper degree of caution, unquestioning acceptance of the word of the mother, and the advocate's lack of a degree of scepticism of her client's version of events. In *Y v M* there was a degree of urgency to the case that meant that a full investigation was not possible. It was held that this was more an error of judgment than incompetence or misconduct.

14.11 Presenting the law

Lawyers are expected to know the law when they come to Court. In presenting an argument a lawyer is expected to have researched the law and not simply be depending on statements of others, whether in textbooks or of researchers. It is the lawyer's duty to assist the Court in determining the law applicable.

A lawyer must disclose all relevant authorities and legislation to the Court even where they do not support the position of the client.[94] The rules provide:[95]

> The practitioner has an obligation when conducting a case to put all relevant authorities known to the practitioner, whether decided cases or statutory provisions, before the Court — whether they support the practitioner's case or not.

The lawyer is entitled to argue why such law can be ignored or overruled. The duty to disclose all relevant cases is important as the Court (usually composed of generalist Judges) often relies heavily on the advice of specialist lawyers on points of law. Even where the authority comes to light after the conclusion of the hearing the lawyer should disclose its existence to the Court.[96] The duty extends to any relevant authority and is not limited to binding authorities. Cases from lower or equal Courts or from other jurisdictions should be put before the Court if they are on point. This duty to bring all relevant authorities to the attention of the Court must be viewed realistically. It is not to be translated as a duty to bring every authority that has considered the matter in question to the attention of the Court. Such a course of action simply overburdens the Court with needless detail. In mounting a legal argument the lawyer is expected to use judgment in putting only those cases that will assist the

94 *Hardie v Booth* [1992] 1 NZLR 356.

95 In the commentary to r 8.01. See also *Glege Sugar Refining Co Ltd v Trustees of the Port and Harbour of Greenock* [1921] WN 85, 86 (HL).

96 Rule 8.01(5), Practice Note [1968] NZLR 608.

Court in making its decision before it. The cases should be more than peripherally relevant.

There is also a duty to refrain from mounting groundless arguments. A lawyer should not pursue a point of law wholly without merit. To do so suggests either an improper purpose or a lack of competence. There are some areas of the law where no room for argument exists. The ABA Model Rules provide:[97]

> A lawyer shall not bring or defend a proceeding, or assert or controvert an issue therein, unless there is a basis for doing so that is not frivolous, which includes a good faith argument for an extension, modification or reversal of existing law.

A lawyer may argue against existing precedents or for a change in the law (where the Court has the power to effect such a change). This may include making arguments that are not likely to succeed. However, provided that there is a legitimate basis for the argument and it is possible that a rational person could accept that the arguments put forward lead to the result sought, the lawyer will be acting properly.

In *DaSousa v Minister of Immigration*[98] it was found that an application for entry permits, and the application for review subsequent to the refusal of entry was doomed to fail: "to a legal practitioner familiar with the provisions of the Act and Regulations there should have been no doubt that ... Mrs DaSousa did not qualify for the grant of such permits".[99] In *DaSousa* French J noted that it was not the fact that the claim failed which led to disciplinary action (in the form of an order of costs) being made against the advocate, but the fact that the bringing of the action amounted to a serious dereliction of duty. The application amounted to such a dereliction because it reflected "a serious failure to give reasonable attention to the relevant law and the facts".[100]

DaSousa was relied on in New Zealand by Giles J in *McDonald v FAI (NZ) General Insurance Company Ltd.*[101] The facts giving rise to that case are complex. The plaintiff was a victim of the fraud of a former solicitor who had since been bankrupted. Compensation for losses suffered at the hands of the former solicitor were sought from the solicitor's insurers and from the law society. A claim for costs against the advocate was made on the basis that the claim against the insurer was wholly without

97 Rule 3.1.
98 (1993) 114 ALR 708 (Federal Court of Australia).
99 *DaSousa v Minister of Immigration* (1993) 114 ALR 708, 710.
100 *DaSousa v Minister of Immigration* (1993) 114 ALR 708, 713.
101 *McDonald v FAI* [1999] 1 NZLR 583, affirmed by the Court of Appeal as *Harley v McDonald* [1999] 3 NZLR 545.

merit and doomed to fail. The claim had failed on a number of counts. In light of these failures the Court found that "there never really was any prospect whatsoever of success against FAI".[102] It was noted on appeal that counsel in that case was not even aware that the case was without merit and "had no grasp of the essential issues". Counsel was guilty of "incompetence to such a degree that she was in serious dereliction of her duty to the Court".[103]

There is a distinction between a case that is wholly without legal merit, and a case for which no precedent exists, or for which a contrary precedent exists. There are numerous examples of cases in which an advocate has successfully argued that the Court ought to depart from existing law, or create a new rule. The mounting of a novel legal argument is not of itself misconduct, even if the Judge who hears it refuses to extend the law in the way suggested. In *Abraham v Jutsun* Denning MR noted that it is an advocate's "duty to take any point which he believed to be fairly arguable on behalf of his client. The advocate is not to usurp the province of the Judge".[104] There are, however, two situations where an argument that is not consistent with existing law may amount to misconduct: if the advocate misleads the Court as to the law, or if the argument is so without foundation as to show bad faith or incompetence on the part of the advocate.[105] The statement of Denning MR in *Abraham v Jutsun* was mitigated with the caveat that it is improper for an advocate to present the law to the Court as something it is not. When making an argument against authority, the existence of the contrary authority must be brought to the attention of the Court. Harman LJ took a similar stance noting that it cannot be misconduct merely to take a bad legal point unless the advocate knows that the argument is flawed and conceals the flaw from the Court.[106] It has been held to be improper conduct to ignore contrary precedent and to cite misleadingly from cases.[107]

Any novel argument mounted must have a degree of merit to it. It must be conceivable that a Court would agree with the submission. It must be within the jurisdiction of the Court to make the order sought. It must be possible for the argument made to lead to the order sought. If the

---

102 *McDonald v FAI* [1999] 1 NZLR 583.

103 *Harley v McDonald* [1999] 3 NZLR 545.

104 *Abraham v Jutsun* [1963] 1 WLR 658, 663, followed in *Utah Construction and Mining Co v Watson* [1969] NZLR 1062, 1065.

105 As to the duty to put all relevant authorities before the Court see r 8.01 of the Rules of Professional Conduct for Barristers and Solicitors including cls 4 and 5 of the commentary.

106 *Abraham v Jutsun* [1963] 1 WLR 658, 663.

107 *A-Abart Electric Supply Inc v Emerson Electric Co* (1992) 956 F2d 1399 (CA) (decided under r 11 of the Federal Rules of Civil Procedure).

application is wholly misconceived[108] or simply fallacious[109] it demonstrates a degree of incompetence on the behalf of the advocate which warrants the Court taking disciplinary action. If the arguments which are put forward also serve a collateral purpose such as the delaying of the inevitable exercise of remedies the Court will give short shrift to the advocate who makes them.[110] If an argument has no basis in existing law and no realistic argument can be made that the law can and should be changed, sanctions will be imposed.[111] If the advocate can show that reasonable research was done into the point of law that is being argued this will assist in showing that the argument is non-frivolous. The mere fact that after research a mistake as to the law is made that would have been revealed with extended research will not, of itself, be enough for an order to be made.

14.12 Lawyer zeal and proper conduct

It is central to the role of the advocate that the advocate acts zealously in the interests of the client. In a trial the interests of one litigant will ultimately prevail over those of the other, and it is the advocate's task to argue that the interests of his or her client ought to so prevail. Such a duty of zeal exists within a framework which requires that lawyers act properly and with courtesy as well as obeying the professional and procedural rules applicable.

It is not acceptable to "save the client by all means and expedients, and at all hazards and costs to other persons".[112] While there are no legal duties to others in the conduct of litigation[113] there are professional duties which require that the lawyer bear in mind the interests of persons other than the client alone. Not only must the lawyer assist the Court in its endeavours, but also bear in mind the interests of third parties, for example, a lawyer must be careful of making allegations of misconduct against others unless there are good grounds for such allegations. The mere fact that the client has stated the allegations to be true will not usually be sufficient.[114]

---

108 As in *DaSousa v Minister of Immigration* (1993) 114 ALR 708.

109 As in *McDonald v FAI* [1999] 1 NZLR 583.

110 *Henrickson v Grierson Jackson Securities Pukekohe Ltd* (1992) NZ Conv Cas 191-419, 191-442.

111 *Gutterman v Eimicke* (1989) 125 FRD 348 (New York Court of Appeal).

112 These are the famous words spoken by Lord Brougham in defence of Queen Caroline and were in fact part of a veiled threat to reveal the existence of an illegal prior marriage of the King to a Catholic, which would have meant the surrender of the throne: *Proceedings in the House of Lords, Trial of Queen Caroline* London, Duncan Stevenson & Co, 1820, vol 2, p 7.

113 *New Zealand Social Credit Political League v O'Brien* [1984] 1 NZLR 84 (CA); *Gordon v Treadwell Stacey Smith* [1996] 3 NZLR 281, 293 (CA).

114 Rules 8.2 and 8.4; *Y v M* [1994] 3 NZLR 581.

A lawyer is also prohibited from taking improper advantage of a mistake or slip of the other side. There will be situations where a lawyer's client will benefit from decisions made by the other party such as not to call a particular witness, or not to plead a particular cause of action. Such advantages are the natural result of the adversarial process and (while able to be criticised) may properly be exploited. However, there are situations where a lawyer may make a mistake (rather than an error of judgment) of which a lawyer may not take advantage. Consider, for example, a situation where a statement of claim has been served and the lawyer for the defendant has advised of the intention to file a defence, but fails to do so in the required time period. Under the rules of Court in the absence of a defence a judgment by default may be applied for, however, such an application would be taking advantage of the slip by the lawyer in failing to file the defence on time. The proper course would be to advise the lawyer of the expiration of time and forewarn of an intention to seek default judgment if no defence is filed.

There is no duty to assist the other client or the lawyer. The line between such assistance and taking advantage of a slip can be fine. In *Chamberlain v Law Society of ACT*[115] the Court seemed to make a distinction between active exploitation of a mistake and passive acceptance of the benefits. In that case a claim had been made for the sum of $25,557.92 by the Revenue. The counsel for the defendant agreed to a consent order admitting liability for that amount. The reason for the consent was the fact that the other lawyer, in drafting the claim had inserted the sum in error and it ought to have read $255,579.20. The result was that once the consent order had been made a claim for the balance owed was barred by the doctrines of issue estoppel and res judicata. It was held that in actively exploiting the mistake (that is, proposing the consent judgment) the lawyer was guilty of misconduct. It was suggested in the judgment that if the lawyer had simply done nothing in the hope that default judgment for the mistaken sum was entered there would have been no misconduct.

The fine distinction shows the tendency of the Court to accept mercenary tactics of lawyers that do not assist in the disposal of a case on its merits. The knowing silence of a lawyer in the face of such an obvious mistake seems to run counter to the basic duty of a lawyer to the administration of justice, no matter how passive the acceptance of the advantage.[116] The distinction between active and passive advantage taking often becomes artificial in reality when a silence can be as communicative as a positive statement.

115 (1993) 118 ALR 54.

116 *Ernst & Young v Butte Mining plc* [1996] 1 WLR 1605.

Particularly problematic is the situation where the other party is a litigant in person (that is, is unrepresented). While a lawyer should treat such an unrepresented party with courtesy and fairness there is no duty to assist the other party.[117] If lawyers were to assist the unrepresented party to the detriment of their own client it would be a breach of their duty of loyalty. Lawyers might, however, render assistance to expedite the proceedings where this is in the interests of their client. This might include pointing out deficiencies in documents or procedure, which if left unremedied would cause delay or inconvenience. Lawyers should not take advantage of the lack of experience or expertise of the unrepresented party in seeking to gain advantages by misleading them, or suggesting that a certain course is usual where this is not the case.

A related duty is the duty of a lawyer to conduct himself or herself with decorum and treat others with courtesy.[118] A lawyer should not make derogatory statements about other counsel, and should use the appropriate forms of address where relevant. The findings of other Courts should be dealt with respectfully, even where it is argued they were wrongly decided. The reason for this is to ensure that the Court and its procedure is held in high regard as well as effecting the disposal of cases efficiently and unaffected by personal animosities. There are also practical reasons for dealing with other members of the profession and the judiciary with courtesy. It is likely that one will have repeat dealings with many people, and it is important to be thought of as fair dealing.

These duties which effectively lessen the loyalty that may legitimately be demanded by a client from the lawyer must be viewed with caution. Pressure from other counsel, third parties, and (frequently) the Courts to take a course of action that is more advantageous or convenient to them at the expense of one's own client should be resisted. While a lawyer should exercise careful judgment in all aspects of the conduct of a proceeding if, in the lawyer's judgment, a certain step is in the interests of the client and not obstructing the administration of justice it should be taken. The fact that it causes extra work for the Court, inconveniences the opponent, and delays the final resolution of the matter should not stand in the way of the legitimate pursuit of the client's interests.

117 Rule 7.1.

118 Rules 6.01, 7.01, 8.03.

Part Five

Duties in Legal Practice

Chapter 15

Duties in the Conduct of a Legal Practice

15.1 Introduction

As well as the duties owed to clients and to the administration of justice the professional rules impose a number of duties on practitioners regarding the way in which they conduct their practices and the manner in which they treat each other. Some of the rules such as those dealing with the manner in which lawyers may advertise, or the names of practices, will overlap with the requirements of the general law which prohibit misleading conduct.[1] Other rules such as the duty to honour undertakings are important to ensure that the foundation of mutual trust upon which the efficient operation of the legal profession depends is maintained. Other rules are aimed at the maintenance of the position of the legal profession. Such rules include the duty to report unqualified practitioners, and the prohibition on fee sharing.

An associated body of rules is that of etiquette. Those rules, usually unwritten, describe the protocols and traditions that exist in the legal profession. They include forms of address, proper attire, conduct in Court, seniority of advocates and numerous other details concerning accepted conduct of practitioners. While some of them may be useful, many of them are valued as simply traditional. Because most of them have little or no bearing on the role and function of lawyers they are not separately considered in this work.

In many of the areas discussed in this chapter there is a good argument that the regulation is superfluous. For example, a number of rules concern the names which firms may adopt. Such matters are arguably dealt with better by the general law. If the firm's name is misleading it will fall foul of the Fair Trading Act.[2] If it too closely resembles the name of another firm the tort of passing off will provide a remedy.

1 Such as s 9 Fair Trading Act 1986.
2 Sections 9 and 14 Fair Trading Act 1986.

Similarly, rules which require lawyers to be courteous seem largely redundant in the modern profession. While there remain good practical reasons for a practitioner to adopt such a course the prospect of a disciplinary action for breach seems remote.

15.2 Courtesy

Practitioners are required to treat each other with courtesy and respect. The commentary to r 6.01 provides: "A practitioner shall treat professional colleagues with courtesy and fairness at all times but consistent with the overriding duty to the client". While lawyers are expected to be loyal to the interests of their client, they ought to do so in an even-tempered and independent manner. Even where a lawyer agrees with his or her client's cause, and the conduct of the other litigant is considered unreasonable, a lawyer should treat the other party with courtesy and recognise that lawyer's independence from the client's cause and conduct.[3]

The rule might be seen as serving a number of purposes. First, it ensures that the lawyers remain detached from any animosity that may exist between their clients. This independence is a vital ingredient in the ability of a lawyer to make useful judgments and advise the client on the best course of action. It encourages a degree of cordiality amongst members of the profession. This encourages a sense of collegiality between lawyers which is at the heart of the traditional view of the profession. The knowledge that one will be dealt with politely and fairly by other practitioners also assists in the effective resolution of the business at hand. Where the business is contentious as in the case of litigation this is especially helpful. It is far more likely that a dispute will be settled by the intercession of two lawyers who are able to discuss matters freely than where the lawyers themselves are infected by the acrimony of their clients. It also ensures that lawyers do not disparage other members of the profession and thereby bring the profession into disrepute.

The duty of courtesy is owed between all practitioners regardless of age or experience. A junior practitioner should not be disparaged or ridiculed for mistakes, or intimidated by senior practitioners. While much is learnt by junior lawyers by instructions and advice given by senior practitioners, this should be done in a collegial manner.

Associated with the duty to treat other practitioners with courtesy is the duty to respond to correspondence or calls from other practitioners.

---

3 Rule 6.01 commentary (5) provides: "Practitioners should not communicate or correspond in an atmosphere of acrimony or discourtesy" notwithstanding the nature of the relationship between their respective clients.

When a lawyer is particularly busy, or where the problem is particularly intractable, there is a temptation to refrain from taking action or responding to correspondence. Such actions (which may also be negligent) may cause considerable extra work for the other practitioner, and are, of course, a breach of common courtesy.

It may be appropriate to record telephone conversations. Such a practice will avoid later disagreement about the contents of the conversation. The law society has given guidance in respect of taping telephone conversations by observing that:[4]

> It is an invasion of a person's privacy to tape a conversation without that person's consent. It is unprofessional and discourteous for one practitioner to do so in respect of another practitioner or an employee of another practitioner. If a practitioner wishes a conversation by telephone or otherwise to be taped the specific consent of the other practitioner or employee must first be obtained.

Presumably, similar principles will apply to the taping of conversations with non-practitioners, and the taping of exchanges other than by telephone.

15.3 Harassment

It is not possible to deny that harassment including sexual harassment exists in the legal profession. Evidence exists of harassment within firms, between practitioners, and by judiciary towards counsel, counsel to judiciary, and judiciary to judiciary.[5] There is no specific reference to harassment in the rules, however, they do state:[6]

> No practitioner shall discriminate against or treat unfairly any other practitioner by reason of the colour, race, ethnic or national origin, sex, marital status or religious or ethical belief of that other practitioner.

It is also illegal to discriminate on grounds of sex, race, marital status etc pursuant to the Human Rights Act 1993.[7] On these grounds unwanted

---

4 Rule 6.01 commentary (7).

5 G Gatfield *Without Prejudice* Wellington, Brookers, 1996, 233, 237. For a UK perspective see C McGlynn, "Sex Discrimination at the Margins" (1996) NLJ 146.

6 Rule 6.01 commentary (2). Contrast the position of the English Bar which in 1996 adopted an "Equality Code" dealing with all areas of discrimination and harassment in legal practice at the bar, also the NSW Bar Association's EEO Policy (1995) in which the Bar Council "condemns all forms of sexual harassment, discrimination on the grounds of sex or sexual preference, and sexist behaviour of any kind".

7 Sections 21, 22 and 36 Human Rights Act 1993.

and inappropriate behaviour towards other lawyers which amounts to discrimination will also amount to misconduct. It seems to be widely believed within the profession that discrimination on the basis of gender occurs.[8] A firm or profession in which harassment occurs is dysfunctional. If the necessary trust and respect between members is missing the quality of the service rendered to clients will suffer along with the personal lives of the victims of the harassment.[9]

While the claim that harassment will amount to misconduct is uncontroversial, the victims of harassment will very rarely seek to remedy the situation in any formal way. The seriousness of such complaints is frequently underestimated, particularly by senior members of the profession. There is an unwillingness to make a complaint against a lawyer for fear of the legalistic response to the complaint, which will only exacerbate the problem. The fact that it is frequently necessary to prove that the harassment occurred (with consequent ramifications for the harasser) means that making the complaint can be an arduous and possibly damaging task. Even if the harassment is proved, the consequences for the victim (such as transferring within a firm, or being marked out as a complainant) can be nearly as harmful as the harassment itself.

While there appears to be scope within the rules and disciplinary process to take action in the case of harassment, it is unlikely to occur. It is not surprising that there are no instances of harassment between lawyers that have been the subject of disciplinary action. Victims of harassment will remain unwilling to take action in an official sense but will resort to strategies of avoiding, ignoring, or deflecting the harassment. In serious cases it appears that lawyers will resign to escape the harassing environment.[10]

The disciplinary process is an inappropriate forum for dealing with harassment. While in the future complaints may be made to the law society the large majority of incidents will pass unremedied. Engaging in harassing behaviour is inappropriate and amounts to professional misconduct, however, a change of culture is necessary rather than a change in the Rules to remedy the worrying incidence of such conduct.

8 In a recent survey of the profession 31% of employed lawyers considered that there were not equal opportunities for women in the profession and the majority of women believe it is harder for women to progress in the profession. *Polls of the Profession and the Public — Summary— The New Zealand Law Society* Wellington, MRL Research Group, 1997, 62.

9 See the comments in E Nosworthy, "Ethics and Large Law Firms" in C Parker and C Sampford *Legal Ethics and Legal Practice* Oxford, Clarendon Press, 1995.

10 G Gatfield *Without Prejudice* Wellington, Brookers, 1996, 233, 253.

15.4 Contacting opposing clients

A lawyer may not contact a person who is represented by another lawyer other than through the lawyer in any but the most exceptional circumstances.[11] To do so is a breach of professional courtesy. There are also sound reasons of principle behind the rule. The rule seeks to prevent a lawyer from circumventing the protection afforded by the other party's lawyer and obtaining an unfair advantage. One reason a lawyer is retained is to ensure that no concessions or admissions are made, and no information is disclosed, except on good grounds. If a client is contacted direct the judgment of the lawyer in making those decisions is dispensed with and a significant reason for retaining the lawyer rendered useless.[12] The prohibition on contacting another lawyer's client also extends to any agents of the lawyer.[13]

There will be occasions when such contact is permitted. It is permissible to contact the opposing client to ascertain whether the client is represented, and if so, who the lawyer is. However, such an inquiry should extend no further. The rules also provide:[14]

> If a practitioner has tried unsuccessfully for a reasonable period to obtain a response from the other practitioner in the matter, then it may be appropriate for the client of that other practitioner to be approached. This action should, however, be regarded as most unusual and be used only in extreme circumstances. In any event, the action should be taken only after advice to the other practitioner of the practitioner's intention to do so.

This exception contemplates a situation where the other practitioner is not responding to communications (and is, therefore, in breach of the duty of courtesy). This may be due to some supervening event such as illness, or the lawyer may have ceased acting for the client (although in the latter case the other lawyer should have been informed). Before any contact with the other client is appropriate the lawyer should have made attempts at contacting the lawyer already, informed the lawyer of the intention to contact the client directly, and have given the lawyer an

---

11 Rule 6.02. See also Leubsdorf, "Communicating with Another Lawyer's Client: The Lawyer's Veto and the Client's Interests" (1979) 127 U Penn LR 683.

12 G Dal Pont suggests that the rule also protects against the lawyer undermining the relationship between the client and their lawyer by making disparaging remarks etc. However, it is suggested that (except where retained for the purpose of a possible negligence claim) it is unprofessional to cast aspersions on the competence or conduct of another practitioner in any event. See G Dal Pont *Lawyers' Professional Responsibility in Australia and New Zealand* North Ryde, NSW, Law Book Information Services, 1996, 437.

13 See South Australian Professional Conduct Rules, r 10.3.

14 Rule 6.02, para 2 of the commentary.

opportunity to respond. Where the lawyer in question is a member of a firm, it may be appropriate to contact another member of the firm who will be able to take the matter in hand if the other lawyer is incapacitated or otherwise unavailable.

In the first instance, it may be appropriate simply to inform the clients that no response has been forthcoming from the lawyer and asking the clients to confirm that the lawyer is still representing them. It is also advisable to inform the other practitioner that such contact has been made.[15] Even where the above steps have been taken, the action of contacting an opposing client direct should only be taken in the most exceptional circumstances. If for example some step is to be taken which the other client requires in order to be given the opportunity to be represented to ensure justice is done (such as an application for an urgent injunction) such contact may be warranted. It is important that the motivation of such a communication is to ensure that the failure of the other lawyer does not unjustly prejudice his or her client's interests rather than to embarrass the other lawyer.[16]

That it is in the interests of the contacting lawyer's own client that the contact is made is not a reason for circumventing the other client's lawyer. There may be circumstances where it is considered that the other lawyer is unnecessarily prolonging proceedings, not passing on offers of settlement, or giving unfounded advice as to the strength of a claim. The fact that the opposing lawyer is conducting the case in a manner that is considered inappropriate will not usually be a reason for contacting the other client direct. Such problems should be dealt with by other avenues. There may be grounds for an application to the Court to strike out a claim or defence that is without foundation. Alternatively, if the conduct is clearly inappropriate, it may be proper (and sometimes required) that the matter be brought to the attention of the law society.[17]

There is no bar on one client contacting the other client direct. Such contact may lead to progress in a dispute where the efforts of the lawyers have failed. This is recognised by the rules, which provide: "A practitioner may suggest to a client that an approach by that client to the other practitioner's client might be appropriate or useful".[18] Such contact should not be used as a way to circumvent the rule prohibiting the lawyer contacting the client and thereby seeking to obtain an illegitimate advantage. It would be inappropriate for a lawyer to advise a client to

15 This is the approach of the Law Council of Australia's Model Rules, r 23.1.

16 The Australian Capital Territory *Guide to Professional Conduct and Etiquette* para 20.03 requires that the interests of the other practitioner's client will be severely prejudiced if the communication is not made without delay.

17 See also r 6.03.

18 Rule 6.02, para 1 of the commentary.

obtain admissions, gain information that is privileged, or suggest that aspersions be cast on the conduct of the other lawyer. Such a communication between clients may be useful in circumstances where the other lawyer is not passing on information to the client, or is misrepresenting matters and inflaming the situation.

15.5 Unrepresented persons

An associated problem is the manner in which a lawyer ought to deal with parties who choose not to retain their own solicitor. A lawyer must interact with persons who choose to conduct their own affairs, and certainly should not seek to confuse the other party with unnecessary technical language or obfuscation.[19] There is a danger that an unrepresented party will look to the opposing lawyer for guidance on the appropriate course to take or assistance in technical matters. [20] While it may be appropriate for a lawyer to give assistance to ensure a proceeding advances smoothly in the interests of the lawyer's own client there are dangers in permitting an unrepresented person to rely on the opposing lawyer in any way. A lawyer should avoid giving any substantive advice (except the advice to retain their own lawyer) as to do otherwise would be to create a conflict of interest. The ABA Model Rules deal with the matters as follows:[21]

> In dealing on behalf of a client with a person who is not represented by counsel, a lawyer shall not state or imply that the lawyer is disinterested. When the lawyer knows or reasonably should know that the unrepresented person misunderstands the lawyer's role in the matter, the lawyer shall make reasonable efforts to correct the misunderstanding.

The lawyer must deal with the opposing litigant in a way which is in the interests of his or her own client, and in a manner which does not give the impression that the lawyer is unbiased in proffering assistance to the other litigant.

15.6 Conduct in trade

There are a number of restrictions on the manner in which lawyers may run their business, and the kinds of business in which they may engage. The rules are in addition to the requirements of the general law requiring fair dealing, minimum standards, open competition, and accurate information.[22] Some of the rules may be construed as aimed at the

---

19 Rule 7.01.

20 Rule 7.01, paras 1 and 2 of the commentary.

21 Rule 4.3.

22 Such as the Fair Trading Act 1986, Consumer Guarantees Act 1997, and the Commerce Act 1986.

protection of the public or clients. The rules also serve the purpose of the protection of the reputation and market of the legal profession as well as limiting unfettered competition between practitioners.

15.6.1 *Advertising*

The rules concerning the manner in which lawyers may advertise exist in addition to the rules of the general law, and the special rules that concern the content and accuracy of advertising in the media.[23] Many of the rules concerning the manner in which a lawyer may advertise simply restate the statutory prohibition against engaging in misleading or deceptive conduct in trade in the context of the legal profession. The other rules are concerned with the maintenance of the dignity of the profession. Lawyers were prohibited from advertising on the basis that it was unprofessional to tout for business and to seek to obtain clients on a market-oriented basis. While this view is no longer held there are still considerable restrictions on the manner in which a lawyer may obtain clients.

The prohibition on tasteless or base advertising is contained in r 4.01:

> Advertisements to or any other communications with any person relating to the services of a practitioner or of a firm of practitioners must be consistent with the maintenance of proper professional standards.

The commentary continues to prohibit obtaining testimonials or endorsements obtained by offering reward, and prohibiting any comparative advertising which denigrates other lawyers. The standard of "the maintenance of proper professional standards" is vague.[24] Guidance may be obtained from some of the particular rules imposed in other jurisdictions. The ABA Model Rules prohibit any dramatisations, and practitioners may not advertise in terms that are simply "self laudatory", and the advertisement ought not to use voice-overs by celebrities.[25] The English *Guide* prohibits reference to any success rates, or the making of any direct comparison with other identifiable solicitors.[26]

Many lawyers practise in particular fields largely to the exclusion of other kinds of work and as such are specialists in the particular area rather

23 Such as those of the Broadcasting Standards Authority and the Advertising Standards Complaints Board.

24 See further Virginia Shirvington, "Advertising: Is it Ever At Odds With Professional Ethics?" (1996) 34 (6) LSJ 31 which discusses the position in New South Wales.

25 ABA Model Rules 7.2.

26 *Guide to the Professional Conduct of Solicitors* Annex 11A; Solicitors Publicity Code 1990. See also Council of the Law Institute of Victoria *Guidelines on Undesirable Advertising* in *Members Handbook* Victoria, Law Book Co, loose-leaf, 24 March 1988, para 3-1000.

than generalists. Many professional rules, New Zealand's included,[27] prohibit lawyers from claiming special expertise unless it can be established. Lawyers who do not claim special expertise may still advertise as "practising in the area of..." and are, therefore, not making an explicit claim to special expertise.

15.6.2 *Firm names and letterheads*

The rules also give guidance on the manner in which the firm may be presented to the public by its name and stationery. The name of a firm should not "be misleading as to the nature or structure of the firm; bring the profession into disrepute; or be unfair to other practitioners or the public".[28] The requirement that the name not bring the profession into disrepute requires that the name not be vulgar, however, exactly what this would require is difficult to contemplate.

The commentary to the rules gives some guidance as to the other requirements of the rule. A name should not give the impression that it has many partners when this is not so, or that it is a legal aid agency, or that it incorporates all the legal practitioners in an area when such claims are false. Where a firm operates a branch under a different name (as is often the case) the branch name must incorporate a disclosure of the relationship with the parent firm.

The duty to represent the nature of the firm accurately is reinforced by r 2.02 which requires that on any stationery used or publications issued by a firm, the structure of the firm, and the status of its members is accurately represented. Where a person is mentioned on a letterhead it should be clear what is his or her status in the firm. Whenever a letter is sent from a firm, the status of the person who sent it should be clear. In addition to the signature the designation of the writer should be shown.[29]

15.6.3 *Soliciting work*

The problem of lawyers seeking retainers from clients in inappropriate circumstances (that is, ambulance chasing) is perhaps not as great in New Zealand due to the absence of claims for personal injuries. Lawyers have traditionally been expected to refrain from actively seeking clients, and certainly to refrain from encouraging litigation. This view has been

27 Rule 4.02. That rule also permits the district law society to investigate claims of expertise and require a practitioner to desist from such claims if they are unfounded.

28 Rule 2.01.

29 Ruling 1/98 of the New Zealand Ethics Committee ruled that it was inappropriate for a practitioner qualified in another jurisdiction to sign letters as "Barrister of England and Wales" when in fact her status within the firm in question was that of law clerk.

replaced with a view that accepts that lawyers, like other professionals, may seek to retain clients, and that it is not necessarily improper to encourage people to enforce their rights by Court action if necessary. The profession restricts the manner in which approaches to prospective clients may be made. The rules provide:[30]

> A practitioner must ensure that approaches to persons who are not existing clients, are made in a manner which does not bring the profession into disrepute. Approaches must be made in accordance with proper professional standards and not in a way that is intrusive, offensive, or inappropriate.

One of the main reasons behind such a limit on the manner in which a lawyer may communicate with prospective clients is the reputation and prestige of the profession as well as possibly reducing competition between practitioners. It also has the effect of protecting the public from offensive advances, by limiting contact that is intrusive, offensive, or inappropriate. Where a client chooses to change practitioners, the former practitioner is expected to accept this with some grace. They should not exert pressure, influence, or persuasion to restrain the client from leaving.[31]

15.6.4 *Whistle blowing*

Lawyers are required to report other lawyers who breach their professional obligations to the law society.[32] This will obviously place some lawyers in a difficult position. Lawyers are encouraged to consider the profession as a community of like-minded individuals with common interests. This is particularly the case in respect of members of the same firm whose ties of collegiality and friendship may be particularly close.[33] It is problematic when one member breaches the rules and another member is expected to report the infringement and effectively initiate the disciplinary machinery. There is a tendency amongst lawyers to seek to resolve such problems without recourse to the formal disciplinary procedures and they generally prefer to seek a pragmatic solution.[34] The majority of complaints regarding members of the profession are received from members of the public.

Rule 6.03 states the obligation to report misconduct of other practitioners to the law society:

---

30 Rule 4.03. Compare the strict approach of the *Guide to the Professional Conduct of Solicitors* Annex 11A; Solicitors Publicity Code 1990 which in cl 3 prohibits unsolicited communications in almost all circumstances.

31 Rule 6.05 including para 1 of the commentary.

32 Rule 6.03.

33 See the observations of B Davidson, "A Practitioner's Duty to Report Breaches of Rules of Conduct by Colleagues" *LawTalk* 464, 1996, 6.

34 See the steps taken in *McKaskell v Benseman* [1989] 3 NZLR 75.

> Subject always to the rights and duties pertaining to practitioner and client privilege there is generally an obligation on every practitioner who has grounds to suspect defalcations or other improper acts by another practitioner to make a confidential report at the earliest possible time to the President or the Council of the District Society.

A breach of the rule will be a serious matter. In *Weston v Law Society*[35] a solicitor was struck off for failing to investigate the firm's transactions or reporting the matter where his partners had transferred money from the trust account to meet firm liabilities. This is notwithstanding that the practitioner was not guilty of dishonesty and had no actual knowledge of the wrongdoing (although it appeared a blind eye had been turned).

Two things are immediately striking about the rule itself. The first is that the rule is stated in equivocal terms. It is prefaced by an exception and states that there is generally an obligation to report misconduct.[36] The second observation is that it appears to require only reports of serious misconduct as the obligation is only to report "defalcations or other improper acts",[37] the implication being that the other improper acts will be of a similar seriousness as defalcations. The fact that only serious matters must be reported to the society (and arguably only matters as serious as mishandling of trust funds) calls into question the rationale behind the requirement. While there is obviously an element of protection of the public, it does also seem to be driven by the need to protect the profession from certain of its own members who if left unchecked will cause irreparable damage to the reputation of the profession.[38]

15.6.5 *No conflicting business interests*

Perhaps the least respected of all of the rules governing the manner in which a practice is conducted is the prohibition on lawyers conducting a business which is incompatible with that of the practice of law. It is not uncommon for lawyers to have many and varied business interests

---

35 (1998) Times, 15 July.

36 Compare the equivalent ABA Model Rules, r 8.3: A lawyer having knowledge that another lawyer has committed a violation of the Rules of Professional Conduct that raises a substantial question as to that lawyer's honesty, trustworthiness or fitness as a lawyer in other respects, shall inform the appropriate professional authority. See also r 19.03 of the English *Guide to the Professional Conduct of Solicitors* which imposes a similar duty.

37 In some jurisdictions the obligation is expressly limited to the reporting of misdealing in trust account funds alone. See Legal Professional Regulations 1994 (NSW) r 69(1), Rules of the Queensland Law Society Incorporated (Qld) s 92.

38 This is the view of H W Arthurs, "Why Canadian Law Schools do not Teach Legal Ethics" in K Economides *Ethical Challenges in Legal Education and Conduct* Oxford, Hart, 1998, 105, 112.

which will have varying degrees of proximity and compatibility with their legal practice. It is certainly arguable that the rule no longer accords with the manner in which lawyers practise, and the expectations of lawyers as to what is proper conduct. The rule tends to be construed narrowly as prohibiting only those activities which are in clear conflict with the role of the lawyer.

The original rationale of the rule was the setting apart of lawyers as professional people. While they were astute in business they were not business people themselves and could act and advise wholly independently. Lawyers were expected to devote all their professional time to the furtherance of the interests of the client rather than the pursuit of business interests. In such an environment there could never be a fear that the business interests of a client could be at odds with those of the lawyer. It also ensured that there was no overlap between the business and professional interests of the lawyer that might give rise to confused or conflicting duties. The prohibition on incompatible business interests also ensured that the urgent need for cash did not give rise to a temptation to defraud clients. A number of instances of serious fraud have occurred when lawyers engaged in speculative businesses have succumbed to the temptation to borrow money to temporarily support a failing venture, but the money has never been recouped. This led to the New Zealand Law Practitioners Disciplinary Tribunal stating:[39]

> This Tribunal wishes to send a clear message regarding involvement of practitioners in commercial activity combined with their professional practice. Involvement in commercial activities can often impinge on the practitioner's judgment and efficacy as a lawyer. Where a practitioner engages to a significant extent in commercial endeavours, particularly if those commercial endeavours are of an entrepreneurial nature, there is a real risk of the practitioner losing objectivity and judgment. There is also a very real risk of the public perceiving a conflict of interest, even if no such conflict exists.

While some of these reasons are reflected in the wording of the rule and its commentary, the main effect of the rule seems to be a prohibition on conducting a business or profession other than law, intermixed with that of law.

The rule itself provides:[40]

---

39 Comments of the Chairman of the Disciplinary Tribunal, NZLS *Annual Report* 1993.

40 Rule 2.03. See also *Holden v Marlborough District Law Society* (High Court, Wellington AP 213/93, 16 February 1994, Eichelbaum CJ, Doogue and Neazor JJ).

> A practitioner shall not, while the holder of a practising certificate as a barrister or solicitor or as both, engage in a business or professional activity other than the practice of law unless the business or professional activity:
> (i) Will not detract or have the potential to detract from the standards of independence and professionalism a client is entitled to expect from a practitioner;
> (ii) Does not have nor has the potential to have a harmful effect on the privilege or confidentiality attaching to communications between a practitioner and a client;
> (iii) Would not of itself have the potential to create a conflict of interest on the part of a practitioner.

While r 2.03(3) proceeds to expressly prohibit multidisciplinary practices, the rule is clearly of wider scope. It is not only the matter of a direct conflict of interest that is of concern, but also any loss of independence. Any business activity which suggests that a lawyer's sympathies will threaten the independence required is a prohibited activity. The history and difficulties with the current rule are described in a report concerning multidisciplinary practices:[41]

> That rule was drafted in its present form in 1992, in the wake of the *Renshaw Edwards* [defalcation] fiasco. It was a time when lawyers were being enjoined to "stick to their knitting", at least with respect to lending activities. The rule has proved extremely difficult to apply in practice, which led the New Zealand Law Society Ethics Committee to ask that the whole question of what services lawyers may provide be the subject of careful inquiry. One can safely predict that, whatever the outcome of this inquiry, rule 2.03 will require amendment.

More obvious are those situations where the business activity gives rise to a possible conflict of interest, or where there is a risk that confidences will be breached. It is often difficult in practice to anticipate situations where such problems might arise. Where a person is part-owner of the business and also acts as its legal adviser, problems of conflict, lack of independence, and loyalty are foreseeable.[42] It is advisable to effect a clear division between the role of businessperson and lawyer and avoid any confusion. The Courts have generally construed any arrangements against the lawyer. In *Sims v Craig Bell and Bond* the Court refused to accept that a lawyer could relax the duties owed to others by claiming that the lawyer was acting in a business capacity when the roles are unclear.[43] Conversely, in *Solicitors Liability Committee v Gray & Winter*[44] the Federal Court of Australia construed the facts against the lawyers in finding that lawyers were acting as entrepreneurs and when they were

41 NZLS *Discussion Paper — Multidisciplinary Practices and other Related Matters* , April 1999, para 2.28.

42 *Day v Mead* [1987] 2 NZLR 443; *Sims v Craig Bell & Bond* [1991] 3 NZLR 535.

43 *Sims v Craig Bell & Bond* [1991] 3 NZLR 535, 545 per Richardson J.

44 (1997) 147 ALR 154.

liable to a third party for negligence their professional indemnity insurance did not cover them.

There are also inherent conflicts which arise where a lawyer seeks to mix entrepreneurial activities with the practice of law. This is especially the case when the activities involve the participation of members of the public who may perhaps trust the lawyer in the belief that he or she is acting in a professional capacity. It has been observed: [45]

> It has not been material to consider whether it is possible for the role of a professional adviser and the role of an entrepreneur properly to coincide or overlap, but the appearance of solicitors performing these respective roles in the present case leads me to invite attention to significant differences between the two functions. These … arise because the field of professional activity is co-extensive with a lawyer's professional duty. That duty is to give advice as to the meaning and operation of the law and to render proper professional assistance in furtherance of a client's interests within the terms of the client's retainer. It is a duty which is cast upon a lawyer, as a member of an independent profession, whether his services are sought with respect to the operation of taxing statutes, the provisions of a contract, charges under the criminal law or any other of the varied fields of professional concern. It is a duty which arises out of the relationship of lawyer and client. But activities of an entrepreneur … [fall] outside the field of professional activity; those activities are not pursued in discharge of some antecedent professional duty. Entrepreneurial activity does not attract the same privilege nor the same protection as professional activity; and the promotion of a scheme in which particular clients may be advised to participate is pregnant with the possibility of conflict of entrepreneurial interest with professional duty.

Where lawyers provide services which might be offered either by a lawyer or by another professional (such as financial advice or employment advocacy) they must do so in the capacity of a lawyer. Such work is often referred to as unreserved legal work in distinction to reserved legal work (such as appearing for clients in the normal Courts or admitting wills to probate) which non-lawyers may not undertake. Non-lawyers often provide unreserved legal work under the auspices of a limited liability company and obtain the commercial advantages of using that entity. Where lawyers provide services which would normally be provided as a lawyer they must do so under the auspices of a legal practice. It is also prohibited for a lawyer to provide such services through another entity in a capacity other than that of a lawyer.[46] The rationale for this approach is stated by the Ethics Committee of the NZLS:

45 *Leary v Federal Commissioner of Taxation* (1980) 32 ALR 221, 240 per Brennan J.

46 Ethics Committee *Practitioner Engaged in Other Business* Ruling 1/99.

> If we permitted lawyers to do unreserved legal work outside their legal practices, then many lawyers would choose to move all such work to separate companies. Such work could then be done with the benefit of limited liability through a corporate entity, something not permitted by the Law Practitioners Act 1982. Clients would not have the benefit of numerous consumer protections contained in that Act. That would not be in the public interest. Clients might not appreciate that their work was "unreserved legal work" and that their "lawyer" was not wearing his or her "legal hat" when undertaking work for them. Lawyers would be tempted to fudge the distinction between their legal practice and their non-legal practice (still doing legal work).

Also problematic is the situation where a lawyer is a director of a company, or member of a local body organisation. A client of the lawyer is likely to have interests opposed to those of the organisation of which he or she is a director.[47] The rules deal with the problem by providing:

> A practitioner who is a director or member of a body corporate (which term includes, but without any attempt to be exhaustive, a local authority or a public board or authority) must not, without the consent of the body corporate, make use of information received in that capacity to the extent that advantage would result to a client or the practitioner personally and disadvantage to the body corporate.

Where the lawyer has an interest that might give rise to an appearance of conflict of interest it is certainly advisable that the interest be disclosed to the client in accordance with the normal rules applicable. In the event that there is an actual conflict of interest a lawyer may be required to refuse to act.[48]

The rule limiting the business activities of lawyers is, in its current form, outdated and fails to take account of the reality that not all lawyers are able to gain a comfortable and secure living from the practice of law alone. It may be unreasonable to restrict lawyers to professional activity alone. This is the tentative view arrived at by a committee of the law society which considered the matter along with the question of multidisciplinary practices when it stated:[49]

---

47 Rule 1.11. At the time of writing a new r 1.12 is under consideration. That rule deals with the protection of information of lawyers who have previously held public office and prohibits such practitioners from acting for a party in connection with a matter relating to information gained while in office.

48 Pursuant to r 1.03, particularly para 3 of the commentary.

49 NZLS *Discussion Paper — Multidisciplinary Practices and other Related Matters*, April 1999, para 9.6.

> The Committee's tentative view is that there should be no restrictions on the work that practising lawyers can do outside their legal practices, subject to the two qualifications mentioned, namely:
>
> - There should be a rule intended to ensure that clients are fully aware of the distinction between the legal practice and the other entity and are fully aware of the implications of the distinction between the two service providers.
> - There should be a rule that, if the service the lawyer wishes to provide is a service normally provided by practising lawyers, then that service must be provided (if it is to be provided at all) by the lawyer within his or her legal practice, and not by the lawyer outside his or her legal practice.

This accords with the approach of other jurisdictions that place few limits on the business activities of lawyers. The approach of the ABA Model Rules is to deal with the problem in the context of the normal conflict of interest rules, but with special provision for business dealings with clients.[50] The English position is to regulate the manner in which other business may be conducted, but without prohibiting engaging in business.[51] The fact is that many lawyers engage in varied business activities which, on scrutiny, would be likely to breach the rules. Much of some lawyers' work involves acting in a commercial rather than legal capacity. The time may have come to update the rule in accordance with the modern practice of law and the expectations of those who try to make a living from the profession.

15.6.6 *Duty not to resile from commitments*

Much of the work within the legal profession proceeds on the basis that other members of the profession will act honourably. While this does not necessarily mean that they will act with outright frankness it does require that lawyers adhere to their professional word whatever the circumstances in which it was given. A lawyer must not misrepresent the facts. A lawyer should be able to rely and act on information given by another lawyer with impunity.[52]

Undertakings

One of the most useful devices in the practice of law is that of the solicitor's undertaking. In many situations a minor problem could hold up or possibly frustrate a transaction or proceeding. Lawyers frequently vouch that they will take certain actions to overcome the failure. For example, a lawyer might undertake to arrange service of an affidavit of

50 ABA Model Rules, r 1.8.

51 See r 3.20 of the English *Guide*, r 5 Solicitors Practice Rules 1990 and the Solicitors' Separate Business Code 1994.

52 Rule 6.01, para 3 of the commentary. See also *Bristol & West Building Society v Fancy & Jackson* [1987] 4 All ER 582 where it was observed that financiers are entitled to rely on information provided by solicitors and solicitors will be liable if the facts warranted to exist are not in fact the case.

documents to avoid the need for an application being made to the Court, or may undertake to obtain and deliver a duplicate certificate of title that has been mislaid to enable a sale of a property to be settled. If such an undertaking has been given by lawyers they are bound to honour it. A failure to do so will be an incident of misconduct.[53] Rule 6.07 affirms this position:

> Every practitioner has a professional duty to honour an undertaking, written or oral, given in the course of legal proceedings or in the course of practice; and this rule applies whether the undertaking is given by the practitioner personally or by a partner or employee in the course of the practice.

Such undertakings should be honoured according to their spirit and should not be construed or drafted in a technical manner with a view to avoiding their intent.[54] The undertaking will be enforceable whether given orally or in writing, though for obvious reasons it is advisable to record such things in written form.[55] A firm will be held liable for the undertakings of any of its partners or staff.[56]

The reasons for the rule, which requires the strict adherence to undertakings, are pragmatic. Undertakings are common throughout legal practice and the continued efficient working of legal practice requires that such undertakings be honoured regardless of other supervening circumstances. The additional reason for the strict application of the rule is the maintenance of the integrity of the legal profession. Members of the profession must be seen as wholly trustworthy in that, once they have undertaken a particular course of action, they can be depended on to act accordingly. The fact that the duty to honour undertakings is strict means that even where there has been an error or oversight by the lawyer, circumstances have changed radically, or to adhere to the undertaking will cause hardship, the lawyer will still be required to adhere to the promises made.[57]

Enforcing undertakings[58]

Undertakings may be legally enforceable according to the ordinary rules of law as giving rise to a contract or an estoppel.[59] However,

53 See also r 18.05 of the English *Guide*.

54 *Re W P Roberts* (1856) 26 LT (OS) 239. An ambiguous undertaking will be construed in favour of the recipient: r 18.07 of the English *Guide*.

55 Rules 6.01, para 4 of the commentary.

56 *Burbery Mortgage Finance Ltd (in rec) v O'Neill* [1994] BCL 1750. See also P Webb, "Solicitor Undertakers Beware" [1995] NZLJ 36.

57 *Re C* [1982] 1 NZLR 137.

58 A more detailed discussion of the jurisdiction of the Court to enforce undertakings can be found in G Dal Pont *Lawyers' Professional Responsibility in Australia and New Zealand* North Ryde NSW, Law Book Information Services, 1996, 433-451.

undertakings will be enforced by the Courts as an aspect of the inherent jurisdiction to supervise the profession regardless of whether they give rise to any cause of action in law or not.[60] Defences that might be available in a legal action will not be available when the Court is exercising its disciplinary jurisdiction in enforcement.[61] Because a breach of an undertaking is an incident of professional misconduct, the Courts in their supervisory jurisdiction of the profession will enforce such undertakings. Because it is an exercise of the inherent jurisdiction of the Court over its officers it will not be constrained by technical rules and will approach the issues in a broad manner.[62] Such an application will be heard summarily, which means that the usual pre-trial procedures will be dispensed with. Although the action of a Court is disciplinary and punitive, it can have considerable remedial benefits for the third parties to whom the undertaking was made.[63] The Court may order the lawyer to pay any legal costs incurred by a failure to adhere to an undertaking,[64] as well as damages suffered by the client due to such a failure.[65]

When such an application is made to the Court, the Court will be concerned to establish that the undertaking was made in the capacity as a solicitor, rather than in the course of personal affairs. An undertaking that is given in the context of a transaction being conducted on behalf of a client, expressly or impliedly required to be a solicitor's undertaking, or given under the auspices of a legal practice, will almost certainly be regarded as given in the capacity of a lawyer.[66] To avoid any doubt in such matters such undertakings should be drafted clearly and the capacity in which they are given stated explicitly. In other circumstances it may be appropriate for a lawyer to undertake on behalf of the client that certain steps will be taken.[67] It is important to make clear that the

---

59 However such discussions are left to texts in those areas.

60 *Re Grey* [1892] 2 QB 440, 443 per Lord Esher MR; *Gill and McAsey v Wainui Timber Co Ltd* [1992] 1 NZLR 1, 4 per Richardson J (CA); and r 6.07, para 9 of the commentary.

61 *Countrywide Banking Corporation Ltd v Kingston* [1990] 1 NZLR 629, 638 per Wily J, although His Honour does note that the existence of legal defences may be a consideration as to whether the Court ought to exercise its discretion not to order enforcement.

62 *Australian Guarantee Corporation (NZ) Ltd v East Brewster Urquhart & Partners* [1990] 2 NZLR 167.

63 See *Countrywide Banking Corporation Ltd v Kingston* [1990] 1 NZLR 629 where the bank successfully applied to the Court to enforce an undertaking to repay a $400,000 mortgage.

64 *National Westminster Finance v Bryant* [1989] NZLR 513.

65 *Australian Guarantee Corporation (NZ) Ltd v East Brewster Urquhart & Partners* [1990] 2 NZLR 167.

66 *Countrywide Banking Corporation Ltd v Kingston* [1990] 1 NZLR 629, 635, 636 per Wily J.

67 See r 6.07, para 5 of the commentary.

client rather than the lawyer is bound, and to ensure that the client has authorised the lawyer to make the undertaking given.

A Court will not order that an undertaking be enforced unless it is capable of being performed.[68] The reason for such an approach is that if lawyers fail to comply with an order to adhere to an undertaking they will be in contempt of Court and liable to imprisonment.[69] If the undertaking is unable to be performed the third party will have to seek a remedy through channels other than the disciplinary jurisdiction of the Court. The failure to perform the undertaking will still amount to misconduct in respect of which a complaint might be made to the law society.[70]

If all the grounds for ordering that the undertaking be honoured are present the Court still has a discretion as to whether or not to make such an order. The Court, in exercising that discretion, may take any relevant matter into account including the surrounding circumstances, the existence of a defence if the claim were made in law, the conduct of the other party, the effluxion of time, and so on. In exercising the discretion the Court will weigh the prejudice or injustice in ordering the honouring of the undertaking against the public interest in ensuring that parties may rely on undertakings given by lawyers.[71]

Payments

Associated with the lawyers' duty to honour their undertakings in all circumstances, is the duty not to stop payments once they have been initiated. In many forms of payment such as by cheque or electronic transfer there is a period of time after the cheque has been delivered, or the order to transfer given, in which the cheque may be stopped or the order reversed. A lawyer should not reverse such a payment in any but the most exceptional circumstances.

When a lawyer hands over a trust account or bank cheque, or informs another party that an order for electronic transfer has been made, the other party is entitled to assume that payment once made may be relied upon. Rule 6.04 emphasises the importance of this, particularly in respect of payments made from the lawyer's trust account or by bank cheque. It is customary to accept bank and trust account cheques (and electronic payments from trust accounts) as guaranteed forms of

68 *Re McDougall's Application* [1982] 1 NZLR 141.

69 *Peart v Bushell* (1827) 2 Sim 38, 57 ER 705, 39, 705 per Hart V-C.

70 See r 18.03 of the English *Guide, which* provides that "An undertaking is binding even if it is to do something outside of the solicitor's control".

71 *Countrywide Banking Corporation Ltd v Kingston* [1990] 1 NZLR 629, 639 per Wylie J.

payment. This is distinct from non-trust account cheques that are recognised as able to be stopped in the normal manner.

Rule 6.04, which prohibits the stopping of such payments other than in exceptional circumstances, is limited to situations where a practitioner has given the cheque or written verification of electronic payment to another practitioner. The implication is that where the order is one to pay a lay person it is permissible to stop the payment. This limitation of the duty to relations with other practitioners seems insupportable. Promises to pay, as with any other promise or undertaking by a lawyer, should be considered as inviolate regardless of the identity of the party to whom they are given. It would demonstrate a strange inconsistency if a lawyer were permitted to stop a trust account cheque given directly to a third party, but were prohibited from doing so if that cheque were given to the third party's lawyer.

The circumstances in which it will be permissible to stop a payment order even when it is made from a trust account or by bank cheque will be rare indeed. If the cheque itself is a forgery it will be able to be stopped as it is a nullity.[72] The fact that the consideration on the faith of which the cheque is drawn has failed will not warrant (or be a legal basis for) the cheque being stopped.[73] It is possible to countermand a trust account cheque prior to it being finally and irrevocably paid by the bank.[74] Such a step might be taken in the event that it becomes clear that the client's own cheque deposited into the trust account and on the faith of which the trust account cheque is drawn has bounced.[75] If the holder of the cheque received it in good faith and for valuable consideration there will be a valid claim for its value.[76] Stopping a cheque in such circumstances would almost certainly amount to misconduct as the third party has relied on the trust account cheque as a vouchsafe that the client has sufficient clear funds to meet the cheque.

The rules are of little assistance in such cases as they simply provide that:[77]

> The circumstances that would justify stopping such a cheque, or cancelling or reversing or amending such an order for payment, would need to be truly

---

72 Section 24 Bills of Exchange Act 1908.

73 At least in the case of bank cheques: *Yan v Post Office Savings Bank* [1994] 1 NZLR 154.

74 *H H Dimond (Rotorua 1966) Ltd v Australia and New Zealand Banking Group Ltd* [1979] 2 NZLR 739; s 75 Bills of Exchange Act 1908.

75 To write a trust account cheque in such circumstances would be extremely foolish and in breach of r 5(4)(a) Solicitors Trust Account Rules 1996.

76 Section 29 Bills of Exchange Act 1908.

77 Rule 6.04, para 1 of the commentary.

exceptional. Such a step is not likely to be justified in the absence of clearly proper and legal grounds for doing so.

The rule states, rather obviously, that if a payment order or cheque is to be stopped there must be legal grounds for doing so. In addition to the existence of a legal justification it must be proper to do so. No guidance is given as to the circumstances in which it would be proper.

Some assistance may be gleaned from the English *Guide* which provides that in cases where a cheque may be properly stopped notice of the intention to stop payment must be promptly given.[78] There is a suggestion that if notice is not given before the third party has committed himself or herself to an action in reliance on the receipt of the funds then it will not be permissible to stop the cheque. The mere fact that the recipient of the cheque is a lawyer who has paid it into the trust account and informed the client accordingly will not of itself prevent the cheque being stopped.[79]

15.7 Barristers sole[80]

Barristers in New Zealand occupy an apparently anomalous position in the fused profession. Any barristers are qualified to act as solicitors as well as barristers, however, they voluntarily place themselves under certain restrictions which attach to the position of barrister. The essence of those restrictions is that they confine their practice to work connected with Court proceedings and refrain from engaging in the transactional work which typifies a solicitor's practice.[81] There are some minor benefits attaching to such a choice. A barrister is relieved of the obligation of administering a trust account, and is not required to contribute to the solicitors' fidelity fund.

A practitioner's choice to practise as a barrister sole is essentially a choice to specialise in the area of litigation, and often in a particular kind of litigation. The existence of a large body of practitioners who choose to practise as barristers demonstrates the efficacy of such specialisation. The advantages to a client in the employment of a barrister extend beyond merely the expertise of the barrister. There are a number of rules and conventions governing practice of a barrister, most of which are

78 Rule 17.02 of the English *Guide*.

79 Commentary to r 17.02 of the English *Guide*.

80 The current rules relating to barristers sole are under review by a special joint committee of the New Zealand Law Society and the New Zealand Bar Association and there may well be changes in the near future. Advocates' immunity is considered in para 11.5.

81 Barristers also engage in some non-litigious work such as the giving of legal opinions, and acting as mediators or arbitrators.

drawn from the English tradition in which the professions of barrister and solicitor are quite separate. Whether those restrictions are appropriate in the New Zealand environment certainly bears scrutiny.[82]

15.7.1 *Barristers' intervention rule*

One of the most important rules governing the practice of barristers is that "a barrister sole must accept instructions only from a solicitor and may not accept instructions direct from a lay client".[83] This means that, except in limited circumstances,[84] a barrister may act for a client only through the mediation of a solicitor. The rationale behind the rule is the protection of the special independence that a barrister has. In jurisdictions where the professions of barrister and solicitor are quite separate the independence of a barrister is held in high regard. They consider themselves to be more detached than the solicitor. Such a view comes from the manner in which barristers work. Usually a barrister will only be retained once it is clear that a matter will go to Court, and the barrister will not deal directly with the lay client. Any meetings between the barrister and the lay client will be held in the presence of the solicitor. The solicitor is seen as an intermediary (and buffer) between the lay client and the barrister.

There has been some recent criticism of the rule requiring litigants in need of the services of a barrister having to employ a solicitor as an intermediary.[85] The claim to a special independence presumes a corresponding lack of independence on the part of practitioners who do not practise as barristers sole and such a disparity is not apparent in

---

82 The numerous rules and conventions surrounding the practice of a barrister are beyond the scope of this work (and are not reproduced in the rules). A useful source of the rules is the Code of Conduct of the Bar of England and Wales, although those rules and conventions apply with some variations in New Zealand to account for the peculiarities of the fused professions and the development of different (typically less stringent) practices.

83 Rule 11.03; *Kaye v Auckland District Law Society* [1998] 1 NZLR 151; *Time Ticket International Ltd v Broughton* [1996] 2 NZLR 176.

84 Those exceptions are contained in r 11.04 and are where the barrister is (i) instructed to act in a judicial or quasi-judicial capacity or is instructed by a person or body acting in such a capacity; (ii) instructed by the Society or a District Society; (iii) instructed by: (a) a registered patent attorney (b) a lawyer practising overseas (c) an Official Assignee or Official Liquidator; (iv) acting as a revising barrister pursuant to any enactment; (v) (a) assigned to a legally aided person (b) acting as a duty solicitor (c) providing assistance to a legal advice service operating on a non-profit basis (d) advising a legal aid committee (e) acting under a Detention Legal Assistance Scheme; (vi) advised in any other case by the Ethics Committee of the Society that he or she may act.

85 It is understood that the rule is currently under consideration by a special joint committee of the New Zealand Law Society and the New Zealand Bar Association.

reality. It is also obvious that such a barrier between a client and barrister is not regarded as essential as much Court work is undertaken by practitioners who practise in the joint role of barrister and solicitor.

The requirement that where a barrister is to be employed it is necessary to also retain a solicitor to instruct a barrister on behalf of a lay client also imposes a further burden of costs on the client. A solicitor is expected to file documents, write, send and receive correspondence, and accept service of documents. This role means that further work is created by the need for considerable exchange of information between barrister and solicitor.[86] This inconvenience is sometimes circumvented by practitioners evading these rules and using a solicitor simply as a "post-box" to ensure superficial compliance.[87]

In the New Zealand context there appears to be little justification for the continued retention of the referral rule where it simply adds to the cost of legal assistance, and is not required when dealing with a person practising as a barrister and a solicitor. The rule has been relaxed in some Australian jurisdictions albeit with the requirement that the barrister inform the lay client of the disadvantages of retaining a barrister alone.[88] There may be cases where it will be in the client's best interests that a solicitor be retained. In such cases there are good reasons for allowing a barrister to decline the work unless the client agrees to the use of a solicitor. Where direct access to barristers is permitted it is usual to permit barristers to insist that a solicitor be retained if this is in the client's best interests.[89] Such circumstances may arise in a complex case where the resources of a firm of solicitors are needed to manage the case, or where the client is particularly difficult and to do the work properly a buffer is needed between barrister and lay client.

There is a proposal to abolish the compulsory intervention rule, though barristers would still be free to require clients to use a solicitor as an intermediary. The proposal is part of a significant reform package.[90] The following discussion should, therefore, be read bearing in mind any reforms which have occurred since the publication of this work.

---

86 See generally rr 11.10, 11.11 and 11.12.

87 See the criticisms aimed at a barrister who had in substance circumvented the rule requiring an instructing solicitor in *McDonald v FAI* [1999] 1 NZLR 583, 589, 590 per Giles J.

88 New South Wales, Queensland and the Australian Capital Territory have adopted r 80 of the Australian Bar Association's Advocacy Rules which permit such direct access. See also the Direct Professional Access Rules of the Bar of England and Wales.

89 Rule 1 of the Direct Professional Access Rules of the Bar of England and Wales.

90 Letter, President of the Law Society to all practitioners, 20 October 1999, and the attached paper.

15.7.2 *Barristers' fees*

Like any professional person a barrister renders bills to the client for work done. Because of the referral rule, that client is almost always the solicitor who instructed the barrister. However, a curious and anachronistic rule prohibits a barrister from suing for fees. The obligation of a solicitor to pay a barrister is one which is "owed in honour not in debt".[91] The rule has arisen from the customary practice of the English profession and is, somewhat perplexingly, considered by some as of considerable importance. Tipping J in *Atkinson v Pengelly* stated:[92]

> While the English rule [that barristers cannot sue for their professional fees] might be thought in some quarters to be commercially anomalous, the rule is of considerable antiquity and can fairly be said to be a fundamental feature of the relationship between a barrister and his clients, both lay and professional.

It is difficult to see how the inability to sue for fees can be regarded as a foundation of the professional relationships of a barrister and it is suggested that little would change if the rule were done away with.

The rule is particularly anomalous in New Zealand because it has been held that lawyers who practise as both barristers and solicitors may sue for all their fees in the normal manner.[93] This results in the farcical situation which renders one professional's bills unenforceable at law simply because he or she has chosen to practise as a barrister sole rather than as a solicitor as well. While a barrister may not sue for fees, the solicitor who is liable for them may sue to recover the amount from the client.[94]

Where a solicitor instructs a barrister, the solicitor is prima facie bound by the rules to meet the barrister's fees regardless of whether or not the

---

91 *Atkinson v Pengelly* [1995] 3 NZLR 104, 110 per Tipping J.

92 *Atkinson v Pengelly* [1995] 3 NZLR 104, 111 per Tipping J. That case concerned a claim by a barrister to a lien on the proceeds of litigation. The claim was refused on the basis that if there was no ability to establish a legal claim, no lien could be supported.

93 *Robinson and Morgan-Coakle v Behan* [1964] NZLR 650; *Wyatt and Cohen v Willis* (1909) 29 NZLR 58. The distinction is on the basis that a solicitor may, when suing to recover for his or her own fees, sue for the fees of the barrister as a disbursement. See s 140 Law Practitioners Act 1982.

94 Section 140 Law Practitioners Act 1982. It appears that the solicitor may sue for the fees even where it has been agreed that the lay client will pay the barrister direct and the solicitor will not be responsible for them: *Findlay v Webb Morrice and Partners* (High Court, Auckland, AP 82-SW99, 6 September 1999, Robertson J).

solicitor has been put in funds by the client for this purpose.[95] The rule will be displaced where there is an agreement between the solicitor and barrister that the payment of the barrister's fees is dependent on some other eventuality (such as payment by the client). In the absence of such factors it will be misconduct for a solicitor to fail to pay the professional fees of a barrister whom he or she has instructed.

15.8 Professional cooperation with non-lawyers

The market for services provided by lawyers is a competitive one. One of the examples of this is the provision by non-law firms, particularly accountants, of some services traditionally provided by law firms. Tax and corporate planning are good examples of this. Lawyers have also become more ready to offer, within the framework of a law firm, advice of a non-legal nature concerning such diverse areas as investment, property management and development, and planning. The provision of such advice may involve the employment of non-lawyers within the law firm. There are a number of rules which bar the creation of what have become known as multidisciplinary practices (MDPs) where professionals of different kinds enter into a partnership and form a firm with a broad range of expertise. There has recently been a questioning of whether the prohibitions on such practices are in the interests of the legal profession or the public and the law society has taken the step of issuing a discussion paper on the problem.

15.8.1 *Prohibition on non-lawyer partners and business*

There is no express prohibition in New Zealand against entering into a partnership with non-lawyers. However, the provisions of the Law Practitioners Act 1982 and the rules make it clear that such associations are not permitted. It is an offence under the Act to practise as a solicitor or barrister unless properly qualified.[96] More explicitly, r 2.03(3) and (4) provides:

> (3)… a practitioner shall not, while the holder of a practising certificate as a barrister or solicitor or as both, become a partner of a firm or shareholder in a company that practises a profession other than law, or that proposes to practise another profession as well as law, …
>
> (4) Where a practitioner or firm provides or intends to provide to clients, services ancillary to legal services, such ancillary services must be solely in connection with and concurrent to the provision of legal services, and be provided by the practitioner or firm or by an entity in which the practitioner or firm has a controlling interest, so that the activities of a practitioner in the provision of such services will be and remain subject to the provisions of the Act and all rules and regulations made under the Act.

95 Rule 6.08.
96 Sections 54, 64, 65 and 66.

The effect of the rule is to prohibit a lawyer practising law in a professional firm other than a law firm.[97] The rule also has the effect of prohibiting a law firm from offering non-legal services as a core part of its business.[98]

15.8.2 *No fee splitting/sharing*

An associated rule is the prohibition on splitting fees with non-lawyers. Once again under the New Zealand regulatory structure the prohibition is not explicit. Any arrangement whereby a lawyer agreed to split fees, or grant a profit share to an employee who was not a lawyer would amount to an evasion on the prohibition on entering into partnership with non-lawyers. The prohibition in other jurisdictions is explicit.[99] The prohibition is hinted at in r 4.04:

> A practitioner must not directly or indirectly offer to, or receive from, a third party, a reward or inducement, whether financial or otherwise, in respect of services rendered or to be rendered to the client.

The rule amounts to a prohibition against arrangements between professionals whereby a client requiring diverse services is referred to an associated professional, either in return for a fee or as part of an understanding that the other professional will reciprocate if a client of the other professional requires the services of the first professional. As such reciprocal agreements are frowned upon by the rules, more formal arrangements of fee sharing will be prohibited as a more serious example of giving or receiving benefits in the referral of clients between professionals of different disciplines.

15.8.3 *Rationale for the prohibitions*

The prohibition on close associations with professionals from other disciplines is premised on the assumption that in such associations there is a danger of a conflict of interest between the lawyer and the client. In the event that a client needs the services of another professional the existence of a referral arrangement presumes that the client will be referred to that other professional. In some cases this may not be the best professional for the client's needs, however the existence of a

---

97 Compare the explicit English provisions which in r 14.02(6) of the *Guide* provides: "A solicitor shall not enter into partnership with any person other than a solicitor, a registered foreign lawyer, or a recognised body". The rule is drawn from r 7 Solicitors Practice Rules 1990.

98 This prohibition is also effected by other legislation that grants monopolies to other professions such as the Real Estate Agents Act 1976. See further *Lewis v Real Estate Institute of New Zealand Inc* [1995] 3 NZLR 385.

99 For example the English provisions in r 14.02 of the *Guide* drawn from r 7 of the Solicitors Practice Rules 1990. In *Mohamed v Alaga & Co (a firm)* [1999] 3 All ER 699 a contract for fee splitting in breach of the rule was held to be illegal and unenforceable.

financial incentive for the referring practitioner may well cloud his or her judgment in the matter. The receipt of a benefit from the referral also amounts to the receipt of a profit arising out of the fiduciary relationship with the client and will be in breach of the duty not to receive a profit other than that agreed in the retainer.[100]

These objections do not tie in with the realities of modern business practice. In the first place, the problem of referrals to other professionals is not restricted to professionals of other disciplines. No lawyer is able to meet the needs of every client and this means that there will be numerous instances where lawyers refer their clients to other lawyers. When the lawyer is a member of a firm there is a tendency to refer the client to a member of the firm more proficient in the required area of expertise. A more proficient and appropriate lawyer may be found outside the firm, but no one seriously objects to such in-firm referrals. The availability of a wide range of expertise and the associated support network within one firm is one of the main reasons that some clients will choose larger firms. Where the client is referred to another lawyer outside the firm (a barrister is the most obvious example) the lawyer will most likely refer the client to a barrister whom the lawyer knows in a professional capacity, and has some kind of working relationship with.

When a lawyer does have to refer a client to another professional it is business reality that they will be more likely to refer the client to a profession with whom they have an established relationship. Such networks of relationships are a valuable professional asset and are fostered by lawyers and other professionals alike. This is recognised in the commentary to r 4.04:[101]

> While the offering of direct payments or benefits for the advancing of work is proscribed, it is not intended that the rule should prohibit the usual professional associations that develop between practitioners and third parties, i.e. those associations which may involve social exchanges, the mutual referrals of work, or small gifts such as calendars or pens.

This illustrates the fact that in the light of the prohibition on overtly financial arrangements in respect of referrals, practitioners are often the recipients of collateral benefits such as gifts and entertainment which are intended to foster the professional relationships between different professional firms.[102] Such relationships are useful for clients as well as

100 See also r 3.02.

101 Para 2.

102 Such activities are particularly prevalent in respect of relationships between real estate agents and lawyers because of the significant amount of cross-referrals that may occur.

practitioners. The existence of a relationship between various professionals means that it is not necessary to blindly choose another professional on the basis of advertising, or other essentially unreliable information. A lawyer, as a professional who regularly works with other professionals, is in an ideal position to judge the proficiency and integrity of those others. Provided the lawyer refers work only to other professionals who are regarded as competent and honest, the existence of mutually financial beneficial relationships would seem to be a side issue (providing they are disclosed to the client). The rules as they currently stand take a cautious approach in prohibiting such financial relationships to ensure that merit is the primary basis for such referrals.

15.8.4 *The case for multidisciplinary practices*

Business reality is the foundation of the pressure to amend the rules and associated legislation to enable lawyers to form partnerships with other non-lawyer professionals.[103] The law society has defined MDPs as: "a business in the form of a partnership or a company, formed by members of various occupations who share the profits of the business. It can include the members of any profession".[104] There are a number of advantages claimed by proponents of MDPs. These include efficiencies gained which result in lower cost of professional services, greater convenience to the consumer, more effective completion of work involving cooperation between professionals, making lawyers more competitive as against other professionals (particularly accountants), encouragement of specialisation, increased client bases of firms, and ultimately making firms more profitable.[105]

15.8.5 *The challenges of MDPs*

There are concerns whether MDPs are likely to deliver the predicted benefits. Of more relevance to this work is the question of what impact such practices would have on the professional conduct of members of such firms. Some of the dangers are identical to those mentioned above in respect of fee sharing and non-law practices concerning a conflict of interest between the interests of the client and the practitioner. An associated problem is the risk of over-servicing clients. That is to say, a

---

103 See N D Israel, "Multidisciplinary Practices" [1996] NZLJ 381 for a discussion of the emergence of such practices world-wide.

104 New Zealand Law Society *Discussion Paper — Multidisciplinary Practices and other Related Matters* April 1999, para 2.9.

105 It is of note that in jurisdictions where such practices are permitted they have not proliferated. This may be due to the fact that clients associate quality legal services as being provided by a law-dedicated firm. It also appears that there is no evidence of lower costs being handed on to consumers (but this is to be expected as long as the market is dominated by law-only firms with higher cost structures). See New Zealand Law Society *Discussion Paper — Multidisciplinary Practices and other Related Matters* April 1999, paras 4.15-4.19 and the reports cited therein.

practitioner may be tempted to encourage a client to obtain other services such as financial advice that he or she would not recommend but for the fact that the practitioner's firm will profit by giving such advice. This risk seems negligible, and no different in principle from similar risks that exist in a law firm to over-service a client by providing services which are not needed, or not needed in the depth that they are given.

The law society's discussion paper also identified a possible tension between the interests of the firm and the overriding duty of the lawyer to the administration of justice. There are undoubtedly instances where a lawyer is under pressure to subvert the duty to the administration of justice to more immediate pressures. For example, a lawyer might be pressured to take a case that is hopeless or an abuse of process, or to turn a blind eye to inadequate discovery or client wrongdoing. It is hard to see how these pressures would be compounded merely due to the fact that the lawyer is in partnership with other non-lawyers. The suggestion is that "this pressure might arise not through the dishonesty of non-lawyer members but through their simple ignorance of lawyers' ethical obligations". This may be overstated. The other members of the firm will be professionals, and the concept of overriding professional duties will be familiar. Similar problems in other jurisdictions have been addressed by overt statements of the lawyers' overriding duties in legislation.[106]

It is also claimed that the proffering of advice by an MDP would cloud the issue of legal professional privilege. While privilege is granted in respect of all communications made in respect of the conduct of litigation, outside the litigation situation it is only those communications made between lawyer and client for the purposes of giving legal advice that are privileged. If advice is given of a legal or quasi-legal nature that is generated by a non-lawyer member of an MDP it is unlikely that privilege under the current rules would attach. More problematic is the case where the advice proffered was composed by both lawyers and non-lawyers in the MDP. Certainly if MDPs are to proceed there will be

---

106 Section 27 of the Courts and Legal Services Act 1990 (UK) was amended in 1999 by inserting the following:

(2A) Every person who exercises before any Court a right of audience granted by an authorised body has—

(a) a duty to the Court to act with independence in the interests of justice; and

(b) a duty to comply with rules of conduct of the body relating to the right and approved for the purposes of this section;

and those duties shall override any obligation which the person may have (otherwise than under the criminal law) if it is inconsistent with them.

That section is designed particularly to deal with the issue of employed lawyers rather than MDPs.

a need for clarification of the rules of privilege. It will be important to ensure that privilege is not inappropriately extended to cover communications that do not warrant such protection on the public policy grounds on which the doctrine is based. The problem is largely technical and requires the formulation of clear rules to cover the various problems of privilege and confidentiality which may arise in an MDP environment.

There is also a danger in MDPs that professional regulation becomes difficult because the members of the firm do not belong to any single professional body. The anomalous situation might arise that different professional obligations will bind practitioners depending on what profession they belong to, notwithstanding the fact that the work they are completing is identical. The governance of the conduct of non-lawyer members of MDPs needs to be addressed. Numerous options exist including the universal application of the Law Society Rules, the development of an independent set of MDP rules, or each profession's rules applying to the different members of the MDP.[107]

The concept of a multidisciplinary partnership does not sit well with the existing regulatory framework governing the practice of law. However, it is rash to suggest that the practice of law in a partnership with non-lawyers is incompatible with ethical and responsible legal practice. While the emergence of such practices will require a significant shift in the manner in which law firms are regulated, and the conception of the proper way to conduct a legal practice, these are regulatory rather than ethical hurdles. The ethical challenges of practising are broadly similar whether the lawyer practises alone, alongside other lawyers, or alongside accountants and investment advisers. The suggestion that other professionals, if in partnership with lawyers, would tend to drag down the ethical standard is unfounded and presumes that other professionals are either less ethically aware or more dishonest than lawyers. Neither can be shown to be the case.

107 New Zealand Law Society *Discussion Paper — Multidisciplinary Practices and other Related Matters* April 1999, ch 6 .

New Zealand Law Society

Rules of Professional Conduct for Barristers and Solicitors©

5th Edition
1998

Contents

Introduction

The purpose of this publication is to provide guidance for practitioners in the practice of law in New Zealand. This is not to be considered an exhaustive code or treatise. It is rather a definition of the bounds within which a practitioner can practise the profession. Observance of those bounds, and managing all aspects of practice within them involves the acceptance of the basic principle of professional responsibility.

The Council of the New Zealand Law Society has approved and adopted this publication of a set of rules and commentaries on those rules under the rule-making powers in section 17 Law Practitioners Act 1982. There is a professional obligation on every practitioner to observe and comply with the rules that follow in the course of practice in New Zealand. There is a corresponding duty on the council of each District Law Society to enforce those rules.

The provision of guidelines is more complex in New Zealand than in a number of other countries including most of the "common law" countries. In many other jurisdictions one is either a barrister or a solicitor and the functions of each branch of the profession are clearly defined. We therefore find in places such as England and New South Wales that the Bar on the one hand, and the solicitors' branch of the profession on the other are subject to different codes of conduct and their members are members of different professional organisations.

By contrast with such jurisdictions the profession in New Zealand has sometimes been referred to as "fused". This is a misconception. A practitioner in New Zealand is enrolled as a barrister and solicitor. From that starting point there is flexibility in our modes of practice. By far the greater number of our members take out practising certificates as both barrister and solicitor and practise as such either alone or in partnership, or in employment with other practitioners or in commerce or government. As holders of such certificates they are entitled to engage in the practice of any type of law including court and tribunal work. It is quite usual to find law firms that cover the whole scope of legal service to their clients. Many members who prefer to practise in the courts remain as partners in their firms and are able to take instructions direct from members of the public or, if the occasion arises, from another practitioner.

Other members of the profession, referred to in this publication as "barristers sole", prefer to take out practising certificates as barristers only. Having done this they have become subject to the constraints of what have been called the "Barristers' Rules". These constraints require a mode of practice somewhat similar to those of barristers in New South Wales and other places, particularly in as much as with certain exceptions, the barrister is not able to accept work direct from the public. The client must normally come to the barrister through a practising solicitor. Far from being an anomaly in a jurisdiction where a practitioner is on the Roll as both barrister and solicitor, the preference shown by those who wish to practise as barristers sole serves to demonstrate the flexibility of our modes of practice when compared with those in other countries.

The differing modes of practice in New Zealand inevitably affect any attempt to enunciate the principles of professional responsibility. Guidance in this field must have regard to the different types of practice. The Society has long recognised that while the general rules of practice must apply to all members of the profession, there are some that apply to those who practise as barristers and solicitors on the one hand, and others that apply to those who practise as barristers sole on the other hand. While this publication will of necessity include rules and commentaries for those who practise as barristers sole, some of those principles will apply equally to barristers and solicitors who do barristers' work in a firm. In like manner, much of the general area of the publication applying to practitioners generally will apply to those who practise as barristers sole.

The sanctions for infringements in the field of professional responsibility are set out fully in Part VII, Law Practitioners Act 1982 which deals with the complaints and disciplinary processes both at national and district level. There are concepts in Part VII that find no definition in the Act or in this publication. These include "misconduct in his or her professional capacity" and "conduct unbecoming a barrister or solicitor". Several sections of the Act deem a practitioner in particular circumstances to be guilty of misconduct in a professional capacity. Otherwise, the assessment of whether there has been a breach of acceptable conduct by a practitioner is one for a district society complaints committee, a district disciplinary tribunal, the NZ Law Practitioners Disciplinary Tribunal or the Court.

Any attempt to compile an exhaustive code purporting to define exclusively the rules for a breach of which a person could be subject to the disciplinary processes of the Act would be self-defeating. The proceedings of the New Zealand Law Practitioners Disciplinary Tribunal and the Disciplinary Committee that preceded it, have demonstrated clearly that a charge of misconduct in one's professional capacity need not be tied to any specific rule of ethics or to the Solicitors Trust Account Regulations or Rules. First the Committee, and later the Tribunal, have had the task of deciding whether any particular act or omission forming the basis of a charge of misconduct comes within the concepts of Part VII of the Act. In each case it is a question of fact having regard to the circumstances of that case.

Practitioners must, however, be aware that a breach of a rule as elaborated by a commentary in this publication, could well put the practitioner in jeopardy.

It is reiterated therefore that this publication, to the extent possible, defines the bounds within which a practitioner may practise the profession. Within those bounds the prime responsibility of a practitioner is his or her own sense of professional responsibility. The preservation of the integrity and reputation of the profession is very much a matter for individual members.

Many practitioners are not in private practice either as barristers or solicitors. They practise their profession in salaried employment in commerce, the state service or elsewhere. Some of these practitioners, although salaried, have a right, by agreement with the employer, to conduct a private practice as well. To the extent that an employed practitioner conducts a private practice, that practitioner is bound by the provisions of the Solicitors' Trust Account Regulations 1998, the Solicitors Trust Account Rules 1996, and other obligations in the same way as any other private practitioner. No matter which branch of legal work the salaried practitioner engages in, and whether or not private practice is combined with the salaried occupation, the contents of this publication apply to every practitioner.

Additional guidance can be obtained from the publications of the profession in other countries. Three of these are:

- The Guide to the Professional Conduct of Solicitors - The Law Society of England and Wales
- Model Rules of Professional Conduct - American Bar Association
- The International Code of Ethics - International Bar Association

Rulings and Opinions on the Meaning and Effect of the Rules and Commentaries

On 29 August 1997 the Council of the New Zealand Law Society passed the following resolution:

That there be approved a system for the production of rulings and opinions on the Rules of Professional Conduct for Barristers and Solicitors as proposed and that it be published in the Introduction to the Rules and in LawTalk.

(2) That there be new Rules 9.6 and 13.5 of the New Zealand Law Society as follows:

9.6 Pursuant to s.17(2) of the Law Practitioners Act 1982 the Council hereby empowers itself to give rulings in respect of the application of any rules made under s.17 of the Law Practitioners Ace 1982 and requires that such rulings be observed by practitioners.

13.5 Pursuant to s.15 (4) of the Law Practitioners Act 1982 the Council (without prejudice to Rule 10.15.2 of the New Zealand Law Society which delegates certain of the Council's functions and powers to the Board), delegates to the Ethics Committee of the New Zealand Law Society the power to give rulings in respect of the application of the Rules of Professional Conduct made under s.17 of the Law Practitioners Act 1982 and Commentaries thereto. Applications in this regard by practitioners must be referred through the relevant District Law Society Council unless there is an emergency or the practitioner reasonably suspects that the Council might not be in a position to deal with the matter objectively or where it fails expeditiously to deal with the matter. Rulings of the Ethics Committee are to be observed by practitioners. The Council of the District Law Society or the practitioner concerned if not satisfied by any such ruling by the Ethics Committee nay apply within 21 days of the notification of the ruling to have it reviewed by the Board. The decision of the Board will be final."

In making this resolution the Council accorded the following meanings to the words "rulings" and "opinions":

Rulings

Rulings in respect of any rules made under s.17 may be given by the Council pursuant to s.17(2)(h). Rulings are binding decisions as to the proper and intended application of the Council's rules - the application in individual instances or situations of the generally stated rules. A ruling may be of general application or apply only in respect of a specific fact situation. The scope and ambit of a particular ruling will be determined by the context in which the relevant issue arose. The NZLS, District Law Societies and practitioners affected should all be bound by such rulings and observe and apply them in practice.

Opinions

Opinions are statements not amounting to rulings, either as to the meaning and effect of a rule of the NZLS or with regard to any other applicable ethical principle. "View" and "interpretation" have like meanings. Opinions, like rulings, may be of specific or general application. Neither law societies nor practitioners are bound by opinions.

Procedure

Rulings

Applications by practitioners for rulings must be referred through the relevant District Law Society Council unless there is an emergency or the practitioner reasonably suspects that that Council might not be in a position to deal with the matter objectively or where it fails expeditiously to deal with the matter.

Rulings of the NZLS Ethics Committee are to be observed by practitioners. If the Council of the District Law Society or the practitioner concerned is not satisfied by any such ruling by the Ethics Committee that Council or practitioner may apply within 21 days of the notification of the ruling to have it reviewed by the NZLS Board. The decision of the Board will be final. All rulings whether made by the NZLS Ethics Committee or the NZLS Board will be published in Law Talk and in the Rules of Professional Conduct, (for which see Appendix IV in this publication).

Opinions, etc

Individual practitioners should normally apply for an NZLS Ethics Committee opinion through the relevant District Law Society which should first try to deal with the question itself rather than simply pass it on. Regard should be had however to the need for a single national treatment of matter having implication for practitioners outside the district's jurisdiction. Practitioners should not approach the NZLS Ethics Committee directly unless they reasonably suspect that the District Society might not be in a position to deal with the matter objectively or where that Society has failed expeditiously to deal with the matter. If any party finds an opinion unacceptable that party should apply to have the matter referred to the NZLS Ethics Committee for a ruling.

While opinions are not binding on recipients practitioners should be aware of the possible negative consequences of failing to observe them.

The Ethics Committee intends to record all of its significant opinions in a form readily accessible by practitioners.

General

When forwarding applications for rulings or opinions to the NZLS Ethics Committee, District Societies should clearly identify the issues and summarise the arguments on both sides. Care should be taken to ensure that all parties to the issue have been given the opportunity fully to state their cases.

This publication is administered in the Directorate of Standards of the New Zealand Law Society.

Definitions

In this publication:

"**the Act**" means the Law Practitioners Act 1982.

"**the Society**" means the New Zealand Law Society.

"**the District Society**" means the District Law Society in which the Act, these Rules or any other Rules under the Act vest jurisdiction in the particular matter.

"**Barrister sole**" means a practitioner who holds a practising certificate as a barrister only, and practises on his or her own account as a barrister.

"**Counsel**" is used where appropriate to refer to a Practitioner carrying out the functions of counsel.

"**Practitioner**" means any person enrolled as a barrister and solicitor of the Court, as defined by the Act; and unless the context requires otherwise in the case of a practitioner practising on his or her own account or employed by a practitioner so practising, includes any partner, employee or employer of the practitioner.

Chapter 1

Practitioners' Rights, Duties and Responsibilities Generally: Independence of Practitioners: Conflicts of Interest

1.01 Rule

The relationship between practitioner and client is one of confidence and trust which must never be abused.

Commentary

(1) The professional judgment of a practitioner should at all times be exercised within the bounds of the law solely for the benefit of the client and free of compromising influences and loyalties.

(2) The practitioner should never seek an advancement of personal interest or position at the expense of a client.

(3) The relationship of confidence and trust may be breached where a practitioner and client enter into a sexual relationship.

[This Rule 1.01 incorporates the amendment made by NZLS Council resolution on 15 and 16 April 1993 which came into effect on 1 October 1993.]

1.02 Rule

A practitioner as a professional person must be available to the public and must not, without good cause, refuse to accept instructions for services within the practitioner's fields of practice from any particular client or prospective client.

Commentary

(1) It would be improper for a practitioner to accept instructions unless the matter could be handled promptly with due competence and without undue interference by the pressure of other work or other obligations. Instructions for work which is outside the field of competence of a practitioner should be either declined or, with the consent of the client, referred to another practitioner.

(2) The complexities of modern legal practice mean that a practitioner is unlikely to be competent in all fields of practice. A practitioner should not hesitate to explain to a client or a prospective client that the client needs the services of a practitioner more experienced in the appropriate field of practice.

(3) Where the commitments of a practitioner would not allow sufficient time to be devoted to the matter, those commitments would be good cause for refusing to act.

(4) Any refusal to act must not be based on the race, colour, ethnic or national origins, sex or creed of the prospective client.

(5) If a client is eligible for legal aid the practitioner has a duty to draw that fact to the client's attention.

(6) A client should receive the same standard of service whether the client is legally aided or not.

(7) Nothing in this rule or commentary shall prevent a practitioner contracting for a general retainer by accepting a payment in return for which the practitioner remains available to receive instructions from the payer and agrees not to accept instructions that would conflict with that obligation. A barrister sole would need to make a retainer contract through an instructing solicitor.

[Note: at the time of writing new rules 3.05 and 3.06 touching on practioner duties where clients are legally aided or eligible for legal aid have been proposed][1]

---

[1] **Proposed new Rule 3.05**

If a client or prospective client may be eligible for legal aid in a matter where a practitioner proposes to act, the practitioner must investigate whether that person is likely to be eligible. If the practitioner concludes that legal aid may be available, the practitioner must explain the advantages and disadvantages of obtaining a grant of legal aid.

Commentary

1. The advice that the client or prospective client is likely to be eligible for legal aid should preferably be in writing. (That requirement will not apply, however, to duty solicitors when acting in that capacity). It would be good practice for the practitioner to provide a copy of the Legal Services Board's booklet on legal aid.

2. The explanation of the advantages and disadvantages of obtaining a grant of legal aid need not be in writing. Among the matters which should be explained are:

(i) applicable legal aid rates and cappings:
(ii) the advantage of being legally aided with respect to potential liability to pay the other party's legal costs;
(iii) the review of bills by the District Legal Services Sub-Committee;
(iv) the fact that legal aid may cover the cost of mediation;
(v) the statutory charges;
(vi) possible delays in the conduct of the litigation;
(vii) possible restraints placed on expert assistance;
(viii) the fact that in criminal cases counsel of choice is not normally available to a legally aided defendant.

1.03 Rule

A practitioner must not act or continue to act for any person where there is a conflict of interest between the practitioner on the one hand, and an existing or prospective client on the other hand.

Commentary

(1) The rule is based on the premise that a person who occupies a position of trust must not permit his or her personal interests to conflict with the interests of those whom it is that person's duty to protect.

(2) The rule is intended to protect a client in situations where the interest or position of the practitioner would or could make the practitioner's professional judgement less responsive to the interests of the client.

(3) The existence of a personal interest of a practitioner should be disclosed to the client or prospective client irrespective of a perceived lack of conflict. The practitioner should consider carefully whether a personal interest is directly or indirectly in conflict with the interests of the client, and refuse to act if there is any such direct or indirect conflict.

---

3. If the client is likely to be eligible for legal aid and proposes to apply for legal aid, the practitioner is bound to accept instructions on legal aid if he or she is prepared to work at legal aid rates, has the time, and the job is within his or her competence (see Rule 1.02)

4. The practitioner may not offer to act and may not agree to act at the legal aid rate/capped amount instead of making application for legal aid unless the practitioner has complied with Commentary (2) and the client having been so informed has declined to apply.

5. A client should always receive the benefit of the practitioner's best efforts, having regard to the time and funding available

Proposed new Rule 3.06

A practitioner may decline to act where a client will be legally aided if the practitioner believes that:

a. the legal aid rate or the likely legal aid rate is not fair remuneration;

b. the grant of legal aid in the particular case has been capped at an unacceptably low figure.

In declining to act the practitioner must, however, at that time advise that there are other competent practitioners who are likely to be willing and able to do the work on a legal aid basis.

Commentary

1. Declining to act for the reasons stated in this rule constitutes "good cause" for the purposes of Rule 1.02.

As a consequence of these new rules existing Rule 1.02 will be amended by deleting existing Commentaries (5) and (6) and substituting the following as Commentary (5):-

> (5)For legal aid considerations, see Rules 3.05 and 3.06. Declining to act in accordance with Rule 3.06 constitutes "good cause" for the purposes of this rule.

(4) A practitioner may not enter any financial, business or property transaction with a client if there is a possibility of the fiduciary relationship between practitioner and client being open to abuse. This applies even if the practitioner does not propose to act for the client in the particular transaction.

(5) It impossible to detail all the situations which arise where a practitioner should not act or where independent representation or advice must necessarily be obtained under this rule. One example would be where a practitioner borrows money from a client other than a client whose normal business is lending money. It is not then enough to offer independent advice to the client. The solicitor must sever the relationship of solicitor and client in that matter and ensure that the person concerned receives independent and competent advice. If the client refuses to take independent advice, the transaction should not proceed.

(6) The rule will usually apply to any interest or dealing through the practitioner's family or relatives or any company, trust, partnership, or other body in which the practitioner has or exerts a material measure of control or influence. It will also include interests which are not personal in the strict sense but representative in character such as directorships and trusteeships.

(7) In the context of this rule the word "client" must be given an extended meaning. It will, for example, ordinarily include any company, trust, or other body in which the client has a significant interest or exercises a material measure of control.

(8) See also Solicitors Trust Account Regulations 1998, Reg.6.

1.04 Rule
A practitioner shall not act for more than one party in the same transaction or matter without the prior informed consent of both or all parties.

Commentary
(1) A conflict of interest does not exist between parties simply because the practitioner is acting for more than one of them.

(2) A practitioner should exercise careful professional judgement to ensure that a conflict of interest does not exist and is not likely to arise.

(3) It is difficult to guard against conflicts of Interest through clients being represented by different practitioners in the same firm. There is a danger that information may be imparted by one client to a practitioner in the firm to which the firm should not have access, having regard to the interest of another client who is represented by a different practitioner in that firm. Firms should establish systems to prevent such events occurring.

(4) A potential conflict of interest is a situation which without care, could well lead a practitioner into a breach of fiduciary duty.

NOTE: As a corollary to this rule, there is likely to be a conflict in a practitioner acting for an authority, a tribunal, statutory body, parliamentary committee, or other related body, and also appearing for a party before any such body.

[This Rule 1.04 incorporates the amendments made by the NZLS Council resolution of 9 April 1992 which came into effect on 1 August 1992.]

1.05 Rule

A practitioner must not act for a client against a former client of the practitioner when through prior knowledge of the former client or of his or her affairs which may be relevant to the matter, to so act would be or would have the potential to be to the detriment of the former client or could reasonably be expected to be objectionable to the former client.

Commentary

(1) In some circumstances, a practitioner could face a very difficult situation through acting or continuing to act against a former client. Knowledge acquired while acting for the former client is confidential and privileged (see Rule 1.08) and yet the practitioner is bound to disclose information received which relates to a present client's affairs (see Rule 1.09). Such a situation is likely to give rise to a conflict and in those circumstances it is not proper for the practitioner to continue to act.

(2) This rule can apply, for example where a practitioner has acted for:

(i) Both borrower and lender in the transaction;
(ii) A husband and wife;
(iii) Members of a partnership;
(iv) Directors and shareholders in a company;
(v) A number of members of a family;
and is subsequently invited to act for only one or more of those parties against the other party/parties.

(3) In acting for both a lender and a borrower in a loan transaction, notwithstanding the prior informed consent of both or all parties, a practitioner is in a situation of potential conflict. If enforcement steps are taken against the borrower (including the issue of a Section 92 Property Law Act Notice) the practitioner should not continue to act for both or all parties. In some circumstances the only proper course may be to act for neither the borrower nor the lender (whether Nominee Company or otherwise) nor any other parties, such as guarantors, when enforcement steps are taken.

(4) Practitioners are referred for further guidance to:

(i) an article by Miriam R Dean and Christopher F Finlayson - [1990] *NZLJ* 43;
(ii) Re *A Firm of Solicitors* [1992] 1 All ER 353 (CA)

(iii) *Black v Taylor* - [1993] 3 NZLR 403 (CA)

(5) In addition to ethical and common law liability for breach of fiduciary duty, practitioners who use personal information obtained in connection with one client in acting for another may be in breach of the Privacy Act 1993 (refer to information privacy principle 10).

[This Rule 1.05 incorporates the amendments made by NZLS Council resolution on 14 and 15 April 1994 which came into effect on 1 August 1994 and the amendments made by NZLS Council resolution on 8 November 1996 which came into effect on 1 July 1997.]

1.06 Rule

Where a practitioner advises a client on either an appropriate investment of the client's moneys or the borrowing of moneys by a client, the practitioner must act as an independent adviser and where appropriate advise the client on a representative range of investments or sources of loan moneys as the case may be.

Commentary

(1) Without limiting the general application of this rule, its provisions apply to the following circumstances:

(i) where one of the potential lenders to the client is a client of the practitioner or the practitioner's firm, or a solicitors nominee company of which the shares are owned by the practitioner or the practitioner's firm;

(ii) where one possible avenue of investment for the client is a solicitors nominee company of which the shares are owned by the practitioner or the practitioner's firm or another client of the practitioner or the practitioner's firm;

and practitioners must always have regard to the provisions of Rule 1.04.

(2) The provisions of this rule may not apply where a client has, prior to instructing the practitioner, already made firm and specific arrangements independently of the practitioner for an appropriate avenue for the lending or borrowing of money.

(3) Practitioners are referred for further guidance, particularly in regard to the need for the fully informed consent of clients, to the judgment of the Privy Council in *Clark Boyce* v *Mouat* [1993] 3 NZLR 641.

[This Rule 1.06 was adopted by NZLS Council resolution on 9 and 10 April 1992 (initially as Rule 1.11 subsequently renumbered as 1.07 and later again as 1.06) and came into effect on 1 August 1992. It now incorporates the subsequent amendments made by NZLS Council resolution on 14 and 15 April 1994 which came into effect on 1 August 1994.]

1.07 Rule

1. In the event of a conflict or likely conflict of interest among clients, a practitioner shall forthwith take the following steps:

(i) advise all clients involved of the areas of conflict or potential conflict;

(ii) advise the clients involved that they should take independent advice, and arrange such advice if required;

(iii) decline to act further for any party in the matter where so acting would or would be likely to disadvantage any of the clients involved.

2. Once a situation of the type described in paragraph 1.07(1)(iii) arises, it is not acceptable for practitioners in the same firm to continue to act for more than one client in a transaction, even though a notional barrier known as a Chinese Wall may be or may have been constructed. Such a device does not overcome a conflict situation.

Commentary

(1) Practitioners are referred for further guidance to *Farrington* v *Rowe McBride & Partners* [1985] 1 NZLR 83 (CA) and *Clark Boyce* v *Mouat* [1993] 3 NZLR 641 (PC).

(2) In taking the steps under paragraph 1(i) of this rule practitioners should note the duties under Rule 1.08 and under the Privacy Act 1993.

[This Rule 1.07 (formerly Rule 1.05) was adopted by NZLS Council resolution on 14 and 15 April 1994 and came into effect on 1 August 1994 and incorporates the amendments made by NZLS Council resolution on 8 November 1996 which came into effect on 1 July 1997.]

1.08 Rule

A practitioner has a duty to hold in strict confidence all information concerning the business and affairs of the client acquired in the course of the professional relationship, and should not divulge such information except where:

(i) the client expressly or impliedly authorises the disclosure;

(ii) the practitioner is reasonably seeking to establish or collect his or her fee;

(iii) the practitioner is defending himself or his or her associates or employees against an allegation by the client of malpractice or misconduct or against a criminal charge;

(iv) the information relates to the anticipated or proposed commission of a crime (and where the anticipated crime is one involving the possibility of physical injury to another person, disclosure is mandatory);

(v) the information is or has become public knowledge;

(vi) disclosure is required by law;

(vii) disclosure is required by order of a court;

(viii) disclosure to the practitioner's professional indemnity insurer is required in order to maintain or secure the practitioner's cover;
(ix) the practitioner forms the view that there is a serious and imminent risk to the health or safety of the client;
(x) the practitioner has an overriding duty to a court or tribunal.

Commentary
(1) Confidentiality and privilege of client information are among the prime principles of professional practice. A practitioner must bear in mind that confidentiality and privilege belong to the client and not to the practitioner. Generally any request by a third party for personal information held by a practitioner on a client file should be referred to the client or refused pursuant to s.29(1)(f) of the Privacy Act 1993 on grounds that disclosure of the information would breach legal professional privilege.

(2) It is not practical to list all circumstances where disclosure may be required by law. Examples include however:
(i) disclosure of information indirectly arising from compliance with a search warrant issued under s.198 of the Summary Proceedings Act 1957;
(ii) disclosure of information contained in books of account and accounting records where such records are seized pursuant to s.198A of the Summary Proceedings Act; see too s.35A of the Evidence Amendment Act (No.2) 1980;
(iii) disclosure of information to the Commissioner of Inland Revenue in certain circumstances: see ss.17 and 20 of the Tax Administration Act 1994;
(iv) disclosure of information relating to money laundering in certain circumstances: see ss.15 and 19 of the Financial Transactions Reporting Act 1996.

(3) If a practitioner is of the opinion that the information in question is subject to legal privilege or that for some reason an order or warrant requiring disclosure of information ought not to have been made or issued, he or she should discuss with the client the possibility of making an application to have the order or warrant set aside without unlawfully obstructing its execution.

(4) In any circumstances where disclosure is justified, a practitioner should nonetheless be concerned not to divulge more information than is required of him or her for the purpose.

(5) Where exception (iv) applies, the appropriate body to which disclosure should be made is usually the Police and, in cases of urgency or threatened personal injury, the likely victim or his or her solicitor.

(6) Where a practitioner is in possession of information received from joint clients, the consent of both or all the clients is required to waive the duty of confidentiality.

(7) A practitioner practising on his or her own account or as a partner in firm may, unless the client directs otherwise, disclose the client's affairs to partners (if any) and employed practitioners and, to the extent necessary, to employed law clerks, legal executives, non legal staff such as secretaries and filing clerks, and to others whose services are utilised by the practitioner.

(8) A practitioner who is employed by a practitioner practising on his or her own account or by a firm of practitioners may always disclose the client's affairs to his or her employer. Such a practitioner may not agree to accept instructions or directions from the client on any other basis. The extent to which the employer may then, generally or in a specific case, permit further disclosure will be determined by application of paragraph (7) of the commentary to this rule and any further disclosure will be subject to the client's direction otherwise.

(9) Where exception (ix) applies, the practitioner may disclose to a health agency or health professional whatever information is necessary to assist in the care and treatment of the client. Disclosure to others must be only to the extent necessary to minimise the threat to the client's health and safety.

(10) A practitioner's duty continues even after the client has ceased to be the practitioner's client. Following the death of the client or former client, the right to confidentiality passes to the client's personal representatives and can be waived only by them.

(11) Difficulties often arise in relation to a practitioner's duties when a client becomes insolvent. Upon the liquidation or receivership of the company client, authority is vested in the liquidator or receiver, who is entitled to information and documents relating to the company. Authority to permit disclosure to others thereafter vests in the liquidator or receiver. If a practitioner has also acted in the past for directors or shareholders in their personal matters, care must be taken to ensure that confidentiality in respect of such personal matters is maintained.

(12) Where a client is adjudicated bankrupt, the practitioner formerly acting for that person cannot claim privilege if summoned to give evidence under ss.68-70 of the Insolvency Act 1967, as the bankrupt's privilege has passed to the Assignee. Where the bankrupt takes professional advice in relation to the bankruptcy proceedings themselves, however, his or her privilege in this connection does not pass to the Assignee and may be claimed by the bankrupt. In those circumstances, disclosure of information obtained in the course of those instructions would not be authorised.

(13) Information not to be divulged by the practitioner in terms of this rule will include the fact of having been consulted or retained by a person, unless the nature of the matter requires such disclosure.

(14) Rule 8.01 will be relevant where exception (x) applies.

[This Rule 1.08 was adopted by NZLS Council resolution on 11 April 1997 and came into effect on 1 July 1997 and incorporates the subsequent amendments made by NZLS Council resolution of 27 March 1998 which came into effect on 1 May 1998.]

[Note: At the time of writing new rule 1.08A is proposed [2]]

1.09 Rule

In most circumstances, a practitioner is bound to disclose to the client all information received by the practitioner which relates to the client's affairs. There are certain exceptions which include cases where one of the reasons set out in ss.27-29 of the Privacy Act 1993 provides good reason to refuse a request from the client for access.

Commentary

(1) A practitioner should take all reasonable steps to prevent a situation arising where confidential information is received on the basis that it is not to be disclosed to a client.

(2) If a practitioner receives information on a basis of confidence as against the client, then a conflict of interest may have been created. If such a situation seems to have arisen, the practitioner must advise the client of it and of the client's right to seek independent advice. It then becomes a matter of professional judgement on the part of the practitioner as to whether or not to continue to act in the particular transaction in the interests of the client.

---

[2] Proposed new Rule 1.08A :

"A practitioner has a duty to do his or her best to ensure that a valid claim for legal professional privilege is not inadvertently waived or waived without the client's consent."

Commentary

1. A privilege holder can waive his or her privilege directly by intentionally disclosing protected material or consenting to his or her lawyer doing so. He or she can also waive privilege by implication. An implied waiver occurs when, by reason of some conduct on the part of the privilege holder or his or her agent, it becomes unfair to maintain the privilege. The rationale is that the holder of the privilege should not be able to abuse it by using it to create an inaccurate perception of the protected communication. What is fair depends upon the facts of each case. Privilege is waived where a privileged document is made available to an opposing party in litigation. Privilege may also be waived where privileged material is referred to in any affidavit filed in a proceeding by the privilege holder or by his or her agent.

2. The fact that the privilege is the client's privilege means that in cases where a practitioner acts for more than one party, it is necessary to establish which client holds what privilege in respect of which information. If there is a joint privilege, both persons who hold the privilege must consent to the waiver. Even in the case of a joint retainer, however, a communication made to a practitioner exclusively by one of the clients may only be waived by that client.

(3) If having so considered the matter the practitioner decides that it would be wrong to continue to act in the matter, the client must be advised accordingly. The client should be told to seek the services of another practitioner and that the first practitioner in those circumstances will not act in any way against the interests of the person who becomes the former client.

(4) One example of a difficulty which can arise for a practitioner in the observance of this rule, is when in matrimonial proceedings, a practitioner becomes aware of the address of the client's alienated spouse in circumstances where the practitioner knows the alienated spouse would not wish the client to become aware of the address. An undertaking not to disclose an address in such circumstances without the consent of the client could mean that a practitioner is in breach of the rule. Generally as to the disclosure of the address of a client, see Rule 1.10.

(5) While there is a general duty at common law to disclose all material matters to the client, there may be certain circumstances in which it may not be appropriate to disclose all information (see *McKaskell v Benseman* [1989] 3 NZLR 75.)

(6) It is important to note that the fact that fees are outstanding does not provide a good reason to refuse a request for access to personal information. While the Privacy Act 1993 does not prevent a practitioner from claiming a lien over original documents, the client will still be entitled, under that Act, to obtain access to the personal information contained in any file or paper. The client is entitled to insist on receiving a copy of any document containing personal information at reasonable cost notwithstanding that a lien has been claimed.

The following quotations from the judgment of Jeffries J will assist practitioners:

- "A primary obligation of the fiduciary is to reveal all material information that comes into his possession concerned with his client's affairs. The emphasis is on what is material or essential. That is a matter of judgement by the solicitor on the facts of each case, for certainly he is not obliged to pass trifling and insignificant detail."
- "Lawyers, as well as other professional men, as part of their practice, have to convey not infrequently to clients unwelcome, bad, and even at times, devastating information. The greatest care should always be taken on the occasion of such communication, but, nevertheless, it must be done."

[This Rule 1.09 and amended commentary was adopted by NZLS Council resolution on 8 November 1996 and came into force on 1 July 1997.

1.10 Rule

A client's address and any information which might indicate the client's residence or business are part of the confidential information held by a solicitor on behalf of the client. They must not be disclosed without the client's consent.

Commentary

(1) Practitioners should be aware that the standard required under this rule exceeds that in the Privacy Act 1993. A permitted disclosure under one of the exceptions to information privacy principle 11 of that Act may still be in breach of this rule. There are some statutory exceptions for example the Financial Transactions Reporting Act 1996.

[This Rule 1.10 incorporates the amendments made by NZLS Council resolution on 8 November 1996 which came into effect on 1 July 1997.]

1.11 Rule

A practitioner who is a director or member of a body corporate (which term includes, but without any attempt to be exhaustive, a local authority or a public board or authority) must not, without the consent of the body corporate, make use of information received in that capacity to the extent that advantage would result to a client or the practitioner personally and disadvantage to the body corporate.

Commentary

(1) If in a practitioner's capacity as a director or member of a body corporate, the practitioner comes into possession of information detrimental to the body corporate, then the practitioner should not subsequently act for a client in connection with any relevant matter affecting the body corporate.

(2) A practitioner should be careful not to act for a client in circumstances which could give the impression that the practitioner's membership or directorship could be used for the advantage of the client.

(3) A breach of this rule may also involve breaches of principles 10 and 11 of the Privacy Act 1993.

[This Rule 1.11 incorporates the amendments made by NZLS Council resolution on 8 November 1996 which came into effect on 1 July 1997.]

[Note: at the time of writing a new rule 1.12 has been proposed][3]

---

[3] **Proposed new Rule 1.12**

A practitioner who, while in public employment or in national or local politics, had substantial responsibility for confidential information relating to a matter must not, after leaving public employment or politics and returning to legal practice, represent any other party in connection with that matter, without the consent of the practitioner's former public employer, the relevant Minister of the Crown, or the local authority, as the case may be.

1.12 Rule

1. A practitioner must accept legal responsibility for his or her actions. Subject to the following provisions, a practitioner must be prepared to meet any liability arising out of any act, error or omission in the course of the practitioner's professional duties or business. A practitioner shall not exclude by contract his or her liability to a client except as provided by this rule.

2. In order for a practitioner to take advantage of the provisions of this rule permitting limitation of liability the practitioner must:

(i) have in full force and effect valid professional indemnity cover for civil liability (apart from fraud or dishonesty of the practitioner or any partner) arising in New Zealand out of any act, error or omission in the course of the practitioner's professional duties or business:

(a) to a minimum of two million dollars ($2,000,000) per claim per sole practitioner or firm (or such other amount as the Council of the Society may from time to time prescribe); "the stipulated minimum cover"; and

(b) with a deductible (if any) up to a maximum amount of twenty thousand dollars ($20,000) (or such other amount as shall from time to time be prescribed by the Council of the Society) per claim in respect of each sole practitioner or each partner in a firm; and

(c) "providing cover for the fraud or dishonesty of employees to a minimum of $250,000 per claim per sole practitioner or firm (or such other amount as the Council of the Society may from time to time prescribe)", and

(d) providing that all claims arising out of any one act, error or omission are deemed to be one claim; and

(e) meeting any other terms of cover as may be stipulated from time to time by the Council of the Society.

(ii) ensure that the policy effecting the professional indemnity cover is obtained through a sound and reliable brokerage;

(iii) use his or her best endeavours to maintain such cover (with the original or some other insurer) for at least the stipulated minimum cover for at least 6 years from the date of the contract of limitation;

(iv) ensure that the limitation of liability will not be in respect of an amount less than the stipulated minimum cover;

(v) fully advise the client of all aspects of the contract of limitation including:

(a) the actual level of the practitioner's professional indemnity cover or, alternatively, confirmation that the level extends to or exceeds the stipulated minimum cover; and

(b) the minimum terms of cover otherwise required under this paragraph of this rule; and

(c) the practitioner's obligations under this rule.

(vi) ensure the client is aware of the provisions of paragraph (13) of the commentary to this rule.

3. A practitioner must be able, on inquiry by the council of a District Society:
   (i) to demonstrate that any contract of limitation is fair and conscionable, having regard to the parties involved, the nature of the transactions and any other relevant circumstances which were or ought reasonably to have been known or in contemplation when the contract was made;
   (ii) to demonstrate that the practitioner took all reasonable steps to ensure that the client understood and accepted the terms of any contract of limitation;
   (iii) to demonstrate that the practitioner's professional indemnity cover complies with the provisions of paragraph 2 of this rule.

Commentary
(1) The provisions of paragraph 2(i) of this rule represent only the minimum terms of cover which the professional indemnity policy must have for the purposes of this rule. The cover can, of course, be wider. Details of any additional terms of cover stipulated under paragraph 2 (i) (e) will be published, or can be obtained from the Executive Director of the Society.

(2) Although not essential for the purposes of this rule (unless the Council otherwise stipulates at any time), the Council recommends that the terms of cover should preferably include as well:
   (i) Cover for innocent partners against liability arising from the fraud or dishonesty (actual or constructive) of their other partners;
   (ii) Specific cover in respect of activities and functions commonly or sometimes fulfilled by practitioners such as services as directors, secretaries, trustees, executors, personal representatives, receivers, liquidators and officers of charities;
   (iii) Cover in respect of past partners;
   (iv) Provision for a minimum period of notice of 90 days for the exercise of any right of cancellation of the policy, whether by the insurer or the insured;
   (v) Provision that non-disclosure or misrepresentation by the practitioner or anyone else in his or her firm in the insurance proposal will not invalidate the policy in respect of innocent persons not committing or condoning the same.

(3) The broker who arranges professional indemnity cover should preferably be a member of the Corporation of Insurance Brokers of New Zealand.

(4) Paragraph 2 (v) of this rule requires that a practitioner must advise the client of the level of his or her professional indemnity cover or provide confirmation that this extends to or exceeds the stipulated minimum cover required under the rule so that the client is aware of this in the context of any contract of limitation. The rule allows, of course, a higher limitation of liability than the minimum cover stipulated in paragraph 2(i)(a), and also

allows a practitioner to have a higher level of limitation than the professional indemnity cover. On the other hand, the limitation of liability may be for an amount less than a practitioner's professional indemnity cover. However, in all cases a practitioner must otherwise have the minimum terms of cover stipulated in paragraph 2 (i) and make the appropriate disclosure. Paragraph 2(v) also requires the client to be fully informed as to the terms of the rule generally. Accordingly, the client should be made aware of paragraph 2(iii) for instance.

Paragraph 2(vi) requires that the client is made aware of paragraph (13) of this commentary.

(5) If a practitioner wishes to take advantage of the provisions of this rule, it is recommended that he or she obtains a certificate or a written confirmation from his or her brokers that the terms of cover of the policy comply with the terms of paragraph 2 (i). Specific, commonly excluded civil liabilities, (e.g. for a practitioner's trading debts or for loss or damage to property or for death or personal injury) would be acceptable.

(6) The level of the prescribed minimum amount of insurance cover required in order to render limitation of liability by contract ethically acceptable is an indication that the Council considers the element of risk in a transaction must be substantial or unusual before liability for that risk may be limited by contract. Limitation of liability would not normally be appropriate, for instance, for everyday conveyancing or domestic transactions. Where, however, the risks are substantial or unusual or the transaction is likely to be difficult or complex or one involving a large sum of money or high value of property, it may be unreasonable to expect a practitioner to be in a position where the personal assets of the practitioner and his or her spouse or family could be at risk, without the ability to limit that liability. It is also permissible for a practitioner to limit his or her liability on an on-going basis, covering a series of transactions or all transactions.

(7) The reference in paragraph 2(i) of this rule to the requirement that a practitioner must have in full force and effect valid professional indemnity cover for the minimum prescribed amount is intended to ensure that such cover is effective, that the practitioner genuinely believes this to be the case and that he or she has taken all reasonable steps to ensure that such cover will not be denied because of, for instance, material non-disclosure or misrepresentation or non-payment of the premium.

(8) The reference to the requirement that a practitioner must use his or her best endeavours to maintain such cover for at least 6 years, is intended to ensure that cover is available for any claim made during the usual contract/tort limitation period for a claim and that practitioners will maintain such cover, until there are genuine or special reasons precluding this. Such cases are likely to be rare and would have to be justified on inquiry by the Council of a District Society It is, however, obviously desirable that the cover be maintained for longer than 6 years, especially since the breach giving rise

to a claim may not occur and so the relevant limitation period may not commence until an indeterminate time after the contract of limitation has been entered into. Practitioners should also be aware that professional indemnity cover is invariably on a "claims made" basis (i.e. the cover applies to claims notified during the period of the cover, not to when the default giving rise to the claim occurred). Practitioners should also ensure that their obligations under the rule continue to be properly fulfilled consequent upon a dissolution of the firm or the retirement of a partner. The cover need not be effected continuously with the same insurer throughout the period but any policy replacing a previously held policy must be fully retroactive. More than one insurer may be used.

(9) The rule is subject to the general law relating to contracts being voidable or unenforceable as being unfair or unconscionable. The general law relating to the lack of capacity on the part of a contracting party will also be applicable. The rule will also be subject to the general fiduciary obligations of practitioners. A practitioner should also be mindful of other statutory provisions, including in particular the Fair Trading Act 1986, which applies to the provision of services. Further, no limitation will be effective where there has been fraud or theft, or other material dishonesty on the part of the practitioner

(10) The terms of any contract of limitation of liability must be brought clearly to the attention of the client and fully understood and accepted. It would be preferable that they are confirmed in writing. If a practitioner has any doubt about the degree of understanding of the client or the appropriateness of any proposed limitation then the practitioner should see that the client is independently advised. It would be preferable that any such independent advice was appropriately recorded and the acceptance or otherwise of it confirmed in writing. If such independent advice is offered to and declined by the client, again it would be preferable that this be confirmed in writing. The onus will be on a practitioner, on inquiry, to satisfy the Council of a District Society that the client properly understood and accepted the terms of any limitation of liability.

Accordingly, it is suggested that the terms of a contract of limitation should expressly include:

(i) the amount of the limitation of liability;

(ii) the level of the practitioner's professional indemnity cover which is in full force and effect, or confirmation that the cover extends to the required minimum;

(iii) confirmation by the practitioner that the terms of the cover otherwise comply with the requirements of paragraph 2(i) of this rule;

(iv) confirmation as to compliance with the practitioner's obligations, both present and future, under paragraph 2(ii) to (iv) inclusive of this rule;

(v) confirmation that the client understands and accepts the terms of the contract and, if appropriate, that the client has received or has had the opportunity of receiving independent advice about the contract;

(vi) confirmation that the client is aware of and accepts the provisions of paragraph (13) of the commentary to this rule.

It may of course, be appropriate for other matters to be provided for in the contract in any particular case.

(11) Nothing in this rule affects a practitioner's right to seek to limit his or her liability to persons who are not clients.

(12) This rule is not designed to affect the normal ability of a practitioner to qualify any advice or opinion given on a particular matter such that it is made clear that the practitioner is not unreservedly accepting or cannot accept responsibility for the advice or opinion. That may be appropriate, for instance, where the relative law is genuinely uncertain or complex or where there may be unknown material facts.

(13) It should be clearly understood that neither the Society nor any District Society shall be liable for any matter relating to or arising out of this rule or commentary, whether in respect of any contract of limitation or professional indemnity policy or otherwise."

[This Rule 1.12 was adopted by NZLS Council resolution on 27 July 1990 and came into effect on 1 September 1990. It now incorporates the subsequent amendments made by NZLS Council resolution on 3 November 1995 which amendments came into effect on 1 January 1996.]

Chapter 2

Conduct of Practice Generally

2.01 Rule

The name of a practitioner's firm must be one which is not likely to:

(i) be misleading as to the nature or structure of the firm;

(ii) bring the profession into disrepute; or

(iii) be unfair to other practitioners or the public.

Commentary

(1) The name of a firm must be consistent with the requirements of professional standing.

(2) The name of a firm must not be misleading nor should it unfairly describe the firm. It should not, for instance, give an impression to the public that the firm is multi-partnered and broadly based when in fact it might be a very small firm.

(3) When using a name such as Foxton Legal Clinic or Taihape Law Service, care should be taken, if confusion is likely to result, to use an express

disclaimer to show that the office is not a public legal aid agency. The disclaimer should be so worded as to avoid any misleading implications. The same principle would apply if a firm called itself Fairfield Solicitors' Centre unless all solicitors in Fairfield were in fact members of the Centre.

(4) Where a branch or division of a firm is operated under a name different from that of the firm itself, there must be adequate disclosure of the association between the branch or the division, and the firm. An appropriate disclosure would be:

"Eketahuna Conveyancing Centre
-a branch of C D & E,
Barristers & Solicitors,
Masterton"

(5) In cases of doubt whether a name or proposed name comes within the terms of this rule, a practitioner should refer the matter for decision to the council of the District Society.

[This Rule 2.01 incorporates the amendments made by NZLS Council resolution of 15 November 1990 which came into effect on 1 February 1991.]

2.02 Rule

On a firm's letterhead or any other publication or literature issued by a firm, or in an advertisement of a firm's services, a firm must see that neither the public nor other practitioners are misled about the structure of the firm or the status of any person named in such letterhead or publicity.

Commentary

(1) If the names of partners, consultant partners, consultants, or associates or any of them are shown, their status should be indicated.

(2) If a person whose name is included is not a partner, consultant partner, consultant or associate this should be made clear by the use of appropriate expressions such as "legal executive", "office accountant", "practice manager".

(3) A practitioner who holds a practising certificate as a barrister only and is employed by another barrister must not do anything to lead the public or other practitioners to believe that the practitioner is practising as the employer, or as a barrister sole.

(4) A firm must ensure that the public, and other practitioners dealing with a principal or an employee of the firm, should know the name and status of the person with whom they are dealing. A letter should therefore at least show the name of the partner responsible for the matter concerned, or the name and status of the person dealing with it if that person is not the partner responsible. See also the ruling by the Society in Appendix IV.

[This Rule 2.02 incorporates the amendments made by NZLS Council resolution on 14 April 1990 and 15 and 16 November 1990 which came into effect on 14 April 1990 and 1 February 1991 respectively.]

2.03 Rule

1. A practitioner shall not, while the holder of a practising certificate as a barrister or solicitor or as both, engage in a business or professional activity other than the practice of law unless the business or professional activity:
(i) Will not detract or have the potential to detract from the standards of independence and professionalism a client is entitled to expect from a practitioner;
(ii) Does not have nor has the potential to have a harmful effect on the privilege or confidentiality attaching to communications between a practitioner and a client;
(iii) Would not of itself have the potential to create a conflict of interest on the part of a practitioner.

2. If a practitioner intends to engage in a business or activity in terms of paragraph 1 of this rule, and any of the conditions will or may not be complied with, the practitioner must surrender his or her practising certificate to the District Society. If there is doubt as to whether any of the conditions will be complied with, the practitioner must refer the matter to the District Society for a decision as to whether he or she may engage in such business or activity while retaining a practising certificate.

3. Without limiting the general application of paragraph 1 of this rule, a practitioner shall not, while the holder of a practising certificate as a barrister or solicitor or as both, become a partner of a firm or shareholder in a company that practises a profession other than law, or that proposes to practise another profession as well as law, except that practice as a registered patent attorney or as a principal of a firm practising as patent attorneys, shall not be a breach of this rule, so long as the firm practises no profession other than law or that of patent attorneys.

4. Where a practitioner or firm provides or intends to provide to clients, services ancillary to legal services, such ancillary services must be solely in connection with and concurrent to the provision of legal services, and be provided by the practitioner or firm or by an entity in which the practitioner or firm has a controlling interest, so that the activities of a practitioner in the provision of such services will be and remain subject to the provisions of the Act and all rules and regulations made under the Act. The provision of such ancillary services will be subject to the provisions of paragraphs 1 and 2 of this rule.

Commentary

(1) It is important that the public should have confidence in the competence, integrity and accountability of practitioners as members of a largely self-regulating profession. Any diversification of practitioners into fields outside the practice of law will in many circumstances undermine those attributes.

(2) The prohibition in paragraph 3 of this rule against a practitioner becoming a principal of a firm or company that practises a profession other than law, is a recognition that such participation by the practitioner is very likely to lead to a breach of one or more of the conditions set out in paragraph 1.

(3) In not making a general prohibition against a practitioner engaging in a business or professional activity other than the practice of law, paragraph 1 of this rule recognises that some practitioners while practising law, have been so engaged in activities such as company directorships. The central point is that in the interests of the profession and the public, the
practitioner must take scrupulous care to comply with all aspects of this rule. Equally, the Society and the District Societies must be vigilant in seeking to ensure compliance. Practitioners must, of course, also comply with the law in regard to any other business or professional activity. In addition, practitioners should be aware of section 16 of the Real Estate Agents Act 1976, considered in *Real Estate Institute of New Zealand (Incorporated) v Lewis and Callanan.* CA.(242/94) 31.08.95.

[This Rule 2.03 was adopted by NZLS Council resolution on 17 July 1992 and came into effect on 1 February 1993. It now incorporates the subsequent amendments made by NZLS Council resolution on 3 November 1995 which came into effect on 1 January 1996.]

2.04 Rule

A practitioner must ensure that each separate place of business is at all times under effective and competent management by a practitioner who is qualified, in terms of s.55 of the Act, to practise on his or her own account as a solicitor, whether in partnership or otherwise.

Commentary

(1) A practitioner must bear in mind that, irrespective of the status or qualification of an employee of the practitioner or firm, where such employee is responsible for the management of a place of business of the practitioner or firm, no part of this rule or commentary can derogate from the ultimate responsibility of the practitioner who is a principal of a firm or a sole practitioner, for the acts or defaults of the employee. If, therefore, a practitioner who is otherwise qualified and is not a principal of a firm has the management of a place of business of the firm, that practitioner must be under effective and regular supervision by a principal or principals of the firm.

(2) Where because of illness or other similar emergency this rule cannot be complied with, that circumstance shall be reported to the District Society and appropriate arrangements shall then be made to ensure compliance with this rule to as great an extent as possible during the existence of the emergency.

[This Rule 2.04 was adopted by NZLS Council resolution on 11 April 1991 and came into effect on 1 January 1992.]

Chapter 3

Relations: Practitioners and Clients

3.01 Rule

A practitioner shall charge a client no more than a fee which is fair and reasonable for the work done, having regard to the interests of both client and practitioner.

Commentary

(1) Charges must be fair and reasonable in all the circumstances. Practitioners are referred to the Society's Costing and Conveyancing Practice Manual. The "Principles of Charging" set out in the manual are:

> *1. The charges by practitioners for all professional work shall be calculated to give a fair and reasonable return for the services rendered, having regard to the interests of both client and practitioner. Such charges shall take account of all relevant factors and in particular:*
>
> > *(a) the skill, specialised knowledge, and responsibility required*
> > *(b) the time and labour expended*
> > *(c) the value or amount of any property or money involved*
> > *(d) the importance of the matter to the client and the results achieved*
> > *(e) the complexity of the matter and the difficulty or novelty of the questions involved*
> > *(f) the number and importance of the documents prepared or perused*
> > *(g) the urgency and circumstances in which the business is transacted*
> > *(h) the reasonable costs of running a practice.*
>
> *The relative importance of the factors set out above will vary according to the particular circumstances of each transaction.*
>
> *2. A practitioner shall be at liberty to charge less than an amount calculated in accordance with the principles set out in Paragraph 1.*

(2) A practitioner must bear in mind at all times the provisions of Part VIII of the Act dealing with the revision of costs.

(3) A client who expresses dissatisfaction about the amount of a fee and continues to do so after having the matter explained, must be advised of clients' rights under Part VIII of the Act.

(4) The rule is drafted in terms which contemplate the possibility of charging a contingency fee. The following points should, however, be noted in that regard:

> (i) It may be that, in some circumstances at least, the common law rules against maintenance and champerty may still apply, so as to

invalidate an agreement for a contingency fee. In the absence of clear and current authority on the point, the Society draws the possibility of invalidity to the attention of practitioners.
(ii) If, however, a practitioner assumes the validity of a contingency fee arrangement in a particular case, then the quantum of the fee would, nonetheless, be subject to revision under Part VIII of the Act and the provisions of this rule.
(iii) Rule 18 of the International Code of Ethics published by the International Bar Association provides a point of comparison:

> "A contract for a contingent fee, where sanctioned by the law or by professional rules and practice, should be reasonable under all the circumstances of the case, including the risk and uncertainty of the compensation, and subject to supervision of a Court as to its reasonableness."

The attention of practitioners is drawn to *Mills v Rogers* [1899], 18 NZLR 291 (CA)."

[This Rule 3.01 incorporates the amendments made by NZLS Council resolution of 11 April 1991 which came into effect on 1 August 1991.]

3.02 Rule
A practitioner must not receive a reward, whether financial or otherwise, of which a client is unaware, in respect of services rendered to the client.

Commentary
(1) Practitioners must at all times observe the provisions of the Secret Commissions Act 1910 and make appropriate disclosure to a client.

(2) Where a practitioner sends an account to a client and that account includes a payment which has been, or is to be made to an agency company or other body in which the practitioner or members of the practitioner's family has or have an interest, then that interest must be disclosed on the account; and for the purposes of this Commentary the term "practitioner's family" shall include:

(i) The spouse of the practitioner or of any of the practitioner's partners;
(ii) Any child of the practitioner or of any of the practitioner's partners.

(3) Where disbursements are included in an account sent to a client, the disbursements should reflect only actual payments by the practitioner and must not include any undisclosed fee charged by the practitioner.

(4) Practitioners are referred, in relation to inducements to or from third parties, to Rule 4.04.

[This Rule 3.02 incorporates:-
(a) The amendments made by NZLS Council resolution on 5 August 1994 which came into effect on 1 October 1994, and

(b) The amendments made by NZLS Council resolution on 12 April 1995 which came into effect on 1 August 1995.]

3.03 Rule
If a practitioner has reasonable grounds to doubt the bona fides of a client, then the practitioner is entitled to make inquiries, the form and extent of which would be a matter for the professional judgement of the practitioner in the circumstances of each case.

Commentary
(1) In exercising professional judgement under this rule the principles of the Privacy Act 1993 must be complied with. However the application of the Privacy Act is affected by specific provisions in the Financial Transactions Reporting Act 1996 which must be complied with.

[This Rule 3.03 incorporates the amendments made by NZLS Council resolution on 8 November 1996 which came into effect on 1 July 1997.]

3.04 Rule
No practitioner shall give an undertaking or assurance, (whether in writing or otherwise), that moneys invested in any security arranged through the practitioner's trust account will be repaid before the time at which the moneys are due for repayment according to the provisions of the security, or until a definite arrangement has been made for such moneys to be repaid by the borrower or to be advanced on the security by another client.

Chapter 4

Information about Legal Services: Dissemination

4.01 Rule
Advertisements to or any other communications with any person relating to the services of a practitioner or of a firm of practitioners must be consistent with the maintenance of proper professional standards.

Commentary
(1) The advertisement or communication must not be false, misleading or deceptive, or likely to be so.

(2) The advertisement or communication may indicate a field or fields of practice in which the practitioner is prepared to take instructions (but see Rule 4.02 below).

(3) If any advertisement or communication contains or refers to testimonials, endorsements or the like about a practitioner or the services offered, the practitioner must be able to show on inquiry that such testimonials or endorsements were not provided for monetary or other reward. The

genuineness and veracity of any testimonials or endorsements may be tested on inquiry.

(4) The advertisement or communication must not be comparative in relation to other practitioners so as to denigrate them, either individually or as a group. For further reference see Rule 4.03.

(5) The advertisement or communication by a Barrister sole must make it clear that members of the public may instruct a Barrister sole only through a solicitor.

(6) A practitioner must not consent to, nor permit, being mentioned (whether by name or in any other identifiable way), in an advertisement or other promotion by a third party, which is misleading in relation to the legal services offered.

[This Rule 4.01 was adopted by NZLS Council resolution on 11 April 1991 and came into effect on 1 August 1991. It now incorporates the subsequent amendments made by NZLS Council resolution on 14 and 15 April 1994 which came into effect on 1 August 1994.]

4.02 Rule

1. A practitioner must not, in any advertisement to, or any other communication with any person, claim to be a specialist or to have special expertise in any field or fields of practice unless such a claim is capable of verification on inquiry.

2. The council of a District Society may at any time after such a claim has been made, call on the practitioner to verify the claim.

3. The council of a District Society, having considered any material put forward by the practitioner in support of the claim, shall advise the practitioner whether or not it considers the claim has been satisfactorily verified, and if not, the council shall require the practitioner to cease forthwith the making of such a claim.

Commentary

(1) The Society does not have a scheme for certification of specialists. There are, however, practitioners who may properly be described as specialists, whether or not they hold themselves out as such.

(2) A valid claim by a practitioner to be a specialist or to have special expertise in a particular field of practice depends on a number of factors which may be taken into account. While an assessment of a practitioner's claim will depend on the particular facts and circumstances, the following factors may be taken into account in trying to gain an overall impression:

(i) the academic qualifications of the practitioner;

(ii) the number of years of experience the practitioner has had in the field of practice;

(iii) the proportion of the practitioner's total working time involved in the field of practice;
(iv) the level of success achieved by the practitioner in the field of practice;
(v) the importance or significance of the matters in respect of which the practitioner has practised in the field;
(vi) an assessment by a number of the practitioner's peers to establish whether or not the practitioner is regarded by other practitioners as a specialist or as having special expertise in the field of practice;
(vii) such other matters as are relevant in all the circumstances.

(3) A practitioner will therefore need to consider carefully any claim to be a specialist or to have special expertise. Alternative indications such as "practising in the fields of ."or" undertaking legal work in ."may be more accurate and satisfactory". The term "specialist" as used in this rule means "a practitioner having special expertise". The other connotation of the term, to denote "the area in which the practitioner principally practises", would be satisfactorily met by the indication of a field or fields of practice.

[This Rule 4.02 was adopted by NZLS Council resolution on 11 April 1991 and came into effect on 1 August 1991.]

4.03 Rule
In offering services direct to members of the public other than by normal advertising channels, a practitioner must ensure that approaches to persons who are not existing clients, are made in a manner which does not bring the profession into disrepute. Approaches must be made in accordance with proper professional standards and not in a way that is intrusive, offensive, or inappropriate.

Commentary
(1) A direct approach should not misrepresent the standard of services provided by other practitioners or firms or by the practitioner.

(2) An approach by a barrister sole must be made clearly on the basis that a client can instruct a Barrister sole only through a solicitor.

(3) The manner of such approaches, their frequency and the surrounding circumstances may be taken into account in assessing the propriety of the practitioner's actions.

4.04 Rule
A practitioner must not directly or indirectly offer to, or receive from, a third party, a reward or inducement, whether financial or otherwise, in respect of services rendered or to be rendered to the client.

Commentary
(1) A financial arrangement between a practitioner and a third party whereby that third party refers work to the practitioner or is recommended by the

practitioner, is likely to involve a conflict of interest, with a practitioner having loyalties to both the client and the third party. That conflict of interest will often be irremediable under Rule 1.07.

(2) Although the rule is cast in absolute terms there is a line to be drawn between two situations. While the offering of direct payments or benefits for the advancing of work is proscribed, it is not intended that the rule should prohibit the usual professional associations that develop between practitioners and third parties, i.e. those associations which may involve social exchanges, the mutual referrals of work, or small gifts such as calendars or pens. There could, nevertheless, be instances where indirect benefits may create a conflict of interest, or involve a breach of Rule 1.01.

(3) Practitioners must at all times observe the provisions of the Secret Commissions Act 1910 and make appropriate disclosures to a client. For further reference see Rule 3.02.

[This Rule 4.04 was adopted by NZLS Council resolution on 5 August 1994 and came into effect on 1 October 1994.]

4.05 Rule
A practitioner may not, without the specific consent of a client, give any interview or make any public statement relating to the client or the affairs of the client, whether or not the client is involved in a matter of public knowledge.

Commentary
(1) The solicitor/client privilege may not be broken without the consent of the client. That consent is not something to be obtained by representatives of the news media. It is to be given only after proper discussion between the practitioner and the client.

4.06 Rule
A practitioner must not, either by advertisement or personal representation, give clients or the general public the impression that the practitioner is running a financing or banking business rather than or as well as providing legal services.

Commentary
(1) If a practitioner wishes to advertise that moneys are available for investment, the advertisement must make it clear that the moneys belong to the clients of the practitioner and not the practitioner.

(2) Any reference to a solicitor's nominee company must refer to it being a bare trustee which does not borrow money or lend money in its own right.

(3) If a client wishes to borrow money, it is permissible for the practitioner to advertise on the client's behalf indicating the amount required and the type of security that will be available.

Chapter 5

Handling of Clients' Moneys

5.01 Rule

A practitioner must observe strictly the requirements of:

(i) Part VI of the Law Practitioners Act 1982
(ii) the Solicitors' Trust Account Regulations 1998
(iii) the Solicitors' Trust Account Rules 1996
(iv) the Solicitors Nominee Company Rules 1996

Commentary

(1) Failure to comply with the above requirements may amount to professional misconduct.

[This Rule 5.01 was adopted by NZLS Council resolution on 27 March 1998 and came into effect on 1 May 1998.]

5.02 Rule

There is a continuing obligation on a practitioner to ensure that the solicitor's nominee company operated by the practitioner is at all times conducted in accordance with all rules, rulings and directions of the Society relating to such companies and from time to time in force, and also in accordance with the provisions contained in the Company Constitution.

Commentary

(1) Failure to comply with the above requirements may amount to professional misconduct.

(2) The obligations of the Solicitors' Nominee Company Rules 1996 apply to each practitioner whose firm operates a solicitor's nominee company whether or not that practitioner personally is actively involved in the operation of the solicitor's nominee company.

(3) Guidance notes have been promulgated for practitioners to assist them in observing the Solicitors' Nominee Company Rules. Practitioners have a duty to be fully conversant with these notes and to be aware of their importance in the proper operation of the nominee company.

[This Rule 5.02 was adopted by NZLS Council resolution on 27 March 1998 and came into effect on 1 May 1998.]

5.03 Rule

A practitioner instructed on behalf of any person to invest money within the meaning of S.169A of the Act (except where Section 169A(4) applies) shall advise that person that the Solicitors' Fidelity Guarantee Fund shall not be applied in reimbursing any person for any loss relating to that money.

Commentary
(1) The enactment of S.169A of the Act in 1993 substantially reduced the degree of protection afforded by the Solicitors' Fidelity Guarantee Fund under the provisions of Part IX of the Act and it is important that any person (whether or not a client) instructing a practitioner to invest money within the meaning of S.169A is made adequately aware of the implications of that provision prior to investing.

[This Rule 5.03 (then numbered 5.04) was adopted by NZLS Council resolution on 23 July 1993 and came into effect on 1 October 1993.]

Chapter 6

Relations Between Practitioners

6.01 Rule
A practitioner must promote and maintain proper standards of professionalism in relations with other practitioners.

Commentary
(1) A practitioner shall treat professional colleagues with courtesy and fairness at all times but consistent with the overriding duty to the client.

(2) No practitioner shall discriminate against or treat unfairly any other practitioner by reason of the colour, race, ethnic or national origin, sex, marital status or religious or ethical belief of that other practitioner.

(3) There are many occasions when a practitioner needs to rely on information given by another practitioner. Professionalism demands that such reliance should not be misplaced. Whether the information is given in writing, or orally, or is in the form of an oral or written undertaking, the practitioner receiving the information or undertaking is entitled to be able to rely and act on it with impunity.

(4) Wherever possible oral undertakings should be avoided in favour of written undertakings - see Rule 6.07(2) following.

(5) Practitioners should not communicate or correspond in an atmosphere of acrimony or discourtesy notwithstanding the nature of the relationship between their respective clients.

(6) While it is not always possible to take telephone calls from another practitioner, such calls should be returned at the earliest opportunity.

(7) It is an invasion of a person's privacy to tape a conversation without that person's consent. It is unprofessional and discourteous for one practitioner to do so in respect of another practitioner or an employee of another practitioner. If a practitioner wishes a conversation by telephone or otherwise

to be taped the specific consent of the other practitioner or employee must first be obtained. Practitioners should also note privacy principles 2 to 4 of the Privacy Act 1993.

[This Rule 6.01 incorporates the amendments made by NZLS Council resolution on 8 November 1996 which came into effect on 1 July 1997.]

6.02 Rule
It is only in very exceptional cases that a practitioner should communicate either directly or in writing with the client of another practitioner in relation to a matter in which the practitioner is, or has previously been dealing with the other practitioner.

Commentary
(1) A practitioner may suggest to a client that an approach by that client to the other practitioner's client might be appropriate or useful.

(2) If a practitioner has tried unsuccessfully for a reasonable period to obtain a response from the other practitioner in the matter, then it may be appropriate for the client of that other practitioner to be approached. This action should, however, be regarded as most unusual and be used only in extreme circumstances. In any event, the action should be taken only after advice to the other practitioner of the practitioner's intention to do so.

6.03 Rule
Subject always to the rights and duties pertaining to practitioner and client privilege there is generally an obligation on every practitioner who has grounds to suspect defalcations or other improper acts by another practitioner to make a confidential report at the earliest possible time to the President or the Council of the District Society.

Commentary
(1) A practitioner may receive information in professional confidence from a practitioner who is a client. In any such case the practitioner/client privilege applies and there is a duty of silence imposed on the practitioner. A practitioner should where appropriate encourage a client to consent to disclosure to the President or Council of the District Society unless such encouragement is contrary to the practitioner's professional duty to the client.

(2) A somewhat similar situation exists with the FRIEND system operated by some District Societies. A member of the FRIEND panel might receive in confidence from a fellow practitioner, information that should be reported to the District Society. The member of the panel should, in such a circumstance, advise either disclosure by the other practitioner or that the other practitioner should take advice on a full professional basis. Members of such panels may have to consider whether the fellow practitioner should be advised that full practitioner/client privilege attaches to their communications right from the outset.

(3) It is not possible to itemise all the indications there might be of improper conduct on the part of a practitioner, but such circumstances as an extravagant mode of living, an undue involvement in property transactions, the dishonour of cheques or delay or procrastination in effecting settlements might be sufficient to indicate that all is not well with the practitioner's practice or with the practitioner's firm.

(4) If a practitioner does give his or her name, or other information which might enable identification, that information may, under the Privacy Act 1993, be available to the practitioner to whom the allegation relates.

[This Rule 6.03 incorporates the amendments made by NZLS Council resolutions on 8 November 1996 and 11 April 1997 which came into effect on 1 July 1997.]

6.04 Rule

Unless there are exceptional circumstances, a practitioner shall not:

(i) Stop a trust account cheque drawn on a solicitor's trust account payable to another practitioner; or

(ii) Stop a bank cheque payable to another practitioner; or

(iii) Cancel or reverse or amend an order for payment made to another practitioner by means of electronic transfer from a solicitor's trust account;

once the cheque or printed verification of the electronic transfer instructions has been handed or despatched to the other practitioner.

Commentary

(1) The circumstances that would justify stopping such a cheque, or cancelling or reversing or amending such an order for payment, would need to be truly exceptional. Such a step is not likely to be justified in the absence of clearly proper and legal grounds for doing so.

[This Rule 6.04 was adopted by NZLS Council resolution on 8 November 1991 and came into effect on 1 January 1992.]

6.05 Rule

A client has an unequivocal right to change from one practitioner to another.

Commentary

(1) A practitioner has no proprietary interest in a client. It is permissible to inquire why a client is changing but it is not permissible to exert persuasion, influence or pressure on the client to return to the practitioner.

(2) On a change of practitioner an authority to uplift specific documents should be acted upon without undue delay subject only to any lien that the holding practitioner may claim. It is however recognised that documents may be required for a short time for costing purposes.

(3) Even when a practitioner does have a lien over documents the urgency of a situation may demand that as a matter of courtesy, that practitioner will make the documents available to the client's new adviser on receipt of an appropriate undertaking as to the payment of the practitioner's fee. Where a client requests copies of documents containing personal information the lien cannot be relied upon to refuse the request (see rule 1.09)

(4) Efforts should be made in the interests of the former client and of the profession to facilitate the transfer of files on a change of practitioner. There could be circumstances, such as a revision of costs, where delays might occur which would be harmful to the client's interest unless the file was handed to the new practitioner against appropriate undertakings.

(5) A circumstance might arise where the practitioner whose client wishes to change to another practitioner, has given undertakings to settle and pay settlement moneys and hand over documents. In such a situation, a practitioner should decline to hand over documents and moneys to the new practitioner until he or she receives from the new practitioner a personal written undertaking to honour the terms of the undertaking already made.

(6) Practitioners are referred to the following references which might assist to clarify situations as they arise:

(i) Documents and Papers Being Handed Over

- Halsbury - Laws of England
- Cordery on Solicitors
- "The Guide to the Professional Conduct of Solicitors", The Law Society (England and Wales)
- *Marshall v Macalister* [1952] NZLR 278
- "Ownership and retention of legal records and files - guide lines" by the Society's Property Law and General Practice Committee published in "LawTalk" 400 on 6 September 1993 These guidelines reflect an opinion by Mr. R.P. Smellie Q.C. which is available from the Society.

(ii) Liens for Unpaid Costs

- Halsbury - Laws of England
- Cordery on Solicitors
- "The Guide to the Professional Conduct of Solicitors", The Law Society (England and Wales)
- "Privacy Act v Solicitors Lien", article in LawTalk 452 April 1996, page 11.

[This Rule 6.05 incorporates the amendments made by NZLS Council resolution on 8 November 1996 which came into effect on 1 July 1997.]

6.06 Rule

Where a practitioner becomes aware of a potential claim for negligence, the practitioner must advise the client to seek independent advice in connection with the matter, and must inform the client that the practitioner can no longer act in the matter unless the client, having been independently advised, requests it.

Commentary

(1) A practitioner is entitled to ensure while informing the client of the client's
rights, that the practitioner does not make any statement that may prejudice any insurance cover held by the practitioner.

(2) A practitioner who is requested to hand the relevant papers to a new practitioner instructed by the client should, as a matter of prudence, take copies of relevant papers which may be material in the practitioner's defence.

6.07 Rule

Every practitioner has a professional duty to honour an undertaking, written or oral, given in the course of legal proceedings or in the course of practice; and this rule applies whether the undertaking is given by the practitioner personally or by a partner or employee in the course of the practice.

Commentary

(1) The honouring of an undertaking involves the joint and several responsibility and liability of all the partners of a firm.

(2) While a professional undertaking may be given in writing or orally, it is prudent for practitioners to express an undertaking in writing if it is at all practicable. An oral undertaking has the same effect as one in writing but may raise evidential problems as to its content or existence.

(3) If circumstances require an oral undertaking to be given, it may be that a contemporaneous note, transcript or written confirmation recorded by either practitioner may be necessary as conclusive proof of its existence. If the recipient confirms or accepts the terms of an oral undertaking and these are not promptly repudiated by the giver of the undertaking, this would be likely to constitute sufficient evidence of the existence and terms of the undertaking.

(4) An undertaking should be given expressly and not merely by implication. For example, a vendor's practitioner's undertaking that rates will be paid on settlement should be express rather than implied from a settlement statement.

(5) If a practitioner gives an undertaking "on behalf of my client X", the practitioner may in some circumstances be held liable personally on the undertaking and not the client X. Practitioners should be very careful about accepting undertakings worded in that way. The result might be that the undertaking is found to bind neither the practitioner nor the client.

(6) A practitioner should try to ensure that an undertaking is precise and unambiguous in its terms An ambiguous undertaking will generally be construed in favour of the recipient.

(7) A practitioner may not escape liability on an undertaking by pleading that to honour it would be a breach of a duty owed to the practitioner's client.

(8) Practitioners are referred to:

(i) *Udall v Capri Lighting Ltd (in liquidation)* [1988] QB 907
(ii) *John Fox v Bannister. King and Rigbeys (Note)* [1988] QB 925
(iii) *AGC v Brewster & Ors - Fisher J Rotorua* CP92/89 19-12-89

The cases consider the inherent jurisdiction of the Court to control solicitors, a jurisdiction which arises from their role as officers of the Court. In New Zealand this jurisdiction is also affected by legislation. he judgments concern losses suffered by clients following a practitioner's failure to honour an undertaking. It is noted that the judgments "re-emphasise the importance of solicitors' undertakings, and that they should be neither given nor treated lightly". In the New Zealand context, regard should be had to Part VII (ss. 94 & 138) of the Act.

(9) A practitioner should be aware of the power of the Court in particular cases to compel the performance of an undertaking.

See:

(i) *Re McDougall's Application [1982]* NZLR 141
Per Hardie Boys J.

- "The undertaking was incapable of being performed and for that reason the Court would not enforce it."
- "The jurisdiction is based upon the right of the Court to insist and require that its officers observe a high standard of conduct. It is a jurisdiction of punitive and disciplinary nature and does not exist for the purpose of enforcing legal rights (*Re Grey* [1892] 2 QB 440). It is a summary jurisdiction, by which the solicitor is deprived of many of the advantages of a defendant in a trial. Therefore it ought to be exercised only in a clear case *(Geoffrey Silver and Drake v Baines* [1971] 1 All ER 473, 475; [1971] 1 QB 396, 402, per Lord Denning MR)."

(ii) - *National Westminster Finance New Zealand Ltd v Bryant* [1989] 1 NZLR 513 where Smellie J. followed McDougall. but ordered performance of the undertaking.

[This Rule 6.07 incorporates the amendments made by NZLS Council resolution on 11 April 1991 which came into effect on 1 August 1991.]

6.08 Rule

A practitioner who instructs another practitioner in the role of counsel or in any other capacity in any matter shall, unless agreement to the contrary is reached, become responsible personally for the prompt and full payment of the fee of the instructed practitioner.

Commentary

(1) This rule must be read subject to the right of the instructing practitioner's client to require the fee to be revised under Part VIII of the Act.

(2) A practitioner may not delay payment because the client has not paid the amount of the fee to the practitioner.

(3) The relationship of the practitioner to the instructed practitioner is that of a professional client, who may be looked to for the fee accordingly.

(4) Practitioners are referred to Rule 11.08 for guidance as to the duties of counsel in relation to fees.

(5) If a practitioner needs to instruct another to appear on a matter, the client's prior consent should be obtained. Principles 3 and 11 of the Privacy Act 1993 may be relevant. In exceptional cases where alternative counsel need to be instructed urgently to avoid sudden non representation, the exception to those principles which permit actions necessary for the conduct of court proceedings may possibly apply.

(6) Practitioners are referred for further guidance to *Atkinson v Pengelly & Ors* [1995] 3 NZLR104.

[This Rule 6.08 incorporates the amendments made by NZLS Council resolution on 8 November 1996 which came into effect on 1 July 1997.]

6.09 Rule

1. A practitioner (practitioner A) closely related to another practitioner (practitioner B) shall not act for a client in a matter directly adverse to a person who practitioner A knows is represented by practitioner B, except upon consent by the client after consultation regarding the relationship.

2. For the purposes of this rule:

   (i) two practitioners are closely related if one is to the other the parent or sibling or if they are married or living as partners on a domestic basis;

   (ii) a practitioner is not to be regarded as "acting for a client" solely because a partner in his or her firm or an employee reporting to another partner in his or her firm is acting for that client. This rule applies only where the practitioner with the close relationship is himself or herself engaged in the matter, whether directly or as supervisor or adviser.

3. Where practitioner A and practitioner B are both retained by their respective clients before the conflict is known, then, in the absence of clients' consent to their continuing to act, the practitioner retained later in time shall cease to act. With the client's consent, that practitioner may hand the instruction to another partner in his or her firm (if any), provided that the practitioner so handing does not thereafter in any way act for the client. The

problem is not resolved, however, by the practitioner briefing counsel if the practitioner continues to act as instructing solicitor.

Commentary

(1) The relationship between two practitioners, even thought not of a character as to bring it within this rule, may be such as to render it unwise for one or both to continue to act in a matter because of perceived conflict.

[This Rule 6.09 was adopted by NZLS Council resolution on 27 March 1998 and came into effect on 1 May 1998.]

Chapter 7

Relations with Third Parties

7.01 Rule

A practitioner, when acting for a client in a matter where the other party is acting in person, should treat the other party with courtesy and fairness.

Commentary

(1) Where the other party submits a document that is faulty in some respects the practitioner may within reasonable limits amend the document and advise the other party accordingly.

(2) Where, however, the document is deficient to the extent that it cannot be rectified by a few simple amendments, the practitioner is entitled to and should return it to the party with an appropriate covering letter.

(3) If a practitioner has reason to believe that another party to a conveyancing transaction is represented by a person unqualified in terms of S. 65 of the Act the proper course is for the practitioner to refuse to deal with such person.

(4) A practitioner should not request an unrepresented party to execute a contract or other document under circumstances known to the practitioner that will place that unrepresented party in an unfair position through being unsure or unclear as to the entitlement to take legal advice, or having had no opportunity to seek legal advice.

7.02 Rule

A practitioner has a duty, subject to availability, to administer oaths or take declarations, but must not do so in respect of a contentious matter or proceeding in which the practitioner is involved .

Commentary

(1) When administering an oath or taking a declaration the practitioner must while the person is present:

(i) make sure the person is who he or she says

(ii) ascertain if the deponent or declarant knows what is being declared or sworn

(iii) check with the person the exhibits noted in the document.

(2) A practitioner should when taking affidavits also have regard to the requirements of the High Court Rules. See Part V of the Second Schedule to the Judicature Act 1908.

(3) A practitioner only administering an oath or only taking a declaration is not responsible for the contents of the document and need not read it.

(4) If for good reason, extraneous or otherwise, the practitioner suspects an affidavit or declaration to be false then the practitioner should decline to administer the oath or take the declaration as the case may be.

(5) It is not acceptable for a practitioner to take an oath or declaration in the absence of the deponent, nor is it acceptable for a practitioner to request another practitioner to do so.

7.03 Rule

A practitioner who:-

(i) instructs another person, for example an accountant, valuer or engineer to prepare an assessment valuation or report or to provide other services; or

(ii) engages an expert witness

shall, in the absence of any agreement to the contrary, be liable for the prompt payment of the proper fee of the person so instructed, or the witness, as the case may be.

Commentary

(1) Except where the matter is funded on legal aid the practitioner is not relieved from liability merely because the client or a third party has not paid the amount of the fee to the practitioner. In the absence of agreement with the person so instructed or the witness ("the instructed person"), the practitioner has personal responsibility for payment.

(2) Practitioners should be precise as to fee arrangements at the time the instructed person is retained. Where a fee or formula for fixing a fee (eg. an hourly rate) has been agreed in advance, then that agreed fee or a fee fixed in accordance with that formula will be the proper fee for which the practitioner will be responsible under this rule, Otherwise the proper fee is the instructed person's reasonable fee. If there is a dispute about the reasonableness of the fee, the practitioner should promptly pay the amount which the practitioner considers reasonable and attempt to negotiate prompt settlement of any balance.

(3) Where the matter is funded on legal aid, the practitioner should inform the instructed person of that fact at the outset. The instructed person should be asked to supply his or her terms of engagement and an estimate of the cost.

The practitioner should then refer the proposed terms to the relevant District Legal Services Subcommittee for approval. Once that approval is obtained, the practitioner must inform the instructed person of the full terms of that approval and the terms of payment. The practitioner should also inform the instructed person that his or her liability for the instructed person's fee will be limited to the amount paid by the District Legal Services Subcommittee in terms of the approval given or any subsequent increase approved. The instructed person should be informed that there may be some delay in having any invoice paid. The practitioner is responsible for promptly referring any invoice from the instructed person to the relevant District Legal Services Subcommittee.

(4) All fee arrangements with an instructed person should be in writing.

(5) The provisions of this rule will also apply in circumstances where a practitioner has made a personal commitment to be responsible for the fees and expenses of a non-expert witness.

[This Rule 7.03 incorporates the amendments made by NZLS Council resolution on 27 March 1998 and came into effect on 1 May 1998. It now incorporates the former Rule 8.03.]

7.04 Rule

A practitioner must make all reasonable efforts to ensure that legal processes are used for their proper purposes only and that their use is not likely to cause unnecessary embarrassment, distress or inconvenience to another person's reputation, interests or occupation.

Commentary

Examples of the operation of the rule are:

(1) A practitioner should not issue a statutory demand under s.218, Companies Act 1955, knowing that the debt is bona fide disputed, and should make reasonable inquiry from the client as to the existence of any such dispute.

(2) A practitioner should not register a notice of interest under s.42, Matrimonial Property Act 1976, or a caveat under s.137, Land Transfer Act 1952, knowing that there is no "registrable interest" on the part of the client to be protected pursuant to either Act, and should make reasonable inquiry from the client as to the existence of any such interest.

(3) A practitioner, in arranging service of a document on a person, has a clear duty to the client to make all reasonable efforts to effect service promptly or to seek substituted service, but the practitioner must try to effect service in such a manner and at such a place as to avoid causing the person being served unnecessary embarrassment and as to avoid as far as possible any damage to the person's reputation, interests or occupation.

(4) As to service in New Zealand generally, see Rules 192-218, High Court Rules.

[This Rule 7.04 was adopted by NZLS Council resolution on 9 April 1992 and came into effect on 1 August 1992.]

Chapter 8

Court Proceedings and Practice

8.01 Rule

In the interests of the administration of justice, the overriding duty of a practitioner acting in litigation is to the court or the tribunal concerned. Subject to this, the practitioner has a duty to act in the best interests of the client.

Commentary

(1) A practitioner must never deceive or mislead the court or the tribunal.

(2) The practitioner must at all times be courteous to the court or the tribunal.

(3) The practitioner, whilst acting in accordance with these duties, must fearlessly uphold the client's interests, without regard for personal interests or concerns.

(4) The practitioner has an obligation when conducting a case to put all relevant authorities known to the practitioner, whether decided cases or statutory provisions, before the court - whether they support the practitioner's case or not.

(5) If a point of law which affects the case is discovered by the practitioner some time after the hearing but before the decision has been given, the practitioner has a duty to bring it to the attention of the court and to provide a copy of the reference to the practitioner acting for the other party or parties in the matter.

(6) See also Practice Note [1968] NZLR 608 regarding the correct procedure as to submitting further information to the court after the conclusion of the hearing.

(7) A practitioner should not make any statement to the news media relating to proceedings which have not been concluded, which may have the effect or may be seen to have the effect of interfering with a fair trial.

(8) In this area generally practitioners should be aware of the law relating to contempt of court, and the severe sanctions that can be imposed.

The following points should be specifically noted:

(i) A publication will amount to contempt if it is likely to prejudice the trial or conduct of the action.
(ii) A publication may constitute a contempt if it is likely to interfere with the proper adducing of evidence, either by discouraging witnesses from coming forward or by influencing them in the evidence that they are prepared to give. An example would be a publication attacking or criticising a witness or disparaging a party in proceedings.
(iii) Contempt of court in a civil action extends also to conduct that is calculated to inhibit suitors from availing themselves of their right to have their legal rights determined by the courts. An example would be a publication which is likely to bring pressure to bear on one or other of the parties to an action so as to prevent that party form prosecuting or defending the action.
(iv) In criminal proceedings it is a serious contempt to publish the criminal record of an accused, or to comment on the previous bad character of the accused or to publish a confession. It is also a contempt to publish any comment which imputes guilt to or asserts the innocence of a particular accused.
(v) In general no publication can amount to a contempt of court in proceedings unless at the date of the publication the proceedings are either pending or imminent. A prosecution may be said to be pending at any time after a person has been charged or if it is obvious at the date of the publication that a suspect is about to be charged. It remains pending until the proceedings are finally concluded and no further appeal is possible. Civil proceedings are pending immediately the originating documents are filed in the Court. A contempt may be committed until an appeal has been heard or the time within which an appeal may be lodged has expired.

(9) Whether or not civil or criminal proceedings are pending or imminent, a practitioner must not discuss a client's affairs without his or her consent: see Rule 4.05 and Commentary (1).

[This Rule 8.01 incorporates the amendments made by NZLS Council resolution on 14 and 15 April 1994 which came into effect on 1 August 1994 and the amendments made by NZLS Council resolution on 27 March 1998 which came into force on 1 May 1998.]

[At the time of writing there are proposed a new rules 8.01A and 8.01B] [4]

[4] **Proposed New Rule 8.01A**
It is a breach of a practitioner's duty to the Court and an abuse of process for a practitioner to allow a client to claim privilege in the absence of reasonable grounds for doing so.
Commentary
1.Legal professional privilege exists to protect the confidentiality of:-
(a)Communications of a professional nature passing between practitioners and their clients the dominant purpose of which is the seeking or giving of

8.02 Rule
A practitioner must exercise care in court about naming persons not involved in the proceeding, and must refrain particularly from making scandalous or unnecessary allegations against such persons.

Commentary
(1) If it is necessary to name a person in a way which, if published, might damage that person's reputation or character, the court should be asked to receive the name and information confidentially in writing or in chambers.

(2) A practitioner must also bear in mind the power of the court to prohibit publication of a particular part of evidence given in a case where potentially damaging evidence has been given without there having been a prior application to receive it in confidence.

(3) Practitioners who disclose personal information which is not necessary for the conduct of court proceedings may be in breach of privacy principle 11 of the Privacy Act 1993.

[This rule incorporates the amendments made by NZLS Council resolution on 6 November 1996 and came into force on 1 July 1997.]

8.03 Rule
Subject to the interests of the client, a practitioner must in the conduct of litigation, as in all legal dealings, treat other practitioners with courtesy.

Commentary
(1) Except in cases of urgency or where an ex parte application is justified, a practitioner must not discuss the merits of a case or matter with the judge or other presiding officer either formally or informally, without the consent of the other practitioner; and such discussion should be held only in the presence of the other practitioner unless he or she consents otherwise. In any event,

---

legal advice as to rights or obligations (commonly known as "solicitor client privilege"); and

(b)Information brought into being by practitioners or clients for the dominant purpose of use in current or anticipated litigation (commonly known as "litigation privilege").

2.Legal professional privilege does not attach to communications between a practitioner and a client made confidentially for the purpose of legal advice if that advice is sought or given in furtherance of or to facilitate, criminal, fraudulent or other unlawful purposes. This is irrespective of whether the practitioner was a party to or ignorant of those purposes.

Proposed new Rule 8.01B
It is in breach of a practitioner's duty to the Court and an abuse of process for a practitioner knowingly to fail to discover a relevant document
Commentary
(1) Practitioners are reminded that the duty to discover relevant documents is a continuing one up to and including the time of judgment.

natural justice demands that generally there should not be unilateral communications with a court or other tribunal.

(2) Disparaging or derogatory remarks or comments are not to be made in court or in chambers about another practitioner.

[This Rule 8.03 was previously numbered 8.04.]

8.04 Rule
A practitioner must not attack a person's reputation without good cause.

Commentary
(1) This rule applies equally both in court during the course of proceedings and out of court by inclusion of statements in documents which are to be filed in the court.

(2) A practitioner should not be a party to the filing of a pleading or other court document containing an allegation of fraud, dishonesty, undue influence, duress or other reprehensible conduct, unless the practitioner has first satisfied himself or herself that such allegation can be properly justified on the facts of the case. For a practitioner to allow such an allegation to be made, without the fullest investigation, could be an abuse of the protection which the law affords to the practitioner in the drawing and filing of pleadings and other court documents. Practitioners should also bear in mind that costs can be awarded against a practitioner for unfounded allegations of fraud.

(3) If necessary, a practitioner must test the instructions which have been given, by independent inquiry, before making such allegations.

(4) Practitioners are referred for further guidance to:
(i) *Gazley v Wellington District Law Society* [1976] 1 NZLR 452,
(ii) *McKaskell v Benseman* [1989] 3 NZLR 75

[This Rule 8.04 was previously numbered 8.05.]

8.05 Rule
No practitioner engaged in a proceeding, criminal or civil, has the sole right to call or discuss the case with a witness.

Commentary
(1) If an expert witness has, to a practitioner's knowledge, been retained by the other party, the practitioner should not without the consent of the practitioner acting for the other party, approach the expert witness. To do so could possibly lead the expert witness into a breach of fiduciary duty.

(2) Subject to paragraph (1) above, it is permissible for a practitioner acting for one party to interview a witness or prospective witness at any stage prior

to the hearing whether or not that witness has been interviewed by the practitioner acting for the other party or called as a witness.

(3) Practitioners acting as defence counsel are referred to Rule 10.08.

(4) A practitioner who calls a witness at a hearing may discuss matters with the witness at any stage up to the commencement of cross-examination. If discussion with the witness is sought during the course of cross-examination or re-examination, this can only be permitted with the consent (for good reason) of the judge and opposing counsel. This applies even during adjournments of the hearing.

[This Rule 8.05 was previously numbered 8.06.]

8.06 Rule
A practitioner must not act as both counsel and witness in the same matter.

Commentary
(1) If there is any reason for a practitioner to think that he or she may be required as a witness in a matter, the practitioner should decline to act as counsel.

(2) The same principle applies to making an affidavit in a contentious matter where the practitioner is acting as counsel.

(3) If, having started to act as counsel, the practitioner finds it necessary to make an affidavit in respect of the matter concerned, then the practitioner must immediately retire from the position of counsel, unless the court, in the particular circumstances, directs that it is still appropriate for the practitioner to continue to act.

(4) Even where an affidavit might appear to be in respect of a formal or non-contentious fact, it is prudent for the practitioner to have it made and sworn by some other person.

(5) Where a practitioner, having already accepted instructions as counsel, becomes aware that a partner or employee of the practitioner might be called as a witness for the client, the practitioner must exercise care and professional judgement in deciding whether or not to continue as counsel in the matter.

(6) The constraints expressed above apply to the same extent where a practitioner acts as both solicitor and counsel.

[This Rule 8.06 was previously numbered 8.07.]

8.07 Rule
In litigation matters, as in the course of other aspects of practice, a practitioner must avoid a conflict of interest.

Commentary
(1) In civil proceedings a practitioner should ensure that parties with different interests are not represented by the same practitioner, whether or not counsel is or are briefed.

(2) Even if there is a perceived, though remote possibility of a conflict arising, the possibility should be avoided by declining to act.

(3) The provisions of this rule apply where two or more persons are charged jointly in a criminal matter.

(4) Rules 1.03 and 1.04 apply, where the context allows, to practitioners engaged in litigation.

[This Rule 8.07 was previously numbered 8.08.]

8.08 Rule
Subject to any question of privilege which may arise in a particular case, a practitioner must disclose to all interested parties such information regarding the execution of a will and the circumstances surrounding it as he or she would be obliged to give if subpoenaed as a witness.

Commentary
(1) This rule applies in, for example, claims under the Family Protection Act 1955, where in addition to providing information concerning the execution of the will and the circumstances surrounding it, the practitioner should disclose the initial instructions in relation to the will and any earlier wills.

(2) The claim of privilege by the former practitioner of a deceased in respect of proceedings involving the estate of that deceased does not attach to:

(i) former revoked wills of that deceased in the possession of that practitioner - *Re Moore* [1965] NZLR 895;
(ii) documents recording relevant inter vivos transactions to which the deceased was a party - *Carmichael v Goddard* [1979] 2 NZLR 586;
(iii) all relevant information concerning the reasons for the dispositions made by the deceased - *Re Cross* [1981] 2 NZLR 673 - an interview with the deceased a couple of weeks or so before his death.

(3) The attention of practitioners is also drawn specifically in this connection to:

(i) *Bullivant v Attorney-General* [1901] AC 196, 206;
(ii) S. 11 and S. 11A Family Protection Act 1955;

(iii) W M Patterson - "Family Protection and Testamentary Provisions in New Zealand" - (Butterworths) Chapter 8.

(4) See also for guidance in relation to a practitioner's response to a subpoena duces tecum:
National Employers' Mutual General Association Ltd v Waind & Hill [1978] 1 NSWLR 372.

(5) A request by a family member for information relating to that person derived from the execution of a will, will be an information privacy request under information privacy principle 6 of the Privacy Act 1993. As such the information must be disclosed unless one of the reasons in Privacy Act provides good reason to withhold it, for example where the disclosure of the information would involve the unwarranted disclosure of the affairs of another individual, would breach legal professional privilege, or prejudice the safe custody or rehabilitation of that individual (where the person is in custody).

[This rule incorporates the amendments made by NZLS Council resolution on 6 November 1996 and came into force on 1 July 1997. It was previously numbered 8.09.]

8.09 Rule
A practitioner appearing for a party shall not seek or agree to a consent order without the client's authority, preferably to be obtained in writing.

Commentary:
(1) Where a practitioner appearing for a party informs the court that he or she consents to an order on behalf of the party, the court and the other counsel and client are entitled to rely on the authority of counsel.
Carrell v Carrell [1975] 2 NZLR 441.

(2) The rule applies whether:
(i) the client is present and makes no demur; or
(ii) the client is absent.

(3) The rule also applies particularly in respect of orders made under S. 170, Family Proceedings Act 1980.

(4) Where, unknown to the other party's counsel, a practitioner's usual authority has been expressly limited by instructions but the practitioner has nevertheless entered into a compromise without authority, the court in its discretion may set aside the compromise and the orders based on it.

[This Rule 8.09 was previously numbered 8.10.]

[At the time of writing there is proposed a new rule 8.10][5]

GUIDANCE

Complaints against the Judiciary

Where a practitioner feels that he or she has been unjustly censured by a judge, the practitioner should report the matter to:

· the head of the court of which the judge is a member; or

· the president of the practitioner's District Society, who shall pass on the complaint to the head of the court of which the judge is a member.

Chapter 9

Advocate for Prosecution

9.01 Rule

A practitioner prosecuting a criminal case must do so dispassionately and with scrupulous fairness.

---

[5] **Proposed new Rule 8.10**

(1) Subject to paragraph 2 of this rule, a practitioner shall not appear as counsel before a judicial officer who is that practitioner's parent, spouse, sibling, child, parent-in-law, or child-in-law, unless:

i. all parties to the hearing consent; or

ii. the urgency of the matter renders such appearance necessary in the interests of justice, or

iii. the appearance is with respect to a formal application; or

iv. the appearance is with respect to an interlocutory matter not determinative of any substantive rights.

(2)Nothing in paragraph 1 applies to practitioners in their capacity as duty solicitors.

(3)In this rule:

i. "judicial officer" means a Judge or Master or Justice of the Peace or Community Magistrate and includes any other person required to act judicially;

ii. "spouse" includes a person living as that practitioner's partner on a domestic basis.

Commentary

1. The relationship between a particular practitioner and a particular judicial officer, even though not of a character as to bring it within this rule, may be such as to render it unwise for that practitioner to appear as counsel before that judicial officer, either generally or in a specific case, without the consent of all parties to the hearing.

2. Practitioners are reminded that judicial officers reserve the right to disqualify themselves from hearing a matter on the grounds of their relationship with a counsel whether or not the circumstances are covered by the express terms of this rule.

3. Practitioners should advise the court or tribunal at the time of applying for a hearing or being granted a hearing date, whichever first occurs, if there is a particular judicial officer who should not hear the matter either because of the bar imposed by this rule or for any other reasons. It would be an abuse of procedure for practitioners to defer advising the court of the bar to a time when the effect of advising of the bar would or might lead to an adjournment of the matter.

Commentary
(1) While it is the duty of prosecuting counsel to use every known fact to support the prosecution, there is also a corresponding responsibility to advise the defence of any factors in mitigation.

(2) Expressions of opinion should be confined to those required for the fair presentation of the
case.

(3) Counsel for the prosecution should also bear in mind their obligations in relation to the right of the defence to information and the provisions of Rule 10.08 regarding the interviewing of witnesses. Particular note should be taken of;

> (i) *R v Mason* [1976] 2 NZLR 122.
> (ii) *Commissioner of Police v Ombudsman* [1988] 1 NZLR 385 C.A. The effect of this decision is that exercise of a criminal defendant's right to personal information will not ordinarily prejudice the maintenance of the law (and fair trials), as shown by the traditional disclosure of prosecution information for indictable (jury) trials. The practice should be disclosure on request of police briefs of evidence, witness statements or notes of interviews containing information about the defendant. This would generally apply only after criminal proceedings have been commenced, and information may be withheld if a specific risk (such as fabrication of evidence or intimidation of a witness) is shown; disputes should be determined as incidental or preliminary matters by the trial court.

(4) Prosecuting counsel owes the same duty to the court as counsel appearing in all other matters to quote all relevant cases and statutory provisions whether for or against the prosecution case.

Chapter 10

Advocate for Defence

10.01 Rule
1. On a plea of not guilty counsel for the defence has a duty to see that the prosecution discharges the appropriate onus to prove the guilt of the accused, and to put before the court any proper defence in accordance with the client's instructions.

2. Counsel may not wantonly or recklessly attribute to another person the crime or offence with which the client is charged, provided that if facts or circumstances arising out of the evidence or reasonable inferences drawn from them, raise a reasonable suspicion that the crime or offence may have been committed by another person, such a line of defence may be proper.

Commentary

(1) Counsel should examine the facts that the prosecution will prove before advising the client about an appropriate plea. If the client's decision is to plead not guilty, counsel must act conscientiously in presenting the case for the accused.

(2) Defence counsel should bear in mind the judgements of the Court of Appeal in *Commissioner of Police v Ombudsman* [1988] 1 NZLR 385, C.A. concerning access by the accused to certain information held by the prosecution (see paragraph (3) (ii) of Commentary to Rule 9.01).

(3) Counsel for the defence has the same general duty of counsel to the court to disclose all cases and authorities bearing on the matter whether or not they support the defence.

(4) Although counsel may present a technical defence available to the client, counsel must not invent or participate in the invention of facts which will assist in advancing the client's case.

(5) Whatever the view of counsel about the guilt or innocence of the client or of some third person, the clear duty of counsel is not to mislead the court by allegations not supported by evidence.

10.02 Rule

Counsel must not in the course of making submissions or cross-examining a witness say or lead a witness to say anything that might mislead the court. In particular, counsel must not make any statement to the court or put any proposition to a witness that is not supported by reasonable instructions, or that lacks factual foundation by reference to the information available to the court.

Commentary

(1) Counsel has a particular responsibility to the court when cross-examining a witness, not to put to the witness allegations in the form of questions which counsel knows that the witness does not have the necessary information or knowledge to answer, or where there is no justifiable foundation for the question.

10.03 Rule

Subject to Rules 1.02, 1.03 and 1.04 counsel has, on receiving instructions, a duty to defend a person on a criminal charge, whether or not counsel has formed a belief or opinion about the guilt or innocence of that person.

Commentary

(1) It is not for counsel to assess the guilt or innocence of the client. That is a matter for the court. There could well be cases where counsel feels reasonably sure of the client's guilt, but is still under a duty to put the prosecution to the proof and is free to submit, if justified, that there is insufficient evidence for a conviction.

(2) If a client tries to put before the court evidence which to the knowledge of counsel is false, counsel should cease to act.

10.04 Rule

1. Where counsel has been instructed to defend a criminal charge and before or after the proceedings have started the client makes a confession of guilt to counsel, counsel must bear in mind:

(i) a trial is for the purpose of finding whether the accused person is guilty or not guilty, and not whether the accused is innocent;
(ii) it is for the prosecution to call evidence to justify a verdict of guilty;
(iii) a "crime" is a defined offence committed by a person of sound mind and understanding.

2. In such circumstances, counsel may continue to act only if the plea is changed to one of guilty or if not, within very strict limitations. Counsel must not put forward a case inconsistent with the confession.

3. If the plea is to remain one of not guilty, counsel may conduct the defence by putting the prosecution to the proof, and if appropriate, assert that the prosecution evidence is inadequate to justify a verdict of guilty; but must not raise any matter which suggests that the client has an affirmative defence, for example an alibi. Counsel may, however, proceed with a defence based on a special plea such as insanity, if such a plea appears in counsel's professional opinion to be available.

Commentary:

(1) This rule applies to a case where there is a clear confession that the client committed the offence charged.

(2) No rule can deal with doubts raised in counsel's mind after he or she has been instructed to act on a not guilty plea, by inconsistent statements by the client which might suggest to counsel that the client is guilty. Counsel can deal with such a situation only in the light of all the circumstances and pursuant to counsel's professional judgement and duty as an officer of the Court.

10.05 Rule

Counsel must, in advising the client on a plea, or as to whether or not to give evidence, traverse all relevant aspects of the case and seek to ensure that the client makes an informed decision.

Commentary

(1) Although counsel has a clear duty to advise on a plea, the client has the sole right to make the decision whether to plead guilty or not guilty.

(2) In all cases, but particularly where the client might have difficulty making a decision on a plea, it is prudent for counsel to take written instructions on the plea. To have the client's decision so recorded might well assist counsel if in the course of the proceedings or on appeal, the client decides to change the plea. Likewise, it is prudent for counsel to take written instructions as to whether or not the client is to give evidence on his or her own behalf.

(3) In giving advice on a plea, counsel's clear duty is to the client and the court. The interest of the practitioner or any potential benefit to the practitioner by way of fee or otherwise, is quite irrelevant to the nature of the plea.

10.06 Rule
Where counsel is told by the accused that he or she did not commit the offence, or where counsel believes that on the facts there should be an acquittal, but for particular reasons the client wishes to plead guilty, counsel may continue to represent the client, but only after warning the client of the consequences and advising the client that counsel can act after the entry of the plea only on the basis that the offence has been admitted, and put forward factors in mitigation.

10.07 Rule
Defence counsel must not disclose a client's previous convictions without the client's authority.

Commentary
(1) Should the court raise the question of previous convictions with counsel, counsel should inform the court that it is not entitled to ask such a question and that counsel will not answer the question.

(2) See also the ruling by the NZLS Council in Appendix IV.

10.08 Rule
In criminal, as in all other proceedings before the court, no practitioner or party has the sole right to call a witness or discuss the case with a witness.

Commentary
(1) In a District Court prosecution, counsel may interview any person who might be called as a witness by the police prior to the court hearing save that counsel would be unwise to interview complainants in sexual offences or members of the police without first notifying the prosecutor of counsel's intention.

(2) In indictable matters, where counsel wishes to interview any Crown witnesses after the lower court hearing but before the trial, counsel should notify the Crown solicitor of counsel's intention to do so.

(3) Where a prosecution witness is interviewed, counsel should bear in mind the possibility of subsequent accusations of tampering with the evidence to be

given by that witness. Depending on the circumstances of the matter, including the nature of the offence and the importance of the witness in the case, consideration should be given to carrying out the interview in the presence of an independent and reputable person.

(4) As a general rule, particularly in cases involving allegations of sexual offending, a practitioner should not interview a child complainant or child witnesses unless the interview is conducted in the presence of an independent and reputable person who is able to ensure that the child is not pressured or unreasonably distressed by the event.

[*Notes from Ethics Committee*
This matter had been considered fully by the Ethics Committee and the Criminal Law Committee prior to being reported to the NZLS Council. The matter first arose out of an expression of concern by the Care and Protection Resources Panel of the Department of Social Welfare. The concern of the Panel was that the interviewing of children who may have been the subject of sexual abuse should be carried out by persons who have the appropriate specialist abilities. It was pointed out that there is already a great deal of pressure on children in sexual abuse cases and that pressure can often come from family members who do not believe the child or who may have a vested interest in ensuring that a prosecution does not proceed. The Panel believed a procedure must be set in place to deal with the situation. They were aware that it is possible to audit interviews with children where transcripts or videos of the disclosure interview can be made available. The Panel then referred the matter to the Society.]

(5) Counsel has a responsibility when interviewing a prosecution witness to ensure that nothing is said or done to intimidate the witness.

(6) It should be remembered that while a practitioner has the "right" to interview anyone, so also has the person the "right" to refuse to be interviewed. No one is obliged to make a statement, if he or she does not wish to do so, when interviewed by a solicitor, counsel or anyone else. It follows that in interviewing prosecution witnesses, both courtesy and self-interest are usually served by making arrangements for the interview through the police prosecutor or Crown solicitor.

(7) Any difficulty in gaining access to a prosecution witness should be promptly brought to the attention of the Court.

(8) The attention of practitioners is drawn particularly to *R v Mason* [1976] 2 NZLR 122 where it was held:

> Where the police have interviewed a person who can give evidence on a material subject and the prosecution does not intend calling that person, then whether the prosecution considers the person credit worthy or not, the person's name and address must be made available to the defence.

(9) Attention is also drawn to *Commissioner of Police v Ombudsman* [1988] 1 NZLR 385, C.A.

(10) See also paragraph (3) of the Commentary to Rule 9.01 in this connection.

(11) A practitioner must be careful to avoid treating a potential witness in an overbearing or misleading way in regard to that person's right to decline to be interviewed.

[This Rule 10.08 incorporates the amendments made by NZLS Council resolution on 16 April
1993 which came into effect on 1 October 1993.]

GUIDANCE
Practitioners are referred for further guidance in the duties of defence counsel to ARCHBOLD: "CRIMINAL PLEADING EVIDENCE AND PRACTICE" which contains extracts from the Code of Conduct for the Bar of England and Wales.

APPENDICES
Counsel are referred to the following appendices to this publication for important information about;
(i) "Alibis": APPENDIX I

Chapter 11

The Practice of Barristers

NOTE: As *stated in the preface, many of the rules in this publication apply to practitioners generally in whatever capacity they might be acting. The rules in this chapter apply particularly:*

(i) to practitioners who have a practising certificate as a barrister only (a barrister sole);

(ii) to practitioners who have a certificate as a barrister and solicitor but have been briefed to act as a barrister by a practitioner not in his or her own firm or employment.

11.01 Rule
A barrister sole may not practise in partnership.

Commentary
(1) A barrister sole may employ another practitioner who holds a practising certificate as a barrister only.

(2) Barristers sole may practise from sets of rooms or chambers, and join with other barristers sole in sharing secretarial and support services for their practices.

11.02 Rule
No person holding a practising certificate as a barrister and solicitor shall hold himself or herself out as practising as a barrister sole.

Commentary
(1) A practitioner in practice with a certificate as a barrister and solicitor is subject to the provisions of the Solicitors' Audit Regulations and the Solicitors' Trust Account Rules, and may hold trust moneys on behalf of clients. This is inconsistent with the nature of the practice of a barrister sole.

11.03 Rule
Except in the circumstances prescribed in Rule 11.04, a barrister sole must accept instructions only from a solicitor and may not accept instructions direct from a lay client.

11.04 Rule
A barrister sole may act or advise without instructions from a solicitor where the barrister sole is:

(i) instructed to act in a judicial or quasi-judicial capacity or is instructed by a person or body acting in such a capacity;
(ii) instructed by the Society or a District Society;
(iii) instructed by:
 (a) a registered patent attorney
 (b) a lawyer practising overseas
 (c) an Official Assignee or Official Liquidator;
(iv) acting as a revising barrister pursuant to any enactment;
(v)
 (a) assigned to a legally aided person
 (b) acting as a duty solicitor
 (c) providing assistance to a legal advice service operating on a non-profit basis
 (d) advising a legal aid committee
 (e) acting under a Detention Legal Assistance Scheme;
(vi) advised in any other case by the Ethics Committee of the Society that he or she may act.

[This Rule 11.04 incorporates the amendments made by the NZLS Council resolution on 5 August 1994 which came into effect on 1 October 1994.]

Commentary
(1) Because, in New Zealand, the nature of the practice of a barrister sole may not be readily understood by the public, it is in order in the event of a potential client approaching the barrister sole direct, for the potential client to be told that the barrister sole would be prepared to accept instructions, but that they must come through the medium of a solicitor.

(2) It is not proper practice for a barrister sole to accept instructions from a duty solicitor. A practitioner serving as a duty solicitor has no continuity of

appointment as such, and does not have the normal facilities of a solicitor's office available when carrying out those duties. Where it seems necessary to the duty solicitor, a legal aid assignment can be sought or solicitor's instructions to a barrister arranged in the normal way.

11.05 Rule

A practitioner, having made the decision to practise as a barrister sole, must be in a position of complete professional independence and be available to accept instructions within his or her fields of practice and subject to other professional obligations, from any solicitor wishing to brief the barrister sole for a client.

Commentary

(1) Nothing in this rule derogates from Rule 1.02 or the commentary to that rule.

11.06 Rule

A barrister sole must not do anything to induce persons to suppose the barrister sole retains a connection with any law firm of which he or she was previously a partner or employee or to suppose that there is any connection between the barrister sole and that firm or any other practitioner.

Commentary:

(1) While a barrister sole may receive briefs from a firm of which he or she had been a partner, the link with the firm must be demonstrably severed.

(2) The degree of objectivity and independence required of a barrister sole negates the notion of any indication or implication that there is any connection with the former firm or any other firm or practitioner.

11.07 Rule

1. A barrister sole must not have an arrangement which restricts the complete freedom of a solicitor to instruct any counsel the solicitor or the client selects.

2. This rule does not affect the right of a barrister sole to accept a general retainer from a solicitor on behalf of a particular client.

11.08 Rule

When being instructed by a solicitor, a barrister shall if requested, state what the fee will be, or if that is not practicable, give a carefully considered estimate.

Commentary:

(1) Where the brief relates to a protracted matter, it is good practice to send fee notes periodically to the instructing solicitor.

(2) It is improper for a barrister to set the fee by reference to the fee charged by the instructing solicitor.

(3) Refer to Rule 6.08 in this connection.

11.09 Rule
A barrister must treat all practitioners with courtesy and fairness.

Commentary
(1) A barrister should neither accept nor continue with a retainer or brief in a matter on which the barrister knows or discovers that another barrister has been retained or briefed previously, until he or she communicates with the instructing solicitor and inquires whether there is a satisfactory reason for the change of counsel.

(2) Nothing in this rule derogates from the entitlement of the lay client to a free choice of counsel to be instructed by the practitioner.

11.10 Rule
A barrister should keep his or her instructing solicitor reasonably informed of the progress of the brief. Normal relations between an instructing solicitor and a barrister require the barrister to seek the consent or the solicitor before interviewing the client or witnesses.

Commentary
(1) The consent of the solicitor could be either a specific consent obtained for each occasion or a general consent given at any stage.

11.11 Rule
Correspondence between parties on matters relating to litigation should normally be carried out between the instructing solicitors.

Commentary
(1) Counsel may correspond with the court, instructing solicitors and other persons such as experts.

(2) Counsel may on appropriate occasions correspond with other counsel, but the risk will be that the correspondence may become relevant to the litigation, thus placing counsel in an embarrassing position.

(3) Counsel should avoid corresponding with lay clients, as this is the prerogative of the instructing solicitor, unless that solicitor consents to such course, either generally or on a specific occasion.

11.12 Rule
A barrister should not normally file documents in court, or in the course of proceedings, show his or her rooms or chambers as the address for service. There may however, be exceptional circumstances where it is practicable and necessary to do so. One exception would be where the barrister is not instructed by a solicitor in accordance with Rules 11.03 and 11.04.

Appendix I

ALIBIS

When considering matters relating to "Notice of alibi" under s.367A Crimes Act 1961, a practitioner should be aware of and have regard to the following extract from Police General Instructions:

C150A

(1) Whenever an alibi is put forward by a defendant concerning a matter in respect of which summary proceedings have been commenced, it shall be the duty of the investigating member to ensure that the alibi is inquired into as thoroughly as possible and the result of the inquiry fully reported to the prosecutor.

(2) When particulars of alibi witnesses are notified in accordance with the provisions of s. 367A of the Crimes act 1961 the member in charge of the case shall institute a "Query Persons" (Q.P.) transaction and notify the Crown Prosecutor of their criminal record, if any.

(3) (a) Alibi witnesses whose particulars have been advised in accordance with s.367A are not to be interviewed by the Police except at the request of the Crown Prosecutor.

(b) Whether or not the Crown Prosecutor has requested that alibi witnesses be interviewed, inquiries shall be made of persons other than those whose particulars have been supplied to confirm or rebut evidence in support of an alibi. The result of these inquiries is to be forwarded to the Crown Prosecutor.

(4) When the Crown Prosecutor requests that alibi witnesses whose particulars have been supplied be interviewed, the following procedure is to be adopted:

(a) The defence solicitor should be told of the proposed interview and given a reasonable opportunity to be present.

(b) When an accused is not represented an endeavour should be made to ensure the witness is interviewed in the presence of some independent person not being a member of the Police.

(c) When the defence solicitor is not present at the interview and so requests, a copy of a witness's signed statement

taken at any such interview is to be made available to him through the Crown Prosecutor.

(5) Particulars of, and statements from, witnesses interviewed for the purpose of rebutting evidence of an alibi witness should only be made available to the defence at the request of the Crown Prosecutor.

Appendix II

Deleted by resolution of the NZLS Council 1999

Appendix III

INTERNATIONAL CODE OF ETHICS
First adopted 1956, this edition 1988

PREAMBLE
The International Bar Association is a federation of National Bar Associations and Law Societies with full or sustaining organisation members and individual members. Most of the full or sustaining organisational members have established Codes of Legal Ethics as models for or governing the practice of law by their members. In some jurisdictions these Codes are imposed on all practitioners by their respective Bar Associations or Law Societies or by the courts or administrative agencies having jurisdiction over the admission of individuals to the practice of law.

Except where the context otherwise requires, this Code applies to any lawyer of one jurisdiction in relation to his contacts with a lawyer of another jurisdiction or to his activities in another jurisdiction.

Nothing in this Code absolves a lawyer from the obligation to comply with such requirements of the law or of rules of professional conduct as may apply to him in any relevant jurisdiction. It is a restatement of much that is in these requirements and a guide as to what the International Bar Association considers to be a desirable course of conduct by all lawyers engaged in the international practice of law.

The International Bar Association may bring incidents of alleged violations to the attention of relevant organisations.

RULES
1. A lawyer who undertakes professional work in a jurisdiction where he is not a full member of the local profession shall adhere to the standards of professional ethics in the jurisdiction in which he has been admitted. He shall also observe all ethical standards which apply to lawyers of the country where he is working.

2. Lawyers shall at all times maintain the honour and dignity of their profession.
They shall, in practice as well as in private life, abstain from any behaviour which may tend to discredit the profession of which they are members.

3. Lawyers shall preserve independence in the discharge of their professional duty.
Lawyers practising on their own account or in partnership where permissible, shall not engage in any other business or occupation if by doing so they may cease to be independent.

4. Lawyers shall treat their professional colleagues with the utmost courtesy and fairness.

Lawyers who undertake to render assistance to a foreign colleague shall always keep in mind that the foreign colleague has to depend on them to a much larger extent than in the case of another lawyer of the same country. Therefore the responsibility is much greater, both when giving advice and when handling a case.

For this reason it is improper for lawyers to accept a case unless they can handle it promptly and with due competence, without undue interference by the pressure of other work. To the fees in these cases Rule 19 applies.

5. Except where the law or custom of the country concerned otherwise requires, any oral or written communication between lawyers shall in principle be accorded a confidential character as far as the Court is concerned, unless certain promises or acknowledgements are made therein on behalf of a client.

6. Lawyers shall always maintain due respect towards the Court. Lawyers shall without fear defend the interests of their clients and without regard to any unpleasant consequences to themselves or to any other person.

Lawyers shall never knowingly give to the Court incorrect information or advice which is to their knowledge contrary to the law.

7. It shall be considered improper for lawyers to communicate about a particular case directly with any person whom they know to be represented in that case by another lawyer without the latter's consent.

8. A lawyer should not advertise or solicit business except to the extent and in the manner permitted by the rules of the jurisdiction to which that lawyer is subject. A lawyer should not advertise or solicit business in any country in which such advertising or soliciting is prohibited.

9. A lawyer should never consent to handle a case unless:

- (a) the client gives direct instructions, or
- (b) the case is assigned by a competent body or forwarded by another lawyer, or
- (c) instructions are given in any other manner permissible under the relevant local rules or regulations.

10. Lawyers shall at all times give clients a candid opinion on any case. They shall render assistance with scrupulous care and diligence. This applies also if they are assigned as counsel for an indigent person.

Lawyers shall at any time be free to refuse to handle a case, unless it is assigned by a competent body.

Lawyers should only withdraw from a case during its course for good cause and if possible in such a manner that the client's interests are not adversely affected.

The loyal defence of a client's case may never cause advocates to be other than perfectly candid, subject to any right or privilege to the contrary which clients choose them to exercise, or knowingly to go against the law.

11. Lawyers shall, when in the client's interest, endeavour to reach a solution by settlement out of court rather than start legal proceedings.

Lawyers should never stir up litigation.

12. Lawyers should not acquire a financial interest in the subject matter of a case which they are conducting. Neither should they directly or indirectly acquire property about which litigation is pending before the court in which they practice.

13. Lawyers should never represent conflicting interests in litigation. In non-litigation matters, lawyers should do so only after having disclosed all conflicts or possible conflicts of interest to all parties concerned and only with their consent. This Rule also applies to all lawyers in a firm.

14. Lawyers should never disclose, unless lawfully ordered to do so by the Court or as required by statute, what has been communicated to them in their capacity as lawyers even after they have ceased to be the client's counsel. This duty extends to their partners, to junior lawyers assisting them and to their employees.

15. In pecuniary matters lawyers shall be most punctual and diligent.

They should never mingle funds of others with their own and they should at all times be able to refund money they hold for others.

They shall not retain money they receive for their clients for longer than is absolutely necessary.

16. Lawyers may require that a deposit is made to cover their expenses, but the deposit should be in accordance with the estimated amount of their charges and the probable expenses and labour required.

17. Lawyers shall never forget that they should put first not their right to compensation for their services, but the interests of their clients and the exigencies of the administration of justice.
The lawyer's right to ask for a deposit or to demand payment of out-of-pocket expenses and commitments, failing payment of which they may withdraw from the case or refuse to handle it, should never be exercised at a moment at which the client may be unable to find other assistance in time to prevent irreparable damage being done.

Lawyers' fees should, in the absence or non-applicability of official scales, be fixed on a consideration of the amount involved in the controversy and the interest of it to the client, the time and labour involved and all other personal and factual circumstances of the case.

18. A contract for a contingent fee, where sanctioned by the law or by professional rules and practice, should be reasonable under all circumstances of the case, including the risk and uncertainty of the compensation and subject to supervision of a court as to its reasonableness.

19. Lawyers who engage a foreign colleague to advise on a case or to co-operate in handling it, are responsible for the payment of the latter's charges except express agreement to the contrary. When lawyers direct a client to a foreign colleague they are not responsible for the payment of the latter's charges, but neither are they entitled to a share of the fee of this foreign colleague.

20. Lawyers should not permit their professional services or their names to be used in any way which would make it possible for persons to practise law who are not legally authorised to do so.
Lawyers shall not delegate to a legally unqualified person not in their employ and control any functions which are by the law or custom of the country in which they practise only to be performed by a qualified lawyer.

21. It is not unethical for lawyers to limit or exclude professional liability subject to the rules of their local Bar Association and to there being no statutory or constitutional prohibitions.

International Bar Association,
271 Regent Street,
London W1R 7PA,
England
Telephone: 00 44 (171) 629 -1206
Fax: 00 44 (171) 409 - 0456

Appendix IV

RULINGS BY THE SOCIETY
(Given pursuant to s.17(2) of the Act)

RULING BY THE NZLS COUNCIL ON 8 NOVEMBER 1991

Rule(s) concerned: 10.07

Subject: Counsel for Defence: disclosure of charges pending.

Terms of the Ruling
Where a practitioner, appearing for a client in respect of a charge, becomes aware before or during the hearing that there are or may be other charges pending against the client, then, provided nothing the practitioner says will be incorrect or intended to mislead the Court, the practitioner must not disclose to the Court the existence or possible existence of the other charges. The provisions of Rule 10.07 apply by analogy to these circumstances.

RULING BY THE NZLS ETHICS COMMITTEE on 5 March 1998

Rule(s) concerned: 2.02

Subject: Disclosure of status of practitioner within a firm.

Terms of the Ruling
The Ethics Committee has been asked to give a ruling as to whether it is in order for a barrister of England and Wales, Miss X, working in New Zealand as an employed clerk of a New Zealand firm of barristers and solicitors, to sign correspondence on that firm's behalf as a "Barrister of England and Wales", or alternatively "Barrister of the High Court of England and Wales".

Commentary (4) to rule 2.02 of the Rules of Professional Conduct provides as follows:

> "A firm must ensure that the public, and other practitioners dealing with the principal or an employee of the firm, should know the name and status of the person with whom they are dealing. A letter should therefore at least show the name of the partner responsible for the matter concerned, or the name and status of the person dealing with it if that person is not the partner responsible".

When that commentary refers to a person's "status", it means that person's status within the firm. Miss X's status within the firm is that of a "law clerk". Accordingly, if Miss X is to sign correspondence on the firm's behalf, it is necessary that her status as a "law clerk" be referred to.

It is by no means uncommon for principals to have their qualifications printed on the firm's letterhead. While it would be unusual, it would not be improper for any employee of the firm to put any qualifications he or she may have after his or her name. Such qualifications may be a degree or a certificate or a status in a foreign jurisdiction, e.g. Barrister of England and Wales. The use in correspondence of such qualifications is optional. What is mandatory is disclosure of the status within the firm of the letter writer.

Accordingly, the Ethics Committee rules that it will not be sufficient for Miss X simply to sign correspondence on her firm's behalf as "Barrister of England and Wales" or alternatively "Barrister of the High Court of England and

Wales". If she signs correspondence, she must also state her status within the firm, namely "law clerk".

RULING BY THE NZLS ETHICS COMMITTEE on 30 July 1998
Rule concerned: 2.04.

Subject: Separate place of business and supervision of staff.

THE Ethics Committee was originally asked to give a ruling on the basis that a qualified legal practitioner (M) was employed by a law firm (Mc) on the basis that he would:

- Work one day a week from the offices of Mc and the remainder of the time from his home.
- Continue working as a private investigator for a company in which he had a financial interest.
-

The committee was subsequently advised that M no longer proposed to work as a private investigator and that he no longer had a financial interest in a company carrying out financial investigations. It was therefore not necessary for the committee to make a ruling in this regard.
Subsequent discussions and correspondence with M and Mc has revealed that M's situation was not as originally proposed. The situation was set out in Mc's letter to the NZLS dated 28 July 1998 and is as follows:

- M spends two full days per week at the premises of Mc.
- On other days he is at the office of Mc for at least an hour unless he is precluded from doing so by reason of a court commitment.
- M seeks advice on new files from his supervising partner and other staff and the partnership is aware of his file commitments.
- M rarely interviews clients at home. All new clients are interviewed at the offices of Mc. He only sees clients at his home if they are unable to attend the offices of Mc.
- All correspondence is channelled through the offices of Mc. Apart from routine correspondence, M's correspondence is checked by his supervising partner.
- Sometimes M receives faxes or email messages at home but these are documents rather than correspondence. All are filed on the appropriate file at the premises of Mc.
-

The only rule the committee has needed to consider is Rule 2.04 which provides:
"A practitioner must ensure that each separate place of business is at all times under effective and competent management by a practitioner who is qualified, in terms of s 55 of the Act, to practice on his or her own account as a solicitor, whether in partnership or otherwise."

The committee rules on the basis of the information contained in the material supplied for its consideration that there is no breach of this rule on the part of Mc because:

- M's home is not a separate place of business.
- Even though M is working from his home for approximately three days per week, he is being adequately supervised by Mc.

RULING BY THE NZLS ETHICS COMMITTEE in February 1999

Rule discussed: 2.03

Subject: Separate Business

The Auckland District Law Society has sought a ruling on "whether a practitioner who holds a practising certificate as a barrister and solicitor is engaging in a business or professional activity other than the practice of law if the practitioner separately carries on the business as an employer's or employee's representative under the Employment Contracts Act".

Some legal work only practising lawyers can legally do; in this ruling, we call such work "reserved legal work". Other legal work practising lawyers do, not only in competition with each other, but also in competition with non-lawyers: in this ruling, we call such work "unreserved legal work". Much of the representative work under the Employment Contracts Act 1991 is work of this latter category.

The dividing line between reserved legal work and unreserved legal work is a difficult one to draw and not all lawyers would agree on where it is to be drawn. It principally turns on the rather vague prescriptions contained in sections 54, 64 and 65 of the Law Practitioners Act 1982. But representative work under the Employment Contracts Act is clearly on the "unreserved legal work" side of the dividing line: see section 59 of that Act.

A practitioner (as defined in the Rules of Professional Conduct) who wishes to do only unreserved legal work has a choice. He or she can elect to take out a practising certificate and do unreserved legal work as part of his or her legal practice. Alternatively, he or she can elect not to take out a practising certificate and do the work under another banner, eg "bargaining agent" or "Employment Contracts Act representative". If he or she chooses the latter option, he or she must take care not to hold himself or herself out as a practising lawyer. What the practitioner may not do, however, is operate or be employed in both a legal practice and a non-legal practice doing unreserved legal work.

If we permitted lawyers to do unreserved legal work outside their legal practices, then many lawyers would choose to move all such work to separate companies. Such work could then be done with the benefit of limited liability through a corporate entity, something not permitted by the Law Practitioners

Act 1982. Clients would not have the benefit of numerous consumer protections contained in that act. That would not be in the public interest. Clients might not appreciate that their work was "unreserved legal work" and that their "lawyer" was not wearing his or her "legal hat" when undertaking work for them. Lawyers would be tempted to fudge the distinction between their legal practice and their non-legal practice (still doing legal work).

The answer to the question posed is therefore that a practitioner holding a practising certificate as a barrister and solicitor may not carry on a separate business as an employer's or employee's representative under the Employment Contracts Act. The work of an employer's or employee's representative is legal work (albeit unreserved legal work) and, if a practising lawyer wishes to do it, the lawyer must do it within the legal practice he or she operates or in which he or she is employed.

The question was posed in light of rule 2.03. That is not the applicable rule, however, because the nature of the "other" activity here is not an "activity other than the practice of law". Here the practitioner wants to practise "law" partly through a legal practice and partly through a separate business. Neither the framers of the act nor the framers of the rules ever envisaged that such would be permissible.

New Zealand Law Society

Rules of Professional Conduct for Barristers and Solicitors

Index

Index